ANTHONY
Fokker

ANTHONY

THE FLYING DUTCHMAN
WHO SHAPED
AMERICAN AVIATION

MARC DIERIKX

SMITHSONIAN BOOKS
WASHINGTON, DC

Text © 2018 by Marc Dierikx

This book may be purchased for educational, business, or sales promotional use. For information, please write: Special Markets Department, Smithsonian Books, P.O. Box 37012, MRC 513, Washington, DC 20013.

Published by Smithsonian Books
Director: Carolyn Gleason
Senior Editor: Christina Wiginton
Editors: Duke Johns and Gregory McNamee
Designer: Jody Billert
Cover design: Bart van den Tooren

Library of Congress Cataloging-in-Publication Data
Names: Dierikx, M. L. J., author.
Title: Anthony Fokker : the Flying Dutchman who shaped American aviation /
    Marc Dierikx.
Other titles: Anthony Fokker. English | Flying Dutchman who shaped American aviation
Description: Washington, DC : Smithsonian Books, [2018] | Includes bibliographical
    references and index.
Identifiers: LCCN 2017034700 (print) | LCCN 2017050282 (ebook) |
    ISBN 9781588346162 (eBook) | ISBN 9781588346155 (hardcover) |
    ISBN 1588346153 (hardcover)
Subjects: LCSH: Fokker, Anthony H. G. (Anthony Herman Gerard),
    1890–1939—Chronology. | Fokker, Anthony H. G. (Anthony Herman Gerard),
    1890–1939—Influence. | Air pilots—Netherlands—Biography. | Aeronautical
    engineers—Netherlands—Biography. | Aircraft industry—United
    States—History—Chronology.
Classification: LCC TL540.F6 (ebook) | LCC TL540.F6 D5313 2018 (print) |
    DDC 338.7 62913334092 [B]—dc23
LC record available at https://lccn.loc.gov 2017034700

Manufactured in the United States of America
23 22 22 20 19 18   5 4 3 2 1

CONTENTS

1

NEW YORK, NEW YORK
DECEMBER 1939

Among the shopping public, the heavyset, middle-aged man wearing his suit in a state of disarray, an advancing baldness hidden under the brim of his hat, does not immediately stand out. That this is the world's first aviation multimillionaire is not apparent by sight. The streets are busy in New York this first day of December 1939. Although the war in Europe—now three months old—is far away, New Yorkers hasten to department stores such as Saks Fifth Avenue and John Wanamaker. For weeks they have been luring customers with advertisements that this may well be the last time they stock imported luxury items. Expectations are that the Christmas sales will be 10 percent higher than in 1938.[1] The splendid fall weather is beautiful for shopping; in anticipation of winter, which has been exceptionally slow to set in, New York relishes an autumn that goes on and on. Indeed, it is so warm and dry that city mayor Fiorello La Guardia has announced special precautions to supply Manhattan's trees and plants with extra water—something normally done only in the heat of summer.

La Guardia, nicknamed "the little flower" after his first name, has an eye for nature. Since his appointment as mayor almost six years ago, he has had Central Park restructured and replanted. And it is not just flowers and plants that he loves. As an aviation enthusiast, former pilot, and bomber commander in the Great War, he is also the driving force behind the creation of a new airport. After two years of construction and $40 million in costs, this is his big day: at three minutes past midnight he is to welcome the first scheduled airliner—a flight from Chicago.[2] With this event the New York Municipal Airport will officially become operational on the beach of the borough of Queens. Several leading personalities from the world of aviation have been invited to witness the event. Among this select group is Anthony Fokker.

ℂ

It is already past midday when the porter opens the door of the former Viceroy Hotel at Park Avenue and 59th Street for Fokker. In the luxurious hallway, where marble and gold glisten in the lamplight, his appearance seems slightly incongruous. Yet he feels at ease in this environment. He knows the building, although it has changed much since its grand opening in 1929. In the wake of the Great Depression, the owners reconditioned the thirty-two-story building. Its 525 rooms have been made into apartments to be sold individually. What has not been sold has been leased. Even Delmonico's, a well-known specialty restaurant once frequented by wealthy New Yorkers, is no more.

It is quiet in the hallway when Fokker reports to the reception desk. In his somewhat awkward, Dutch-riddled English, he tells the receptionist he has come for his appointment with doctor Robert Cushing. In anticipation of the gathering at the airport this evening, he has traveled from his house in Nyack in upstate New York to seek release from his persistent splitting headaches. From the lovely village on the southern bank of the Hudson River, the drive to Manhattan has taken some forty-five minutes. The road through the rolling, wooded landscape high above the river is well known to him. Since moving into his mansion Undercliff Manor in the summer of 1937, he has often driven this route. His old house in the woods near Alpine appears unchanged as he passes. At Brookside Cemetery, just outside Englewood, New Jersey, much has remained the same as well; from the road he can see Violet's grave on the high grounds, where he buried his second wife after she met such a tragic death. He has driven here hundreds of times, when he still had his factories at the Teterboro Airport and in nearby Passaic, New Jersey. His German companies closed long before. Only the Dutch factory is left, far away in Amsterdam. He interferes with it as little as possible and prefers to spend his time on one of his boats.

Outside Englewood, Fokker turns left across the new George Washington Bridge that leads to New York. From the high bridge he can see Riverside Drive with his former apartment on the corner of 101st Street, which he abandoned after his wife's death in 1929.

He arrives late for his appointment with Dr. Cushing. Being late is something Anthony Fokker relishes—the prerogative of an *homme arrivé*. Even President Warren Harding had to wait thirty minutes for him at the White House seventeen years ago.[3] There is no need to rush anyway: Cushing has seen him often enough. His ailment has been the same for years: chronic sinusitis, a condition he has picked up after many years of flying in open cockpits. Today his face is again taut. Breathing through the nose exhausts him. It almost appears as if the congestion in his forehead presses on his eyes more than usual. His whole head feels heavy, and even his neck is rigid.

Doctor Cushing's practice is pleasantly light and spacious. Its low-slung sofa suggests an ordinary living room rather than a doctor's office. This is no coincidence;

Cushing caters to an affluent clientele and wants his patients to feel at ease. His specialty, osteopathy, is a relatively new, alternative treatment in 1939, aimed at providing relief for patients suffering from reduced flexibility of body tissues and bone structure. The treatment involves special manual techniques.

As is customary, Cushing asks his patient to lie down on the sofa. He will manipulate Anthony's skull, vertebrae, forehead, and nose with his hands. These maneuvers are meant to improve the circulation and the pulsations of brain fluid, stimulating the cerebral membrane and the membrane of the spinal marrow. The technique should—at least temporarily—reduce the headaches and make the patient feel better. Although the manipulations are not painful in themselves, their duration makes the treatment unpleasant. Therefore it is better to sedate the patient, so that he will be able to relax fully. Cushing applies nitrous oxide (known as laughing gas), a commonly used anesthetic that is both fast and effective. Anthony receives a cap over his nose and mouth and is instructed to take a deep breath to relax. A wondrous feeling of tiredness descends upon him, and within seconds he floats into a deep sleep.

With great care, Dr. Cushing then feels and manipulates Anthony's skull. For an hour his hands apply pressure in several places to equilibrate the bodily functions and restore the mobility of the bone structures. When the treatment is over, he waits for the patient to wake up. Today it takes longer than expected—much longer. Whatever the physician tries to bring his patient around, nothing happens. Hours pass. Finally there appears to be no other option but to call for an ambulance, which brings him to Murray Hill Hospital, a mile away in midtown Manhattan. This hospital caters to the rich and famous who live in the Murray Hill district. Cushing holds a position there. While preparations begin at New York Airport for the landing of the first scheduled flight, Anthony Fokker sails into the undetermined sphere between heaven and earth.

ᛪ

In the days that follow, worries mount at Murray Hill Hospital.[4] Examinations reveal that Fokker's loss of consciousness is not so much an unforeseen effect of the anesthetic, but rather is directly linked to a much-feared bacterial infection, pneumococcus meningitis, which causes encephalitis. The bacteria must have invaded from Anthony's sinuses and colonized his nose and throat cavities, subsequently entering his bloodstream. Now it has affected the membrane that normally protects the brain and the spinal cord. Severe headaches and stiffness of the neck are the symptoms that accompany this condition. In 1939 an effective treatment does not yet exist, although experiments with an antimeningitis serum have been conducted by the Rockefeller Institute for Medical Research since 1904.[5] Failing a serum, the disease persists, pulling the patient into a downward spiral of semiconsciousness and unconsciousness. The complications increase: in Holland, newspapers report of pneumonia on top of everything else.[6] Semi-oblivious, Anthony Fokker is fighting for his life.

JAVA, NETHERLANDS EAST INDIES
APRIL 1890

It had taken Anna Fokker-Diemont half the day to reach the government hospital in Blitar with her horse and carriage. The wet western monsoon had taken hold of Java, and the roads were covered in puddles and mud. For months the clouds hung low around the slopes of the Kelud volcano, where she had her home on the coffee plantation Njoenjoer with her husband, Herman. She had chosen a dry day for her trip to Blitar, and thanks to the dispersing clouds she could now enjoy the landscape with its rice terraces. The route was beautiful. The first part, along the horse track that the planters had built connecting the model gardens of Kali Tapak and the tea and rubber plantations of Gogo Niti and Senggrong, had taken her to the village of Wlingi. From Wlingi the great Postal Road curved for some twelve miles through desas, across bridges, and through rice fields and dry land.[1]

Blitar, one of the strongholds of the Dutch colonial administration on eastern Java, was a quiet town with about nine thousand inhabitants. Its wide avenues joined at the central grass square, which was lined with trees. The town was known for a mild climate that lent itself to the recovery of the sick and ailing. A Dutch civilian physician resided at the government hospital on the edge of town. Here modern medical care could be provided to European women in childbirth.

It was best for expectant mothers to make the journey early, rather than await the first signals of labor on a plantation. At Njoenjoer, Anna would have been dependent upon the assistance of the *doekoen baji*, the native midwife. Midwives were few in number in the Kediri district, and Anna, like other Dutch women, had no faith in them whatsoever.[2] To give birth to her first baby, her daughter Catharina (nicknamed

"Toos") she had traveled all the way to the district capital Kediri to be certain of the services of Herman van Buuren, one of the few European doctors in the area, who specialized in childbirth issues.[3] Now she was to have her second child. Fortunately, everything went well on Sunday, April 6, 1890, and after some days recuperating in a Blitar hotel, Anna returned home to Njoenjoer as a proud mother with her infant son "Tony"—Anthony Herman Gerard Fokker in full.

ℭ

Now that the rain season was nearing its end, the intensity of the precipitation lessened by the week. In June the dry eastern monsoon would make Kediri's coffee shrubs bloom, covering the volcano's planted slopes in white flowers that spread an intoxicating sweet smell. Then the red coffee berries would ripen until October, when it would be time to harvest them before the rains returned in November.

In the last quarter of the nineteenth century, coffee growing had boomed in the Dutch East Indies. In Europe coffee had become a popular drink. Growing and trading it was lucrative, since this took place under the protective umbrella of colonial rule. The Netherlands Trading Company (Nederlandsche Handel Maatschappij, or NHM) had obtained a monopoly on exports in 1824. Until recent years growing export crops had been the prerogative of the state, but in 1870 new agricultural laws had come into force that allowed for private farms and plantations. After tea, sugar, and rubber, coffee growing had seen a quick rise since then. The climate on the volcano slopes of eastern Java proved eminently suited for it. In fact, the district around the provincial town of Kediri had effectively become known as "coffee country."

Without exception these coffee farmers were Dutch. Most of them had settled with the support of the NHM, which provided capital and supervised businesses. Coffee plantations were often quite large agricultural estates of 250 to 1,000 acres. Planters obtained land cheaply, under government leasehold contracts for a seventy-five-year term, as the colonial authorities claimed ownership of all the island's nonproductive soil. Annual turnover in such an enterprise would easily run into several hundred thousand guilders (more than $100,000). Planters often had two hundred to three hundred employees working for them, mostly native people.[4]

One such planter was Herman Fokker, descended from a wealthy family of shipowners and merchants from Middelburg in the southwest of Holland. For many generations the Fokkers had worked in the colonial trade. Herman was born on January 26, 1851, as the seventh and youngest child of the merchant and tanner Anthony Herman Gerard Fokker (1809–1874) and his wife Maria van den Broecke. Herman's father Anthony—the combination of first names Anthony Herman Gerard was a family tradition—was then vice president of the Middelburg Chamber of Commerce and a deputy commissioner of the NHM.[5]

Expectations were that Herman would follow in his father's footsteps. But young Herman did not fit well within the small circle of Middelburg's social and business elite. Unlike his brothers, who made careers in law, commerce, and science, he had trouble completing his education and even prided himself in adopting an anti-intellectual attitude. His unruly behavior strained on family relationships considerably, until his father resolved to send Herman to a boarding school in Germany, hoping that foreign experience might bring improvement. It did not work. However, the Fokkers were not the only wealthy family to struggle with such problems. The accepted solution was to encourage an unruly son to leave for the East Indies, in hopes that he would "calm down."

And so Herman boarded one of the ships of the Rotterdamsche Lloyd destined for the Dutch East Indies' capital Batavia (Jakarta), soon after the death of his father on August 27, 1874. There he was met by his senior brother Anthony (born 1842), the secretary of Batavia's Plant and Zoological Garden. Encouraged by his brother, Herman Fokker went to work "in the coffee" as an overseer. While Herman sweated on the plantations, his brother Anthony made a rapid career for himself in the years that followed. On March 18, 1878, Anthony even became a full board member of the "Factorij" in Batavia, the Dutch East Indian branch of the NHM—a very select grouping, which consisted of only two members and a president.[6]

Brother Anthony's new prominent position soon came in handy. In October 1879 their mother, Mary Fokker—van den Broecke, died in Middelburg. Herman now had a substantial inheritance to deploy. In consultation with Anthony, who of course had very good contacts in the colonial administration, the brothers decided that Herman should invest his money in a coffee plantation. Given the high profits they expected, this seemed a sensible decision. It took a while before the brothers had located a suitable site, but on September 29, 1880, Herman Fokker acquired a leasehold on about 500 acres on the southern slope of the Kelud. He was not alone there: in all, sixty-four planters were farming around the small provincial town of Wlingi.[7] Njoenjoer, as it was known locally, was situated on a sloping terrain, rising from 1,300 to 1,500 feet in altitude. It was located between the streams of the Semoet and Soeso Rivers, adjacent to the horse track leading from Wlingi to the hamlet of Semen, higher up the Kelud slopes.

ᑫ

The task awaiting Herman on his new property was not an easy one. To begin with, the land had to be cleared and prepared for planting. This meant removing and then burning the existing trees and shrubs. Thereafter, the ground had to be leveled and organized into proper plant beds to obtain a structured plantation in which the coffee seedlings could grow. Not before 1883 was he ready for the first coffee plants to be put into the ground. In three years, he planted 175 acres with as many as 113,567 coffee shrubs. Then patience was called for, because three years were required before a coffee bush would yield enough berries to be harvested.

Meanwhile, the opportunity arose to increase the size of the plantation with another fifty acres in May 1885. After preparations, Herman planted a further 95,441 shrubs in 1888 and 1889 that provided berries by 1891. By Herman's own estimate this resulted in a harvest of more than 30,000 pounds of coffee in 1893, with a market value of about 60,000 guilders (then approximately $24,000) in Batavia. Yet the costs were significant as well: from the beginning of the plantation in 1880 Herman spent 265,385 guilders on Njoenjoer, partly on an expensive Lidgerwood pulping machine that turned out a complete disappointment.[8] Moreover, the 1888 and 1889 plantings suffered considerably from the dreaded coffee leaf disease, a fungus that devastated entire harvests on Java and against which virtually nothing could be done with the knowledge of the day.[9]

In his first years at Njoenjoer, Herman Fokker was more than busy making the place work, but by 1888 things had progressed enough that he dared leave his plantation temporarily in the care of the garden superintendent he had hired a year and a half before. On January 13 he embarked in Semarang on the steamer *Prince Alexander* of the Netherlands Indies Steamship Company, destined for Batavia. Exactly two weeks later, he left from there for the Netherlands, onboard the *Samarang* of the Rotterdamsche Lloyd. His intent was to return with a bride to keep him company in the remote planter's house. In 1888 a Dutch woman on a Javan plantation was still fairly uncommon. Most coffee farmers looked for affection closer to home and lived in concubinage with native women.[10]

Yet Herman Fokker had searched for love within his own family circle. In late February he set foot on Dutch soil in Rotterdam and was engaged forthwith with his twenty-two-year-old cousin Anna Diemont, sixteen years his junior. It was an arrangement that had been proposed by letter and that suited both parties. The links between the Fokker and Diemont families went back for generations. Three months previous to Herman's arrival, Anna's mother had passed away, and now she only had her older brother August left as next of kin. Her father, a theologian and preacher in the Walloon Reformed Church in Arnhem, had died in October 1884. Herman and Anna exchanged their initial vows on March 18. The wedding ceremony itself was held in Arnhem eleven days later. On March 31, local newspapers carried a brief message of gratitude that Mr. and Mrs. Fokker-Diemont wished to thank their friends and relatives "for the evidence of interest experienced in their marriage."[11]

The young couple took three months to get used to each other before Herman embarked in Amsterdam on June 23 aboard the *Princess Marie* for his return trip to the Dutch East Indies. For his young bride, this journey took too long. Prompted by family members who had preceded her, Anna chose the comfort of the boat train that ran along the French coast, and she joined Herman onboard in Marseille.[12] Four weeks later they put in at Tandjung Priok, the Batavia port. They were met by Herman's brother Anthony and his wife, Susanne, who offered them several weeks of hospitality in their spacious Batavian villa, overlooking the central square opposite the palace of the governor-general. Not before late August 1888 did the couple finally arrive at Njoenjoer. It was there, in the simple planter's house with its wide galleries and its wide cantilevered roof that Herman had built, that their marriage took shape.

Colonial roots: Anna Fokker-Diemont and Herman Fokker with their children Toos (blurry and barely visible, front left) and Tony (in front of his mother), house staff, and their Dutch overseer on the veranda of their house at the Njoenjoer coffee plantation, Java, Netherlands East Indies, 1892. **COLLECTION SMEULERS, BRONKHORST, THE NETHERLANDS**

֍

For Tony and his sister Toos, their early years on Njoenjoer were a source of fond memories. In the small circle of the plantation the two children of *tuan* and *nonja*, mister and missus, held an exceptional position, constantly guarded by their caring *babu*, the native nurse. Little by little they expanded their territory, from the dark interior of the planter's house with its plastered bamboo walls to the shaded galleries around it. In their "outdoor living area," father had his own recliner, mother her rocking chair. The dining table was outside as well. Well apart from the house stood the kitchen, full of smells and sounds, where the staff prepared meals. On the forecourt Tony and Toos played between the drying beds for the coffee berries and the "establishment," the workshop that housed the coffee peeling machinery. When the machine was not working, as happened intermittently, native women sorted and picked the coffee berries and bit them open with their teeth to rid the beans of their skin. Before long the barns and the nursery for coffee and cocoa plants also became part of their world. The stable was one of their favorite spots; here the Fokkers kept two riding horses, a few cows and calves, chickens, ducks, and even a monkey named Kees.[13] A bit farther

9

away, on the edge of the yard, stood a watermill, powered by a drainage pipe that Herman Fokker had linked to the Soeso River. It also served as a bathhouse. The yard's little fountain with its pointed red roof, a remarkable detail that Anna captured in a delicate oil painting she made of Njoenjoer in June 1892, also operated from the water pipe.[14] On the other side of the house, about 160 feet up the hill, the overseer's house was located, and near it the kampong where Njoenjoer's workers lived. Beyond that point the coffee gardens stretched, with high and low coffee shrubs interspersed by cocoa plants. High above this, specially planted shade trees rose with their bare trunks. To little Tony this was the most wonderful place he could possibly imagine: "it was like paradise."[15]

Life on Njoenjoer was less carefree, however, for Herman and Anna. Owing to leaf disease, to which the "Java" coffee variety that Herman had planted was particularly susceptible, the coffee harvests from 1888 were disappointing.[16] In the disaster year 1890, the entire harvest on Java collapsed because of this blight, plunging by 80 percent. The next two years were better, but in 1893 the harvest dropped again, this time by 61 percent.[17] Meanwhile, local competition increased rapidly. Every year brought new plantations, bringing pressure on prices.[18] In 1893 a kilo of coffee fetched 13 percent less than the year before.

Herman Fokker regarded these developments with growing concern. He reacted by putting excessive demands on his workforce, for which he was publicly scolded in the regional newspaper.[19] But unlike most other members of the Kediri Agriculture Society, he was not completely dependent on the income from the plantation. On many long evenings Herman and Anna sat on their veranda discussing what to do. Amid the typical sounds of the tropical night that seeped in through the matted windows, Tony and Toos heard the seriousness in their parents' voices. They thought that mom and dad were worrying about the options for their education. This was not so. In April 1893 Herman asked his brother Anthony to have the NHM send an appraiser to bid on Njoenjoer. He himself believed that the plantation, in which he had invested a major part of his inheritance and so much of his work effort, would be worth around 175,000 guilders ($70,000). But although the appraiser acknowledged that Herman had done his utmost to make the plantation a success, he did not see fit to exceed an evaluation of 150,000 guilders ($60,000).[20] That was way short of what Herman wanted, and the result was that no sale materialized. Herman then tried selling the property privately, placing an ad for Njoenjoer in the *Locomotief*, Semarang's trade and advertising newspaper, in December 1893.[21]

Meanwhile, the decision to leave had been taken. Because they were financially independent, Herman and Anna could afford to depart, even without selling the plantation. Moreover, Herman's brother Anthony, his powerful mentor in Batavia, was also due to leave for the Netherlands with his family in May 1894. Given the circumstances, it did not seem to be a good idea to remain in Wlingi, hoping for better times. After four months of almost continuous rain that came with storm winds heavy enough to cause trees to be uprooted, berries thrashed, and the harvest again threatened, Herman and Anna Fokker left for the Netherlands with their two children at the beginning of the dry season of 1894. Furniture and household goods were, as was the colonial custom, auctioned off to interested parties.

Yet the sale of the plantation itself still did not come about. For several years after his departure, Herman continued to be listed as the entrepreneur and administrator of Njoenjoer. Meanwhile, he tried to find a buyer in the Netherlands. It took him until March 1896 before he finally agreed to an offer, but the 160,000 guilders he now hoped to get still did not materialize. A group of eleven Dutch investors from The Hague, revolving around the affluent Evers family and united in the 's-Gravenhaagsche Koffie Cultuur Maatschappij (the Hague Coffee Culture Company) that had been founded six months before, eventually paid him 120,000 guilders ($48,000) for the plantation.[22] That, incidently, was also Njoenjoer's 1897 tax value. One Philip Evers, son of the main founder of the Coffee Culture Company, became the new planter.[23] Even then things did not go well at Njoenjoer. In 1898 the plantation was no longer listed in the *Government Almanac*. That year several leasehold operators pulled out of the Wlingi district altogether. The eruption of the Kelud volcano in May 1901 destroyed what was left of the plantation. By 1911 the estate had become run down and almost overtaken by wilderness.[24]

ᛢ

The Fokkers' 1894 journey from Wlingi to Batavia was a quite a trip. The first stage brought them to Malang by carriage, a distance of about forty miles. From there a train service ran to Surabaya, where they boarded a steamer for Batavia. A day later the Fokkers reached Batavia's port Tandjung Priok. On May 16 they embarked on the steamship *Van Diemen*, a freighter with passenger accommodation of the Royal Packet Company, that brought them to Singapore, the first stop on the long voyage to Holland. From the railing of the ship's sail-shaded stern, they watched the tropical Dutch East Indies recede and slowly become smaller. But if the adults viewed the scene with mixed feelings, for Tony the world aboard the mail ship with its pounding engines was just another big adventure. The journey left him with a lasting fascination for boating and ships.

NAARDEN, HOLLAND
MARCH 1918

The first day of a fresh army recruit started with waiting and idleness. From half past eight in the morning until three in the afternoon, the new conscripts bided their time in an exercise of obedience and patience. At last Tony Fokker was assigned to the ninth company of the Second Regiment of Fortress Artillery at Naarden, about fifteen miles southeast of Amsterdam. The journey from Haarlem to the Naarden-Bussem rail station was by train. From there the fortress was half an hour's march. Tony used the opportunity to get on a friendly footing with his sergeant by offering him a handful of expensive cigars that he had brought on purpose—to which the sergeant proved "most susceptible," Tony wrote in a letter to his mother.[1] Once in Naarden, the recruits were fed first. After that the troops were aligned in the parade ground in front of the Promers barracks and addressed by the commanding officer. Then they were dismissed to the quartermaster, where everyone was issued the customary dark blue tunics, white pants, blue cap, and dark greatcoat of the fortress artillery. A short-sticked shovel and a handful of personal items completed the gear. Tony found his fork, spoon, and mess tin all equally greasy and dirty. Only the food itself—potatoes with beans and meat—proved passable and even "most edible."[2]

The barracks themselves gave Tony a shock. The Naarden fortress, inhabited by 630 soldiers and a hundred officers and situated under more than eight feet of earth, represented a completely foreign, hectic world. Once past the gate with its fierce-looking lions that held the royal coat of arms, "Je maintiendrai," a long, dark vaulted corridor led away from civilian existence. In the bomb-free brick passageway every footstep echoed. The corridor divided the complex in two. There was a cold draft. Here privacy did not exist.

Tony was given one of the fifty-six low wooden sleeping bunks in one of the barracks' six dormitory caverns, and introduced to his "sleeping mate" on the bed next to his. As a mere soldier, his own private space was no larger than a section of planking attached to the wall at the far end of the dormitory—and the "rock hard straw bag" that formed his bed.[3] In the middle of the dormitories, bare wooden soldiers' tables stood, with planks to sit on attached to the legs. Chairs were provided only in the sick bay. There was a single, stinking communal toilet and wash facility for the whole garrison. Only the officers had better accommodations, meaning they had their own chairs to sit on.

Tony found these circumstances very difficult. He longed for home. Discouraged by the spartan conditions, he tried to file for a medical discharge that same day. But in "the small cubicle all the way in the back in the dark" of the sick bay, where the military physician examined him, his "skewed leg" was given no attention whatsoever.[4] The doctor barely listened to his complaint of having uneven legs. Undeterred, Tony inquired about the opportunity to have a second examination later that week. His request was summarily dismissed. A soldier's existence was proving to be nothing like the protected civilian life in Haarlem that he had just left.

⸙

Haarlem, twelve miles west of Amsterdam, was a city beloved by returning colonials. Since their arrival in 1894 it had been the residence of the Fokkers. In June of that year, Herman, Anna, Toos, and Tony had finally set foot in Holland after a sea voyage of about five weeks from Batavia. With the years of hard work in the tropics behind him, Herman Fokker now found time for his cigar, good company, and a game of billiards. But for the children Haarlem was a strange, cold world they did not know and did not understand. For Tony the move meant "leaving everything behind."[5] He and Toos had trouble feeling themselves at home in their new surroundings. The children acted withdrawn and behaved shyly.

In many respects the Dutch city on the Spaarne River was the opposite of Njoenjoer and Wlingi. Its streets were paved and narrow, and its high stone houses made Tony and Toos feel small. Only the trees and the grass of the Haarlemmerhout park, on the outskirts of the city, reminded them of Java's lush greenery. Luckily, the Fokkers passed their first summer in a hotel along the Haarlemmerhout, because the house that Herman had bought was not yet ready when they first arrived.[6] The Hotel Widow van den Berg was the final stop of the horse-drawn tram from the station. It had been built in 1889 at the most beautiful spot in the park, with a big fountain in front and overlooking a deer pen. Widow van den Berg also had modern amenities such as private balconies for each room. For that reason it was especially popular among summer guests.[7]

The quiet environment of the Haarlemmerhout helped the children adjust. Then, on August 1, Herman registered himself and his family as the new residents of Kleine Houtweg number 41 (now 65), just outside the city center.[8] Number 41, a typical Dutch townhouse of the period, had few features that stood out. It was about twenty-five feet wide and forty feet deep, located on the edge of the old town. Initially it had been designed as a somewhat stately town mansion, but in the course of construction it had been divided into two residences that essentially mirrored each other. It overlooked the Frederiks Park, a view of which Herman soon became fond.

ℱ

For little Tony, moving to Haarlem was not easy. In contrast to the house on Njoenjoer, where the inside and outside interlaced and where the children had their own foal that moved in and out of the house like the dog did, the doors at Kleine Houtweg were usually closed. The building did not even have a front yard. Visitors were shown straight into a small vestibule that doubled as a hallway, or into the adjacent antechamber. A door with decorated glass panes gave access from the vestibule to a narrow corridor that split the house in two. The left side held the antechamber, the basement entrance, and the kitchen and pantry, primarily intended for the small house staff. On the right side of the corridor was the living room, with en suite dining. From there double doors led to a hundred-foot-deep garden where the children could play with the sheepdog Max. Between the hallway and the dining room was a niche containing a toilet and built-in stairs that led to the second floor. At the top one entered a small, somewhat dark landing that gave access to three bedrooms, a guest room, a bathroom, and—luxurious for the time—a second toilet. Behind a closed door on the landing a second staircase led to the attic. The attic's rear included three small bedrooms for the kitchen help and two maids. Their chambers were separated by a walkway from the spacious storage room in the front.[9] For a modest-sized family such as the Fokkers it was a large house, equipped with such modern conveniences as a bathroom with running water. Yet none of this appealed to little Tony. He later remembered the house and garden as constricted. The Dutch climate did not help. For the first time in their lives, the children had the strange experience of snow.

What Haarlem had in abundance was water. A mere 650 feet from the house was the canal that separated the old city from the new expansion where the Fokkers lived. On the quays at the weigh house and along the Spaarne River, ships moored daily to load and unload. Few were seagoing vessels; most ships were inland barges and other freight carrying vessels rigged with sails. But for young Tony, water and ships exerted an irresistible attraction.

The same could not be said of school. At the nearby elementary school Tony proved himself a mediocre student. In his own words, "School and I didn't agree at all. Active, high-spirited, full of inventive ideas with a practical turn to them, I found study a boring routine, monotonous in the extreme, something which the teachers did little to make more interesting. Herman Fokker's little boy, Tony, soon became a byword and a hissing to the irritated pedagogues. . . . It has since seemed to me that most of the teachers showed a lack of imagination and of any real teaching ability when they attempted to force a square peg into a round hole."[10] Despite his ingenious methods for spying, about which he boasted in his autobiography, he invariably ended at the bottom of his class, yet only had one year in which he was not promoted to the next grade.

At home the storage room in the attic was Tony's preferred spot. Here he built his own little world, which gradually took shape from all sorts of loose objects that he gathered. He was a creative child, with a special gift for tinkering. Before long the floor of the attic was filled with miniature rail tracks constructed from tiny strips of metal. He ran self-built toy trains on these with his friends, and later undertook experiments with electricity, miniature steam engines, and Bunsen burners that ran on gas he illegally tapped from a pipe that ran to their neighbors' house. Tony also showed prospects as a tradesman; his mother preserved an early "bill" from the "Electro-Technical Bureau Fokker & Co." for the total amount of 40 cents, charged for soldering caps on some lead piping.[11] The water also beckoned, although his father refused to buy him the small boat he longed for. Undaunted, at twelve years of age Tony managed to build his own small canoe in the attic storage room. Herman Fokker, who encouraged his son's tinkering activities from time to time, was sufficiently impressed to have the canoe hoisted out the attic window and brought to a nearby wharf to seal the vessel's planks and have it painted.

Ქ

No matter how much agony Tony suffered in primary school, his years of secondary education proved worse. In the summer of 1903 his father registered him at the municipal Higher Civilian School (HBS), which offered a five-year program. The school had a good reputation, and Tony had to pass an exam to get in. To the relief of his parents, he was accepted. From September 1903 until December 1908 a good part of his life took place within the high walls of this institution. The school was located on a square just behind Haarlem's city hall, a mere ten minutes' walk from Tony's house. It was an imposing building, with hollow-sounding corridors and classrooms high enough to enable an amphitheater arrangement in the biology and the physics rooms so that pupils had a better view of demonstrations and tests. Since the school's founding in 1864, the number of pupils had risen considerably. When Tony began classes, about two hundred students were enrolled, which resulted in a lack of space and classrooms. To address the problem several adjacent houses were added to the school building, creating further organizational discomforts. Some classes, such as drawing and arts, were taught in former living rooms, garden rooms, bedrooms, and the like that could be reached only through a maze of passageways and stairs that were never built for the number of persons using them. Such classes seemed at the end of the world, as a former pupil later remarked. Eventually a second school building was opened in a nearby converted gas factory in September 1907. But overall the facilities remained substandard throughout.

Tony Fokker was an unmotivated student, and his results showed it. Although he was conditionally promoted after his first year, he ended that year failing in no less than six subjects: geography, history, Dutch, German, French, and even draftsmanship.[12]

The school principal, Hotse Brongersma, resolved to sit him in the first bench in every class so that his teachers would be able to keep an eye on him. More often than teachers later cared to remember, he was disciplined because of pranks and even suspended for several days—which was much to Tony's liking as it provided him with extra time to spend on his various hobbies.[13] There was nothing he liked better than playing hooky, and he was seldom in search of excuses to do so, honoring the adage high on the wall in his biology class: "Knowledge means much. Character means more." In a commemorative issue of the school paper, published on the occasion of the school's sixtieth anniversary, he recounted how he would hide out until the concierge was back from his rounds to report absentees; then Tony would reappear, panting and pretending to be out of breath, his hands oily from the chain of his bicycle that had supposedly broken, begging to be stricken from the absentee list and allowed to rejoin his class. If the concierge allowed this, Tony would quietly escape to spend his day on the Spaarne River.[14] More than once he had to report to "the boss," Brongersma—an "old and grey gentleman" who ruled the school with dignity.[15] Once Brongersma summoned him on the customary free Wednesday afternoon; Tony daringly protested "that I didn't understand why the headmaster would sacrifice his own free afternoon to rob me of mine, thus punishing himself without having committed any wrongdoing, which I found completely illogical . . . an argument that he found so right that he released me on the spot."[16] Such occasions were, of course, exceptional. He would have to repeat his fourth year as well, after showing a report card with no less than ten subjects in which he had failed. In his autobiography he noted, "History and languages—I couldn't have cared less. Speech practice I found gruesome."[17]

In the end gymnastics was the only subject in which Tony demonstrated real talent. For geometry and physics his grades were passable, but only just. Yet in algebra, chemistry, mechanics, history, and modern languages he came nowhere near passing.[18] Pranks were more his thing: stink bombs, shooting pellets. As results did not improve, father and son Fokker threw in the towel at Christmas 1908, at the end of a disastrous first semester of his second year in the fourth grade (the equivalent of an American student's freshman year).[19]

ᖆ

Tony was glad to close the school doors behind him. As he put it, "I've learned all that I can."[20] Instead he focused on his big hobby, water sports: rowing his skiff, sailing his small *dory* class sailboat, which required great concentration to avoid capsizing. For his boundless enthusiasm he had already been elected second commissioner of Haarlem's Rowing and Sailing Club at the annual meeting on February 22, 1908. Contemporaries called him a daring sailor. At the Amsterdam *dory* races "Fokkie," as he was fondly called at the club, won several prizes.[21] Water was his big passion, and there was no risk he would not dare to prove it. Once he connected a long plank to the roof of the boathouse and laughingly rode his bicycle over it into the Spaarne. Spectators cheered as he reemerged and swam ashore with his bike in hand.[22]

On dry land the attic remained his domain. Here he pondered various experiments and in the process developed a new interest: aviation. In 1909 aviation was still a new phenomenon that was conquering Europe rapidly. Spectators flocked by the hundreds of thousands to spectacular air meets, even if they had to travel for days to get there. The newspapers were full of the latest events and achievements. On June 27 the very first airplane took off from Dutch soil. Boys dreamed of an exciting career as an aviator. Soon Tony was among those who wished to learn all about flight. Technical knowledge about aviation, however, then existed only in the heads of less than a thousand people worldwide, and it remained inaccessible to a nineteen-year-old school dropout without qualifications. Yet Tony paired a creative mind with a keenness that was way above average, working with what information that did reach him to expand his understanding of the phenomenon of flight. He tried to gain some firsthand knowledge of aerodynamics. From celluloid he cut small basic airplane-shaped models and launched them from the attic window. He constructed representations of the steering mechanisms of planes that he had read about and had seen photographs of in newspapers.[23]

He also embarked on an engineering adventure with his friend and classmate Frits Cremer, another unruly spirit who shared a history of bad behavior and came from an affluent family.[24] Herman Fokker's means, however, could hardly compare to those of Jacob Cremer, Frits's father, who had been chairman of the board of the NHM and of the Deli Company, which traded in colonial goods such as tin, tobacco, and other commodities, and who had also been the nation's Minister for Colonial Affairs. The Cremers lived in an enormous mansion on their private estate outside Haarlem, Duin en Kruidberg. Jacob had the house and grounds specially built and furnished to meet his every demand as a millionaire.

It was there that the two young friends embarked upon the development of an idea that had been in the back of Tony's mind for some time: a car tire that would minimize the risks of springing a leak. Frits was ideally suited as a partner in such a venture. The Cremers possessed two automobiles, and Jacob had no objection to lending his aging 1904 Peugeot Type 66 to the boys for their experiments. In the garage of Duin en Kruidberg, the boys had plenty of room to tinker to their hearts' content. Air-filled rubber tires were prone to puncture on the badly paved roads of the day. The solution that Tony and Frits tried to develop was a steel shackle belt that would be attached to the wheels by a system of springs and torsion rods. This effort might be classified as a form of "reverse engineering": going back to the massive wheels that had been used on carriages and coaches, with modifications. The garage space and the project budget had to come from Jacob Cremer, yet Tony's father Herman was prepared to file the patent application on May 24, 1909.[25] In the meantime Tony and Frits had the time of their lives trying to make the old Peugeot go as fast as it possibly could. They practiced alongside the railroad tracks, the car's leather sides taut in the wind, trying to keep up with the fast train into Amsterdam, and had themselves photographed as racing drivers, standing next to the vehicle.[26] For over half a year the boys tinkered away at the Peugeot before the project ran aground. They found that a patent similar to theirs had already been filed in France.[27]

The disappointment over the car tire was only the beginning of bad news. In December 1909 Tony and Frits were called up for military service, a distinctly unappealing prospect for the pair. They attempted to simulate flat feet at their medical examinations, but both young men were found to be physically fit.[28] Tony was drafted in March 1910, and for him there was no option but to obey. The Cremers were in a much better position to dodge the draft. Jacob Cremer launched an appeal, and on his father's instructions Frits left on a world tour with his older brother Marnix and a distant cousin. For a year Tony and Frits were almost completely out of touch with each other. When Tony reported for duty at the Naarden barracks, his friend was dancing at the Penang Golf Club in Malaysia. Indeed, Frits's departure had been so unexpected and quick that the two friends hardly had time to say their goodbyes. Frits wrote to his father from Malta to inquire what had become of the automobile tire scheme.[29] Until December 1910 Jacob Cremer remained involved in proceedings to exempt his "frail son" from military service.[30]

¶

Naarden itself, a small fortress town with about four thousand inhabitants, surrounded by earth walls and moats, was a bitter disappointment for Tony. Centuries of occupation by rotating garrisons had left its traces in the streets. Although the town was one of the key strongholds in the water defenses southeast of Amsterdam, contemporary photographs show it to have been in poor repair. Within the town's high earth walls, both the bigger and smaller houses were built low to shield them from gunfire. On many houses the brickwork showed traces of soot and of humidity. Window frames and doors were in need of a fresh layer of paint. Only the main street, with the town hall and church, was presentable. The "murderous" steam tram that ran from Amsterdam to Laren passed through the street to the Utrecht gate. Except for military movements—guns and supplies being moved around—this practically summarized all traffic there was in Naarden. For a city lad from Haarlem, the small garrison town was less than boring: it was "a hole to hang yourself."[31] Unlike his fellow conscripts, Tony hardly appeared to notice the pub-like recreational facility that stood next to the parade ground in front of the Promers barracks.

Weeks went by with the usual drills and exercises for the new recruits, weeks in which Tony did his utmost to get noticed in a negative way by falling out of step as often as he dared. Although his grades for gymnastics had been the highest on his report cards at school, he now pretended not to be able to run because of his flat feet.[32] The coincidence that he had caught a bad cold and thus coughed continually worked to his advantage. He was sent to the sick bay to recuperate, a recovery that was encouraged by confining patients to a strict diet of bread and milk. Yet Tony persevered in his act. His performance was convincing enough for the doctor to send him

Tinkering with an automobile: In 1909 this was Tony Fokker's favorite way to spend the day. To stay abreast of punctured tires, Tony and his friends "reverse engineered" a wheel with a steel shackle belt, attached by a system of springs and torsion rods. The goal was to make the customary bicycle pump superfluous. **FOKKER HERITAGE TRUST, HUINS, THE NETHERLANDS**

to the Naarden military hospital for examination. Although conditions there were a step up from those in sick bay—the hospital wards had real beds instead of wooden bunks, and there was a table with chairs for recuperating soldiers who were allowed out of bed—the diet of milk, water, and rice did not agree at all with Tony. He begged his mother, "Please send me some butter and cookies and *lots* of sugar (dark brown and white) and some sausages in *a tin*? A little money please ± 2,50."[33]

Getting an early discharge proved difficult, however. The military doctor took hardly any notice of Tony's complaints and prescribed strict bed rest, plus weekend detention. He was not allowed off the hospital premises and was confined to its enclosed garden even on Sundays, which he feared would be "boring to death." His subsequent plea to be allowed to visit his sister in Amsterdam for a couple of hours was grudgingly granted, and he was allowed to visit his sister on a Monday evening.[34]

That visit proved a prelude to a speedy return to civilian life. When he jumped off a moving tram in Amsterdam, he lost his balance and fell, badly bruising his ankle on the curb.[35] The immediate result was that he was taken to the Amsterdam military hospital, where all they gave him were wet bandages.[36] Again he was prescribed bed rest. The game lasted for two more weeks, while Tony complained in whining letters to his mother that the charade was taking up the time he had planned to spend on reequipping his sailboat. "My chocolate powder is all gone now and the sugar too," he wrote to his mother. "Please send, or better bring a whole lot, the sooner the better. I am completely out of things. I gave the guy who inspects the postal parcels a cup of my *choc*, although he is not allowed to take this. Sic! I'm really not splashing it about, but the cups here are really big and the bread is barely buttered and dry."

Mama also sent him money. Tony needed little encouragement to use that to further his early release, promising his ward sergeant twenty-five Dutch guilders—about twice a man's weekly wages then—to help him obtain a discharge. His letter continued:

> *Help of your ward sergeant is worth its weight in gold. To remain good friends with him is really a prerequisite, because if such a man is against you, there is no escaping. I've promised him 25 guilders if he gets me a discharge. (A boy from another ward has done the same in similar circumstances). It looks like a lot at first sight, doesn't it, but don't forget what you're gaining with this and his help is the main cause that things are going so quickly for me (well quickly for here, that is, mind you). He is ward sergeant and assistant to the doctor in all operations, hence makes good money, so you can't send him off with a small bribe. Anyways, I'll be cheaper off here than in Naarden. Patience alone is now the cue.*[37]

The money would prove well spent for Tony. The financial massage helped procure his medical discharge. It was the first time money enabled him to wriggle out of commitments, and it was a lesson that would stay with him. Dreaming of a career as an aviator, he returned home in the automobile his parents gave him for his twentieth birthday.

MAINZ, GERMANY
JULY 1910

The decision had been his father's, and Tony found it terrible. School in Germany sounded like a expulsion order. Nonetheless, Herman had stood his ground and ordained that it was time that his son should finally learn a trade. As he himself had attended a boarding school in Germany, this was where Tony ought to follow. To ease the suffering at least a little, Herman had agreed that Tony's friend and neighbor Tom Reinhold could accompany him in his search for lodging. In the last week of July the boys took a train from Haarlem, Holland, to Cologne, Germany, where they looked around under an overcast sky full of rain clouds and then finally boarded the river steamer to Mainz.

In his autobiography Fokker noted, "The thought of going away to school frightened me to death. Feeling very much as if I was leaving for the end of the world . . . I don't remember when I ever was so discouraged."[1] To a boy for whom the Dutch North Sea coast between the villages of Katwijk in the west and Domburg in the southwest of the country had hitherto represented the far ends of the familiar world, Germany was an unknown country where people spoke a language he barely understood. The Rhineland dialect with which people greeted him sounded nothing like the German he had learned at his Haarlem high school. Everything was different in Germany: the landscape with its mountains and river valleys, the cities and villages with their unfamiliar architecture, the culture of beer and wine. Even the food had an unusual taste. Tony developed a lifelong preference for Dutch cookery. What had driven his father to send him here, where he was so much left to fend for himself? Of the river journey and the beautiful landscape along the Rhine, he later remembered little other than that he had felt more dejected with each mile covered.

G

July 1910 had turned out to be an overcast, wet, and cool summer month. It had been two months since Tony had come back from the Naarden fortress to live with his parents in Haarlem. Life suited him fine, tinkering in the attic storage room, playing with Max the dog, or sailing with old friends on the Spaarne River. But what was to him a perfectly enjoyable way to bide the time was agony for his parents. Day after day they saw young Tony in complete idleness: without a school diploma, without work, and without much purpose in life. Even his mother, who had secretly entertained hopes that Tony might somehow end up at the Delft Polytechnic, was at the end of her wits. Matters were made worse when other family members started to ask questions about young Tony, or tried to interfere: "The whole family began concentrating intensely upon my career, except me. I hadn't thought much about it, and resisted their efforts."[2]

Meanwhile, Tony himself had more or less decided he wanted to become an aviator. He just lacked the courage to tell his parents about it. The idea had grown on him since January 1909, when he had visited the eighth edition of the annual Brussels Automobile Show with his father. He had been fixated by the three Belgian airplanes that were on display there amid the automobiles: the machine of Jean de Crawhez, Pierre de Caters's triplane, and Adhemar de la Hault's *orthoptère*—a peculiar apparatus that its inventor hoped could fly by simulating the wing movements of a bird.[3] Flying: that was what he wanted! He would have preferred to have been allowed to depart for France immediately upon his return from military service, to attend the flying school of airplane constructor Antoinette in Châlons-en-Champagne near Reims, the center of the French aeronautical effort. There young daredevils were instructed in the art of flight—for a hefty price.

Tony later complained that "I received no encouragement from my parents. They viewed flying as most people did at the time, as the shortest way to the cemetery."[4] Indeed, the life expectancy of pilots was limited in those days and could be counted in months rather than years. Herman Fokker flatly refused to contribute to an adventure that would inevitably lead to his son's death. Between father and son many a difficult hour passed discussing Tony's future, without any resolution in sight. In June Herman's patience ran out; he insisted that Tony should go to Germany and learn a trade, no matter what. After considering the episode of tinkering with the Cremers' old Peugeot, Herman believed that Tony should be trained in automobile technology. A decision had to be forced, he thought, because "I did not tolerate him around the house as a loafer."[5] In the end father and son agreed that Tony would be registered for a course in automobile technology at the Technikum in Bingen, some twenty miles west of Mainz.

G

The Rheinisches Technikum was housed in an imposing four-story building on the outskirts of Bingen, between the vineyards along the Rhine and the Klopp Castle. It had been founded in 1897 as a private college for the sons of the well-to-do and was renowned in and beyond Germany for its training in electrotechnology and mechanical engineering. In 1910 as many as three-quarters of the school's pupils came from abroad.[6]

Herman Fokker was satisfied with the education he had selected for his son: did not electricity and things mechanical precisely match Tony's activities in the attic? Besides, the Fokkers had friends living in Bingen—the Koning family—who could help Tony get settled and might offer him advice and assistance if necessary.

But when Tony arrived in Bingen on July 30, his first impression of the school building made his heart sink. The Technikum was even larger and more imposing than his school in Haarlem, where he had felt so miserable. Was this really where he had to register? It looked as if there were no other option. Yet his father had not enlisted Tony for the Technikum itself, but for a chauffeurs' course associated with it—a private initiative of the school director, Hermann Hoepke. His registering for the chauffeurs' course had everything to do with the fact that Tony did not possess a high school diploma. Contrary to the Technikum itself, the chauffeuring course required no prior qualifications, and whereas the school itself possessed several automobiles, the chauffeurs' course was only sparsely equipped. To Tony the whole setup looked like a swindle to exploit young people's wishes to learn to drive and maintain a car. A short walk around the premises was enough to convince him that this situation was not for him. He wrote to his mother:

> In the afternoon we had a look around in the chauffeurs' school, a small square garage with two automobiles, 1 rickety 4-cyl, and one 1-cyl, beyond that an assortment of old iron, cars of at least ten years old, not in driving condition and without tires. Everything listed in the prospectus is inflated in such a way that I am astounded. There was just a single turning lathe the size of a sewing machine, no forge. . . . The whole prospectus is humbug and it would be throwing good money away to attend. . . . One only learns here how to drive, plus what's required for the government driver's license. . . . Anyway, we are not going to the chauffers' course, it's a waste of money. Pity I am here now.[7]

However, Tony and his friend Tom Reinhold, who had accompanied him to the school, dared not tell director Hoepke what they thought of the chauffeurs' course, and so Tony signed up for it. Afterward he left it to his parents to write to the principal and ask to have his registration papers back, "as there has been a change of plans. . . . If he doesn't agree by any chance, he can whistle for his money anyway, as he cannot exercise control over a minor in Holland who does not have the legal power to sign a contact, so the whole thing will be void anyhow."[8] Herman's acquaintance in Bingen, Mr. Koning, came up with an alternative. He directed the boys to a similar school in Mainz, the Erste Deutsche Automobil-Fachschule (First German Automobile Trade School). Since January 1907 this had been an independent branch of the Technikum in Aschaffenburg. The two friends took the train to Mainz, where they were met in the adjacent locality of Zahlbach by the school's director Rudolf Kempf. Tony was immediately impressed: "much better [than] Bingen . . . better known . . . has a much better reputation."[9]

The drivers' course of the Automobile Trade School had begun in November 1904. Since then more than a thousand candidates had received their training there. The school was supported by the larger German automobile manufacturers and had been authorized to issue driving licenses in May 1910. Initially the trade school's activities had focused on mechanical engineering courses for the automobile industry, but in the latter years the side curriculum of the driving school had taken off. The course took no longer than four weeks. Every first or fifteenth of the month, new entrants were welcomed to start the course, which consisted primarily of an introduction to the automobile engine and to the car's various mechanical and body parts. Cars in those days were prone to failure, and owners had to be able to make their own repairs on the spot.

The trade school had also started a course for owners of powered boats in April 1907, and in October 1909 a third course was added on aeronautical technology. This was advertised as the Fachschule für Flugwesen (Aeronautical Trade School). Like the other specialized courses, the Aeronautical Trade School was very much a hands-on affair: in the school's workshop the participants joined in the construction of a genuine airplane. In May 1910 the school went one step further and advertised that it would offer flight instruction as well. This pilots' course had as its broadly phrased aim "to offer future professional pilots, future engineers and airplane constructors the opportunity to get acquainted with the design and construction of the airplane."[10] A course of four to six weeks was considered sufficient for this objective. Compared to the training courses offered in France, the tuition was modest: 500 marks (about $120). According to Fokker's autobiography, the actual costs for the course were double that amount, as students were required to provide an equivalent security deposit. Although the total investment was thus considerable, it was nonetheless an amount that Herman Fokker might be willing to pay for his son's fascination with flight. How to proceed from there was a matter to be decided at a future moment. Meanwhile, this opportunity was the chance of a lifetime.

⸸

It took some imagination to recognize more than the driving school in the assorted sheds and buildings near the former Carl Ludwig Marx paint factory in Zahlbach, just outside Mainz, of which the Aeronautical Trade School was a subsidiary. The basic training consisted of driving around the school grounds with a "propeller vehicle," a contraption that was powered by an airplane engine. But there was more: in October 1909 the first group of trade school students had started on the construction of an airplane. Soon they discovered that the grounds at Zahlbach were not big enough for maneuvering the machine, let alone taking off. In April the school had therefore erected a wooden shed at the army parade ground of Dotzheim near the village of Nieder Walluf, just across the Rhine outside Wiesbaden. The Dotzheim terrain measured 1,600 by 1,400 yards—big enough even to fly, which of course was the final goal. On July 21, 1910, the commander of the Wiesbaden garrison officially agreed to the use of the parade ground.[11] So Tony Fokker had arrived just at the right moment.

He was excited: this was just what he wanted. Nonetheless, he took care not to show his eagerness to his parents, nor report on the school's aeronautical curriculum, lest they would put a sudden stop to his participation. He wrote to his mother, "The only thing left for me to do now, is go home and then decide whether I shall go to the Technikum or to the Trade School in Mainz, which will begin in October."[12] In anticipation of his parents' answer to this question, Tony and Tom waited in Mainz and Wiesbaden for a few days before collecting the answering letter in Rüdesheim, across the Rhine near Bingen. It turned out that Herman Fokker had agreed to the change of plans, and in early October Tony Fokker signed up as one of the twenty-three students who had taken the course in aeronautics since 1909.[13]

In the meantime, part of the aeronautics course had moved from Zahlbach to the shed at the Dotzheim parade ground in August 1910. The trade school's one and only genuine airplane, a Farman biplane with a pusher engine, was hauled through the streets of Zahlbach and Mainz the day after the city had been featured as a staging post for the First German Overland Flight from Frankfurt to Mannheim. The shed at Dotzheim was thereafter identified by the rather inflated name of "Fliegerhalle" (Pilots' Hall). Subsequent taxi trials at the parade ground soon proved that the only airplane engine that the trade school possessed would not be powerful enough to get the plane off the ground. Moving across the field at some speed was all it was capable of. In other words, the machine was too heavy, although a project was already under way to construct a lighter version of the Farman. The man to coordinate the effort was Bruno Büchner, the Aeronautical Trade School's recently appointed teacher.

Although he was an engineer, cyclist, and racing driver, Büchner did not yet possess a flying license. But he could nonetheless boast of some experience in aeronautics. He professed to have taken lessons in France at Louis Blériot's flying school and then to have worked at the Anzani airplane engine factory. Büchner had also been involved in experiments at Berlin's showcase Johannisthal airfield and at Bork near Magdeburg, after earlier successes in speed contests and in repairs of vehicles.[14]

Even before classes started, Tony found out that Büchner and a second trade school teacher had plans to travel to Paris with their seven students to visit the second International Aeronautical Salon at the Grand Palais from October 15 to November 2. Tony immediately sent a letter to his father begging to be allowed to join the outing. The 150 marks that this would cost were, he wrote, "not too much and not too little. However, I have been unable to save this amount from my monthly allowance and would therefore like to be sponsored as it is for my study."[15] He offered to combine the return journey with a visit to his parents in Haarlem, hoping to convince them of the sound reasons for his preference to go into aviation. Not an easy task, as a skeptical Herman had lost patience with his unruly son by now. On a specially inserted page, Tony begged his mother, "Speak well for me. I shall come home no matter what, even if I have to pay for it myself. But if coming home is really absolutely unwanted for keeping the peace or something like that, then write me as soon as possible and I will go back to Mainz from Paris with the rest. . . . Write me back *as soon as possible* or send me a telegram (. . .) OK—if all is well and I can go *and* come home, *half*—if no payment will follow, but I can come home, *not*—if I should *not come home*, but proceed to Paris on my own expenses."[16] To Tony's intense frustration, Herman refused even to consider the plan, and in the end Tony was forced to cancel the whole trip for lack of funds.

Despite his initial enthusiasm, the trade school's aeronautical curriculum turned out not to be quite what Tony had expected when it started, after a week's delay, on October 24, 1910. With its duration of only six weeks, the training was short even by the standards of the day. Nonetheless, it formed Tony's introduction to the coveted status of aviator. His plans had evolved in the months that had passed. Initially he had only aspired to acquire knowledge of how to build a plane, but after coming to Dotzheim he now hoped to learn to fly one. Knowledge was his first priority now.

The training at the trade school consisted of a theoretical introduction in the classroom in Zahlbach, where students were familiarized with the basics of construction theory, followed by a practical sequence at the workshop in Dotzheim. The first four weeks were primarily spent in the classroom, learning about engines, electrotechnology, propellers and their construction, and airplane design. After that barely two weeks remained for actual practice, which was largely spent working on the lightweight version of the Farman biplane. Together with his six fellow students, Tony labored on the construction challenge. The idea was that the new machine would receive an engine that would power a pulling rather than pushing propeller.[17] But would it be possible to fly with this new airplane? The course was scheduled to end by mid-December, so there was not much time to find out. A stronger engine would improve the chances of achieving flight, but such engines were expensive. Purchasing costs ran into the thousands of marks. Fortunately, one of Tony's fellow students managed to locate an airplane engine that had more horsepower than the first one. It thus appeared that the project could proceed.

On November 5, however, less than two weeks after the start of Tony's course, the trade school received bad news: the military garrison issued instructions that all flying activity would henceforth be prohibited within a radius of six miles from the fortress of Mainz. This sudden move was instigated by the recent discovery of the potential of aviation—and of aeronautical espionage—by the German military. It appeared that their interest would preclude any flying by the trade school students at Dotzheim. Moreover, the decree singled out foreign pilots especially. Although the school's director, Rudolf Kempf, was offered the chance to finish the ongoing course, the end of the school's aeronautical training was now suddenly in sight.

Of course this decree dominated the talk of the day among the students, who believed their chances of becoming aviators were evaporating. A sense of urgency pervaded. All the students' muscle and effort were put to work getting the lightweight biplane ready for flight before the decree's deadline. Thanks to the stronger engine, the new airplane indeed left the ground. Its pilot Bruno Büchner, however, who was to obtain the fifty-third German pilot's license on February 3, 1911, did not dare risk anything beyond a short hop into the air. The plane came down with a bang, badly damaging the machine. Perhaps the effort to reduce weight had compromised the plane's structural rigidity.[18] But since the primary goal of the trade school was to provide know-how and experience in airplane construction, this crack-up did not seem as disastrous to the school as it must have to the students. Tony was bitterly disappointed. In his autobiography he would inflate the story of Büchner's flight to an utter failure that resulted in the complete loss of the machine, but perhaps his tears were real: "All I could say was, 'It is terrible,' and sniffle. . . . I was thinking only of myself, and those letters I had written my father."[19]

In the meantime a third plane remained unfinished. This was a simple monoplane based on the practical knowledge that the students had gained in Dotzheim. One less wing meant a considerable savings in weight. Possibly the trade school's engine would be strong enough to allow such a machine to fly. Contrary to the school's earlier planes, there was no design to follow for this monoplane, and it was developed on the basis of ideas that emerged on the spot. Tony Fokker, the group's most eager participant, provided quite a few ideas himself. And although his notions were instinctive rather than based on actual know-how, they did turn out to be useful. He soon came to believe that in fact the entire design of the monoplane was his.

ꟼ

On December 20, after the course had been completed, director Kempf formally received the written orders banning further flights. For the Aeronautical Trade School, which relied for a substantial part of its revenue on students from abroad, the decree came as a severe blow. All flying activity around Mainz came to a halt. Although Kempf entertained the idea of moving the aeronautical section of the trade school elsewhere, instructor Büchner packed his bags to continue his career with the firm Aviatik in Berlin.[20]

Tony saw his chances of learning to fly going up in smoke. Yet he refused to give up his dreams. Frustrated, he claimed his security deposit back from Kempf, now that he would be unable to complete the course and obtain a flying license.[21] For him there was no plan B. Meanwhile, his fellow student Franz von Daum, a retired first lieutenant in the German army from Breslau, came up with a remarkable plan to buy the half-ready monoplane from the trade school and move it to a different location where the machine might be finished. Although in his fifties, Von Daum was intent on learning to fly and was willing to spend serious money. It was an attractive proposition for the school, given that it was unlikely to be able to continue its aeronautical activities in Mainz. Nevertheless, Von Daum operated with caution: a junior partner willing to risk his neck in the adventure would certainly be an asset. This became the basis for an unlikely bond between the former professional soldier Franz von Daum and the draft dodger Anthony Fokker.

It was a bond to their mutual advantage. For Von Daum the investment in the monoplane was a relatively cheap way to attain his goal, now that the Aeronautical Trade School seemed as good as dead. In his young and eager assistant he saw a keen helping hand, willing to take risks. For Tony, the offer from the affluent retired officer was a gift from heaven. He almost could not believe his luck. The matter did require another begging letter to his father, as Von Daum wanted some financial input from his partner. To Tony's surprise, Herman Fokker, perhaps glad that his son had finally found a cause worth fighting for, made a thousand marks available without making a fuss. Tony used this money, together with the deposit that had been returned to him and whatever means he had saved from his allowance, to invest in his share of the partnership. The fact that neither he nor Von Daum possessed any technological know-how beyond the short course they had just completed did not appear to be a major issue. The monoplane was already partly finished; Von Daum and Tony ordered the missing parts from a woodworker in Wiesbaden.[22]

Awaiting further developments regarding the no-fly zone around Mainz, Von Daum managed to obtain temporary permission to continue using the Dotzheim parade ground and the Pilots' Hall. But the two partners soon had to admit that their project exceeded their technical competence. They therefore engaged Jacob Goedecker, an engineer who had acted as a construction consultant with the trade school.[23] Eight years older than Tony, Goedecker was a mechanical engineering graduate of Aachen University, where he had studied with professor Hugo Junkers. Junkers, in his turn, had undertaken various tests and projects with his Aachen colleague Hans Reissner, among them the design of new wing constructions for airplanes. After finishing his degree at Aachen, Goedecker had started working on a plane of his own in an empty shipyard in the village of Nieder Walluf some six miles to the west of Dotzheim, in August 1909. By April 1910 Goedecker's project had proceeded far enough to have the machine transferred to the parade ground of Grossen Sand in Gonsenheim, just outside Mainz on the other side of the Rhine, where the plane could be tested. There was also ample space for an aircraft shed. Although Goedecker had initially limited himself to taxiing the plane across the field, he saw his pilot Paul Lange take his *Taube* (Dove) into the air before the month was out. From then on Goedecker's shed carried the large white lettering, "Flugmaschinen Werke" (Airplane Works). Construction was not limited to Goedecker's own designs; it also included work for others. The deal with Von Daum and Fokker was that Goedecker would help them in constructing the monoplane, in return for which

Tony would act as Goedecker's demonstration and test pilot once he had his flying license.[24]

For the time being Von Daum and Fokker's main concern was to get their plane ready for flight. This proved far from simple. They had ordered various parts from different suppliers: from local woodworkers, from Goedecker, and from the carriage factory of Georg Kruck in Wiesbaden. Fitting and assembly posed problems. They also still faced the issue of finding an alternative airfield outside the Mainz area. If Tony, a foreigner, was to fly the plane, it had to be relocated. Even Gonsenheim was too close. Von Daum remembered that air meets had been held in Baden-Baden in June and July. On the occasion of the Iffezheimer Rennwoche (Iffezheim Race Week), the airfield of Baden-Oos had welcomed the ultimate wonder of German aeronautical technology: the enormous airship Zeppelin LZ-6. The Deutsche Luftschiffahrts-Aktiengesellschaft (DELAG: the German Airship Service Ltd.) had established one of its operational bases at Baden-Oos. However, the LZ-6 had been lost on September 14, 1910, going up in smoke as the result of a fuel accident in the airship hangar. It meant the field's enormous shed now stood empty.

The two pioneers sought shelter there. Without mentioning his junior partner, Von Daum wrote to Baden-Baden's mayor, Reinhold Fieser, known as a fierce supporter of aeronautics, asking for permission to use the airship hangar as a temporary base to test his monoplane. The matter was, he wrote, somewhat urgent, and he hinted that he had several offers from other airfields willing to welcome him. Hence he needed a decision forthwith.[25] On December 9 Von Daum came to Baden-Baden to meet with Fieser. He said it was his intention "to initiate trial flights, strictly for sports purposes, from the city airfield with the flying machine he himself had built, possibly as early as the next week."[26] Fieser had no objections and was even prepared to negotiate with DELAG for a cheap lease of the airship hangar on behalf of Von Daum for an initial period of four weeks, if this could put Baden-Baden on the aeronautical map again. On December 19 the two partners took up lodgings in the luxurious pension Landhaus Rösch in the Schützenstrasse on the outskirts of Baden-Baden, near the airfield. Von Daum liked to be comfortable. The next day he and Tony descended to the facilities at Baden-Oos.[27] There the plane that Von Daum had transported in parts from Mainz lay waiting for them to be reassembled. Von Daum estimated that this work would take about four weeks. He hoped they would be able to start within the next few days.[28]

Not before the end of January 1911 was everything more or less ready for the first test flight. Left to their own resources, it had taken the two partners longer than expected to assemble their flying machine. Several specially ordered parts had also been late in delivery. In the meantime Tony and Von Daum discussed the unknown options for controlling and steering the machine while still on the ground. Beyond that there was the question of how to control the machine in flight. Like most early planes, their machine had no means of directional control other than wing warping.

The coveted status of aviator: Anthony (in the rear) with a passenger on his second *Spider* plane at the Grossen Sand in Gonsenheim near Mainz, Germany, in the spring of 1911. The *Spider* did not have brakes, and assistants had to hold the plane before takeoff. **FOKKER HERITAGE TRUST, HUINS, THE NETHERLANDS**

Tony, who like Von Daum regarded the monoplane as his own, dismissed any reservations his partner expressed, professing to be more than willing to take the risk of flying it. In trials he managed to make several short hops into the air, some as long as a hundred feet. It made him ecstatic: the machine could actually fly! In three months' time he had progressed from a complete novice to the coveted status of aviator—and this on a machine that had incorporated ideas of his own.

There soon was a price to be paid for this rapid success. For weeks Tony exerted himself, sweating away in the cold, drafty airship hangar. Countless times he and Von Daum swung the engine into life, after which the plane would start to move by itself, with Tony chasing it on foot, gasping to catch up and climb onto the moving machine. On top of these efforts he braved wintry weather while racing across the field on top of the plane at a speed of some forty to fifty miles per hour. On February 3, 1911, Tony was forced to take the train home to his parents in Haarlem to recover from a bad case of pneumonia.[29]

Franz von Daum, who regarded the monoplane as *his* and who had thus far furnished most of the money, remained behind in Baden-Baden. Understandably, he took the control stick once Tony was out of sight. His flying adventure, however, ended with a resounding bang when the plane hit "the only tree on the whole airfield"—or so Tony cared to remember years later (the only trees at the Baden-Oos airfield were off the actual landing area). Von Daum informed him of the crash by telegram, after which Tony hastily returned. On February 23 he inspected the wreckage and had to admit that the plane looked beyond repair.[30] Their dreams of flight lay in shatters. The mishap had its effects on the relationship between the two partners, which took a turn for the worse. In a letter to his mother, Tony referred to Von Daum's "generally known stupidity." By necessity the two pioneers moved back to Mainz, where Kempf's continued protests to the military authorities had resulted in the lifting of the restrictions on flying. With other ex-students of the trade school, Karl Schumm from Germany and Arthur Grünberg from Estonia, Tony moved into a small cottage in the woods near Gonsenheim's Grossen Sand: "The three of us live here at the 'Krimm' (Crimea), and it is good to live a bit cheaper again, although the circumstances are fairly bad. . . . The soup tastes like petroleum and there is *spinach* here every day."[31]

In the six weeks that followed—a record, according to Tony's letter—a new and improved machine was constructed in Goedecker's workshop, an activity paid for but shunned by a remorseful Von Daum. By the second week of April the new plane was ready for its first tests. This time Tony managed to stay airborne for several hundred yards, after which his seat on top of the fuselage gave way in a hard landing.

Soon after, the group in the "Crimea" was augmented by a Dutch friend of Tony's whom he knew from the annual holidays on the beach at Katwijk with his parents. Arnhem-born Bernard de Waal and Tony had characters that matched. Both had unruly minds and a history of problems at school.[32] Like Tony, Bernard hoped to learn the aviation trade with Goedecker, who now had plans to open his own flying school at the Grossen Sand that spring. Meanwhile, fine tuning the second Fokker–Von Daum plane took time. Not before early May was the machine ready for its first official test flight. On May 4, 1911, Tony risked the dangerous maneuver of attempting to make a turn. With success he rounded the airfield three times and managed to attain a height of about 150 feet.[33] Twelve days later, around half past seven in the evening of a rainy May 16, Tony felt sure enough of himself to test his skills as a pilot. Before a sizable crowd and two representatives of the Sports Commission of the Deutschen Luftschiffer Verband (German Association of Airshipmen) he steered his *Spider* into the air at the red flag on the airfield that marked the testing stretch for his licensing flight. To qualify he had to make two flights of about three and a half miles each. At a height of 300 feet, completing a pattern of five figure eights was required. To register the flights, the Sports Commission had erected two poles at Grossen Sand, 500 yards apart. Tony was to circle these while making the figure eights. At the final landing he was ecstatic: he could now officially register as an aviator. To celebrate he flew an extra round around the airfield with Von Daum in the passenger seat.[34] On June 7, 1911, he received Germany's pilot's license number 88.

Trying to follow suit, Von Daum was less successful. On May 30 he made a bad landing with the *Spider*, again damaging the plane. While awaiting repairs, Tony went to work for Goedecker as promised and started giving flying lessons. The partnership with Von Daum did not survive the new damage. On June 12 the *Mainzer Anzeiger* carried the news that Fokker would no longer use the Von Daum plane and was to have his own machine built at Goedecker's.[35] He was now earning money as a pilot and therefore wanted to have a machine of his own. Tony seized the opportunity of the latest crash to end the cooperation. Two days before, he had demonstrated his rapidly growing flying confidence as Goedecker's participant in the Deutscher Zuverlässigkeitsflug am Oberrhein (German Reliability Flight in the Higher Rhine Area). He received a silver cup as a prize for his performance.

A few months later Tony also represented Goedecker in the army autumn maneuvers near Mainz, flying Goedecker's *Sturmvogel* (Storm Bird). He attained the participants' highest endurance record by covering a distance of thirty miles in a single day, a feat then considered exceptional. Yet it was the German Goedecker, and not the Dutchman Fokker, who was knighted for the results achieved with the *Sturmvogel*.[36]

HAARLEM, HOLLAND
AUGUST 1911

At the end of the afternoon of August 31, 1911, all of Haarlem's residents were on their feet to witness a unique event. For the annual celebrations of Queen Wilhelmina's birthday, the organizing committee had planned something truly special. Apart from the usual concert, cabaret shows, bicycle races, and a fair that lasted several days, the committee had contracted a flying demonstration from one of its own townsmen, Anthony Fokker. The weather cooperated: it was sunny all day, with hardly a gust of wind. Expectations were running high when the covers of the improvised tent hangar of Fokker's *Spider* were lifted. Anthony, Frits Cremer, and Tom Reinhold stood up from their reclining garden chairs in front of the airplane tent and put out the cigarettes they had been smoking in their guise as cool aviators. Now the machine was moved into the open. Just after half past five, when the bicycle races had ended, Tom Reinhold turned the propeller to start the engine. The plane came to noisy life in a cloud of dirty smoke. After posing for a photo with three members of the organizing committee, Anthony climbed onto the machine in his dark brown sweater, which "looks like the thing has already seen twenty-five years of aeronautical service." He strapped himself onto the airplane seat and put on his gray flying cap and goggles. The public was on its toes not to miss any of the excitement to come. Their patience was tested, because it was two minutes to six before the plane took its starting position in a corner of the improvised airfield and the "all clear" signal was given. Anthony revved the engine and started his takeoff. The photographer who had been waiting to document the event keeled over backward into a wet ditch. Bystanders laughed and cheered.

For a moment it appeared that the plane would not leave the ground, but then Anthony was airborne. At a height of about a hundred feet, he made the *Spider* turn, dived down for a mock landing, and then was off again, disappearing in the direction of the nearby coast. At low altitude he approached Haarlem's "Adriaan" windmill, rounded it, and then descended again in the general direction of the improvised airfield from where he had taken off. He landed his machine. The demonstration had lasted less than seven minutes altogether.[1]

In front of the tent in which the aircraft had been stored, his mother was anxiously waiting to hug him upon his safe return. The public was overjoyed. Those who had found a place near the tent stormed at Anthony to shake his hand and congratulate him on the extraordinary achievement. Afterward the dapper aviator was lifted off the ground, shouldered, and then carried along the grandstand by a group of boy scouts, to be covered in three wreaths: one from the Queen's Day Association, one from the Spaarne River Rowing and Sailing Club, and one from his former tennis friends. Again he had to pose for a photo, which took longer than he cared for. "This is even more exerting than flying," he joked. He was presented with a "flycycle," a bicycle dressed up as a flying machine with a tail of red and white flowers. He tried to ride it but keeled over on the bumpy ground—to the delight of the public. "Too much wind!" he quipped. Asked whether he was going to make a second "altitude flight," the young aviator professed that he wanted to, but only after the engine had been checked first, because he was not satisfied with the way it had run.

But by half past six everything was back in order, and a second flight could be attempted. This time Anthony managed to get his plane up to a height of about 330 feet, where he turned another few circles for a couple of minutes, trailing a cloud of dark smoke from burned oil. He managed another landing. After that, Anthony walked off with the announcement, "Gentlemen, the show is over." The journalist from the local newspaper covering the event, who had been to other flying displays before, was most impressed by the young pilot's sense of calm resolve.[2]

¶

The driving force behind this spectacular initiative was Herman Fokker, now proud of his son's aeronautical achievements despite his earlier skepticism. As a member of the organizing committee, he had convinced his colleagues of the soundness of contracting his son's flying display, pricey though it was. On August 23, Fokker's *Spider* had arrived by train from Mainz to be taken to the fairgrounds at 't Huis ter Spijt. Tony's friends Tom and Frits had traveled along with the machine to help assemble it.[3] Their task was not an easy one. In Haarlem none of the members of the organizing committee had any experience with aviation. It was only with considerable trouble that Tom and Frits had managed to convince them that the terrain selected for the flights, measuring about thirty by ninety yards, was too small. The meadow was also surrounded by ditches. But the most dangerous obstacles were the covered grandstand and a series of flagpoles that were part of the festive preparations. It took quite a bit of persuasion to make the organizers agree that removing them was necessary for the terrain to be used for flying. Finally the organizers agreed to fill in the ditches at both ends of the meadow and create a longer runway. Several of the flagpoles were also removed. Costs for the event were in danger of getting out of hand.

During all of these adjustments, the young pilot contracted to perform the flights, Anthony Fokker, remained absent. He still had some flights to perform under his contract with Goedecker in Mainz and only arrived in Haarlem the following week. Not before Wednesday evening, August 30, were the three friends done and the machine deemed ready for its first test flight. The *Haarlems Dagblat* reported that

> At the aerodrome Fokker tinkers with his engine around seven in the evening. He has said more than once that he is not yet ready to fly, but has the engine started all the same. The machine bumps, lurches across the terrain to the edge with the shed. There he turns the plane again toward the field. It appears a few flagpoles beside the hangar might hinder the machine in its course. They are quickly pulled out of the ground. The blades of the propeller make another few irregular turns and then the unsteady sounds make way for the reverberating and strong rattle of the engine. From the corner with the shed the machine speeds away across the field toward Klever Lane. Then it is off the ground and floats across the street.[4]

Happy shouts blew across the field. Anthony circled the improvised airfield twice, then made a few figure-eight turns. Three minutes and a hair-raising landing later, the *Spider* was back on the ground again. Anthony wiped the sweat off his forehead. His handmade four-cogged brake had held.[5]

The climax of the flying displays followed on Friday evening, September 1, the day after Queen's Day. Around 6:50 p.m. Anthony was back in the air. This time he dared venture farther away from the improvised field, and his plane reached an altitude of about 1,200 feet above the city. In a wide curve he approached the market square and rounded the tower of the St. Bavo church—to the thrill of the Haarlemmers who again flocked to see their local hero in flight. More than satisfied with the attention and praise, he got into a white automobile decked with purple hyacinths and drove off to his parents' house.[6] That evening Anthony was the guest of honor at a dinner party in the Hotel Roozen, paid for by the organizing committee.

Buoyed by the success of his earlier flights, he staged a third and even a fourth demonstration flight the next day. The fair emptied out on the sound of the *Spider's* engine. Spectators witnessed Anthony putting both hands into the air to demonstrate how easy it was to fly his plane. For his final flight he passed low over the Spaarne Rowing and Sailing Club and over his parents' house. Upon landing, spectators and officials again ran to congratulate him. The praise appeared to flow endlessly. Weeks after the event, journalists were still writing about it. "I had not thought," Fokker later confessed to a reporter, "that I would leave this place without having ended up in a Haarlem ditch with my plane. I must be more skilled than I thought." In his autobiography he commented, "I will always remember this reception as the biggest satisfaction I ever got out of aviation. For me it remains the high point of my life."[7]

ᴦ

The *Spider* that Anthony used in Haarlem was already his third plane. It had only been ready from early August. Its construction had evolved from the monoplane built at the Aeronautical Trade School the previous year. Anthony simplified the construction of the metal frame under the wings that acted as a support for the plane's bracing wires. The new design used the trapezoid-shaped support of the landing gear to connect the many cables. On top of the wings the triangular construction of the metal "bracing towers," from which the airplane derived its name and which acted to increase its rigidity, had also been simplified. Now all the wires connected in a single metal support mounted on top of the fuselage. The arrangement was an attempt to reduce the risk of structural failure and was one of the important simplifications that distinguished Fokker's planes from those built by Goedecker under his own name.

The new version of the *Spider* also did away with wing warping for making turns and used a tail rudder for steering. The position and sweepback of the wings was also different from the two earlier examples. The new *Spider* had dihedral wings: the tips were higher than the wing root, which lowered the aircraft's point of gravity and improved stability, albeit at the cost losing some of its maneuverability.[8] Anthony also strengthened the machine's tail. Only the fuselage had largely remained the same. This consisted of two wooden beams held together by metal crossbars. On top of this a four-cylinder engine was bolted, with a simple seat for the pilot behind it. The aircraft had no bottom: the pilot—who wore a small compass strapped to his thigh—could see the ground between his legs.

Anthony's third *Spider* was still powered by the only aeroengine that he possessed. The fact that it could be mounted on the new plane was a small miracle in itself, given that Von Daum had crashed twice with the machine in February and June. By sheer luck the engine had remained intact, although the propeller had been broken and had to be replaced. After the second crash Franz von Daum, lucky to walk away without serious injuries, had decided he had done enough flying to last him a lifetime. He had allowed Anthony to buy him out of the project for a mere 1,200 marks (then approximately $285)—money that again came from Herman Fokker, who by the end had invested a grand total of about 183,000 marks (about $43,000) in his son's aeronautical adventure.[9]

After Von Daum's second crash, a new machine had to be built at short notice. Anthony lacked the time and the staff to undertake the job on his own. Eager to show himself as a hometown boy made good, he had immediately accepted the invitation from the Haarlem committee.[10] With Goedecker's people he now spent long hours constructing the new *Spider*. This also seemed the logical moment to incorporate the various changes and improvements that he had come up with so far. He himself referred to the new machine as "Type B." The plane had to be ready to fly by mid-August at the latest, but so far things were not going the way he wanted—not at all. Anthony was anxious and impatient. Several parts made from molded aluminum were delivered late, retarding the construction process even further. Deferrals in arrangements with Goedecker also delayed matters.[11] Anthony coped by keeping busy. In the first weeks of August he made twenty-seven flights in Goedecker's *Sturmvogel*.

Meanwhile, the day of his planned departure to Holland was getting near. Therefore Anthony was pleased when his friends Tom Reinhold and Frits Cremer, the latter back from a trip around the world, showed up in Mainz. Both were keen to learn to fly the *Spider*. Frits even posed as Anthony's first customer and "ordered" a plane for himself. As usual Frits relayed the bill for this expensive gesture to his father. By now the final construction of the machine required haste, since no more than two weeks remained until the contracted demonstration in Haarlem. Oblivious of the construction problems Anthony was facing in Mainz, the organizing committee expected him to honor the contract. It had financially guaranteed the rail transport of the plane, insured it, and was now finishing preparations of the airfield. The schedule was tight, but the new *Spider* was indeed finished in the nick of time.

ℭ

With his successful hometown demonstration, Anthony had struck a sympathetic chord with his father. The "secure and elegant" flights surpassed Herman Fokker's wildest expectations.[12] As a token of his appreciation, he gave his son an expensive silver pocket watch with a commemorative inscription, but what counted even more for Anthony was the promise of continued financial support—to a maximum amount of 50,000 guilders ($20,000), no less.[13] All the same, he was glad to be able to earn something extra piloting Goedecker's plane. Thus he boarded a train back to Mainz from Holland on September 5 so that he could be Goedecker's participant in the autumn maneuvers of Germany's 18th Army, scheduled to be held between Mainz and Diez starting September 16. Anthony not only needed the money this would bring, but he also craved the attention of the press, which would surely bring him requests for further demonstrations. He badly needed contracts, as money tended to slip through his fingers like sand. On September 14, Frits had wrecked the reassembled *Spider* in a curve that turned out too low. Frits was lucky he was able to tell the tale, because the plane itself had been reduced to smithereens. This meant that, three months after the latest Von Daum crash, yet another machine had to be built. Between August and December Anthony was forced to use about 11,000 guilders ($4,400) of his father's credit.[14]

Meanwhile, participating in the army maneuvers was no easy task. It required expert navigation, which was his weak point. The weather did not help. Flying the Goedecker *Sturmvogel* on the afternoon of September 18, he encountered an unexpected strong headwind on his way to Diez and had to return to Mainz. But at a quarter to six he was ready for a second try. At a height of 2,500 feet he crossed the Rhine,

The first crash: In the early evening of October 5, 1911, disaster struck. Upon Tony's landing at Gonsenheim, a gust of wind caught the *Spider* and caused a crash. He sent his mother this photo card summarizing the damage. The two parallel lines at the center bottom indicate where Tony hit the ground. His health insurance immediately revoked his policy. **FOKKER HERITAGE TRUST, HUINS, THE NETHERLANDS**

to be caught in headwinds again an hour later. The receding light and a rising fog made it impossible for him to locate the Diez airfield, and he had to make an emergency landing in a recently harvested wheat field near the village of Lohrheim, some three miles south of Diez, to ask utterly surprised and excited locals for directions. With the dusk settling, there was not enough daylight time left to fly the remaining stretch, and he was obliged to spend the night with friendly farmers before continuing to Diez the next morning.[15] Fortunately for him, his flying hours were paid for, because by late September even the key to his money box had broken from excessive use.[16]

Anthony's fiscal pressures also had consequences for his relationship with Goedecker. Although they got along fine personally, financial and technological disagreements were on the rise. It bothered Anthony that he was under contract to relinquish one-third of his earnings to Goedecker. It had also become evident that Goedecker was prioritizing the work on his own designs over the construction of the new *Spider* for Frits Cremer. Maintaining business relations with Goedecker also meant that all sorts of things had to be documented on paper. In October and November alone, this requirement involved over a hundred pages of correspondence, Anthony wrote in despair to his father. With his limited knowledge of the German language, he hated having to put things in writing. Under the circumstances he was struggling to find the time to fly.[17]

Perhaps his reduced flying schedule was for the best, because he hurt his knee when he crashed his *Spider* on October 5. In fact, he was lucky that he had not been killed outright. Upon landing at 5:40 p.m., his plane was caught by a gust of wind and blown over sideways. The *Spider* somersaulted, and both wings broke off. The engine stuck in the ground, and the tail folded forward over the bent and cracked fuselage. Anthony himself was ripped free from the seat he had tied himself to and smacked into the sparse grass of the Grossen Sand. To everyone's surprise, he had not broken any bones. With a sense of youthful immortality, he sent his mother a picture postcard, indicating where he had lain amid the wreckage.[18]

The young flyer was fortunate to have suffered no more than a sore knee. His health insurance company thought so too, and immediately annulled his coverage. As notorious damage claimants, aviators were no longer welcome as customers.[19] To make matters worse, yet another *Spider* now had to be ordered from Goedecker.

Nonetheless, Anthony's activities were beginning to draw attention from the German aeronautical press. The journal *Luftsport* (Air Sports) repeatedly wrote about his flights for Goedecker and about his own remarkable plane. On Grossen Sand he was accosted by Georg Gischel, the representative of the Dixie Aeronautical and Nautical Engine Company. Gischel advised him to think about moving to Berlin and offered his company's support in the process. It fit Anthony's plans perfectly, as he had been harboring doubts about his continuing cooperation with Goedecker, now that their diverging interests were beginning to show more clearly. And although Jacob Goe-decker argued that he saw no reason for Fokker to move, and Anthony himself felt that "saying is easy, following it up rather less so," he and Frits Cremer boarded the night train for Berlin on November 29, 1911, for a reconnaissance mission.[20] Berlin, in the center of German aviation, might offer a breakthrough for a young foreign pilot. Suddenly, setting up shop for a small enterprise of his own loomed on the horizon.

BERLIN, GERMANY
MAY 1912

Finally it was the turn of Lt. Willy von Schlichting of the Railway Battalion. All afternoon he had been waiting for his chance to go up into the air as a passenger. Yet it was hardly flying weather that Saturday, May 25. Rain clouds hung low over Berlin, and there was quite a bit of wind. Nonetheless, demonstrating aviator Anthony Fokker needed extra income and thus took his chances. Payment was by the minute, and there was a lot of money to be made. The director of the Johannisthal Airfield, Georg von Tschudi, had set aside no less than 40,000 marks in prize money for the Johannisthaler Frühjahrsflugwoche (Johannisthal Spring Flying Week) that was to be held May 24–31, 1912.[1]

The signs for the event had been bad. The day before, Johannisthal's twenty-seven pilots, united in the Bund Deutscher Flugzeugführer (Alliance of German Aeronauts), had taken the unprecedented step of going on strike. The surprising action was directed against Von Tschudi's refusal to appoint an airfield physician to provide first aid in the case of a crash, which happened frequently. Von Tschudi found such a functionary wholly superfluous: in his view, the aviators flew at their own peril, or at least at somebody else's risk, and therefore ought to look after themselves. That Friday, the opening day of the event, matters between him and the pilots had come to a head. Witnessed by a great number of grumbling spectators who had arrived expecting to see the performance of the latest planes and the popular heroes who flew them, the pilots had flatly refused to take off unless they were promised the services of an airfield doctor. It was the first strike in the short history of aviation, and Anthony Fokker took part in it, having previously registered to fly two of his machines in the Spring Flying Week. When the airmen threatened to remain on the ground the next day too, Von Tschudi had given in, pressured by a public that was sympathetic to the pilots' demands and ready to demand their money back. Starting Sunday, May 26, a military doctor would henceforth be on standby at Johannisthal to tend to pilots in need of first aid.[2]

Reassured by Von Tschudi's promise, Anthony had started flying that Saturday with a journalist from the *Berliner Lokalanzeiger* as his passenger. Over the Tempelhof exercise grounds they had been caught by "colossal rainstorms" and had become quite wet. Undaunted, Tony had dared undertake a second flight, this time with an Italian officer who expressed an interest in his machine because of Fokker's claim that his plane could even fly under adverse wind conditions.

Now the rainclouds hung low over Johannisthal. While other aviators took care to put their machines in shelter, and the public on the grandstand began to make for home, Willy von Schlichting followed Anthony's instructions and carefully positioned himself in the forward seat on top of the plane. With a take-off run of about forty yards, the *Spider* went up in the air. Fokker later recalled:

> Before I knew it I was back at 400 meters, where we floated like on the surface of a smooth mirror. Suddenly I hear a metal sound and I see that one of the wing's bracing wires has snapped and is hanging down. But the wing construction is so strong that it did not break, despite the broken wire. I descended slowly and saw the wing veer up and down in the winds. I asked Lieutenant Von Schlichting to put his foot on the wing's forward beam for security, something he did not manage to do for long as he was frightened apparently. I was still lowering the plane and still thought that I could put it down safely when at 10 to 15 meters above the ground a heavy gust of wind hit the wing and broke it. I saw the machine collapse, yet I remained inside the fuselage and braced myself with my legs on the rudder; my passenger, however, stood up at the very last moment. A second later the plane was lying on its side with the engine half buried into the ground, the wings folded up like a harmonica, and its bodywork on its side.[3]

Anthony was thrown from the wreckage; Von Schlichting was not so lucky. He landed under the machine and was killed instantly. With a terrible crash Anthony hit the ground, where he remained prostrate with a wound to his head and a half-collapsed lung. Spectators soon surrounded him, hurrying near to witness the disaster at close range. Again he had his good fortune with him, although the airfield doctor was still a day away. After some four minutes, he came to. He asked the people around him, "I am unhurt; where is my passenger? Is he wounded? I want to see the plane!" But bystanders held him back, telling him that Von Schlichting had only suffered minor injuries. It was the next day before anyone dared tell him the truth of his passenger's demise. Anthony was brought by car to the house of Lt. A. B. C. von Bose, a Dutch friend who had appeared at Johannisthal with his wife only a month before to take flying lessons with Fokker. At Von Bose's he remained prostrate and in bed all the next day, suffering from a minor concussion, several broken ribs, internal bleeding, and pain all over his body. But already on Monday there was no holding him back any longer: he just had to go to the airfield. A journalist from the *Berliner Zeitung* was more than happy to show the spot of the crash, where his plane had remained since Saturday with a splintered propeller, a crushed fuselage, and a broken right wing. Only the tail was virtually undamaged.[4] The event clearly stuck with Anthony; eighteen years later, the minutes before the crash were still imprinted in his memory. He told his biographer, Bruce Gould, that the episode was the worst experience he had gone through in his entire flying career.[5]

G

Because everyone agreed that Fokker was not to blame for the accident, he was able to return to flying before long. But the Spring Flying Week and its potential revenues were lost for him: the crash meant that he ended second to last in the field of participants, with a total flight time of only one hour and ten minutes. The winner of the event, the Russian Vsevolod Abramovitsj on his Wright machine, totaled thirteen hours and twenty minutes.[6] He pocketed 4,244 marks for this achievement. German contestant Willy Rosenstein made over 6,000 marks that week, but there was a special bonus awarded for German pilots. By comparison, Anthony's 203 marks and 67 pfennig was a mere handout.[7]

Two weeks later, on Sunday morning, June 9, Fokker had recovered enough to be present at the start of the Berlin to Vienna air race. Three German and three Austrian pilots competed for the honor and prize money. As a foreigner, he was not allowed to enter, but he nonetheless managed to catch the eyes of the fifty to sixty thousand spectators who had come to witness the takeoff at Johannisthal in the early hours of the morning. Around six o'clock he flew one of the other three *Spiders* that had recently been delivered to him, making figure eights in an extremely low-flying maneuver over the airfield. The crowds cheered enthusiastically: he was back![8]

Since his decision back in November to make a dramatic new start in Berlin, half a year had passed. The remarkable plane on which he had been officially granted patent rights on January 26, 1912, attracted attention, and Anthony proved himself to be a demonstration pilot ready to go to every extreme.[9] Within a short time the name Fokker became synonymous for spectacular stunt work—the very thing Johannisthal was renowned for and which drew crowds from the city.

The airfield had opened its gates for the first time in September 1909 and had been conceived, like most early flying centers in Europe, as a commercial air racing venture. The Flug- und Sportplatz GmbH Berlin-Johannisthal (Air and Sports Ground Berlin-Johannisthal Ltd.) had shareholders and a board that signed for the organization of the various public events staged there. The field measured approximately 500 by 1000 yards. At its corners wooden pylons indicated the boundaries of the flight trajectory. Between the grassy middle section, where the landings and takeoffs took place, and the wooden grandstands around it, a wide sandy expanse had been kept free over which the planes made their rounds. In races the aviators

Stunt pilot: In December 1911 Tony launched his flying business in Berlin, the center of German aviation. Initially he tried to make a name for himself by giving spectacular flying demonstrations. The Johannisthal air shows drew hundreds of thousands of spectators each year. The pilots received part of the visitor fees.
FOKKER HERITAGE TRUST, HUINS, THE NETHERLANDS

would fly the circuit around the pylons. In a central "targeting house," their rounds and flying times were clocked and registered with the aid of a specially designed machine. Aviators or constructors received a share in the proceeds according to the number of minutes they stayed in the air. Such a share could easily amount to thousands of marks, depending on the event itself.

Johannisthal, home to more than twenty German aircraft constructors that had their own workshops there, welcomed hundreds of thousands of visitors, an annual turnover that ran into the millions.[10] On racing days the normally quiet suburb would change into a cauldron of tens of thousands of people flocking from Berlin and other parts of Germany, eagerly anticipating a spectacle. From the center of the city, the eleven-mile journey out to the southeastern suburb took about fifteen minutes by train. From the station, the public then had to walk another fifteen minutes to get to the airfield. Tickets came in several categories: the more expensive ones cost one mark and provided access to the seated, covered grandstands and to the restaurant; the cheaper ones cost thirty pfennig for the 100 thousand nonseated places along the flight track.

Anthony, Frits Cremer, and Bernard de Waal initially planned to set up shop in Johannisthal and offer flight instruction there. They relied on the cooperation of the Dixie Engine Company, from whom Fokker rented hangar space. For the necessary technical support, Anthony brought along one of Goedecker's mechanics, August Nischwitz. He hired him on a six-month contract for a weekly wage of thirty-five marks.[11] Operating a flying school made good business sense. It meant that the Fokker airplanes would be more likely to find customers, as freshly licensed pilots usually ordered a plane of the make they had learned to fly. A number of companies had their base at Johannisthal. Setting up a flying school was easy in those days: permits did not yet exist, and pilots-to-be learned at their own risk. Flight training was expensive and easily cost 3,000 marks, plus another 1,000 as collateral in case the machine was damaged or destroyed in the instruction process.[12] The latter risk was considerable and exceeded the 1,000 marks limit, which explains why Fokker had to earn extra money with flying displays to keep his business afloat.

For the time being he was the only one of the four who could provide instruction, as he alone had a flying license. Bernard de Waal was practicing, as was Frits Cremer, whom Anthony did not encourage, because "he cannot get the hang of landing. He is not sensitive enough and doesn't have the lifestyle to keep his nerves and body in proper shape."[13] Indeed, flying implied risks well understood by Fokker, who saw one of his new friends crash to his death that very month; Anthony dropped flowers from his airplane at the funeral on February 19. Hence the arrival of a second licensed pilot toward the end of the month was good news. Holland's very first aviator, twenty-five-year-old Jan Hilgers, had been looking for a job in aviation since his Dutch employer, Verwey & Lugard had folded in The Hague in December. Anthony felt an instinctive connection with the new arrival. Like himself, pilot and technician

Hilgers had been born in the Dutch East Indies, in Probolingo on Java in December 1886. Hilgers was hired as a constructor, draftsman, and pilot and quickly became Fokker's "first assistant."[14]

Anthony understood very well that as a new arrival at Johannisthal he would require spectacle to make a name for himself. In December and January the German trade journal *Flugsport* reported that he had made quite an impression with his first flying display on December 27, 1911, when he had demonstrated the maneuverability of his plane despite its unusual design.[15] On Sunday, February 4, he defied the freezing cold and made a five-mile flight to the Grosser Müggelsee lake outside Berlin. There he managed to land on the frozen surface. Skaters and pedestrians strolling on the ice cheered as he took off for his return flight. Two weeks later, on February 19, he attempted to break the German altitude record, without success. His plane did not climb above 7,200 feet, but at least he got his name in the papers.[16]

His flights were also noticed in business circles. Two Berlin investors, Erich Schmidt-Choné and Adolph Borchard, contacted Anthony with an ambitious proposal for a serious investment in Fokker aircraft. It was almost too good to be true—which in fact it was. Still inexperienced in the world of finance, Anthony was easily convinced that their promise of 100,000 marks to launch a full-fledged Fokker company was firm. He readily signed a contract in which he relinquished his patent rights for his automatically stable monoplane, as well as the control of his company-to-be. In exchange the bankers promised him 20,000 marks in short-term credit to set up a company. Thus it came to be that Schmidt-Choné and Borchard, and not Anthony Fokker, signed the founding documents of Fokker Aviatik GmbH (Fokker Aviation Ltd.) on February 6, 1912. Borchard was listed as director.[17]

Fokker's risky business was now officially registered at the Chamber of Commerce in Berlin-Charlottenburg under number 10360. The ties with Dixie Motors were severed. The Chamber of Commerce papers identified Fokker Aviatik as located in Johannisthal's shed number 10 at the Alte Startplatz (Old takeoff grounds)—one of the sixteen companies located there. The name on the new sign read "Fokker Aeroplanbau" (Fokker Airplane Construction) to distinguish the new upstart from its competitor Aviatik that was already located at the airfield. Initially, the activities of Fokker Aeroplanbau were limited to the assembly of planes ordered from Goedecker in Mainz, which arrived packed in crates. Altogether some ten to fifteen planes were thus assembled.[18] But there was a catch to the agreement with the investors: the money they had promised for the new company would only be paid when Fokker landed an order from the German military. Anthony hoped he would be able to sell one of his more original concepts: a plane that was easy to assemble and disassemble and could be towed behind a car. Advancing army units would be able to take such a plane with them and use it for reconnaissance.[19]

The development for such a plane took longer than anticipated, and when the army did not immediately place an order, the two investors pulled out on May 7,

Fokker Aeroplanbau: A glimpse at the Fokker shed at Berlin's Johannisthal airfield. In 1912 Fokker employed about twenty-five people. The airplanes were built in Mainz at Goedecker's and then transported to Berlin for assembly. At the time Fokker relied on supplemental income from giving flying lessons to the well-to-do. **COLLECTION MICHAEL SCHMIDT, MUNICH, GERMANY**

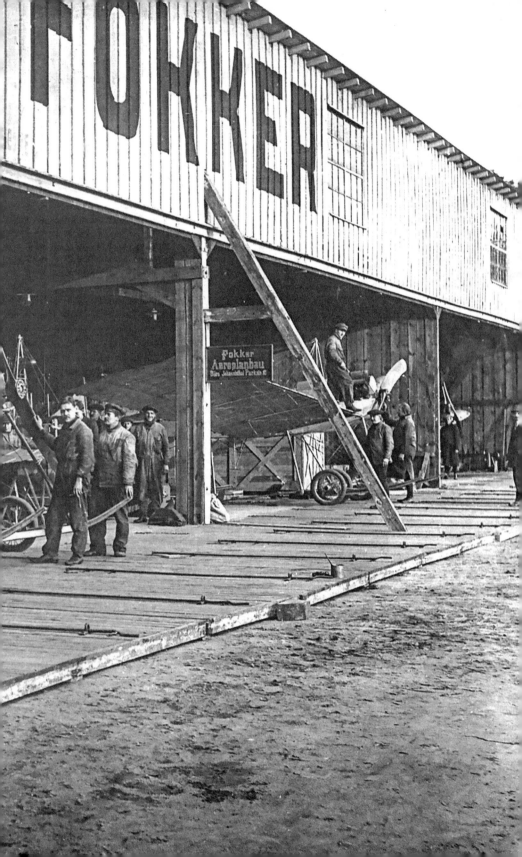

leaving Fokker in charge but nearly ruined. To make things even worse, he had another flying accident early that month, when the undercarriage of his plane suddenly gave way and the machine somersaulted. Again he was lucky to survive. Nonetheless, such accidents were bad publicity, and several of his flying pupils left for the competition. The loss in revenue meant that he had to ask his father again for extra money, this time to buy out Schmidt-Choné and Borchard. To Anthony's relief, Herman Fokker again made a bank credit available in the sum of 50,000 Dutch guilders, despite his objections to his son's wild plans.[20]

Because shed number 10 proved to be too small when four *Spiders* that Anthony had ordered from Goedecker were delivered, Fokker Aeroplanbau moved to the larger shed number 6 at the Neue Startplatz (new starting grounds) in the summer of 1912. The new facilities measured fifteen by fifteen yards, had double doors, and were quite a bit more spacious. They could fit four to five planes. Fokker rented the shed for 400 marks per month. In 1913 his business expanded further as demand increased for flight training. Fokker hired three more sheds to park planes overnight.

Competition remained fierce at Johannisthal, and in 1912 Anthony was on his own. Initially the other aviators shunned the young Dutchman. Apart from being foreign, he struggled with his cash-flow problems. Twenty years later, his experiences with his competitors at Johannisthal still echoed in his autobiography's unfriendly depictions of other pilots, such as the successful German flyer Willy Rosenstein, who worked for Rumpler-Luftfahrzeugbau GmbH.[21] Nonetheless, Anthony managed to arrive first in a return flight from Johannisthal to the Berlin suburb Bückow on March 3, beating his competitors Abramovitsj and Rosenstein.[22]

⚘

Anthony had a shield screwed to the support that divided the entrance to the Fokker hangar, referring potential customers to his "office" in the suburb of Überschöne-weide at Park Strasse 50 at the corner of Park and Kaiser-Wilhelm-Strasse. Even for a fledgling company, it was a peculiar arrangement, as the office was located at the aviator's café Senftleben. The establishment, a mere two minutes' walk from the airfield, was run by Max and "Mama" Senftleben. Like the other houses in this part of Überschöneweide, the three-story structure had been built between 1907 and 1909. Since it had opened its doors, Senftleben had become the favored watering hole for the Johannisthal aviators, the place they gravitated to in the evenings.

Anthony was one of about ten flyers who rented modest lodgings at Senftleben. He occupied a room on the second floor and conducted business at one of the café tables in front of a large round mirror in the bar on the ground floor. This was the Centrale für Aviatik (aviation center), where pilots and airplane manufacturers held office—in the vicinity of one of the few telephones that could be found in Über-schöneweide in 1912. Days began early at Senftleben, as the tranquil air of the dawn was considered best suited for flying lessons. Often Anthony would ride his *Spider* with an empty stomach, sauntering back to Senftleben's for breakfast after his morning flight. In the evenings the latest news, gossip, and experiences were exchanged and discussions held on various topics, while the alcohol flowed freely and the bar filled with cigarette smoke. Those who withdrew from the discussions often spent their time playing cards. In all, it was a colorful group of young people—the average age was around twenty—who gathered at Senftleben's on a daily basis. At the zenith of their fame, and often on the eve of a premature death, they pursued life and lust to the fullest. Young women, enchanted by the "gods of the sky," or simply out for the money the pilots spent while they could, were an essential part of the entourage. Evenings at the table for the regulars were prone to get out of hand, especially when Anthony's new friend, the ever teasing propeller tradesman Friedrich Seekatz, and his "society for the undernourished" were present.[23] In 1913 the German pilot Willy Hahn wrote that "the women . . . really went mad when they laid eyes on the pilots, coming on in groups, going from hand to hand."[24]

Within this merry environment Anthony Fokker remained somewhat of a marginal figure, whose means were invariably tight. Not only did he feel his father's pressure to be parsimonious, but he was a monomaniac in the way that aviation dominated his every move and thought. In the alcoholic gaiety of the evenings at Senftleben he stood out, because he did not drink. Alcohol never was his thing. Even a strong cup of coffee was too much for him. He preferred "Fokker coffee": two-thirds warm milk, one-third coffee, with an abundance of sugar, a predilection from his childhood years on the coffee plantation. Perhaps this was the reason why other pilots often referred to him as "das Fokkerschen" (little Fokker). For a while it appeared his frugality might serve him well. A bond negotiated with the Berlin entrepreneur and pilot Hans Haller enabled him to put his activities on a more secure footing. Haller took care of Fokker's meager corporate finances, while Anthony focused on technology and flying: a division of responsibilities that would reoccur throughout his career.[25]

Nevertheless, 1912 turned out to be yet another difficult year. It was a good thing that Anthony was still under contract with Goedecker. In February and March 1912 Anthony was involved in trials of Goedecker's new machine at Johannisthal. The new plane had wings made of steel piping and an aluminum-clad fuselage. Between April 3 and 14 the machine was demonstrated at Berlin's Allgemeine Luftfahrt Ausstellung (General Aerospace Exhibition). Anthony would have loved to participate with his own aircraft as well, but he lacked the means to pay the starting fee. In a letter to his father he voiced his frustration that he had to restrict himself to placing an advertisement for Fokker Aeroplanbau in the *Berliner Zeitung*—and even that proved to be more expensive than he had thought.[26] He made barely enough money to keep his head above water. Anthony had to make an all-out effort to persuade his father to give him yet another loan:

> *You cannot understand how painful it is for me not to be able to make it clear for you and convince you of the necessity to provide me with company funds as substantial as you can afford financially. . . . That I have achieved*

these results, and not only that, but have obtained know-how and a base to stand independently at all times, because I have, if no high school diploma, made a name for myself, which is worth more to me than a diploma, all of this I owe to the fact that you gave me your trust and provided a first and later a second *credit, for which I am most grateful to you. Because I do not have the gift to act as a learned merchant and administer these credits in a tradesman's way I hope that you will be convinced that I am always cautious and* correct *in the way I handled things. For my own person I have made very few demands and I have devoted all of my power and time to work toward realizing my ideas and theories, and have been successful at that too so far. Believe me, I have had difficult times and I still have them, but I hope to be able to conquer the difficulties. I am struggling with the means that I have, hoping you will supplement them.*[27]

But for the time being, costs ruled the endeavor, and orders for the construction of planes were few. In March Anthony had missed out on a possible order from Holland, because he happened to be in Mainz when a government representative from The Hague visited Johannisthal. In shed number 10 there was no one available to demonstrate the *Spider*. A British commissioner who came to visit the Allgemeine Luftfahrt Ausstellung also called in vain. Fokker's first strengthened *Spider*, intended for use as a reconnaissance plane, still had to be transported from Mainz. Thus, performing at air shows remained Anthony's main source of income.

Meanwhile, work continued in Mainz at Goedecker's to improve the *Spider*. Apart from a more powerful 100-hp engine, the plane received a more enclosed aluminum fuselage to boost its reliability. Because of such changes Fokker's fragile machine came to resemble the more robust *Taube* variants that were built by his competitors Rumpler, Albatros, and LVG.

Anthony mentioned in a letter to his father that he had recently heard of generous new credit options approved by the German parliament, which would allow the army to order larger numbers of aircraft. Until then he continued to depend on private commissions. Airplanes represented a weak market, and having a good name for oneself was of prime importance. Accidents hit home hard and immediately created problems. Therefore it was something of a disaster when one of Fokker's wealthier customers, Baroness Marcella Leitner, ruined the machine on which she was learning to fly on April 26. Shortly after 8 a.m., her plane turned over on the ground as she was trying to land. Anthony, onboard as her instructor, again escaped unhurt. He felt no relief, however, after his lucky escape: "In her stupidity she makes a steering error, so that the airplane spins and keels over sideways and cracks up. The whole thing was not as bad as it seemed and it was nothing like a real crash. I myself remained inside the fuselage and was able to step out. The baroness was also still inside, and the whole thing was on its flank. But instead of sticking her arms out, she has herself drop on her shoulder and broke her collar bone. . . . I don't know if she will continue to take lessons, though I think she will. Anyway, I don't care, I'd prefer if she would sod off; teaching women to fly is a thankless and futile endeavor, they belong behind their needlework."[28]

That unkind remark did not do Leitner justice. Although she was one of his most generous customers, Anthony failed to understand why the baroness, who indeed turned out to have a broken collar bone and had to be taken to hospital, did not try to get up on her own accord after the accident. The aircraft itself was badly damaged. But even when Fokker stayed in full control of the airplane himself, accidents were common. A week later he somersaulted when the undercarriage of his *Spider* gave way again. That did not discourage him from taking off on May 9 with no less than three passengers and ninety pounds of extra weight onboard to circle the airfield several times.[29]

After that Anthony had to hurry back to Mainz. Goedecker had booked him as a pilot for the Deutsche Zuverlässigkeitsflug am Oberrhein (German Upper Rhine Reliability Flight) on May 16. Mainz was a long trip from Berlin. Via Halle and Bebra, with a stopover in Frankfurt, it took him nine and a half hours by train. The return journey took almost as long, but by May 19 Anthony was back in the air above Johannisthal.

ᚷ

Facing financially stronger competitors, Anthony Fokker was struggling. He lacked the means, the people, and the know-how to develop his *Spider* further. The number of students for his flight training school was smaller than he had hoped for. Worse, his father was losing patience with his son's exploits and wanted to cut his funding. The day before Anthony's crash with Von Schlichting, Herman wrote to him, "I'll be curious just how long it will take you to burn those 50 thousand. You're excellent at *spending*, as if that were an art. The way I look at it you will go bankrupt this way. If you continue on your own, you will do just that and I will *not* help you, even if you stand on your head."[30]

Indeed, the latter was precisely what happened to Anthony on June 27. With one of his new pupils, a Lieutenant Rütscher of Germany's Imperial Navy, he had circled low over Johannisthal several times before indicating that Rütscher should land the plane. But the lieutenant miscalculated, hit the ground too hard, tried to pull up again, and stalled the aircraft. The *Spider* hit the ground with its tail first and then toppled over on its back. Both Fokker and Rütscher found themselves trapped under the plane. But whereas Anthony was again lucky enough to crawl away from the wreckage without injury, Rütscher had to be taken to the hospital with a concussion and wounds to his back and head. He had the dubious honor of taking one of the first rides in the airfield's new ambulance and would not fly again. The aircraft was a total loss.[31]

Clearly a stronger construction might limit the damage caused by such accidents. Anthony considered changing his construction methods. Earlier in June he had struck up conversation with a mechanic working for the Johannisthal flying school of the Frenchman Gabriel Poulain. In 1905 Reinhold Platz, born in Cottbus on January 16, 1886, had been one of the first people in Germany to embrace the new technology of autogenous welding of steel tubes. For the Berliner Sauerstoffabrik (Berlin Oxygen Factory), he had traveled the country for several years giving demonstrations of the new welding technology. Thus far it had not found much use in aeronautical construction, where wood remained the dominant material.[32] After his two recent crashes, Fokker, who had thus far shunned away from welded connections because they would be more difficult to repair when damaged, recognized the possibility of building a more robust plane without the penalty of additional weight. In December 1912 he was able to add Platz to his team. It was the start of a long, intensive cooperation between them.

Anthony had been experimenting since February with the concept of a plane that would be easy to assemble and disassemble. The idea originated with the savings that could be achieved by being able to ship *Spider*s in a standard wooden crate measuring fifteen by three feet. Fokker was also still toying with the idea of an airplane that could be towed behind a car.[33] The latter idea also appealed to the German army, whose tacticians were pondering the use of planes for reconnaissance over battle terrain. After a first round of talks in February, army officials invited Fokker to demonstrate an improved, more robust version of such a reconnaissance plane at the Döberitz exercise and proving grounds on the other side of Berlin. For this demonstration Anthony came up with a towable version of his *Spider* that could be assembled and disassembled quickly.[34] An additional requirement stipulated that the machine should be able to cover the twenty-five-mile distance between Johannisthal and Döberitz in a single flight. This was an interesting but taxing idea for Fokker, who was forced to make an emergency landing on the delivery flight when a water hose became disconnected from the engine. Trouble traveled with him: once the hose was fixed and he was airborne again, he lost his way in the low clouds and could not find Döberitz. It took him a second emergency landing—this time to ask for directions—before he was finally able to make the delivery.[35] Fortunately, the army paid up soon thereafter, as Fokker Aviatik was scraping the bottom of the barrel four months after it had been founded. It was obvious that something had to be done to boost revenue—and soon.

7

ST. PETERSBURG, RUSSIA
SEPTEMBER 1912

Two high-ranking Russian army officers introduced her to him and asked whether he might take her up for a spin as a passenger sometime. Anthony was immediately smitten by the exuberant twenty-four-year-old-singer and revue dancer with her pitch-black hair and dark blue eyes. Even as he shook her hand at the St. Petersburg airfield he was falling in love, head over heels. Moreover, she was an aviatrix!

Although Anthony did not speak a word of Russian, this did not stand between them, as she turned out to be fluent in German and in French. In the Dutch edition of his autobiography, Anthony noted, "I thought . . . she could not fly well enough, even though she possessed a pilot's license, and offered her to accompany me to Johannisthal, so that I might 'teach her how to really steer my plane'"—quotation marks for a double meaning. When she came back the next day to make the promised flight, "she looked even lovelier than yesterday. She could talk about airplanes, and airplanes were all the conversation I was capable of, even though I was also in love with her." "Perhaps," Anthony wrote exclusively for his Dutch readership, "there was a bit of self-ishness in my maintaining that she needed more flying lessons, because I was, honestly speaking, in love with her, just like that, at first sight." Maybe the flying lessons were truly necessary, because critics mentioned more than once that Anthony's *Spider* was not so easy to fly.[1] Anthony was on cloud nine when she reappeared the next day for the promised flight: "My method of teaching Ljuba Galantschikoff to fly was a little rough, but effective. She would sit in the plane's forward seat, with the stick and engine controls within reach. . . . To signal her what to do, I would grab the back of her coat, push her forward, jerk her back, pull and yell at her, and after just a few flights she was ready to land without help."[2]

Theirs was a passionate relationship that started at a flying pace. Ljubov Alexandrovna Golantschikova, usually identified as Ljuba Galantschikoff, was born on April 21, 1888, as the daughter of the postmaster of Viljandi in Estonia, Alexander Golantschikov, and his wife of German extraction. In 1909 Ljuba had arrived in St. Petersburg to take a course in bookkeeping, yet office work did not agree with her. The world of the theater, of cabaret, was what appealed most. She had talent as a dancer and soon joined an amateur group. After one performance she was offered an engagement by the manager of the St. Petersburg Folies Bergères, a dance company that showed at lot of leg at the Villa Rodé, a slightly disreputable but popular café chantant with a stage for cabaret, located behind the famous Peter and Paul Fortress. At this club, which catered to the well-to-do, almost anything was possible for the right amount of money. Dancing was exactly what Ljuba wanted, and she readily agreed. She began performing at the Villa Rodé with a singing and dancing act, and her looks and talent created something of a local attraction. Placards soon appeared in the streets with her new stage name: Molly Morée.

Perhaps it had always been her dream to learn to fly, but this rich man's pastime was far beyond her means. Flying was, above all, as expensive as it was hazardous. The first time Ljuba came in touch with flight was when the First Russian Aviation Week had its kickoff at the Kolomjazhsky race track on April 27, 1910. Much of St. Petersburg society worked itself into a frenzy because of the event, and the fever of flight also touched Ljuba. She managed to get herself introduced to several of the pilots, all young men her own age. Mikhail Efimov, a former electrician and racing cyclist from Odessa, became her favorite. She persuaded him to take her up into the air. After that, flying became her passion. With the money she earned and saved over the winter, she registered for flight training with the First Russian Aviation Society in the spring of 1911.[3] A pupil was required to pay a deposit of 600 rubles, on top of which came the actual flight training, which cost another 500 rubles. For a dancing girl, these were more than hefty sums. But Ljuba was lucky in that a drunken admirer, Prince Vladimir Rachevsky, who had more than a soft spot for her, had publicly promised to pay for her tuition. His patronage made her flying adventures quite a bit more affordable.[4] Ljuba proved herself a quick and motivated pupil. In the mornings she would travel the twenty-eight miles to the Gatchina airfield south of St. Petersburg, journeying back to the city for her evening stage performances. On September 29, 1911, she became the third woman in Russia to obtain a flying license: number 56, on a Farman biplane.

For Ljuba it was a dream come true, and she did her utmost to obtain contracts for flying demonstrations. In May 1912 this brought her to Riga (Latvia) with two other Russian pilots. There she became the victim of a bizarre accident on May 2: several of the spectators threw sticks at her plane as she came in low overhead to

Frl. L. Galanschikoff auf Fokker-Eindecker.

Ljuba Galantschikoff: In August 1912 Fokker tried to interest the Russian army in his planes by participating in a flying competition in St. Petersburg. He fell in love with the spirited vaudeville dancer, singer, and pilot Ljuba Galantschikoff. In Berlin she subsequently became one of his most important publicity assets, although her interest in the quirky Dutch aviator soon waned. **FOKKER HERITAGE TRUST, HUINS, THE NETHERLANDS**

land, hitting the propeller and damaging the controls. The flight ended in a crash. Miraculously, Ljuba survived, although she suffered face, foot, and internal injuries. It took her months to recover her confidence.[5] Nonetheless, there was no denying her aviator's blood. Perhaps the young Dutchman with the high-pitched voice might be persuaded to help her advance? He might even allow her to make a solo flight, she hoped. After several more test flights together, during which he shouted further instructions to her through a piece of metal tubing he had installed between the two cockpits, the amorous Anthony could hardly deny her such a request. He watched her with deep anxiety when she took off to do her first solo rounds on the *Spider*. To his immense relief, Ljuba skillfully maneuvered the plane down for a safe landing. Yet her bold promise to buy the plane came to naught. Her earlier crash in Riga had robbed her of her income.

The fact that Anthony and Ljuba had met at all was the result of a fluke. In the spring of 1912 the small band of Fokker employees in Johannisthal had been strengthened by aviator and technician Arthur Friedrich Grünberg. Born in May 1881, Grünberg came from Tallinn in Estonia, then part of Russia. Fokker and he knew each other from Mainz, where they had camped out in the little cottage near the Grossen

Sand. Since then Grünberg had worked as a demonstration pilot for one of Fokker's competitors, Albatros. His arrival at the small Fokker outfit effected a certain east-ward reorientation.

Grünberg hoped that Anthony would appoint him as his sales agent in Russia. Interest in the military applications of aviation was on the rise there, pushed by an investigation by the Russian Ministry of War. Something was about to happen in Rus-sia's aeronautical circles, that much soon became clear, because the Russians launched an ambitious scheme to train a considerable number of pilots. In the summer of 1912 the main conclusions of a report became public, proposing a budget for the purchase of about thirty airplanes for a total of 1.6 million rubles. Rumors had it that an even larger number of purchases was under consideration: it seemed likely that the czarist army might buy as many as 400 planes between 1913 and 1915.[6]

Meanwhile, a large aeronautical exhibition was organized in St. Petersburg in August and September 1912, along with a five-week competition to select the most suitable planes for the army. Baroness Marcella Leitner, who had kept her faith in Fokker's plane despite her accident in April, proposed to enter the competition. For each participant 2,000 rubles were available as compensation for transporting a fly-ing machine to St. Petersburg. Anthony was all ears to the proposal, especially since the baroness volunteered to cover all costs.[7] It seemed there was hardly anything to lose and much to gain by entering. But rather than send a foreigner, he chose to send his fellow countryman and chief pilot Jan Hilgers and his personal mechanic Hans Schmidt along with Leitner. They were supposed to offer flying demonstrations along the way to Russia, which might bring in one or two extra production orders.

In June 1912 Hilgers and Leitner got on the train with her *Spider*, which had been repaired since her accident. Hilgers and Leitner flew their first demonstrations in front of the beach pavilion at Pärnu on June 29. Four weeks later, on July 21, they performed in Tallinn. This latter event was so successful that several more flights followed on July 27 and 28, together with Marcella Leitner. To everyone's horror, the flights ended with yet another accident, which damaged the machine.[8]

The damage threatened a disaster for the fragile finances of Fokker Aeroplanbau. To have a chance of winning the Russian competition, the *Spider* of course needed to be in perfect order. Anthony decided to travel to St. Petersburg himself to person-ally take charge of the situation. The previous month his friend Bernard de Waal had successfully passed the test for his pilot's license at Goedecker's in Mainz. He had received his papers on July 15, which meant that Anthony could now leave the flight instruction at Johannisthal to him. Early in August he obtained a visa for Russia and booked passage on the Nord Express from Berlin to St. Petersburg.

⨎

The superluxurious express train of the Compagnie Internationale des Wagons-Lits left from Berlin's Schlesischer Bahnhof around 7:30 a.m. Via Schneidemühl (Piła) and Königsberg (Kaliningrad) in East Prussia, it covered the 460 miles to the

Prussian-Russian border station of Wirballen (Kybartai) in eleven and a half hours. It was a comfortable but expensive journey, because the Nord Express consisted exclusively of first-class carriages. Upon arrival at Wirballen (now in Lithuania), dusk was beginning to set. All passengers had to disembark while their luggage was taken from the baggage compartment to be checked.

The procedure at the border took several hours. Slightly bewildered, Anthony Fokker tried to find his way amid the travelers and baggage porters in the station's inspection hall. Anthony had arrived at the end of the world as he knew it. Never before had he been so far away from home. The signs on the station were in unintelligible Cyrillic. He had to put his watch an hour forward to Russian time. Even the rail track itself ended here. After customs procedures all passengers changed to a Russian train, its wooden carriages waiting for them across the platform on a different railway gauge. Finally all were aboard, and around eleven o'clock the Nord Express set itself in motion for its nightly journey to St. Petersburg. This took another sixteen hours, as the speed on the Russian part of the itinerary was lower than on the German track. Toward 4 p.m. of the following day the train finally rolled into St. Petersburg's Vitebsky station.

St. Petersburg was unlike any other city Anthony had visited. Europe's most unhealthy capital was surrounded by an ever-expanding ring of heavy industry that colored the air with dust and ashes. From the window of his compartment, Anthony saw the landscape change from forests and fields to industrial sites. Metal companies, railway industry, weapons factories, and shipyards proliferated. These industries were surrounded by endless slums where the majority of St. Petersburg's two million inhabitants lived in squalor.[9] It was not a pretty sight. Once the train had finally stopped along Vitebsky's platform and Anthony had disembarked, the impact of the white modern train station could hardly have been bigger.

Vitebsky was the pride of Russian railway architecture. Finished in 1904, the station was like a jewel in the eye of the beholder. No other station in St. Petersburg was so lavishly decorated. Arriving passengers flocked toward the platform hall, painted and sculpted with Jugendstil art. From there a stairway led down to the main hall, which was even more richly decorated. In the crowd of passengers, porters, coachmen, and taxi drivers, Anthony tried to find his way to the exit, anxious because he did not understand the language or customs of the city. Once on the square in front of the station his adventures started for real.

A carriage brought him to the hotel and restaurant Alt-Riga, a modern middle-class establishment on Novy Pereulok Street in the Admiralty District. This was where Jan Hilgers and Hans Schmidt had checked in after their aborted Baltic adventure with Marcella Leitner. The ride to Alt-Riga highlighted St. Petersburg's remarkable mixture of old and new: cartwheels and horse-drawn carriages, but also electrical trams and motorcars. Anthony's first impressions of the city were discomfiting: "Russia was like nothing I had seen. The luxuriant beards, the meaningless jargon, the happy inefficiency of everyone; the Slavic-Oriental architecture, the unaccountable mixture of magnificence and filth, struck me as a nightmare."[10] The rich upper class flaunted a lifestyle of which Anthony could only dream, with exceptionally large houses, city palaces, restaurants, theaters, and cafés. On and around Nevski Prospekt well-to-do citizens showed themselves in their best clothes. This was where the larger banks and luxury shops were located. In the city on the banks of the Neva River, money seemed to flow like water. Anthony soon regarded this conspicuous consumption with a mixture of contempt and regret. After two weeks in St. Petersburg, he wrote to his sister Toos, "Petersburg is a shitty city, if you have money it is another thing, *but I am poor.* . . . With a ruble [2.16 marks] you can do just as much here, or rather just as little, as with a mark in Berlin, consequence is spending lots of money."[11]

In the meantime Fokker made an effort to cultivate the Russian officers of the selection committee. A substantial sum loomed at the end of the competition: 55,000 rubles for the top three winners.[12] Making a good impression, however, was not easy: "Nowhere did one find the accustomed reaction either to thought or deed. It left me confused, and despite my customary optimism, I soon became convinced that Russia and I would not get along."[13] Russian aerodynamic expert Georgiy Botezat decreed that the concept of Fokker's automatically stable *Spider* deviated too much from common practice to stand a chance of winning the competition, which also stung. Nonetheless, Anthony made several demonstration flights in rapid succession. He flew from the exercise grounds at St. Petersburg's Korpusnoy to the Gatchina airfield and back. He also treated the Russian War Minister, Gen. Vladimir Sukhomlinov, to a flight as his passenger.[14]

The competition, in which nine Russian-built aircraft and four foreign examples participated, was poorly organized. Both the rules and the various parts of the contest were messy. Adverse weather conditions also had a negative effect. Major and minor accidents happened almost every day. The event lasted much longer than Anthony had anticipated, and his finances dwindled by the day. "Soon I learned what was meant by Russian efficiency," he later recalled. "[They stretched out] the demonstrations, in the expectation that others would arrive to join in. They encouraged us to fly and applauded our skill and experience, but that was all."[15]

From its start on August 21, the contest at Korpusnoy dragged on for weeks. At the time, Anthony initially remained optimistic: "In business, I can expect the best here, as my airplane puts all competitors in the shade. I have already finished the various tests. Take-off, climb, gliding down etc., demonstrate, assemble, flying with max. loads, like flying with Hilgers for 1½ hours and show that we can land on bad fields."[16]

Anthony believed that Vsevolod Abramovitsj, whom he knew from Johannisthal, was his biggest competitor. Abramovitsj had come up with a remarkable promotional scheme to fly his Berlin-built Wright machine all the way to St. Petersburg, an exceptional feat in those days. He even took a passenger to act as navigator: Karl Hackstetter, a well-known German balloonist. They were followed on their flight by a ground crew in a motorcar that carried gasoline, spare parts, and provisions. What Abramovitsj and Fokker did not know was that it had been decided beforehand that only planes that had been built in Russia would qualify for receiving military orders.[17] Therefore the German entries remained outside the competition. It was unfortunate that Anthony, who did his utmost to outclass Abramovitsj in dangerous stunt flying, failed to register the Russians' built-in bias. The Leipzig-based company Deutsche Flugzeug-Werke (DFW), which had entered two planes, failed to land orders for the same reason. Their machines were disqualified, even though their pilot Heinrich Bier was the first participant to complete all parts of the flying contest.

The main protagonists were therefore all Russian entries, such as the Dux factory from Moscow, which had entered two planes. Their aviator, Adam Haber-Włyński from Poland, was also quick to complete the trials. Ivan Steglau, a successful entrepreneur who had made his fortune providing water and sewer piping, entered one aircraft: a part-metal, welded biplane with cantilever, triplex-clad wings. Fokker showed a lot of interest in the design. But Steglaus's plane lost its propeller in flight and crash landed. Bad luck also chased the Russian Vasily Hioni, whose machine ended in a ditch. The St. Petersburg engineering professor Yakov Gakkel was present with two machines. Initially his planes were considered favorites to win the contest. But his aircraft were plagued by all sorts of engine malfunctions, and Gakkel was unable to complete the tests in time. (Years later evidence would come to light that Haber-Włyński had bribed Gakkel's mechanic to pour acid in the engines.) Thus the laurels went to Igor Sikorsky, who had his workshop in St. Petersburg. Sikorsky, who badly needed to win, took no chances and remained on the airfield to sleep in his plane's transportation crate, so that he could report to the officers of the selection committee first thing the next morning and take to the air as soon as possible. To give him every opportunity to meet the requirements, the duration of the competition was extended. This was, of course, much to the dislike of Anthony Fokker, who could hardly afford to remain in St. Petersburg to await the final decision. Not surprisingly, Sikorsky cashed first prize for his achievements: 30,000 rubles.[18]

Anthony had remained optimistic about his chances of success right up to the last. As one of the first to complete all required parts of the contest, he believed the prize should have been his. In the German aeronautical press and in Dutch newspapers, reports mentioned a pending Russian order of ten *Spiders*. Anthony even dreamed of opening a subsidiary in St. Petersburg. He thought the good news for him was only "a matter of time and form."[19] His entry had never stood a chance, but he was about the last person to arrive at this conclusion. He lacked the means to pay bribes to the czarist bureaucracy. If Fokker's was a fine plane and its pilot well versed in the art of keeping it aloft, that did not mean he could convince the selection committee that was to choose the winning entry. Later he angrily noted in his autobiography that St. Petersburg was rife with corruption: "Before you could see an official in his office, it was necessary to send in your visiting card wrapped in a ten-ruble note, otherwise your card got no further than the porter. . . . The secretary of the department expected . . . a larger banknote to rouse him from lethargy. Then if you wanted to talk to the General himself, you had to see the executive officer with a really important bribe, and finally the General would only sign a contract if there were enough banknotes folded in it."[20] Of the three aircraft types that were eventually ordered, only that of the winner, Igor Sikorsky, was truly developed in Russia. The other two were Russian variations on French Nieuport and Farman designs. The criticism in the Russian press at the official end of the competition on September 7 was severe: the participating planes were designs that already existed and that contributed nothing to the development of military aviation in Russia. None of them could genuinely be considered a military design. What Russia needed first and foremost, if it wished to count in aviation, was to set up its own aviation industry.[21]

⌘

From a business perspective, the Russian adventure had ended for Fokker in a deception. The weeks in St. Petersburg had been expensive and had not produced any sales. In the end Anthony had to leave because his money ran out. For the time being he left the *Spider* in the care of Jan Hilgers and Hans Schmidt. Nonetheless, when he boarded the Nord Express for his return trip to Germany on September 19, his head was in the clouds because Ljuba had, after some persuasion, agreed to accompany him to Berlin. Anthony could not have been happier. For him the train journey was like a romantic dream.

Once back in Berlin a peculiar triangular relationship developed between Anthony, his airplane, and Ljuba. On September 30 they made a momentous flight together. Around four o'clock they took off, rounded the Johannisthal airfield to excite the public, and then disappeared into the sky. They flew right across Berlin. Then Anthony decided to show Ljuba what his machine could do and climbed all the way to an altitude of 6,500 feet. From there they made a high-speed descent, coming in for a hair-raising landing just in front of the grandstand. Both made sure Anthony's new pilot got noticed. In the weeks after her arrival she proved herself to be a rapid pupil, although she never managed to accumulate enough money to be able to buy a *Spider* for herself. Before the month was out, she had made fifteen flights on Fokker's planes, remaining in the air for forty-eight minutes. The following month she was registered to take off no less than fifty times, with a total flight time of three hours, eleven minutes.[22] Very conscious of the publicity value of a young, attractive female aviatrix in his outfit—the Berlin papers described her as "picture pretty"— Anthony hired Ljuba as a demonstration pilot. It also enabled him to spend more time with her. Before long Ljuba became known as "the Pushka" (Russian for "cannon," a customary designation for successful pilots in those days).

On November 12 she made an attempt to better the altitude record for women, then held by the German pilot Melli Beese, one of Fokker's competitors at Johannisthal. She managed to climb to 2,400 feet, but was then forced to land. For the time being Beese's record of 2,800 feet held, but Anthony was impressed. That evening he wrote to his friend Tom Reinhold that she made her turns better than Hilgers or Cremer, and had descended in a long circular glide that he described as *tadellos* (impeccable).[23] Ten days later, in the mid-afternoon of November 21, Ljuba finally did break the women's altitude record—and by a wide margin too. Her flight in a specially prepared *Spider* up to 6,600 feet was a daring feat, as pilots' lore had it that flights above 4,500 feet were exceptionally dangerous and could lead to hallucinations, heart palpitations, headache, and sleepiness. In a thirty-minute climb Ljuba managed to set her record. She enjoyed the view and afterward relished the memory of the flight, although she would later complain that the cold so high in the air had made her legs and arms numb.[24] Luckily for her, the descent went considerably quicker: she spiraled down in six and a half minutes and landed her plane safely. A group of admirers, Anthony in the lead, awaited her by the Fokker hangar with enthusiasm, laurels, and admiration. Ljuba hardly managed to answer the many questions put to her; the cold had numbed her facial muscles, something that sips of an alcoholic beverage during her descent had not been able to avert.[25]

ℱ

Business, on the other hand, remained problematic. Although Anthony had enough commercial spirit to apply for patents for his automatically stable *Spider* and for a range of minor inventions related to aeronautical construction, he was still scraping the bottom of the revenue barrel. In mid-September 1912 he had to conclude that he had sold no more than five aircraft and that the net result of his trip to St. Petersburg was that his father's entire loan of 50,000 guilders was now exhausted. Providing more flying lessons brought no quick solution either, although Anthony believed they still held earning potential. One reason was that Heinrich von Preussen, the brother of Emperor Wilhelm II, had launched an aviation appeal in April 1912. His massive campaign, the Nationale Flugspende (National Air Subscription), aimed to expand the number of aviators from which the German army could draw in times of crisis. Twenty manufacturers were selected to give flight training, to be reimbursed by public funds of 7 million marks. Despite his status as a foreigner, Fokker qualified as one of them.[26]

Being selected for the Nationale Flugspende did not alter the fact that too little money was coming in. Fokker now had twenty-four people on his staff to pay.[27] Costs were spiraling. To Anthony's panic, his father chose this moment to pull the plug. Anthony's repeated pleas and warnings that if his father withdrew he stood to lose his complete investment remained unheeded. Herman Fokker refused to bankroll his son any longer. To him, the 50,000 guilders he had provided represented the full amount he was willing to risk in his son's career:

> *If you understood anything about business you would know that all businesses can go wrong. If I would now be so stupid to keep furnishing you until I would have invested, for example, half or three-quarters of my estate in your*

venture, and your business went belly-up, then I would not only be forced to go hungry or find myself a job in my old age, but I also have a wife and daughter who would be dragged down in the demise. I would act like a criminal if I were to risk their future for your pleasure. . . . Perhaps I would have risked more than 50,000 guilders if I would have received proper monthly accounts of the capital used, which it was your duty to provide, but now I have been forced to set a maximum. . . . Now I have received notice from the bank that you have used up that maximum, from which obviously follows that the 50,000 guilders have been used up and that the bank will not provide any more money. And neither will I, of course. This is what I meant when I stated before that you never seem to understand what the word "maximum" means.[28]

To make matters worse, Anthony's love life was on a downhill slope as well. In and around Johannisthal, he paraded "his" Ljuba as "my Russian girlfriend from St. Petersburg," but her interest in the monomaniacal Dutchman, with his strange behavior and shrill voice, was waning quickly. Ever since returning to Berlin, Anthony was preoccupied by his business troubles. Partly out of uncertainty when facing Ljuba, his conversation with her was reduced to a single topic: flying. On the other hand, Ljuba was only too happy to relish the attention of Johannisthal's other young airmen, and soon she attracted a small crowd of male admirers. When on the ground, Anthony was defenseless against the competition: "I worked hard and was then often so tired that when I visited her that I dropped asleep instead of telling her what a lovely babe she really was. And if I happened to be awake, flying was, for lack of a better one, the only topic of conversation every time."[29]

To raise more cash, Anthony had to fly as often as possible. He took up where he had left off as a demonstration pilot. In the Autumn Aviation Week that started on October 5, he made sure people noticed him by finishing first in the altitude competition, leveling out at 9,300 feet. His *Spider* did not feature at the head of the field in comparative speed trials for monoplanes or in takeoff run tests. But he managed to finish third in trials to drop an object on a target from the air. The next day he got his name in the papers by flying a passenger all the way to Hamburg.[30]

As Anthony's funds grew tighter, his plans to promote business got wilder. Early in October Jan Hilgers, freshly arrived from St. Petersburg, took a train for Holland to approach Anthony's wealthy uncles in Haarlem with a proposal to invest in an expedition to the Dutch East Indies and sell planes there. He failed to raise the money but proceeded with the plan regardless—to the intense anger of Anthony, who had been so careless as to suggest he would contribute financially.[31] Hilgers forced Anthony to sign an agreement on December 20, 1912, in which Fokker supplied two planes for the venture, plus spare parts. Hilgers's part of the deal was to fund the sea transportation to Java, organize a demonstration tour, and pay the deposit of 2,000 marks for the two planes. Eight days later, he and his tour manager Peter Klingenspoor boarded the steamer *Suevia* of the Hamburg-America Line's East Asian Freight Steamer Service, destined for Surabaya. On its stern the ship carried two *Spiders* in their transportation crates, plus another crate with spare parts. The plan was to provide aerial displays in the Dutch East Indies, Siam, and Australia.[32] Hilgers and Fokker had agreed to split the proceeds on a fifty–fifty basis. At the end of January 1913, Hilgers arrived on Java, where he was able to produce a letter of recommendation signed by the Dutch Minister for Colonial Affairs, Jan de Waal Malefijt. The initial results of the endeavor were hopeful. In Surabaya the community raised 18,000 guilders to stage an aviation week with flying displays in February. A month later, however, disaster struck. One of the two *Spiders* was lost in a crash at Semarang. A second crash followed on April 2. Hilgers tried to repair and reduce the weight of the aircraft, but without success. The scheme eventually cost Anthony Fokker another 40,000 guilders.[33]

ૌ

Meanwhile, Anthony continued singing praises of his beloved Ljuba's flying displays in letters home.[34] Thanks to her altitude record, she was now one of the star performers at Johannisthal, and with her theater background and her liberated attitude, she was like a magnet to the young fliers in Café Senftleben. One of her admirers there later wrote, "When she dances the Krakowiak in her red Russian leather boots, there is not a pilot who will think of airplanes or engines."[35] Anthony saw how the Berlin aviator Gustav Adolf Michaelis—in his own words, "a good-looking guy who owned a 100 hp motorcar and knew how to handle women"—was taking his place in Ljuba's arms. Toward the end of 1912 Michaelis and Ljuba had embarked on a passionate love affair, a development that Anthony seemed helpless to prevent. He sent his mother a photo card of himself with a slightly pathetic message: "The following image represents . . . Tony at Joh[annisthal]. Skinny from worries and hunger. Post[card] received. Adio—regards to Dad and Toos."[36]

The love between Ljuba and Gustav was not fated to last. On May 27, 1913, Michaelis's plane crashed. The badly wounded pilot was taken to hospital, where he died of his injuries five days later. Ljuba was heartbroken, but Anthony could not bring himself to overcome his wounded pride and comfort her: "I was angry, I was jealous, and I was too proud to show my feelings. When a woman looked at another man I would do anything, rather than admit that I was still interested in her. Even if I felt miserable, I would not show it to her."[37] However, Johannisthal was full of other young aviators who were all too eager to comfort Ljuba, and it was not long before she found herself in the arms of the Frenchman Léon Letort. Letort had arrived on Johannisthal after a direct flight from Paris on July 14. With that morning's Parisian newspaper under his arm and a bag full of prize money, he walked into Café Senftleben and into Ljuba's life. At 4:30 a.m. on July 27, he and Ljuba took off in his fast Morane-Saulnier monoplane, in an attempt to win the 10,000 marks available for the fliers who would be the first to cover the distance between the German and French capitals. Fokker escorted them part of the way in his own plane and then sadly watched them fly off into the distance. It would be thirteen years before he and Ljuba next met. As it turned out, the Berlin-Paris record was not broken. Rains along the route forced Léon and Ljuba down near Hannover, and in Cologne they remained grounded for two full days.

In an effort to drown his sorrows, Anthony plunged into Berlin's night life and had himself photographed with several cheerful young ladies in an apparently very bright mood. He noted in his autobiography in 1931 that "for six weeks I totally lost my head and participated in the unruly life of the other aviators; I went out with them in Berlin at night looking for traditional pleasures. . . . For the first time in my life I learned something about women. I visited nightclubs and met the kind of women there that I didn't know existed. I found them enchanting, merry and ravishing. It was impossible for me to treat them in the fashion that the other aviators did, so casual, without recourse to their true feelings. I liked hearing them speak about their life and I studied their character. More than once I helped a girl whom I admired to find a different, less unworthy source of income."[38]

SCHWERIN, GERMANY
JUNE 1913

Along with Anthony Fokker, garbed for the occasion in a formal dinner jacket and top hat, Frits Cremer was looking his best on Sunday afternoon, June 22, 1913. After quite a bit of hesitation and several tries, Frits had finally obtained his flying license on November 1, 1912. Since then he had not really been in the spotlight, but this was to be his day of fame as a pilot. From the 250-foot-long and 33-foot-high grandstand, 1,500 spectators cheered at him. For a long time his friend Tony had secretly doubted him: "he is a weakling and will never really become much better."[1] But now the local press celebrated Frits as one of the contenders in the North German aerial circuit flight Lübeck–Schwerin–Wismar–Lübeck. The event was to mark the official opening of the Schwerin-Görries airfield. Despite his already dubious track record of crashes, Frits now started a new occupation as head of the Fokker Flying School in Schwerin. It was an odd choice for the position, and the fact that Anthony had asked him was probably more revealing of their close relationship than of Frits's capabilities as a pilot and flight instructor. Young Frits did not possess a stable personality and was forever plagued by physical ailments that stemmed from a medical operation several years before. To make matters worse, he was also continually pursued by financial problems. Time and again his rich father had to bail him out. His family worried about him constantly.[2]

Today, however, was a special event for him, juiced up even further by a flower show, the proceeds of which were intended for charity. The Schweriner damsels had flocked en masse for the festivities. The local paper reported that that the participating daredevil airmen were much sought after by the city's young women and were proving themselves to be adept seducers. Frits relished the attention, and the event brought him a new girlfriend but no prize for flying. Anthony's familiar adversary Willy Rosenstein was also present with his Gotha Stahltaube plane and came in first at the finish in Lübeck the next day. But Frits had made a name for himself in Schwerin. The only dissonant note that afternoon was that one of the participants flew his airplane into the ground.[3]

ᵞ

Upon closer inspection, Schwerin, with its forty thousand inhabitants, was not a likely place to play a role in the history of aviation. The sleepy capital of the state of Mecklenburg, surrounded by lakes and marshes, it was not known for its industrial activity. The city was dominated by the imposing palace of the grand duke, situated on a small island at the water's edge. Even from afar, the palace's many windows, towers, and gold-clad roofs commanded attention. Otherwise, the main products from Schwerin were bricks, furniture, and pianos, all of which were made on a small scale.[4]

Around 1910 a handful of entrepreneurs and city officials with ambition had begun focusing on the newly emerging technology of flight. In the eyes of Schwerin's vice mayor, Otto Weltzien, the key figure in this group, opportunity beckoned. The flat landscape around Lake Schwerin appeared well suited for the construction of an airfield. In November 1912 Weltzien was present at the birth of the Mecklenburgische Flugplatzgesellschaft Görries-Schwerin (Mecklenburg Airfield Society Görries-Schwerin), which bought a number of acres of land a few miles southwest of the city. The society was able to pay the hefty price of 416,000 marks ($99,000).[5]

With that deal completed, the next question was how to put the grounds to use. This was no easy matter; all of Germany currently counted no more than about 250 aviators. The majority of them were active around the aeronautical center of Johannisthal. In February 1913, therefore, Weltzien took a train for Berlin, hoping to make connections there that might prove useful in luring aeronautical activity to Schwerin. At first there was not much interest in his ideas. After all, what could the residential city of Grand Duke Friedrich Franz IV offer other than some level fields?

The concentration of aeronautical activity in Berlin was encouraged by the Nationale Flugspende (National Air Subscription). The German army, with its headquarters in Berlin, was the main customer. If the army had bought a mere twenty-eight new aircraft in 1911, purchases increased fivefold the next year and reached 461 in 1913. The acquisition program focused on two general types: Type A were slow but stable aircraft of the *Taube* configuration, while Type B referred to more agile biplanes. Production numbers of either type were more or less equal in 1912. They were powered by similar engines, usually a six-cylinder, water-cooled Argus, Daimler, or Mercedes, because the army had ordained that standardization would be beneficial for a rational and economically viable army air service. The *Taubes* were stable and easy to fly, which made them eminently suited for officers, whose lives were especially valuable. The *Taube* was a slow and not particularly maneuverable plane, but since army aircraft were conceived to be used exclusively for reconnaissance, this limitation was not considered problematic. The army's orders were awarded to ten different producers, among which were Fokker's immediate competitors at Johannisthal: Rumpler, Albatros, and LVG (Luftverkehrsgesellschaft). These firms built about five hundred machines, mostly used for pilot training.[6] As a result, space at Johannisthal was becoming precious.

Although Fokker's *Spider* was also automatically stable, his "foreign" machine hardly featured in German military planning. In December 1912 the army ordered no more than two airplanes from him, which was remarkable in itself, since the official guidelines dictated that the army was to buy German machines only.[7] The young Dutchman, known for his aerobatics, was primarily regarded as someone who might train pilots, not as an aircraft constructor. Nonetheless, it was as constructor and company director that Fokker was listed in the trade register of Berlin-Köpenick on December 7, 1912, after signing the papers for his first military contract. The seat of his company thus moved from the suburb Charlottenburg to Köpenick, at a stone's throw from Johannisthal. Business now turned more serious, and Anthony moved out of the saloon at Senftleben to rent a small office a little further down the street at Parkstrasse 18. Next to director Fokker, the Berlin entrepreneur and aviator Hans Haller was registered as having power of attorney.[8]

Fokker's company capital, again provided by his family circle, totaled 40,000 marks. He later remembered how his father had initially refused to participate, stating that he "would not put up with being undressed to assist his son before going to bed." This had resulted in a major financial crisis for Anthony, which he had managed to resolve through a "long and expensive intercommunal telephone conversation with his uncle Eduard in The Hague." Indeed, to whom else could he turn to secure funding for his expensive and risky venture? But Anthony's uncles and aunts were none too secret about enjoying the crazy flying exploits of their young nephew, and they could afford to invest in his fledgling venture. Eduard put up 20,000 marks himself "to prevent the name Fokker from being tainted by financial difficulties." In the end Herman gave in as well and provided the other half of the capital.[9]

Now that Fokker had become a contracting party to the German army, the General Staff officer in charge of rationalization of the aircraft industry, Capt. Franz Geerdtz, decided to investigate whether Fokker might be interested in Weltzien's quest, thus freeing more capacity at Johannisthal. The matter proved easy to arrange. Having unsuccessfully campaigned thus far to attract manufacturing interest, the Schwerin Airfield Society came up with a generous offer to rent the entire facility to Fokker for a modest fee.[10] For Fokker, strapped for cash as usual, the offer was a godsend. He was also short of hangar space at Johannisthal, and this was obstructing his plans to increase production of his own aircraft. He was hoping for more orders from the German military, and perhaps from Holland too. Weltzien's offer provided the opportunity to expand his venture without having to make substantial further investments of his own. It also represented a good moment for ending his association with Goedecker in Mainz. In the past year his own technical expertise had grown, and he now had some people working for him who could help with calculations and design drawings.

Schwerin was everything Berlin was not. It had the friendly proportions of the province instead of the impersonal air of the big capital city: distances were smaller, streets narrower, squares enclosed. The city officials showed engagement and were accessible, even to a young foreigner. Anthony was going to be the only aircraft constructor there. And Schwerin had another asset: it was situated on the shore of Lake Schwerin, and since the spring of 1912 Anthony had been following Goedecker's lead in developing a floatplane. The vast lakes around Schwerin seemed to provide an ideal environment for such an activity—and perhaps a market too. Water sports were almost "in Anthony's blood." He saw air and water as a perfect combination, even though he had crashed his first prototype of a flying boat upon landing, one year earlier. The idea of building airplanes that could be launched from water stuck with him. On January 15, 1913, he wrote from Berlin to his mother, "As a sign of life this card. As usual 'super busy' working extra hours on the water plane, which is coming along nicely and will turn out tip top. The details take up most of the time. Really cold here, no flying weather for weeks, which I don't regret, as it means no disruptions. Van Heyst [a Dutch military pilot] will be sent to Berlin by Dutch War Ministry, begin of deliveries to the army. For now, adio, Tony."[11]

By February 9 the floatplane was nearly finished. Only the wings still had to be attached. Four days later Anthony made the first test flight from Müggel Lake in Berlin. The ease with which the airplane lifted from the water, despite carrying a passenger and 150 pounds in ballast, surprised him. Nonetheless, several adaptations to the plane were needed before he embarked upon a second test flight. By April he could be seen flying above the Spree River regularly. He even entered his latest machine in an aeronautical contest over the bay in Monaco, although he eventually decided not to participate. Anthony hoped he had finally found his niche in aviation. He advertised his floatplane in the Johannisthal journals.[12]

Meanwhile, pilot training remained the cornerstone of his enterprise. In April 1913 the venture employed twenty-five mainly young, enthusiastic people. The bookkeeper was the oldest employee at the age of thirty-six. Fokker's flying school listed eight officers and three private customers. The generous conditions of the National Air Subscription in which he participated meant that they brought about 88,000 marks in revenue, although the company had to make provisions for the risk of material damages out of its own pocket.[13] For the rest of his revenue Fokker relied on flying displays. Unfortunately, these had proved insufficient to cover the enormous losses caused by the misadventure in St. Petersburg and Hilger's departure to the Dutch East Indies. It must have been a relief that the flying school gradually started to attract more customers, now that Fokker could leave some of the instruction to his friends Frits Cremer and Bernard de Waal. The latter had come over from Goe-decker in February 1913. In short: Fokker Aeroplanbau was beginning to show some modest growth potential.

This development had not escaped Captain Geerdtz; it was what encouraged him to bring Weltzien and Fokker together. At the end of March both parties came to a provisional agreement, although it was not until June 17 that the city council gave its blessing to the deal that put Schwerin on the map in aeronautical development.[14] Geerdtz guaranteed Fokker thirty army customers per year, which would provide the company with a secure income of 240,000 marks. This was the chance Anthony had hoped for. He would now be able to leave his ceaseless financial worries behind. The Mecklenburg Airfield Society also did quite nicely: it could look forward to receiving 5 to 6 percent of the fee for every pilot that passed the licensing exam. It also could count on visitors' fees and revenue from renting the hangar space at Görries.[15]

For a brief moment it looked as if the deal would not materialize after all, because Anthony suffered yet another crash at Johannisthal in early May. On takeoff his machine somersaulted again. He was thrown from his seat and landed some forty feet away from the plane. He had dislocated his shoulder, and the airfield doctor had to be summoned to put his arm back into position.[16]

The accident meant that flying was out for several weeks, and thus it was Bernard de Waal rather than Anthony who took off from Johannisthal for a planned demonstration flight to Holland on May 13. Mechanic and copilot Franz Kuntner accompanied him. With no more than a railway map tied to their upper legs, the two men managed to cover the 360-mile distance from Berlin to Holland's only airfield, Soesterberg, in sixteen hours (of which six hours and twenty minutes were spent in the air). At Soesterberg, and a week later also at a rainy The Hague, De Waal demonstrated the *Spider* before Dutch military officials, hoping to stimulate sales. The single flying machine of the Dutch armed forces was also flown at The Hague on the same day. Despite the rain, the event drew several thousand spectators. As the father of the designer, Herman Fokker was given special treatment. He was one of the few civilians taken up for a short flight. De Waal and Fokker's newly appointed representative at home, Lieutenant Von Bose, were laureled after the demonstration by the chief of the General Staff, Cornelis Snijders. As a token of appreciation they also received a silver chalice. With his arm in a sling, Anthony shared in the success via the telephone line from Berlin.[17]

Several days later, disaster struck again: en route for a flying display in Nijmegen on the Dutch-German border, De Waal's engine quit, and he had to make an emergency landing. As happened so often in the early days of flight, his airplane somersaulted and had to be written off completely. De Waal was lucky to emerge from the wreckage with no more than a black eye.[18] Yet the story was bad publicity for Fokker, and no sales resulted.

In the same month of May, the German army showed renewed interest in Fokker's idea of a plane that would be easy to disassemble and move by road. Designs

The Fokker Flying School: In nearby Görries, the Schwerin airfield was proud to welcome Fokker. His Flying School brought revenues from ticket sales at the large visitors' grandstand that could accommodate up to 1,500 people who came to watch the flying spectacle. **FOKKER HERITAGE TRUST, HUINS, THE NETHERLANDS**

by Albatros, LVG, and Fokker were evaluated. To the surprise of more than a few observers, it was Fokker who landed the sales order on June 11, 1913. His design was found to be more robust and easier to move by motorcar than his competitors' projects. The army contracted him to deliver four M.2 reconnaissance aircraft before August 15. Daimler constructed the transportation vehicles.[19]

�

On June 1, 1913, the Fokker Flying School opened at the Görries airfield with twelve pupils. Anthony rented from the Airfield Society the hangar space necessary to house the six training aircraft his company possessed. The machines represented a cross section of the various models he had built thus far: the flight line ranged from the 1911 two-seater to the M.4 *Stahltaube* model, recently built to military specifications. Meanwhile, talks were arranged between Schwerin city officials and Fokker to determine a location where aircraft might also be constructed. Defying the apparent logic of focusing on Görries, where the flying school was located, Anthony preferred a site by the water, where he hoped to build floatplanes as well. After the first successful trials on the Müggel Lake in Berlin, he was convinced that flying from water was going to provide the niche he was looking for. And although his corporate finances hinged on pilot training at Görries, building floatplanes was the way in which he wanted his enterprise to develop. The city council offered him an unused plot at the Hintenhof outside Schwerin's city limits, an unpaved dead-end street that ran behind the Jewish cemetery. The spot was right on the lakeside and thus fit Anthony's growing fascination with floatplanes. The only objection came from the local sports fishing society, which was dead set against noisy airplanes in their quiet backwater. The fight they put up lasted a year and ended without result. In the meantime the city council had been most generous to Fokker and even agreed to build him a large wooden shed. In November 1913 it offered to disown a second plot on behalf of Fokker and thus enable him to expand his factory shed in the future and obtain direct company access to the lake.[20]

Building the shed and laying the rails leading to the water took time. Not before October 1 was Fokker able to move into the new facilities. Some months later, Fokker's company director, Hans Haller, initiated talks with the city of Schwerin to obtain permission for future expansion at the Görries airfield, which he hoped might even have its own rail connection. This would be important as the starting point for shipping aircraft throughout Germany.[21] For the time being Anthony maintained a part of his flying school and a repair facility at Johannisthal under the guidance of August Nischwitz. All summer the young entrepreneur traveled to and fro between Johannisthal and Schwerin to arrange the various details of the move. On October 4 he himself also moved, leaving the warm, friendly atmosphere at Senftleben's behind. He rented a furnished apartment on the first floor of a newly finished house on the corner of Scharnhorststrasse (now Walter Rathenau Street) next to the army barracks, about six hundred feet from his factory at the Hintenhof.

The Fokker factory: In the spring of 1913 the city authorities of Schwerin, north of Berlin, made Fokker an attractive proposal to move his activities there. As an incentive, the city offered several workshop buildings along the shore of Lake Schwerin. Fokker intended to build floatplanes there. Several of these buildings from the world's oldest airplane factory can still be visited today. **FOKKER HERITAGE TRUST, HUINS, THE NETHERLANDS**

From now on Anthony, only twenty-three years old, was an entrepreneur and factory director first, and a pilot second. For a factory director, his lodgings were truly modest. The gray, cement-plastered building on number 2 had few distinctive characteristics. Although Anthony worked long hours and would often only come home to sleep, he nonetheless wanted to have his friends around him. In the new and as yet unfamiliar entourage of Schwerin, it was important to re-create something of the Senftleben ambience. Frits Cremer, who had initially stayed at Hotel Nordischer Hof, and designer Carl Palm joined him at number 2. Bernard de Waal followed shortly after, bringing his unruly pet capuchin monkey, Cuckoo. Architect Richard Thiede joined them from Berlin, where he had worked at Johannisthal. He now became responsible for the construction of the various buildings and sheds that Fokker occupied on the Hintenhof and on Görries. The five of them were entrusted to the care of Frieda Grabitz, their landlady.[22]

With the new facilities and employment for fifty-five people, Fokker Aeroplanbau was beginning to resemble a real factory. Yet to achieve progress in airplane construction was far from easy. Neither the newly developed M.3 nor its successor the M.4 became a success. They were unstable in flight and difficult to handle. The same could be said about the W.2 floatplane, which broke in half after a few test flights above the Schweriner Innensee. This spelled failure for Fokker's chief constructor,

Carl Palm, whom Anthony replaced with his assistant, Martin Kreutzer, at the end of 1913. Even if the aircraft itself was improved as a result of the change, Anthony was still easily incensed when encountering critiques of his floatplane achievements a year later.[23]

Meanwhile, a remarkable new pupil had registered at Görries in October 1913. Born on April 30, 1897, Alexander von Bismarck was the second cousin of Germany's Iron Chancellor. Although just sixteen years of age, he had already decided to risk his health, life, and considerable fortune in the air. Alexander knew Anthony Fokker from a distance: young Bismarck had spent his childhood on his mother's estate near Wiesbaden. He and Anthony felt an instinctive bond, and both were equally obsessed with speed and flight.[24]

But there was more that connected them. In July Anthony had not only seen Ljuba and Letort depart for Paris, but he had also made a close inspection of Letort's airplane. With its 50-hp air-cooled rotary engine, the Morane-Saulnier Type H was the latest in aeronautical technology, far surpassing anything that flew in Germany. French aviators won one air race after the other thanks to the slender, lightweight machine and its remarkable engine. Fokker had not been the only one at Johannisthal to take a special interest in the plane. Several German constructors were competing to obtain production rights for the Morane, or were sneaking around with sketchbooks and slide rules to uncover the French design secrets.

In the early days of aviation, copyists were just as important as people with original ideas. Anthony Fokker was no exception. Variations on the Morane appeared as aircraft types from four different German manufacturers. Fokker followed another, more practical course. Bismarck and he agreed that Bismarck would buy a Morane in France and pursue options from there. (That way Fokker's name would remain outside the deal.) Late in 1913 Fokker and Hans Haller traveled to Paris on behalf of their client. They returned with a severely damaged Morane-Saulnier Type H that they had been able to buy for the bargain price of 500 marks.[25] The intention was that the airplane would be repaired in Schwerin. Fokker used the reconstruction project to learn all there was to know about the Morane and develop his own version of the plane. Ideas were embraced as they popped up. While Schwerin was covered in ice and snow that prevented flying in mid-January 1914, Anthony and his small circle bent over the Morane in their hangar at Görries. Gradually a new version of the design took shape. The fuselage was stretched by about three feet and was constructed from welded metal piping to improve rigidity. This had a beneficial effect on the aircraft's behavior in flight. Fokker also extended the wings.

On January 31 Fokker boldly indicated to the German military authorities that he was working on a new monoplane that would have a lightweight rotary engine.[26] Such an engine, a French invention, had a considerably better power-to-weight ratio than the water-cooled Argus, Daimler, and Mercedes engines that were customarily used

Industrial espionage: Early aviation developed on the basis of copying the ideas of others. Early in 1914, Fokker's improved copy of the French Morane-Saulnier, which he lovingly described as his "first baby," became Germany's most agile reconnaissance plane. Anthony even dared to fly loops in it. **FOKKER HERITAGE TRUST, HUINS, THE NETHERLANDS**

in Germany. Despite poor weather conditions, Alexander von Bismarck had achieved his flying license on January 17 on a *Spider* that he owned. However, that plane was lost on February 10 in a crash that resulted from a bad landing, just when Grand Duke Friedrich Franz IV came to inspect the airfield. The only thing that remained of the machine was the aluminum body work; young Bismarck himself escaped scot-free.[27] For months he had to fly the school's older aircraft. Not before May 11 had the development of the Morane copy proceeded far enough that Fokker dared draw up a delivery contract for the machine that Bismarck had ordered. He sold the machine, now indicated as M.5, for 8,452 marks and 95 pfennig ($1,998.34).[28]

Before that, Fokker had built his own personal M.5 so that he would be able to test the machine himself. At the time no one commented on its likeness to the Morane. Well into 1915, reports referred to the similarities as something normal and evident.[29] For Fokker, however, the M.5 represented a radical break with the past. The design sacrificed automatic stability to maneuverability and was of overriding importance in the technological evolution of the Fokker designs. By the end of April the new machine was more or less ready. Anthony held the highest expectations and was planning a series of flying demonstrations with the M.5. In recent months his big example had become the Frenchman Adolphe Pégoud, the "man without nerves" and the only pilot in Germany who dared the dangerous maneuver of the loop, perceived as the most daring stunt imaginable. From October 23 to 25, 1913, Pégoud had excited several hundred thousand spectators at Johannisthal with this stunt. After pocketing 180,000 marks (about $42,550) in flying fees, he had left again for France at the end of the month.[30] But in March 1914 Pégoud was back, performing the same maneuvers. Fokker, whose public reputation depended on his performances as a stunt pilot, could not afford to pass up the challenge, especially after Pégoud had again drawn huge crowds at Johannisthal. Now Anthony finally had the plane with which he could dare make the dreaded loop. Equaling Pégoud's maneuver became his biggest ambition, even if he was scared to lose his life in the attempt. His first loop etched itself into his memory. Later he confessed (exclusively to his Dutch readership) that

> I set my teeth and thought "Someday you must die, it might as well be now." With that, I pushed the nose far down, picked up speed until the wind whistled through the guy wires, and pulled up sharply on the elevator. The plane staggered fearfully, turned over like a flash on its back, and for a moment my feet slipped off the rudder as we hung there, upside down. I prayed for my straps to hold. Then over we came in a steep dive toward the ground, out of which I pulled as rapidly as possible. In a minute the airplane was back again in normal flying position. I had flown my first loop and was still alive![31]

Anthony next embarked on a demonstration tour that took him and his new monoplane to Frankfurt and other German airfields. To draw attention—and orders— he took considerable risks in seeking the limits of his machine's capabilities, including the dangerous loop, then known in Germany as the *Schleifenflug*. It was no surprise that his spectacular airshows and the exceptional maneuverability of his plane soon drew attention in military circles. On June 1 the chief of the General Staff, Gen. Erich von Falkenhayn, came to inspect the new wonder machine at Johannisthal. Anthony dared risk a loop with Bismarck on the passenger seat. The spectators were much impressed. There was even talk of erecting a bronze statue of Fokker to commemorate his *Schleifenflug*. That same month, at a two-day demonstration in Kiel, Fokker performed a *Kerzenflug* (a near vertical climb), a daring nosedive, a corkscrew maneuver, and a landing without engine power. Those daredevils ready to risk their lives along with the pilot were invited to sign up for special nosedive flights with a passenger onboard. All this was not without danger. On June 13 a cylinder head on Fokker's machine exploded in an airshow in Wanne, near Gelsenkirchen in the west of the country. Anthony barely managed an emergency landing, and the plane was badly damaged.[32] Nonetheless, he refused to be discouraged and continued his circuit of flying displays.

In the meantime his company was slowly taking root. On May 14, 1914, the company had officially been moved to Schwerin. The sheds at Johannisthal were gradually emptied and transferred to the Zentrale für Aviatik.[33] The company's move had consequences. To maximize the growth potential offered to Fokker's company in Schwerin, the corporate capital would need considerable expansion. But few German investors seemed likely to invest in a risky venture run by a twenty-four-year-old youngster from abroad, without diplomas or other professional papers, hardly any serious business experience, and operating within a small market? Anthony had little other choice but to turn again to his circle of family members. His father set up another meeting in Haarlem in December 1913 with uncle Anthony senior, uncle Eduard, and Jacob Cremer. It was a decisive moment for the young entrepreneur. For the first time he could sit down at the table as the director of his own company, with men who were used to deciding on sizable business investments, and discuss possible expansions in his enterprise. Thanks to the revenues from pilot training and the German army's recent down payment on the ten aircraft it had ordered, Anthony was now able to present a company prognosis that was backed up by investments of his own: he was able to put 90,000 marks (about $21,300 dollars) on the table. This made an impression. Uncle Eduard, who had once before translated the trust he had in his nephew's venture into hard cash, proved himself generous again: he put up 60,000 marks (then about $14,200). Uncle Anthony committed 30,000 ($7,100), to which his wife, Susanna, added another 20,000 ($4,730). Glad that his "unruly" son Frits had finally found a calling in life, Jacob Cremer offered to invest 40,000 marks ($9,500). Moreover, he brought in two further investors: Constand von Schmid, a retired chief administrator of the Deli Company (a Sumatra-based trading and distribution firm), who put up 15,000 marks ($3,550), and Jan Everwijn, the former chief of the Dutch Ministry of Agriculture, Industry, and Commerce, who committed 10,000 ($2,365). Frits Cremer himself also joined in with 35,000 marks ($8,275), so that he now became part owner of his friend's company.[34] Thus a total of 300,000 marks was on the table (just under $71,000), meaning that Herman Fokker could, for once, abstain from further investment and limit himself to filling the glasses and proposing a toast to the future of aviation.

Anthony had by now learned to be careful and prudent with the means put at his disposal. No more than a quarter of the committed funds were used to augment the company capital. After completing the move to Schwerin, the founding papers of his new Fokker Aeroplanbau GmbH (Fokker Aircraft Construction Ltd.) were registered with the Schwerin Chamber of Commerce on July 7, 1914, under number 1069.[35] On the eve of the Great War, twenty-four-year-old Anthony Fokker thus found himself at the helm of a well-capitalized corporate venture that employed fifty-five people and had twenty-four aircraft for its flying school.

STENAY, FRANCE
JUNE 1915

Anthony Fokker had already been in the northern part of occupied France for several days. Now he found himself in a German trench at the front line of the war with an officer of the Air Corps. It had not been his outright intention to inspect the war personally, but the former soldier of the Dutch Second Regiment of Fortress Artillery had accepted the offer to do so. Now he was going to see actual combat with his own eyes:

> We left the motorcar about two kilometers behind the actual front lines, and walked by a circuitous route through the trench area. This section was under fire regularly, I was told, at about eleven o'clock in the morning, and so it was suggested that I return before that hour. . . . The French were . . . easily visible . . . not more than 1,500 feet away. I found the situation so interesting that time slipped by quickly. It was 10:30 before anyone realized it. The commander urged me to go at once, saying he would send a soldier back with us as far as the motorcar, which had been left at the far side of a ruined village. On the way through the trenches we were delayed, partly because of my curiosity. Just before reaching the abandoned village the expected artillery fire opened up. The screaming of shells as they approached; the bursting roar as they hit; the blasting of earth, bricks, and trees simply frightened me to death. I began dodging with every detonation, even though my mind told me that once the explosion was heard, it was too late to dodge. With one accord we started running, catching our feet in stray bits of wire, falling down in the mud, and getting up even more scared. My arms were covered with filth clear up to my shoulders where I had plunged headlong into the muck. In a few minutes we were dripping. Exhausted with running, we dropped into an abandoned dugout to catch our breath. As soon as we had stopped panting, we saw that the shelter offered little protection, for only a few timbers formed the roof, and shells were dropping on all sides of us. The soldier who had brought us out of the trenches was paying not the slightest attention to all the firing, and was as near to laughing as a German soldier could come to mocking a superior officer. It made me feel pretty small, but nonetheless afraid.[1]

At the front: On June 13, 1915, Fokker demonstrated the latest development in airplane armament at Stenay, just behind the front line in northern France. His synchronized machine gun would revolutionize air warfare. German Crown Prince Wilhelm (in a white uniform, talking to Fokker behind the fuselage) was much impressed by the new weapon.
N. V. NEDERLANDSCHE VLIEGTUIGFABRIEK FOKKER, LIQUIDATED 1996

What had brought Anthony to France on June 11, 1915, was a revolutionary new invention that he and his technical staff had come up with. It promised to change the war in the air beyond recognition. Traveling in wartime had been a bewildering experience. As his train continued farther into France, he saw more and more signs of fighting: damaged houses and villages, bridges that had been blown up and then provisionally repaired. Toward the end of the journey the thudding noises of guns and explosions had pressed themselves upon Anthony's ears—ominous sounds he had not heard before with such intensity. Stenay, his destination, was less than twenty miles from the front. In that small provincial town on the River Meuse, Crown Prince Wilhelm, commander of Germany's Fifth Army Corps, had made his headquarters in the luxurious late nineteenth-century Château des Tilleuls in September 1914. In the subsequent months the look of the town had changed: the majority of its four thousand inhabitants had left or fled. German uniforms dominated the narrow streets, which had been given new German names. Stenay had a military command post, officers' quarters, a military hospital, and even a German field bookstore.

Anthony's real destination was not Stenay itself, but the repair facility for damaged aircraft, located near the princely château to the north of town.[2] There the airplane he had brought on the train from Schwerin was reassembled and readied for testing. This was not just another flying machine: it was the world's very first fighter aircraft, and it would change the war in the air completely. No other airplane was equipped with a fixed, forward firing machine gun that the pilot could aim by steering his own airplane toward enemy aircraft. Prince Wilhelm, who had an interest in the possibilities of military aviation, had requested that the machine and its inventor visit him in Stenay for a flying display that might convince him the new discovery worked. Such potential royal acclaim meant a lot to Fokker. If he played his cards right, he could achieve a critical breakthrough as an aircraft producer.

In recent months his life had changed completely: from display stunt pilot to factory owner to industrialist deeply involved in the war. That Sunday morning, June 13, 1915, Anthony proudly explained the workings of his new fighter plane to Prince Wilhelm, who had arrived early on the airfield in his impeccably white uniform and who made no attempt to disguise his surprise at the young age of the inventor. On the veranda of the Château des Tilleuls, Anthony had himself photographed in the uniform of a lieutenant of the German Air Service, so that no one would be able to question his dedication to the German war effort later on. He used his piloting experience to stage a number of spectacular nose dives, firing bursts into the Meuse. Wilhelm was suitably impressed; the synchronized machine gun was a revelation to him. As Anthony rode in the prince's gray Mercedes to the château for a celebratory ham and sherry lunch, he knew he had landed support from the highest echelons of power.[3] For his invention he would later be decorated by Emperor Wilhelm II with the Iron Cross.

In August 1914 the outbreak of the war had taken many by surprise. At the beginning of that beautiful summer, few had thought it possible that the international tensions among Germany, Austria-Hungary, Serbia, Russia, France, and Britain would soon hold all of Europe in a deadly grip. While army columns moved and trainloads of soldiers and equipment rolled toward the borders, considerable numbers of well-to-do citizens were still enjoying their holidays on the North Sea beaches. Few had more than a vague idea of what a modern war would mean. Expectations were that the fighting would be short and localized. Civilians tended to look back to the Franco-German War of 1870–71, which had been decided quickly in several large battles. Nonetheless, many German citizens were anxious. The start of military skirmishes led to a bank run on cash savings and hoarding of foodstuffs and other goods that were perceived as likely to become scarce. Anthony himself bought six pairs of shoes.[4]

Anthony's deepest worries, however, concerned his business affairs. The demand for reconnaissance aircraft was skyrocketing. The German army was ill prepared for aerial warfare, and in the first month of fighting, almost half the available aircraft were lost over the front. The army had to buy every airplane it could get. Naturally Fokker wanted his piece of the cake. The question was how to increase production without having to invest too much money in a war that was expected to end by Christmas. He counted himself lucky that the city of Schwerin had offered to fund an expansion of his workshop facilities on the lakeside just before the outbreak of hostilities.[5] For the time being he resorted to hiring more workers. Every week the local papers featured advertisements in which Fokker offered jobs. Training took place on the job and was limited to a week. The task of guiding the new workers and overseeing factory expansion resided with Heinrich Liebig, Fokker's supervisor. Anthony knew him and August Nischwitz from the days they had cooperated at Goedecker's workshop in Mainz. Extra help in setting up something resembling series production of aircraft came from Anthony's friend Friedrich Seekatz.

That autumn the German advance in the West was brought to a halt, and the war took on the character of static combat conducted from reinforced trenches. Reconnaissance missions on horseback became almost impossible. As a result the airplane rapidly gained in importance, creating an exceptional opportunity for Fokker. Although the larger producers such as LVG, Aviatik, and Albatros were responsible for the majority of Germany's military aircraft, the war also created demand for Fokker's agile, lightweight machines such as the M.5 single-seater and the M.8 two-seater. Although frontline pilots praised the flying characteristics of both types, technical problems prevented larger numbers of them from being ordered. There was little that Anthony Fokker could do about this; he had to work with the materials and equipment that were available in Germany. Yet the lightweight rotation engines from the Oberursel factory that powered his designs—copies of the French Gnome and Le Rhône rotaries—were notoriously unreliable. Pilots joked about the Oberursel Gnom as meaning "Geht nie ohne Monteur" (Never runs without mechanic).[6]

Pilots flying Fokker planes were warned to stay on the German side of the trenches on their reconnaissance missions. Meanwhile, Anthony did his utmost to land as many orders as he possibly could. In August he made promises to a delegation from the Austro-Hungarian Air Corps on a procurement mission in Berlin. To meet demand he even thought of opening a second production line in Berlin, although talks about this led nowhere.[7] Thus Fokker continued to build his aircraft in Schwerin, which certainly was cheaper than the capital city.

₲

Fokker now had enough money to pursue the more pleasurable things in life, but time to spend it was short. Since moving to Schwerin, he had taken up his old sailing hobby again. He joined the local water sports club Schweriner Segler-Verein 1894 and the rowing club Obotrit. The latter had an additional attraction in that its membership was open to women. Of course the youthful, rich bachelor, pilot, and factory owner drew quite a bit of female attention, especially at parties and outings, even if he did not always quite know what to do with the ladies' flirtatious attentions.[8] By way of escape he took his friends out for sailing trips on the lakes.

At a jetty behind his factory he kept several boats. If the weather was right, he could be observed sailing the various lakes around Mecklenburg's capital, but what he liked best was boat races. Speed fascinated Anthony, not just in the air or on the road but also on the water. Together with his Dutch friend Bernard de Waal, he developed a special racing boat that lay shallow on the water. The craft was driven by an aircraft propeller. With this "glide boat" he managed to attain speeds of up to twenty-five mph. In the winter, Anthony would go ice sailing on Lake Schwerin. He obtained even higher speeds with his car, a Peugeot Torpedo sports model, which he had fitted with a 100-hp engine, three times the standard capability.[9] All the same, his personal desires did not appear to extend far beyond sleek boats and flashy cars, and until 1916 he shared the house on Scharnhorststrasse with his friends. Eventually their circle became less tight, a gradual process that coincided with the increase of Anthony's responsibilities as director while the factory expanded.

Even though he built his aircraft in Schwerin, Anthony spent quite a bit of his time in Berlin, where new army commissions were decided. The twenty-four-year-old foreigner, with his high-pitched voice and thick Dutch accent, did not have an easy time there. At the beginning of the war in 1914, Fokker was primarily known as a stunt pilot, not as an aircraft constructor. To boost his image as a serious businessman, he moved into one of Berlin's most prestigious hotels that autumn. Hotel Bristol was located on Unter den Linden, the city's most prominent boulevard, less than a hundred yards from the famous Brandenburger Tor (Brandenburg Gate). With its 350 rooms, the capital's foremost international hotel provided temporary lodgings to Europe's royalty, leading politicians, entrepreneurs, and top artists such as actress Sarah Bernhardt and opera singer Enrico Caruso. Pedestrians strolling along Unter den Linden could recognize it from afar, thanks to its Bordeaux-colored decorative shields on the ground floor and the imposing cupola that dominated the roof above the hotel's central staircase. Visitors entered into a large hallway with a thick red carpet, flanked by marble pillars and plaster ornaments. From there they could see the glass-covered winter garden and hear the soft sound of water running in its electrically lighted fountain.

Anthony loved this ambience. For guests preferring peace and quiet, there were separate rooms on the ground floor as well. The hotel had an exquisite restaurant, luxury jewelry, tobacco, and gift shops, a bank, a café, and even its own variety theater. Most rooms featured mahogany furniture upholstered in silk, carved wooden desks, lace curtains, murals, and paintings depicting landscapes. Owner Conrad Uhl provided completely upholstered luxury apartments, mostly rented out to foreign guests who wished to stay in Berlin indefinitely.[10] Anthony rented such an apartment on the first floor, plus rooms 163, 164, and 165 as office space for his company. The office arrangement proved temporary. By mid-1916 the Fokker administration had expanded so much that the rooms at the Bristol had become too cramped. Therefore the Fokker Flugzeugwerke (Fokker Aircraft Works), as the company had called itself since January of that year, moved to rented offices across Unter den Linden at number 56. This became the location of the Fokker Zentralbüro (Fokker Central Office), where the various strands of the firm's ever-expanding activity intersected at the desk of company director Wilhelm Horter.

Anthony's own apartment, with a sofa, chairs, and a bedroom with adjoining bathroom, was not merely meant as a place to stay in town. It also presented an operating base for sorties into the Berlin nightlife that Fokker liked to offer to airmen on leave from front duty. He became widely known for the effort he devoted to amusing his guests. An evening out often started with *Flieger Tee* (pilots' tea) at the Bristol or the adjacent Hotel Adlon. From there the company would head into town for the night. In the first years of the war Berlin remained an entertainment oasis, at least for those who had money to spend. Cultural activities and nightlife largely continued as they had before the war, with theater and films that amused audiences and upheld morale. Cafés poured beer as in normal times, and good food could be enjoyed in restaurants, if at rapidly increasing prices.[11] Fokker's care of his "customers" went even further: "We did our best to show the flyers a gay time. . . . What they wanted most, and what we tried to give them, was gaiety, charm, diversion, the society of pretty girls, the kind of a good time they had been dreaming about during their nightmare stay at the front. Berlin was full of girls eager to provide this companionship."[12]

Fokker's rising number of aircraft orders ensured that his company attracted more and more attention from the authorities. Was a defense industry with a Dutch owner to be trusted in wartime? On October 16, 1914, the government issued a decree that all foreign companies were to be placed under German supervision. This regulation affected hundreds of enterprises. Each foreign corporation now received an official supervisor who acted as a representative from the government and who also

Expansion at Görries: During World War I the Fokker Flying School at Schwerin-Görries was militarized and enlarged. Several new hangars and company buildings were constructed at the airfield, not just to house the extra training aircraft but also for the final assembly and testing of fighter aircraft built at Fokker's lakeside factory. **COLLECTION MICHAEL SCHMIDT, MUNICH, GERMANY**

held power of attorney.[13] Although Anthony pointed to native-born Hans Haller as his business partner, the authorities were not satisfied. In December 1914 Fokker received an urgent "advice" from the military authorities to apply for naturalization and become a German citizen. The subtext of the request could hardly be misread. Anthony quickly filed a request to become a German citizen. His reply was accompanied by a letter in which he urged for a speedy treatment of his case, so that the whole matter might be settled upon his return to Germany after spending Christmas with his parents in Holland. At home he worked out a deal with his uncles, buying them out so that his company would become wholly German-owned once he obtained his new passport.[14]

Upon his return from Haarlem, Anthony Fokker had finally become his own boss. Nonetheless, the administrative and legal procedures for transferring the shares took another year. As a token of confidence that everything would continue to proceed as planned, Anthony was issued a German passport on his birthday, April 6, 1915. His transfer of nationality was a fairly public event: the Dutch newspaper *Telegraaf* reported on it in March, even before Anthony received his new passport. Nine months later his restructured company, now renamed Fokker Flugzeugwerke GmbH (Fokker Aircraft Works Ltd.), was registered at the Schwerin Chamber of Commerce on January 28, 1916. Anthony Fokker was listed as the sole shareholder.[15]

In the meantime the Fokker company had witnessed tremendous growth. The number of employees had doubled. Both at the Hintenhof and at the Görries airfield, architect Richard Thiede had supervised the construction of several large workshops. Nonetheless, Anthony harbored doubts about the duration and the outcome of the war, and steered a parsimonious course. He managed to strike an advantageous deal with Mayor Weltzien, who also presided over the Mecklenburg Airfield Society, for the construction of additional buildings at Görries. The rental agreement provided for a fixed lease at several hundred marks per month plus a compensation of about 150 marks for every airplane delivered from the Fokker premises. It all meant that Fokker could expand further, without having to invest serious money.[16]

This arrangement suited both parties. For Fokker it was cheap: the fixed rate was low, and the fee on the aircraft could be surcharged to the military authorities in Berlin. For the Airfield Society the deal entailed rising income as the numbers of aircraft ordered from Fokker increased. Anthony soon disengaged from the process and left it to his advisers—administrators and technicians with whom he was personally acquainted—to hammer out the details. Outsiders were few in the Fokker company, and only started to arrive in 1916 when the Inspektion der Fliegertruppe (Inspection of the Air Corps, known as IdFlieg) sent specialized engineers from Berlin to review construction drawings and their underlying mathematical formulas.[17]

Nonetheless, the organization of the Fokker company was seriously flawed. Changing from the construction of individual machines to series production proved difficult and time-consuming—no surprise, considering that the factory had been set up to turn out about twenty-five aircraft per year.[18] Although Fokker's fifty-six employees did their best to boost production and managed to deliver the first of a series of forty M.8 reconnaissance aircraft in October, no more than twenty-three M.8 aircraft were transported from Schwerin in 1914. Fokker's production remained well below that of better-organized companies such as Aviatik and LVG, even though the score was not exceptional. The German aircraft industry was in no way prepared for the demands of war.[19] At Fokker's competitor Rumpler, things got out of hand completely; Rumpler managed to produce only half of its assigned orders. To address the issue, several meetings were convened between representatives of the army, the aircraft industry, and the government. These resulted in a concerted effort to raise nationwide production to 200 aircraft per month. At Fokker's factory a time clock was introduced to improve worker punctuality. He hired experts from the Schwarz-kopf torpedo factory to organize production. Yet the German engine manufacturers were unable to deliver more than 170 engines per month. In 1914 and 1915 several dozens of Fokker aircraft stood idle at Görries awaiting engines.

Meanwhile, pilot training gradually changed in character. In the winter of 1915 the Fokker Flying School was taken over by the military.[20] In response Bernard de Waal, Anthony's trusted friend and confident, was put in charge of the Fokker workshops at Görries, where his job was to flight test all the Fokker aircraft that were rolled out. Fokker's other friend, Frits Cremer, had relatively little to do, and he decided to move back to Holland with his wife, Dora van Spengler. For the time being they moved into the house adjoining the stables at his father's mansion, Duin en Kruidberg, near Haarlem.

Fokker's initial factory buildings were cramped and proved ill-suited for series production. Anthony tackled this by buying and erecting several standardized wooden prison barracks to serve as factory sheds. Their prime attraction was that they came cheap. Toward the end of the war the permanently guarded complex encompassed nine larger and smaller buildings. Various parts of the assembly process were sepa-rated. For the wooden wing construction, tree stems had to be sawed to the correct dimensions, a process that produced considerable dust and had to be undertaken apart from the welding of steel tubes for aircraft fuselages because of fire hazard. The steel tubing itself proved difficult to come by. Covering the frames with fabric was no longer done under the same roof, and the construction of the wooden wings, the individual parts of which were glued together, was also relocated to a different build-ing. While carpenters worked on the assembly, already completed wing frames were hung out to dry over their heads.

The assembly process was largely done by hand, demanding skill and, above all, people. In 1915 the number of employees was already in the hundreds, with repeated ads in the papers offering high wages for fitters, metal workers, welders, and mechan-ics. By the end of the war their number would be about 1,850. As the numbers of aircraft ordered rose, the factory became increasingly pressed for space.[21] In 1915 a part of the wing production was relocated to the piano factory Perzina, located in a monumental four-story building in the middle of Schwerin. Grand pianos and aircraft wings both required precision construction, but the production process remained bumpy. The development of new aircraft types depended on the experimental department, located in a separate shed that was kept under lock and key. There various static stress tests were undertaken, using sand bags for weight. Wings were supposed to be able to withstand stress loads of up to 5,000 kilograms (11,000 pounds).[22] Although construction drawings were made, there was no discipline in the factory to consult these for each new aircraft part. Parts (and even complete aircraft) were made and assembled "on sight."

The whole process, spread out among buildings at Hintenhof, Perzina, and Görries, was haphazard. The fuselage and the wings were joined at Görries. The engine was installed last, after which a plane was ready for flight testing. Keeping tabs on what was happening in the company became an increasingly demanding task, and Fokker's administration, largely staffed by women, grew ever bigger. To keep even a semblance of coordination and overview, the telephone became indispensable. This applied especially to Anthony himself, who showed a definite preference for the telephone over written communication. To show just how modern he was, he had himself photographed and filmed using the latest communication devices.

Since the production process was so fragmented, organizing a proper quality control proved difficult. Indeed, Fokker's expedition chief continued to ship aircraft that had parts missing. In 1917 Friedrich Seekatz, by then head of Fokker's subsidiary in Budapest, where they built planes for the Austro-Hungarian forces, repeatedly complained of machines delivered without provisions for armaments. Others arrived without a rear wall for the engine, without engine cowling, or missed other vital parts. Seekatz also found that the engines did not always fit the airframes.[23] At Görries aircraft were readied to be shipped to the front by train. Even this stage was far from easy, as Fokker and the Reichsbahn (the German national railway company) argued from May 1914 to December 1918 about the cost of a direct connection from the Fokker works at Görries to the rail network.[24] Communications between various parts of the Fokker company were chaotic. Complaints soon became supplications. Always looking ahead and busy trying out new ideas, Anthony preferred not to answer such pleas.

New ideas were tried at a surprising pace, since aircraft development at Fokker Flugzeugwerke was done on the basis of hands-on experience and practical experiments. The mathematics behind the constructions, necessary to satisfy the IdFlieg military technicians in Berlin, came second, or so Anthony believed. Proper design drawings were made on the basis of aircraft that had already been tested. Even if Fokker and his designers, Martin Kreutzer and Franz Möser, deviated little from common practice, his competitors were quick to label him as a "tinkerer." In the course

of the war Fokker tried over 110 different aircraft models, an average of a new prototype every two weeks. Among these no strange ideas were barred: a plane with five
wings—a triplane arrangement at front and a biplane set of wings at the rear of the
fuselage—may not have promised much success, but it was tried out all the same. In
January 1917 Fokker even proposed to develop a small airplane for the navy, suited for
operations from submarines despite its wooden wings. He conducted several discussions about the project with the chief of the German submarine service.[25]

৭

"Tinkering," however, formed the introduction to Fokker's greatest triumph. In the
early months of 1915, the air war over the Western Front became a reality as a result of
a change in French tactics. Specialized hunting squadrons were sent up with a mission
to try and stop German reconnaissance flights over Allied lines. From now on pilots
shot at each other, even if their weapons were mere pistols or carbines, or carried
gunners in a second cockpit.

Several constructors, on both sides of the front, had already been working to
develop a more effective way of firing at the enemy. After months of tests, the French
aviator Roland Garros, a former test pilot at Morane-Saulnier, and his mechanic Jules
Hue had discovered the beginning of a solution. They fixed a Hotchkiss machine gun
atop Garros's aircraft, just in front of the cockpit. By steering his plane Garros could
now engage the enemy in battle, which increased the chances of hitting something.
Of course it was imperative that the bullets fired from the machine gun would not
hit his aircraft's wooden propeller. This Garros and Hue achieved by reinforcing the
rear of the two propeller blades with a steel wedge that deflected the relatively small
number of bullets that struck the blades. (The firing speed of the gun was limited.)
This system, however crude, was something of a success. Between April 1 and 18, 1915,
Garros managed to shoot down three German aircraft over the Western Front—an
exceptional success in those days.[26]

On April 18, however, Garros's luck ran out. The engine of his machine was hit by
shots fired from the ground just as he had crossed the German lines. He was forced
to land and was taken prisoner before he could manage to set his plane alight. His
damaged machine was then sent to the German military testing facility at Döberitz
near Berlin. Because the French were dominant in the air, the investigation of Garros's ingenious device received top priority. But what the Germans discovered was
that simply copying Garros's invention would not do. French bullets had copper
points, whereas German ones had a point made from a harder chrome alloy, which
shot propellers to smithereens in tests. In May several German aircraft constructors
who were known to have experimented with fixed forward-firing synchronized arms
were invited to Döberitz to review Garros's invention in practice. Among them was
Anthony Fokker.

The young new German was not an obvious choice, given the fairly marginal
position he occupied in German aircraft production. Yet it was known that he had

been experimenting in Schwerin with his chief mechanic, Heinrich Lübbe, to develop a synchronizing mechanism since the end of 1914. Fokker and Lübbe hoped to synchronize the revolving propeller with the gun's firing mechanism.[27] The basic principle of this idea had been the intellectual property of aviation pioneer August Euler since July 1910. In May 1912 Euler had received a patent for his invention. Apart from the Euler patent, a second patent was later issued that specifically dealt with the issue of synchronization: in July 1913 the Swiss aeronautical engineer Franz Schneider, who was the director of technology of Fokker's Johannisthal competitor LVG, had filed an application for this. Schneider's patent related to a system in which the machine gun's firing mechanism would be blocked mechanically every time a propeller blade would pass in front of the gun's barrel. The German Patent Office took a year to arrive at a judgment on this invention before granting Schneider patent rights on July 10, 1914.[28] But even if aircraft engines achieved no more than 1,200 rpm in 1914, this still meant that a two-bladed propeller would need to jam a firing mechanism 2,400 times each minute. In practice no time would remain to fire the gun, and Schneider's patent therefore appeared unusable. Yet Fokker and Lübbe recognized the potential behind the idea. Around Christmas time they set to work with a small team. Five months later they had arrived at a reasonably workable solution.

On May 19 Fokker and the other aircraft constructors arrived at Döberitz to acquaint themselves with the Garros invention. Anthony must have been pleased to note just how far away the French were from cracking the problem. After months of experimenting, however, he was about to make a breakthrough. All he needed was a compact, lightweight gun that might be fixed to a plane's fuselage. With his usual flair he assured the army officers present at Döberitz that it would not take him long to solve the synchronization problem. With a lightweight machine gun, ammunition, and the propeller from Garros's plane on the back seat of his car, he drove back to Schwerin. Everything was now in place for the final test.

Fokker, Lübbe, and their assistants briskly went to work. There was some urgency to their efforts, because the invention would not only be of military significance; it also reeked of money. The system the Fokker team came up with was a variation on the Schneider patent. Instead of mechanically blocking the firing mechanism itself, Fokker allowed the gun to fire constantly once the trigger was pulled. To avoid hitting the propeller, the Fokker team fitted a cam to the engine shaft that would activate an interrupter every time the propeller turned in front of the barrel. This mechanism prevented the gun from firing for a brief moment. The cam was fitted in such a position that the bullets remained away from the propeller, staying within two imaginary half circles. A comparatively simple mechanical system of connected rods transferred the cam's impulse to the gun: they called this system the *Stangensteuerung* (rod drive).[29]

With most of the work already done, the firing trials could be conducted quickly with the gun that Fokker had brought. This was just the kind of hands-on approach in which Anthony excelled. On the little stretch of land between the factory and the lake, a fuselage was placed with both the engine and the gun mounted. But instead of using the propeller, the Fokker team fitted a wooden disk on which the outline of the propeller had been painted. In this way, the pattern of the bullets could be traced. After repeated firing tests and more than a few wooden disks, the team worked out the ideal location for fitting the cam on the engine shaft. Fokker was able to drive back with his plane in tow, two days after leaving Döberitz.[30] This was the invention that would revolutionize air warfare.

The military evaluation commission demanded several live demonstrations before they were ready to believe that the invention truly worked. The army command took a similar view. Therefore Fokker's demonstrations could not remain limited to Döberitz. He was asked to display the world's first real fighter aircraft and its synchronized gun before skeptical officers serving at the front in northern France. After all, they would be risking their lives flying with a synchronized gun. So it was that Anthony put his new airplane on a train in Schwerin on June 11, 1915, to travel to the front for a live demonstration of the new invention. To be sure that nothing could go wrong because of an unforeseen technical mishap, he also took a second airplane with him. The work Fokker had done on easy assembly and disassembly of aircraft now proved its value. The evening after his demonstration in Stenay, June 13, he and his machines traveled to Douai, 140 miles northwest of Stenay, closer to the front. There he was able to give a second flying display the following day. Besides himself, he had Lt. Otto Parschau, one of the pilots who had learned to fly at his school in Schwerin, fly the second machine. From the air they fired several bursts of fire into targets on the ground. Germany's top pilots of the time, Oswald Boelcke and Max Immelmann, who witnessed the performance, could hardly believe their eyes. When Anthony returned to Germany several days later, he left his armed fighter plane in Boelcke's hands.[31]

By then Anthony's presence in Schwerin was urgently required. All aircraft of Fokker's E-series of monoplanes were to receive urgent modifications to arm them with a fixed forward-firing machine gun. Even before the end of the month, the first five armed Fokker fighters were operational over the front. In Schwerin everything was readied for series production of the world's first operational fighter aircraft. Depending on the type of engine fitted, the Fokker aircraft were identified as E.I, E.II, and E.III. Before production was discontinued in mid-1916 because these monoplanes had become obsolete, about 415 fighter aircraft had left the factory in Schwerin.[32] Fokker and his machines had become legendary, and the money poured in like never before.

♀

Aeronautical engineer August Euler, who had been the first to patent the concept of a synchronized gun in 1912, was not happy with this turn of events. He refused to transfer his rights to his junior competitor. A court case loomed. Both aviation pioneers, who knew each other, felt regretful. On August 18, 1915, Fokker visited Euler at his home in Frankfurt to try and settle the matter. Their conversation lasted less than an hour; Fokker was pressed for time and was expected back in Berlin with a result. The two pioneers agreed that Fokker would pay Euler a compensation of 2,000 marks per aircraft. Two days later Fokker had a meeting with IdFlieg officials, when it transpired that his promise to Euler was made on the assumption that IdFlieg would foot the bill itself. But the IdFlieg officials found 2,000 marks excessive. Thereupon Fokker developed second thoughts as well. He subsequently maintained that it was not *him* who had infringed on the Euler patent but rather IdFlieg, which was responsible for generating the aircraft orders and signed off for converting the planes to take the machine guns. In this new line of thinking he was backed up by the War Ministry, which forbade Fokker and Euler to settle the issue between themselves. Instead they were to await a settlement proposed by the authorities.[33]

But Berlin was slow in drawing up a settlement. This was particularly annoying for Euler, since Fokker was the one receiving public acclaim for the invention that was to turn around the war in the air. It took until January 1916 for a meeting to be arranged in Berlin between Hauptmann von Loewenstern of the War Ministry, Euler, and Fokker's general director Wilhelm Horter.[34] After this, silence ruled; all parties remained unhappy. Meanwhile, IdFlieg made a plea to Fokker to settle the issue on his own account. Passing through Frankfurt on May 5, 1916, Anthony called Euler to schedule a visit with him that evening. At around 10 p.m. Fokker rang the doorbell with a once-only offer to pay 300,000 marks (then approximately $54,500) in compensation, plus 500 marks ($90) for each new airplane to be fitted with the synchronization system in future. Euler smelled money, for by now Fokker's system was being used by other manufacturers as well. This time they spoke for an hour and a half, again without reaching an agreement. But Euler contacted Fokker the next day, saying he was ready to consider the offer after all. In the end the synchronization mechanism would bring Euler close to a million marks.[35] Yet Fokker stood to make a far greater amount of money. By the end of 1915 about 400 fighter aircraft had already been fitted with synchronizing gear, and orders were on the increase steadily.

For Fokker, the synchronizing mechanism did not only bring money. In Germany he became more famous than he already was, celebrated in fact as a national hero. At a festive rally in the Hotel Bristol on July 7, 1916, to commemorate the German motor sports heroes of the prewar era, he proudly featured as the keynote speaker. He referred at length to the contribution made by August Euler, who was present in the audience. The two heroes of invention shared the enthusiastic applause between them.[36]

Meanwhile, it proved not at all easy to produce the synchronizing gear in greater numbers and according to a standardized process. As soon as the army started ordering synchronizers for other than Fokker aircraft, the company ran up against the limits of its production capacity. Army officials demanded that Fokker move production of the synchronizing gear to Berlin and link it up with the production of machine guns at the Deutsche Waffen- und Munitionsfabriken (German Weapons and Munitions Factories) in Berlin-Spandau.[37]

On June 22, 1916, Fokker had a contract drawn up to rent production and floor space at the F. H. Zimmermann Maschinenfabrik in the Berlin quarter Reinickendorf-Ost. It was a typical Fokker solution that demanded no investments. For the modest amount of 15,000 marks per year (then $2,700), plus another 4,000 ($730) for the use of the machinery present in the Zimmermann factory, a new Fokker subsidiary was set up: the Fokker Flugzeugwaffenfabrik (Fokker Aircraft Armaments Factory). The arrangement was temporary. The contract Fokker and factory owner Gustav Lüderitz signed stipulated that Fokker could end it three months after the war. The Zimmermann workforce was also taken on. For them the new employer meant a real change of routine: Wilhelm Horter, who supervised armaments production from Fokker's central office in Berlin, introduced strict demands of punctuality, work attitude, and profitability. As in Schwerin, a time clock was introduced to improve worker discipline. The weapons system itself was developed further under the supervision of Lübbe, without any involvement from Fokker personally, although subsequent new patents were registered in his name as owner of the company.[38]

Thus a *Zentralsteuerung* (central steering) system went into production at the end of 1916, which solved the issue of converting Fokker's synchronizing gear for use on different aircraft. Horter protested strongly against attempts to spread the production of the synchronizer gear and share it with other manufacturers such as Albatros.[39] The ultimate success was garnered in July 1917, when Fokker received notice from the commander of the German Air Corps to deliver synchronizers for all German fighter aircraft, plus several thousand extra for the Austro-Hungarian Air Corps. By the time the war ended, nearly 42,000 synchronizer gears had left the Reinickendorf factory.[40]

🦅

Although he held the actual synchronization patent, Franz Schneider was initially left out in the cold. It soon became evident, however, that this was going to be a business that would run into the millions. Through his employer, LVG, Schneider initiated legal proceedings against Fokker for breach of patent. Before the court in Berlin he indicted both Anthony Fokker personally, as well as the Fokker Fleugzeugwerke GmbH. Anthony immediately hired three heavyweight patent lawyers to protect his interests. In a countersuit they charged that the Schneider patent should be labeled null and void, because his invention had never been proven to work in practice.

Although Fokker's advisers told him that his case was weak in legal terms, he dug in for the fight as long as it might last. With money flowing in from the army's orders, he could afford to have his solicitors put in extra-long hours. At his instruction they did their best to slow the proceedings every chance they got. Nonetheless, he was convicted twice by the Royal Chamber Court in Berlin, in June 1917 and in March 1918, for patent infringement and sentenced to pay a fine of 1 million marks in damages (approximately $150,000). Both times Fokker, who genuinely believed that his synchronizer solution deviated substantially from the Schneider patent, refused to pay and went higher up the legal ladder to have the verdict overturned, even though he knew that he was likely to lose his appeals. Meanwhile, his lawyers dragged the proceedings as much as possible. When the war ended in November 1918, a final verdict was still nowhere in sight. In fact, the legal wrangling would last until September 1933, when Schneider, by then reduced to poverty as a result of the global economic crisis and having embraced the fascist movement in his search for support and solace, saw his latest attempt to sue Fokker under the German poor law dismissed by the Berlin District Court. Schneider was even required to pay the court's legal charges: another 1,000 marks (about $300). After a dispute lasting seventeen years, the invention of the synchronizer gear was finally Fokker's.[41]

On the Allied side, Fokker's armed monoplanes soon became the topic of the day, especially since the Germans publicly exploited their military successes. The nation's ace pilots—Immelmann, Boelcke, Von Richthofen, Udet, Goering, and others—became icons of the war effort, in which countless foot soldiers perished anonymously. The qualities of the individual Fokker airmen received systematic praise in the German press. At the same time Fokker's discovery had to be kept secret for as long as possible. Hence German pilots received specific instructions not to cross Allied lines in their Fokker aircraft, for fear of losing the advantage of the synchronized guns. In January 1916 reporters for the British newspaper *Manchester Guardian* wrote with ill-concealed admiration of the effectiveness of the latest German air war tactics. Noel Pemberton Billing, a member of the House of Commons and founder of the Supermarine aircraft works at Southampton, openly criticized British aerial policy on March 22, speaking of a "Fokker Scourge" that made Allied pilots into "Fokker Fodder."[42]

ᑫ

If Fokker's fighter aircraft were now heralded for their weapons system, their maker continued facing issues with his image, most particularly with his young age. The twenty-five-year-old factory director found it difficult to gain entry into the social circles that mattered in Germany. Neither a moustache nor a three-piece designer suit with matching cap had the desired effect.[43]

Even in his office Anthony searched for the right attributes that would underline his position as director. In December 1915 he had a series of photographs taken of himself in his guise as the director in his office, carefully rearranging various objects around him time and again to get the setup just right. Such an office ought to have a certain panache that suggested its occupant was well-educated and familiar with the ways of the world. Possibly this required the presence of art objects, but Anthony was no cultural connoisseur. However, his three-year-older niece Annie Fokker, daughter of his artistically inclined uncle Abraham, a former colonial administrator in Kediri, was a sculptor. In wartime, a framed photograph depicting one of her seated nudes

The public image: Being so young for an industrialist, Fokker was highly sensitive to everything connected with his public image. In 1915 he had a series of photographs taken in his office to demonstrate his entrepreneurial status. For each photograph he selected and moved the objects on his desk, such as the photos of his mother (left) and of his close friend Bernard de Waal (right). **COLLECTION SMEULERS, BRONKHORST, THE NETHERLANDS**

was easier arranged than transporting the sculpture itself. The photo was displayed in front of an embroidered tapestry with motifs that reminded Fokker of his family ties in the Dutch East Indies. Next to the image of the sculpture, Anthony displayed a photograph of one of his biplanes dangling from a set of antlers. In front of him on his desk he surrounded himself with the latest instruments of office technology: a Parlograph dictaphone, a typewriter, and a telephone.[44] He also made sure he displayed his Iron Cross decoration. On the left and right, and lighted by electric lamps that had only recently been installed at the Hintenhof, he placed photographs of his mother and of his friend Bernard de Waal. Both were carefully positioned facing away from the young director, so that they would be recognizable in each of the set of photographs taken. Yet Anthony was not entirely satisfied with the results. He had a film taken in the same office environment, from which he removed all the glistening distractions, keeping only the telephone as a symbol of modernity. This time he also stressed his own position by having a secretary hand him some papers to be signed.[45]

As a result of the war, life had become difficult for most Germans. The nation had entered the conflict without sufficient preparations. The distribution of grain and bread soon became especially problematic: statistics showed a reduction of 43 percent per capita between 1914 and 1917 as a result of the Allied sea blockade that virtually stopped all food imports from the United States. The army, encompassing 16.5 per cent of the entire population, needed so much food that not enough was left for civilians. In the autumn of 1914 the first protests were staged against the insufficient availability of bread. It was difficult to distribute the food that was available, because of fuel shortages. In the second half of the war the daily ration of food provided only 60 percent of the calories required for normal functioning. To make things worse for the average citizen, winters came early and were severe.[46] For weeks Schwerin remained snowed in and frozen. Gasoline was in ever shorter supply. For purposes of distribution, and to keep tabs on who used what, a detailed administrative system was set up. Even Fokker could not escape these difficulties. He spent more and more of his time in Berlin, where he held long conferences with IdFlieg officials on technical problems experienced at the front with several of his aircraft types.

For distraction and entertainment, Fokker kept dogs. In later years he especially remembered his long-haired black dachshund Ziethen (identified as Zeiten in the American edition of his 1931 autobiography): "Zeiten tagged at my heels, looking critical when I stopped to examine anything, and trotting along contentedly on his splayed legs when I seemed pleased. He was the most intelligent dog I've ever seen." Curiously, there was something strange and disquieting in Fokker's treatment of animals. Every morning started with "a spanking on account" for the poor animal, as "he did enough mischief every day to do for a dozen dogs."[47] With clearly visible pleasure, Anthony had himself filmed in 1915 while he was alternately holding Ziethen by the tail and by the ears, as if he were a live doll.[48] He also enjoyed letting the dog ride and balance on the hood of his Peugeot racing car as he drove, actively trying to dislodge it. Ziethen did not live to see the end of the war.

10

SAINT-QUENTIN, FRANCE
AUGUST 1918

August 1918 had started out as a cool month, but now the days warmed quickly. The summer weather and the clear blue skies encouraged Anthony Fokker to travel on top of the train he was riding. On August 21, he sat down in shirtsleeves with a group of soldiers in the midday sun on the roof of a third-class railway car transporting German troops to the Western Front. The atmosphere was boisterous. The soldiers passed around fruits, food, and drinks as if they were on a school outing. Only the military uniforms and the assorted guns indicated they were traveling to war. Anthony enjoyed shooting some film images of the passing scenery. Upon arriving at the small field station in northern France, he stood wide-legged on top of the car to watch the troops getting off the train.

This was the first time Fokker visited the front for other than business reasons. Perhaps even these were now secondary, because Anthony was in love. In the village of Ham near Saint-Quentin he hoped to speak with Lt. Gen. Curt von Morgen, once a military explorer in German West Africa and now commander of the 1st Reserve Corps. He intended to ask him for the hand of his daughter, Elisabeth, whom he had been courting for almost two years. To make the trip, Anthony had needed an official reason, which related to a series of recent accidents involving Fokker airplanes that had fallen from the sky for unknown reasons. The crashes had raised doubts about the wing construction of Fokker's latest fighter model, the E.V. Anthony had insisted on participating in the crash investigation commission sent out by the Inspektion der Fliegertruppe. The team was headed by Lt. Friedrich Mallinckrodt. In Bernes, west of Saint-Quentin, they were warmly welcomed by the commanding officer of

Jagdgeschwader 1, Hermann Goering, one of Fokker's friends and allies in the air corps.

Anthony's conversation with General Von Morgen went smoothly. The general was pleased that such an excellent candidate had presented himself for his only daughter. Proudly he recounted the successes his troops had achieved at the front that month and how they had incapacitated the latest Allied weapon, the tank.[1] This was something Anthony wanted to see. With Von Morgen's cooperation a visit was arranged to a former no-man's-land where a crippled and shot-up British tank had been left behind in the barbed wire. Curious as always and apparently oblivious to the scent of death, Anthony wriggled himself inside to examine the latest battle weapon. With evident enthusiasm he had himself filmed in the open hatch on top of the tank, leaving through the hole where a German shell had hit, killing its crew. For the time being the war, still raging on a mile or so away, appeared forgotten.[2]

Yet Fokker's visit to the front later became even more informal, encompassing a nude swimming party in the Somme. The ruined town of Saint-Quentin, where not a house was left standing, formed a bizarre backdrop. In the best of moods, having received Von Morgen's blessing, Anthony grabbed the chance to push Hermann Goering well under water—something few people would be able to repeat later on.

ᕫ

Such a relaxed state of affairs had become the rule between Fokker and the aviators at the front. Where other manufacturers focused on good relations with the central authorities in Berlin, Anthony had done his utmost to become the favorite of the pilots at the front. He visited them whenever he could. The atmosphere of comradeship, of young men connecting through aviation, greatly attracted him. Here he could escape from his daily chores as company director and from the continual pressure of competition, which he would bemoan later in his autobiography.[3] Flying created a bond, just as age did. Fokker was the only aircraft producer who was of the same age as the pilots flying his machines. Certainly at the beginning of the war he personally knew all those who flew his aircraft, having trained them at Johannisthal or Görries. They were his natural allies in the German military procurement system, and he liked them to think of themselves as his customers. Several pilots traveled especially to Schwerin from the front to await delivery of their new airplanes. Fokker encouraged such commitment and liked the pilots to think each plane had been custom built for them. A number of pilots struck up a correspondence with Fokker's office in Schwerin, reporting on their experiences in flight and combat, and making suggestions on how to improve handling characteristics.[4]

Anthony attached great value to such direct contacts and encouraged them. When frontline pilots visited him in Berlin while on leave, he made sure their every wish was catered to. With some of "his" pilots—Oswald Boelcke, Max Immelmann, and later the flyers of "Richthofen's Circus" such as Ernst Udet, Kurt Wolff, Konstantin Krefft, Werner Voss, Manfred and Lothar von Richthofen, and Hermann Goering—he developed a personal friendship. Such well-known pilots usually defended his aircraft when their design was called into question—something that occurred with alarming frequency. And even though he refused to touch liquor himself, he enjoyed keeping his flying comrades well lubricated. Whenever he was present in a restaurant or officers' mess, the schnapps went hand to hand at his expense.

ℭ

In April 1917 Anthony had stayed for several weeks in Kortrijk (Courtrai), Belgium, as the special guest of "Red Baron" Manfred von Richthofen's Jagdgeschwader 1, best known as the "Flying Circus." Fokker had arrived there with a mission. Two months previously, news had reached Berlin of a British plane that reportedly possessed superior climbing characteristics. A good rate of climb was deemed of crucial advantage in aerial combat, and so the appearance of the Sopwith Triplane demanded a German reaction. With the support of IdFlieg, the frontline pilots demanded a response loud and clear. IdFlieg approached several aircraft firms to come up with a comparable machine, Fokker among them. Yet Fokker went about this mission in quite a different fashion than his competitors. Rather than first assembling a design team, he took a train to the front at Kortrijk. There Von Richthofen's "Flying Circus" was up against the triplanes of a French naval squadron. Anthony hoped to be able to examine a downed Sopwith Triplane personally and gain firsthand knowledge of its construction details. While waiting for such an opportunity, he amused himself by filming daily life at the Kortrijk airfield. He had to wait for several weeks before he was able to inspect a machine that had come down behind the German lines. Upon his first examination of the triplane, Anthony was not impressed. He noted that the construction of the machine's third wing had inherent weaknesses. According to him, the risk of material breakage of the extra upper wing constituted a hazard in diving maneuvers.[5]

Once back in Schwerin, Fokker and his new chief constructor and *Werkmeister* Reinhold Platz, who had become responsible for the research department a year before, began work on a Fokker answer to the Sopwith design. They had at their disposal a recently augmented team of two technical draftsmen and about twenty other staff members, all secluded from the factory proper by a door that was kept permanently locked. For an experimental department, their supplies were sparse: two drawing tables, manually operated carpentry tools, a sawing stand with several sawhorses, and a ten-foot-long, T-shaped girder on a stand, on which stress tests could be carried out using adjustable weights.[6] As usual at Fokker's, aircraft development was approached through practical experimentation. Platz later dared to be honest about it: "Of the statics probably generally applied in aircraft construction I understood nothing. Neither did I know the . . . static break formulas."[7] All decisions were based on experience and gut feeling. The guiding principle was to arrive at a design of exceptionally low weight, which had to be maneuverable above all.[8]

The Fokker team cooperated with a Swedish engineer working in Germany, Villehad Forssman, who was attached to the engineering firm of Brüning in Hanau.

Forssman and Fokker had known each other for several years; before 1914 Forssman had run a patent bureau at Johannisthal. On April 1, 1916, they had met again in Berlin. Forssman, by then working as a consultant for Brüning, had drawn Anthony's attention to a new type of wing that he was trying to develop in cooperation with Brüning. It would be a wing that no longer required bracing wires for its rigidity and would be clad with a plywood veneer cover. The combined effects of these innovations promised a stronger wing, better capable of withstanding the dynamic forces applied to it in an aerial dogfight, especially the forces that came with high speed dives. These thick "veneer wings" were stronger than the constructions that Fokker had used thus far for his monoplane fighters. Their specific wing profile meant that the Forssman wings would offer reduced drag as well. In short: the new wing had better flying characteristics than the traditional cloth-covered surfaces that Fokker had been using. In fact, with this wing it would even be possible to make steep turns at low speeds. No wonder that everything to do with this new development was shrouded in secrecy. Fokker was cautious lest his competition could get wind of the new technology. On the basis of experience gained in 1916 with several monoplanes and biplanes, it was decided to equip the D.VI Fokker biplane that was under construction for the Austrian Luftfahrttruppe with an additional cantilevered upper wing.[9]

Anthony's personal involvement with the development of the triplane did not extend far beyond this. His strong points lay in the contribution of new ideas and in flight testing new aircraft, not in going over calculations. Moreover, the contracts that IdFlieg had negotiated with Fokker stipulated that he would personally test fly each new design.[10] In mid-June Anthony left Schwerin for Berlin and then Budapest, to visit his friend Friedrich Seekatz, who had become sales manager at the Hungarian machine factory Magyar Altalanos Gepgyar (MAG). Anthony was a major shareholder in this company that built Fokker aircraft under license. His particular reasons for visiting were to discuss aircraft deliveries and to give air shows. While the work on the new triplane proceeded in the Schwerin construction office, Anthony gave a spectacular performance of his daredevil piloting skills. As the grand finale of an aerial display on June 26, he flew his M.21 biplane under Budapest's Elisabeth Bridge across the Danube.[11]

Meanwhile, the choice of a suitable engine, one of the most important moments in the development of a new airplane, proceeded at Schwerin in typical Fokker fashion. After several less successful designs, IdFlieg had excluded Fokker from receiving prime-quality water-cooled Mercedes and BMW engines in 1916. Yet Anthony had cunningly managed to counter this setback, at least partially, by acquiring a majority interest in the Oberursel engine factory near Frankfurt.[12] Right from the start it was evident that the new fighter would be powered by one of the lightweight air-cooled rotary engines that Oberursel produced: the recent 110-hp UR.II, even though a more powerful Siemens engine was also available. Using the Uberursel engine was something of a double-edged sword. Fokker could control its supply, and it would contribute to his personal profit, but it was relatively weak and consumed an enormous amount of fuel. To use the engine for a top-rate fighter, the Fokker team was forced to focus on keeping the triplane as light as it possibly could be. This need reinforced the importance Fokker attached to new wing constructions, which he saw as breakthrough discoveries.[13]

Nonetheless, lightweight construction held risks, as experience had already indicated. Fokker's D.III biplane fighters, of which several hundreds were built, had to be returned from front duty in December 1916 because of wing failures.[14] Since the German army command had no immediate use for the machines thereafter, Fokker was allowed to deliver a number of D.III fighters to the Dutch military in the summer of 1917—machines that had been returned to Schwerin for overhaul. To swing the deal, The Hague sent a lieutenant of the air service, Jacob Duinker, to Fokker in April 1917. They met at the Hotel Bristol in Berlin. The actual delivery and shipment of the aircraft was supervised by Holland's top pilot, Lt. Willem Versteegh, who arrived in Schwerin early August to test the aircraft and would stay there until the deal had been completed in October. Sixteen D.III fighters were exported by rail to Holland and eventually arrived at the country's only military air base, Soesterberg. Fokker earned 369,000 Dutch guilders ($155,000) with the transaction.[15]

Months before that, on August 7, Fokker's new triplane was ready for static stress testing at the Adlershof facilities near Johannisthal. Expectations were high, as was the time pressure. On July 14 Fokker had already received an initial commission for twenty preproduction aircraft. The F.I, soon redesignated the Dr.I (for *Dreidecker*, meaning triplane) came through the stress tests without many problems. On August 16 IdFlieg's Central Procurement Commission gave the green light for series production. Five days earlier the first two F.I machines had been expedited to the front. Anthony traveled with the aircraft and staged a demonstration flight in Kortrijk on August 25 before the highest authority on procurement affairs, Gen. Erich Ludendorff.

Von Richthofen, Germany's prime air ace, also subjected the Dr.I to a personal test. He was enthused over the small, agile fighter and demanded that his newly formed Jagdgeschwader 1 be equipped with the Fokker triplane. On September 3 he brought down his sixtieth opponent, and Fokker was perhaps his most satisfied witness. Proudly, he let himself and Von Richthofen be filmed by the wreckage afterward, clad in the British pilot's flying attire and merrily chatting away with the downed airman, who was lucky to have escaped with his life after eight bullets had grazed him.[16] Suddenly Fokker was back in the limelight as the producer of important combat aircraft.

Von Richthofen's right-hand man, Werner Voss, also wanted such a machine at the earliest possibility. At the beginning of September he accompanied Fokker on his return journey to Schwerin, where Anthony put him up as his personal guest. On September 18 his new machine stood ready for him at Görries. Voss was full of praise after his first test flight, which he included in an official report. Fokker knew how to

Famous friends: Anthony Fokker (second from left) talks with German flying aces Kurt Wolff and "Red Baron" Manfred von Richthofen (both to the right of Fokker) and their technician Konstantin Kreft before test flying the new Dr.I triplane at Kortrijk (Courtrai) near the Western Front in Belgium, August 1917. **COLLECTION MICHAEL SCHMIDT, MUNICH, GERMANY**

reciprocate: the next day he took Voss and his father to Berlin, treating them to all the pleasures that a rich man with connections could still arrange, despite the war. Werner Voss then traveled back to the Belgian front near Kortrijk, where he was soon shot down in his new Dr.I in a dogfight with several British aircraft.[17] Nonetheless, Fokker's small triplane became legendary because of its quick rate of climb and maneuverability.

An order for no less than 320 aircraft followed shortly after. Demand for the new fighter exceeded Fokker's production capacity, which was already strained because of a standing order for the construction of a considerable number of Allgemeine Elektricitäts-Gesellschaft (AEG) training aircraft that had been allocated to his factory after the earlier unsuccessful Fokker fighters. To cope with this dramatic increase in demand, Anthony outsourced all the wing production for the Dr.I to the Perzina piano factory in the Schwerin city center. That move had been in the making ever since Fokker had first diverted parts of his wing production and the construction of propellers to Perzina. But the new demands on Perzina came at a peculiar time. For months the company had been in turmoil. In March director Daniel Huss had been arrested on charges of bribery and for delivering poor-quality, unsuitable material to the army. Since then he had been convicted and sentenced to ten months of imprisonment. To end the chaos, Anthony decided to bring Perzina fully under his own control. He paid nearly 2 million marks for the company. In late August the piano factory became an integrated part of the Fokker Works, initially charged with wing production for the Dr.I.[18] By mid-October the first seventeen triplanes had been delivered to the Fliegertruppe, scheduled to be operational over the front no later than December 1, 1917.

The war dictated that everything had to be done at an enormous pace, and it was expected that the 400 employees of Perzina would keep up with increased demand. But the Perzina factory had never been built for industrial series production. Located in a monumental building in the middle of the city, it lacked sufficient floor space for the twenty-three-foot aircraft wings workers were now supposed to turn out by the hundreds. The factory became ever more congested, while the number of different parts and products that were made there increased. Work went up to ten hours per day, plus a minimum of six hours overtime on Saturday and Sunday. Anthony was proud to announce that his company had managed to increase production in this way without hiring extra staff.[19] The consequences, however, shortly became clear: efficiency and workmanship decreased. Fokker failed to keep sufficient tabs on this.

Indeed, Fokker had several other distractions. He was already deeply engaged in another project: the development of a fighter for the German Navy that would use floats to operate from water—one of his old dreams that had not yet come to fruition. To help his ideas along, he had bought the Deutsche Flugzeug Werke in the coastal city of Travemünde on the Baltic Sea for 200,000 marks on August 20. This move swiftly led to disappointment. The Travemünde City Council saw no value in an expansion of airplane production. In fact, they ordered a no-fly zone over the city. The development of the naval aircraft itself was marred with technical problems related to the floats. The planned factory expansion therefore came to naught, and on September 20 Fokker resold the facilities to the Hanseatische Flugzeugwerke Karl Caspar from Hamburg.[20]

It was not long before he had to apply himself to the triplane again, because within weeks after their introduction over the Western Front, several of the new fighters fell out of the sky. Eyewitnesses reported that their top wings had broken off—accidents that appeared to resemble crashes with Fokker's earlier E- and D-models. A special investigative commission was urgently dispatched to the front to trace the cause of the accidents. The reason for the crashes was determined fairly quickly: the great haste involved in the aircraft's production had resulted in sloppy and incomplete application of humidity-protecting varnish on the wing spars and ribs. Conditions at the front, where aircraft were housed in tents and in makeshift wooden sheds, had led to an accumulation of humidity inside the wings that reduced the adhesive effects of the natural glues used in the construction process. Several airmen lost their lives in

In the Perzina factory: During the war, Schwerin's leading piano factory Perzina switched from building grand pianos to building airplane wings. Fokker bought the company in 1917 and used its facilities to construct wings for his Dr.I triplane. As the war went on, more women joined the German armaments workforce.
COLLECTION MICHAEL SCHMIDT, MUNICH, GERMANY

the resulting crashes. All Dr.I aircraft were grounded, and in November 1917 Fokker replaced all wings for the machines with new ones that had been properly varnished against humidity. The production of the Dr.I was seriously delayed as a result.[21]

G

The problems with the triplane compounded difficulties in which Anthony was already entangled, and which were to a considerable degree of his own making. Yet these challenges were typical of the war's peculiar development of aircraft technology, stemming from a meeting in Berlin on December 16, 1916, between IdFlieg's Maj. Felix Wagenführ, professor Hugo Junkers, and Fokker. Wagenführ, whose ultimate goal was the founding of one nationwide *Reichsflugzeugwerke* (state aircraft industry), convened the meeting that brought the two aircraft constructors to one table.[22] His initiative led to a strange amalgamation of industries and personalities.

Hugo Junkers, born in 1859, was thirty-one years older than Fokker. Since the middle of the 1890s, Junkers & Company had made a fortune producing gas heating appliances. He also occupied a professorial chair in mechanical engineering at the University of Aachen. There he had been deeply involved in the development of a metal cantilever wing for aircraft. After years of experimenting, his first plane equipped with such a wing, designated the Junkers J.I, had become ready for testing in December 1915. Lt. Friedrich Mallinckrodt of the air corps made the first flight in the machine on December 20, but this first practical all-metal aircraft design did not go into production as planned in the subsequent months. Instead Junkers, an uncompromising and perfectionist academic, kept changing and improving the design at his factory in Dessau. Wagenführ, who held overall planning responsibility for German aircraft production, began to lose patience with Junkers. What was necessary, in his view, was a fair dose of practical insight, the kind that Fokker excelled in. And thus the theorist Junkers and the practitioner Fokker ended up at the same table. Anthony immediately showed keen interest.[23]

The Junkers J.I, and its derivative, the J.II, were conceptually revolutionary aircraft, years ahead of their time. Knowledge of their construction details was limited to the small circle of Hugo Junker's staff members and some of his factory workers. He planned to build an armor-plated plane that could be used in close air support over the battlefield to attack targets on the ground. Anthony, test pilot par excellence, instinctively grasped the design's far-reaching innovations and quickly proposed that he and Junkers join forces to develop the two prototypes into aircraft that could go into series production. Although his company had no experience with all-metal designs, what he could offer was experience with series production, which Junkers lacked.

At the meeting it was decided that Fokker would visit Dessau, seventy miles south of Berlin, to inspect the two Junkers aircraft. The next afternoon he boarded the train for Dessau, arriving there that evening. The next day he was shown around by Junkers's company director, Kurt Lottmann. Anthony proved himself a keen guest indeed, deeply interested in the specialized construction of the machines. Four days later, on December 22, he was allowed to make a test flight with the J.II from Adlershof near Johannisthal. When he landed about a half hour later, he proclaimed himself most satisfied with the plane's flying characteristics. Moreover, he proposed to buy the licensing rights for production of the J.II. The base price that Junkers wanted for this, 500,000 marks (approximately $68,700 at the time), posed no problem for Fokker. Nonetheless, an agreement was not forthcoming, since Junkers demanded an additional 15 percent commission per aircraft for the use of his patents. His aeronautical experiments were proving very expensive, and he was in constant need for new funds. His demand, however, was rather steep for Fokker.[24] The two constructors did not reach agreement, and the meeting was adjourned in a prickly atmosphere.

In January Anthony made several telephone calls to the Junkers factory to set a date for a new meeting, but Hugo Junkers wanted none of it and told his spokesmen to relay that he was in bed with a cold.[25] Now Fokker also began to backtrack, indicating that he saw various financial and technical problems with the proposed cooperation. Days went by before the reasons behind Fokker's sudden reservations became clear in Dessau and started a severe row. On December 18 Fokker had asked Junkers's engineers to explain nearly everything there was to know about the design and construction of the new aircraft. After consultations with his own people in the Hotel Bristol, he had decided that he preferred to use this information for the further development of the wooden cantilever wing that he and Forssman had been working on, instead of building aircraft for yet another competitor.

Upon learning this, Hugo Junkers almost exploded with rage: he could not find words to describe the depth of his loathing for Fokker's lack of personal integrity. He immediately went on a search for alternative funding.[26] But the harm was already done. On the insistence of Wagenführ, a second meeting between the two adversaries was scheduled at the Hotel Bristol on February 2, 1917. Now Fokker was the one to play hide-and-seek. He sent a message down to Junkers in the hotel lobby, claiming that he was ill, and left it to his manager, Wilhelm Horter, to calm things down. Horter pretended he did not know what had previously passed between the two men and tried to convince Junkers that the Fokker Works were only interested in acquiring the patent rights for Junkers's cantilever wing construction.[27]

IdFlieg, where Wagenführ was primarily interested in applying Junkers's discoveries, supported Fokker in these maneuvers. On strict instructions from Wagenführ, the two entrepreneurs entered into further negotiations. After months of difficult discussions, an agreement was finally reached on June 16, 1917, in which Fokker gained permission to produce and develop aircraft according to Junkers's designs. The deal included the use of the cantilever wing construction. Fokker agreed to pay the 500,000 marks that he had offered earlier, plus 10 percent of the sales price of every machine that the Fokker Works would turn out under the contract with Junkers until the end of the war—and 7.5 percent for every airplane built after the end of hostilities until February 1, 1925.[28]

On August 24 IdFlieg also managed to have the two parties agree to the foundation of a joint venture, Fokker-Junkers Werke AG Metallflugzeugbau (Fokker-Junkers Works Co. Metal Aircraft Constructions). This was not quite what Anthony wanted. He would have preferred to get a large industrial concern onboard, such as AEG or the steel conglomerate run by industrialist Hugo Stinnes, to obtain a more secure financial footing. But Junkers would agree to none of this.[29] Hence the founding papers that were signed on October 20, 1917, only mentioned Fokker and Junkers. Both invested 1 million marks ($173,300), to which the army added another 630,000 marks ($109,000) in short-term credit, bringing the corporate means to 2,630,000 marks total ($282,300). Junkers paid his share by incorporating all the nonfixed assets of his heating appliances factory, Junkers & Company. Fokker, on the other hand, was able to pay his share in cash. It was indicative of the distribution of power within the new company that Fokker, and not Junkers, became general director. Not surprisingly, the deed was signed at the office of Fokker's lawyer, Hugo Alexander-Katz, in Berlin.

The stated aim of the Fokker-Junkers Works was to start production of the all-metal aircraft designed by Junkers, for which they would now hold all patent rights. For Junkers the new enterprise meant financial support of his research in aerodynamics. He also retained the right to use his patents outside the joint venture in Junkers & Company. For Fokker the matter was more complicated: apart from the right (or duty) to start up a production line of Junkers aircraft, he received the coveted patent rights for Junkers's cantilever wing construction. For the sum of 250,000 marks ($43,330) plus 9 percent of the net price of every airplane sold, Fokker Flugzeugwerke in Schwerin could henceforth make use of the knowledge gained from the linkup.[30]

Setting up a production line to build Junkers aircraft in large numbers was no easy matter in a country now suffering from shortages of just about everything. Aluminum was very hard to come by in Germany. Besides, neither Fokker nor Junkers had any experience with series production of all-metal aircraft. (Indeed, no one had at that time.) It demanded machines and tooling for working large and small metal parts and a specialized labor force. The complexity of the Junkers designs was another obstacle. In March 1917 IdFlieg had placed an advance order for fifty armored J.4 aircraft for the Western Front near Kortrijk in Belgium. But the first two aircraft were not delivered until October.[31] Clearly dissatisfied with the delays in getting the J.4 production line up and running, IdFlieg repeatedly threatened to break the sales contract and pay a much lower price per aircraft. Further problems followed after delivery: repairs to aircraft damaged in combat proved difficult and time-consuming. Early in December Fokker and Wagenführ agreed to make an all-out effort to increase production and have eight aircraft ready by the end of that month. In 1918 production was then to expand further. But what was the value of such a promise coming from a company that was marred with trouble at the top? The relationship between Junkers and Fokker was characterized by distrust, ill will, and suspicion. Both entrepreneurs were out to do business with the cantilever wing construction, but on their own terms and at each other's expense.[32]

Fokker stood to gain the most. Early in 1917 he and Franz Möser had developed their own cantilever wing, made out of wood and both lightweight and strong. The V.17, V.20, V.23, and V.25 prototypes, each borne by a single cantilever wing, were closely related to the Junkers J.7 and J.9. The progress from rough general ideas to an actual wing followed the same pragmatic trial-and-error method that had been used with other Fokker designs and constructions.[33] In the end the various development processes came together in a revolutionary-looking biplane with two cantilever wings and a radically streamlined fuselage, the V.1 (V standing for *Versuchsmaschine*, or test machine). But continuing problems with the production of powerful aircraft engines meant that Fokker could not locate a suitable engine for the V.1. Poor downward visibility from the cockpit also made the machine difficult to land. Despite its ultramodern features and looks, the V.1 was found unsuitable for military use. But if production orders were not forthcoming, the practical use of the wooden cantilever wing had been proven. Hugo Junkers resented the way in which Fokker had obtained this technology. Despite their forced cooperation, he filed a lawsuit over Fokker's breach of the patent for this type of wing, which had been granted to him on December 22, 1916, just as the talks with Fokker had begun. The suit would drag on until 1940.[34]

Given the enforced character of their cooperation, there was no stopping Fokker. Neither theory nor practice could remain hidden from his sight. According to the terms of the Fokker-Junkers Works joint venture, Anthony made a test flight with the new J.7 on December 4, 1917, to examine the plane's handling characteristics. Upon landing, he hit a deep hole in the grass airfield with one of the wheels, cracking the undercarriage. This damage set the development of the J.7 further back. Hugo Junkers, who suspected malicious intent on Fokker's part, was furious, but he was unable to back out of the cooperative venture.[35] That the 2,000-strong workforce of the Junkers-Fokker Works managed to complete 227 armored ground-attack aircraft in 1917 and 1918, plus 41 ultramodern Junkers D.I fighters, was, in the end, largely due to the organizational talents of Wilhelm Horter, because the two constructors continued to use every opportunity to make life difficult for each other. In March 1918 even Wagenführ had to admit that it might be best to split up the joint venture. To effect this separation became Junkers's principal mission in the remaining months of the war.[36]

ᚷ

Apart from relations at the top, material work conditions deteriorated rapidly as well. There was little that Fokker could do about this. Stocks of all raw materials were being depleted in Germany. Even routine maintenance, such as fixing a leak

Front deployment: Starting in August 1917, the extremely maneuverable Fokker Dr.I triplane was used over the Western Front. Piloting his personal bright red machine, Von Richthofen became world famous. Here ground technicians work on two Fokker Dr.I aircraft at the base of Jagdgeschwader 1, better known as "Richthofen's Flying Circus," in the spring of 1918.
COLLECTION MICHAEL SCHMIDT, MUNICH, GERMANY

in the roof of one of Fokker's factory buildings in Schwerin, or filling the potholes in the street in front, became problematic.[37] In December 1916 the whole country had been mobilized for the war effort, and all men between seventeen and sixty who did not serve in the army were conscripted for labor duty. Growing numbers of women were also detailed to serve in the war industry. At Fokker they represented nearly a third of the workforce.[38] Food rations were becoming smaller and smaller, and many products could only be obtained as *Ersatz* (substitutes). The bread supply shrank. The potato ration went down by nearly a third in January 1917. A growing number of products could only be obtained on the black market—and commanded extortionate prices while inflation went through the roof. That winter German houses were cold because of a lack of coal, and also dark, since the electricity supply was curtailed. In Schwerin the authorities decreed that heating would only be allowed after 5 p.m. and was not to exceed 18 degrees Centigrade (64 degrees Fahrenheit). The winter of 1917 would go down in public memory as the "winter of despair."[39] The authorities began to worry over a growing discontent among the population.

But for those who could afford to spend money, life continued much as if these shortages did not exist. This was certainly the case for Fokker, although he later wrote that he hoarded food and had to top off his sugar supply—Anthony was a sugar addict—before he would go on a journey. When it became difficult to obtain sweets and chocolates in Germany, he had his friend Friedrich Seekatz ship him a suitcase full of exquisite Kugler chocolates from Budapest.[40]

Fokker did his best to look after his employees. Workers at risk of being sent to the front could turn to him for exemption from military duty. Advertisements boasted that wages at the Fokker Works were above average. In April 1917 he made a donation of 20,000 marks to the Olga Foundation in Schwerin, which sought to assist newborn children and toddlers, groups that were especially at risk in a society plagued by shortages. Fokker also started a program to buy food for his employees, since bread, butter, and other foodstuffs could only be obtained on ration cards and at high prices. The metal of the German coins became more precious than the denominations they represented. The government resorted to the introduction of paper money as a substitute, but this only pushed inflation further. At the beginning of 1917, workers took to the streets in many cities demanding higher wages. To address their discontent, several larger companies distributed special vouchers to replace the government's currency. In April 1917 Anthony followed this example and introduced 16,250 marks ($2,800) of Fokker emergency money into circulation. The notes carried his signature. Later on he claimed pride in this curious arrangement. Very little of that "Fokker money" passed through his own hands, though. It was intended for use within the company and for daily shopping in a select number of Schwerin shops that had agreed to accept Fokker's one-, five-, and fifty-pfennig vouchers. At the factory cashier's office the vouchers could be reclaimed for genuine marks.[41]

᚜

Fokker's role as a director had by then created a distance between him and his staff. When the war started, Anthony had known all of his forty employees on a personal basis. In those days the company had almost resembled an extended family. But since August 1914 the atmosphere of comradeship had faded. He himself wrote of an "inhuman accumulation of labor, which has descended upon me as a result of the growth I managed to achieve for my companies."[42] His craving for companionship and friendly chats had been replaced with a desire for peace and quiet. In the spring of 1916 he moved with his friend Bernard de Waal from the Scharnhorststrasse to a roomy apartment on the first floor of a relatively new but nondescript house in the center of Schwerin. Initially he rented Schelfstrasse 25, but from 1917 until 1927 he held the house in ownership.[43] There was something odd to this arrangement, because although Anthony owned the house on paper and paid property tax, he never transferred the sales price. Meanwhile, housekeeping duties were the domain of the widow Frieda Grabitz, who also provided the cooking. In his autobiography Fokker referred to her as his "landlady." She was an excellent cook, and her meals were lauded by Fokker's guests.

The house in Schelfstrasse not only provided peace and quiet. It also provided an environment in which he could work as and when it pleased him, without recourse to others. As time went on his lifestyle became less and less compromising, his general conduct increasingly restless. Anthony was not only devoted to his work; he grew addicted to it. If and when it suited him, or when he felt he needed to, he could keep working day and night. In one of his scarce letters to his father, he wrote, "I do not have time for marriage yet, and would give a woman little of myself, as I'm engrossed in my work, which is more than ever 'pastime' for me and the development of which is my life's objective. . . . The money is therefore no more than a tool for me, one that is indispensable for a development, such as I have in mind. For myself, I use a minimum, as much as needed, just what pleases me, without throwing it out by the handful to luxuries, such as hundreds of war profiteers do in Berlin or with you. But I have everything that I need for the relaxation of body and spirit."[44]

Women, however, remained enigmas, on whom Anthony would have temporary crushes. How to express such feelings was something that troubled him. In *The Wind and Beyond*, aerodynamist Theodore von Kármán, one of the directors of MAG, later remembered:

> He was . . . *constantly embroiled in love affairs. I remember that once we traveled by train from Vienna to Budapest for an important conference. When the train arrived at the station in Budapest, I looked around for Fokker. He was nowhere to be seen. "Where is Herr Fokker?" I asked his assistant anxiously. "Oh," he said, "Herr Fokker has left the train." "But I told him it was an important meeting of the Board of Directors. What happened?" The assistant smiled. "Herr Fokker met a pretty girl and left with her. He anticipated you might get angry," he added, "so he told me to tell you that a meeting of the Board of Directors will take place every month. But if you let a beautiful young lady slip through your fingers, you will never get her back again."*[45]

Repeatedly Anthony would name a boat after his latest muse, evidenced in his sailing yachts *Pushka*, *Hana*, and *Tetta*. The *Tetta*, his latest acquisition, named after his fiancée Elisabeth von Morgen, was a fairly big boat that slept several adults and had about 90 square yards of sail. But he did not sail all that often. In the spring of 1917 he missed the opening of the season because of his extended visit to the Western Front; for the same reason he passed over the sailing regatta in August.[46]

Three boats for just one person? Anthony liked to bend the unusual circumstances of the war in his favor, acquiring luxury possessions at a fraction of their normal price. Apart from the *Tetta* he also owned several smaller racing vessels, which he liked to name after himself. In June 1917 he bought the twenty-three-foot *Melusine* from one of the board members of Berlin's elite sailing club, the Verein Seglerhaus am Wannsee, when such expensive vessels went down in price because of the worsening economy. Some weeks later he renamed it *Fok.III*, his third racing boat. But for a fanatic water sports person like Fokker, this was not enough. A month later he bought a fourth vessel, the *Heinmück*, of similar rigging, which he renamed *Fok.IV*. Now that he had so many boats, he decided to become a member of the Seglerhaus am Wannsee, where he kept the two latest additions to his fleet. That same July, he passed the ballot of the elite club, which had been founded in 1867. He proved himself an eminent sailor and soon became a popular club member, not just on the water but also on dry land. He particularly liked to stage viewings of his private movies in the clubhouse, which still was something of a special occasion in those days.

The various technical requirements of the club he found troublesome, however. The club's secretary had to remind him repeatedly of his membership duties and of various rules. Rules and regulations were never his thing, and especially not now that he had become a wealthy man. Anthony showed more interest in the various sailing events, which continued as if the war never existed. Meanwhile, the price of yachts continued to decline. In the spring of 1918 Anthony was therefore easily tempted to add a *Fok.V* to his collection. Then on a visit to Hamburg he found an even greater treasure: the beautiful, slim, twenty-foot yacht *Schelm*, which had been built in 1912. He acquired it at a bargain price, renaming it *Pushka* and entering it in the Süddeutsche Regatta on the Starnberger See in Bavaria, which was to be held from July 20 to 23, 1918. In that final summer of the war, Anthony managed to find quite a bit of time to spend on the water. For a contest that took place on the Wannsee from September 17 to 22, 1918, he personally put up the prize money.

Meanwhile, the news of the war was becoming increasingly grim. As a witness at the front toward the end of August he was able to judge for himself that things had taken a turn for the worse. Germany's supplies of men and equipment were spread ever thinner. If the war would be lost, he would have to write down his possessions, that much was obvious. It appeared prudent to sell off some of his recent sailing investments while he could, in favor of hard cash. He therefore sold the *Fok.IV*, which he had not used much, in September.[47]

In the autumn of 1917 Anthony bought a luxurious seagoing yacht, the forty-nine-foot *Senta*, which combined sails and an engine. He acquired the *Senta* from Duke Ernst II of Sachsen-Altenburg. To his father he wrote, "Why I'm already buying a yacht *now*? All yachts are bought up by foreigners, and at crazy prices. For years to come it will be impossible to build new yachts for lack of materials. That's why I bought one *now*. Just the keel of the ship is presently worth 24,000 marks in materials. If I sell it to an expert I stand to make 30,000 marks for it immediately, meaning my whole sailing stuff will be free, but I will not sell it because I cannot sail in money and when I've had another ship built I can sell it at a late profit.... Such a ship is an expensive pet object, but I've now come so far that this no longer matters...."[48]

Sailing met several objectives. Apart from providing an informal backdrop for business transactions, it also served as Anthony's favorite environment for relaxation.

The exclusive ambience of aristocratic sailing clubs offered him an introduction to the more privileged classes of society. Sailing was in itself a relatively low-cost pastime as far as memberships fees were concerned, suiting Anthony's general parsimony. To the alarm of the club's secretary, he repeatedly managed to "forget" to pay the required fee for the *Stander Zertifikat*, the customary payment for running the club's little triangular red-and-black flag. In 1918 the annual contribution to the Seglerhaus am Wannsee amounted only to a modest 120 marks (about $15). Fokker liked to indulge in the expenditures that his status as a millionaire allowed him. But he was less interested in such details as keeping his ships' paperwork in order so that he could participate in races.[49]

℘

That last summer of the war, Anthony's priorities lay elsewhere. In the spring of 1916 he had met the twenty-year-old Sophie Marie Elisabeth von Morgen, the daughter of Lt. Gen. Curt Ernst von Morgen and his wife Maria Guthmann, who had passed away in July 1910. Anthony had met the attractive brunette, born in Zehlendorf on August 12, 1895, on the Wannsee. Just outside Berlin, the Wannsee was a beloved location for the city's affluent classes to relax. On the shore of the lake Sophie's grandparents had a large estate, with their own private jetty for mooring sailing yachts. After her father remarried in January 1914, and especially after his return to active service once the war broke out, Sophie (or "Tetta," as she was known to friends and relatives) had spent a lot of time with her grandparents. She developed a particular fondness for sailing. Rather than obtaining an official introduction, Anthony had first admired Tetta from a distance until chance offered itself for a direct meeting. For reasons that remained unexplained, he later wished to share his recollection of how they met only with his American readership:

> I had taken up my old hobby of sailing and had bought a six-meter yacht for racing. I noticed how skillfully Miss von Morgen handled her fast yacht and formed a liking for her, but was too shy to seek her out until an accident gave me an opportunity. She was standing in the bow of her yacht ready to pick up a buoy when a sudden dip of the boat threw her overboard. I happened to be nearby and thought it was a good moment to show my interest, so I jumped overboard to rescue her. This was entirely unnecessary, because she was one of the best swimmers around the lake, as I well knew. But the result of my rescue was that she invited me to change my clothes at her grandfather's house, and borrowed dry ones from her brother. After that I was invited to dinner, and the rest was moonlight.[50]

Thus the romance that he had longed for began with the kind of physical contact that would normally have been impossible at a first encounter. The lake brought them together in more ways than one. Deep waters flowed between the general's athletic daughter and the brazen young Dutchman, with his high-pitched voice. Like Anthony, Tetta loved physical activity. In this respect they formed a perfect match. Besides, the youthful industrialist was an excellent catch. It was no surprise that he was welcomed with open arms into the stately home that Tetta's grandfather, the wealthy cement manufacturer Robert Guthmann, had built on the slopes above the Wannsee in 1885. Under the beautiful ceilings and surrounded by chic wood paneling, the two young people developed an affair that followed the rhythm of Anthony's visits to Berlin. For Fokker Tetta also represented exciting social prospects. Both her father and her grandfather had the kind of connections in the Berlin establishment that he lacked. The atmosphere of the Guthmanns' stately home reminded him of the ambience of the Cremer residence in Santpoort in Holland, which he admired. He relished the thought that his next arrival at the large house along the Sandwerder, in his flashy car, would be anticipated with delight.

ꝗ

In 1916 and 1917 Fokker was recognized not only as Schwerin's biggest employer, but also as one who paid fair wages.[51] Nonetheless, as in so many other places in Germany, discontent was brooding among his workers beneath the surface. In his director's office in the corridor of the annex in front of Halle 2, Fokker knew or noticed very little of this. He was spending a good deal of his time in Berlin, away from the factory. In July and August 1917 there had been minor food uproars in Schwerin, with workers gathering in the marketplace to demand higher bread rations. Fokker's nearly 1,800 employees had played a visible role in this unrest. But with Fokker's approval the demonstrators had been bought off with pay raises and more liberal food rations. Still, the Fokker Works were hit with a strike at the end of January 1918, as labor unrest spread over Germany. On January 31 about 800 Fokker employees demonstrated in the city center in favor of ending the war, demanding a further pay raise to keep up with the ever increasing costs of living, and the right to vote.

The strike did not last half a day. Fokker's management and the Mecklenburg authorities managed to smother the discontent with new promises. Seven Fokker employees who had played leading roles in the protest were arrested and immediately sent to the front. The city of Schwerin was put under military rule. These strategies brought a return to normal conditions, although they did not improve workers' morale. As before, Fokker tried to mitigate the situation by raising wages. Yet he felt that his grip on the situation was becoming less sure, as general conditions in Germany worsened further. Apart from food and raw materials, staffing was now a major problem. The Fokker Works came to rely increasingly on female workers, who were being actively recruited in newspaper campaigns. Meanwhile, the army increased pressure to raise production. On July 10, 1918, Fokker was forced to relinquish his directorship of the factory in favor of a government-appointed supervisor, Karl Hackstetter.

Two months later, in September, conditions took another turn for the worse. In several of Mecklenburg's defense contractor establishments, workers went on strike, demanding not only better conditions but political reforms as well. The authorities reacted tensely, issuing a general ban on strikes and threatening those who refused to comply with military tribunals. In the final months of the war substantial numbers of workers were commandeered into the army and sent to the front, which led to further unrest. Weeks went by before conditions returned to a semblance of normality.[52] Few people now believed that the war would end in victory for Germany. Even the General Staff was convinced that there was no hope of winning the final battles.

11

BERLIN, GERMANY
NOVEMBER 1918

On the morning of Saturday, November 9, 1918, a freight train from Ludwigslust pulled into the shunt yards of Berlin's Lehrter Bahnhof. As soon as the train stopped, Anthony Fokker climbed down and made himself scarce. He needed to get away as quickly as possible in his borrowed army uniform, without attracting attention. The revolution was everywhere now. In a matter of days, the world that he knew had suddenly collapsed, and since then his life had been filled with dangers and threats. The evening before he had fled Schwerin in a hair-raising motorcycle ride to Ludwigslust, where he had finally hid himself in the train.[1] But here in Berlin dangers were rampant as well. The sounds of uproar and agitation blew across the tracks. He was tired, at the end of his wits. His nerves were shattered. Yet staying at the railway depot was not an option. Where could he go? Would he be safe in his customary residence at the Hotel Bristol? He began to walk, gambling on the anonymity of the big city with its 2 million inhabitants.

Once outside the station he became part of a moving mass of excited demonstrators. That very morning news had broken that Emperor Wilhelm II had abdicated. Toward midday more than 100,000 people from Berlin's suburban factories assembled and moved toward the Reichstag building, less than ten minutes' walk from the Lehrter Bahnhof. There, in the center of power, the freshly appointed Social Democratic chancellor Friedrich Ebert frantically conferred about Germany's future now that the war had been lost. Outside the masses called for peace, a demand that was interspersed with general cries of uproar. Red flags, the color of the revolution, were flying above the demonstrating masses. The situation was tense and unclear: would

Stress testing, Fokker style: In August 1918 Anthony again visited the Western Front, this time to check on problems with glued connections in the wooden wings of his D.VIII fighter. Ever the showman, he enlisted servicemen to demonstrate that there was nothing wrong with his machines' constructional strength. **COLLECTION MICHAEL SCHMIDT, MUNICH, GERMANY**

the police and the army interfere to restore order? At the front of the crowd, signs were carried imploring "Brüder! Nicht schiessen!" (Brothers! Don't shoot!)

To everybody's surprise, indeed nothing happened. At the police headquarters on Alexanderplatz, officers even removed their weapons and joined the protests. The result was an almost festive sense of relief that the anticipated confrontations did not occur. Toward four o'clock the idea took root to occupy the Royal City Palace at Berlin's central avenue, Unter den Linden. There Karl Liebknecht, a socialist and a declared opponent of the four-year-old war effort, delivered a speech. He had been released two weeks earlier from jail, where he had served time for his open protests against the war. From the palace balcony he now declared revolution. After years of war and hardship, such words fell on fertile ground. There would be no stopping developments now.[2]

⚓

Few had been prepared for such a turn of events, and Fokker less than most. Politics and government were topics of which he took no notice. Indeed, his interests hardly extended beyond aviation and sports. His attention and energy had always been focused on his company and its aircraft. Now that he had been forced to hand over the daily running of the factory to Karl Hackstetter in July, he had his hands free to concentrate on the development of his new monoplane fighter, the E.V (usually designated as the D.VIII). In the spare time that remained, his primary concerns were love and matrimony, now that his future father-in-law had approved of his relationship with Tetta. They spent hours together on or near the water. The salon and the guest rooms of the luxurious Seglerhaus am Wannsee became a sort of second home for them. But even in this privileged and secluded world the war had finally intruded. After it had already been proven difficult to gather crews for the annual sailing championships in September 1918, the Reichskommissar für Fishversorgung (Government Commissioner for Fish Supply) had issued a decree in October that the club's boats were to be turned over to the government as fishing vessels. Anthony was called upon to contribute to the fishing program.[3] He did not bother to reply.

Meanwhile, Berlin was adrift. The Western Front was about to collapse. Supreme Commander Gen. Erich Ludendorff had admitted as much to Emperor Wilhelm at the imperial headquarters in Spa, Belgium, on September 29. Five days later, on October 4, the cabinet, headed by Prince Max von Baden, proposed a truce. It was a step that found widespread support among the civilian population, where an antiwar movement now flourished, sustained by the political left.

A number of commanders in the field, however, did not agree with Von Baden's step. There was resentment within the highest ranks of the military, reflecting an ongoing power struggle with the civilian government. The supreme command of the Imperial German Navy schemed to initiate a final confrontation with the Allied fleet. This plan prompted strong reactions among the sailors. What started on November 3 as a localized uproar in Kiel of sailors who refused to put out to sea for an unwinnable battle mushroomed into a full-scale revolution that engulfed other German cities within days. By November 5 the unrest had already reached Lübeck, home of the Von Morgens.

The next day the uprising reached Schwerin. Here the unrest began in the dead of night, with 180 members of the Landstorm militia resisting an order that they be moved to the front for duty. Toward 3 a.m., the local garrison commander Luiz von Liliencron sent a detachment of recruits to the Landstorm barracks near the palace of Grand Duke Friedrich Franz IV with orders to march them off. But the Landstorm members refused to budge. After it had become known that the government had proposed a ceasefire to the allies, it was clear to all that the war was nearly over. Who would then agree to be sent to the front to risk his life? Nonetheless, the disobedient Landstorm troopers were summoned to hand in their rifles and put themselves at the disposal of the military authorities. An intense discussion resulted, which ended when the commanding officer of the recruits indicated he would not have his men open fire on the Landstorm. This was celebrated as a victory for the rebels.

The Landstorm militia then decided to march on the large infantry barracks on the other side of town, several hundred yards from Fokker's house in the Schelfstrasse. It appeared that the soldiers of the garrison had also had enough of the war. After heated discussions, a majority of them chose to support the Landstorm. By 5:30 a.m. the entire barracks of the grenadier complex had been occupied by mutinous soldiers. In groups they blocked and guarded crossroads, putting up machine guns in the street. Then the unruly soldiers marched to the nearby Fokker factory to claim support from the workers there, who were known to have harbored discontent since the strike of January 31. Together both groups moved to the arsenal, the monumental weapons depot on the edge of the city center.

Later that morning several companies of the 89th Infantry Reserve Battalion also marched into the Fokker workshops at the Görries airfield, ordering the workers who were present to join them. In a demonstration march on the city center, the gathered soldiers and workers demanded peace, food, voting rights, and the abdication of Grand Duke Friedrich Franz IV, *the* symbol of the old order. Now the ghost was out of the bottle: on the arsenal building a red flag was hoisted. But Commander Von Liliencron was in no mood to give in that easily and surrender the town. In an attempt to calm the situation, he appeared at a gathering in the city square, accompanied by a large marching band. This show of musical force resulted in laughter, which fitted the otherwise nonviolent if chaotic day. Nevertheless, the revolt in Schwerin proceeded in similar fashion to those in other German cities. Banks and postal and telegraph offices were occupied, as was the train station. In the evening a joint workers and soldiers council was chosen, which acted as a new city council. One of its first decisions was to release all political prisoners from jail and incarcerate all representatives of the former authorities instead.[4]

Thus Anthony Fokker woke up in a different city from the one in which he had fallen asleep the previous night. And if not a single shot had been fired, the sounds of excitement, of voices and marching feet beneath his window as the troops moved from the barracks to the arsenal, would have awakened even the tightest sleeper. After a night full of worries, he had nowhere to go when a delegation of soldiers and workers reported at the front door of his house. Even though he lived relatively modestly, the address of Schwerin's biggest employer was generally known. Everybody knew the owner of the flashy Peugeot sports car that habitually parked in front of Schelfstrasse 25. At the door Anthony was told that his workers wanted money and that he was to consider himself under house arrest until further notice. The revolution was not even half a day old. How would this end?

Things got considerably worse. In the afternoon of the next day representatives of the workers and soldiers councils reached agreement with Grand Duke Friedrich Franz about his abdication and the resignation of his government. Henceforth the council of workers and soldiers would be the city's official authority, a development that the grand duke officially condoned in the interest of maintaining the peace. That evening a widely distributed extra issue of the *Mecklenburgische Zeitung* appeared in which Friedrich Franz confirmed that a new government had been formed. At Fokker's house, a second delegation of workers and soldiers arrived and demanded that Anthony give them access to his bank accounts, because the revolution had to be paid for. "I was more affected by the horrors of the revolution than by the whole war," he later recalled. "They shattered my nerves. No one knew from day to day whether he was rich or poor; whether he would even escape with his life."[5]

Fokker was now summoned to appear before a workers council, which convened in the arsenal building. There he was told that his workers expected to be paid, even though the Fokker Works had come to a sudden full stop. If he did not pay up, he would be shot, the soldiers threatened. But meeting such a demand was no easy matter. The banks in Schwerin had been taken over by the workers and soldiers council and had stopped functioning. All that Anthony could manage was to distribute the petty cash that was available in the factory offices. After promising that he would telephone Berlin and ask his contacts there to send more money, he was escorted back to his house. Two soldiers posted themselves at his front door to ensure he would not go anywhere. He found himself "solely at the mercy of irresponsible dictators."[6]

§

As an employee, his friend Bernard de Waal did not face such an ordeal. Loved and appreciated by almost everyone for his good nature, "Papa" de Waal was just as much taken aback by the recent developments as his friend, but at least he was allowed to come and go as he pleased. In Anthony's apartment the two friends debated what to do. Anthony was determined not to robbed by the workers council, but he was scared and anxious about his personal safety. He and De Waal devised a plan for sneaking Anthony out of Schwerin, even though the train station had been taken over by the rebels.

That evening, after dark, Bernard collected his Vulkaan motorcycle and waited for Anthony several streets away from the house. Once dusk had settled, Anthony put on the military uniform of his housekeeper Frieda Grabitz's son, stuffed several thousands of marks in his boots, and sneaked out the back door. His youth now served him well: there was nothing unusual about a young man in military uniform. Hastily he walked the dark streets to where Bernard was waiting for him with the motorcycle. Leaving Bernard behind to look after the house and the factory, he made a wide detour to avoid the city center and then took the long straight road to Ludwigslust, the next town on the railway line to the south, which was reportedly not yet occupied by revolutionary forces. Perhaps he might be able to board a train to Berlin there. He later remembered that "through the night, afraid to show a light, I raced at forty miles an hour, fearful that at any moment I would hit something and break my neck, or run into a revolutionary patrol."[7] In Ludwigslust he hid the motorcycle in the garden of an empty house and found his way to the station, aided by the darkness. He dared not enter the building, for fear that someone might recognize him. Instead he hid along the railroad tracks, hoping for a chance to climb aboard a freight train headed for Berlin. Thus he managed to reach the German capital toward the end of the next morning.

He dared not take the risk of staying in his usual rooms at the Hotel Bristol. Although the Bristol was reasonably close to the Lehrter Train Station, that would be the first place anyone would look for him in Berlin. The same could be said of the house of Tetta's grandparents at the Wannsee. So instead he rang the doorbell of one of his friends in Berlin's arts entourage, Mia May, a popular film star and singer. Two years before, Mia (née Hermine Pfleger, a baker's daughter from Vienna) had become a celebrity after her performance in the blockbuster movie *Die Sünde der Helga Arndt* (The Sins of Helga Arndt). With her wealthy husband, film director and studio boss Julius Mandl (known as Joe May), a descendant from an Austrian family of arms manufacturers, Mia May lived in the center of Berlin in a large house that was a favorite watering hole for artists and friends.[8] Anthony, Mia, and Joe were friends, and he was in good and safe hands with them for the time being.

That evening, November 9, the Reichstag building was taken over by force and occupied. Prisons that had held people convicted for political offenses opened their doors. Early the next morning, Emperor Wilhelm II crossed the border from his headquarters in Belgium into Holland and asked for asylum. Germany was essentially without a government, without central authority, and with cities that had been partly taken over by the revolutionaries. Unter den Linden was decked with red flags in several places. By contrast, the public services such as trams and the underground rail system continued to function more or less normally. That afternoon an assembly of revolutionaries appointed a council of soldiers and workers at the Circus Busch. Most of its members were affiliated with the Ebert government—the Council of People's Delegates in the new terminology—which had come to incorporate the more revolutionary wings of the Social Democratic movement. Although all positions of power and authority at the top changed hands to accommodate revolutionary elements, Berlin began to function more or less normally. People went about their business.[9]

𝓖

Anthony tried to return to normalcy as well. He soon moved back into the Bristol, although he was careful not to take undue risks and was accompanied by four sailors who served as armed bodyguards whenever he went out.[10] For the time being there could be no returning to Schwerin and his factory. Communications were disrupted, and news was scarce. He was equally in the dark about what was really happening in Berlin. Anthony found it difficult to fathom the problems that were coming his way. On November 11, these suddenly became bigger as well.

Just after 5 a.m. that day, the French, British, and German military commanders of the Western Front met in a French railway carriage, parked in the woods near Compiègne halfway between Paris and Saint-Quentin, for the signing of an armistice to end the war. The conditions to which Germany had to agree were abundantly clear. In general terms they stipulated that the Germans must pull out of all occupied territories forthwith. In Western Europe, German troops would have to withdraw to behind the Rhine. The German fleet was to be surrendered, and the peace agreement with Soviet Russia that had been signed earlier that year was to be annulled. Some conditions were very specific indeed. Article 4 of the armistice read, "Surrender in good condition by the German armies of the following equipment: 5,000 guns (2,500 heavy, 2,500 field), 25,000 machine guns, 3,000 trench mortars, 1,700 airplanes (fighters, bombers—firstly all D.VII's and night-bombing machines)."[11]

This meant the death blow to the Fokker Works. The Fokker D.VII fighter represented the pinnacle of Anthony's ceaseless efforts during the war years. The machine possessed flying and handling qualities superior to anything the Allies could put against it and had brought Fokker to the top of the German aircraft industry. In front reports to Berlin, ace pilot Hermann Goering reported that the D.VII, equipped with the 185-hp BMW IIIa engine, was superior to all Allied aircraft. The development of this remarkable fighter, intended as a successor to the Dr.I triplane, had started in September 1917 and had proceeded at an amazing speed through several prototypes that were equipped with different kinds of engines.[12] This time all the pieces of the puzzle had ended up in just the right place.

Fokker's D.VII, with its alternative Mercedes or BMW engines, had won the comparative flight trials that had been organized, for the first time, at Adlershof from January 20 till February 12, 1918. The design had left the competition—the Pfalz D.VIII, the LFG Roland D.VI, and the Siemens D.III—behind at a comfortable distance.[13] The trials themselves were a consequence of the public admiration for Germany's crack pilots, which went so far as to give them a say in the army's aircraft procurement.

A select group of Germany's best pilots had been invited to participate in the selection process at Adlershof. The winner of the competition could look forward to substantial production orders. Fokker's good relations with the fighter pilots now paid off: his D.VII entry received the support of Manfred von Richthofen and other top-scoring pilots. This result had required quite a few hours of nightly tinkering to incorporate last-minute changes. Until the last moment Fokker and his mechanics had been working to get the prototype just right. Reinhold Platz later remembered the frenzy of the process: "Fokker telephoned me from Berlin on a Saturday night. 'The machine is superb, I'd like to have another one, with the 180-hp Mercedes, but the trials will only last another 14 days. Can you still make it?' The aircraft needed to be completely redesigned to take this engine, but we managed."[14]

After the pilots had been able to evaluate the D.VII, the representative of the General Staff, Fritz von Falkenhayn, a good friend of Von Richthofen, took Fokker aside. Seated in his staff car, he asked Anthony how fast he would be able to set up series production. Von Falkenhayn mentioned an initial order of at least 400 aircraft. Such numbers presented Fokker with a problem, because his factory in Schwerin was already stressed to build a series of training aircraft. Von Falkenhayn, however, dismissed his reservations as "details"; after all, the new fighter could also be built under license in other factories. Anthony suddenly realized he was looking at a commission reaching 10 million marks or more.[15] Indeed, from early in February, orders for the D.VII mushroomed. Contracts at Schwerin mentioned up to 1,000 aircraft. To produce the fighter in sufficient numbers, IdFlieg commissioned Albatros to build D.VIIs as well as Fokker. By the time of the ceasefire in November, about 800 aircraft were already being deployed at the front, although no more than 300 of them came from Schwerin.[16]

The D.VII's special mention in the armistice agreement pulled the rug from under Fokker's company. It took a while before the gravity of what was happening sank in at the Fokker Works. A catalog published by Fokker at the end of 1918 even mentioned that higher praise was hardly possible than the special armistice mention.[17] But there was no escaping the consequences of the war's being lost. The aircraft industry was hard hit by the Allied demands. Suddenly nothing was secure or safe anymore, not even bank balances. In defeated Germany the value of Fokker's ventures and investments plummeted. In these uncertain circumstances inflation raged. Like other Germans who had become wealthy because of the war, Anthony tried to secure his money before the nation was submerged completely in revolution.

༆

Within days of the signing of the armistice, Fokker began bombarding IdFlieg with proposals that would at least return the 1.5 million marks that he had invested in the joint venture with Junkers. Eventually Wilhelm Horter managed to massage IdFlieg into providing a settlement agreement up to 1.8 million marks. This sounded better than it actually was, since it quickly became evident that the army no longer had

Nose dive: In November 1918 the armistice agreement spelled out that all Fokker D.VII fighter aircraft (such as this plane, completing a loop) were to be turned over immediately to the Allies. The special mention of Fokker's most successful fighter was a prelude to the demise of his activities as an airplane constructor in Germany. **DEUTSCHES MUSEUM, MUNICH, GERMANY**

the financial means to honor such promises. The money to dissolve the Junkers-Fokker joint venture could only come from Hugo Junkers, who was persuaded early in December to buy Fokker off for a lump sum of 1.49 million marks and thus gain full control over Junkers-Fokker. Junkers thereby distanced himself from the forced cooperation that had brought him nothing but headaches, and became boss in his own house again. On December 9 Felix Wagenführ personally signed off the agreement, after which the split between Fokker and Junkers became final on April 24, 1919.[18]

But what was to be done with the extraordinary sum of money resulting from this transaction? Anthony had no clear answer. To keep abreast of inflation he began to buy foreign investment papers at random, trying to change as much of his German marks into foreign currency as soon as possible. This was no easy matter; the mark was currently under huge pressure, and Berlin authorities were desperate to prevent a bank run. The export of securities from Germany was expressly forbidden. Foreign currency could only be bought under the strictest conditions, and the transfer of funds abroad became a shady business that primarily enriched the bankers involved. Therefore Anthony tried to change his money into bonds and other long-term securities. With the assistance of two brokers he bought many thousands of coupons, hoping to be able to cash these at some point in the future.[19]

Soon the sheer physical volume of the money became a problem, as Fokker's funds filled a collection of bags and trunks. Friedrich Seekatz, whom Anthony had called back to Berlin in March 1918 to act as a general technical adviser, later remembered how he had counted and stacked piles and piles of 100 mark banknotes on the living room carpet of Tetta's aunt's house in the chic Tiergarten quarter. They were packed into the carpet to be shipped to Holland.[20] Seekatz was also instrumental in obtaining the cooperation of the British Red Cross in Berlin, receiving permission to conceal some of Fokker's funds in their safe.

Anthony feared that his assets would be confiscated, and not everything could be transferred into cash and concealed. It therefore appeared best to invest in property, at least temporarily. For 1 million marks Fokker bought the house of a former director of the Dresdner Bank at Bellevue Strasse 31, a stone's throw from Potsdamer Platz in the center of Berlin. The price included the furniture of the house and a number of bronze sculptures and paintings. It would prove a bad investment. The house was expropriated in 1923 and sold at only half its value during the course of one of the gun synchronization lawsuits that Franz Schneider and Luftverkehrsgesellschaft (LVG) filed against Fokker. Anthony also bought a country estate near Woltersdorf at the Kalksee (Chalk Lake) nine miles east of Berlin. Joe and Mia May had an estate there too and entertained plans to build a large film studio at the location. For Fokker, a movie fan, this was an attractive setting. He and Tetta also planned to use the house as a summer residence and enjoy the Kalksee for water sports. For another 220,000 marks he bought the twelve-room apartment of the Hungarian consul, who had become nervous because of the revolution and wanted to sell his German holdings while there was time. In December 1918 Anthony moved to the apartment, since he no longer trusted that the Hotel Bristol's conspicuous luxuries would be left alone by the revolutionaries. To spread his assets further he bought a property in Bavaria and invested in Berlin's new Scala Variety Theater.[21]

ᚷ

When the worst of the unrest appeared to be past, Anthony dared to venture into the streets again, although he kept his bodyguard. Through acquaintances of Seekatz's he managed to obtain provisional identity papers, issued by the new authorities.[22] The general situation in Berlin, however, remained uncertain. Chancellor Friedrich Ebert, supported by the General Staff, schemed to have the army disarm everyone who had helped overturn the old institutions. This counterrevolution was to take place before December 16, because that was the day when a general assembly of soldiers and workers councils was to convene. But on December 6 matters got prematurely out of hand. An army unit arrested and imprisoned the committee of Berlin's soldiers and workers councils, which had thus far cooperated with Ebert's government. Shootouts took place in several parts of the city. For a while it appeared as if this would end in a military coup d'état, but as the days passed the situation calmed down. Many soldiers, fed up with the army, ignored orders and simply went home. The central council of workers and soldiers could thus convene without problems on December 16. The meeting demanded abolition of the military command structures—something that was not negotiable for the Ebert government or for the General Staff. The Supreme Army Command henceforth encouraged the formation of volunteer units that were supposed to block the demands of the revolutionary central council meetings.[23]

Fokker grew increasingly nervous as a result of such developments. It would be better and safer if he were to leave Berlin, but how and where to? On December 12 he convened a meeting at the Hotel Bristol to discuss his options. Both Wilhelm Horter and Maj. Hans Bartsch were present. At the War Ministry, Bartsch had recently become responsible for the German Air Corps. Anthony asked him whether the War Ministry would be prepared to let him leave. Bartsch did not appear unwilling.[24] So Anthony reported to the Dutch legation on the Voss-Strasse two days later to ask for a Dutch passport. He told the consul, Jacob Wolff, that he had plans to resettle in Holland. With a Dutch passport he would be able to cross the border without problems. Wolff indicated that although he was sympathetic to the request, he still would have to apply for permission from The Hague through official diplomatic channels. Wolff told Anthony that the grounds for his request would have to be legally verified: did Fokker still possess the Dutch nationality on which he based his petition? Stories that he had become a German citizen were widespread. Wolff would first have to confer with the Ministry of Foreign Affairs in The Hague.[25]

Anthony was disconcerted; clearly this process was going take time. The next day he met again with Bartsch at the Bristol. This time he asked Bartsch whether it would be possible to annul his German nationality. The major indicated he would do his best but could not make any promises as to how long it might take. Days passed, during which the situation in Berlin with the central council of workers and soldiers became increasingly grim. Anthony decided to risk traveling to Schwerin and try to get an exit visa for Holland stamped into his German passport.

ᵠ

The revolution had continued in Schwerin too, but had lost its sharp edges. On November 14 Grand Duke Friedrich Franz had signed his abdication and left with his family to find shelter in Denmark with his sister, Queen Alexandrine. After that Schwerin had returned to relative tranquility. The local workers and soldiers councils had become divided ideologically, and their influence was waning. Since early December the city had prepared for the election of a new civil assembly just after Christmas. Talks had been continuing since October 1916 between the Fokker Works, Mayor Otto Weltzien, and the Airfield Society about changes in the lease contract for the factory buildings and the sale of the grounds below them beside the lake, as if no revolution had ever occurred. The various documents on the talks even mentioned the start of series production of civil aircraft.[26]

On December 16 Anthony could therefore report at the Schwerin police station without any problems, although he was cautious enough to have the Dutch consul, Hans Friese, accompany him. It must have been a relief to him that he received a permit without problems to go on a business trip to Rotterdam between December 18 and March 17, 1919. All Friese needed to do was to countersign the document as a witness. But would Fokker's passport hold up, given the uncertain conditions in Germany? Anthony had his doubts. In consultation with his legal advisers in Berlin he asked the War Ministry to annul the German nationality that he had received in 1915.[27]

Meanwhile, the Fokker Works were on a downhill slide. Because of the armistice all army contracts had been canceled. In Anthony's absence the management of the company had felt obliged to lay off about one-third of the workforce.[28] Further measures appeared inescapable, but which ones? Anthony himself would have preferred to leave things as they had been and to focus on building aircraft for exports. In a letter to the state government he wrote, "I stand before the decision to expand my industrial enterprise in Schwerin on a grand scale."[29] His letter was accompanied by a plea to help resolve the issue of his nationality, because the Fokker Works might have better growth possibilities as a foreign enterprise. To warm the authorities to this idea, he hinted at investments that might run into the millions.

This plan, if it was ever serious, was subject to substantial doubts. It was still uncertain whether there would even be a future for an aeronautical industry in Germany. In conversations with employees, which Anthony could now conduct fairly normally, the idea gradually took root that it might be an option to move part of the factory to Holland. Other companies that had worked for the German war industry were considering similar options. Fearing a complete dismantling of Germany's industries, the authorities in Berlin were willing to cooperate with such plans. Dornier soon transferred part of its production to Switzerland and Italy. Several parts of the airplane constructor Rohrbach disappeared across the border to Denmark. Fokker's former partner Junkers oriented himself toward Sweden and the Soviet Union.

For Fokker, Holland offered the most attractive refuge. The news from his mother country was tempting. It was common knowledge that the procurement of aircraft for the Dutch Army Air Corps (LVA) had been problematic for years. To build an effective Dutch air defense, the army needed about 200 fighter aircraft. However, the Dutch national producer, the Nederlandsche Automobiel- en Vliegtuigenfabriek "Trompenburg" in Amsterdam, had proven to be completely unable to develop modern aircraft. To make things worse, the aircraft that Trompenburg managed to deliver had only arrived after considerable delays. Everyone knew that the LVA wished to be rid of the Trompenburg contract.[30]

Early in January 1919 Trompenburg suffered another setback when the company was hit by labor unrest. The end of the war meant the end of defense contracts, and Trompenburg was forced to contemplate massive cutbacks in staff.[31] Perhaps Trompenburg's director, the Dutch aviation pioneer Henri Wijnmalen, might be interested in a cooperation with Fokker? Was this the export market Fokker had referred to in his letter to the authorities in Schwerin? First and foremost, it had to be established whether the German War Ministry would allow factory equipment to be moved to neutral Holland. And thus Anthony traveled back to Berlin.

¶

In Berlin another powder keg ignited on December 24. That morning there was an armed encounter at the Schlossplatz in front of the royal city palace. The "People's Navy Division," about 1,000 revolutionaries from the group that had started the sailors' mutiny at the beginning of the previous month, had occupied the chancellor's office and effectively placed the Ebert government under house arrest. The sailors demanded deferred pay and various reforms, and then decided to march on the royal palace. At 7:45 a.m. they were met by hastily assembled army units that were still loyal to the government. The sailors took cover in the stables of the royal palace at Unter den Linden. The exchange of fire between the two groups lasted until after midday. Large numbers of Berliners gathered to see who would win. Fokker, who was in the streets that morning, had to take cover in the recesses of the walls of the Prussian State Library.[32]

The navy rebels emerged from the battle victorious, and a crisis of power was the inevitable result. In the first weeks of the new year, the power of the Ebert government slipped further. There was another wave of strikes, and strategic buildings were occupied. The Dutch envoy, Willem Gevers, reported to The Hague on January 9, "While I write this letter, shots are fired everywhere. Tonight there was a violent shootout in the Voss-Strasse just in front of the legation, the traces of which are still visible on the houses across our building."[33] In the end Ebert had no alternative but to mobilize all remaining loyal troops. Between January 9 and 12, the revolution was smothered in blood. Hastily formed volunteer units of pro-government soldiers moved into Berlin, and on January 15, 1919, they occupied the city center and some of the surrounding quarters.[34]

ᓀ

For Fokker this new spiral of violence was the last straw. By now he knew that he enjoyed the tacit support of the German War Ministry for his plans to move to Holland. With Wilhelm Horter he approached the Government Taxation Bureau, a department specially formed to supervise the sale of surplus war material, to ask for their cooperation. His request was quickly acknowledged. Moreover, a special representative to accommodate Fokker was designated in the person of his friend Hermann Goering, which made things both easier and cheaper. Through the mediation of Seekatz, a highly profitable arrangement was hammered out: Fokker would be allowed to buy back those aircraft and engines already paid for by the army but still present at Fokker's facilities in Schwerin. The arrangement was duly reported to the Allies by the German negotiators of the armistice conditions in Spa, and the Allies made no objections.[35] Thus Fokker bought back ninety-two D.VII fighters and a hundred rotary engines. Now it was time to find out whether they could be sold in Holland.

The man for this confidential mission was Bernard de Waal, who had returned to his native country in mid-December. On December 21 he met with the commander of the Dutch Air Corps, Col. Hendrik Walaardt Sacré at the Soesterberg airfield.[36] From telephone contacts with Henri Wijnmalen in Amsterdam, it was learned that Trompenburg was ready to collaborate. All Fokker needed to do was to push ahead. In Schwerin his chief of shipping, Heinrich Mahn, received instructions to make preparations for transporting the aircraft.

On January 14, 1919, Anthony and Tetta received the required official notice from the Berlin police commissioner of no objection to their intended marriage.[37] Anthony insisted that the wedding should take place in Holland, which would reinforce his claim for Dutch nationality. It meant that Tetta had to hurry to apply for a visa. She had to take a swift leave from her friends and relatives, none of whom would be able to witness her wedding because of travel restrictions for German citizens.

ᓀ

While Horter applied himself in Berlin buying back aircraft and engines, turmoil hit Schwerin. On the night of January 5 a group of rebel sailors occupied the arsenal and the postal and telegraph office for several hours. The newly elected local authorities managed to restore law and order, but the future for the Fokker Works and its 1,800-strong workforce looked grim.

Anthony considered continuing the Schwerin operation with about 250 people who would primarily concern themselves with building boats. His idea, rooted in his sailing hobby, produced a lot of uncertainty. At the end of January a delegation of seven employees traveled to Berlin to talk with Horter and Fokker about their plans for the future. In view of the sharp rise in unemployment in the Schwerin area, they requested a financial compensation during a period of up to six months after severance to allow sufficient time to find alternative employment.[38] Anthony, however, said he was unable to give them what they wanted.

Meanwhile, Heinrich Mahn was practically on his own in his preparations for the planes' transport to Holland. Even Anthony had no idea of the details. Organizing freight cars was the biggest problem to overcome, as the German railways were facing shortages in rolling stock. Fortunately for Mahn, clear-cut instructions regarding the export of goods were not yet in force in those parts of Germany that had thus far remained beyond Allied control. Border restrictions applied primarily to the import of goods into Germany from neutral countries. Allied regulations held that no German goods were to be exported without special permission. But in early 1919 most of the control measures that the Supreme Allied Economic Council was to impose via the Inter Allied Trade Commissions still had to be implemented. Consequently, Fokker and the Berlin authorities were more or less free to do as they pleased.[39]

₲

By February 16, preparations had proceeded far enough for Anthony and Tetta to undertake the journey to Amsterdam themselves. Only a few days before, Anthony had driven a carful of suitcases, bags, and his rug with the hidden money, along with bonds and securities worth millions of marks, all the way to Travemünde on the shore of the Baltic. There he had delivered his precious cargo onboard his powered sailing yacht *Hana*. Captain August received secret instructions to try and sail the valuable cargo to Holland, dodging the Allied controls on shipping. The seabound operation was possible because by late December most of the mines in the German coastal waters had been cleared. Following Anthony's instructions, the *Hana* put out to sea.

But not all matters were finalized. Once in Holland, Anthony would need funds while he waited for the *Hana* to dock. For this another daring plan was devised. A sum worth about 1 million Dutch guilders, in foreign currencies, was crammed into an unobtrusive old bag belonging to the cook of a diplomatic legation in Berlin who had permission to travel to Holland. Anthony and Tetta bought first-class tickets for the same train. Before they went on their journey, they visited Consul Wolff one last time to obtain entry permits now that they would both be traveling on German passports. Wolff complied with their request.[40] Nonetheless, Anthony was sweating profusely when the diplomatic luggage was taken from the train's baggage compartment at the last station before the border, Bad Bentheim. International travelers were forbidden to take more than fifty marks' worth of cash across the Dutch border. Luckily the German customs officers did not undertake a closer inspection. With a final stamp in their German passports, Anthony and Tetta crossed into Holland near Oldenzaal.[41]

HAARLEM, HOLLAND
MARCH 1919

Finally, the moment had arrived. On March 25, the small party set out in three automobiles from Herman Fokker's house at Kleine Houtstraat to the Haarlem City Hall.
It was a sunny Tuesday morning, around eleven. At 41° Fahrenheit (5° Celsius), it was
cold for the time of the year. The first car, a modern, enclosed Peugeot, carried Tetta
and Anthony, the happy bride and groom. In the second, older automobile sat the
groom's proud parents, Herman and Anna Fokker. The third car held Toos and her
husband, Geert Nijland.

For an international wedding, the affair was remarkably Dutch. General Curt
von Morgen was on the Allied list of suspected German top military staff and was not
allowed to leave the country. His wife, Rose Lee Bolbrugge, and Tetta's three brothers
(Ernst Robert, Heinrich Joachim, and Hans Georg) had also been denied permission
to travel to Holland, and Tetta's other family members and friends were absent as
well. Even the postcards to wish her well had been held up at the border.[1]

For the occasion, Anthony had a dark gray suit made. Over it he wore an open
coat in the same color with a wide, dark fur collar. This way his simple white carnation stood out well. Rather uncharacteristically, he wore a black bowler hat to complete his outfit. Tetta, too, was dressed in modest gray: a layered dress that reached
down to her booted ankles, its top lined with white embroidered lace. A plain pearl
necklace graced her neck. Over this she wore a wide black coat lined with dark fur. A
peculiar, outsized large carnation hung down from a pin that prevented the lapels of
her coat from opening. The only playful element of her outfit was a light, flat hat with
a wide brim, laced with a black ribbon. The attire was chic yet distinctly unfestive,

as the local paper noted. "Oh, just getting married in a bit," Anthony had remarked earlier that morning when people passing him in the street inquired where he was heading with the three-piece suit under his arm.[2]

The ceremony at the large oak table in the old reception room of the city hall was just as somber. Asked whether there were any objections to the marriage, Herman and Anna Fokker said they had none. The city clerk kept it brief, as requested. Two witnesses signed the marriage certificate: Frits Cremer, who had come home from Germany in the middle of the war and had lived at his parents' estate since, and Geert Hoekstra, a young general practitioner from Utrecht.[3] It was only when they left the reception room that Anthony let on that the ceremony and the solemn vows touched him too: he donated a thousand Dutch guilders to the city's poor.[4]

When they reappeared, some twenty-five Haarlemmers, young and old, had gathered at the bottom of the staircase of the city hall so as not to miss anything of the wedding of their famous townsman. Passing by, Anthony merrily lifted his hat but did not slow his pace. A uniformed chauffeur held the door of the car open for him and Tetta. In just twenty-five seconds, the bride and groom were gone. There was no wedding in church to follow the civil ceremony, as was the custom in the country. Doubtless to the regret of his mother, a reverend's daughter, Anthony had chosen to stick to the civil, administrative ceremony only. Religion meant little to him, and the whole wedding party had been organized to accommodate his wishes.

A reception followed, held in the back garden of his parents' house on Kleine Houtweg, despite the cold. Anthony needed the light to have the event filmed, having hired a crew and camera to document it. Mother Anna was brief in her congratulations. Father Herman, in one of his customary informal suits and chomping a half-smoked cigar, was warmer in his wishes. In the short time that they had come to know each other, Tetta had taken a liking to her unconventional father-in-law, who did his best to charm and tease her and pretended to wipe a little tear from his eyes now that his unruly son was finally wed. Made up of the small circle of Anthony's uncles and aunts and an occasional invited friend, the queue of well-wishers was short. Nonetheless, it was rather special that Prince Hendrik, the queen's husband and an acquaintance of Anthony's from the entourage of the Grand Duke in Schwerin, Hendrik's brother, came to present his best wishes. Frits Cremer, as one of Anthony's oldest friends, closed the roster of guests. Only the next day did the local paper carry the "absolutely only official message" that the marriage had taken place, including a spelling error in Tetta's family name.[5]

⚓

Up to then, the couple had spent their days in Holland as the guests of Anthony's parents at Kleine Houtweg. Now that they were married, Anthony wanted his privacy. In anticipation of finding a suitable house to live in, they moved to an apartment in the Hotel de l'Europe in Amsterdam, an expensive hotel located on Rokin, one of the city's most prestigious streets. Anthony was used to living in hotels and furnished

A very Dutch ceremony: On March 25, 1919, Tetta von Morgen and Anthony were married at the town hall of Haarlem in the Netherlands. It was a modest and very Dutch affair. None of Tetta's family were able to attend, owing to Allied travel restrictions for German citizens.
AUTHOR'S COLLECTION

homes. It was in his interest to settle in Amsterdam, where he would be close to his new business associate, Henri Wijnmalen, Trompenburg's director. In the past few weeks, the contacts between the two entrepreneurial pilots had developed rapidly. Six days after his arrival in Holland, on February 22, Fokker and Wijnmalen signed an agreement that Fokker would provide 98 D.VII fighter aircraft, 118 C.I reconnaissance planes, and a supply of BMW engines so that Trompenburg could fulfill a contract with the Dutch armed forces. The deal involved the sum of 6,406,000 marks (then $195,000).[6] Wijnmalen profited greatly. He was eager to be rid of the old air corps contract and focus his company's activities on building motor cars instead.

For Fokker, the contract presented a golden opportunity: finally a buyer had presented itself for the stock of the superfluous fighter aircraft he was amassing in Schwerin. Trompenburg might serve as the official importer of the transports that Heinrich Mahn was organizing. Even the administration of the rented railroad carriages now became impeccable, since the German railways had an elaborate system by which they kept track of all rolling stock and what they had carried.[7]

On the planes thus exported, Fokker paid the taxes due in Schwerin.[8] The deal was entered into the books as a normal international business transaction between two companies and remained outside the scope of the weapons exports ban that was issued by the Armistice Committee in Spa on March 14, 1919.[9] Anthony Fokker, who was only marginally involved in the organization of the exports, could not even recall Mahn's name later.[10]

The first transport of forty railcars crossed into Holland on March 18, a week before Anthony's wedding, accompanied by all the necessary legal documents. The railway companies fully cooperated, which was helped on the Dutch side by the coincidental fact that Frits's father Jacob Cremer had presided over the joint boards of control of the two Dutch railway companies until just a few weeks before the transport. The train itself ended at a siding in the Amsterdam Petroleum Docks.[11] After March 18 three more transports followed. On May 17 part of the company stocks and factory inventory were shipped, along with two C.I reconnaissance aircraft. On June 10 another twenty-nine C.I aircraft followed, and on June 19 there was a smaller, final train transport of 11 C.I machines. According to Fokker's own estimate, some 220 aircraft were transported from Schwerin to Holland: about 120 D.VII fighters, more than 60 C.I reconnaissance aircraft, and a number of D.VIII machines and some other planes, including Anthony's personal two-seat D.VII. Along with them, some 400 aircraft engines went by train, as did a substantial part of the production tools and stores.[12]

On April 11 the Dutch cabinet discussed the issue, agreeing that Fokker would assume the responsibilities of the Trompenburg contract. Criticism of the government's readiness to accept former German war materials was waved aside. The government and the army's Munitions Bureau, which supervised the procurement of war materials, maintained that the terms of the agreement between private parties

Sonderzug mit 35 Fokker-Flugzeugen an die Westfront
13.7.1918.

1351.

Transportation by train: After a contract was signed between Fokker and the Dutch manufacturer Trompenburg, four trainloads of Fokker aircraft rolled across the German-Dutch border between March 18 and June 19, 1919. In both countries the authorities lent full cooperation. In Germany export duties were paid over the aircraft, which Fokker had bought back from the military authorities. **COLLECTION MICHAEL SCHMIDT, MUNICH, GERMANY**

did not concern them.[13] Foreign Minister Herman van Karnebeek informed the British ambassador to The Hague, Robert Graham, that the government could not be expected to supervise all imports from Germany by private parties and enterprises.[14]

Nonetheless, the government maintained that the matter at hand concerned the sales contract, drawn up before the Armistice, between the government and Trompenburg. Under the terms of the agreement, Fokker was to deliver the aircraft separate from a set of Clerget rotary engines. These were already held in storage by Trompenburg to be used for the contracted aircraft. Because they were completely unsuited for the D.VII or for the C.I, they were superfluous to begin with. The engines were taken on by the armed forces in order to be demolished immediately. Fokker, by contrast, offered his aircraft with BMW engines that came free of charge. It took a while before the details of the contract were hammered out, but by the end of June the parties agreed in principle. The actual deed for the Fokker aircraft then remained in the pipeline until January 2, 1920: Fokker was to deliver ninety-two D.VII machines at a unit price of 10,692 guilders ($4,193), with an additional ninety-two C.I aircraft at 12,784 guilders ($5,013) each. On top of this, Fokker paid Trompenburg 167,960 guilders ($65,866) as a fee for the company's cooperation, plus 47,040 guilders ($18,447) in compensation for costs incurred.[15]

As the organizer of the special train transports, Mahn felt shortchanged. He had hoped that Fokker would at least be there to welcome the last trainload at the Dutch border station of Oldenzaal and hand him an amply filled wallet for his efforts. None of that happened. Moreover, in the summer of 1919 he was railroaded by Reinhold Platz, who considered himself company manager in Schwerin, after a row over a typewriter that had gone missing. A decade later, the conflict still raged in Mahn's mind.[16]

ℭ

Initially, all those who participated in the Trompenburg deal expected to gain quite a bit of money. Fokker paid Trompenburg 1,368,080 guilders ($536,500). He himself stood to gain 2,159,792 guilders (approximately $847,000) in additional income. The LVA had no reason to complain, either; it was to receive first-rate fighter aircraft for a rock-bottom price, with engines even delivered free of charge. Yet, early in 1920, the Netherlands' government decided on big cuts in defense spending. Instead of buying 190 aircraft, it decided to buy no more than twenty D.VII fighters and sixty C.I reconnaissance aircraft. This was a major disappointment for Fokker, who now suddenly found himself left with a large quantity of unsold fighter aircraft. The value of the new contract was proportionally lower, too: 600,000 guilders ($207,000).[17] But the aircraft themselves appeared on Fokker's books at no more than 9,000 marks each (then as little as $158).[18] For the 184 aircraft that were exported to Holland, this amounted to a total of 298,000 guilders ($102,759), equaling Fokker's profit for the aircraft. The total proceeds of the arms sales were just over 300,000 guilders ($103,000).

On top of this was the money that Fokker had managed to bring across the border. According to his own estimate, he rescued about a quarter of his personal fortune of 30 million marks (some $3.8 million), which still amounted to some 7.5 million marks (then about $954,000).[19] After a first sleepless night in Holland, he had even been able to collect the money-stuffed suitcase in The Hague. Both the locks had sprung open, but to his immense relief the bundles of money were still inside. In the days that followed, he had driven to the port of Den Helder in the north of the country, where he had anxiously awaited the arrival of Captain August and the *Hana*—in vain, as it turned out. Only when he had nearly given up hope of ever seeing his yacht and his money again did he receive a message at his hotel in Amsterdam that his ship had finally come in and was safely moored along the quayside. Captain August had successfully managed to evade the remaining British sea blockades.[20] Anthony deposited the money at the Unie Bank voor Nederland en Koloniën, conveniently located within walking distance of the Hotel de l'Europe in Amsterdam's prestigious Nieuwe Spiegelstraat.

Regaining his Dutch nationality proved more problematical. That difficulties loomed had already become evident when Tony and Tetta had reported to the Haarlem City Hall on March 4 to comply with administrative requirements connected to their intended marriage. They were asked difficult questions. In December consul Jacob Wolff had sent enquiries from Berlin to the mayor of Haarlem, Anthony's last known place of residence in Holland, for a "Declaration of Dutch Nationality." Turning over such a document was a legal requirement for issuing a new passport. But before providing such an official statement, the mayor had been obliged to trace Fokker's antecedents.[21] Doing so, interim mayor Johan de Breuk had learned that Fokker had been naturalized as a German citizen. With this information, it became impossible for him to issue the required official declaration. Anthony, who had not counted on such "trivial" administrative problems at all, was outraged because of these "obstructions." He had lived in Germany for more than eight years, but he considered himself Dutch. In December 1914, he had regarded the issue of his citizenship as a purely pragmatic thing. Circumstances had dictated his choice to become German. Now matters were just the other way around. Anthony denied having obtained his German citizenship of his own free will. After consultation with his council Jacques Oppenheim, a prominent law professor at Leiden University and an acquaintance of his uncle Eduard, he maintained that he had been coerced to cooperate in the nationality change, which he now said he had never recognized. In support of his argument, Anthony pointed to the letter of the German War Ministry dated January 13, 1919, which confirmed that his German nationality would be annulled.[22] This decision had been communicated to consul Wolff in Berlin.[23]

Mayor De Breuk remained firm. The law left him no room to maneuver. It stated that Dutch nationality was automatically lost through naturalization into foreign citizenship. Coercion was not mentioned in the law, and as interim mayor, De Breuk was hardly in a position to reinterpret the law on his own authority. He referred the case to the province's Queen's Commissioner.[24] Frustrated, Anthony appealed to Oppenheim, hoping he would be able to effect a breakthrough in the matter. Oppenheim, however, saw insufficient legal precedent for such a course of action. Anthony then tried a different approach. If Oppenheim could not help him, then maybe his family relatives could. After all, uncle Eduard had been a prominent member of Parliament and was still well connected in government circles. Anthony himself had been introduced in Schwerin to Prince Hendrik, brother of Grand Duke Friedrich Franz IV and husband to Dutch Queen Wilhelmina. Maybe he could help in the matter? It so happened that Hendrik had a warm interest in flying and had become the patron of the Royal Netherlands Aeronautical Society (KNVvL).

The outcome of this was that the issue of Fokker's nationality ended up at the desk of Prime Minister Charles Ruys de Beerenbrouck. After some further consultation, the Prime Minister sent Anthony his assurances that the matter would be resolved favorably. On Anthony's wedding day, the Cabinet decided to put legal impediments aside. Justice Minister Theo Heemskerk informed Anthony of the outcome. Thus Anthony was to receive a new Dutch passport. It was a peculiar decision, and it was whispered that it had been taken at the express wishes of Prince Hendrik.[25] The exceptional nature of the case was evidenced by the fact that Dutch nationality did not extend to Tetta von Morgen, although article 5 of the Law on Dutch Citizenship stipulated that the nationality of a lawfully wedded female followed that of the husband. It was also a sign that the government held high expectations for Fokker and believed that he would found a new Dutch aeronautical industry that would be an asset to Dutch neutrality and autarky.[26]

⚘

Even behind closed doors, business came before pleasure. The dream of sailing the world in the *Hana* that Anthony and Tetta had entertained in Berlin evaporated. A week after they had moved into Hotel de l'Europe, Anthony's personal D.VI machine arrived on the train from Schwerin, and he had it readied to fly from an Army airstrip just north of Amsterdam. Several enthusiastic reporters witnessed him making his famous aerobatic maneuvers. He announced his intention to found a large aircraft factory in Holland.[27] That he was serious about starting anew in his native country was illustrated two weeks later, when, around 7 p.m., the Air Corps duty officers at the Soesterberg aerodrome were alarmed by the sound of an approaching airplane. Moments later, Bernard de Waal and his flight mechanic, Karl Pohl, landed their C.I reconnaissance plane. They had left Schwerin early that afternoon without telling anyone where they were going. Hours later, mist and a malfunctioning compass had got them lost over the north of Holland, forcing them to make an emergency landing near the town of Meppel when their fuel ran out. Pohl was interned and then extradited to Germany because of his illegal border crossing, while De Waal was welcomed with open arms by his old aeronautical friends and soon reunited with Anthony.[28]

On April 29, 1919, Fokker reported as promised at the Haarlem flower pageant. From the military exercise grounds at Halfweg, between Amsterdam and Haarlem, he took off for a series of spectacular flying demonstrations over his home town. Above the Frederikspark, in front of his parents' home, he made several loops so that they could see his stunts from their front window. After landing again at Halfweg, he and Tetta got into a white car decorated with dark blue hyacinths and joined the flower pageant, chased by groups of excited children who yelled after their hero, "Long live Fokker!" The enthusiasm of the organizers was almost boundless. Anthony was presented with a special jury prize, which he received with laughter, stating it had been a pleasure to see Haarlem again from above.[29] A week later, admiration and fascination for the city's very own airman resounded in a poem printed on the front page of the *Haarlems Dagblad* newspaper:

The swallow parts the air,
The seagull turns with a wing to spare,
The lark rises fast,
The eagle floats high past,
The vulture dives steeply to the ground,
But Fokker, fast, unbound,
Flies, turns, flashes to and fro,
As secure as all birds do.[30]

Giving flying displays was one thing, but setting up a complete new company was something else. Above all, it required time. Initially, Anthony had intended to start a flying school on the beach at Scheveningen near The Hague. The plan did not progress beyond a series of plane rides for tourists, watched anxiously by the local police. The risk to the public that these flights by "Fokker's Air Tourism" presented was soon deemed far too great, and they grounded Fokker's recently hired Dutch pilot, Willem van der Drift, ending the venture.[31] A second plan to open an "airplane garage" in The Hague also came to nothing.

Every train that arrived from Schwerin made a decision on the future more urgent. At the end of May, Anthony took Tetta along to Soesterberg to witness the delivery of the first C.I aircraft to the Dutch Air Corps. He also took her up for an extended aerobatics display, flying all the way to the Dutch North Sea coast and back.[32] Meanwhile, Anthony's days became crammed with preparations for his new company. Meetings with officials, industrialists, bankers, and investors filled his days. He spoke at several fundraising events to convince the public of the great future that was in store for aviation, not just in commercial air traffic but also in aerial photography of unexplored regions of the earth. Along with this "big future," he also envisioned something like a "small future" for aviation; whenever he found the time, Anthony tinkered with his new friend Willem van der Drift on the construction of a lightweight glider that could be towed behind a powered plane.[33]

Anthony also worked on his public image, sponsoring such things as the construction of a facility in Haarlem for patients suffering from tuberculosis. He also acted as co-organizer of a lottery to collect more funds for patients suffering from the then-incurable disease. Building on the idea that the reduced air pressure at higher altitudes above the clouds might have beneficial effects, Anthony came up with a plan to take patients on special flights.[34] For the Haarlem sports week, organized on the occasion of peace festivities, Anthony offered to give a flying display, with proceeds going to charity. A lottery was organized in which participants could win the privilege to accompany Fokker on one of his flights. In all, 2,028 lottery tickets were sold, which brought in 1,200 guilders ($470). His father managed to persuade him to lend his name to a raffle to collect money for the victims of the eruption of the Kelud volcano on Java, which had occurred on May 20. After all, the Fokkers had worked the slopes of the Kelud at Njoenjoer for years.[35]

The winners of the lottery were to be taken on their flight on June 24, but that day did not suit Anthony, and he sent Van der Drift instead. Haarlemmers were disappointed that he did not show. In a letter to the editor of the *Haarlems Dagblad*, he answered his critics:

> *The possibility that I might have other demands on my time and would have to send a replacement is something I expressly told the organizers in advance. . . . The public completely disregards the risks a pilot runs in such performances, not to mention that he that gives such demonstrations purely for the benefit of the committee that organizes the festivities. After all, I am personally fully responsible for any accidents, to the pilot as well as to other persons or properties, even without considering possible damage to the value of my plane and of my name. Every demonstration results in a desk full of requests from enthusiasts of all ages and sexes . . . to hold a similar demonstration, preferably in the North and in the South of the country at the same time. It is purely for charity and for Haarlem interests that I agreed to this aerial demonstration, by exception, which I hope has lived up to expectations.*[36]

ᚳ

Anthony's departure to Holland had not entailed a sudden and complete disconnection from his German past. In Berlin, Wilhelm Horter explored possible new options for the Fokker Works, which resulted in an effort to earn money in commercial aerial photography. But the time was not right for such an endeavor, and Luftbild GmbH was dissolved before 1919 was out. Nonetheless, the Fokker Central Office at Unter den Linden continued to function, even if layoffs turned out to be unavoidable. At the end of the year, only Horter and Fokker's private secretary, Martha Moslehner, were left. The expensive office across from Hotel Bristol was sold off, and the Fokker Central Office moved to rather more modest dwellings in the suburb of Charlottenburg.

In the first postwar months, Schwerin still employed some 800 people, but their number fell rapidly. In February 1919, a large part of the remaining workforce was sent home. Fokker did his best to preserve his reputation as a good employer, and those who were laid off received three months' pay on top of the legally required severance money.[37] The compensation was also intended as an encouragement for other workers to leave. Between April 1919 and June 1921 the number of employees diminished from 680 to 140.[38] Those who were kept on received compensation for the general increase in prices, although their job security did not extend beyond August.[39] Fokker interfered as little as possible in what went on in Schwerin. Yet he indicated again that he intended to continue to build aircraft there, even if he had no firm plans for how to effect this. But since company revenues were gravely disappointing, paying those who remained behind soon presented serious problems. Clearly, new measures were called for.

For starters, it had to be decided who would be in charge, exactly: former balloonist Karl Hackstetter, who had been appointed by the War Ministry in July 1918; Fokker's own general manager, Carl Burgtorff; the head of sales, Richard Just; chief technology officer Curt Neubauer; engineer Reinhold Platz; or somebody altogether different. Fokker, who always preferred to work with people whom he considered personal friends and acquaintances, appointed his new brother-in-law, Hans Georg von Morgen, as general director.[40] This appointment did not go down well with the company employees, many of whom considered the company to be overstaffed at the top anyway.[41] Only in June did Anthony Fokker bring himself to intervene personally in the affairs of the company, when it could no longer be denied that some 4.5 million marks had evaporated in Schwerin since the beginning of the new year.[42] Fokker became convinced that there was no other option but to shut down the company, preferably as early as September 30, 1919. But that idea denied the new conditions that had emerged from the revolution, which required the cooperation of a council of employee representatives as well as permission from the local authorities. Neither occurred.[43] Nonetheless, Von Morgen tried to clean up shop, which resulted in the departure of Hackstetter and Neubauer in October. The more laid-back Platz fared better. He received permission to dedicate a small team of technicians to the development of a commercial transport plane. Most of the other remaining employees were transferred to the company's new department of motorboat construction—a short term proposition the management came up with, inspired by Anthony's love of sailing. As lessor of the factory buildings, the Aerodrome Company gave the green light for this change in manufacturing.[44]

Consequently, Fokker's obligations to his factory workers continued. Money primarily came in the shape of a promise of government compensations for orders that had been annulled because of the end of the war, 3.2 million marks in all. It was to be spent on back payments to Fokker's workers and in recompense for the rapidly rising costs of living. Anthony Fokker was personally charged to put up an equivalent amount so that all employees would receive their due.[45] Such local arrangements at his expense took Anthony by surprise, and he was very much opposed to them. Government compensations were in the end limited to aircraft that were left behind in Schwerin or dismantled as a result of postwar actions instigated by the Allies. They did not amount to the promised sum and only totaled 350,000 marks.[46]

One arrangement that did come true was with Junkers. In April 1919 Hugo Junkers took over all assets and debts of the Junkers-Fokker joint venture to continue the company under the name Junkers Flugzeugwerke AG (Junkers Aircraft Works Plc.). According to Fokker's own estimate, the enforced cooperation had cost him a million and a half marks, which represented but a modest sum for the acquisition of a wing design and construction technology that brought him many times that amount in profits. Junkers, on the other hand, was fully compensated by the German government and ended up paying nothing at all.[47] Nonetheless, the two rivals were not quite done with each other yet. Until the end of the 1930s they were entrenched in legal proceedings over patent rights, a conflict that soon spanned the Atlantic. Fokker kept a special account to pay his patent lawyer from Berlin, Paul Brögelmann, who continued to be busy with the various cases.[48]

In Schwerin, talks with the Aerodrome Society over the sale and trade of various plots of land continued, even though in 1919 the Fokker Works had run out of the funds required for such property transactions and indicated its loss of interest in such matters. For the Aerodrome Society, in its turn, this presented a very disappointing turn of events, and reason for legal action.[49] But if the maneuvering with property rights was complex, matters became substantially thornier in September when Fokker received a deferred claim from the German tax authorities. The state seized all of his remaining assets in Germany in payment for a total sum of 14,251,000 marks in unpaid taxes (then worth $434,000) that, the government claimed, had remained at the end of the war.[50] For such cases a complex set of rules, dues, and payment facilities existed. Often payment was effected in the form of goods that were either seized or sold under duress.[51] However, the sum of more than 14 million marks was well beyond the average scope of such tax suits. If the Fokker Works, sued in conjunction with its owner, wished to have any kind of future at all, it was imperative to cut all ties with Anthony Fokker forthwith—at least formally.

Anthony therefore parked his company shares with the Unie Bank in Amsterdam, which thus became financially responsible for running the Fokker Works in Schwerin while acting as a shield against claims that emerged from his ownership. Despite this arrangement, however, he intervened in company affairs from Amsterdam. To emphasize the legal changes that resulted from the bank deal the Fokker name was changed to the more neutral-sounding Schwerin Industrial Works (SIW: Schweriner Industrie Werke) on January 23, 1920. Thus SIW, of which the Unie Bank acted as major shareholder, severed all ties with Anthony Fokker. Yet the company could not avoid being dragged into the legal proceedings surrounding the dissolution of Fokker's German affairs. After protracted negotiations through Fokker's lawyers in Berlin, an agreement was hammered out with the German tax authorities regarding a reduction of the deferred tax claim to some 6 million marks (then worth $105,000).[52] Until an agreement could be signed, Anthony discovered to his dismay that he could not travel to Germany, even on his Dutch passport. If he had been unable to leave Germany without special permission since becoming a German citizen in 1915, he was now stuck with his German wife on the other side of the border.

In the meantime, the Unie Bank appointed another Dutchman, Jacob Lioni, as a supervising administrator to SIW. This was done on Fokker's advice. Fokker and Lioni knew each other from the First Air Traffic Exhibition Amsterdam (ELTA:

Eerste Luchtverkeer Tentoonstelling Amsterdam) that had been held in August 1919. Lioni, a decommissioned Air Corps lieutenant, had been one of the exhibition's administrators.[53] In turn, the city of Schwerin, which hoped to keep the local aircraft industry afloat, came up with a proposal for a profitable real estate trade-off in return for which SIW would receive better access to the lakeside. After all, the company was now building boats. In July 1920 this resulted in a complex deal between the city, the Aerodrome Society, and SIW.[54] At and around the Görries aerodrome a similar property arrangement was reached. Because SIW no longer needed the land, several large plots were sold off at Fokker's behest. A small number of houses that Fokker had bought near the aerodrome during the war were also sold.[55]

Despite his ban from Germany, Anthony's private affairs in the country also continued. He kept his membership in the Wannsee Sailing Club, with which he exchanged a series of letters in the spring of 1919 over the conditions of membership. That correspondence went through the Fokker Central Office in Berlin. Since he could no longer enjoy personal possessions that remained in the clubhouse, he had them sent to Amsterdam in August.[56] Such trivia took a long time to arrange, perhaps because of Anthony's uncertainty whether Amsterdam was the best place to send them to. Although now legally again a Dutchman, Fokker continued to invest in Germany as well. The world of the stage and of filmmaking especially fascinated him. On May 3, 1919, he was among a select group of entrepreneurs that invested in founding the Scala Theatre in Berlin. It opened its doors a year later and would shortly attain top billing in onstage variety shows. In the 1920s, Berlin was to become world-famous for its entertainment. Fokker's contribution was substantial; he controlled half the votes on the Scala's board.[57] He also remained as owner of the Perzina building in Schwerin and of the smaller Adolf Nützmann piano factory. The buildings themselves were rented to the Berlin entrepreneur Otto Libeau, a manufacturer of furniture and musical instruments. Anthony also continued his shareholding in the engine manufacturer Oberursel.[58]

ℭ

His prime interests now focused on the Netherlands. In the first week of May 1919, he opened an Amsterdam office at 84 Rokin, built in 1883 as a richly ornamented edifice with three floors, a roomy attic, and a basement. Fokker rented the first two floors for his new company's administrative staff. In doing so, he stuck to the pattern that had evolved in wartime Berlin. Anthony had a keen eye for whom to keep close. He rented the top floor of his office to Prince Hendrik. For years, Hendrik kept a personal pied-à-terre in Amsterdam above the Fokker offices.[59] Realizing that his German past would not easily be forgotten, Anthony made sure that his new company emanated a Dutch character.

To bring the new company about financially, his old Haarlem circle of family and acquaintances once again stepped in. Through the intervention of Jacob Cremer, he managed to get support from the former governor-general of the Netherlands East Indies, Joan van Heutz, who also took up the position of chairman of the board of the new Dutch Fokker company. The other members of the board reflected whom Fokker had met and spoken with since his arrival in the country: Cornelis Vattier Kraane, the director of the Nederlandsch-Indische Steenkolen Handel-Maatschappij (Netherlands Indies Coal Trading Company) and of the Amsterdam based trading company Blaauwhoedenveem Vriesseveem; the millionaire and investor Frits Fentener van Vlissingen, a key figure in Dutch enterprise and finance, who was also involved in the ELTA exhibition and acted as one of the founding fathers of KLM; Johan van der Houven van Oordt, a former secretary general of the Ministry of Colonial Affairs; the banker Daniël Patijn; and Anthony's uncle Eduard. To avoid the politically sensitive name "Fokker," the new company took the neutral name NV Nederlandsche Vliegtuigenfabriek (Netherlands Aircraft Factory Plc.). On July 21, 1919, the founding papers were signed before a notary in Amsterdam. The Unie Bank, with whom Anthony had opened an account to park the money he brought from Germany, acted as founder of the company, together with the stockbrokerage Patijn, Van Notten & Company. Both the Unie Bank and Patijn, Van Notten & Company invested 275,000 guilders. Anthony Fokker remained consciously shielded from view at the signature of the founding papers and was referred to only as company director.[60] The total founding capital of the company was registered as 1.5 million Dutch guilders ($600,000). The founding papers stated the purpose of the venture as "the production of, and trade in, aircraft and fast-running boats, and parts thereof, and everything that is connected with such; the foundation and operation of flying schools, airports, landing strips, and repair workshops, either under its own account, or on the account or with participation of third parties, and organizing and providing airshows. The operation of traffic in the air for persons, letters, goods, and so on, the provision of aerial photography for exploration and for topographical purposes, either under its own account, or on the account or with participation of third parties."[61]

Ultimate control over the company resided with Anthony Fokker. For all their expertise and resounding names, the members of the new board of control would have hardly any influence. In the months following the official signature, Anthony took over nearly all the shares of the group of founders. This gave him complete control over the Nederlandsche Vliegtuigenfabriek, soon known far and wide as the Fokker Factory. This development was to have far-reaching consequences. Fokker's way of conducting his business affairs was impulsive and unstructured; most of the time he was absent from the office, traveling across Europe on business. Over the years the company capital and his private capital became so entangled that no one could tell what was what. His financial manager, Frederik Elekind, whom he had inherited from Trompenburg, had a full-time job keeping even a semblance of order.[62] Although Anthony put himself on the company payroll for a modest 18,000 guilders annually, he declared expenses well over 50,000 guilders per year. Most of these were travel costs, connected to his many business trips.[63]

G

Of course, Anthony presented himself at the largest aviation spectacle ever organized in Holland, the ELTA, held in August 1919. Queen Wilhelmina officially opened the festivities. Two Air Corps lieutenants signed up for the organizing effort, Albert Plesman and Marinus Hofstee. They had managed to get substantial financial support for the venture from business circles, from local authorities in Amsterdam, and from the government in The Hague. The ELTA festivities lasted full six weeks and drew over half a million paying visitors from all over the country to the marshy fields north of Amsterdam where the event was held. For Anthony, it presented an ideal opportunity to show off his skills as an aerobatics pilot and demonstrate his aircraft before a national audience.

On Sunday, August 3, he made sure all public attention focused on his personal, bright red D.VI biplane, which he flew over the ELTA terrain as well as over the 24-hour cycling tournament at the Stadionbaan elsewhere in Amsterdam. The races were specially interrupted so that all might see and enjoy his aerial performance. The national newspaper *Algemeen Handelsblad* reported with awe:

> One saw the red wings, one saw under the lower wing the letters FOKKER. For a second the light of the sun setting touched the machine, and it was as if a golden miracle buzzed in the last light of the day. Then the aviator descended. For a moment he was out of sight. But suddenly he leapt with roaring sound over the wall of the stadium and came in low over the center field. We cheered. He greeted. And again and again he came back, suddenly carving upward through the blue sky, then again rolling, flying loops, coming down in a tailspin, sharply turning on a wing, and then zipping back full speed, all along the stadium, so low that the grandstand eliminated the machine from view. It was fantastic. It was frightening and yet grand. It was awesome and touching.[64]

Anthony himself was rather soberer on the matter of his performances. Over the years flying had become for him "one of the most boring and unexciting pastimes. I seldom fly longer than ten, fifteen minutes and I fly . . . when something has annoyed me intensely, or when I have to test a new airplane, because then I only have to concentrate on the technical characteristics of the machine. From time to time I derive pleasure from letting the aircraft make strange movements, but all these 'miracles' are in the end not more than proof of the technical perfection of modern aircraft. . . . Bravery is really not necessary for such aerial maneuvers."[65]

That did not apply to everyone. From the flights she made with Anthony Tetta returned pale and fragile. In the few photographs that remain she gave the appearance of an extra in the wrong movie scene in her thick leather flying coat and with her helmet on. Nonetheless, she managed the required smile for the cameras, be it somewhat timid. Anthony also took his parents up for a ride. On August 9, he even made a loop with his father onboard. Herman Fokker was truly impressed:

You lose all notion of time and speed and direction, speeding forward, suddenly a colossal turn to the left, to the right, descending at an angle, then you see the water, then ships, blocks of houses, the parking grounds, the exhibition, the aerodrome with next to the commercial stalls this square black mass that is supposed to be people . . . suddenly he really gives full throttle, your speed becomes enormous and then you go up and stand on your head, seeing nothing but sky, so you look up to see the earth and there you see Amsterdam upside down. . . . It all goes so incredibly fast that you just cannot understand. I later heard that one of the loops had gone wrong because the engine had stopped and we fell down vertically. . . . To have experienced something like this, is beyond imagination.[66]

Anthony, however, soon tired of demonstration flights. In the third week of August he packed his bags and departed for the seashore at Domburg in the southwest of the country for a quiet holiday with Tetta. After the closure of the ELTA, he rented the grounds from the city of Amsterdam and bought the wooden exhibition buildings to act as his new factory buildings. Thus, the Nederlandsche Vliegtuigenfabriek started its business activities on September 16, 1919.[67] The location, however, was far from ideal and in fact wholly unsuited for airplane construction since the factory had no airstrip of its own. During Fokker's life, all aircraft had to be taken from the ELTA facilities to Schiphol Airfield by barge for final assembly in Fokker's hangar there. Flight testing then followed. It was a cumbersome procedure, but then again the ELTA facilities came cheap, which for Fokker was paramount.

Having delivered his first series of aircraft to the Dutch Air Corps, Fokker was left with the question of what to do with the remainder of the aircraft he had brought from Germany, 140 machines in all. As a temporary solution, they were stored in a large warehouse in the Amsterdam docks so that they would at least be shielded from the weather. Meanwhile, Anthony devoted himself to get his new company running. This took quite a bit of time since he did not really have an idea of what he wanted with the new endeavor. In January 1920 the organization, then employing eighty-eight people, was still in a quandary.[68]

Quite a few of Fokker's early band of employees in Holland, the supervisory staff in particular, had been recruited at Fokker's German companies and at the Fokker Central Office in Berlin. The most important among them was Wilhelm Horter, who now became general manager in Amsterdam. From Schwerin came Bernard de Waal. Anthony appointed him to supervise the flight testing facility at Schiphol Airfield. In 1921, he also brought Reinhold Platz to Holland as his head of construction. This was a decision with far-reaching consequences, because at the beginning of the 1920s, Platz, never educated as an airplane engineer, had reached the limits of his capacities. Bruno Stephan, Fokker's deputy director from 1925 to 1935, described Platz as a narrow-minded man with "really limited mental capacities" who showed little understanding or respect for theoretical aerodynamics and disregarded all ideas that transcended his personal understanding.[69] His presence and final responsibility in design and construction acted as an impediment to technological innovation, which put Fokker's market position under increasing pressure.

Meanwhile, Horter's first concern was to sell the remaining stocks of D.VII and D.VIII fighters abroad. It was obvious that the company would depend on exports if it wished to survive in a small country like Holland. Yet initial foreign sales efforts largely remained unsuccessful. Anthony then presented the idea to convert the planes to sports aircraft and machines for aerobatics, but that did not work either. The German inventory remained with the factory until Anthony managed to bring in Friedrich Seekatz as head of sales in June 1921.

13

NEW YORK, NEW YORK
NOVEMBER 1920

Wednesday, November 10, 1920, was cold and foggy when Anthony and Tetta finally set eyes on New York, fourteen months after their passports had been validated for the United States. The voyage onboard the *Noordam* of the Holland-America Line had been pleasant but slow. The steamer had taken twelve days, a long time to cross the Atlantic from Rotterdam, where they had embarked on October 29.

Anthony and Tetta had sailed in the company of Frits and Dora Cremer and Fokker's new engineer Robert Noorduyn and his wife. The setting indicated that the trip was not just meant for enjoyment. Noorduyn, three years Anthony's junior, had been born in Nijmegen, near the German border. In high school he had become deeply interested in aviation and in the construction of model airplanes, with which he undertook flight trials. Noorduyn had a knack for technology and managed to find a job in the embryonic aviation business. During the war he had worked in Britain as a draftsman for the aircraft constructors Armstrong Whitworth and the British Aerial Transport Company. Now he was to become Anthony Fokker's sales agent in the United States. Like Frits Cremer, his mother was British, and he spoke English fluently, unlike Anthony. In the past days the six young people had distinctly enjoyed the ambience of first class aboard the *Noordam*. Tetta in particular appeared to be in her element and used her charms on the ship's captain to persuade him to join in fun and games on the first-class promenade deck, where Anthony's camera recorded the passengers entertaining themselves with a game of shuffleboard. There was a lot of time for such activities, for life aboard the 550-foot ship had a calm rhythm that went from meal to copious meal, followed by time spent on the conversation deck and evening entertainments of light music and variety shows.

Now their destination was finally in sight. It gave a special feeling: America, land of unbound opportunities and new chances! Anthony was not the only one to point his film camera at the city's skyline in the cold and fog as the ship slowly sailed past the Statue of Liberty in the direction of Ellis Island, the gateway to the United States for the less fortunate immigrants on the lower decks. From the stern of the ship, he filmed a group of new arrivals being taken off the ship by a lighter. Ellis Island was for them alone, while those traveling in first class found that the immigration formalities were limited to filling out a sizable packet of paper forms onboard. What they did not escape from were import duties, to be paid in the customs hall on the Hoboken pier opposite New York. These were levied over all goods and luggage brought into the country, including the trunks that contained them. The inspection was rigorous.[1]

On the pier, reporters were waiting for Anthony and Tetta. Nearly every arriving ship was met by curious journalists interested in the stateroom passengers who sought to enter the United States. Anthony was immediately surrounded by journalists. He proudly allowed himself to be photographed with Tetta at the end of the gangway, a pair of binoculars on his chest. The "wizard of airplane construction" had reckoned with such interest.[2]

ᚴ

Preparations for the trip went back to April 10, 1919. That Thursday night, two American officers in civilian attire, Major George Brett and Lieutenant Gordon Keller, had reported to the reception desk at the Hotel de l'Europe in Amsterdam for a long conversation with Anthony Fokker. They were part of a larger American effort to study Fokker aircraft for possible use in the United States.[3] The subject of the meeting was to find out what his plans in aviation were since leaving Germany. Even though the communication was marred by Anthony's poor English, he still managed to convey that he considered the prospects of developing a company in Holland to be small. Therefore he was "very desirous of going to the United States." Moreover, he believed the two officers intended to deliver a standing invitation for him to move there.[4] Although it turned out that this was not the case, the idea had stuck with him since. It had formed the background to his critique of the lack of commitment on the part of the Netherlands' government, which he accused of indecisiveness with regard to his aircraft.

The interview that carried Anthony's harsh words had been printed in the widely read *Telegraaf* newspaper days before he boarded the *Noordam*. He had a point to make: after all, the twelve D.VII fighters that he had planned to deliver to the Dutch East Indies Army (KNIL) were still awaiting delivery at his factory. Instead of ordering Fokker aircraft, KNIL had suddenly awarded the contract to the British armaments firm Vickers because its Avro and De Havilland aircraft were offered at cheaper costs. The affair had hit a raw nerve with Fokker, who felt cheated in an already parsimonious deal. Besides, he argued, he could hardly be expected to build a flourishing aircraft manufacturing industry based solely on commercial orders from the newly founded Dutch national airline, KLM. The two aircraft they had ordered did not in any way represent a real business proposition. Holland was just too small for the aircraft industry that he envisioned, and he thought he had better set his sights on the emerging market in the United States and seek his fortune there.[5] Upon his arrival in New York, journalists quoted him as saying, "I am out for business all over the world. Air transport is of the greatest international importance, and its possibilities must he studied everywhere. I have my eye on transatlantic air travel as well as on transcontinental service."[6] On the latter subject, Anthony entertained a distinct vision: the next important breakthrough in aeronautical construction would be to build aircraft able to carry large enough payloads to enable profitable operations. He said he expected a future in which all-metal landplanes would cross the ocean regularly, although he did not rule out the possibility that other construction materials might also be used.

That same afternoon, Anthony and Tetta took a room at the Waldorf Astoria Hotel in Manhattan, on the corner of Fifth Avenue and 33rd Street. The richly decorated, iconic grand hotel, with its 1,500 rooms, was the most luxurious in the world and internationally renowned among the rich and famous for its superb amenities. Even Berlin's Hotel Bristol looked pale by comparison.

Like everybody else who arrived in America the first time, the experience of New York was overpowering for Anthony and Tetta. The high-rise buildings with their abundance of electric lighting made the streets appear narrower than they were. On Fifth Avenue, brightly lit shops lured customers. Leaning from the window of their suite at the Waldorf Astoria, Anthony filmed various street scenes. The large number of cars in the road must have been striking. Automobiles appealed to him, as did the abundance of food, American eating habits, the more liberal dress codes, and the entertainment that appeared to be on offer everywhere. Even then, Times Square, with its cinemas, theaters, and brightly lit billboards, acted as a magnet for visitors. Films showed as early as eleven in the morning. Theater shows were sold out evening after evening, and good seats required reservations. In the Hippodrome elephants danced the foxtrot while large baskets carrying flower girls adorned in tight flesh-colored bodysuits were lowered from the ceiling. Every day brought new attractions.[7] Anthony and Tetta were thrilled. They thoroughly enjoyed New York's touristic highlights. Anthony recorded the imposing Brooklyn Bridge on film. From Battery Park they watched the *Noordam* leave again for Holland and waved farewell to the ship.[8]

Nonetheless, the touristy part of the journey did not last. With Frits Cremer and Bob Noorduyn, Anthony embarked on a tour of the American aviation industry. Major Virginius Evans Clark, a leading aeronautical engineer with the U.S. Army Air Service, went with them to take care of the necessary introductions. The three Dutchmen spoke with government officials, prominent figures in aviation, and various people with a corporate background on the possibilities of forging American business interests with Fokker in some form. By train they traveled through the frozen American landscape from city to city. In a letter to the staff he and Tetta employed at their new house in Amsterdam, Anthony praised the amenities of American hotels. The central heating was so good, he wrote, that he could travel with only a small suitcase carrying a minimum of clothing. A tuxedo, two matching shirts, three to five other shirts, a dark suit and a sporting plus-four with winding cloth to cover his lower legs, black pajamas, and two underpants were all he needed. For outdoors he had brought a formal coat and his fur-lined flying jacket. The rest of his luggage had had left in the care of the Waldorf Astoria.[9]

In Washington, Anthony exerted himself in compliments. The Navy building was the biggest he had seen in his life, he claimed, and the Library of Congress the most beautiful, "far superior to any building I have ever seen in Europe." The occasion required optimism: "I am more than ever convinced that in five or ten years we shall cross the ocean in less than a day as safely in giant airplanes as we do now in liners, and more comfortably."[10] He was introduced to the Secretaries of War, of the Navy, and of Agriculture, with whom he vainly pleaded for special privileges to deliver aircraft.[11] He also visited various aircraft factories and research establishments: in Buffalo, Dayton, and Detroit. On the basis of these visits, Anthony concluded that America actually did not have any commercial transport aircraft and that the industry had come to a standstill after the war. Such circumstances had to present business opportunities for Fokker. In his conversations he sketched the advantages of the very large transport aircraft that his men were working on in Holland, the F.IV. Before the month of December was out he managed to sign a contract for the delivery of two such aircraft to the Army Air Service. In classic Fokker style, the basic design excelled in its simplicity: it was to be a substantially enlarged version of the F.III airliner that had just become ready in Schwerin. The contract furthermore specified the construction of two armored aircraft suited for attacks against ground targets (later identified as PW-5). Making these sales was encouraging, and Anthony began to anticipate a bright future for himself in the United States. On December 9 he took care to have several military aeronautical inventions patented in America. Toward the end of his visit, it appeared that it would be feasible to raise enough local capital to found an American Fokker company.[12]

As a result, Bob Noorduyn received instructions to prepare the grounds for an American sales organization in New York, the Netherlands Aircraft Manufacturing Company. Initially this was a rather informal venture, although Anthony had helped select the corporate location with great care: Noorduyn rented office space at 286 Fifth Avenue, a prestigious venue. The plan was that Noorduyn would work on the development of ideas for an American future for Fokker. Frits Cremer also was to stay behind. He would act as Fokker's confidential representative and build on political and business contacts that his father Jacob, the former Netherlands envoy in

Washington, had left behind when he returned to Holland in May 1920.[13] Frits's task was not an easy one. He was very much bent on proving himself in business, partly to impress his father that he had now shed his daredevil pilot's image and had finally acquired what it took to be successful by himself.[14] Yet he and Noorduyn did not get along, and before long they were fighting over pecking order in the American Fokker organization.

Frits and Bob finally chose to maintain separate offices in New York. It was a development Anthony preferred to ignore. Thus he could pretend not to notice how life was now becoming a struggle for Frits, both within the small Fokker outfit and beyond. His private investments in various American aeronautical ventures all went wrong. It put a further strain on relations with the more cautious Bob Noorduyn, who soon had some successes to show for his efforts.[15] Anthony let his friend Frits fend for himself. On January 8, 1921, he, Tetta, and Dora Cremer (who later rejoined Frits in New York in June 1921), boarded the steamer *Rijndam* bound for Holland. In the booked-up environment of first class, a mixed international company of seventy-nine passengers, they met the Dutch oil trader George Gleichman, with whom Anthony struck up a lifelong friendship.[16]

ᚷ

For Anthony and Tetta, the American trip formed the close of a busy year. On January 3, 1920, the paperwork for the purchase of a detached house in Roemer Visscherstraat, prominently located next to the entrance to Amsterdam's Vondel Park, had been approved by a city notary. The house, built in 1894, was Tetta's project. Long discussions had preceded the acquisition, because Anthony had already bought a house at the Valeriusplein. But a house in a row, even if it was a luxurious one and had twelve rooms, was not at all to Tetta's liking. As a result, the house on Valeriusplein was put back on the market in March 1920 to be sold, without the Fokkers' even spending a day in it.[17] Tetta paid for the new villa with her own money. The daily view of the park from the upstairs windows was to her worth 100,000 Dutch guilders, a hefty sum for its time. But the costs went up higher still: Tetta had modern heaters, fixed washbasins with running water, and a special water heater for the bath installed. She also made sure the house was decorated with new carpets, linoleum, new runners on the stairs, curtains, and marquisettes.[18] It must have been a relief to her to be able to close the hotel door behind her. On January 19 she moved in to supervise the workmen she had hired to prepare the place. Anthony did not follow until three weeks later, on February 10. According to the Dutch custom of the day, the city administration recorded that he was the main proprietor.[19]

Roemer Visscherstraat 47 was a stately villa, clad with white plaster. It may have reminded Tetta of her parents' home in Lübeck, Germany. The house had a large basement, a first and second floor, and an attic with bedrooms for the house staff under a black tiled roof. Visitors entered the house through a small elevated entryway decorated with floral designs on stained glass-paneled doors. Beyond the doors,

The prototype: The first Fokker F.II airliner, model for all subsequent Fokker transport aircraft, at Schwerin's Görries airfield. On March 25, 1920, Fokker's friend and confidant Bernard de Waal flew the aircraft from Schwerin to Holland. Near Drachten, however, the motor gave out, and he had to make an emergency landing. **DEUTSCHES MUSEUM, MUNICH, GERMANY** a staircase curved up to the bedrooms on the floor above and to the kitchen and the servants' quarters downstairs. Anthony and Tetta had a spacious living room with a wooden porch and a large balcony at the back of the house, overlooking the park. The corner that was left was just big enough for Anthony to use as a modest home office. Anthony was very particular about his privacy and had the garden at the back and at the sides of the house surrounded by a high wrought-iron fence. His mother, Anna, took charge of hiring the house staff, but for head of the household Tetta was adamant that she would make her own choice. She had her personal companion, Christine Döppler, come over from Germany with the cook, Frieda.[20]

At the beginning of 1920, Anthony himself was chiefly occupied with getting his new factory equipped and running. He had bought the former ELTA halls from the exhibition organization for 800,000 guilders (then about $294,000).[21] The ground below the buildings was rented. The halls themselves, rather big initially for the small Fokker workforce, were used to store the aircraft brought from Schwerin until assembly for the Dutch Air Corps, the Navy, and prospective foreign buyers. This way the new staff could gain experience in aircraft construction. Meanwhile, Anthony conducted talks with the city of Vlissingen in the southwest of the country, which tried to interest him in empty factory space they had available in the vicinity of the Souburg airstrip.[22] But his first concern was the delivery of twenty D.VII fighters for the Dutch Navy. Not before April 1920 was he able to announce that he was ready to start assembly of the aircraft that had been ordered for the Air Corps, although the government's reduction of the order continued to bother him.[23]

Along with these military assignments, Anthony entertained plans to start a flying school. With prewar Görries as an example, he approached the incumbent administrator of KLM, Albert Plesman, in December 1919 to find out whether they might cooperate in this. Plesman and his board of directors were not enthusiastic. They told him that KLM preferred to charter aircraft from Fokker for taxi flights when needed. This idea, too, came to nothing; Fokker's aircraft were built in Germany, and the KLM board feared political repercussions if one of the machines were to land at a foreign airport.[24] For the same reason, Fokker did not receive a contract from the Dutch postal authorities for his projected international airmail service to London.[25]

Nonetheless, the future possibilities for international air services beckoned. This was the very idea that Anthony had embraced when he decided to go with Reinhold Platz's plan to develop an airplane that would be suited to carry several passengers. Platz's initial idea provided for passengers to be seated in open cockpits as was the custom in military observation aircraft, but the concept was soon traded in for a design with an enclosed cabin.[26] This became the V.45 (V=Versuchsflugzeug, or trial aircraft), ready for its first flight in October 1919. With its thick cantilever wing and enclosed passenger cabin, the V.45 was a revolutionary machine. At a time when most aircraft were biplanes and airplanes with passenger accommodation needed several engines to fly, a single 185-hp engine sufficed for the V.45. Its design blended the concepts of Forssman and Junkers. The only feature of the plane that was perhaps less deviant from the usual construction standards was the fuselage, which was made of welded steel tubes covered with aircraft linen and wood. Behind an open cockpit for the pilot and a navigator, or occasionally an extra passenger, the machine seated four people crammed together.[27]

Fokker had good reason to believe that KLM would be the ideal launching customer for the F.II, as the production version of the V.45 became known. If he managed to sell the aircraft to the new Dutch national airline, it would emphasize the solid Dutch character of his enterprise in Amsterdam. The Koninklijke Luchtvaart Maatschappij voor Nederland en Koloniën (KLM: Royal Airline Company for the Netherlands and Its Colonies) had been founded on October 7, 1919, by a conglomerate of large trading banks, financiers, and shipping lines. The new company possessed no aircraft of its own. Competitors were plentiful from the start, although in that day and age it was impossible to make money in commercial aviation. With the support of national governments, airline companies were founded in several European countries as (expensive) expressions of national prestige. Evidently, this development presaged the possibilities of a new market that might extend beyond Holland itself. Fokker's main problem was now how to get the airplane from Schwerin to Amsterdam and warm KLM to the concept. Since he himself could not enter Germany because of the ongoing dispute with the German authorities over his tax debts, Anthony sent his trusted friend Bernard de Waal to Schwerin on a reconnaissance mission in March 1920.

On Thursday afternoon, March 25, De Waal started with the F.II from Görries for what was to be an extensive test flight with the new aircraft. But once airborne, he set course for the Netherlands and soon disappeared beyond the horizon, as he had done a year before with the C.I reconnaissance plane. He again failed to reach his destination. As evening fell, the engine quit over the town of Drachten in the north of Holland. An emergency landing in a meadow was the inevitable consequence. The aircraft came to a standstill in a ditch, from which a recovery crew from the Fokker factory in Amsterdam had to rescue it. To transport the machine, it had to be disassembled on the spot. That Saturday Anthony and Tetta drove all the way from Amsterdam to supervise the work.[28] In the end the airplane arrived in Amsterdam on a barge.[29] In the months that followed, Anthony made numerous test flights with the F.II, which resulted in various improvements on the aircraft.

Meanwhile, Fokker did all he could to convince KLM to buy the plane. Not only did he boast of the technical characteristics of the machine, but he also exhausted himself on patriotic arguments to entice KLM to do business with his Netherlands Aircraft Factory. To lure Plesman in, he offered the F.II for the rock-bottom price of 27,500 Dutch guilders (about $9,500).[30] The comparable British De Havilland DH-18, a single engine biplane with a cabin that also fit four passengers, cost two and a half times that amount.[31] Plesman was bound to accept such a generous offer, especially after KLM's pilot, Walter Hinchcliffe, made a trial flight with the machine from the Soesterberg airfield on June 17 and came back much impressed with the aircraft's handling characteristics. KLM soon placed an order with Fokker for two F.II aircraft.

However, what Anthony had carefully avoided mentioning was that the F.II had not been developed in Holland, but in Schwerin, and that it was also going to be built in Germany. In his discussions with Plesman, he had referred to the aircraft as the first achievement in commercial aviation of his Netherlands Aircraft Factory. At the small KLM office in The Hague, nobody had any knowledge of the arrangements between Amsterdam and Schwerin. The perspective of the KLM board did not yet extend beyond the border. Only after the signing of the sales contract did word reach Plesman that the two aircraft he had ordered would not be constructed in Amsterdam but in Germany. For him and his board members, this was a serious blow. They accused Fokker of deceiving them on purpose. After all, operating German aircraft could have big repercussions for the airline. What if Belgium, France, and Britain would refuse to issue landing rights because KLM used former enemy aircraft? It appeared entirely possible that the aircraft could be confiscated in Brussels, Paris, or London. But the sales papers were signed.[32] Anthony, for his part, decided that the anxiety would probably blow over and kept his distance in the meantime.

KLM took delivery of the first F.II on August 25, 1920. A little over a month later, Walter Hinchcliffe dared take it on a trial flight to London. It was to be a memorable adventure. Five times Hinchcliffe had to turn back to Amsterdam's Schiphol Airfield because of various mechanical malfunctions. It took him more than two days to reach London. To the relief of Plesman and his fellow board members, the aircraft was not seized as war booty, and Hinchcliffe touched down again with the F.II at Schiphol on October 5.[33]

And yet there was a peculiar smell to the whole affair. In the small Dutch aviation world, Anthony Fokker and Albert Plesman were stuck with each other. They understood this only too well. Neither felt comfortable with the situation. The eccentric war-tainted millionaire Fokker and the authoritarian former Air Corps lieutenant did not get along. Possibly their very different backgrounds played a role too. Plesman, the seventh child of small shopkeepers from The Hague, had been chosen as "administrator" of the new airline venture because of his exceptional drive to make the ELTA into a success. He was a bully who got excited easily and liked to use strong language. Plesman almost couldn't help feeling personal resentment against Fokker, his privileged family background, and his slick ways of conducting business.[34] On his side, Fokker failed to appreciate what Plesman stood for. While pleased with the publicity that the "Dutch" combine Fokker-KLM produced, he did not fully recognize the chauvinistic nature of the association. He knew that KLM, which was dependent on government subsidies for its survival, had no realistic alternative but to buy Fokker aircraft. Yet he did not take in that KLM expected more than just value for money from his company. This caused constant friction. Anthony was often fickle in his contacts and was given to wriggling out of deals that appeared done to the observer. Along with that, quality control was a constant issue at the Netherlands Aircraft Factory, and this created numerous problems in itself.

The issues surrounding the sale of the F.II were still fresh when the next conflict announced itself. Early in October 1920, Fokker told Plesman that he was working on a hugely improved version of the F.II. The new plane, designated F.III, was to have more or less the same takeoff weight and the same engine, but it would have a longer wing span for increased lift. By widening the fuselage, the cabin could provide for five seats instead of four while also offering marginally more leg room. It was an idea that Anthony had recently passed on to Reinhold Platz. The pilot was moved farther up the nose of the aircraft to be seated right next to the engine. This improved the downward view from the cockpit, which translated into better safety upon landing.[35] These changes increased the attractiveness of the aircraft.

Plesman was immediately interested in the new design and announced that he wanted to buy as many as eight of these machines. He also hoped to trade in the F.II aircraft, which KLM had thus far hardly used, for the new F.III type. With the new equipment KLM wanted to start scheduled operations in the spring of 1921. Anthony Fokker considered the latter proposition risky. The new machine was then only in its first stages of development, and it was questionable whether it would even be ready in time for the planned opening of KLM services in March. Nonetheless, he urged Plesman to place an advance order for the new F.III so that KLM would be certain to be the first to fly this new, more economical type. He put pressure on his business partner: only if he had a signed order before leaving for New York could he guarantee KLM the coveted status of "launching customer." To lure Plesman, Fokker told him that he would offer him the F.III at a special discount and even suggested he might be willing to buy back the F.II aircraft that had already been delivered to KLM.[36]

Under considerable pressure from the government to cover at least one-third of KLM's annual losses from the company's reserves, Plesman received instruction from his board to buy the more economical F.III as soon as possible. Together with the tension exercised by Fokker's pending departure to the United States, the order gave rise to misunderstandings. Fixed on drawing KLM across the threshold and thus reducing his own financial risks in developing the F.III, Fokker again suggested he might be willing to buy back the two F.II aircraft from KLM at the price Plesman had paid for them. He attached great value to strengthening the groundwork for his new enterprise, especially now that the expected orders from the Dutch armed services were not forthcoming. The latter presented Fokker with a big problem. In June 1920 he wrote to the Dutch War Ministry, "We wish to appeal to Your Excellency for support, be it not in the form of a subsidy, but in the form of a commitment, that Your department will place aircraft orders, if at all possible, with us, and will also procure the necessary test aircraft, to be built by us, if these are acceptable to the State."[37]

Convinced that Fokker's buyback suggestion constituted a real promise, a very satisfied Albert Plesman made a verbal agreement with Fokker to buy two F.III aircraft straight off the drawing board. The whole transaction therefore appeared to be a done deal, and Anthony left for New York according to plan. But in his absence a difference of opinion soon arose. In December, Fokker's Dutch sales manager, Hendrik Nieuwenhuis, told Plesman—to the customer's dismay—that he knew nothing of the agreement to exchange the F.II for F.III aircraft. Plesman was perplexed.[38] When Anthony Fokker returned to Holland on January 18, 1921, he too pretended to have no recollection of the deal. He took the position that the agreement between him and KLM did not extend beyond the airline's firm commitment to buy two F.III aircraft. He denied ever having suggested that he would take back the older machines and insisted on delivering the F.III machines as agreed before his American trip. After an exchange of angry letters and a screaming row between the two men at Fokker's house in Amsterdam's Roemer Visscherstraat, Plesman was left with no option but to keep the two F.II aircraft and the two F.III machines on top of this. It did not, however, resolve their differences. After the new aircraft had actually been delivered, a most irritated Plesman reported to his board that "the Netherlands Aircraft Factory tries, to deliver bad materials, like old tires, bad airscrews, bad windows etc. The Administrator [Plesman] has already complained repeatedly to the factory about this."[39]

For Fokker it was not easy to address such complaints. In Schwerin the construction of the aircraft was done with the limited means that were still available or could be bought. SIW chronically lacked all sorts of materials. Incorporating improvements that were suggested in Amsterdam was no easy matter. It was typical of the unstructured work routine at Fokker's factory. While he was in America, the various changes that Anthony had suggested earlier were first put on paper in provisional construction drawings. Afterward, a full-scale mock-up of the redesigned fuselage was built in Amsterdam. This formed the basis for a more precise blueprint of the new aircraft, which was sent to Schwerin. There it was Platz's responsibility to build the actual prototype, a process that took place beyond view, or interference, from Amsterdam. After the new airplane was ready and had been test-flown in Schwerin, it was disassembled, crated, and sent to Holland by rail for reassembly in Fokker's flight hangar at Schiphol Airfield. The whole development process had taken less than a month. On November 20, 1920, one of KLM's pilots made a test flight with the new machine and reported that it behaved satisfactorily in the air. But because Fokker was still the ultimate test pilot of the machines that carried his name, further flight testing was postponed until his return from New York.

After he arrived back in Holland on January 18, 1921, a single test flight sufficed for him to reject various parts of the construction of the fuselage, engine installment, and the aircraft's rudder, ailerons, and elevator. This showed Fokker at his best: suggesting changes on the basis of his vast practical flight experience. When the Dutch Bureau of Aeronautics (Rijksstudiedienst voor de Luchtvaart), which was responsible for the aircraft's airworthiness papers, later examined the F.III, it found that the changes that Fokker had proposed resulted in a machine that was safer and easier to fly for less experienced pilots. After the changes had been incorporated, Anthony made another series of test flights, which resulted in further modifications. Finally, new blueprints were produced and sent to Schwerin, where the series production was planned.[40]

Anthony held high expectations for the future of the F.III and had a series of commercials filmed for the aircraft. In some of them he featured himself as the aircraft's pilot in a flight suit. Before production of the F.III had to be stopped at SIW because of an Allied ban on German aircraft production, Fokker shipped some twenty aircraft from Schwerin. The German government approved of this in writing. In the end, production had to be discontinued, and the remaining machines were transported to Holland by train to be completed by staff that had traveled with them from Germany. There was a price to be paid by SIW for this expensive arrangement, since labor costs proved substantially higher in the Netherlands. SIW found it was left to pay 15 million marks, which was duly paid from the company's ever-dwindling reserves.[41]

❦

Even without such solutions, Anthony's relation with his German past was problematical. In December 1921 matters became more complicated. That month Fokker received notice from the German military tax authorities (Reichsmilitärfiskus) charging him with embezzlement of some four million marks between 1916 and the end of 1918. What was the case? Like most warring countries, the German government had issued special war bonds, or *Kriegsanleihen*, to raise capital for the war effort. To encourage the acquisition of bonds, a special arrangement had been made by which both companies and private individuals could ask for a cash advance for the payment of bonds. This advance came in the shape of a loan, which remained interest-free in its first month. After that period, the loan was to be converted into war bonds and altered into a regular loan that carried between 4 and 5 percent interest. Because the bonds were also issued at a 5 percent interest rate, investing in them was promoted as a patriotic act, not as a guaranteed safe investment. In September 1916 Anthony Fokker had therefore asked the military authorities for a cash advance of 1 million marks. A second advance, 3 million marks, had been made available to him in 1918. But when the military tax inspectors reviewed the case in December 1920, they found that Fokker had never used the 4 million in advances to acquire war bonds. So where had the money gone, and why had Fokker never paid a penny of the 252,000 marks in interest that was due?[42]

The case had first come to light shortly after Fokker had left Germany. It was now necessary to arrive at some settlement. On May 31, 1919, Wilhelm Horter, then still in Berlin, sent the assistant sales manager of the Fokker Central Office, Otto Borde, with 4,047,000 marks' worth of war bonds to the military tax inspector with instructions to pay off the 4 million that had gone missing between 1916 and 1918. But since there was no file that documented that Fokker had transferred the cash advances into war bonds—something that was probably only done at the end of 1918 in the process of liquidating Fokker's bank accounts—Borde's visit gave rise to all sorts of difficult questions, among them where these bonds had come from. There was another catch: the tax inspectors explained Borde that the value of the bonds had plummeted. After all, the war had been lost. It meant that the real value of the papers that Borde carried was no more than 3,966,060 marks. Borde countered that not all of the bonds' interest coupons had been cashed. At a value of 33,725 marks, this reduced the difference to a mere 215 marks.

Not quite knowing how to handle such a case, the tax inspectors had in the end accepted the bonds as payment. Their superiors, however, took an entirely different position: because there were no official documents stating that Fokker had acted timely in transferring the cash advances into war bonds, they maintained that the bonds could not be accepted as payment for the loans. The advances had been made available to Fokker in cash, and for this reason they demanded that they be returned in cash. Besides, it had been established that the total value of the bonds was less than the sum of the cash advances and that the government had never received any of the 252,000 marks Fokker owed in interest. On the contrary, the military tax inspector concluded that Fokker had evidently cashed part of the dividends on the bonds. Such an act was deemed "to constitute contempt for any sense of patriotism."[43]

Finding out what had actually happened took time, and it was June 1922 before Fokker's legal and fiscal advisers had their defense ready. They held that the cash advances to Fokker had never been intended to be converted into war bonds. By September 1916 the administrative system of the German armed forces had become so slow that it was no longer possible to pay Fokker for aircraft delivered within a reasonable time period. This had caused cash flow problems for the company, which Fokker had tried to resolve with the cash-advances-for-war-bonds scheme. When these cash advances materialized, all parties concerned agreed that they in fact referred to back payments and were not actually intended to be converted into war bonds. In fact, a verbal agreement had been reached that the cash advances would, for this reason, remain without interest, although the official documentation stated that interest would be charged. Claiming overdue interest was therefore not justified, Fokker's legal counsel argued. To fortify their case, the lawyers produced a witness, a former clerk of the military payments office, who was prepared to make a statement under oath to this effect before the court. Accepting the bonds by way of repayment of the cash advances had already been a mistake, the lawyers held, but the consequences of such an error were to be borne by the authorities, who were not supposed to propose such arrangements in the first place.

Around this nucleus of arguments, Anthony's Berlin lawyers arranged a thick smokescreen to divert attention from the heart of the matter: had the cash advances really been interest-free, and did Fokker have the right to keep his hands on the money for such a long time?[44] The lawyers next produced an unpaid bill of 350,000 marks for aircraft and company supplies that had been destroyed in 1919 by order of the Weimar government as part of Germany's enforced disarmament.[45] This complicated matters even further. The military tax inspector therefore proposed to dismiss the case, provided that the Schwerin Industrial Works agreed to drop the claim for 350,000 marks. The state even offered to pay 91 percent of the legal costs that Fokker and SIW had been forced to make to defend themselves. This would have put an end to the case, had the German mark not crashed, which necessitated conversion of all fees and dues into the new Reichsmark currency. Not until September 1926 was the matter finally settled.[46]

14

On the afternoon of June 27, 1923, Anthony crossed the German-Dutch border near Oldenzaal. Anger, disappointment, and sorrow filled his mind. In Berlin, where the Fokkers had stayed on holiday since April 22, Tetta had finally told him in a cloud of bitter reproaches and cigarette smoke that she wanted the marriage to end. She had found the comfort she needed to cope with a failed relationship in the arms of Anthony's German test pilot, Friedrich Mallinckrodt, she told him. For a while now, they had secretly been lovers. Now that she had confessed, the drama was complete.

Friedrich Mallinckrodt had been born in Zehlendorff near Berlin in 1891 into a politically influential German family. Just like Tetta, he had spent much of his youth on the shores of the Wannsee. Anthony, who was the connecting link between the two lovers, had met Friedrich for the first time in 1916 as one of the military test pilots for Junkers aircraft. Later that year Mallinckrodt had been transferred to the Western Front near Verdun, where he was seriously wounded in the pelvis and one of his legs late in April 1917. His recovery had taken months, after which the army had reassigned him to IdFlieg in 1918, where he played a role in the performance tests of the D.VII.[1] Later that year, in August, he had been part of the investigating committee that had looked into the crashes of Fokker's D.VIII fighter. Since then they had run into each other from time to time in Berlin. That was how Mallinckrodt had met Tetta.

Once home in Amsterdam, Anthony was still beside himself. He took the telephone and rang Julius Keizer, a solicitor who held office at the city's prominent Heerengracht and who had arranged other legal issues for him in the past. As far as Anthony was concerned, a meeting in person really could not wait until the next day. That very afternoon he had Keizer file for divorce with the District Court in Amsterdam.[2] In legal terms the requisition read "that petitioner has had to experience, that respondent has had during the marriage between [the] parties communion in the flesh with other men, or at least with one other man, and is thus guilty of having committed adultery."[3]

Anthony was completely beside himself. Days passed before he regained some grip on life. A meeting with his senior management designed to brief him about the affairs of the company during his prolonged absence in Germany, which had been scheduled some time before, now did not suit him at all. An undated and unsigned later narrative biography written by a sailing friend who must have known Anthony quite well contained an eyewitness passage that read:

Mister Fokker, here are the people from the factory that have arrived for the meeting, as you requested. They are all here, seated next door. The voice of his secretary sounds flat as always, but with a resonance of impatience with the fact that he has had to repeat this three times already.

Oh well. Conference. Yes, yes, I know, I said so, but right now I don't feel like it. We can also do it tomorrow. No hurry. Send them off. I'm going away for a few days. Sailing. I want something else right now than this eternal hassle over business.

Mr. R [Pieter Reeringh, the company secretary] is really confused for a moment. Fokker is never like this, always wanting to know what's on, with his well-tuned head for business that never lets off. There has to be something depressing him. Let him have his diversion. Later on, after he's come back, things will be different. He'll be fresh and sharp as ever and things will run smoothly as usual. And Mr. R quietly leaves the room to tell the people from the factory that they'd better leave now and wait to be summoned anew. . . .

Behind the door that is now closed Fokker sits. Hands under his head, two deep wrinkles right across his forehead. He is troubled. Nothing of importance to the business, and certainly no financial worries, but he frets over other things, which concern his soul. Things are not good between him and his wife. Is he himself not to blame that things are not always as they should be? Has he not always given preference to his own interests, has he not lived within himself too much and has left the needs of his wife pass him by as if they were of little consequence? Sure, she doesn't budge, ah she needn't complain in that department, but in all the others? He is confused in his inner self. He is not as sure of himself as normally. The uncertainty is suffocating him. Because he knows much of the blame is on him. Very much. But what the hell, he can't help being the way he is. Shouldn't other people take him just the way he wants them to? After all, he is Fokker!

His struggle is a battle of so many. And he is not fighting it, lets himself be led to contemplation, pondering the pros and cons. What else can one do? What. . . . Oh to hell with it all. Fokker has thought about it, has said it aloud as is his custom in more instances. He presses the bell. Twice. A spirited maid appears promptly. Fokker does not even look up, remains seated with his fists under his chin and mumbles something to himself. He wants his gear to be readied. He is going sailing for a few days. The car has to be brought around. No, that's not necessary, he'll take the small car that is parked in the garage next to the house. He'll leave it at the marina. Anything else? No. Just, call Frieda in for a minute, will you? The girl disappears quietly. Momentarily Frieda enters. Impassive—she has heard this so often—she hears that Fokker is not hungry yet. Dinner time has long passed.

Tetta Fokker-von Morgen: Like her husband, Tetta had a mind of her own. Being confined to duties in and around the marital home, as was then customary in Holland, was not for her. Anthony's workaholic behavior drove her into the arms of Fokker's German test pilot Friedrich Mallinckrodt. The marriage ended in 1923, but in Anthony's eyes Tetta remained his true love. **AUTHOR'S COLLECTION: FILM STILL**

There is no one else in the house. He is truly lonely. Just give me something to take away. Cold. You've always got something prepared for me. No, not chicken. Some caviar. Yes, and some bread too. No, I don't want anything on it. And don't forget to pack some mineral water. Yeah, yeah, I'm going away for a few days. Back on Monday. There's a race then. Yes, I will participate myself. With the Catch Me. *Yes, tell madame if she comes home.*[4]

But Tetta did not come home. That summer Anthony spent much time on the water—alone, left to his own thoughts, trying to find his balance again. His marriage had stranded, and for this Anthony bore a considerable part of the blame. Reserving time to have a life together had been truly difficult for him. Business and aeronautics took precedence. Tetta had indicated early on that she had no intention of settling for a secondary existence as a subservient housewife, a role into which she was repeatedly forced in Amsterdam. She did not share Anthony's absolute dedication to flight. On occasion she accompanied him—at the ELTA the "sports couple"

Among the "high society": Tetta and Anthony visit with Germany's former Emperor Wilhelm II at his place of exile, House Doorn, near Utrecht. Although Fokker hated social engagements, he gladly made exceptions to visit royalty. In Holland, Prince Consort Hendrik (the husband of Queen Wilhelmina) became one of his friends, maintaining a pied à terre above Anthony's offices in Amsterdam. **COLLECTION SMEULERS, BRONKHORST, THE NETHERLANDS**

attracted special attention by flying loops in Anthony's two-seat D.VII—but she took no particular pride in such performances. Sailing was much more her thing. For her, doing something together as a couple in the ambience in which they had first met was a highlight. They were at their best exerting themselves with the crew on Anthony's two-masted seagoing yacht *Hana*, or on his smaller yachts for inland sailing contests. Together they participated in races, pushing their boat to the limits. Rowing, canoeing, and swimming were things they enjoyed together.[5] For a quieter pastime there was the thirty-six-foot-long powered luxury yacht *Honey Moon* that Anthony had custom-built in Amsterdam in 1919 after German designs.[6] Only on the water did Anthony manage to disengage from his many duties. And Tetta too was more playful then, merrier. When on their boat she was game for anything he could think of, like water skiing together on a rough cut wooden plank. Nonetheless, she necessarily spent much time alone in the house at Roemer Visscherstraat. Countless hours she dedicated to hand-knotting a large, multicolored tapestry with the Fokker family coat of arms. But Anthony showed no interest in such pastimes and even refused to keep the tapestry after their divorce.

The silence of the house and the lonesome activity of the needlework did not agree with Tetta. To her Amsterdam was and remained a foreign city. She missed her family, friends, and acquaintances, whom she was unable to look up until after her first year of marriage, when something of a solution to Anthony's problems with the German tax authorities was beginning to come into view. Not before March 22, 1920, did they set foot on German soil together for a three-day visit.[7] She had to attend the wedding of her brother Hans Georg in Schwerin on June 11 alone because Anthony was preoccupied with the sale of the F.II airliner to KLM, a contract on which the future of the company hinged. As his business took root in the Netherlands, the demands on Anthony's time increased. Plans and tensions mounted. In a sudden fit of anger, he drove three cyclists off the road in July 1921. It landed him in court with a six-month suspension of his driving license and a fine of 150 guilders.[8] Anthony was not one for social graces and avoided calls beyond family and friends, although he was happy to make an exception for a visit to the former German Emperor Wilhelm II at his Dutch residence-in-exile, Doorn House.[9] Tetta had imagined life together very differently.

ᘐ

The trip around the world that Anthony had held out to her never materialized, and this was one of the precipitating factors for that later divorce. Instead, Anthony soon focused all his attention on aeronautics. After arriving in Holland he initially reverted from company director to test pilot. It was still not uncommon for him to put the aircraft that were built under his name through an extensive and rigorous personal test-flight program. Nonetheless, the preoccupations that came with the position of director caught up with him before long. The advance of gliding, in which Anthony became interested in 1919, was one of the developments that offered a diversion. Here was an area of flight in which practical experiments ruled as if it were still 1910.

In June 1919 he risked the stunt, then unheard of, of having himself towed into the air in an engineless plane at the Soesterberg airfield.[10] Eight months later he told American reporters that he believed gliding was going to be *the* sport of the future.[11] Building a glider aircraft was therefore one of the tasks that awaited Reinhold Platz upon arrival in Holland. In June 1921 Fokker had him travel from Schwerin to the small town of Veere, in the southwest of the country near his ancestral town of Middelburg, to take charge of the new subsidiary of the Fokker company there. In this quiet Dutch backwater, Fokker proposed starting a new experimental department. For a small amount of money he was able to obtain a leasehold from the Dutch Navy at a former repair facility for ships. As long as he promised to leave the typical townscape intact and built the houses for his employees elsewhere, he was free to do as he liked there.[12] Since the area had numerous high sand dunes as well, it was an ideal environment for experimenting with engineless flight over the beach.

Initially Platz restricted himself to observing the in-flight behavior of several large experimental airplane models he had made out of steel tubing and linen as they sailed down from the sand dunes toward the sea. But after Anthony and Bernard de Waal had driven Anthony's big eight-cylinder Cadillac from Amsterdam to the German mountain ski resort town of Gersfeld on August 18, 1921, things began to flow. There they met up with Hans Georg von Morgen, who had arrived from Schwerin, and Bertus Grasé, researcher and test pilot at the Dutch Government Aeronautical Service.[13]

Gersfeld, some 125 miles east of Frankfurt at the foot of the Rhön mountains, was the location of a slope called the Wasserkuppe, the most prominent meeting point for German glider pilots. As a new "sport" gliding had its roots in the postwar Allied ban on the construction of powered aircraft in Germany. With professional military and civil aeronautics grounded, an amateur movement of private pilots who tried their hand at unpowered flight had sprung up and developed rapidly.[14] Gliding activities were particularly popular in student circles. War veterans of the Air Corps often attended meetings. The annual Rhön Segelflug Wettbewerb (Rhön Gliding Contest) at the Wasserkuppe was not just a sporty event, but also a social gathering where old friends could meet. What Anthony and Bernard hoped to find there was a reminiscence of the bygone Johannisthal days. Anthony recalled, "It reminds me of the first years of aviation, the nucleus of enthusiasts . . . already working away at dawn with just one single thought on their minds, flying *without* [an] engine from the ground up. . . . Just like the first flights then were merely small jumps, crazy in the eyes of the masses, I see in gliding from the slopes of the Rhön the dawn of a new period in aviation!"[15]

Gliding itself was not quite as innocent as it appeared. Anthony and Bernard satisfied themselves with merely observing, but they noticed that several high-ranking civil servants were present to watch. The German army was also interested in what was taking place at Gersfeld, which was also evidenced in erecting various sheds for aircraft and several army tents where less well-off participants could spend the night. Nonetheless, the gliding itself appeared primarily a sports event. The trick was to use the ascending winds that blew over the Wasserkuppe to stay in the air for as long as possible. Flying times were measured in minutes and seconds.[16]

Driving home at the end of the contest, Anthony was certain that he would take up gliding. The return journey turned out to be more eventful than they had anticipated. For Dutchmen traveling from Germany to the Netherlands, strict customs regulations were in force in 1921, forbidding the export of all goods. Everybody was checked thoroughly to prevent smuggling. Even shoes had to be taken off for inspection. Nonetheless, Anthony arrived back in Amsterdam full of enthusiasm: at least this was *real* flying again, the way things had been before the war. Besides, gliding exerted the kind of dangers that Anthony knew well. The understanding of the ascending winds and thermals that was necessary for engineless flight was still limited. Gliding seized his imagination.

ᘓ

At the Seventh International Aeronautical Exhibition, the prestigious biennial international event that was held in Paris on November 12–21, 1921, the Netherlands Aircraft Factory revealed its owner's new hobby. In the Grand Palace at the Champs Élysées, Fokker presented two aircraft at the Salon: one was the new F.III that was displayed in KLM colors, the other an engineless development of the D.VIII fighter from the final months of the war. It was the airplane in which Anthony had been towed into the air in 1919.

As a participant in the exhibition, the primary objective of which was to underscore France's leading role in aviation, Fokker caused considerable commotion. Even in the weeks leading up to the event, French papers commented it was a disgrace to invite a former enemy to show his latest inventions. Comments spoke of "a scandal to come and exhibit in Paris . . . these sinister birds that caused us so much harm."[17] When President Alexandre Millerand opened the exhibition, there was instant trouble at the Fokker stand. The Parisian newspaper *Le Matin* reported on "outraged protests of former combatants, of the mutilated and of war victims" and police had to be called in to prevent the public from tearing apart the airplanes on the spot. Albert Plesman, present to promote the interests of KLM, managed to quiet things down by suggesting to the organizers that they mask the name "Fokker" on the aircraft. All this was very much to Anthony's liking. He again demonstrated his fine nose for publicity and positioned himself near his aircraft as visibly as possible, only too ready to answer criticism with wit. When someone in a small group of French flyers remarked, "Oh yes, the Fokkers! I shot down about twenty of them!" Fokker leaned in amicably and answered "Aha, good, then you're one of my best friends, my dear. Because for every Fokker that was shot down I had to build a new one!"[18]

The next day the French undersecretary for aviation, Laurent Eynac, himself a former war pilot, visited the Salon. When Eynac approached the stand of the

Netherlands Aircraft Factory, the secretary of the Dutch Aeronautical Society, Isaac van den Berch van Heemstede, stepped forward and announced in a loud voice, "Mr. Undersecretary, I have the honor to present to you the famous constructor, Mr. Fokker."[19] The result was pandemonium in the French delegation. Fokker had already been warned the day before that it was not a good idea to appear at the show again, but now there was no denying his presence. From the midst of the French group someone shouted angrily, "*à bas les boches!*" (down with the krauts!). The French newspaper *Le Journal*, which had a reporter on the scene, wrote that Fokker stepped forward, extending his hand to greet Eynac. The Frenchman's face froze, and he turned on his heels to avoid Fokker's handshake. Teeth clenched, he walked briskly from the scene.[20] To prevent further unpleasantness, Fokker was again urgently advised to stay away in his own best interests and of French-Dutch relations generally. In Paris, a motion was carried in Parliament to prohibit Fokker from participating in the Salon and from ever showing his face again in the Grand Palais—"utter exaggeration," according to Fokker in an interview with Dutch journalists:

> The only thing that has annoyed me, has been the fact that some—businessmen and others—have reproached me for a lack of tact. But judge for yourself. Last year, shortly after the war therefore, the Netherlands Aircraft Factory received an invitation to exhibit at the Aeronautical Salon. It was because of tact that we abstained from participating. Some months ago we received an invitation to register for the present Salon. I assured myself of the cooperation of the French Air Ministry and personally cleared the matter of participating with the management of the exhibition. . . . I protested against taping off the name Fokker, but for practical reasons and to smooth things with the management, I did not exert myself in this matter, especially since it turned out that the whole incident resulted in the most welcome free advertisement that I could imagine as a manufacturer.[21]

But trouble was not over yet, because on November 25 Anthony showed himself again after all. He appeared at the exhibition in the company of a Dutch naval officer, Hans Steensma, and spotted the American naval attaché whom he knew at the stand of the French aircraft constructor Henri Potez. Potez was just trying to explain something to the American, but was having big trouble because he spoke no English. Fokker recalled, "So he asked me a few things and before I knew it I was sort of acting as an interpreter. Potez, who didn't know who I was, later heard that Fokker had been at his stand. And he came to argue with me about it. That is to say: he wanted to, but he didn't get very far because members of the security police, some of whom were constantly present near my stand, made it clear to him he'd better not make a fuss! So far the whole affair had hardly drawn any attention from the public, despite Mister Potez's loud voice. Besides, it was nearly six o'clock, the hour at which the exhibition closes."[22]

But newspapers picked up on the rumor of a row anyhow, spread the story, and thus gave birth to new agitation. The next day several visitors tried to attack Fokker. This time Anthony panicked. He tried to calm things down, but he could not remember the right words and resorted to repeating a terrified "I don't know any French!" Nobody believed him, and the police had to intervene and escort him off the premises so that he would not be hurt. Even at the close of the exhibition there was another incident. On November 27 the French airplane builder Esnault Pelterie had the two Fokker aircraft seized, claiming they represented an infringement on his patent of a pilot control stick that could be moved in every direction. Fokker was forced to call on the services of the Dutch Ministry of Foreign Affairs to come to some arrangement with Pelterie.[23] Not surprisingly, the Netherlands Aircraft Factory was not invited to the next Paris Aeronautical Salon, which was held from December 15, 1922, to January 2, 1923. An official Dutch protest, printed in the French newspapers, remained without effect.[24]

℘

It did not matter to Anthony Fokker. Since the previous Salon he had come to focus his efforts on developing his business interests in the United States. The first of five F.III aircraft that he had shipped to America had attracted the press attention he craved for when it made a passenger flight over New York on July 22, 1921. It had carried a select group of people from the Netherlands' legation in Washington.[25] Fokker announced a plan to start building aircraft in the United States at a former Colt Firearms factory in Hartford, Connecticut. Noorduyn had prepared for this in contacts with the local Chamber of Commerce. On August 6, Bert Acosta, a well-known pilot, landed in Hartford with a small delegation in one of the seven Fokker aircraft present on the North American continent.[26] But in the months that followed the required finances did not materialize, and the plan fell through. Starting a business in the States appeared more difficult than Anthony had imagined. For lack of air transport activities it also proved impossible to find buyers for the F.III machines, despite Acosta's efforts in a well-publicized demonstration tour.[27] The market for military aircraft looked more promising, however. Two two-seat versions of the D.VII were shipped to the United States in 1921, along with a D.VIII fighter. Fokker also managed to draw attention to the improved version of the D.VII, the D.IX, which received the Army Air Service designation PW-6 (Pursuit, Water-cooled, model 6). Next to these sales, Bob Noorduyn managed to land an order for a further development of the D.VIII, an armored reconnaissance fighter that was identified as the Fokker F.VI (PW-5). Early in 1922 Fokker delivered two prototypes, followed by a modest series of ten aircraft in May.[28] Nonetheless, the going was tough. In Congress a "buy American" attitude was on the rise, which had its repercussions for the interest of the American armed forces. General Mason Patrick, chief of the Army Air Service in Washington who held final responsibility for aircraft procurement, was increasingly reluctant to place orders abroad.[29]

General Patrick's hesitation had only limited effect on Fokker's position in the United States. He was fortunate to be able to build on personal relations. In December

1921 the American war hero General William (Billy) Mitchell, a staunch advocate of air power, had arrived back in Europe with his assistant, Captain Clayton Bissell, and aviation pioneer Alfred Verville. Mitchell, a charismatic but also highly controversial figure in the American defense establishment, had been sent overseas on a four-month assignment so that his supporters might redress a serious scandal after charges regarding his mental stability. His mission, "smacking as much of adventure as of hard work," had been to report on advances in European aeronautics.[30] After preparing for their task by a familiarizing themselves with the pleasures of the Parisian society and night life for several weeks, Mitchell and his party embarked upon their real European mission in January 1922. At the end of February they arrived in Holland, visiting the Fokker facilities in Amsterdam and in Veere.

In the best of his former German traditions, Anthony went to great lengths to please his visitors. He correctly judged that fostering good relations with Mitchell might just be of prime importance for his prospects on the American market. After all, Mitchell never tired of pointing out the sorry state, organization, and equipment of the Army Air Service. Convinced that it needed to import the latest in aeronautical technology, Mitchell gave Fokker the distinct impression that he might be willing to open some doors for him in return for the favors Fokker bestowed on him. Hence Fokker pampered his guests, personally driving them around in his car. Through his contacts with Prince Hendrik, Anthony managed to arrange a visit for the Mitchell party to Queen Wilhelmina, something to which Mitchell, who aspired to a lifestyle modeled on European nobility, proved most partial. The time and effort spent would prove more than worth Fokker's while. Mitchell bought the prototype of the C.IV light reconnaissance bomber for the Army Air Service, followed by an order for eight more. His advocacy was also instrumental in landing the order for the PW-5 aircraft. And Fokker also reined in a commission for a training model, designated S.I (TW-4 in the Air Service designation).

As pragmatic as Fokker, Mitchell was receptive to Anthony's approach to aeronautics. Coincidence had it that he was offered a demonstration of the way Fokker incorporated practical knowledge and experience in aeronautical design. When visiting the Fokker establishment in Veere on March 4, Bissell was given the opportunity to make a test flight with the new T.II single engine torpedo bomber that was under construction there for the U.S. Navy. Upon his return, Bissell remarked that the aircraft had been a bit slow to respond to the rudder. Anthony immediately set to work on a solution, presenting it to the American party the next morning. He had given instructions to shorten the fuselage of the aircraft by three feet. Working through the night, Fokker's men had the modified plane ready again for testing by the time the Americans had finished their breakfast. Indeed, Bissell concluded that this had resolved the problem.[31] Mitchell was in awe. He wrote to his superiors: "This man has capabilities which are unlimited in the development of aircraft."[32]

ᕧ

An avid filmmaker: Anthony loved the moving image. He filmed many occasions in his life, or had them filmed. On July 6, 1922, he made recordings of the flight trials of the Fokker T.II torpedo bomber ordered by the U.S. Navy at Washington's Anacostia Naval Air Station.
LIBRARY OF CONGRESS, WASHINGTON, DC

So it was that Mitchell made a personal appeal to Fokker to set up a factory in the United States. Was there some sort of tacit understanding between them that Fokker could count on military orders in return for such an investment? Whatever the answer, Fokker had made an influential friend in the American procurement circle. Both men shared a preference for the unorthodox, loathed anything to do with bureaucratic red tape, and shared a mission to promote the development of aviation.

On May 13, 1922, a little over two months after Mitchell's visit to Amsterdam and Veere, Anthony and Tetta boarded the liner *New Amsterdam* for New York. The forward first-class cabin had been reserved for them so that they would have the maximum opportunity to enjoy the voyage. That was a good thing, since Anthony had been immersed in business affairs right up to the moment of embarkation. It was two in the morning when they boarded the ship as it lay awaiting high tide in front of the sluice gates at the Dutch port of IJmuiden, six hours after the gangway had been raised for the other passengers sailing from Amsterdam. To his mother Anthony wrote jokingly, "a good name is a good key!"[33] On its rear deck the *New Amsterdam* carried the first Fokker T.II torpedo bomber to be tested at the Anacostia Naval Air Station in Washington, plus a D.IX fighter.

The ship arrived in New York on May 27. Fresh on American soil, Anthony read in the newspaper that the famous Indianapolis 500 auto races were scheduled to be held three days later, on May 30. This was something the speedy Dutchman did not want to miss. Impulsive as ever, he had Bob Noorduyn call around to see if any tickets might still be arranged for the event that had officially been sold out weeks ago, with all hotels in Indianapolis fully booked. Tetta did not want to accompany him: her younger brother Heinrich Joachim was a racing driver, and she objected to this high-risk occupation. She insisted on staying in the Waldorf Astoria in New York and spent her time shopping in the stores on Fifth Avenue. But there was no stopping Anthony. That same afternoon he boarded a train at Grand Central Station that would take him to Indianapolis. His fame opened doors, because on May 30 Anthony had himself photographed in the center area of the Indy 500, inspecting the various racing cars. He was in the company of the former American ace pilot and decorated war hero Eddie Rickenbacker, now working for General Motors, who had been a racing driver before the war and was part-owner of the circuit. He had not only provided Anthony with a ticket but even proved willing to share his hotel room with his eccentric former opponent. Within two days they had become friends.[34]

After visiting the Indy 500, the Dutch company reunited in New York. Anthony, Tetta, and Frits Cremer traveled by train into the American heartland. Since January of the previous year Frits had explored the possibilities for business contacts in America and had been able to make connections with several possible financiers, among them the opulently rich New York lawyer Charles Guggenheimer and the bankers Arthur Goldman and Samuel Sachs. Now the time had come to do business.

Early in June the Dutch company traveled to Chicago. This time Anthony tried to strike a better balance between business and pleasure for Tetta's sake.

In Chicago they took in a baseball game and visited the enormous stockyards of the meat packing industry. But it was not long before Anthony was again engrossed in business concerns. After all, he was looking for investors to enable him to open an airplane factory in the Midwest. His German experiences between 1914 and 1918 had taught him that American money would be necessary to avoid ending up as a foreign exception in an otherwise American aviation industry. And there was an added benefit to attracting local capital: he would not have to risk substantial sums of his own money. A location in the Midwest appeared most suited for a factory, since surely any future air route between the East Coast and the West would run through Chicago.

On the advice of Frits Cremer, who had made contact with a group of investors around the Hudson Motor Company in Michigan, Anthony spoke with various potential investors from Chicago and Milwaukee. With a combination of horror and dismay, Frits and Dora Cremer noticed how he antagonized his potential partners because of his bad English, without even knowing it. Frits summarized: "appearance flawed, no manners, doesn't understand the language, and has only left a good impression in Milwaukee where there are a lot of Germans."[35] His wife Dora was of the same opinion: "Fokker ought to take English lessons. His manner of conduct is an absolute disgrace and does no service to himself here in America."[36] Repeatedly he criticized the disorganized state of America's civil aviation. The development of air transport suffered not only from a lack of suitable airfields but also from a lack of regulation. It meant that proper safety standards were missing, a problem that was aggravated because of strong competition.[37] Nonetheless, the Pennsylvania Railroad, then America's largest railway company, declared itself interested in starting an airline company in partnership with Fokker and taking the lead in the development of commercial air transport in the United States.[38] Frits also managed to strike up discussions with major shipping lines and with steel corporations.

Still, time remained for the more pleasurable things in life. The Dutch party visited New York's Coney Island entertainment park, deriving great pleasure from rides in the carousel that had little airplanes.[39] Of course there was also flying for real. A little further along on Long Island Anthony gave one of his famous aerobatics displays at Roosevelt Field with one of the fighters intended for the Army Air Service.[40]

On July 6 the scheduled flight trials of the Fokker T.II torpedo bomber took place in Washington, witnessed by military authorities. Sadly for Fokker, the results proved disappointing. It took Anthony a whole series of test flights in Holland later to find out why the aircraft was so slow to come out of the water at full takeoff weight: after shortening the fuselage, the bomber's floatplanes were no longer located in the optimum position. Amending this shortcoming turned out to be time-consuming, since the Fokker team in Veere found it difficult to produce design blueprints that showed the Navy engineers in Washington how to go about modifying the aircraft.[41]

At the White House: On July 20, 1922, President Warren Harding received Fokker, his friend Frits Cremer (right), and the Netherlands' envoy Jan Hubrecht (center) at the White House. Anthony arrived half an hour late, behaved disrespectfully, and was uninterested in what the president had to say. **LIBRARY OF CONGRESS, WASHINGTON, DC**

But that July 6, such issues were still in the future. Anthony conferred with Secretary of State for War John Weeks and was even invited to the White House to be received by president Warren Harding. Typically, he arrived half an hour late.[42] But even though the Dutch envoy, Jan Hubrecht, who accompanied him with Frits Cremer, respectfully reported to The Hague that he had found it peculiar "to witness how this young fellow countryman put forward, with conviction though not without modesty, to the Head of State his views of what was to be done in this country in the area of law-making regarding aeronautics,"[43] the meeting was not a success. Frits Cremer complained to his father, "Fokker has the bad habit of not allowing others to give their opinion at a conference. With Harding he spoke of nothing but laws, and even if Harding changed the subject, Fokker would revert to the issue of law making. Hubrecht . . . is still not done talking about this."[44]

Still, when Fokker's ship, the *Rotterdam,* left New York on July 22, 1922, there was reason to be satisfied on the net result of the voyage: his plans to start building Fokker aircraft in America and found his own factory to do so were taking on shape.[45] He was convinced that "Americans are rather quicker than Europeans to grasp the advantages of commercial aviation."[46] Chicago, or rather even Milwaukee, where Frits and Dora had now settled with their children, appeared ideally suited as a place of business. In the city on the shores of Lake Michigan, where many inhabitants were of German extraction, Anthony had had long and seemingly productive discussions with local investors.[47] The newspapers reported that he intended to bid for a transcontinental airmail contract as soon as these would become available.[48] It appeared that his mind was made up to turn his back on Holland and Europe and move his international headquarters to Milwaukee. To effect this, an elaborate construction had been set up on paper. To begin with, there was the plan to found an American Airway Transport Company, for which Frits had managed to raise $100,000 in capital. The new company was to start by carrying out market research from Milwaukee. After all, air transport as such did not exist in the United States, and its organization required serious thought and planning. But if the outcome of the surveys were positive and it were possible to raise $2 million in startup capital, the American Airway Transport Company would initiate the construction and operation of airports and airplanes in the United States. The aircraft themselves were to be produced in a subsidiary, the American Fokker Manufacturing Company.

In advance of these developments, Frits was given an option to participate in American Airway Transport and invest $2,000. As a reward for the preparatory work, Anthony promised him a leading position in the company once it started operating.[49] Frits was convinced this was going to be the case and traveled around extensively, talking to people to widen the circle of shareholders. But in the end Anthony proved less confident than he led Frits to believe. Instead, he heeded the advice of Bob Noorduyn, who had become close to Guggenheimer in New York and was working on entirely different plans. Rather than set up American Airway Transport, Noorduyn proposed taking an interest in the small Gallaudet Aircraft Corporation, in which Guggenheimer also participated. Noorduyn was located in New York, and Milwaukee did not appeal to him at all.[50]

It put Fokker in a difficult spot: whom to rely on? After several months of indecision, he finally chose the Noorduyn/Guggenheimer proposal, having reached the conclusion that the Milwaukee study company did not show enough practical progress. Spending most of his time in New York and listening to Noorduyn, he had become convinced that his former German ties were an obstacle to an American Fokker company. As a result, Anthony had developed second thoughts about the Milwaukee proposition. Learning about this, Frits Cremer was outraged at what he considered as a flagrant breach of trust, and he handed in his resignation on the spot. A friendship of many years came to an abrupt and final end.[51]

⚓

What the American adventure did not end was Fokker's romance with gliding. When he arrived back in Holland in early August 1922 after his trip to the United States with Tetta, he instructed Reinhold Platz to build two glider aircraft for him so that he could participate in the Rhön gliding contest at the Wasserkuppe in Germany. Bending their backs as of old, Platz and a group of former Schwerin employees worked on two extremely lightweight aircraft that were easy to assemble and disassemble and could be moved by car. They finished the job in record time. Anthony traveled to Veere to try out the result of their effort. The gliders were taken to the nearby airfield at Middelburg to be tested. Anthony had the first machine tied to the back of his Cadillac automobile with a 300-foot cable and used the car as a tug to pull the glider into the air so that he might gain some experience of how it handled in flight.[52] After just a few test flights Anthony was satisfied and reported at the Wasserkuppe on August 24. This time he was accompanied by Friedrich Seekatz, who, like Fokker, was curious about the progress in gliding. With his team of experienced mechanics, an abundance of supplies and spare parts, and two trucks, Fokker was greeted with reservations. It was clear that the industrialist and multimillionaire was very far removed from the other participants, some of whom had spent their last penny to participate. The FG.1 and FG.2 (FG = Fokker Gleitflugzeug / Fokker Glider) that Fokker brought were several sizes bigger than the entries of the other competitors. The machines had a wing span of 27 and 39 feet respectively. Both aircraft were very light biplanes; one was single seat, the other a two-seater. To save weight Platz and Fokker had reverted to prewar design practices and had chosen wing warping introduced by the Wright Brothers to steer the airplanes, as had been the custom twenty years before. But since the previous year much had changed at the Wasserkuppe. The duration of the flights was no longer measured in minutes but in hours. Not having made any flights that lasted over ten minutes, Anthony wisely decided not to register for the duration contest.

Flying as such was easier. After assembling the two biplanes, everything was set for a first trial flight around 7 p.m. on August 26. The shiny white linen wings shimmered in the evening sun. Six ground crew members helped attach and stretch the elastic rubber rope used to pull the FG.2 into the air. Fokker and Seekatz had decided beforehand to try to make a flight together, since the actual duration contest was over and done with anyhow and they had no hope of breaking the three-hour record. They got onboard and signaled the crew to make a run for it. Then a loud bang: the rubber snapped and suddenly curled around the airplane like a snake. The first starting attempt had failed. Anthony decided to tie his machine behind his Cadillac, pull it back up the hill, and have a second try. Seekatz recalled:

> At the command "go" the boys run. I notice that the machine is off the ground and climbs immediately. At the same moment there is a pull, the nose of the plane points straight down, before me and behind are blocks of rock, the cord is still attached, stuck somewhere, but with another jerk the machine recovers. "Is there something broken?" Fokker yells at me. All steering surfaces are still attached, everything in order, so on we go. But because of the dive we have lost too much altitude and now we cannot profit from the ascending wind. We have to land, there

near that meadow, says Fokker. "Why don't we rather land in that clover field over there?" I suggest, "it is closer to the surfaced road." (. . .) All goes perfect, and we were in the air for nearly two minutes.[53]

A second flight went much better. This time the cord detached immediately. Anthony and Friedrich set a duration record for a double occupancy flight: 12 minutes and 53 seconds. Seekatz filmed the adventure while in the air. It promised more success to come. Anthony was pleased to accept an invitation from the Peacehaven Estate in the British South Downs near Newhaven in Sussex to come and personally give a gliding demonstration. On October 9 he lodged in the Peacehaven Hotel to see that the tent he had brought was put up properly and that his glider was correctly assembled. The day after started with a show before a select audience of glider films that he and Seekatz had taken. After that it was time for the actual demonstration, but because the wind had changed the glider had to be pulled to the other side of the hill first. Not before 4 p.m. were conditions just right. Anthony took off but did not manage to stay in the air for more than 45 seconds.[54] Later that week he also entered the First British Gliding Competition at Itford Hill. In the short stretch of time that had passed since his participation at the Wasserkuppe his experience had risen quickly. On his second flight from Itford Hill he consciously tried to make the best use of ascending winds and thermals to stay airborne longer. He managed to improve his own personal record to 37 minutes and 6 seconds. In the end he came second in the competition and thus missed the £1,000 prize made available by the *Daily Mail* for the event, but nonetheless attracted considerable attention from the British press, claiming, "I could have stayed up as long as I liked. If we have wind as we had today a man could go up at six o'clock in the morning and stay up until six o'clock at night."[55] Even the cinema newsreels took notice.

After that the gliding incentive was suddenly past him. Observing the participants at the Wasserkuppe and at Itford Hill, Anthony decided that his approach to gliding was fundamentally different from that of the other participants who lacked the technical staff that he could bring. Fokker had made his last glider flight, but he instituted a prize instead for a glider flight over horizontal terrain lasting more than twenty minutes.[56] Meanwhile, other issues had come to preoccupy his mind, although he did negotiate the sale of two two-seat glider aircraft to the testing station of the U.S. Army at McCook Field in Dayton, Ohio, in December. In the end that deal did not materialize.[57]

⌫

On November 1, 1922, Fokker's new amphibious biplane flying boat was lowered into the water for the first time in Amsterdam. It was an important moment for him, because the combination of water and air continued to attract him. To celebrate the occasion, Anthony was present himself. Once out of the water he took the pilot's seat. Suddenly water sports had become all-important for him again. He also turned up at the annual meeting of the Royal Netherlands Sail and Rowing Association

(Koninklijke Nederlandsche Zeil- en Roeivereeniging) in Amsterdam's prestigious Amstel Hotel, presenting plans to build a six-meter speed yacht according to the latest know-how so that Holland would be able to harvest international successes in sailing events.[58] His was an interesting plan, although it came at a time in which discord characterized the Dutch watersports world. At the heart of the matter lay the rise of powered yachts and how these ought to be organized nationally and internationally. Sailing associations and clubs both claimed a leading role in this. To work out a compromise, a meeting was held in Amsterdam just before Christmas at which Anthony spoke out. He advised that the owners of powered boats should settle their dispute. After much discussion, a proposal was carried to change the name of the watersports association to incorporate powered boats and form a United Dutch Water Sports Association.[59]

Despite his urge to embrace new design practices, his own new boat, *Puzzle*, was not a success. Although he participated in races organized in the context of the internationally renowned Kaag Week from July 22 to 29, he did not manage to win a single prize with the *Puzzle*. For an extremely competitive man such as Fokker, this was most disappointing. At the final day of the competition he therefore took over the boat of his company secretary Johan Carp, an avid sailor who had hitherto won every single element of the competition with his boat *Willem Six*. Thus Carp watched from the quayside as his boss won the final event on the last day of the contest. Dutch newspapers commented that this turn of events showed that, in the end, the boat was more important for results than the sailor.[60]

℘

In the air, things did not go according to plan either. Again Fokker was denied a commission to build a series of aircraft for the army in the Netherlands East Indies. The order went to his British competitors. Fokker's protests, echoed in Parliament, were to no avail.[61] As the head of Fokker's research and development in Veere, Reinhold Platz was struggling to come up with new ideas that might prove successful. The gliding experiments had been part of that effort. Dealing with the necessity to provide enough lift to carry two persons had already resulted in reverting to the biplane concept that Fokker had discarded several years before. Pressed for innovations, Platz now tried the same approach in a civil transport plane. In his latest project an extra, detachable lower wing could be fitted to enable carrying heavier loads while using the same power plant. His design for the F.V airliner thus carried up to ten passengers in biplane configuration or six in monoplane and at a higher speed.

In April 1923 Fokker and Carp proposed to sell the F.V to KLM for 45,000 guilders ($17,580). Plesman found this price far too high. His airline had thus far only tallied losses and was under pressure to come out from the red. To compel Fokker to lower his prices, Plesman was out to create competition in the Dutch aeronautical industry. In the previous year a new venture, the Nationale Vliegtuig Industrie

(National Aircraft Industry), had been set up in a couple of sheds in The Hague using British money. It was led by the former chief of the Dutch Air Corps, Hendrik Walaardt Sacré. The new company had hired Frits Koolhoven, a Dutch designer who had worked in Britain during the war and who had been struggling to keep a company of his own afloat ever since. It was Plesman's hope he might be able to play the two companies off each other.

Meanwhile, Fokker had also been trying to sell the F.V to the U.S. Army Air Service, a deal that was extremely slow to materialize. But during a visit to the test facilities at McCook Field on November 23, 1923, Bob Noorduyn learned of a competition for a new army transport aircraft. Given the buy-American attitude in Congress, it was likely that an American company would stand the best chance of landing such an order. Noorduyn therefore pushed to finalize the takeover of Gallaudet, a move that was welcomed by Gallaudet's factory manager, Reuben Fleet, a friend of Noorduyn's. If successful, it might be possible to build the F.V in the United States, or so Noorduyn planned.

Nothing came of it. The Fokker plane was simply too expensive. Anthony, never a true supporter of the F.V to begin with, saw failure in the making and decided to lower the base price of the machine to 40,000 guilders ($15,600). This was still 4,000 guilders more than Plesman was willing to consider. Protracted negotiations followed to try to bridge the gap until Fokker instructed a generous offer to be put forward on May 25, 1923: KLM was to be allowed to test the F.V in scheduled service at no charge at all. He announced the development of a new model, the F.VII. He left it to Plesman to work out which of the two designs would suit him best, the F.V or the F.VII. If KLM were to order six aircraft, he offered the F.VII at a base price of 36,000 guilders ($14,000). He let slip that he was thinking of developing a two-engine version of the F.VII, and a three-engine version as well. If KLM placed an advance order for such aircraft, he was even prepared to sell it three planes for a total price of 100,000 guilders (excluding engines).[62] Such a generous offer was more than Plesman could afford to pass up. He gratefully accepted Fokker's proposal, even if it went against his own scheme for competition in Dutch aeronautics.

¶

That summer the district court in Amsterdam pondered over Fokker's request for divorce. After his demand was heard in session on July 4, the court granted a divorce on the grounds of adultery on July 30. Tetta, who had been allowed to absent herself from the proceedings, was ordered to pay the legal charges of the case, 100 guilders.[63]

For Anthony the divorce remained a drama that he found difficult to deal with. On August 3 he was again on the train to Berlin. Did he hope to see Tetta and win her back, despite everything? If so, his suit was unsuccessful. He returned to the Roemer Visscherstraat the next day but traveled back again three days later. In September he went to Berlin twice in a final effort to save what might be saved yet. Nonetheless, the marriage was annulled at the court's order on October 11, 1923.[64]

Anthony and Tetta were both unhappy about this turn of events and did their best to deal with the divorce in a civil and respectful manner. Although they had contracted to marry without communal possession of goods, Tetta consented that Anthony should retain use of the house at Roemer Visscherstraat—at least temporarily. She moved to Berlin herself, where she took residence in an apartment near the city center at Pariser Strasse 59, bordering the artist's quarter of Wilmersdorf. Realizing that the failed marriage was at least partly his fault, Anthony showed humility and volunteered to pay Tetta a lifelong allowance of 200 guilders each month, so that she would retain a steady source of income of her own, no matter what.[65] In the 1930s he granted her use of his chalet in St. Moritz, Switzerland, so that she might have a place to enjoy winter sports. She remained the love of his life, although he would not win her back.

Tetta married Friedrich Mallinckrodt in Berlin on December 18, 1923. Fokker had sacked him on learning of the adultery. Alas, Tetta's new marriage was as unhappy as her first. Within two years it ended dramatically, and at Anthony's request his friends Wim and Nel van Neijenhoff intervened to protect her.[66] In 1927 Tetta married a third time. Her latest husband, Hans Zehentner, was a German hotel owner from Abbazia (Opatija) in Trieste, now part of Croatia. Like Tetta and Malinckrodt, Zehentner's roots were also at the Wannsee, where he had been born.

That summer the unrest of the divorce raged in Anthony's mind. On August 7 he again passed customs at Bad Bentheim, bound for Berlin, where his German lawyer Hugo Alexander-Katz waited for him. There was much to be arranged, both private and business-related. He was still being chased by court rulings in the lawsuit over the rights for the synchronization mechanism, for which he had been ordered repeatedly to pay damages. Anthony continued to refuse to do so.[67]

But even without effecting payment after the latest court ruling, Germany had become an even more complex country for Fokker than it had been since 1918. Payment for the enormous German war debts and the reparation payments to be made to the Allies had pushed the country to the brink of economic disaster. Inflation, which had begun during the war, had taken on an unprecedented shape. Hyperinflation ravaged the country. Complete estates had gone up in smoke—as had what remained of Fokker's German possessions and accounts after he left for Holland in 1919.

Hans Georg von Morgen still ruled the languishing factory in Schwerin, in which the German authorities had now also lost faith.[68] Ernst Robert von Morgen was in New York, in charge of Fokker's financial interests in the United States and listed as a stockholder in Fokker's American enterprises. Even after the divorce, Anthony left them in place. Years later Von Morgen still held the power of attorney for him in New York.

To get away from such concerns he decided to travel on to Sweden. His new Dutch test pilot, Bertus Grasé, was one of the contestants participating in a military air race from Rotterdam to the Swedish port of Göteborg. He had landed there the Saturday before as second in the race after a flight of just over four hours from Rotterdam.[69] The trip brought the sort of distraction Anthony needed. A menu card he signed onboard the steamer from Sassnitz on the German holiday island Rügen to Trelleborg in Sweden read: "Enjoying the party onboard . . . with the two nicest Schwedisch girls on a high sea and under a good dinner."[70] He arrived in Göteborg refreshed, feeling well enough to give a personal flying demonstration in Grasé's plane, incorporating his old spectacular stunts. Swedish Crown Prince Gustav Adolf, present at the scene, was much impressed.[71]

ᛪ

The stormy summer months had had an effect on Anthony's unruly character. He was annoyed at the way the Dutch government dealt with his interests as a national airplane manufacturer. He repeatedly complained that after crashes the maintenance divisions of the Air Corps and the Navy Air Service put together complete new aircraft from the various spare parts they kept, rather than order a new one from Fokker's factory.[72]

After he complained repeatedly and publicly about the lack of interest that the military air service in the East Indies showed for his aircraft, the government had given Fokker a compensation order for ten C.IV reconnaissance planes and ten DC.I reconnaissance fighters. In protest, the East Indies forces had come up with a set of specifications for the C.IV that the Netherlands Aircraft factory could not possibly meet. Maybe this was why the colonial services had insisted on conducting performance trials to ascertain that Fokker's modified C.IVB machine would meet requirements. Knowing all too well that this was not the case, but refusing to lose face over the matter, Anthony was adamant that the C.IVB come out of the trials with flying colors. And he knew exactly whom to engage for the job. A team of specialists from the Netherlands Aircraft Factory was posted to Schiphol Airfield to be on standby at all times to ensure an "untrammeled running of the tests." The specialists worked long days, much longer than those of the military officers present to oversee the proceedings. This did not remain without effect. To register the maximum height attained in a test flight, the army used a barograph. Out of view of the control commission, the instrument was "adjusted" by Fokker's people in such a way that it showed the required results upon inspection after landing. When the procurement committee, which harbored suspicions, had the instrument sealed after the flight for a second examination the next morning, Anthony arranged for the car that was to take them to Amsterdam for the night to break down. Fokker thereupon ensured that the committee members spent the night at his costs at the small KLM hotel at the airport, where they were served ample alcoholic beverages. The next morning a boat appeared in the canal next to the airport hotel to take the committee members back to Amsterdam to freshen up. This too was done without hurry. Fokker made sure the party was served with quantities of food and drink along the way, and most of them got thoroughly intoxicated. While the military staffers were enjoying Fokker's generosity,

Anthony's specialists got hold of the case containing the barograph. With great precision, the seals were broken and the instruments adjusted again to show correct results upon inspection later that day. The speed trials were similarly rigged. To measure a distance of 1,000 meters (3,280 feet) on the airfield, the commission used two long measuring bands. Fokker made sure a section of a couple of yards was cut out in the middle—enough to shorten the distance by some 165 feet, but not enough to be conspicuous. As a result, the C.IVB prototype miraculously matched the requirements, although later series production machines fell short.

That was not all. To be able to compare the test aircraft to other machines that were also undergoing trials, the contract stipulated that its propeller should measure 6.5 feet exactly. Yet Fokker's prototype was fitted with a propeller of 6.7 feet, although the wooden blade itself showed a burn mark indicating the contractual distance. The Fokker team also fiddled with the engine. In several trials Fokker had the engine exchanged for a copy that delivered more horsepower. This obviously involved a lot of work and did not always go as smoothly as planned. On one occasion the activities of the specialists were met with countermeasures when suspicious commission members wrote down all relevant marks and numbers of the engine. Commission members hung around on the airfield until 7 p.m. but were eventually persuaded to return to their hotel. In a cat-and-mouse game, Fokker's people arranged to be back at the Fokker hangar around 9 p.m. A new engine was fitted and the identification plate carrying the serial number removed from the original engine to be welded onto the new engine. After that the specialists sealed the aircraft hangar again. The specifications also required a rate of climb to a certain altitude with a given quantity of fuel. This happened, but Anthony had made sure beforehand that the aircraft's fuel tank was fitted with a small tap that could be operated by one of Fokker's mechanics, who were in on the plot, by pulling a rope from the rear cockpit. Since the fuel quantity would not be measured after landing, the weight of the aircraft could thus be reduced during flight without anyone noticing, improving the rate of climb. Even the cockpit instruments were rigged by Fokker's people.

Thus the real performance figures of the aircraft were a well-kept secret between Fokker and a small circle of confidants. To guard the secret, the protocols of the trial flights and other tests were expressly kept as general as possible. Anthony made sure that interested customers would all receive the same, rigged information.[73] Not before the Government Aeronautical Service (Rijks Studiedienst voor de Luchtvaart) was alerted to the scam by an angry ex-employee of Fokker in 1925 was any action taken to prevent such tricks.[74] It did not improve Fokker's good name, but it had no direct consequences either.

In the sphere of civil aviation things were not that much better. Anthony found it difficult to function within the strict rules and regulations of Dutch society. Small wonder that he and the law-abiding authoritarian former lieutenant Plesman did not get along. Anthony delighted in disregarding the formalist, self-satisfied attitudes that pervaded government branches and business contacts alike. Besides he was uncertain whether he would keep his Dutch factory functioning at all or move his entire operation to the United States. In the latter scenario he saw no special place for KLM as a customer. In September he suddenly wrote to Plesman that there had never been a formal, legally binding agreement about the discounts on the sale of the F.VII, pointing out that his perceived generous offer had not been committed to writing. On second thought, he now proposed drawing up a formal sales agreement for the F.VII to the amount of 61,000 guilders ($23,800) each.[75] Plesman's board was outraged at such a flagrant breach of good faith. Although Plesman received instructions to continue negotiations with Fokker and try to lower the price of the aircraft, the board also decided to search for an alternative supplier for the six aircraft it had agreed to order earlier.[76] But after a month of heated discussions, Anthony just as easily retreated from his latest position and allowed KLM to have the aircraft at 36,000 guilders ($14,000) each, the price he had agreed to at the beginning.[77]

15

DETROIT, MICHIGAN
OCTOBER 1925

Detroit was covered in dense fog on October 4, 1925. Mist had crept up from Lake Erie and made it difficult to find Dearborn's Ford Airport, the location of the finish of the National Air Tour for the Edsel B. Ford Reliability Trophy. The trophy itself was one of the instruments the automobile industry used to mark its branching off into aviation. From the gray sky came the rumble of engines. It increased, receded, and then became stronger. The 35,000 people present at Ford Airport looked up, eager to see which airplane would come in first. Would it be Ford's own contestant in the event, or one of the foreign competitors, Junkers or Fokker? Then plane no. 20 appeared low above the field. With a gracious maneuver, pilot Egbert Lott put the three-engine Fokker on the ground as the first aircraft to complete the circuit. The next two contenders, the Junkers and the Stout entry by Ford, followed within minutes. The spectators cheered, and car horns sounded. For his part, Lott had a nice bonus to look forward to.[1]

The tour had covered a route that took participants over twelve cities in the American Midwest. The event was a reliability contest and did not carry financial rewards. The intention was that participants would adhere as closely as possible to a prearranged flight schedule. Nonetheless, there was a token of appreciation waiting for the first airplane to come in at Dearborn, an almost three-foot-tall silver and gold chalice that had been made available by Ford. On it an engraving read, "This trophy is offered to encourage the upbuilding of commercial aviation as a medium of transportation." All participants who completed the circuit would see their name added to the engraving.

A breakthrough design: Since 1923 Fokker had dreamed of developing a three-engine version of his F.VII airliner. In the summer of 1925 he had two additional engines installed under the wings of a production F.VII and shipped the machine as a demonstration model to the United States. To generate publicity, he entered the aircraft in the Ford Reliability Tour in September 1925. **FLICKR PHOTOGRAPH**

It was 4:45 p.m. when the plane finally came to a standstill. The passengers filed out to participate in the victory. Anthony Fokker was the first to show himself, his face just under control again after experiencing a nasty smack of his head against the cabin wall minutes earlier, when the aircraft had suddenly struck an air pocket and slid down some five hundred feet just before landing. Except for bumping his head, his photo camera had hit him as it fell from the luggage compartment. The top of his head was still sore, but his sense of triumph was not diminished because of it. He had his speech ready, prepared for him by his publicity man, Harry Bruno, who had accompanied him throughout the tour.[2] After his usual mantra on the great future of air transport, Anthony surprised the ten businessmen and executives who had assembled to welcome the airplane by inviting them for a short flight over Detroit, so that they might gain some personal experience of the progress of aviation technology. For this special occasion he offered to pilot the airplane personally. He recognized one of the invited guests as someone connected to the airport and told him to come sit next to him in the cockpit.

After takeoff, when the aircraft had reached an altitude of about 600 feet, Anthony found he had been separated from his guests long enough and suddenly disappeared into the cabin, assuming the man next to him would take over the plane's controls. But while he merrily chatted away with the passengers, the man in the cockpit was bathed in cold sweat. Never before had he held the controls of an airplane. He had tried to stop Fokker from going aft, but amid the noise and the movement of the machine Anthony had taken no notice. No matter how loud he shouted, his voice was drowned in the roar of the three engines. Besides, Anthony had closed the cabin door behind him, and now the stand-in pilot found himself glued to his seat, hands on the stick and feet on the rudder controls. In blind panic he dared not move a muscle. It was full five minutes before Fokker reappeared in the cockpit to take his seat. The whole story came out after landing, to be cursorily dismissed by Fokker as evidence that his machines were really foolproof.[3]

ꟼ

Earlier that week, on September 28, the twenty-four contestants had been waved off one by one by Henry Ford's son, Edsel, personally. In the seven preceding months Ford had poured quite a bit of effort into the organization. In February Congress had agreed to the Kelly Act, which made it possible that commercial enterprises would take over the existing airmail service from the U.S. Post Office. The question was, however, just how reliable such services could be. Against this background a group of businessmen from Detroit had worked on plans for the Reliability Tour. Edsel Ford, who had a keen interest in aviation, was one of them. He donated the prize chalice. Anthony had initially planned to take part in the tour with two aircraft: one a regular single-engine F.VII, and one three-engine variant that had been put together in great haste in Amsterdam after Fokker had telegraphed instructions from New York and had three Wright Whirlwind engines shipped. A three-engine aircraft presented a change of course: since 1923, Anthony's idea of fixing additional engines to the F.VII design had remained shelved because of constant work improving the existing single-engine version.

While the actual construction of the three-engine F.VII was still under way in Amsterdam, Fokker's American business partners agreed to a proposal from Anthony to buy the new plane as a demonstrator, along with a single-engine F.VII machine.[4] On 25 September both Fokker aircraft were ceremonially waved off at Curtiss Field, Long Island, each carrying six passengers. But at the start of the tour in Dearborn only the three-engine plane appeared. The other had been forced to make an emergency landing because of engine problems several hours after takeoff. For Anthony, much rode on the tour. Beyond the finish line a bright future in American commercial aviation beckoned. This was to be Fokker's breakthrough on the emerging market for airliners in the United States. That was why the Fokker team had not risked landing its big machine at some of the smaller aerodromes along the circuit. To be certain to arrive first and thus maximize the benefit of publicity, Fokker had taken a mixed group of eight people with him. Egbert Lott, a twenty-nine-year-old pilot with Fairchild Aerial Surveys, was responsible for the plane, along with two technicians from engine manufacturer Wright: Ken Boedecker and Thomas Kinkade. The rest of the company had featured primarily as passengers, as did Fokker himself.

ᚵ

At the start of the Reliability Tour, Anthony had been in the United States for exactly one week. It had been a busy one, and it had started with delay, since the arrival of the liner *Leviathan* on which he traveled had coincided with that of no less than fifteen other ocean steamers. The New York Port Authority had not had enough customs officers to process so many ships at the same time and the 122 first class "aliens" onboard the *Leviathan* had to wait for several hours before being allowed to disembark.[5] Once he was on dry land, Anthony's first duty had been to take care of the affairs of the Fokker Aircraft Corporation, founded in Delaware on September 16, two days before his arrival, to combine his American interests in advance of plans to set up an American Fokker aircraft factory in Kansas City. When Anthony disembarked it had not been as a mere visitor to the United States, but with the intention to become a permanent resident, even though he preferred that no one know this in the Netherlands. He had left specific instructions for his house staff at Roemer Visscherstraat in Amsterdam to discretely put his Dutch furniture in storage under an assumed name, and he had told them not to involve anyone from the Netherlands Aircraft Factory in the process.[6]

In the past two years much had happened that concerned his American business interests, which had grown quickly. Although civil aviation took a long time to develop, it was evident that Fokker was to play a major role. In May 1923 the first nonstop transcontinental flight in the United States by Army lieutenants Oakley Kelly and John Macready had been made with one of his two F.IV (T-2) transports and had brought Fokker a lot of goodwill in aeronautical circles, even if actual publicity for the

Nonstop coast-to-coast: On May 2–3, 1923, Lts. John Macready and Oakley Kelly made the first nonstop American coast-to-coast flight in a Fokker T-2 (F.IV) transport plane that was built at Fokker's factory in Veere, Holland. Taking off from Roosevelt Field on Long Island, they flew to Rockwell Field near San Diego. Fokker was disappointed by the publicity, which avoided any mention of his name. SMITHSONIAN INSTITUTION, WASHINGTON DC airplane itself had been subdued. The War Department had been hesitant to point to the fact that the flight had been made with a foreign-built plane, and the name "Fokker" was kept out of the news.[7] Hence Anthony and Bob Noorduyn thought it prudent to provide a more solid base to Fokker's American interests. In spite of pressure to come to an early arrangement, it had taken until September 1923 before the necessary preparations were completed.

That month Noorduyn's efforts to found an American production company resulted in the takeover of a small factory near Hasbrouck Heights, New Jersey. The Wittemann-Lewis Aircraft Corporation, which had its premises in a wooden hangar at Teterboro Airport, could hardly be qualified as a major prize in an international takeover bid. Wittemann-Lewis had gone bankrupt toward the end of 1922 in the extremely costly development of a large six-engine bomber for the Army Air Service, the Barling. The machine was named after its designer Walter Barling, an associate of Mitchell's. The factory building was only four years old, but came cheap—with inventory—as a result of the bankruptcy. Late in December 1923 Anthony came to Teterboro for a personal inspection and declared that matters were now heading in the right direction. A week or so before, on December 14, 1923, his American business partners had founded the Atlantic Aircraft Corporation in his absence with the intention to build Fokker aircraft at Teterboro. That month Anthony even made the cover of *Time Magazine* as the latest promise in American business.[8]

His arrival, onboard the luxurious Cunard liner *Berengaria* on Tuesday, December 18, four days after the founding of Atlantic, marked his third visit to the United States. The previous one dated a year and a half back and since then Anthony had focused on his affairs in Europe. He arrived from Britain, where he had given a well-received speech about his construction methods before the Royal Aeronautical Society.[9] As he stepped on American soil, his empire now spanned the entire globe: along with the United States, his companies were building aircraft to orders from several countries in Europe, the Soviet Union, Japan, and Latin America. The Friday before, as the *Berengaria* was approaching the American shore, the governor of New Jersey had officially vetted the freshly signed founding papers for the Atlantic Aircraft Corporation. Finally Fokker had his own American branch, its purposes stated in the most general of terms so that the company would have as much room as possible to play a role in the development of aviation.[10] Noorduyn had been immersed in preparations for a whole year.

Atlantic was the answer to the political pressure that Congress exerted on the American armed forces to exclusively buy American equipment. Intended in part to encourage American producers to develop both military and commercial aircraft, the buy-American program had chiseled away at Fokker's export market. This was the case not only for transport planes but also for fighters delivered to the Army Air Service. In April 1923 trials with Fokker's V.40, also designated as D.X, had already ended with dissatisfied Army officials. The same could be said of the

American version of the C.IV reconnaissance airplane (U.S. designation CO-4). These were developments that appeared to worry Noorduyn a great deal more than they did Fokker, who preferred to go with the flow and could not even be bothered to provide speedy replies to the ever more pressing letters he received from New York about these matters.[11]

As had been the case in the founding of the Netherlands Aircraft Factory in Holland, Anthony had prudently kept his distance from the founding of Atlantic. He had left the signing of the papers to the group of American business partners that Noorduyn had managed to bring together. It was a bit of a peculiar gathering that illustrated that the various prominent businessmen Noorduyn had initially spoken with had since developed doubts about Fokker's American business prospects. In the end, the signatory parties were Frank Ford and George Davis from the consulting and engineering firm Ford, Bacon & Davis, who had made their fortune in the railroad business and now invested $100,000 in the new venture. In return, Frank Ford received a seat on the board. Major Lorillard Spencer, a wealthy businessman from New York who had been chairman of the board of the defunct Wittemann-Lewis Corporation, received $10,000 in shares as a belated recognition of his services rendered for Wittemann-Lewis. Bob Noorduyn and Charles Guggenheimer participated for a nominal amount of one dollar only and also took a seat on the board. The rest of the money came from Fokker himself, who subscribed on December 20, bringing the initial capitalization to $800,000. He also supplied two F.III aircraft, a mail plane without engine, and office supplies and furniture in New York.[12] Uncharacteristically, because he preferred to rent rather than buy property, he also promised ownership of the factory building at Teterboro, which he intended to acquire from Walter Teter's Riser Land Company in the course of the liquidation of Wittemann-Lewis. To provide initial liquidity, Atlantic borrowed $100,000 from Anthony personally. The principal office of the new corporation was in Jersey City.

Fokker had himself appointed in the position of "chief engineer." This gave him the freedom to interfere with technological issues without being distracted by commercial interests. Spencer was appointed as president. In practice Spencer interfered little in Atlantic's affairs, leaving the day-to-day running of the company in the hands of Anthony, as vice president, and Bob Noorduyn, who combined the vaguely defined positions of company secretary with that of treasurer and general manager.[13] His was not an enviable job. Fokker, who soon acquired more than 75 percent of the company's shares, was more than parsimonious in finances and had Noorduyn forever scraping the bottom of the barrel. Time and again Noorduyn saw himself forced to beg Anthony for finances. More often than not such pleas really regarded but a few hundred dollars, for which Noorduyn was forced to wait for weeks because the mail had to cross the ocean twice.[14]

In May 1924 Atlantic started actual production, leasing the factory building and the airfield from the Riser Land Company under an initial three-year contract for a modest monthly fee and using machinery bought from Wittemann a month before for just $6,100. Finances were tight, but for its time it was a reasonably modern factory, equipped for woodworking as well as for metal construction. Its flaw was, perhaps, that it was somewhat undersized for the kind of production volumes that Fokker dreamed about. Yet the factory had its own modest wind tunnel, a weather station and a radio transmitter. To provide a link between the new owners and the small workforce that had been taken over from Wittemann-Lewis, the British aeronautical engineer Francis Archer was allowed to continue his position as factory manager on the basis of a month-by-month contract.[15] Nonetheless, Noorduyn pointed out expressly that it would be Anthony who would call the shots at Atlantic.[16] Wittemann was interesting for Fokker because the company held a provisional contract for revision and partial reconstruction of a series of De Havilland DH-4 biplanes that belonged to the U.S. Postal Service. These former training aircraft were American war surplus and had been built in large numbers before 1918 because their construction was rapid and easy. Now they were part of a large-scale program of the federal government to extend the service life of its mail planes and improve their safety.

To further its contacts with the federal government, Atlantic appointed Halbert Payne, a former captain in the Army Air Service, as a second vice president in charge of government contracts. Through his connections the new company received a major follow-up order from the remodeling program: modernizing over a hundred aircraft fuselages. In the end the total number would climb to 135. This was Mitchell's reward to Fokker for starting his own American factory.[17] According to specifications the original wooden frame of the aircraft was replaced by Fokker's more sturdy construction of welded steel pipes. Despite such a profitable start, Atlantic struggled with startup problems. Six months after the factory opened, the number of employees still stood at fifty-three. The majority of them came from Wittemann. Anthony personally supervised who was doing what on the work floor and also helped set up series production of the De Havilland fuselages. It showed Fokker at his best, spending much time and effort of the factory floor, interfering in all sorts of practical matters. His vast experience resulted in detailed instructions for structural changes to the construction of the fuselage, and a rearrangement of the cockpit instruments. Because of the modest workforce, Atlantic's conversion program made only slow headway, and the DH-4 work was not phased out before 1926.[18]

Fokker had good reasons not to hurry. As American military orders from the Netherlands Aircraft Factory threatened to dry up—in Washington there had been commotion in Congress, and a committee was questioning General Patrick about foreign aircraft procurements—he used Atlantic to assemble aircraft that had been ordered in America but were actually built in Amsterdam. Earlier on Fokker aircraft were delivered at Selfridge Field, Mount Clemens, Michigan, for assembly by the Army Air Service.[19] However, the financial structures of the Dutch and American firms were kept separate. Between the two Fokker firms an elaborate and complex administration of orders and payments existed. Nonetheless, Fokker did not manage to keep his Dutch and American finances apart. He repeatedly instructed his Dutch company to provide services, parts, wings, or even complete aircraft that he needed at Atlantic. Although this went against his own interests—in Holland Fokker was the only shareholder—he saw such work as robbing Peter to pay Paul. His American shareholders formed the select group of beneficiaries of such arrangements.[20]

In January and February 1924 Anthony traveled across the United States, having been invited to give speeches for various chambers of commerce despite his poor English. His favorite subject was the bright future of commercial aviation. In Cleveland, Ohio, he let out that the spread of the airplane would almost be as wide as that of the motorcar. Anthony painted a prospect of one airplane per every thousand people.[21] But his American sojourn was short this time as well. On March 15 he boarded the *Aquitania* for his voyage back to Europe.

ᚷ

Perhaps he would have preferred to stay longer in the United States, where his people were now working on a new fighter for the Army Air Service, powered by a newly developed, secrecy-shrouded, powerful engine. But all his attention—and presence—was required in Holland to steer the work for the largest order the Netherlands Aircraft Factory ever landed. The case was covered in secrets and preparations had been going on for more than a whole year. The origins lay in vague allusions made in Amsterdam in February 1923 by visiting Germans claiming to be interested in military aircraft. A follow-up conversation had taken place in Hamburg in April between Anthony, Seekatz, and the German industrialist and archconservative politician Hugo Stinnes. Stinnes told Fokker and Seekatz he was interested in buying no less than a hundred Fokker D.XI fighter aircraft—and maybe even many more. He indicated the total sale might well amount to about 200 fighter aircraft, but he refused to disclose who the interested party might be.[22] Nevertheless, the sale of a complete air force to an undisclosed party had all the signs of a transaction that might not stand the light of day. Pressing the issue in discussions that lasted into November 1923, Fokker learned that the prospective buyer would be the Soviet Union. This was not a neutral piece of information. The Netherlands had not recognized the Soviet Union and did not maintain diplomatic relations with the Soviets, who had come to power in Moscow in 1917. It made the delivery of top-grade war material into a dubious activity at the very least, even though Holland was formally a neutral country. In 1922 the Germans had signed an agreement with the Soviets at Rapallo near Genoa in Italy, with a secret clause that referred to mutual assistance. Against this background, Stinnes, Fokker, and the Soviets took extreme caution to avoid attracting attention in finalizing the aircraft sale. There was good reason to be careful, since Fokker had already attracted the attention of the intelligence services a year before by selling fifty of its surplus D.VII fighters, three C.I reconnaissance aircraft, and twelve

C.IIIs to Moscow. Seekatz, although not on Fokker's payroll officially, had brokered the deal with a shady Russian arms salesman called Shirinkin.[23]

Such contacts proved instrumental. Hugo Stinnes took care of initial payments. He had a history as a financier of various business deals with the Soviets. In the summer of 1923 the talks with Fokker had progressed far enough that Anthony dared give the green light for the series production of the fighters, even if the contracts still had to be signed. On June 18 the first order was written into the books: forty-four D.XI fighters powered by Hispano Suiza engines and six aircraft equipped with British Napier engines. It was decided to build the aircraft in Fokker's branch factory in Veere, far away from prying eyes of press reporters around Amsterdam. The wings were assembled at Holland's national train manufacturer, Werkspoor, near Utrecht.

Thus production was set up. On July 14, a prototype of the D.XI was presented at the National Flying Day at the Schiphol Airfield, where Anthony personally demonstrated the aircraft's flying characteristics in front of an enthusiastic crowd of 5,500 paying visitors. Fokker's new test pilot Emil Meinecke next flew the D.XI in Moscow in October, after which the Soviet deal was finalized. That same month Anthony was one of the founding members of the Netherlands-Russian Trading Company, Nedrus, quite respectably housed at Amsterdam's prestigious Heerengracht for the purpose of lending a legal appearance to the arms trade in case the press got wind of things. He also was appointed a member of the Nedrus board of directors, presided over by the influential Dutch banker Allard Pierson of Pierson & Company.[24] In advance of the signing of the official delivery contract on December 20, the first aircraft were loaded onboard the freighter *Cleopatra* in Rotterdam on October 30. The wooden crates that contained them were unmarked. Those who were in on the deal went through a spell of anxiety when the local paper, *Rotterdamsch Nieuwsblad*, published a photograph of the ship being loaded, but other than that all remained quiet. Afterward, fine-tuning the financial arrangements covering the deal took until February 26, 1924. The initial contract stipulated that Fokker would deliver 200 combat aircraft: 125 D.XI fighters (at 22,500 Dutch guilders each) and 75 C.IV reconnaissance machines (at 30,000 Dutch guilders each). In total the arms sale was worth 5,062,500 guilders ($1.95 million). A number of the aircraft were to be taken in three shipments to Petrograd (St. Petersburg), while another part was to be transported to Odessa.[25] Although the government in The Hague had gotten wind of the transactions, neutrality ruled, and officials pretended to be oblivious of what was going on. In fact, The Hague relinquished some of its visa restrictions for Soviet tradesmen and even allowed limited credit guarantees for exports to Moscow.[26]

From the point of view of finances, the matter was full of complexities. Fokker received his money in three installments through the London branch of the Guarantee Trust Company of New York. The money originated with the Soviet Trade Representative in Berlin, which opened an account with the Guarantee Trust Company for the purpose. If for any reason Fokker would not be able to make the delivery, the Dutch NHM guaranteed that the funds would be returned through the National Provincial Bank in London. The whole affair reeked of evasion of trading boycotts. To finance the actual construction of the aircraft Fokker took out a credit of 2,250,000 Dutch guilders ($862,000), for which NHM, Werkspoor, Pierson & Company, and the Dutch financier Frits Fentener van Vlissingen acted as guarantors. Of course, they had to be remunerated in turn for the service, charging a fee of 10 percent.

Despite all these respectable parties, Anthony did not have full confidence in the matter. He had a clause inserted into the sales contract that explicitly mentioned that all aircraft would remain the property of the Netherlands Aircraft Factory until delivery in Petrograd or Odessa. He insured himself against possible mishaps for a period of two weeks after delivery. The last airplane was to be taken over and accepted by the Soviets on December 31, 1924, at the very latest. Because he himself was still in the United States in February, he had his financial adviser, Johan Carp, sign the contract.[27]

But was it really the Russians who ordered all these aircraft, and did the money really come from Moscow? Until after the summer of 1923, Anthony had thought he would have to travel to the Kremlin to finalize the deal.[28] This was not the case. Stinnes held his cards tightly to his chest. Moreover, that autumn matters took on a decidedly German character. One day in September Fokker opened the door to strange visitors at his house in Amsterdam's Roemer Visscherstraat: three former German officers, all in civilian attire. One was his old acquaintance Felix Wagenführ, now a director of Hugo Stinnes GmbH. The other two were Wagenführ's engineering associate Walter Hormel and former test pilot Kurt Student as unofficial representatives of the War Ministry in Berlin. Wagenführ had an unusual and most confidential question: would Fokker be in the market to build another fifty D.XI fighter aircraft on top of the Soviet order, to be delivered to Stinnes? From the context of the conversation—and from the fact that Wagenführ requested provision to carry German machine guns on the aircraft—it was evident that these additional planes would not be for the Soviets but were somehow intended for disarmed Germany.[29] In the aftermath of the French occupation of the German Ruhr area in January 1923, the German president, Friedrich Ebert, had insisted that Germany would buy a hundred modern fighter aircraft abroad for the defense of German soil.[30] As the lead figure in a group of industrialists that had joined forces in civil resistance to the French occupation, Hugo Stinnes wholeheartedly agreed with Ebert.[31] Subsequently it became clear that Fokker would be the only producer capable of building such a large series of aircraft. It was clearly time for Fokker to make good on his German debts. After all, the authorities had been keen to cooperate with him in 1919 when he wanted to leave Germany.

On behalf of Berlin, Stinnes ordered fifty D.XI fighters from Fokker, plus another fifty of the updated type D.XIII. With its 570-hp Napier Lion engine, this latter type was at that moment the world's fastest fighter aircraft. Of course Anthony had to think over the proposition. If this came out, it would seriously damage his position as aircraft producer, both in Europe and in the United States. The question to be answered was whether the profit to be made in the short term was worth the risks in the long term. In the second half of November 1923 several more discussions were held in Germany on the matter before Anthony finally dared take a decision and sign the contract that was offered to him.

The aircraft were to form the backbone of an ultrasecret German military training squadron, stationed on Soviet territory. This was Berlin's answer to the clauses of the Versailles Treaty that had dictated that Germany abolish its army, fleet, and air force. From 1919 the new German chief of staff, Gen. Hans von Seeckt, had played a crucial role in operationalizing secret plans to rebuild the armed forces. Von Seeckt's plan was to strive for military cooperation with the Soviets to counterbalance the conditions that the Allies had imposed through the Versailles Treaty. As early as December 1920 a secret Sondergruppe R (Special Section R) was created within the German defense apparatus. This section became responsible for nurturing contacts with the Soviets.[32] As the outcome of bilateral arrangements, Josef Stalin agreed to make three clandestine military training centers available to the Germans on Soviet soil: an army base for experiments with poisonous gases in warfare, a base to practice tank maneuvers, and an air force base.[33] The latter officially housed the fourth squadron of the Red Air Fleet, known to its German pilots as training unit Freier Fall (Free Fall). The base was located near Lipetzk, a Soviet bathing resort on the river Voronezh, 260 miles southeast of Moscow. In exchange for the use of the facilities the Germans paid a hefty sum per year, provided technological know-how, and gave various forms of military training to the Red Army.[34] The aircraft that Wagenführ ordered were to be used by the German training unit at Lipetzk. Anthony, it is thought, personally extracted a considerable sum for his cooperation in this secret venture: 3.5 million Dutch guilders ($1.4 million).[35]

As a sign of German gratitude, Anthony was again decorated with the laurels of the Iron Cross, Second Class, in Berlin on May 7, 1924.[36] In the meantime, great care was taken to avoid prying eyes. The sales contract was made out in the name of Traugott Thiem, a Brazilian subsidiary of the Stinnes Consortium in Rio de Janeiro.[37] When the aircraft were shipped, they were labeled for export to Brazil. In the end the Germans only took delivery of the fifty D.XIII fighters. They were shipped out in June 1925 and imported via Leningrad. Fokker sold the fifty "German" D.XI machines to Romania for a sum of 1.4 million guilders ($560,000). They arrived in Bucharest in the summer of 1925.[38]

It was not the end of the story. In February 1926 Fokker's representative in Bucharest, Jourgea Negrilesti, was charged of having paid 10 million lei in bribes to land the Romanian order and was arrested for refusing to cooperate in the investigation that ensued.[39] Anthony wisely steered clear of the case and turned to his sales representative, Frits Rasch, to clear up the matter. Within a month a warrant for his arrest circulated in Bucharest, although the authorities retracted their steps later when it became evident that the various parties concerned on the Romanian side with the deal had all behaved most irregularly. Several people were court-martialed but in the end acquitted, and the case was smoothed over.[40] Nonetheless, the very scale of Fokker's exports to the East should have been an indication to the Netherlands government that something strange was cooking here. The Hague preferred not to know. Although the exports were reported on in several newspapers, customs officials in the Dutch ports took the formal position that they could only register the *official* destination of the aircraft as mentioned in the export documents. Whether the goods eventually ended up in the possession of the registered buyer was a thing they could not control. Hence the exports took place in semisecrecy. The documents of the forty-eight fighter aircraft that left Holland for Romania by rail mentioned Austria as the final destination. The remaining two D.XI fighters were shipped onboard the freighter *Euterpe* with documents that listed Denmark as the recipient. When asked by reporters, customs officials openly admitted they had no means of knowing whether the *Euterpe* would not continue to the Soviet Union.[41]

ℂ

The reporting on the exports was bad news for Fokker. Not only did it go against Dutch foreign policy in which all dealings with the Soviet Union were kept on a very low footing since formal relations did not exist, but it also might have damaged Fokker's relationship with the Dutch royal family. He owed the return to his Dutch nationality, of which he had grown rather fond, to the intervention of Prince Hendrik. Hendrik was not just one of Fokker's most welcome guests, but he also maintained a residence on the top floor of Fokker's company office at Amsterdam's Rokin. Together with Anthony he had done the honors of removing the starting blocks on the occasion of the official opening of KLM's international scheduled services on April 15, 1921.[42] They saw each other socially from time to time. On September 20, 1923, Anthony had personally collected Hendrik at the Amsterdam docks and welcomed him onboard his private luxury yacht *Honey Moon* to be taken on an inspection tour of the Fokker factory. On April 3, 1924, the royal family again came to visit. Anthony, dressed for the occasion in a tailcoat and a top hat, led the way while young Princess Juliana merrily frolicked along. In the cockpit of the prototype of the new F.VII airliner, Fokker explained to the princess the function of the various levers and instruments. Queen Wilhelmina and her husband looked on with appreciation. That afternoon Anthony was decorated with the House Order of Orange in gold—all the more reason for Anthony to watch his words.[43] Disclosure was given only to the tax inspector.[44]

ℂ

By the end of June 1924 the work on the F.VII prototype had progressed far enough that the aircraft could be test-flown. Time was precious, because the project had been delayed by half a year after it had been discovered that the aircraft's propeller had been mounted too low. A flaw in the design: the propeller would hit the ground as soon as the tail would come up in takeoff.[45] The blueprints had to be altered drastically. There was considerable pressure on the plane's development. Fokker had promised that the F.VII could be used for the proposed first-ever flight from Amsterdam to Batavia in the Dutch East Indies, a project that had been under preparation since September 1922. The aircraft needed to be ready by October.

In search of publicity for his products, Anthony had been involved in the activities of the Netherlands–Indies Flight Committee (Comité Vliegtocht Nederland–Indië) right from the start. A total of 113 companies and private individuals sponsored the grand adventure that was to take place in 1924. The government also contributed. Anthony personally donated 15,000 guilders, plus the use of the aircraft.[46] Initial progress had been slow, since no engine appeared reliable enough to make it through the 9,578-mile flight and Fokker built only single-engine aircraft. Knowing very well that success would bring lots of free publicity and would result in sales contracts for his commercial aircraft, Fokker had played an important role in the technical preparations. Reasons of climate dictated that the autumn months between October and December presented the best time slot for such an endeavor. On October 1, 1924, just after 8:30 a.m., everything was finally ready for the grand departure from Amsterdam's Schiphol Airfield. As the lead sponsor, Anthony had the honors of being the last to wish the crew well and close the aircraft's cabin door. Accompanied by many cheers, KLM's chief pilot, Abraham ("Jan") Thomassen à Thuessinck van der Hoop; mechanic Piet van den Broeke; and pilot Hans van Weerden Poelman of the Air Corps took off in their specially prepared F.VII. Although the engine would, in spite of all preparations, cut out over Plovdiv in Bulgaria two days into the flight and had to be replaced after an emergency landing, the three adventurers finally reached Batavia on November 24, 1924.[47]

Restless as ever, Anthony learned of the news while in New York, where he had arrived on November 7 as a passenger on the *Mauretania*. The past six months had been packed with difficulties. On July 28 his best friend, Bernard de Waal, had died in the Bronovo Hospital in The Hague after unexpected complications of what initially appeared to be laryngitis. He was buried in Arnhem three days later. Anthony had given an emotional speech by the open grave, recollecting how their long and close friendship went back to youthful summers spent by the sea in the Dutch bathing resort Katwijk aan Zee. Bernard's death affected Anthony. After the burial he had retreated for several weeks in solitude on the water. To take his mind off things he had made plans to travel to the Netherlands East Indies in December, but nothing came of it. Instead he took the Cunard liner to New York on November 1 to personally take stock of the developments at Atlantic in Hasbrouck Heights since March of the year. Anthony pondered over the possibilities to expand his American business. Upon arrival in New York he reminded the press of his intention to contribute to the development of commercial air transport in the United States.[48] Again he stated that the airplane would achieve a spread similar to that of the automobile. "Any man or woman who can drive an automobile, can operate an airplane. It is really easier to operate a plane than an automobile," he told the *New York Times*.[49] Advancing the spread of the airplane would become his grand mission in America, as well as building the planes for it. To do so, the capital of Atlantic was more than doubled in December 1924. This new capital was necessary, in part, to pay Fokker for the exclusive right to use his patents and know-how in North America.[50] But before the month was out, he was back on the boat to Europe. On December 17, 1924, the news had reached him from Haarlem that his father had suddenly passed away at the age of seventy-three. With Christmas coming up, it turned out to be impossible to get immediate first-class passage to Europe. The weather conspired against him too, for all the big liners docked in New York days late and covered in ice because of extremely bad weather conditions over the Atlantic.

Anthony's was a strange Christmas that year. Even apart from the extreme cold, a strong wind blew ice rain from the clouds, covering New York's streets in a thick blanket of ice and snow. America's typical Christmas atmosphere largely passed him by. Forced to bide his time, he boarded the *Olympic* at the first opportunity, on December 26, twenty-four hours before the ship sailed. It grieved him that he had not been present to comfort his dearly beloved mother when the flower-decked coffin containing Herman Fokker was lowered in the crematorium of the Westerveld Cemetery on December 20. It was January 5 before Anthony arrived in Holland, still downcast by what had happened in his absence.

⚓

Having assisted his mother for a few weeks in making the various arrangements that had to be made regarding his father's estate, Fokker decided he needed to take a break and relax. On January 25 he boarded the train in Amsterdam for Basel to go on a skiing holiday in Switzerland. His final destination was the chic Kulm Hotel in St. Moritz. The Kulm, overlooking the frozen lake of St. Moritz, had made a name for itself as a watering hole for the rich and famous. Anthony had already been there several times since 1919 to partake in his favorite winter sports, skiing and bobsledding, in the company of the like-minded happy few. For a man of his means, anything was possible. He would have cut himself short had he not hired an airplane for a special skiing trip in the deep snow far off the regular slopes and high up the glacier, in the select company of Italian Prince Karoly Odescalchi; winter sports fanatic David Carnegie, the Eleventh Earl of Northesk; and former ace flyer now turned stunt pilot Leslie Hamilton.[51]

After a detour through northern Italy, he returned to Holland three weeks later, rested and in the best of moods. Uncharacteristically, he even announced that he was willing to participate in a scientific aeronautical research project run by a Dutch engineer, Albert von Baumhauer of the Government Aeronautical Study Service, to develop a helicopter.[52]

That spring Anthony was mostly busy expanding his Dutch successes. The flight to Batavia with the prototype of the F.VII had resulted in Europe-wide interest in Fokker aircraft, particularly in Germany and Britain. He traveled to London several times to confer with the head of British civil aviation, Sir Sefton Brancker. Although the work on the F.VII was ongoing, he gave a flying demonstration with the F.VII at London's Croydon Airport on April 15. It was Fokker's contribution to an ongoing debate in British aeronautical circles about the shortcomings of the De Havilland DH-34 airliner, a machine that competed with Fokker's. The day before Christmas one such DH-34 had stalled and crashed on takeoff from Croydon, killing all seven passengers onboard.[53] Anthony was confident that stalling was practically impossible with the F.VII. He took off with a group of passengers and let the aircraft climb at such a steep angle that the much-feared phenomenon occurred. But contrary to the DH-34, the F.VII did not go out of control and he was able to bring the airplane in for a normal landing. The British aeronautical press wrote in awe: "Fokker pulled the nose right up until the passengers were almost lying on their backs, and, having steadied the machine, the pilot let go of the controls. . . . The machine rolled very slightly from side to side, and sank very slowly, the nose gradually dropping all the while, until a normal attitude had been reached. . . . Mijnheer Fokker pointed out in his little speech [that] the lines operating with Fokker monoplanes have been singularly free from serious accidents, so that . . . the proof of the pudding is in the eating."[54] To journalists of the New York Times, Anthony later explained, "I have always concentrated on making my planes the safest in the world. . . . The English companies had had some accidents with some of their planes, so I took my twelve passenger ship over to show that such accidents are not necessary."[55]

If Anthony was pleased with the praise that came his way in London, he positively beamed three days later at the festivities in Holland to welcome the return of the three airmen who had made the flight from Amsterdam to Batavia. He was the one who held the honor to officially laurel Van der Hoop and his crew at Schiphol Airfield before the press could get to them. After answering questions and posing for photographers and film crews for forty-five minutes, the company left in procession for Amsterdam. Anthony personally drove the third car, containing the flight crew. He seated mechanic Piet van den Broeke next to him. All along the route people had gathered, cheering with enthusiasm. As the vehicles approached Amsterdam spectators amassed into a real crowd. It had been years since Amsterdam had seen so many people about. Just before they got to the city center, Anthony stopped and had all three crewmembers position themselves on the rear of his car, so that everybody would be able to see them.[56]

The spectacle was surpassed a week later, on April 25, when crowds gathered in the Houtrust sporting grounds in The Hague for a national manifestation in honor of the daring airmen. Pageants of musical bands in shining outfits, equestrian schools, sports companies, dancing groups, all turned up for the occasion. At 2 p.m. sharp it was Fokker, donning his best jacket and tie and wearing a top hat, who stepped out of the Paulez Hotel opposite the royal palace, followed by the three airmen. A guard of honor saluted them. In a carriage drawn by four horses decked with feathers and plumes they slowly made their way through the city, accompanied by the cheers of thousands along the route. At the Houtrust sporting grounds twenty thousand people had gathered. Guns fired a formal salute. Toward 3 p.m. Anthony and the three airmen took their places on the main stage. A nearly four-hour-long pageant in their honor passed in front of them. At the end Anthony and the men received special certificates of appreciation that had been carried to The Hague by relay runners from "the four corners of the country." Only around 7 p.m. were the four celebrated aviators able to withdraw themselves for a private dinner at one of the best restaurants that The Hague had to offer.[57]

The attention and praise bestowed upon him was such that Anthony soon began making plans to introduce the F.VII airliner in America as well. On May 16 he boarded the *Berengaria* in Southampton, bound again for New York. When the liner finally docked, eighteen hours behind schedule because of dense fog, he lost no time indicating to reporters that he was now planning to ship his latest airliners to the United States and focus on the development of commercial air transport there.[58]

16

After three-quarters of an hour's flight, Anthony Fokker carefully steered the large three-engine airplane down to land at Teterboro Airport. The clock was striking six in the late afternoon of April 16, 1927. For the first time, the purpose-built Fokker C.2 *America* flew with all of its crew in preparation for the intended historical first nonstop flight from New York to Paris. If things went right, Fokker's name would be written with capital letters in the annals of aviation history and become a household word in the world press. Anthony's gambit for U.S. Navy Commander Richard Byrd and his crew to be the first to cross the Atlantic in the *America* was generally regarded as the most likely candidate in the competition for the Raymond Orteig Prize of $25,000.

In the left-hand seat of the cockpit, Anthony braced himself. The landing was not going well at all. Twenty-six years of flying experience told him that there was a serious problem with the weight distribution in the plane. The tail had the tendency to move upward. He had noticed it on takeoff but had let it pass. The machine would need to be adapted after the test flight anyhow. Now he regretted his decision. Anthony had already instructed copilot Floyd Bennett to trim the horizontal stabilizers in the tail to the maximum position, yet worried whether this would be enough to maintain horizontal control.

Instinctively, Anthony sensed danger and gestured Bennett to move aft and get more weight in the tail. But this was difficult, since Bennett would have to climb over the large central fuel tank that filled the middle of the cabin. With the machine nearly down, such a maneuver did not appeal to Bennett. Meanwhile, Anthony continued the descent and made a low pass over the airfield. Because of the extra-large wing that provided the transoceanic plane with additional lift, its landing speed was higher than usual. But when the wheels touched the ground, the tail of the plane did not sink, as it normally would, but moved up as the airplane reduced speed. In an attempt to counter the imminent danger, Anthony instantly cut the electrical switches and jerked the steering wheel tight to his stomach, to no avail. In a reflex he gripped the steel tubing at the side of the cockpit with his left hand and pulled up his legs. After another hundred feet the inevitable happened: the tail of the airplane pushed the central engine at the front so far down that the propeller hit the ground. Within three seconds the plane somersaulted and landed on its back with an enormous bang and loud cracking sounds. It appeared as if the whole machine would be torn to pieces. The weight of the central engine tore open the cockpit. Anthony fell out and landed on his head. Before he could get hold of his senses, a gust of hot engine oil hit him in the face and ran over his clothes. "Look out for fire!" Bennett managed to cry out from the mangled cockpit, where he now hung upside-down, strapped to his seat. From all directions Fokker technicians came running to provide help.[1]

The material damage to the airplane was considerable, but it could be repaired. Three to four days might suffice, Anthony estimated when he spoke with press reporters later that evening.[2] Nonetheless, it was May 12 before the airplane was completely airworthy again and could be rolled out of the factory. That repair was possible at all after such a serious crash was evidence of the solidity of Fokker's construction methods. The real problem was the immaterial damage. Copilot Bennett suffered a punctured lung, a broken rib, right thighbone, and collarbone, and a skull fracture when pieces of the cracked propeller hit him. He was covered in cuts and bruises from the splintered glass of the cockpit windows. Radio technician George Noville, who had sat in the cabin with Byrd, had struggled out of the wrecked machine with minor internal injuries. Richard Byrd himself fared a little better: a bruise on his head and what looked like a broken wrist.

The crash brought a sudden end to the dream of being the first to cross the Atlantic and land in Paris. Fokker, Byrd, and the other crew members were taken to the Hackensack Hospital for recovery. Obviously, the competition would benefit from their mishap. Earlier that week pilots Bert Acosta and Clarence Chamberlin had already set a new flight endurance record in preparation of an Atlantic attempt. Young Charles Lindbergh also appeared to be ready to risk the big jump. Byrd's plan to leave for Europe early in May, when there would be a full moon, had fallen through in just seconds: after all, the *America* did not have a crew anymore.[3]

ᵷ

Anthony's nomination for the history books lay shattered. But apart from a painful neck, he himself had escaped without injury—again. That same evening he was able to go home to the house he rented in the village of Alpine since April. It was a mere half-hour drive along the Hudson River. There Violet, the woman he had married a month before, was waiting for him.

"The Hangar": In 1926 Anthony moved to the United States and became a permanent resident. Next to the apartment he had on Riverside Drive in Manhattan, he rented a country hideaway in Alpine-on-Hudson, New Jersey, at the edge of Palisades Park. This became his favorite place to relax. Alpine also had a marina where he could moor his Dutch yacht *Honey Moon*, which he shipped to the States. **AUTHOR'S COLLECTION**

The Canadian actress Violet Evelyn Austman was eight years younger than Anthony. The exuberant and spirited brunette, with her remarkable bright eyes, had been born as Helga Austman on March 4, 1898, in Winnipeg, where her father had moved after emigrating from Iceland. With her older sister Clara (Clair) and her younger sister Lillian, she grew up in a family that was dominated by her father, Snjól-fur Austman, a teacher of agriculture, and her three brothers, Johan (Joe), Ingvar (Emil), and Valtyr (Walter). Her Irish mother, Mary Elliott, had died at an early age.[4] Was it Mary who called her Violet, the name she came to prefer after her mother's death? The Canadian census of 1906 registered her under the name Violet. She was a musically gifted, lively, and beautiful girl. In 1910 she even won a beauty contest at Winnipeg beach.[5]

From an early age Violet knew exactly what she wanted. At the age of nineteen she married against her father's wishes and went to live with her husband in Montreal. The marriage was not a success and ended, at Violet's request, in divorce in February 1924.[6] She then followed her brother Walter to New York, where he was building a career for himself as an actor in comic plays. Violet turned out to be something of a talented actress as well, playing minor roles in theaters in New York and Philadelphia. The ambience of vaudeville theater, to which Anthony was also partial, had provided the setting in which they had met late in the spring of 1926. Up to then

Anthony had shared his house in America with Christine Döppler, a friend of Tetta's and head of the Amsterdam household, who had followed him to the United States.[7] Christine left when she found out that Anthony's attentions were wavering; she could not compete with the vivacious actress. Violet was bent on marrying Anthony, and she gave up her profession as actress for it. Was love also involved in her denying her age, and pretending to be two years younger than she really was? She told Anthony she had been born in the year 1900.

On Monday, March 14, 1927, Anthony and Violet were married in a private civil ceremony in New York with only Violet's brother Walter and her sister Lillian present.[8] It was a beautiful, sunny spring day, warm enough for Anthony to take some pictures of Violet in her white dress outside their home in Alpine. The dress itself was a plain design, and its long sleeves were not particularly flattering. Just as on the occasion of his first marriage, Anthony had opposed any kind of frivolity. To appear at least a little chic, Violet had bought a wide coat with a light whitish fur collar. Before they drove to the Registrar's Office together to take care of the necessary formalities, Anthony set up his camera for some extra photos outside in the front yard of the house by his Cadillac. Violet posed willingly.[9] Although she believed that because of the divorces they had both gone through it would be "very difficult to muster up enough courage to go through the ceremony again . . . we are both very glad." From now on the art deco ring with the large, square cut diamond that Anthony gave her would sparkle on her finger. Violet was ecstatic: "Tony and I love each other and are as happy as we possibly can be," she wrote to his mother. Now it was up to her to make the marriage work. To divert her Tony and give him time to recover from the accident, she arranged a trip to Montreal with him the week after the crash so that he could meet the rest of her family.[10]

It was not easy for Violet to lure Anthony away from aviation. In Montreal he barely lasted two days with her sister Clair and her husband James Miller. On March 25 he was already back on his usual track, speaking before the first annual meeting of the American Society of Mechanical Engineers at the Statler Hotel in Buffalo, on the American side of Niagara Falls. Of Violet's plan to travel to Europe together on May 10 and meet Anthony's family in Holland, nothing at all came. His first priority was to see to it that *America* was repaired. This was also of vital importance for his public image. Hence the work went on day and night. The development of his American interests had been at the core of his activities ever since he had arrived in the United States in September 1925. His participation in the Ford Reliability Tour had been of considerable consequence. Finally, the demand for his airliners was on the rise.

ℱ

After a process of several years, the very thing for which Fokker had pleaded ever since his arrival in the United States had finally happened in 1925: the legal constellation of civil air transport was adapted. The Kelly Act had spurred a rapid development of air transportation. To cash in on it, Anthony and his American business partners had prepared the foundation of a production facility in Kansas City, Missouri, in the summer of 1925. It had been his intention right from the start of his American adventure to produce aircraft at a central location in the United States. The plan was to bring together a million dollars in local capital and set up a production facility in Kansas City.[11] This turned out to be a bridge too far. The capital inscription for the new Fokker Aircraft Corporation remained too low and it was therefore decided to move the company eastward and incorporate it in Delaware. There the Fokker Aircraft Corporation was formally founded on September 16, 1925. After that, the activities of the Netherlands Aircraft Manufacturing Company were scaled down. Fokker's other American venture, Atlantic Aircraft, became a subsidiary of the newly established Fokker Aircraft Corporation. The new company took on all of Atlantic's assets. The four business partners in Atlantic—Anthony Fokker, Frank Ford, George Davis, and Lorillard Spencer—were appointed as directors of the new company. From then on Fokker Aircraft coordinated all imports of aircraft, materials, and parts from Amsterdam.

At its foundation the working capital of Fokker Aircraft amounted to $1 million, but the company's aspirations were to increase this shareholding to $1.6 million. For this, new shares were to be issued. For himself, Anthony reserved the right to increase his personal interest in the new company to 33 percent in the next five years—and against a very profitable rate too. The net results of the company were estimated to be at least $500,000 annually, as soon as production reached the projected level of one thousand aircraft per year. These were enormous numbers. Nonetheless, production was to remain concentrated in the Teterboro area, while the company offices continued to be located at 110 East 42nd Street in New York.[12] With this expansion of capital, Fokker hoped to have strengthened his American factories enough to make a serious start at producing aircraft in the United States. With an order portfolio of more than seventy airliners, he was set to attain a dominant position in American commercial aviation.[13]

That same month of October 1925, the prototype of the new Fokker Universal airliner was rolled out. Specially designed to suit the emerging American air transport market, the single-engine Universal had a cabin that could seat four passengers. Bob Noorduyn, by now formally occupying a position as company director, signed off on a design that seemed a step backward from the aircraft Fokker was producing in Amsterdam. Although Noorduyn incorporated the customary fuselage construction of welded steel tubes covered with linen, the Universal had a completely open cockpit as was customary in the aircraft the U.S. Postal Service used. In this respect Noorduyn had heeded to the wishes of pilots that were consulted about the design. A more important deviation was, however, the use of a non-cantilever wing. To reduce the overall weight of the aircraft, Noorduyn had chosen a thinner wing profile, which meant that the wing had to be supported by steel girders connected to the lower tubes of the fuselage. Nonetheless, the Universal, which could also be equipped with floats, was well adapted to serve the American and Canadian markets. Between May 1926 and the end of production in April 1931 forty-five Universals were built at Teterboro. They were sold at $15,000 each.[14] The type was succeeded in March 1928 by the larger Super Universal, which became Fokker's best-selling commercial aircraft. About 217 were produced (including licensed production in several countries), eighty-one of them in the Teterboro factory.

Anthony predicted far more growth possibilities and maintained that many Americans would come to buy their own thousand-dollar plane in the foreseeable future.[15] To help keep track amid these stormy developments, he had hired a new personal secretary, Helen Kay Schunk, in November 1925. Their cooperation began with a chance encounter at the Book-Cadillac Hotel in Detroit. Hiring Helen was a decision that was based, in typical Fokker fashion, on the fact that she had curly blond hair *and* because she announced right from the start that he must not think that she was going to be present at 7 a.m. after Anthony had kept her busy dictating letters until the middle of the night. She found him fascinating, although working for him was exhaustive: "He keeps one always on the alert as, due to his disconnected method of thinking and expressing himself in English, one must learn to read his mind and anticipate his desires."[16] It took Helen months to convince her employer that he should pay her an appropriate salary for the services rendered. However, the long working hours he demanded of her were compensated by the informal way in which he treated her and by the general atmosphere of the Fokker entourage. In her recollection, work was "interspersed with playing the radio, inventing contraptions for the furnace, trying to train 'Bum,' the pet wire-haired fox terrier, in Dutch, German, French, and English; and by servings of hot chocolate and club sandwiches at all hours. Whenever I began to look exhausted, food was ordered, usually with the injunction: 'Now you must write me a memo that I have not starved you.'"[17]

Meanwhile, every room that Anthony entered soon changed into chaos, with all sorts of personal belongings lying around on the floor. He cultivated his eccentricity, and Helen had a busy time keeping up.[18]

On the way back from Detroit, Anthony made a special detour to fly over the Niagara Falls and shoot color film of the remarkable natural phenomenon from the aircraft's cabin. A passenger in his own plane, he preferred to leave the flying to pilots he contracted for various events. But if his public image could benefit from a personal demonstration, he would make an exception.[19] Just such an occasion arose in December 1925 when his public relations manager, Harry Bruno, persuaded him to take part in a return flight from New York to Havana, planned by airline pioneer Juan Trippe. Anthony was not easily persuaded. At that point his trimotor F.VII was a unique airplane of which there was no duplicate in the United States. He was anxious not to take risks with the machine. On the other hand, Trippe, managing director of Colonial Air Transport, possessed an elaborate network of influential friends and contacts in aviation, in finance, and in Washington politics that might just prove helpful to Fokker's business interests in the United States. And so Fokker gave in. Trippe's plans were big: he wanted to set up an air service to Cuba as a first staging point to build a network of services to various Latin American destinations, eventually operated by his legendary creation Pan American Airways.

The specially chartered Fokker trimotor left from New York on December 13. Also onboard was John Hambleton, a New York banker and millionaire friend of Trippe's. Hambleton's wife Peggy joined the party the next day after they had spent the night in Baltimore. Anthony did not fly the machine himself. Persistent sinus complaints made that he shunned the half-open cockpit, especially in the winter months. He took a seat in the heated cabin instead, entertaining his fellow passengers and instructing them in the use of the aircraft toilet, still a novelty onboard American airliners. At the controls of the machine were pilot George Pond and mechanic Ken Boedecker, who had also accompanied Fokker in the Ford Reliability Tour. Pond doubled as navigator so that the airplane would not need to take a third crew member, who would otherwise intrude on the privacy of the elite group of passengers in the cabin. This solution soon turned out to be impracticable. Already on the second day of the flight, Pond lost his way between Baltimore and Augusta in Georgia. He had to make an unscheduled landing in a cotton field and ask for directions which way to fly.

Meanwhile, Peg Hambleton was getting bored. After spending a full day enduring the tremendous roar of the engines and having to shout to be heard above the noise, while the scenery out the window consisted of endless forests and fields, she declared she had enough of the adventure when the airplane reached Tampa, Florida. From there the flight continued with only the five men. On Anthony's instruction the route to Miami took them via Fort Myers over the Everglades Park. Anthony sat glued to the window, watching to spot groups of alligators. Time and again he gestured to Pond to make a low overpass so that he could film the scenery below him.[20]

Once in Miami, John Hambleton, who did not share Anthony's fascination for aerial wildlife filming, decided he too had had enough and left. As the airplane then proceeded to Key West, the last of the Florida Keys, discord developed between Fokker and Boedecker. Since they had made no special preparations for the flight, it had been difficult all along to get enough aviation-grade high-octane fuel for the machine's Wright engines. The further they went, the more this had become a problem. But Anthony knew an answer to this: on his advice the airplane had already been refueled several times with a mixture of 50 percent regular car gasoline and 50 percent benzol. Although Boedecker had objected to this, the engines had thus far run well on this blend. But after landing at Key West Boedecker felt he had taken enough risks, and he said so. Without the correct fuel he declared the flight to Havana across the open sea too dangerous. Anthony was annoyed and accused Boedecker of cowardice. What kind of a mechanic was he, if he didn't even trust his own Wright engines? Boedecker held out, and when the plane finally took off from Key West for its final lap to Cuba, only Pond, Fokker, and Trippe were left onboard. Two hours and five minutes later they reached their destination without problems, landing at the Campo Colombia military base just outside Havana. There they received a full official welcome from the Cuban president, Gerardo Machado. Now that he had left the winter weather behind him, Anthony dared risk giving a personal flying display with the machine, while Trippe probed the issue of obtaining landing rights with Machado.

And so it was that Anthony Fokker, Juan Trippe, and George Pond spent Christmas in the luxurious Sevilla Biltmore Hotel in Havana. It was to be a luscious Christmas. With its Caribbean charm, its famous boulevard with its clubs, the casino, the sweet temptations of Cuban nightlife, and the Marianao beach, Havana was a popular destination for affluent Americans.[21] So far the trip had been successful. Juan Trippe returned with the coveted landing rights in his pocket. But on the way back after Christmas, fate struck. Between Key West and Miami one of the engines gave out, while the other two were beginning to splutter as a consequence of taking on bad fuel. Apparently something had gone wrong when the aircraft was refueled on the Key West golf course that had served as a makeshift airfield. Pond saw himself forced to make an emergency landing on what from the air looked like a more or less dried mud plain, some two hundred yards out of the shore at Key Largo. He should have known better: the soil of the Florida Keys mainly consists of coral. The moment the plane's tires hit the ground, the sharp coral reef ripped up the rubber, and the aircraft came to a stop.

Shaken up but otherwise unhurt, the three men climbed out of the aircraft and onto the reef. The shore was some distance away, but fortunately one of Key Largo's local inhabitants had witnessed the landing and rowed across to take them to dry land before they got all wet. Fokker and Trippe sent their rescuer off to get help, but the man did not return. Dusk set in. Like good Boy Scouts, the men built a fire on the railway track that connected Key West to the Florida mainland and thus managed to stop the next express train, on which they got a ride to Miami. From there Anthony sent Boedecker, Pond, and a team of extra hands back to Key Largo to exchange the aircraft's engines, replace the tires, and build an improvised plank runway. After these tasks had been completed, Pond took off in the F.VII and delivered it without further problems at the Fokker plant at Teterboro Airport for further repairs and a major overhaul.[22]

ℚ

By that time, Anthony was in Europe. In the late afternoon of December 28, 1925, he had sailed from New York on the White Star Liner *Majestic* destined to dock at Southampton. From there he traveled onward to Davos in Switzerland and then to the Hotel Kulm in St. Moritz for his winter holiday. Not before mid-March did he arrive in Holland—to return to his old irritations on the government's policy of ordering military aircraft abroad. In an interview he left no doubt about it that, in view of these developments, America was now his first priority.[23]

In the private sphere things were more nuanced, although he approved of Tetta's brother Ernst's selling the house in Amsterdam. It sold in September 1926 for about half the price Tetta had paid for it six years before.[24] Anthony was glad to be rid of the property. Since his divorce he had become a wanderer in the ways of love. In America he preferred the company of Violet Austman, but while in Europe he loved being seen with a variety of merry and playful women. In St. Moritz he exerted himself in attracting and keeping female attention.[25]

From time to time such escapades brought complications, such as when he left his flashy Lancia Lambda sports car, with its leather winter cover and nickel searchlight, parked for four days in the Dutch coastal resort of Bloemendaal. An anonymous person placed ads in the local papers calling on anyone who had seen Fokker's car there to come forward and get in touch with him at the Schouten & Voskuil bookstore in Amsterdam, a locale that was used more often as a discrete liaison for ladies and gentlemen who wished to conduct their private affairs anonymously.[26]

Meanwhile, Anthony tried to draw the line under his German past. In September 1925 he did not object when his longtime director Wilhelm Horter, in charge of the factory in Amsterdam, announced he wanted to leave since he could no longer endorse company policy. Next, the Schwerin Industrial Works were also liquidated. The various lawsuits against Fokker in the German courts appeared to be petering out as a result of his vast financial reserves, which enabled him to have his lawyers stall proceedings time and again. There was no need any more to keep SIW as a buffer. A year and a half earlier he and the Union Bank in Amsterdam had again employed the services of his old-time partner Hans Haller to set the wheels in motion for liquidation in Schwerin. Anthony's former brother-in-law Hans Georg von Morgen, still nominally SIW's company director, who had remained in Schwerin with his wife, was forced to witness this turn of events.[27] The local authorities were most disappointed. In May 1925, Mayor Weltzien had called on Haller to discuss remaining options for the company. His question was whether Fokker might not be persuaded to a reconsider and keep SIW going and perhaps even revive aircraft construction there. After all, the allied restrictions on German aeronautics that had been imposed under the Versailles Treaty had recently been lifted. Haller had to disappoint him. Fokker was so engrossed in his American plans that he had no interest in reviving his German factory. Then again, the question was whether Schwerin could be made to prosper in the first place.[28] The same applied to Fokker's naval branch in Veere, in the southwest of Holland. With the decision taken to transfer his core business to the United States, and with the production of fighters for the Soviet Union and the secret German air force nearing its end, Fokker had no longer any use for the old navy yard. He indicated his intention to close the Veere plant in June 1926. The buildings, stores, machines, and equipment were to be sold off.[29]

In Amsterdam Fokker also tried to effect a change of course. He had to, because orders were decreasing while the factory and labor costs were rising because of the extra work that was involved in the development of new F.VII variants.[30] The relatively high costs of producing aircraft in Holland also came into this. Costs were incurred in Dutch guilders, whereas Fokker had to compete against producers from what were then called "currency countries" such as France and Italy, which were in a better position to compete internationally, because of the lower exchange rate. An order from Greece was lost because of this.[31] Fokker's new deputy director in Amsterdam, the former chief engineer of the Dutch Army Air Corps, Bruno Stephan, therefore received more leeway to run the company than his predecessor Horter. Stephan was even allowed to expand the factory's technical staff with some trained engineers. This move was at the expense of Reinhold Platz, who was brought over from Veere to Amsterdam and of whom Stephan held a distinctly low opinion: "He did not even bother to learn the language of the country he worked in, hardly ever read, nor studied that what even he could still have grasped, despite his limited education, and his knowledge therefore depended on what he had taught himself, which showed to be insufficient in the long run."[32]

⚘

On April 9, 1926, everything was ready for the official public presentation of the three-engine F.VII at Amsterdam's Schiphol Airport. This was the third machine of the trimotor type to be finished; the first two machines had been shipped to the United States. Despite the hard, chilly wind, a considerable number of spectators had assembled that afternoon, since Fokker had promised to stage a number of free passenger flights with the new airplane. Invited guests and other visitors grouped in and around the party tent that had been set up for the occasion to try and obtain a ticket for one of the flights. Anthony personally saw to it that orderly groups of ten people were formed. Toward 5 p.m. it was time to take the invited guests back to Amsterdam. Several buses were waiting for them, but none of them had a driver present. Fokker drove around the airfield in his Lancia Lambda to gather them personally and get them back to their buses, even holding the doors of his car open for them. Local reporters commented with admiration on such millionaire chivalry, but *Haarlems Dagblad* was puzzled: "Facetious was his correct, self-possessed attitude toward the overexcited behavior of some ladies, who claimed to be extremely interested in modern flight, acted extremely charming, entered the aircraft's cabin extremely thrilled [and] enthusiastically frolicked back to the hangar from the plane."[33]

It was a festive occasion. Acting the true ladies' man, Anthony had his photograph taken, smiling flirtatiously and posing arm in arm with two women, as if they were about to dance. His mother kept a copy. The day after, the three-engine F.VII was turned over to the British Royal Air Force as a transport plane. Avro subsequently built a series under license. Meanwhile, Anthony began to make final preparations to move permanently to the United States. Ten days later he boarded the liner SS *Leviathan* in Southampton and sailed for New York, where his three-engine airplane was about to make history.

During his stay in Detroit in November 1925, William Mayo, Ford's chief engineer and factory manager, had approached Anthony. Mayo was also chairman of the Detroit Aviation Society and was as such in conversation with the Australian airman, ornithologist, and polar explorer Hubert Wilkins. Supported by the American Geological Society and the North American Newspaper Alliance, Wilkins had managed to raise $150,000 to make a flight from Point Barrow in Alaska across the North Pole to the island of Spitsbergen. The idea was to use the 1,900-mile flight to better map the landmass around the polar region. For this, Wilkins wanted to buy a secondhand single-engine F.VIIA from an American owner. The plan brought him and Fokker together. The two men soon discovered they liked each other, and a sense of friendship grew. In the course of their conversations, the option to buy a three-engine F.VII was also discussed. With its larger wing and extra power, the three-engine machine would offer the possibility of taking more supplies. A three-engine machine was obviously more costly, but Anthony had indicated that Wilkins need not worry about this: if the funds from Detroit proved insufficient, he would personally foot the bill for the three-engine machine. Hearing this, Wilkins's enthusiasm increased.[34] The promise meant that he could now count on two aircraft for his endeavor. Subsequently, the airplanes were prepared at the Teterboro factory at Anthony's personal expense. In January 1926 they were both ready. Wilkins was pleased to accept them. By the end of the month he was all set to ship the planes from Seattle to Seward, Alaska, and have them reassembled in Fairbanks. This took until March 11, when both machines were ready for flight testing. The occasion was celebrated by an official christening of the aircraft, a ceremony conducted by two women. They named the single-engine machine *Alaskan* and the three-engine ship *Detroiter*.

That afternoon, mishap struck. The *Detroiter* ran into a snowbank and got stuck even before it had made a single flight. To make things worse, a reporter was hit by a propeller and died on the scene.[35] Further problems followed. It transpired that Wilkins and his team did not have sufficient experience to fly the large Fokker aircraft from the improvised airstrips made of snow and ice. On two consecutive days both machines were damaged upon landing. Repairs would take time.[36]

Meanwhile, the Wilkins expedition had received competition. Flying across the North Pole was taking on the shape of a real challenge in aeronautics. The Norwegian explorer Roald Amundsen was planning to beat Wilkins by steering his airship *Norge* across the pole first. More competitors were on the way. Fokker knew all about them. On February 13, 1926, he had been approached by the American naval commander Richard Byrd, who was backed by Edsel Ford and a group of wealthy individuals, including John Rockefeller Jr. and Rodman Wanamaker. Byrd had made a flight across Greenland the year before and now wanted to try his hand on the North Pole. To do so, Byrd wished to buy the F.VIIA-3m demonstration machine that Anthony had used in the Ford Reliability Tour. Initially he had planned to fly the North Pole in an airship, but the progress of Wilkins's Detroit Arctic Expedition and Amundsen's

To the North Pole: In February 1926 Navy commander and adventurer Richard Byrd asked Fokker to sell him the three-engine F.VII prototype that had participated in the Ford Reliability Tour. Byrd wanted to use the plane as the first to overfly the North Pole. Fokker agreed, convinced that this attempt would generate publicity for his aircraft. **OHIO STATE UNIVERSITY ARCHIVES, PAPERS OF ADMIRAL RICHARD E. BYRD**

preparations had put severe pressure on his plans to be the first to fly the pole. Now he was in a hurry to acquire an airplane suitable for such a venture. Anthony was not keen to part with his demonstration machine. After all, he also had delivered a plane to the Wilkins expedition, and the F.VIIA-3m was his calling card for the emerging airline companies in the United States. The Army Air Service had also proclaimed its interest. On the other hand, Byrd's endeavor enjoyed the support of high-ranking people, including federal authorities, extending all the way to President Calvin Coolidge himself. If Byrd were to be successful, it would again generate a lot of free publicity for Fokker. Against this background Anthony finally agreed to sell the three-engine airplane to Byrd for $40,000. It was a stiff price, considerably more than a new F.VIIA-3m cost in Europe, but Fokker had a strong bargaining position: comparable aircraft simply did not exist, certainly not on short notice. Yet price was not the only issue at stake in the sale. Fokker's second condition was that the name Fokker appear on the aircraft in large, clearly visible letters. At first Byrd frowned on this demand, since he had promised his chief benefactor Edsel Ford to name the machine after his three-year-old daughter Josephine. But pressed for time, the competitive Byrd had little alternative but to give in if he wanted to be the first to fly the pole. He asked Ford to put up the money.

After a short but intense period of preparations, Byrd and his pilot Floyd Bennett took off in the *Josephine Ford* from Spitsbergen on May 9, 1926, to return to the United States as "the first to overfly the pole." Although one of the airplane's three engines had shown repeated problems, Byrd claimed to have navigated the geographical North Pole and had thrown out an American flag there to mark the occasion. Anthony was more than pleased with the success of Byrd's flight.[37] Upon their return to New York on June 23, 1926, Byrd and his men were treated as real American heroes and even received the traditional ticker-tape parade in Manhattan. It was to be several decades before their claim was called into question and eventually declared invalid.[38] Later that same afternoon Byrd was flown to Washington for an official reception in the Washington Auditorium, with various authorities and diplomats. In the company of Coolidge, government ministers, and congressmen, Anthony reveled as one of the guests of honor to celebrate Byrd's apparent achievement.[39] Four days later tens of thousands of New Yorkers assembled at Miller Field, Staten Island, to catch a glimpse of the wondrous Fokker plane.

ᘐ

The wave of publicity generated by Byrd's flight worked to the advantage of Fokker's American interests. For the past year now he had been pondering whether to apply for American citizenship. On June 17, 1926, he filed his application from the Waldorf Astoria Hotel in New York.[40] Anthony had become convinced that his future lay in the United States. Publicity generated by the various flights with his aircraft served him just fine and would support his application. When Richard Byrd approached Fokker toward the end of the year to sell him an improved three-engine machine with which he might attempt to fly the Atlantic to Paris, Anthony was easily persuaded. It was a marked contrast to the reception Charles Lindbergh received when he knocked on the door of Fokker's representative in St. Louis, Roy Russell. Russell hardly gave Lindbergh serious consideration and let him know forthwith that he was not supportive of Lindbergh's plans. Lindbergh later remembered that Russell had mentioned the exorbitant amount of no less than $90,000 for a three-engine Fokker plane—well beyond the means of the small group of supporters on which Lindbergh could count.[41]

Such financial limitations hardly played a role for Byrd. He could rely on deep pockets. In July 1926, Byrd's *Josephine Ford* had been on display at Rodman Wanamaker's prestigious department stores in New York and Philadelphia. Wanamaker also supported Byrd's bid for the Orteig Prize for the first pilot and machine to cross the Atlantic between New York and Paris nonstop. To finance Byrd's endeavor, Wanamaker had founded an American Trans Oceanic Company. Yet Byrd was careful not to raise expectations too high. On his instructions, the company actually gave out a press statement on March 28 that a new Fokker plane had been ordered for the intended flight—not to win the Orteig Prize, but "to help the progress of aviation" by proving that flights across the Atlantic had now become technically and practically possible.[42] These latter pieces of information caused Anthony considerable anxiety: what if one of the other contenders beat Byrd to it and reached Paris first? Yet Byrd was not easily unnerved and maintained that his prime interest in the undertaking lay in proving that the technology was now in place to set up real air services across the Atlantic with large passenger-carrying aircraft. To demonstrate his point, *America* would be the only plane in the race to carry an official bag of airmail.

Although *America* could be repaired after the accident of April 16, the difference in perspective between its constructor and its commander caused considerable animosity between Fokker and Byrd. Immediately after the crash, Byrd gave out a press statement that the flight would now be postponed indefinitely. Such messages were not at all to Fokker's liking. He wanted *his* plane to be the first to arrive in Paris. Yet Byrd, worried about the likely financial consequences of another mishap, took much more time for his preparations than Fokker deemed necessary.[43] His sponsor Wanamaker also fretted about the public image of the venture and repeatedly called for restraint.[44] Only on May 14 was Byrd ready to risk a second test flight with *America*. The day before, the plane had been flown from Teterboro to the Long Island airfield from which other contenders would also take off. Wanamaker had actually rented part of the airfield for Byrd's endeavor, Roosevelt Field. Of the three remaining contestants, the Byrd team was undoubtedly best prepared: two hangars, beautifully whitewashed inside, equipped with a field kitchen, an officers' mess, a radio station, and all possible technical materials needed to prepare the plane. The hangars even had sleeping quarters and an office with telephone extensions for Byrd and for Wanamaker's representative Grover Whalen.[45] All that was now needed was a spell of fair

All tuned up: On April 16, 1927, the favored contender in the race to fly nonstop from New York to Paris, Fokker's C.2 *America*, somersaulted, landing after a test flight. Its crew members, including commander Richard Byrd, were injured. As a result, Charles Lindbergh—not Byrd and Fokker—would write history. Exactly a month after Lindbergh's epic flight, Byrd delivered a press conference in front of his repaired *America*, but he did not take off. Byrd's reluctance to fly exasperated Fokker. **COLLECTION BLÜM, SANTPOORT, THE NETHERLANDS**

weather and a new pilot to replace the injured Floyd Bennett. For this Byrd selected
Bert Acosta, a well-known pilot who had broken the world's endurance record just
a few weeks before. Fokker did not agree. He insisted that Byrd should take his own,
Norwegian test pilot, Bernt Balchen, with them as well. Byrd and Wanamaker hesi-
tated. They preferred an all-American crew for publicity reasons. But after a further
test flight with Acosta and Balchen, which brought to light that Acosta had no significant experience in instrument flying, Anthony was adamant that Byrd should take his
chosen pilot on the flight no matter what. He ordered Balchen to take out citizenship
papers forthwith to resolve the nationality issue. It appeared that only concern over
the weather remained. That very spring America went through the wettest period in
its written history, as storm fronts followed each other in rapid succession.[46]

For Anthony Fokker, wind and rain were no reason not to fly. On May 17 he
personally proved his point. While Byrd postponed the next test flight with *America*
because of adverse conditions, Anthony and his friend William Vanderbilt took off
for a flight over Long Island Sound in Vanderbilt's Fokker Air Yacht.[47] To increase
the pressure on Byrd and his crew, Anthony took up residence in the Garden City
Hotel near Roosevelt Field, where Byrd and the other aviators also lodged. He now
claimed supervision of the technical preparations for the flight. His action put the
matter on edge. Byrd was not happy at all with this turn of events. His influence
appeared to be reduced to determining which emergency food supplies were to
be taken onboard. Letters started to arrive accusing him of having no intention at all
of flying the Atlantic.[48] On May 19 the papers reported that everything was in readiness for the big takeoff now that Fokker's latest contraption, a fifteen-foot slope that
would give *America* just a little extra push upon acceleration, was finished.[49] At a press
conference filmed by Fox Movietone News, Anthony announced that he expected
scheduled services across the Atlantic to become a reality within ten years.

Everything appeared to be under control. To make sure they were still ahead in
the race, Anthony inspected Lindbergh's plane and spoke briefly with its young pilot.
America made two more short test flights that day. This brought a minor problem to
light with the center engine of the plane. That night the Wright Whirlwind engine
was exchanged for a replacement under mounting time pressure. After all, some 3,500
people had been invited the next day, Friday, May 20, to witness the official christen-
ing of the *America* by Rodman Wanamaker's two daughters.[50] To make sure that all
was now in order and that the new engine performed flawlessly, Bert Acosta made a
short test flight with *America* in the early hours of the morning. Nonetheless, the Fokker team was about to lose the race. Just as *America* landed, young Charles Lindbergh
was ready to push the throttle forward for his daring takeoff. Shortly before 8 a.m. he
started his single-engine Ryan plane *Spirit of St. Louis* for the solo adventure that would
earn him a lasting place in the history books as the first pilot to make it nonstop across
the Atlantic to Paris. From the cockpit of *America*, Acosta watched him leave, while

Byrd stood under the wing. Fokker was also present. Behind the wheel of his Lancia Lambda, laden with fire extinguishers in case there was a crash, he raced the little Ryan to the end of the runway and saw Lindbergh lifting his plane off the ground with difficulty to disappear into the mist.[51] He struggled to hide his disappointment: "I am not predicting that he will not reach the other side. On the contrary, I imagine he will land somewhere on the European mainland, but his equipment for navigating is not so complete as it might be. It was an extremely dangerous takeoff. If Lindbergh's plane had carried fifty pounds more, it would never have left the ground."[52]

With that statement, Anthony left Roosevelt Field to spend the day in solitude on his yacht in the Long Island Sound. He did not return to see *America* christened with water from the Delaware River later that Friday. The flood of news about Lindbergh's success that followed the exploits of the daring young pilot in the days that followed truly ruined his mood. Not before June 17 did he reappear at Roosevelt Field, in the company of Violet, to see how things were going. He only stayed briefly and left without speaking to anyone.[53] To him it was an enigma what was keeping Byrd, although still suffering the consequences of his broken wrist, on the ground. Byrd's hesitation—in Fokker's words "something more than ridiculous"—would remain one of the mysteries of the aeronautical year 1927. Anthony's irritation about this led to a heated row between him and Byrd in the hangar of *America* in which Anthony even threatened to buy back the plane and go himself: "If you don't get going I will buy the ship back and get going myself! . . . I'm sick and tired of it. It is a damned shame!"[54] In his autobiography he noted, "Three times we pushed the completely equipped *America* to the top of the fifteen foot hill—with wooden wheel tracks and greased skid slide—which I had devised. . . . I sent word each time to the Garden City Hotel that all was in readiness but the flyers failed to show up. . . . Fed up, I went aboard my yacht in the Sound."[55]

On June 29, 1927, Byrd finally declared that he was ready to depart. The day before Floyd Bennett, still recovering from his injuries, had visited Roosevelt Field, but he was obviously in no state to fly. It left Byrd with no option but to give in to Fokker and take Bernt Balchen as a replacement crew member. Shortly before 5:30 a.m., the heavily loaded *America* made the risky takeoff. Byrd acted as navigator and overall commander of the flight. Rain was pouring down on Roosevelt Field when the machine started, but weather predictions over the ocean were fair. At the very last minute, Anthony had more or less given his blessing to the flight, encouraged, perhaps, by the fact that Byrd had ordered two new aircraft from Fokker for his next adventure: a flight to the South Pole. In the evening of June 23 they had drawn up a sales contract in the Garden City Hotel.[56] Anthony had himself photographed, with the crew and an uncomfortable-looking Byrd, in front of *America*. The mailbag that was brought onboard contained an envelope with Fokker's calling card, on which he had scribbled "greetings via Atlantic-Air Mail." It was addressed to the Dutch newspaper *Handelsblad* in Amsterdam.[57]

After a flight full of incidents and mishaps, *America* was reported over Cherbourg on the coast of France around 7:45 the next evening. Expectations were that the plane would reach Paris around 10:30 p.m. At Le Bourget Airport everything was readied to receive them. The airport's big searchlights were switched on and the police secured the landing area. In spite of the rain, Parisian spectators amassed to witness *America's* arrival. Toward 11 the rain intensified and the clouds lowered. French airport officials fired flares, hoping to attract the flyers' attention. But a malfunctioning compass and a defective radio made that the crew of *America* was unable to locate Le Bourget. Bernt Balchen saw no other option but to make back for the French shoreline, hoping to discover a break in the clouds there.

Chased by bad luck, the four flyers watched the fuel gauges of *America* run low. At 3:30 in the morning of June 30, at the end of a deadly tiring flight, Balchen resolved to put the aircraft down in the sea some two hundred yards from the shoreline near the lighthouse of Ver-sur-Mer on the Normandy coast. A landing in the shallows was perceived to be less risky than to put *America* down on the beach itself, where several fishing boats had been hauled out of the water. This way the lighthouse crew would at least notice them. The plane landed in the water, and the four men were soaked. Byrd made an effort to remove the mailbag from the cabin and take it with him, only to find later that the seawater had made most of the envelopes illegible and that the stamps had washed off.[58]

The question was why the plane had to come that far, but a reconstruction of the flight turned out to be impossible. In the panic that followed the wet landing in the dark, Byrd had forgotten to secure the aeronautical maps and his navigational notes. They were carried off by the seawater. Putting together a proper documented report on the flight thus became impossible.[59] It also meant that the scientific mission that Byrd had set out to accomplish with the flight had failed completely. To make things worse, souvenir hunters dismantled the aircraft within days, as soon as the tide receded.

To Anthony all this was beyond terrible. Such elaborate preparations, such pretentions, such costs, and then no result whatsoever. Besides, newspapers the world over now carried photographs of his plane, wrecked in the surf. The personal animosity between him and Byrd could thereafter only increase. And although Byrd and his crew were honored with a second ticker-tape parade on New York's Broadway upon their return to the United States, his credit with Fokker had evaporated. Byrd had to go to great lengths to get the money to pay for the three-engine F.VIIB and the smaller Universal, needed for his envisioned Arctic expedition, that he had ordered from Fokker in the days before the Atlantic flight. Grumpy and disillusioned, Anthony did not even bother to reply to Byrd's letters and largely let events take their course without him.[60] On Fokker's specific instructions the shipment of Byrd's F.VIIB from Amsterdam was even postponed until full payment for the plane had been received—a thing that, in turn, ticked Byrd off.[61] In Anthony's eyes Byrd's indecisiveness had cost him his rightful place in the annals of aviation history. This was one thing he could not forgive, and it bothered him greatly over the years. In the autobiography that Fokker published in 1931, he elaborated on his low esteem for the American naval commander. His ghostwriter, aviation journalist Bruce Gould, who had previously had a run-in or two with Byrd himself, was glad to help him put his view in print.[62] Byrd seemed unperturbed, but his friends in the press and in Washington were upset to see their hero dismissed as incompetent. It was a development that would have far-reaching consequences.

17

"You're always sleepy! Why don't you talk to me once in a while?"[1] The words that Violet shouted after him were to echo in his head for years to come. But there was no stopping Anthony, even for his wife. As if he hadn't registered her cry, he went into the bedroom of the luxury apartment they rented for $375 per month on the fifteenth floor of 285 Riverside Drive in New York. Exhausted, he fell on the bed and was immediately fast asleep. Such behavior was not uncommon for Anthony when he was tired or was brooding on something. Violet would just have to wait for a bit.

It was clear to Violet that Anthony's behavior had not changed, even though she had been away in a psychiatric clinic for a month and a half. Now she followed him into the bedroom, urging him to at least eat something. She and the cook had especially prepared a nice meal to celebrate her homecoming. Alternatively, they might go out and have dinner together somewhere. But when Anthony was in such a mood, there was no reasoning with him. He was tired and wanted to sleep—and that was the end of it.

Violet had the meal brought to the bedroom, but to no avail. Finally she gave up and decided that she might as well go to bed herself. She asked the maid to fetch a glass of water while she put on her nightgown. The clock ticked half past seven. Outside it was dark. The low clouds overhead held a promise of snow. In her slippers, she stood in the cold of the opened window, watching Anthony as he lay stretched out on his bed. She shivered as a sense of desperate, utter loneliness descended upon her. The despondency that had been robbing her of life's pleasures for months pounded in her head. Was it her fate to go on living like this forever? Would life with Anthony remain a continual, endless waiting for fleeting moments of his attention and love? No, things would not change. Her depression pressed harder on her than ever. Violet felt at her wits' end. The open window seemed to beckon with a promise of release.... Seconds later, Patrolman Edward Davis discovered her body with a fractured skull on the pavement of 101st Street, fifteen stories below.[2]

Meanwhile, upstairs in the apartment, panic had broken out. The maid, returning with the glass of water, immediately sensed that something was amiss. The window was pushed open, and madame had disappeared! She shook Anthony awake. Sounds from the street below drifted up, punctuated by Davis's alarm whistle. The horrible reality of the drama began to unfold. A glance down from the window confirmed anxious suspicions. The telephone rang. It was the house porter calling. A few minutes later Davis and one of his colleagues stood in the hallway of the apartment between the antique German and Dutch furniture and paintings, ill at ease and hats in hand. Their faces were taut. They found Anthony distraught, shaking, and barely coherent, hardly able to answer their questions.[3] While the assistant medical examiner, Charles Sassoon, went about his sad business on the street down below and recorded Violet as deceased, a doctor had to be called to attend to Anthony. What had just happened hit him with tremendous force. He spent most of the next two days in his bed, prostrate and utterly disconsolate.[4]

ᛜ

Earlier that fateful Friday, February 8, 1929, Violet had been dismissed from Presbyterian Hospital in Upper East Side Manhattan, one of the best and most prestigious hospitals in the United States, where she had spent weeks in psychiatric treatment. In December she had herself admitted there because of "a nervous ailment."[5] "Nervous ailment" was a euphemism used in the papers to describe what was then known in the American medical profession as neurasthenia, "a profound physical and mental exhaustion."[6] For months Violet had been suffering from a severe depression that had come with chronic fatigue, nervousness, irritability, emotional instability, headaches and sleeplessness.[7] Her depression had become an obstacle in their relationship. Anthony, extremely egocentric even when on his best behavior, had been unable to cope with the somber listlessness that Violet had shown lately. When her condition worsened after their return from a highly publicized visit to the Chicago Expo on November 30, 1928, Violet had sought help from specialists at the Presbyterian. The standard treatment for neurasthenia in those days was hospitalization and several weeks of complete bed rest, psychiatric treatment, and sometimes electrotherapy. Often treatment was coupled with an abundance of food, the doctrine being that an increase in bodily weight might have a beneficial effect on the patient's general condition.

When Violet was released from the hospital that afternoon, Anthony had not been there to pick her up. Instead he had sent his driver. Arriving home, Violet found that Anthony was not there either. The domestic staff, on the other hand, had been expecting her. Violet was glad to be back, although it was a disappointment to her that Anthony was not present to welcome her. Nobody seemed to know for certain where he was. There was not much else that Violet could do but wait. In the fading light of the February afternoon the otherwise beautiful view of Riverside Park soon worked on her nerves. To have at least something to occupy herself with, she set about preparing a reunion dinner together with their cook. After all, Anthony was always partial to a nice meal. In the early evening the dinner was ready, but Violet and the maid waited in vain for Anthony's arrival. Obviously—characteristically—he had forgotten all about her release from the hospital that afternoon. A telephone call to the factory in Teterboro revealed that he was out on a test flight with the new F.10A trimotor, which was proving tail-heavy. When he finally appeared around seven, an hour and a half after sunset, he had been completely engrossed in his thoughts and did not even acknowledge her presence.

ℊ

That weekend the task of making preparations for Violet's funeral came to rest on the shoulders of Fokker's new company secretary, Herbert Reed. Violet's body was laid out at the Frank E. Campbell Funeral Church on Wall Street, from which other rich and famous people had also begun their final journey. Reed saw to it that the tone in the reporting on the drama became milder. "Suicide" was soon changed into "vertigo victim." Reed was also to thank for that the story disappeared from the newspapers within days, although one carried a photograph of the unhappy couple, along with a diagram of Violet's fall, on February 11.[8] All the same, Campbell was able to proceed in discretion with the funeral procession the Monday following the drama. Violet was laid to rest in the eastern annex of the Brookside Cemetery in Englewood, New Jersey, along the road that connected Fokker's country house in Alpine and the Teterboro Airport.

For Anthony, dealing with what had happened proved traumatic. He had his niece Annie Cottrau-Fokker, a Dutch sculptor, make a surprisingly delicate and diffident memorial to put on Violet's grave: a two-foot-high white marble statue of a young woman huddled against a black granite rock. Knowing that he had failed to provide Violet with a place to seek refuge from the rigors of life, this was his ultimate way to express his sorrow and remorse. Beyond death he tried to show that he had, after all, understood her needs. He saw to it that her gravestone was inscribed "Violet Fokker," the name she had so dearly wished to be called by. And he had the birth year of her wishes engraved: 1900, instead of 1898. This way Violet would remain forever young. His boat, the *Honey Moon*, to which he was so attached that he had had the yacht transported from Holland to the United States, now served as a place of refuge to which he withdrew to mourn her passing. He rechristened it *Helga* in her honor, commemorating her with her official birth name, one of the intimate secrets they had cherished. Between the curtains and the tablecloths that Violet had made herself for the boat, he could sense her near him.[9] For Violet's family, which he knew from visits and joint

The "happy couple": On March 14, 1927, Anthony married again, this time with Canadian actress Violet Austman—an alliance that would end in tragedy. Here the Fokkers pose in their flashy Packard convertible in front of two F.10 airliners outside the factory at Teterboro, New Jersey. **COLLECTION SMEULERS, BRONKHORST, THE NETHERLANDS**

outings, he also tried to make some amends that might soothe their loss. He took in her sister Lillian, five years Violet's junior, who had divorced from her husband and was without a source of income of her own, to live on Riverside Drive.[10]

Violet's death would haunt him the rest of his life. On every visit to his Teterboro factory and every drive into New York City, Anthony passed the cemetery, where Violet's grave atop a small hill could be seen from the road. Often he would think back of their time together. Only in the Dutch edition of his 1931 autobiography *Flying Dutchman*, he commented, "I have always understood airplanes much better than women. I have had more love affairs in my life, and they ended just like the first one, really, because I thought there could be nothing that was more important than my airplanes. I have always buried myself too deep in my own interests to be able to satisfy the women with whom I was in love. I think too egocentrically. I do not express my feelings, on the naïve assumption that their existence must be understood by intuition. Experience showed me this is false. I have now learned, by bitter experience, that one must give a little too; in love one has to use one's brain just as much as in business, and maybe even more."[11]

The drama made him suspicious toward women. Although he spent a passionate night with a woman named Juanita Percy at the Savoy Hotel in London later that year on October 23, he carefully guarded his distance afterward. Perhaps Juanita, a private teacher of English, tried to get too close too soon and made advances that scared him. She did manage to arrange a second rendezvous, in February 1930, as a sequel to his annual winter holiday. They enjoyed the magic while it lasted. Juanita wrote, "In Rapallo—our return drive!!—all the moments spent with you were the biggest joy of my life. . . . Always I long for your sweet gentle caresses."

Something triggered his suspicion in the wording of the letters she sent to his address in Alpine, to his office in New York, to his mother in Haarlem. It made him keep her at arm's length. In love, Juanita struggled with such rebuff: "Silence does not kill my faith—remembering your words 'you rarely write.'"[12] She must have been heartbroken to receive no answer, even though she included a stamped self-addressed envelope for the letter that never came.

⚐

Anthony never was a writer. Nonetheless, by necessity he spent more and more of his time behind a desk. With the surge of his American interests, it could hardly be avoided. The orders for his three-engine aircraft came in faster than the small Atlantic factory could build them. The Fokker concept for three engine commercial aircraft would dominate international aeronautical construction well into the 1930s. In 1928 the Dutch three-engine F.VIIB formed the starting point for the development of the American F.10. This latter model combined a newly designed fuselage and tail section with a Dutch-built F.VIIB wing. Sixty-four of these aircraft were produced, most of them of the further improved F.10A type, which had a greater wing span and a wing produced in the United States.

This design evolution was typical of Fokker's treatment of the aeronautical design process. Just as was the case in Amsterdam, where the costs for research and development had actually been decreasing since 1924, his American enterprise worked with amazingly low budgets.[13] To keep tabs on overhead, Fokker ran his factories with only a small research staff. "Designing" was more geared to modifying and adapting existing models than to the development of completely new aircraft types. This setup enabled Anthony to safeguard his position as director of technology and maintain his ultimate responsibility for new designs that bore his name. As long as the Amsterdam factory managed to keep research and development going on a shoestring, Fokker could afford to focus his efforts in America on building profitable spinoffs of these Dutch aircraft. In Amsterdam and in Teterboro he instructed his technicians to improvise on the basis of designs that had already been proven—precisely the kind of approach he preferred and in which he excelled. In the short term this proved to be very lucrative.

Meanwhile, Anthony's successes had made him into a media personality. He was always willing to address the press in his characteristic mixture of English and Dutch. The high profit margin of the Atlantic Aircraft Corporation attracted attention anyhow. In 1927 the company still worked with the same million dollars with which it had begun, although the Teterboro facility was augmented with a second production unit in nearby Passaic, five miles away.

On Wall Street aviation shares were rising fast, and Fokker, although not officially listed, was no exception. The reputation of his aircraft was pushed up by the publicity surrounding Richard Byrd's transatlantic flight and that of pilots Lester Maitland and Albert Hegenberger to Hawaii on June 28 and 29 of the same year. Thus propelled, Fokker was one of the first companies to attract new venture capital in this undercapitalized sector of the economy.[14] Anthony personally went out to raise new money. In September he entered into discussions with a group of investors from Wheeling, West Virginia, led by William Wilson and Ralph Kitchen, directors of local building firms. They were interested in financing the construction of a new factory. Anthony found it an interesting proposal. Fokker would be able to expand production without the necessity for major investment on the part of the existing shareholders. Wheeling thus presented a solution to Fokker's biggest problem in the aeronautical year 1927: an acute shortage of production capacity. Indeed, for an enterprise that in December 1927 still only employed 266 people, the gap between sales and production was getting bigger by the month.

On October 7, 1927, an agreement in principle was concluded with the Ohio Valley Industrial Corporation of Wheeling. It invested $1.1 million to establish a new holding company, of which Atlantic would become a part. Fokker was personally asked to participate for $163,000. Moreover, he agreed to take out a life insurance policy worth $500,000 in case something happened to him that might jeopardize the further development of the new company. The agreement would earn Wheeling a place in aircraft production.[15] Under considerable pressure to achieve additional production capacity in the short term, Fokker's associates Spencer, Ford, and Davis needed little time to accept the offer from Wheeling. By November 22 the matter was already in the bag. Anthony then traveled to San Francisco with Violet for a week to see whether it would be possible to set up a third factory there, using local resources. Two local entrepreneurs tried to sell him land near the ports between Oakland and Alameda on San Francisco Bay. Yet the financial side of things remained vague, and Fokker kept his distance.[16]

For the time being Fokker's production expansion would therefore be concentrated in Wheeling or, more precisely, in Glen Dale, one of the neighboring municipalities. As a result of the agreements a new company was formally incorporated in Delaware on December 3, 1927. The Fokker Aircraft Corporation of America found its principal investors in Wheeling, where it would also establish its main base of operations. On December 6, Atlantic Aircraft and the earlier Fokker Aircraft were incorporated as wholly owned subsidiaries of Fokker Aircraft Corporation of America through a share swap, yet they continued to exist as individual operating companies. Anthony retained a majority interest in the new corporation, although he owned a smaller percentage than he had done in Atlantic. Chairman of the supervisory board of the Fokker Aircraft Corporation of America became William Wilson, the chairman of Ohio Valley Industrial. Lorillard Spencer was appointed chief executive officer and Ralph Kitchen vice president. The company was established in Wheeling.[17] For $25,000 per year, Anthony had himself put on the payroll as a consulting engineer. In addition, he was to receive 20 percent of the profits to a maximum of $100,000. Although he put his signature to a noncompetition agreement covering the United States, he retained his freedom to engage in core activities outside the North American continent.[18] To compensate for the diminished share he would hold in the new company, the associates decided to drop the name Atlantic completely in favor of the brand name Fokker.

ᛣ

Satisfied that things were moving in the right direction, Anthony and Violet boarded the White Star liner *Majestic* on December 23, 1927, for a visit to the Netherlands. It was to be Violet's first trip to Holland, and Anthony wanted to introduce her to his mother and to the rest of the family. The ship, ornamented with Christmas decorations, was a well-deserved escape after a busy year. Just after midnight the *Majestic* sailed for Southampton from its pier at New York's West 18th Street.[19]

Shortly after New Year's Day the couple arrived in Holland. With his flashy blue Lancia Lambda, which he had picked up from his rented garage in Cherbourg, France, Anthony visited an old friend who had become a reporter for the *Haarlems Dagblad*. The exclusive interview on January 6 had been agreed beforehand by telephone, Anthony's preferred mode of communication. Beaming with pride, he told his old friend that he had been offered a factory for rent in Wheeling, because people in America really believed in the future of aviation: "Enterprising, isn't it? People are like this in other American cities as well. They ought to do similar things in Holland too. But if I were to tell you just how long I had to negotiate with the city authorities in Rotterdam on the lease of a piece of land there."[20]

A few days in Holland, and Anthony was back to his old complaints over the lack of cooperation and aircraft orders from the government: "In the same length of time I can achieve tenfold in America. And that is why I am in America."[21] With his old friend he drove to his factory near Amsterdam, where Anthony beamed with pride when he was recognized by the gatekeeper, although it had nearly been two years since his previous visit. The 350 employees also appeared happy to see him again. He observed their activities with interest and compared their work with the way things were done in the United States. Surprisingly, he advocated less attention to detail in construction: "No plane will last for fifty years. Why then focus on applying such precision in all nooks and crevices? In America they'd say: it costs too much money, it takes too long, it's not necessary. As long as reliability and true quality of the aircraft are good."[22]

Meanwhile, Anthony and Violet had a busy program. Their to-do list first took them to see some of the main Dutch tourist highlights. Next they visited London by plane. In between Anthony had several public appearances. He reveled in showing Violet how popular he was. Thus he set aside the morning after their return from London, January 18, to be decorated by the Dutch Society East and West in The Hague. The society strove to strengthen the bonds with the Dutch overseas territories and wanted to honor him for the role he had played in organizing the first flights to the Dutch East Indies.[23]

After the society's banquet, they left for Rotterdam. There Anthony spoke at a meeting of the Royal Rowing and Sailboat Society "De Maas" that evening.[24] The next evening another decoration was scheduled, this time by the Haarlem Chamber of Commerce, which had been waiting since September 1926 for an opportunity to award Anthony its gold medal for merit. Here too, Violet took a seat in the front row of the audience hall, although she did not understand a word of the praise in Dutch bestowed upon her husband. At the end of the evening, Anthony himself took the stage to deliver a speech. With his hands in his pockets he added a comical note to the high-toned proceedings, reminding the audience that he had insisted that a good number of his former schoolteachers from Haarlem were to be invited so that he could "thank" them for teaching him "exactly as much as was necessary for my later development." Nonetheless, he ended on a more serious note, stating that it was his firm belief that "in the next war the civilians in cities will be bombed from the air. This will produce such abhorrence to war that this kind of fighting will no longer be possible afterwards. In this fashion the airplane will contribute to general peace and fraternization."[25]

With this, Anthony had said just about all he wanted to share. He and Violet spent the remainder of their time in Holland making family visits and tending to various business interests that needed his attention. Foremost on his mind was to coerce the government into allocating contracts to the Netherlands Aircraft Factory. For years Fokker had maintained that a national aircraft industry could only be continued at the cost of procuring national orders. The government's reluctance to do so had been bothering him immensely. He announced that with the expansion of his American business, he was considering moving his complete aeronautical activities to the United States. This would mean effectively closing the plant in Amsterdam and thus robbing neutral Holland of its indigenous aviation industry. The threat worked. After prolonged consultation, Prime Minister Dirk Jan de Geer made a gesture to accommodate Fokker. To maintain aircraft development and production in the Netherlands, the cabinet decided on May 24 that "the costs involved in the development of a certain aircraft type ordered by the government can, in special cases, be partly compensated for the benefit of the enterprise concerned."[26] Always on the move, Anthony had not waited for this verdict. In the evening of January 31, 1928, he and Violet left by train from Amsterdam's Central Station, bound for Paris and then Cherbourg. His mother, Anna; his sister, Toos; and her husband, Geert Nijland, saw them off. In Cherbourg they boarded Cunard's *Berengaria* and stepped ashore again in New York on February 8.[27]

G

While Anthony and Violet were in Holland, construction of the new factory at Glen Dale, West Virginia, had gotten under way. After he returned to the United States, Anthony regularly flew over to inspect progress of the 720-by-1,080-foot building. But despite Ralph Kitchen's optimistic promises, such a large structure could not be readied before April. Instead, Anthony and Violet visited the opening of the All-American Aircraft Show in Detroit that month. Drawing more than 40,000 visitors in its opening week, the show was an illustration of the public's admiration for the stormy development of air transportation in the United States.[28] It appeared evident that Fokker would harvest the fruits of this process. With the prospected opening of the Glen Dale factory and a well-filled sales portfolio, the Fokker Aircraft Corporation of America was now the nation's largest aeronautical enterprise.[29] The future appeared secure. In an interview, the *Los Angeles Times* asked Anthony, "Where, Mr. Fokker, do you expect the next big advance in aviation?" He answered, "No one can say. I think it will be all along the line. More speed and more power with less weight. We will be flying across the country in just night and day. There will have to be some development on the side of flying fields and night flying equipment. The planes will be ready when the other things are."[30]

G

Private prospects also looked promising. It appeared that health, happiness, and money knew no bounds. That month Anthony bought a large property on the edge of the Palisades Park in New Jersey for $16,000 per acre. Pulpit Rock, as the location was called, was to become the spot for the construction of an enormous Fokker mansion, following the example set by his friends the Vanderbilts across the Hudson River at Hyde Park, New York. Once finished Anthony and Violet would have a commanding view over the river valley from the windows of their house on top of the 500-foot cliffs.[31] A month later he signed the papers in Trenton for the founding of the Pulpit Rock Corporation, an investment company that was to be the vehicle for the business side of the plans.[32] Penrose Stout, an architect from Bronxville, New York, who specialized in luxury houses, received the commission to design the mansion. Anthony knew him from aviation circles. Stout had been a pilot in the Great War. The house itself was to be laid out in the style of the classic big British country houses and was to be of monumental proportions. With its nearly 300-foot front, three stories, and several towers, the house was intended as a lasting memento to "the hometown boy [who] makes good" in the United States.[33] Toward the end of 1928 preparations of the building location began in earnest, followed by the first phases of actual construction. But in the months after Violet's tragic death Anthony lost all interest in the project and abandoned it. The building activities did not extend beyond the foundations, groundwork, and walls that would enclose the house's cellars. In all, progress was stopped before the walls were more than three feet high. Anthony sold the property later.

By contrast, the work on the factory building ended on a more positive note. The local shareholders from Wheeling founded an Industrial Land & Building Company, which provided $300,000 for the purpose of construction. On August 9, 1928, the factory was opened officially. Anthony traveled to Glen Dale to perform the ceremony in front of the 4,000 spectators who had assembled on the factory grounds. The prospect was that Fokker Aircraft would grow to employ around 1,000 people, about half of whom were to come from the Wheeling area. The factory itself was leased to Fokker through Ohio Valley Industrial for a modest fee. Yet of the promised $3 million in investments, no more than $800,000 materialized in the end. To bridge the gap, Fokker Aircraft announced a stock issue worth $2.2 million on October 2, 1928.[34] This was to enable further growth of the company on the basis of orders for the Universal, the Super Universal, and various trimotor types. The first airplane delivered from Glen Dale, an F.10A for Pan American Airways, was rolled out on December 12, making its first flight the following day. In total Fokker built more than sixty commercial aircraft at Glen Dale, plus a series of military types.[35]

With the new factory, Fokker Aircraft was well placed to benefit from the aviation boom that had started on Wall Street early in 1928. Fokker's position was further bolstered by several remarkable and widely publicized flights with Fokker aircraft. On May 31 the Australian flyers Charles Kingsford Smith, Charles Ulm, and two other crew members left in the three-engine F.VII-3m they had bought from the Hubert Wilkins expedition. They flew the plane, rechristened *Southern Cross*, from

Oakland in California to Australia. Eight days later they arrived in Brisbane.[36] Later that month, pilots Amelia Earhart and Wilmer Stultz and mechanic Louis Gordon flew their three-engine Fokker *Friendship* floatplane across the Atlantic. Earhart was the first woman to cross by air. Their machine was secondhand as well. Stultz had bought the plane from commander Richard Byrd with money from Amy Guest, the wife of British Air Minister Frederick Guest.[37] After a flight of twenty-one hours in rain and adverse weather, *Friendship* landed near a buoy at Burry Port near Swansea in South Wales.[38] Anthony sent Amelia a telegram with "best wishes and heartiest congratulations" to applaud the achievement.[39]

Between March 1928 and December 1929, a grand total of around $300 million in stock was floated in American aviation shares. The trade in these securities was highly lucrative: in the same period, the total value of the aviation sector went up by a factor of three to around $1 billion. This masked the fact that aeronautics only took 144th place in the ranking of economic sectors in the United States and that the actual value of the aircraft produced was no higher than $90 million—figures that compared unfavorably with the total investments in aviation. To justify such investments some 25,000 private and commercial aircraft would have to be sold in 1929. Total sales, however, did not amount to more than 3,500 machines.[40] Thus the aviation sector presented a high-risk activity. In Europe, where air transportation originated, the airline companies had thus far not earned a single cent in profit. Nonetheless, American investors were prepared to pour money into aviation. In the short term considerable profits were to be expected. Analysts believed that air transportation was going to be *the* transport mode of the near future. Predictions about the "Coming of the Air Age" that would put "an airplane in every garage" were shared far and wide.[41]

Against this background Anthony was increasingly unhappy about the deal he had struck with the new owners of Fokker Aircraft in December 1927. He now insisted that the $25,000 he earned annually was far too modest. Double that amount was, he thought, more fitting, since the value of the corporation continued to go up. He believed it was time to cash in on his successes. On his proposal, his share in the profits was exchanged for the certainty of payments in hand, plus an option to buy extra stock against a fixed (low) course of eight dollars. Was he preparing to take things somewhat easier and retire with Violet to a life as lord of the manor at Pulpit Rock? It looked like it. Anthony also wished to limit the duration of his involvement in Fokker Aircraft from ten to six years. In September 1928 the board had little alternative but to agree to his wishes.[42]

Meanwhile, the board hoped to use the growth expectancy of the company to fund the construction of the projected third Fokker plant in California. The idea was that the new foothold on the West Coast would initially serve as a repair workshop for Fokker aircraft in use west of the Rockies. The plan for the new factory nearly crashed before it got off the ground, for Anthony barely managed to prevent a midair collision above Teterboro on October 21. The flight ended in an emergency landing in a freshly plowed field.[43] Three days later, however, the board proudly announced that $2.2 million in new shares had been placed. A small group of entrepreneurs, led by James Talbot, president of the Richfield Oil Corporation, had invested heavily in the stock issue.[44] The financial point of gravity of Fokker Aircraft thus shifted to California, where Talbot also held a considerable interest in Western Air Express (WAE), an airline that offered passenger service with Fokker aircraft on the profitable route between Los Angeles and San Francisco, although it had lost the Post Office contract for the money-spinning airmail route from Los Angeles to Salt Lake City. WAE's director, Harris "Pop" Hanshue, a former race car driver and garage owner, had ordered three twelve-passenger Fokker F.10 airliners to fly the route. The first results were so remunerative that Talbot and Hanshue were able to raise the capital of WAE to $5 million.[45] Aided by this influx of new funds, the WAE/Richfield combine acquired a controlling interest of about 40 percent of the shares in Fokker Aircraft three weeks later. It was a strategic maneuver to strengthen Fokker's position relative to its main competitor, Boeing. The Richfield entry reduced Anthony's shares to around 24 percent. The company was thus recapitalized, and Fokker Aircraft was becoming big business.

WAE was in turn controlled by Richfield Oil, and this was where the strings were now pulled. James Talbot immediately claimed the position of chairman of the board of Fokker Aircraft and even bought a personal executive plane from Fokker. He appointed his trusted right-hand man Harris Hanshue as chief executive officer and general manager.[46] Within a week common shares in Fokker Aircraft were floated on the Wall Street Curb Exchange for Unlisted Securities, where they went up by 16 percent.[47]

ᛞ

In October 1928 the board of Fokker Aircraft Corporation of America had welcomed the capital injection from the Richfield/Western group unanimously. Anthony had also been pleased. The agreement fit the larger pattern of rapid expansion of America's major industrial concerns into aviation. The Ford Motor Company had led the way. In 1925 Ford had secured a beachhead into aeronautics with the takeover of the Stout Metal Airplane Company and had started its own airline venture. Now several other large investors came forward. The main groups were the Curtiss-Wright Corporation that was in the works of being founded in early 1929, and the Aviation Corporation of Delaware, a holding supported by financier Andrew Mellon. Next to these a third corporation was in preparation, United Aircraft and Transport, a combine of the automobile industry, the National City Bank, the Boeing Airplane Company, and aeronautical engine producer Pratt & Whitney. A fourth, somewhat smaller "raider" on the stock market was Detroit Aircraft, which also combined investors from the automobile industry.[48] Smaller and independent airplane constructors were soon swallowed up. Boeing was one of the few producers that managed to retain most of its corporate freedom of action.[49]

Always on the go: In September 1928 Fokker managed to attract new capital for a further expansion of his corporate activities as the largest aircraft manufacturer in the United States. James Talbot (left), president of the Richfield Oil Corporation, became the company's new CEO. Fokker Aircraft hoped to expand in California in particular. Fokker and Talbot toured the state in the corporate plane, with Violet in tow. **COLLECTION BLÜM, SANTPOORT, THE NETHERLANDS**

Although the course of its shares on the stock market was rising fast, General Motors (GM) remained on the sideline of these developments. Nonetheless, logic had it that GM would also divert into aviation at some point, as Ford had done before. In the spring of 1929 General Motors chief executive officer Alfred Sloan came to focus his attention at Fokker Aircraft. If action was to be taken, promptness was called for, since the whole American aircraft industry appeared to be adrift. Because Fokker was not officially listed on Wall Street, the trade in Fokker shares took place at the Curb Exchange. There Fokker Aircraft Corporation of America became the target of a high stakes takeover fight in April 1929 to gain control of the last major aircraft producer that was not part of an industrial conglomerate. It started when Universal Aviation Corporation, a holding company that aspired to combine aircraft production and airline activities and that already operated Fokker aircraft, acquired about 50,000 Fokker shares worth $1.25 million in two weeks of intensive trading between April 14 and 29, 1929. Universal was late in becoming interested in aircraft production and wished to strengthen its position in this area. On April 22 the actions of Universal resulted in a tenfold increase in the trade in Fokker securities. It was inevitable that Fokker Aircraft would be up next in the takeover business.

In two days' time the price of Fokker shares went up by 23 percent, from $33.75 to $41.75. Then the Aviation Corporation of Delaware stepped in and used its deep pockets to try to buy up Universal. In turn, Universal tried to increase its value by expanding its shareholding in Fokker. If Universal played its cards right and managed to obtain a majority in Fokker through rapid over-the-counter deals in shares that had not yet been floated on the stock exchange, chances were that Universal's value would rise above the limit Delaware had set itself for the acquisition. At the same time, Universal's investment in Fokker would increase considerably.[50]

If Anthony knew of these developments, he cared little for them. What happened on Wall Street was far beyond the limits of his grief-stricken thoughts. Since Violet's death he had lost all interest in his corporate affairs, spending most of his time in the seclusion of his house in Alpine and on his yacht. One of the consequences was that Fokker Aircraft became totally adrift. To make things worse, Anthony's trusted right-hand man, Bob Noorduyn, announced that he wished to leave Fokker's employ. Noorduyn had been dissatisfied for months after his position had come under severe pressure as a result of the arrival of Talbot and Hanshue as new executives. When they took away his powers of attorney, Noorduyn knew his time was up and left to work as general manager for the much smaller Bellanca Aircraft in February 1929.[51] Anthony did nothing to stop him. As usual, when suffering misfortune, he sought solace on the water. Not before April did he feel well enough to enter again into the limelight. But rather than engage with what was happening on Wall Street, he chose to appear to welcome the crew of the small Dutch lifeboat *Schuttevaer* when it arrived in New York on April 19, after crossing the Atlantic. He knew the captain and owner of the little vessel, Jaap Schuttevaer, as one of the members of the Rotterdam Rowing and Sailboat Society. With his two crew members, Schuttevaer had sailed from Rotterdam over a year before in an attempt to cross the Atlantic in their wooden craft. Before they left, Anthony had promised Schuttevaer to take care of him and his shipmates if they made it to New York. Now he made good on this promise. He personally filmed their arrival and even offered the youngest member of the crew, Piet Meyer, a job as steward on his yacht *Helga*.[52]

Meanwhile, in California, James Talbot and Harris Hanshue watched the developments around Fokker Aircraft with growing anxiety. It was a mystery what plans Universal, or Aviation Corporation of Delaware, had regarding Fokker should either of them manage to acquire a majority shareholding. Talbot therefore searched for a more stable financial environment. On May 13 he sent a telegram to Alfred Sloan, asking whether GM would be interested in buying 400,000 shares in Fokker Aircraft that were still kept in portfolio and thus protect the corporation from the hostile raiders on the stock market. Sloan was immediately interested, settling the matter by telegram that same day.[53] Only to outside observers did Talbot and Hanshue pretend that the deal had taken a week of tough negotiating. Sloan was prepared to pay $19.45 per share, which amounted to a total investment of $7,782,000. For this sum General Motors acquired a 40 percent share in Fokker Aircraft. For GM, Fokker came cheap. About $6.5 million was paid in the shape of current account balances of its subsidiary, the Dayton-Wright Company. GM had bought Dayton-Wright, once founded by Wilbur and Orville Wright, in 1919, but in the past six years the company had been all but dormant. The rest of the money paid for Fokker was financed in the shape of a trade-off in Dayton-Wright shares. The transaction meant that Anthony's personal shareholding was reduced further, to around 12 percent.[54]

The whole acquisition did not cost GM a penny, but it brought short-term benefits for all parties concerned except maybe Anthony himself, who would henceforth only be third largest shareholder. Although GM's agreed price for the share package in Fokker Aircraft Corporation of America was less than half of what the stock was worth on the market, the deal still brought over $5 million above the nominal value of the shares at that point. Besides, Talbot wanted to bring Fokker Aircraft under the aegis of General Motors and thus shield it from further speculation and from new corporate raiders. On May 17, the day after the deal with GM was made public, Universal sold its 50,000 Fokker shares, making a profit of $1.9 million on its investment of just a month ago. The position of GM as the new, controlling shareholder was not affected.[55]

ᘐ

In its annual report of 1929, General Motors reported that Fokker was "one of the most important acquisitions or additions to the Corporation's operating properties."[56] Nonetheless, the takeover was to have dramatic consequences. In the boardroom of Fokker Aircraft a new game of musical chairs commenced in which the newcomers from General Motors did best. The losers were the board members from Wheeling, who were ousted right away. Anthony fared marginally better. He retained his title of director of engineering but had to give up his seat on the board. Henceforth he would focus on technology. For everyone but himself it was obvious that his influence would now be greatly diminished. From the old board only Talbot and Hanshue were allowed to stay, but they had to make room for Charles Wilson and Fred Fisher as the new top dogs representing GM. Wilson was appointed vice president of Fokker Aircraft. On July 1 Eddie Rickenbacker, then sales director of GM's Cadillac/La Salle division, was also brought onboard to act as vice president for sales, while GM's export manager, William Whalen, came in as vice president and general manager in September.[57] If Anthony was concerned over these changes, he made little effort to show it, even though Talbot had kept him in the dark about the GM takeover. What exactly was happening in "his" enterprise? Before he knew it there was a complete change at the top of the corporation. His influence appeared to be nullified. Fokker Aircraft was on the move, but Anthony was unsure whether it was moving in the right direction. In the days after the takeover he hurried to reach an understanding with Hanshue that his Netherlands Aircraft Factory would, for the time being, remain outside the direct influence of General Motors.[58]

Nonetheless, the initial results of Fokker Aircraft Corporation of America under its new ownership were encouraging. The reported half-year profit was just under $500,000. Shareholders could look forward to a good 7 percent dividend. Because of the GM deal, the freely disposable cash reserve of the corporation rose to $7,592,232.[59] It enabled the corporation to acquire ownership of the buildings and the grounds on Teterboro Airport, a step Anthony had never been willing to take. The new board considered it important.[60] The executives also managed to land an order for the development of a new twin-engine bomber for the Army Air Service, the XO-27. The old proposals for a plant on the West Coast were also dusted off again. Talbot announced intentions to open a workshop at Los Angeles Airport, where Western Air Express already had an operating base. To humor Anthony, the new board also reserved $30,000 to build a hangar for floatplanes at a location to be decided.[61]

But did General Motors really know what it had gotten into with its 40 percent investment in Fokker? Judging by the rapidity of the decision, this could hardly have been the case. Sloan's actions were prompted by a perspective of strategic competition in regard to what was happening on Wall Street. He was out to link automobile and aviation technology "in view of the more or less close relationship in an engineering way between the airplane and the motor car."[62] But although GM acquired Fokker Aircraft for a bargain price, Sloan would soon come to regret the purchase. Even in the summer of 1929 it was evident that big changes were ahead. Anthony's disastrous year was only halfway through.

18

NEW YORK, NEW YORK
JULY 1931

Things were tense in the General Aviation boardroom on the Friday morning of July 10, 1931. The newly appointed president of General Aviation, Jim Schoonmaker, scrutinized those present in the General Motors Building on New York's Broadway one by one: Charles Wilson, Fred Fisher, and David Whitney, all present on behalf of General Motors from Detroit; Harris Hanshue of Western Air Express; John T. Smith, head of GM's legal services; Merion Cooper, a financial specialist from Fokker Aircraft; and Anthony Fokker himself. The meeting opened with the main point on the agenda: "Employment contract with Mr. A. H. G. Fokker"—conference speak for the fact that Anthony had handed in his resignation earlier that morning.

Two days before, Fokker's lawyer, Wallace Zachry, had announced the decision.[1] Anthony's departure was precipitated by the appointment of Herbert Thaden to become chief engineer and general manager of General Aviation, the name under which GM had continued the activities of Fokker Aircraft after June 18, 1930. Thaden, an engineer and former pilot with the Army Air Service, was to bring new technologies and new ideas. For years he had been working on the development of metal aircraft. In 1929 General Motors had taken over his small Thaden Metal Aircraft Company and moved it from San Francisco all the way to Pittsburgh.[2] Now was the time to make use of Thaden's know-how. If it was up to Schoonmaker, Hanshue, and the other GM representatives, Thaden would become the main technical man at Fokker.[3] This indicated that Fokker's way of airplane construction was regarded as a thing of the past.

Anthony was furious. Several days before, he had leaked to the press that he was seriously considering resigning from the board if GM persisted in appointing Thaden in his place. To add insult to injury, he had not even been consulted, although he was still the largest private shareholder. Schoonmaker's proposal, which fit a year-long pattern of undermining Fokker's position in the company, was utterly unacceptable for him. There was no denying that GM was after full control of Fokker Aircraft. Two weeks before, when discussing investment proposals, Anthony had already been forced to accept that his own candidate for a seat on the board, William Wilson from Wheeling, had been vetoed in favor of GM's own candidate for the position, John T. Smith.[4] Since then it had become impossible to refute that Fokker's role in the company that had originated in his personal aspirations in North America was coming to an end. In the past few days he had been going over the price that GM would have to pay for his departure, one that was surely going to be high. To protect his financial interests, Anthony demanded that GM agree to let him keep his seat on the board of General Aviation until the end of his contract in 1934. Moreover, he insisted that GM pay him $55,000—his annual earnings—cash in hand in compensation for the loss of his position as director of engineering. He also demanded complete freedom to use the production and marketing rights of the brand name Fokker in the United States for his personal benefit. GM would no longer be allowed to carry his name on its aircraft. All contracts with the Netherlands Aircraft Factory were to be canceled forthwith.

Schoonmaker did not flinch. Clearly GM had counted on such demands. He indicated that he had no problems accepting Fokker's conditions, provided Anthony went along with presenting a public version of affairs that would cover up the true nature of the rupture that lay behind Fokker's departure, and thus prevent unnecessary damage to GM's public image. None of the other board members spoke out on Fokker's behalf. His resignation was approved unanimously.[5] The lack of loyalty stung deep. Schoonmaker did not even see fit to say he regretted this turn of events.[6]

Nonetheless, some form of press statement was called for now, and at the end of the meeting the two adversaries took the elevator down to face reporters. The tension of the confrontation still hung between them as they crossed the gleaming hallway of the General Motors Building and stepped out between the high columns that supported its façade. Outside newspaper reporters were already awaiting them. Anthony read a short statement that they had agreed on:

The arrangements which I have just completed with General Aviation Corporation are not to be regarded in any way as a lessening of my interest in the welfare of that company. As a director and large stockholder I shall continue to be personally and financially interested in its affairs. I am now free to devote my energies to my other interests in aviation, particularly to the development of an extensive expansion program which I now have under way for my Dutch Fokker Company. . . . I have plans which I will reveal in a day or two. This move will release me from many details, but my service and advice will continue to be available. I am interested in the development of more airlines such as the line from Holland to Batavia, which uses Fokker planes exclusively; the enterprises which I have built up and which bear my name must be guided by me. I plan to consolidate these world-wide interests and I want to devote my entire time to them.[7]

It sounded hollow. Had he not neglected his Dutch company in the years past, fully convinced that his future and his interests lay in America? Now he had been forced to make room for someone whose ideas had only recently outgrown the garage they emerged from, while Anthony's personal reach in aviation would be reduced to the Netherlands Aircraft Factory, with which he had hardly interfered at all for years. Moreover, he had lost the option to leave his mark on the rapidly growing American air transportation market. The long-term sales prospects for Fokker aircraft in the United States had just evaporated, although he still held on to some hope. To the Dutch brokers who had introduced General Aviation on the Amsterdam stock exchange, Louis Korijn & Co., he telegraphed, "Since I cannot agree to the expansion policy and the views of General Aviation as a subsidiary of General Motors, I have reached an agreement with this company to the effect that a mutually most satisfactory agreement has been reached, in which I have retained all rights to utilize my patents. I am therefore able to found a new American Fokker company, which will come to operationalize the various worldwide aeronautical interests of an International Fokker Company."[8]

The thought was obviously an illusion. In the past two years Anthony had willingly surrendered his aeronautical interests to General Motors, proud "to have closed the biggest transaction in my life." In May 1929 he had even sent his friends Wim and Nel van Neijenhoff a telegram before the deal so that they might use this inside knowledge and could earn a risk-free profit in speculating on the 25 percent rise of the Fokker stock price that resulted from the GM transaction. "It sounds unbelievable and reeks of American 'bluff,' but to see a check of 6.5 million in your own fingers and under your own eyes does not cheat."[9] Until early in 1930 he had entertained plans to sell the Netherlands Aircraft Factory to General Motors for $1.5 million.[10] Now he was glad that the deal had not materialized.

GM was quick to introduce its own people on the board of Fokker to watch over GM's new investment. The process had started in May 1929 and had taken just three months. From July onward, GM called the shots.[11] Alfred Sloan had ruled that the company needed new blood—and new technology. He had wanted to import knowhow of light metal alloys and aluminum construction from Germany and had even traveled to Europe himself to secure cooperation. In Friedrichshafen he had drawn up a provisional agreement with aircraft manufacturer Claude Dornier. Dornier Metallbauten (Dornier Metal Constructions) possessed a vast experience in building aluminum aircraft, offering an obvious way forward, as Sloan realized. In July 1929 Dornier's pride, the giant twelve-engine flying boat Do.X, then by far the biggest airplane in the world, had successfully completed its first flight from its lakeside base on the German side of Lake Constance.

It was indicative of the new conditions that Anthony had remained outside the preparations of contacts with Dornier. He was no fan of the Do.X to begin with, although he did go to see it when it arrived in New York in August 1931, after he left GM. In May 1929 he had consciously chosen not to become a member of the board of the new Fokker Aircraft Corporation of America after General Motors had taken over. In business terms, and seen against the background of his personal interests, this was a remarkable and disastrously bad decision. Yet the drama with Violet had struck deep, and with his new-earned millions in the bank he was adamant to make changes in his life and take things easier from now on: "This is the material success, which is a comfort and a distraction for the misery, which money could not avert, or perhaps even caused, directly or indirectly."[12]

By giving up his position on the board he stepped aside from the general management of Fokker Aircraft, relying on his shareholding and his informal contacts to retain his influence. It meant that he did not hear about the contacts with Dornier until early October. On October 17, 1929, he boarded the Mauretania in New York in search of Sloan's whereabouts in Europe to demand a place at the negotiating table. He was still shipboard on October 22, when Sloan and Dornier signed a memorandum of understanding on the founding of a Dornier Corporation of America under the flag of General Motors.[13] The day after, Anthony caught up with Sloan in the Savoy Hotel in London. Sloan was then already on his way back to the States. In an offhand manner he informed Fokker of his intention to merge the Dornier Corporation of America with Fokker Aircraft in a larger aeronautical division of General Motors. Anthony was outraged at this open demonstration of power. After a screaming row with Sloan, he angrily announced that he was planning to merge "his" American and Dutch companies into a worldwide Fokker organization, although he must have realized that it was already too late to effect such a move.[14] Nonetheless, he was serious. Two days later he and his new girlfriend, Juanita Percy, boarded a KLM flight to Amsterdam, where they were met at Schiphol Airport by his mother and his Dutch company director, Bruno Stephan.[15]

The heated encounter with Sloan served Anthony badly. His position as director of engineering was under pressure anyhow. To those who asked him about it, he defiantly said that he had not found it necessary to keep a library of technical books over the years. He even maintained that he threw new technology textbooks out the window as soon as he had leafed through them.[16] This was an attitude even Anthony could not afford indefinitely. GM's corporate analysts did not need long to determine that all was not what it seemed at Fokker Aircraft. Depending on adaptations of existing technologies rather than on the development of new ones, the long-term prospects of the company did not look good. Engineers who visited the factories at Teterboro and Passaic returned with disconcerting reports of outdated construction methods. The Fokker designs did not keep up with recent developments in aerodynamics and aeronautical construction. It became evident that as director of engineering Anthony exercised a firm grip on all practical aspects of airplane development and production. This was reflected in faltering innovation. Although Fokker did experiment in metal construction on a modest scale, the focus of the company was on enlarging the size of its aircraft rather than on innovating in technology. This was a course that Fokker had successfully followed in Holland and in the United States since the appearance of the F.II in 1920. Still, in the short run there was little room for complaint. Corporate profit was up, as were the freely disposable cash reserves.[17]

Fokker continued along the beaten path. To serve the growth market for air transportation, he had ordered the development of a very large airliner in May 1926. He hoped that operating large aircraft would effect a reduction of the costs per seat mile. This would in turn enable a reduction of ticket prices and thus an expansion of the air transport market as such.[18] By the end of October 1928 the blueprints for the plane were ready. Fokker's new F-32 would be America's biggest landplane. The 72-foot fuselage towered more than 16 feet above the ground; the wings spanned nearly a hundred feet. The giant airplane could carry as many as thirty-two passengers who would travel in luxury, with railway-style seating. Hanshue's Western Air Express ordered six of these F-32s.[19] In March 1929 Universal Air Lines ordered five.

On December 2, 1928, Anthony proudly announced that the construction of the first prototype would begin soon. He expected the machine to be ready for flight testing within four months.[20] He was convinced that the F-32 was going to be Fokker Aircraft Corporation's next big success. On his say-so, twelve F-32 aircraft were put under construction "before the beast has even flown."[21] His confidence in the project was such that he deemed it unnecessary to initiate other new commercial airliners. On Friday, September 13, 1929, the F-32 was finally ready for its first public flying demonstration, with its proud builder present. But although Jim King, the flight inspector at launching customer Western Air Express, was most enthusiastic about the plane's luxury interior, he also pointed to an unexpected technical problem: "Our biggest problem is to cut the noise, as when you increase the horsepower, the noise increases considerably."[22] The noise was caused by the four engines the twelve-ton airplane needed to fly. On either side of the plane's cabin these were mounted under the wing in tandem, the foremost engine driving a pulling airscrew, the rear engine a pusher propeller. This arrangement turned out to be a source of problems, not only because of the noise for the passengers but also because the rear engines tended to overheat easily. If the engines were operated at full throttle for an extended period, the cylinder heads tended to come off and would fly through the cabin wall, thus posing a severe hazard for passengers at the back of the plane. To avoid risks, WAE limited the seating capacity of its F-32s to twenty-eight passengers. The F-32 turned out to be a difficult aircraft to fly as well. Several pilots reported having trouble

An aircraft launch, Fokker style: Expecting a rapid increase in civil air transportation, Fokker pinned his hopes on the development of the giant F.32 airliner. On March 21, 1930, the plane was launched with festivities that included a frivolous dance performance on the plane's wing by the Fanchonettes showgirls. The event made the cinema newsreels.
COLLECTION BLÜM, SANTPOORT, THE NETHERLANDS

keeping the airplane steady.[23] Fokker's own test pilot, Marshall Boggs, even refused to fly under conditions simulating the aircraft's maximum load.[24]

⚓

Unlike in the past, Anthony Fokker was hardly involved in the testing of the F-32. Since his emergency landing the year before and the drama with Violet in February, his interest in flying had taken a definite downturn. Besides, his health was flagging. For many years he had been suffering from repeated, now near-chronic inflammation of the sinus cavities, a common but very painful affliction of pilots. Especially during descent, he was plagued by blocked sinuses, which caused very sharp, stinging pains above the eyes and in the upper jaw. A few years before he had had an operation in Berlin to clear his sinuses and reduce the pressure on his head. It had not brought relief. Although he hated to admit it, he was no longer able to be his own ultimate test pilot. Yet Anthony would have been untrue to himself had he not used the opportunity for a boyish prank. He kept the gray-green substance that came from his forehead in a glass jar, which he liked to show to people (especially female visitors) so that he could enjoy the shocked reactions it produced when he told them where the substance had come from.[25] Nonetheless, he seldom left the house without his box of tissues.[26]

Now that Anthony was no longer responsible for the day-to-day affairs of the Fokker Aircraft Corporation of America, he could devote more time to leisure, leaving his business affairs in the trusted hands of his new personal secretary and business representative, Carter Tiffany. Like almost everybody else whom Anthony chose to work with, Tiffany had a background in aviation. Qualifying as a pilot in 1916, he was injured in a landing accident a year later and spent the remainder of the war as a pilot instructor in the Army Air Service. After 1918 he had managed to remain in aviation. Tiffany and Anthony had met for the first time in 1927 when Tiffany bought two Fokker aircraft in his capacity as vice president of Reynolds Airways. But apart from a love for flight and a joint delight in tinkering with things technological, the two men also shared an important hobby: water sports. In September 1929 Anthony hired Tiffany as his personal representative at Fokker Aircraft to replace Merion Cooper, whom he no longer trusted. But appointing a personal representative without recourse to consulting the GM people on the board went against the understanding reached with GM on Fokker's position in the restructured company. After Anthony had embarked on the *Mauretania* on October 17 in his chase after Alfred Sloan, Tiffany was immediately sacked and Cooper reinstated in his previous position. When Anthony returned in New York on November 28, he in turn was extremely annoyed about this. He felt obligated to Tiffany and took him on as his personal agent and representative. Anthony had an office installed for him at the banking firm of Jason H. Oliphant & Co. on Broadway.[27]

Anthony was in a bad mood anyway that final week of November. Exactly one day before his arrival back in New York, the prototype of his flagship F-32 had crashed.

That afternoon test pilot Marshall Boggs had taken off with the machine from Roosevelt Field on only three of the four engines. The aircraft had not managed to gain height, and crisis had struck when a second engine quit as well. Going down, the F-32 destroyed two houses. It was a miracle that the inhabitants as well as the flight crew survived the crash, which Anthony blamed on pilot error.[28]

The value of his investments had taken a plunge as well. Anthony had been in London when the stock market crashed on Black Thursday, October 24, 1929. Fokker Aircraft shares plummeted with it, falling by 80 percent to a mere $14.12 a share in December 1929.[29] The influx of new capital into the Fokker Corporation had stopped. And what was worse: the sales prospects for the expensive F-32 with its ticket price of $110,000 had dropped as well.[30] Production crumpled and a first wave of reorganizations, instigated by General Motors, resulted in a series of layoffs.[31] To get a better hold on Fokker Aircraft, General Motors used the collapsing stock prices to increase its shareholding to nearly 50 percent.[32] However, such measures had no effect on the sales portfolio on which the prospects of the company hinged. Airlines did not dare risk new orders for the big, expensive Fokker planes, despite the rapid growth of air transportation in the United States, which went from 173,000 passengers in 1929 to 417,000 in 1930. That growth could be traced back to the opening of new routes with smaller aircraft.[33]

ҁ

While America panicked over the stock market crash that caused whole fortunes to evaporate, Anthony was unconcerned. The effect of the GM transaction was that money had ceased to play a major role in his life. Just two weeks after stepping off the gangplank of the *Homeric* he was on his way back to Europe. This time he traveled onboard the new, fast German liner *Bremen* of the Norddeutsche Lloyd, a ship that fascinated him because it carried a catapult mail plane to boost the speed of transatlantic mail deliveries. Tiffany accompanied him to get acquainted with Fokker's European "shop." Arriving in Cherbourg, the two of them first traveled to Switzerland, though, for a relaxing skiing holiday in St. Moritz.

When Anthony stepped ashore again in New York from the gangplank of the *Bremen* on March 11, 1930, the Fokker Aircraft Corporation of America was heading for turbulence. Nonetheless, the F-32 was presented to the public as if there was not a cloud in the sky. On March 21, the first two machines were officially delivered to Western Air Express at Teterboro Airport. Anthony had ordered a professional film crew to record the event in motion and sound. From New York a chartered Greyhound bus brought twenty-eight specially invited "passengers" to board the "Fox-Fanchon & Marco Flying House Party," which was to last all the way from New York to Hollywood, care of WAE. It was to be a memorable flight, for Anthony had engaged the complete female cast of the Broadway musical *Flying High* to celebrate the occasion. After having boarded in respectable dresses and coats, the ten dancing girls climbed on top of the airplane's enormous wing through a hatch in the cockpit roof. Somewhat awkward because of the height, with the cold wind pulling at their skirts and the cameras rolling, the troupe sat down giggling at the wing's leading edge. Underneath, Anthony climbed atop a small movable platform for a public proclamation of the wonders and achievements of the latest machine that carried his name. In his peculiar mixture of English and Dutch, he said, "the cabin has chairs that are very provided and nicely upholstered, wonderful cabinets, a kitchen, and you will have the finest service you can think of in flying across the country—eh, *hartelijk dank* [thank you cordially]."[34]

After that, the top man on the GM board, William Whalen, underlined the significance of the event: "the completion of the biggest landplanes that have been made so far." Actress Grace Brinkley, who played the leading part in *Flying High*, and Mona Fox, daughter of film producer William Fox, christened the aircraft by smashing a bottle of soda water against the engine. Next the merry company sang a song from the show: "Here's to a happy landing—and may you reach your journey's end."[35] Alas, the variety dance on the wing, for which Anthony had hired the dancers, could not be performed because of the wind and the cold. The girls kept their coats on. Then it was time for the company to depart for sunny California. Upon arrival there, Anthony finally got his show. He saw to it that the "Fanchonettes" showgirls, known for their burlesque theatrical dance acts and performances in Hollywood movies, were waiting for the plane's arrival at Los Angeles's Mines Field Airport. Skirts flying high, eighteen of them danced for the cameras on top of the big wing as if they were at the Folies Bergères.

ꟼ

For a while it appeared as if Anthony's life was regaining its color, despite the effects of the economic crisis that could hardly be denied in aircraft construction. To his immense pleasure he even encountered his old love Ljuba Galantschikoff on July 2 at Roosevelt Field, when he arrived there to see off Australia's renowned aviator Charles Kingsford Smith on the last leg of his round-the-world flight in the three-engine Fokker *Southern Cross*. When Kingsford Smith and his crew had left for Chicago and Oakland, Anthony and Ljuba reminisced over old times. After an adventurous time flying in the Russian civil war that followed the collapse of the czarist regime, she had managed to emigrate to the United States and had arrived in New York in the autumn of 1925 with her husband, Boris Philipov. Registering as Luba Phillips, she had managed to get some marginal commissions as a demonstration pilot next to her regular trade as a beautician.[36] Since then they had encountered each other briefly a few times. Anthony had even hired her once for a demonstration flight with passengers, but since the press had not jumped at the idea of a female commercial pilot, he had let Ljuba slip from his attention. Then, in the summer of 1927, Ljuba had tried to get in touch with him again, hoping he might sponsor a transatlantic flight from Newfoundland to Rome in a Fokker machine. However, after Richard Byrd's mishap with *America*, Anthony had been in no mood for further oceanic adventures.[37] But now they met again in the best of moods. In the spur of the moment they decided to borrow a small sports plane and relive old times in a hair-raising demonstration of low-level stunt flying such as they had performed above Johannisthal before the war. Alas the idea did not catch on with the inspectors of the federal Department of Commerce present at Roosevelt Field, who were supposed to supervise and enforce safety in flight. Upon landing, Anthony was arrested on the spot by an irate official for performing dangerous low-flying maneuvers. It developed that his pilot's license had expired years before. The inspectors wanted to jail him, but since the flying maneuvers had been performed without crossing the New York state line, the federal officers had no authority to incarcerate him.[38] Nonetheless, they managed to spoil Anthony's mood by questioning him for two full hours before handing him a $500 fine for flying without a valid license.[39]

ℂ

Even though the board had decided in March 1930 to build four F-32 aircraft per month, this decision soon had to be reversed because of the continuing adverse economic developments. In the end only two aircraft were actually delivered. Despite the ties between Fokker and Western Air Express, Hanshue canceled the other four machines before their construction had even been completed. They were not only expensive to buy, but their performance was also found to be below specifications.[40] Universal Airlines even withdrew its entire order for five aircraft. Fokker did not make a single other sale, and the company was thus stuck with the machines. The last of the seven F-32 aircraft that were built had been intended for Cadillac's CEO Louis Fisher, but it never was sold. Trying, perhaps, to use the luxury potential of the F-32 as a selling point, Anthony had a furniture company in The Hague, H. P. Mutters, which also worked for KLM, come up with a design to furbish the F-32 as a luxurious and richly ornamented "air yacht," but in the end decided he would not use it. The airplane was parked at Glen Dale and scrapped early in 1934. Thus the development of the F-32 turned into a financial drama that undermined Anthony's position within General Motors even further. The airplane's development had been his decision, and the company did not have an alternative design in the pipeline.

Developments at Fokker Aircraft, meanwhile, went from bad to worse. Some weeks after the official presentation of the F-32, sales director Eddie Rickenbacker announced a 20 percent price reduction on all Fokker production models.[41] Aircraft sales had suffered badly from the economic crisis. A new wave of restructuring and confirmation of the dominant position of General Motors as the majority shareholder appeared inevitable. Meanwhile, GM had expanded its shareholding in Fokker Aircraft Corporation of America, using the fallen prices to acquire a majority. On May 21, 1930, the Fokker board unanimously accepted a name change: Fokker Aircraft would henceforth operate under the name of General Aviation Corporation. Its share capital was raised from one to five million common shares. Anthony, who was present at the meeting although it was not his habit to attend such gatherings, dared not vote against the proposal.[42] Subsequently, General Aviation was incorporated three days later as a holding company, owned by General Motors. Thereafter a bizarre legal and corporate play unfolded. Wishing to put an end to Anthony's ability to influence decision making as a substantial minority shareholder, GM had the meeting of Fokker shareholders, in which GM now held a majority, agree to the name change on June 16, 1930. General Aviation Corporation then transferred its activities back to a nominally new (second) Fokker Aircraft Corporation of America through a symbolic transaction.[43] After that GM had the General Aviation stockholders agree to change the name Fokker Aircraft Corporation back to General Aviation.[44] Thus all activities *and* the shareholders were now attached to the holding. Anthony's influence was seriously reduced. It soon became obvious that Sloan and the highest echelons of General Motors wanted to get rid of the Fokker name. Conditions did not improve when the board found out that Anthony had promised Kingsford Smith and his crew $10,000 from the factory's expense account without asking the board's approval first.[45] In the meeting of delegates, Harris Hanshue, the sole remaining WAE representative since James Talbot had been forced to resign, acted as henchman. He forwarded a definitive proposal to strike the Fokker name from GM's corporate slate.[46] It was a very bitter moment for Anthony Fokker, who was unable to prevent the decision. From that moment on he avoided the board meetings whenever he could, although he managed to hang on to his position as director because of his shareholding. Fokker's work environment thus became increasingly complex. To make things worse, the board even initiated discussions on the closure of the two factories in New Jersey.[47]

Looking back, the road that Anthony had traveled appeared quite a bit better than the view ahead. When visiting Amsterdam in December 1929 he had commented about this to his old friend and employee Friedrich Seekatz. Perhaps it was time to draw up the balance sheet of his peculiar walk through life? Seekatz took to the idea and enthusiastically began digging up stories and contacts from the past.[48] Little by little the notion took hold that Anthony should write his memoirs. Yet Fokker was no writer. Instead of taking the pen himself, he decided to hire a ghostwriter, former U.S. Navy pilot Bruce Gould, whom Fokker had met in 1927 as aeronautical reporter for the *New York Post*. Gould had recently published one of the rare books that Anthony had actually read, *Skylarking: The Romantic Adventure of Flying*, and was available on a freelance basis. Together with a stenographer, Gould spent months in Anthony's company. In combination with some of the stories that Seekatz collected in Germany, this resulted in Fokker's "autobiography," *Flying Dutchman*.[49] The book appeared in New York in April 1931 on Anthony's forty-first birthday. It was also meant to symbolize twenty years of Fokker's aircraft development. Anthony's private, hand numbered and gold stamped copies, bound in fine red leather, had the *Spider* and the F-32 imprinted on the cover.

The book had hardly reached the shops before *Flying Dutchman* became the focal point of a high-pitched controversy that made America's newspaper headlines. As so often, Anthony had not really concerned himself with the details of the story that was told and had given Gould a fairly free hand. This had contributed to the fact that Anthony's candid comments on the turn of events surrounding Richard Byrd's oceanic flight had made it to print unedited. But if Byrd appeared to shrug his shoulders at what Fokker had to say about him, his circle of friends and admirers held quite different views. *Flying Dutchman* became the center of a concerted covert action to put the foreigner and alien Fokker in his place.[50] His adversaries within General Aviation were having a field day.[51]

In Holland, the publishing house of Van Holkema & Warendorf was quick to develop an interest in the book. Anthony, pleased, even promised to write an extra chapter for the Dutch edition.[52] In the end he did not manage a whole chapter. His contributions remained limited to some surprisingly frank insertions in which he offered his readers some clue as to why his personal life had been such a succession of unhappy loves. In these added sections it appeared that Anthony was trying to draw up the balance of his past. But if the book was discussed in the corridors of power in Washington, it did not remain without debate in Holland either. In Parliament questions were asked about the fact that Anthony openly admitted to having worn a German military uniform during the war, and a photograph in the book testified to this. Justice Minister Jan Donner did not have a ready answer.[53]

ⴳ

The struggle for control within General Aviation, the adverse results of the F-32 project, the clamor over the contents of his autobiography—Anthony Fokker might have been able to let it all slip had it not been for a single accident with one of the aircraft that carried his name. What did him in as an aircraft constructor in the United States were events that unfolded high above the small village of Bazaar, Kansas, on March 31, 1931. Shortly before 11 a.m., farmhand Charles McCracken was feeding the cattle when he noticed a plane coming down from the skies very fast at an almost vertical angle. Only one of the three engines sputtered, but before the plane hit the ground it too had stopped. He could not see where exactly the plane hit the ground, but the enormous thud with which the Fokker F-10A buried itself in the earth still resounded in his ears when he saw a part of the wing come down just a few seconds later. After he had alerted the authorities by phone he waited by the roadside to show the ambulance from Bazaar the location of the crash. It arrived on the scene, but there was nothing anyone could do. No one onboard had survived.[54]

The accident, however tragic, would have been forgotten quickly had one of the six passengers on the TWA flight not been the famous Notre Dame football coach Knute Rockne, a national sports celebrity at the peak of his career. Even President Herbert Hoover called his death "a national loss."[55]

The news of the "Rockne Crash" and the subsequent investigation into its causes immediately became front-page news nationwide. Indeed, the much-publicized plane accident had a negative impact on the whole American aeronautical industry, which was already going through a difficult phase. Because of the public pressure that came with the celebrity victim, the Aeronautics Branch of the Department of Commerce, responsible for the supervision of air transportation, decided early on to disclose as much information as possible to the public about the crash.

From day one the federal researchers investigating what had happened focused on finding a structural failure in the aircraft. There was some cause to look in this direction, because concern over the construction and flying characteristics of the F-10A had a history as long as the design itself. To begin with, the aircraft's tail tended to sink during flight, and the airplane was slow to respond to its controls. These were precisely the problems Anthony had been brooding on the evening of Violet's suicide, but they had remained unresolved since. After the accident several pilots came forward to admit they were afraid to fly the F-10A. In conditions of turbulence the outer wings of the plane were prone to flutter, which made it very difficult to keep the machine under control. Fear of losing their jobs, however, had prevented the pilots from coming forward with these problems before.[56]

In the months before the fatal crash attention had been called to the wings of the F-10A on more than one occasion. Part of the problem had been that the nature of the wooden, glued wing construction made it difficult to check its internal assembly. Inspection was simply not possible without causing damage. The various components of the wings were glued together, as was the wings' plywood veneer outer surface. In January 1931 the U.S. Navy had tested the F-10A as a transport plane but turned it down for those same reasons of instability. Suspicions against the F-10A had accumulated even before the crash.[57]

Anthony found the attention paid to the wing construction utter nonsense. He personally visited the crash site to take stock of what had happened, along with TWA's technical manager, Jack Frye. Although he could not deny that the wing had snapped, he maintained that this was caused by excessive strain due to the combination of adverse weather and icing. Irritated, he wrote to the investigating committee, "There is no reason to believe that just at this time when weather conditions were unfavorable, a structural failure of the airplane, independent of the weather conditions, could have been the primary cause of the failure of the wing."[58] In defense of his product he claimed that incomplete and contradictory weather forecasts had contributed to the accident. The authorities had failed to warn the pilots of weather conditions ahead. He said the plane should not have been allowed to fly under the circumstances.

Such general comments did not fit the investigation of the Aeronautics Bureau, and Fokker's letter was quickly pushed aside. In his final report, Leonard Jurden, head of the investigating team, concluded that the airplane had come down because of structural malfunctions caused by material fatigue. According to Jurden, the F-10A had flown for up to three hundred hours in turbulent weather conditions and had been tossed about quite a lot. In his view, the continuous wing flutter that occurred under such conditions had led to a spontaneous structural breakup. Jurden explicitly pointed to the fact that several pilots had indicated that the flutter occurred at precisely the spot where the outer wing of the TWA plane had broken off. Besides, his investigation of the wreckage had revealed that something was amiss with the glued construction. In his report he noted "peculiar glue conditions, particularly in the upper and lower laminated portions of the box spars. Some places the glued joints broke loose very clean, showing no cohesion of the pieces of wood. Other places showed that the glue joints were satisfactory."[59]

Two things distinguished the wings of the F-10A from those on the other Fokker models. The wing span of the F-10A was almost eight feet wider than that of the original F-10. This increased span subjected the outer wing to higher forces. But there was another important difference. The regular F-10 had a wing imported from Fokker's factory in Holland, similar to the one fitted on the Dutch-built F.VIIB aircraft. The F-10A, by contrast, was the first model to be made entirely in the new factory in Glen Dale. Bayard Young, an employee who was hired as an apprentice woodworker in July 1928, later wrote of the process of gluing the wing components as "rather exacting when working with wood."[60] Here one of Fokker's repetitive production problems surfaced again: quality control. Since the Fokker wings derived a large part of their strength from the gluing process, their construction demanded utter precision and a very high degree of craftsmanship. Yet the factory in Glen Dale had been set up, in part, to provide employment for local woodworkers from the Wheeling area. They, of course, had no prior experience with airplane construction. From the Jurden investigation it appeared that the high demands of precision were not always met in Glen Dale.

On May 4, 1931, just five weeks into the investigation, the director of the Aeronautics Branch took the unprecedented step of grounding all thirty-five F-10A machines that had been constructed in Glen Dale in 1929. The measures recalled similar restrictions imposed on Fokker aircraft by the German military authorities during the war. Pending the results of a full inspection of the wings of each individual plane and modifications to the ailerons, all flights with the F-10A were banned. The costs of the inspections and modifications were to be borne by the manufacturer, while airlines operating Fokker aircraft received specific instructions to change and update their maintenance procedures to avoid similar mishaps in future.[61]

Anthony fumed that in its ruling, the Aeronautics Branch cast doubt on the construction of all his aircraft because of a single accident. What made things worse for him was that General Motors, which he believed ought to have spoken out to defend its product, kept silent. Before the Rockne crash, not a single similar accident had occurred, although Fokker aircraft were in use all over the world. As soon as Anthony heard of the pending decision, he stormed into the Department of Commerce in Washington, protesting loudly and demanding to be heard by the officials who were deciding on the future of his aircraft. At 4 a.m. that morning he had already issued a press statement on the matter from his room in the Mayflower Hotel, describing the actions that were about to be taken as "hasty, hostile and prejudiced." Denied access to the meeting, he shouted at the top of his voice to the officials, "I'll give each of you $100 if you *ever* see me again." To his immense frustration, Commerce officials refused to speak with him.[62]

Although twenty-five F-10A machines were eventually returned to service, the affair hastened the disappearance of Fokker aircraft from the American skies. Nonetheless, the effects of the grounding order were marginal in the end. Fokker's full concentration of energy and resources on the F-32 project, followed by the changes brought about by the GM takeover, would have made it inevitable that Fokker would be phased out as an American aircraft constructor. General Aviation was bent on bridging the technological gap that had grown with the competition. Thus, its board was preparing to sever ties with Anthony Fokker and the Netherlands Aircraft Factory, where technological development under Reinhold Platz was at a standstill.[63] As an aircraft constructor, Fokker was becoming more and more isolated from international technological developments in the field.

19

THE HAGUE, HOLLAND
NOVEMBER 1933

On Monday evening, November 27, 1933, the Plesman family had a special guest at their table. Anthony Fokker had come to dine with them. He and Albert Plesman had been conferring all afternoon at the top floor of the KLM office opposite the Parliament buildings in The Hague. The two men disliked each other, but their encounter had been friendly. They had spoken at length about the future development of aviation technology and about the recent introduction in the United States of sleek, streamlined all-metal airliners. Plesman had heard about it from his chief pilot, Koene Parmentier, whom he had sent all the way to California to obtain first-hand knowledge of what the Americans had been working on.

Now Albert, his wife, Suze, and their four children sat down for dinner with Fokker at their home. The two men avoided each other as much as they could, so there had to be business on the menu. Inevitably, dinner talk touched again on the revolutionary new airliner that manufacturer Douglas Aircraft had just released, the DC-1. Fokker knew all about it. In California his former business partners, TWA, had signed an initial order for twenty of them. Anthony himself was also convinced of the potential of the new machine, having sent a telegram to Donald Douglas to enquire about the possibilities of obtaining a license for manufacturing rights in Europe just a month before.[1] Plesman indicated he was also very much interested in the design. Perhaps it would be possible that KLM acquire one such machine for evaluation purposes? And maybe this was something that Anthony might arrange as an intermediary? After all, America was uncharted terrain for KLM, whereas Fokker knew the aviation world on both sides of the Atlantic like no one else and had a lot of experience shipping aircraft internationally. Anthony immediately grasped the wider meaning of what Plesman was subtly putting across the table. Almost a year ago he had been warned confidentially about a possible "Americanization" of KLM.[2] The new information did not come as a surprise. All the same, this meant that the issue had probably been discussed at the Dutch ministerial level, or Plesman would hardly have been able to mention the option to buy an American machine. Obviously the Dutch minister, Jacob Kalff, had not raised any objections to the idea.

No sooner than Plesman had said the words when Anthony jumped up from the table, grabbed in his pockets for loose change, and spontaneously threw all the coins he could find, to the utter surprise of Plesman's children: "all he had on him, guilders, quarters, dimes, rolled on the floor of the dining room." He hastily excused himself and ran out to his car, leaving the Plesman family in utter bewilderment.[3]

It was a good thing that Anthony had just extended his American visa in Amsterdam that morning. That very night a telegram went out to Donald Douglas in Santa Monica with a proposal to set up a meeting. After many hectic arrangements Fokker left by train for Cherbourg, France, to catch the next liner that sailed to New York. On November 29 he boarded the *Bremen*. While Anthony relaxed in the soft comforts of his stateroom onboard, Plesman wrote to the Minister with satisfaction, "It really pleases us to note that the Dutch industry is, in this respect, forward thinking and will not linger in outdated concepts and will make an effort to deliver the most economical and purposeful aircraft to KLM."[4]

G

In the previous two years, Fokker had been forced to come to terms with the fact that the only enterprise that he could still call his own was the one in Amsterdam. Although he had continued to reside in the United States and was a board member of General Aviation, the American market was lost to him. In commercial aviation, crisis ruled, while the Army had decided to focus on metal constructions in the summer of 1931.[5] Fokker hardly interfered with company policy, and if he tried to, it was to little effect.[6] As a consequence of the economic crisis and the collapse of the market, General Aviation had been forced to restructure. In October 1931 all three Fokker factories in the United States had closed down: Teterboro became a dance hall, while Passaic and Glen Dale simply shut their doors. Shareholders who still had ties to Anthony demanded an independent inquiry into the serious mismanagement and dubious roles that General Motors and Western Air Express had played to the disadvantage of Fokker—and them. The stockholders' motion to revoke decisions was overruled.[7]

Nonetheless, a restructuring was inevitable. The company activities were concentrated in the former Curtiss-Wright factory in Dundalk, Maryland. Financial results, however, continued to be disastrous: the 1931 loss of $2.2 million was followed by further losses in the years that followed. In April 1933 General Aviation merged with North American Aviation Incorporated, a holding that had been founded on

The adversaries: In a small country like the Netherlands, Anthony Fokker and Albert Plesman, the central figure in the rise of KLM Royal Dutch Airlines, were fated to remain constant rivals. Fokker's interests soon spanned the world, while Plesman's view was predominantly national. This divergence underlay their many disagreements and conflicts. **AUTHOR'S COLLECTION: FILM STILL**

December 6, 1928, with interests that branched out into several aviation-related sectors. Employment at General Aviation sank from 1,300 in 1931 to around 200 in May 1934. As Fokker had vanished as a brand name, General Aviation now also disappeared.[8]

In Germany, too, nothing remained of Fokker's businesses. Unable to save the company from ultimate collapse, Hans Georg von Morgen had been forced to close the factory gates of the Schwerin Industrial Works in 1926. Part of the premises was rented to the local fishing society, while another part became a maintenance workshop for small boats. The former offices were reconditioned to serve as modest housing. All that remained were memories, although the inhabitants of Schwerin sometimes addressed Fokker, especially when money was tight. In the spring of 1930, Mayor Joachim Sachsenbrecker sent him a letter at his address in New York begging for some financial support for the relief of his city's poor. Anthony made 2,000 Reichsmarks (about $500) available for the purpose.[9] A worker whose wife had been committed to a mental asylum received some money to buy coal. A widow had a small operation paid for. An unmarried woman with two children who was seriously back on her rent had her debt paid off. Because the individual amounts were modest, the money went a long way.[10]

In Amsterdam, the Netherlands Aircraft Factory was also sliding downhill. Diminishing sales and reduced earnings blocked investments and the adaptation of new technologies. The conditions under which director Bruno Stephan and his people had to work were characterized by continuous problems. It did not help that Stephan's powers to act as CEO were strictly limited. Any important decisions had to be vetted by Anthony first. But Fokker was absent most of the time—and decidedly parsimonious besides. By incorporating only smaller aerodynamic improvements, new commercial airplanes such as the F.IX, the F.XII, and the F.XVII could be developed for minimal costs. Even the most expensive of the three, the big F.IX airliner, cost no more than 29,145 guilders ($11,752 at the exchange rate of the time) in research and development. That was less than the going price of a single machine. The F.XII and it derivative F.XVIII showed even more remarkable evidence of what could still be done on a marginal budget. Research and development for the F.XII totaled 10,957 guilders ($4,418). But no commercial airplane was ever developed at lower cost than the F.XVIII, which appeared in the books for 794 guilders and 6 cents ($320.18).[11]

Parsimony also ruled in the development of military aircraft. A contract from the Romanian air force for a successor to the D.XI fighters that had been delivered in 1924 met with serious concerns in Amsterdam over the exchange rate of the Romanian leu. Anthony personally instructed that the negotiations be extended as long as possible to discourage Romanian interest in Fokker deliveries or else raise the price. In the end the order for fifty new fighters went to Poland.[12] A sale to the Kuomintang government in Nanking, China, was also aborted. Salesman Frits Rasch was recalled to Amsterdam after a provisional agreement for the delivery of D.XVI fighters and C.V reconnaissance planes had already been signed, on suspicion that the Chinese would not honor payment. In Nanking, Marshall Zhang Xueliang, who ruled most of northeastern China for the Kuomintang, was deeply offended. Before the Netherlands' envoy in China, Willem Oudendijk, he angrily exclaimed three times, "They tried to fool me!"[13] Between 1930 and 1932 the Netherlands Aircraft Factory lost its prominent international position in military aircraft sales. Meanwhile, factory losses were rising annually, peaking in 1935 with a record loss of 3.5 million guilders (just over $1.4 million).[14]

Fokker found it difficult to address these problems. To him the crisis appeared to be temporary. While enjoying a juicy pear for breakfast, he answered a question on aviation developments from a reporter from the Dutch paper *Telegraaf:* "Thank God I don't have reason to complain, but the crisis really has the aeronautical industry in its grip. There is too much chaff among the wheat, too many factories that have no true right of existence and which produce uneconomically. . . . Of course, Sir, the deeper the crisis goes, the more of my competitors will go under. The process of purification is a natural one and saves me money and effort."[15]

But without export orders, Fokker's production collapsed just the same. Mass layoffs were the inevitable result. The number of employees in Amsterdam went down from around 600 in 1929 to no more than 130 in December of 1932.[16] Even Anthony's long-term associate Reinhold Platz did not escape the downsizing. His position as head of research and development had been under pressure anyhow, since he, like Anthony himself in the United States, proved unable to come to terms with the rapid changes in technology. After nineteen years of faithful service, Anthony saw no other option but to let Platz go as of April 1, 1931.[17] The closure of the last remaining Fokker factory appeared imminent. It caused alarm in Dutch government circles, bent on securing an indigenous aircraft industry as an important contribution to Holland's neutrality. To keep Fokker afloat, the government placed an order for ten D.XVII fighters.[18]

The impulse to innovate in aerodynamics had to come from outside. KLM commissioned Fokker to convert one of its seven two-engine F.VIII aircraft to have its engines built into the wing root, in streamlined nacelles, instead of having them hang loose under the wing. Plesman also spoke with Fokker about the development of a future replacement for the Fokker aircraft it operated on the air route between Amsterdam and Batavia in the Netherlands East Indies. His initial thoughts were for a large, possibly four-engine airliner that should be delivered by 1934.[19] Anthony was not enthusiastic. After his American misadventure, he was reluctant to invest in expensive new developments. Besides, after the F-32 mishap he doubted whether there would be a market for the kind of large aircraft that KLM had in mind. Developments in America had made it abundantly clear that the growth in air transport came, first and foremost, from opening new routes. He did not think that Europe, or the colonial air routes would develop differently. Rather than invest in a large airliner, he wanted to focus on a plane that would offer substantially lower operating costs.

Although Anthony was unsure whether he would be able to keep his Amsterdam factory going, he did initiate the development of a next-generation three-engine airliner in the early months of 1932. According to planning, his F.XX was to be ready by April 1934. The machine was to offer seating for twelve passengers and incorporate much improved aerodynamics. Both the wing and the fuselage were of a new, sleek design, with a retractable landing gear. Yet the basic construction of the F.XX would still be from steel tubing, canvas, and wood—relatively inexpensive materials that did not call for investment in tooling. The expenses involved were therefore limited: $32,337. This was roughly one-ninth of the $306,000 that Donald Douglas in California was able to risk (from the reserves accumulated after several years of significant military orders) on the development of his revolutionary DC-1 and DC-2 airliners.[20] Yet Anthony was convinced that his new machine would reach the market as exactly the right plane at exactly the right time. In an interview in the Dutch newspaper *Het Vaderland* on December 21, 1932, he lauded the fact that the F.XX had its roots in the "gradual line of development of Fokker aircraft."[21] However, the limited innovations that were incorporated in the design did not produce a significantly more efficient aircraft. In fact, the retractable landing gear of the F.XX increased its weight and therefore increased fuel consumption—and thus limited the aircraft's range.

Moreover, the F.XX lacked an enthusiastic launching customer. Plesman judged that the F.XX offered only marginal advantages over earlier designs. It took long negotiations to drag him into buying the machine, and then only because Fokker offered a 20 percent rebate on the price. On December 20, 1933, KLM officially took on the F.XX for the equivalent of $35,000.[22]

Plesman would have preferred not to accept the airplane at all. He was convinced that KLM needed a much bigger aircraft. It put Fokker in a difficult position. His best customer wanted a wholly different plane from the one he had built. Other customers also refrained from ordering Fokker's latest development. Only the French carrier Air Orient, which had operated Fokker aircraft for years, showed some degree of interest, but in the end it canceled its order as a consequence of national political and industrial pressure to buy French.[23] In September 1933 Anthony tried to effect a breakthrough for the F.XX in Holland by making a much-publicized demonstration flight with his friend Prince Hendrik. It was to no avail: only one single F.XX was ever built.[24]

By contrast, the sales prospects for a large four-engine aircraft appeared rather better. Although he harbored doubts about the project after his experience with the F-32 in America, Anthony finally agreed to the development of a four-engine successor to the F.XVIII machines that KLM used on its route between Amsterdam and the Netherlands East Indies. Nonetheless, he sent Plesman a personal letter spelling out his doubts about the ambitious project.[25] The subsequent developments would prove him right. The four-engine F.XXXVI, which was to carry sixteen passengers in luxury sleeping accommodations on intercontinental routes, or thirty-six passengers seated in comfort on European flights, would eat up no less than $183,000 worth of investments in research and development. It was Fokker's most expensive airplane project by far, completely out of proportion when compared to what the company had invested before. Again, only one F.XXXVI was ever built, sold to KLM for the equivalent of $81,000. The smaller parallel development of the F.XXII was not a success either. Production of the twenty-two-seat airplane remained limited to three machines that went to KLM and one single aircraft for the Swedish airline ABA. Notwithstanding these poor sales results, Fokker invested a grand total of $370,000 in the development of these four-engine airliners, $187,000 of which was spent on the F.XXII.[26]

✿

It thus appeared that Fokker had lost his commercial and technological instincts since his run-in with General Motors and his disappearance from General Aviation. Where to focus his attention? Should he save whatever could be saved from his

American venture and his influence in General Motors or focus on development in the Netherlands? He remained undecided.

His personal affairs also continued to be unresolved. He kept his application for American citizenship, which had remained undecided since 1926 because Anthony failed to provide the necessary documentation, in limbo for years. On June 26, 1931, he went through the nationalization ceremony together with his friend Bernt Balchen. Now all he needed to do to complete the dossier was sign his citizenship papers and return them.[27] Then the fight in the board of General Aviation raised his doubts again on becoming American. Given his uncertainty about what the future might hold, he could not bring himself to sign. Ill at ease, he traveled back and forth between the United States and Europe, crossing the ocean no less than eight times in 1931 and 1932.

These long ocean voyages were a source of relaxation, an opportunity to escape from his business duties and frolic with business tycoons, leading politicians, top musicians, and stars from the world of the theater and the movies. He befriended socialite and aviation buff Mabel Boll, who had aspired to be the first female passenger to fly the Atlantic. He also struck up a friendship with film producer Howard Hughes, who had made a name for himself late in 1930 with his spectacular film on the air war between 1914 and 1918, *Hell's Angels*. The film sported a good number of Fokker D.VII fighters. Anthony visited Hughes several times in California to discuss particulars of the film. Friendship also sprouted with Charlie Chaplin, who, like Anthony, cherished winter sports in the Swiss Alps.

Many such friendships developed during the long days at sea. Passengers, mostly men, would gather in the first-class smoking salons and dining halls onboard luxury ships decorated like country estates. Travelers exchanged stories and experiences, went for walks on the promenade deck, played games to pass the time, or dozed in the sunlight on deck chairs if the weather allowed. The evenings were filled with light entertainment and music in the ships' theaters. Anthony must have loved it all; he spent more than half a year of his life on the North Atlantic.

On September 2, 1931, Fokker boarded the *Mauretania* in New York, destined for Southampton, England, so he could be present at the aeronautical event of the year: the races for the Schneider Cup, flown with very fast floatplane racing aircraft. Test flights for the event started under an overcast, rainy sky on Thursday, September 10. Four days later, the weather had finally cleared up for the actual races. The sun shone bright on the waters of the Solent between the English south coast and the Isle of Wight, and nearly a million British spectators had the day of their lives watching the grand finale of a fight between British and Italian aeronautical technology that had gone on for years. From the first-class deck of the *Homeric*, moored in the middle of the circuit, Anthony filmed as a British team from Supermarine Aviation won the prize.

A fortnight later he was also a spectator at the air show organized by KLM at Amsterdam's Schiphol Airport on September 29 to celebrate the official opening of the Dutch scheduled weekly air service to the capital of the Netherlands East Indies, Batavia, on the island of Java. It must have been a strange feeling for Anthony to be the guest of honor at the event. While he was lauded for the role his passenger aircraft played in the development of KLM, his employees in Wheeling began their final workday at the Fokker plant before the factory closed its doors for good on September 30. But then again, little was known in Holland about the American drama. For most of his countrymen, Anthony Fokker was still the celebrated and successful aircraft manufacturer, a national hero. Hence the crowds turned up by the thousands that Tuesday to watch the various flying demonstrations. Anyone who was anyone in Dutch aviation was present for the occasion. Even the royal family was in attendance. The prodigal son felt at home. In front of the camera of the cinema news, Anthony carefully said, "It really is a pleasure to see how the air service to the Netherlands East Indies has developed. . . . I personally think that the aircraft presently used, with their undercarriage and engines all outside the wing are obsolete, and I hope that within a few years we will not only have raised the speed to 200 kilometers, 200 miles an hour, but also that we shall have so much space for passengers that the aircraft will equal the comfort of the large steamships."[28]

Likewise the public in Amsterdam's Concertgebouw clung to his every word as he introduced the Swiss physicist and researcher of the stratosphere Auguste Piccard four days later. Piccard was there to give a lecture containing a firsthand account of his balloon ascent to an altitude of ten miles. Fokker painted a visionary image of future passenger aircraft that would race around the world at high altitude.[29] The warm welcome he received everywhere really did him good. At the end of the month he even looked up his old German friends in Berlin to recollect memories of the time his aircraft had been feared over the Western Front. At Berlin's Tempelhof Airport he was filmed and photographed with Ernst Udet, Bruno Loerzer, and other *alte Kameraden* who had drifted in the direction of the Nazi Party, just as their friend Hermann Goering had. It was also time for a small exercise of revenge toward General Motors. Anthony had himself contracted for a commercial by GM's competitor Chrysler and publicly proclaimed that "I have advised my sister to buy a Plymouth automobile, because of the positive results with it in America, and the excellent reputation of Chrysler products in general."[30]

With the knowledge that he had picked up in Berlin of the recent developments in German aviation, the next stop of his trip was in Augsburg, Bavaria. There Anthony initiated talks with the Bayerische Flugzeug-Werke, the producers of Messerschmitt aircraft. He wanted to pursue the possibility of a cooperative agreement between Fokker and Messerschmitt that might help resolve the present financial trouble the German factory was having. Rumors that Fokker was about to take over Messerschmitt stretched all the way to New York.[31] Despite a second round of talks on the issue in May of the next year, nothing materialized. After his sojourn in Bavaria, Anthony traveled on to St. Moritz, Switzerland, where he stayed in the Hotel Kulm, his usual stomping ground. He remained there until after New Year's Day before returning to the United States. Even so, the unrest he experienced would not leave his system. In May 1932 he was already back in Cherbourg, France, where he kept a Lancia Lambda sports car in a special garage. This time he did not use it, for the day after his arrival he boarded a plane in Paris destined for Berlin. Later that spring he traveled across Europe at a more leisurely pace, something he had never had the time for in the past because of his busy schedule.[32]

Was he really bored, or just restless? In June he was already on his way back to the United States. When the *Europa* docked at the Brooklyn Pier, he found a delegation of representatives from fashion store Abercrombie & Fitch waiting for him with a court order to settle an unpaid bill of $1,454. The amount had remained on the books after aviator Charles Kingsford Smith and his crew had visited the exclusive shop to stock up on clothing. Anthony had promised the aviators a credit line of no less than $10,000, to be paid by General Aviation. The board had, however, refused to pay for costs incurred by Fokker, after which the clothing house had gone to court over the matter. Fokker was "amused and disturbed." He claimed he had "never made arrangements for the Australian party, much less for $15 silk pajamas and $12 shoes." Nonetheless, the verdict of the court left no other option but to take out his checkbook before boarding the *Helga*, which lay ready to take him home to Alpine, New Jersey.[33]

Two months later, at the end of August 1932, he was again at the quayside in New York, this time to board the ageing Cunard liner *Aquitania*. A week later the ship docked in Cherbourg. Anthony took the train to Paris, where the possibilities for diversion outside the view of the press were bigger than in New York. But he soon tired of the French capital and traveled on to his beloved Switzerland. By that time he was turning over a plan in his mind to try and buy a chalet in Davos or St. Moritz. Accomplishing this was not as easy as it first appeared and would take time. He left instructions with an agent to look for a suitable house. After a detour that took him to Holland, he embarked again for the return journey to New York on September 23. Apparently he had changed his plans at short notice, for he was unable to obtain stateroom accommodations on one of his favorite British and German ships. Instead, he sailed on the *Île de France*.

Once in New York, restlessness again got the better of him. Within weeks he was back in Holland. In The Hague he signed the agreement with Albert Plesman to develop a four-engine aircraft for KLM's route to the Dutch East Indies. Subsequently, Anthony left again for New York on the *Bremen*, leaving the details of the new aircraft project to his staff in Amsterdam. For them it was clear that efforts had to be made to catch up with new developments in aeronautical technology and that new insights into aerodynamics should be incorporated in the design. Lacking both the funds and the know-how, the Fokker team did not go for radical innovation. Instead, the designers clung to the familiar Fokker concept of a high-wing aircraft composed of a mixed construction of steel tubing, wood, and linen. This created a major challenge with regard to the design and construction of the undercarriage. In view of the recent technical problems encountered in the F.XX design, the Fokker team chose to adopt a fixed yet lightweight arrangement. The enormous, man-sized wheels that protruded on big struts on either side of the fuselage enabled the use of unpaved airfields, which was of importance if the aircraft were to be used on the colonial route. The arrangement, if practical, was not visually appealing and seemed to refute the modernity of the design.

The F.XXXVI was exceptional in more ways than one. For such a voluminous airplane, it had an unusually narrow cockpit. On Anthony's explicit personal instruction, the copilot in the F.XXXVI was not seated beside the captain on the flight deck but askew behind him. In Fokker's view this arrangement improved the all-round vision of the captain, but the arrangement owed as much to the limited space available in the aircraft's streamlined nose. Anthony proudly demonstrated the unusual arrangement to Charles Lindbergh when he visited the Amsterdam factory on November 2–4, 1933.[34]

The sheer size of the aircraft—the F.XXXVI had a wing span of 108 feet, was over 77 feet long, and rose at its highest point, the cockpit, 27 feet above the ground—presented serious technological challenges for its development. Building the aircraft therefore took more time than anticipated. In the original plans the machine was to be ready for flight-testing at the end of April 1933, but setbacks dictated that the first flight could only be made in the late afternoon of June 22, 1934. Test pilot Emil Meinecke later remembered:

> I had already seen the machine in the factory, but once on the airfield, it . . . looked much bigger still. When I moved into the cockpit, it was as if I was already flying, so high above the ground was I. . . . But I was not the only one to think this was a strange plane. All of Fokker's people were a bit daunted by this colossus. It stood there on the airfield, but how could one get the thing into the air? We just didn't dare. . . . Fokker himself was in the country and hung around at Schiphol: he too was a bit impressed by the giant. That evening he was in a good mood and I used the opportunity this provided. In passing I said to him: "Shall we just try her out?" To my astonishment he did not object.[35]

In the subsequent nine-month test period before the plane was turned over to KLM in March 1935, no fewer than seventy-three serious defects had to mended. In the first six months in KLM service the F.XXXVI remained grounded for eighty-six days because of various malfunctions. Cooling problems with the engines meant that the machine could only cruise at 56 percent of its engine power.[36]

This long development period proved fatal for the marketing perspectives of the F.XXXVI, as well as for Fokker's plans to provide a renewed boost for the Netherlands Aircraft Factory as a producer of commercial airplanes. The F.XXXVI and F.XXII projects were initiated in the worst of circumstances, economically, financially, and technologically. Anthony had been skeptical about the F.XXXVI from the very start, but since KLM had declined his offer to deliver F.XX machines while dangling an order for six F.XXXVI aircraft he was left with little option but to continue the development of the four-engine plane.

In 1933 and 1934, crucial years in the history of international aeronautical engineering, the F.XXII and F.XXXVI projects absorbed unprecedented amounts of money for Fokker. The investments were such that they blocked any hope of catching up with engineering trends outside the company walls and in fact increased the gap that was growing between Fokker and his new high-tech competitors in the United States. The cruel irony of Plesman's insistence on the development of the F.XXXVI was that Fokker now repeated the crucial mistake that had cost him his leading position in the United States. When the prototype was finally taken over by KLM on March 16, 1935, aeronautical technology had made an enormous leap that changed aviation completely. To make things worse, the midterm planning at KLM for the route to the Dutch East Indies had also changed. Anthony Fokker was again faced with a commercial airplane for which there was no market.

MONTAUK POINT, LONG ISLAND
SEPTEMBER 1935

Aboard the *Helga* off the Long Island coast at Montauk Point, life was relaxed. Anthony was killing time in the company of his friend Wim van Neijenhoff, who had traveled with him from Holland. In the days past they had filmed whales, which were exceptionally numerous in the coastal waters that year. They had also been hunting sharks and bluefin tuna with one of Tony's speedboats. Almost unnoticed, the other food stocks onboard the *Helga* had diminished. In the afternoon of September 4, Anthony had himself dropped off at East Hampton by his crew so that he could go shopping for supplies. Using the ship's radio, he had arranged for a car to be waiting on the shore. While Anthony and Wim went about their business, the *Helga* sailed ahead to the Montauk Point marina, where they were to board the ship again. Around 7:30 p.m. Anthony stepped out of the car in front of the Montauk Yacht Club. He had taken no more than a few steps before several policemen suddenly blocked his way. Process-server Stanley Ferguson, who had arrived by train from New York for the occasion and had already executed an extensive search by the Coast Guard of the *Helga* earlier that afternoon, stepped forward and announced in his official capacity that the U.S. Senate had issued a warrant for Fokker's arrest. Finally Ferguson had the culprit in custody. But what, in fact, was the charge? Anthony had no idea: "The first thing I knew of an investigating committee wanting me was what I read in this morning's newspapers. I am not running away from anything. I'm merely on a vacation. I came here Friday on my yacht with friends for the bluefishing, and I've been having pretty good luck. . . . I do not know what this is all about."[1]

Six days earlier, on August 30, Ferguson had rung Fokker's doorbell in Alpine-on-Hudson, New Jersey. In his hand he had held a subpoena from the U.S. Senate Special Committee Investigating the Munitions Industry. Chaired by Senator Gerald Nye, a Republican from North Dakota, this committee had been investigating the foreign dealings of the American weapons and munitions industry. Nye had also wanted to interview Fokker, whose name had popped up in the investigation, but Ferguson had found his house empty. When he questioned the staff, Ferguson learned that Anthony had left only a couple of hours before. Alarmed, and suspecting that the committee was finally onto something big and that Fokker had fled on purpose, Nye had ordered a nationwide search for Fokker. Instructions for his arrest had been issued in all states. Border posts along the roads leading to Canada and Mexico had been put on full alert, as were all U.S. ports, since Ferguson and Senator Nye suspected that Fokker might try to flee the country. In Washington, the Justice Department and even Secretary of State Cordell Hull were notified.[2]

Anthony did not have to wait long for explanations about his arrest. In the days that followed, his trusted friend Carter Tiffany informed him that Senator Nye's arrest warrant had its roots in a bizarre weapons deal with the Soviet Union that had gone awry the year before. What gave the case its zing, was that the investigation revolved around the role of President Roosevelt's second son, Elliott. In January 1934 Anthony had met Elliott Roosevelt for the first time in the lobby of the Roosevelt Hotel in Hollywood, where America's rich and famous assembled. Anthony had already been staying there for several weeks. After making a flight in the Douglas DC-1 airliner, he had been negotiating the acquisition of the European sales rights for its successor model, the DC-2. On January 15, he and Donald Douglas had signed an agreement that had given Fokker the exclusive rights to act as Douglas's sales agent for DC-2 aircraft in all European countries with the exception of the Soviet Union.[3] The two aeronautical entrepreneurs, Douglas and Fokker, got along well, both combining their love for aircraft with a passion for sailboat racing. Douglas had even made America's team in the 1932 Summer Olympics in Los Angeles.[4]

Sometime after signing the European contract with Fokker, Douglas had introduced Roosevelt, at twenty-three already known for his extreme opportunism, to the forty-four-year-old Fokker. With his business partners George Stratton and Franklin Lane, Roosevelt had been in Los Angeles for some time, awaiting the arrival of a Soviet trade mission that was expected there in February 1934. Roosevelt had learned about their imminent visit through sources of his at the White House. He had also heard that Stalin's representatives would arrive in California loaded with funds to pay for the acquisition of modern aircraft. Rumor had it that the Soviets were interested in buying at least fifty transport planes that could be converted to bombers easily. For that reason Roosevelt and his associates had bought the sales rights for the Douglas DC-2 in the Soviet Union—even before Fokker turned up. When Anthony, always on the lookout for easy money, learned about this, the matter immediately aroused his interest. Perhaps there was a way in which he might be able to cut into a potentially lucrative deal with the Russians? In that case it would be convenient if he were able to put forward a competing airplane.

The day after he signed his own sales agreement with Donald Douglas, Anthony walked into the office of Robert Gross in Burbank. Gross was just the man he needed to see. Shortly before, he had become commercial director of the ailing Lockheed Aircraft Corporation. Lockheed was a company that Anthony knew fairly well. A year before he had proposed to the board of General Aviation that it might buy Lockheed, then for sale at a bargain price.[5] Since then Lockheed had recovered, helped by a $200,000 loan from the Reconstruction Finance Corporation. In fact, it was now putting the finishing touches to its very advanced Model L-10 Electra.[6] Well informed as usual, Anthony managed to wrangle the sales rights for the L-10 from Gross, together with the exclusive rights to acquire a contract for its license production in Holland at a later stage. And although Gross had initially been suspicious about Fokker's motives, Anthony had managed to win him over to the idea that an association with a well-established European aircraft producer such as Fokker would be in Lockheed's best interests in the long run. A week later the two men agreed to a provisional contract.[7] Anthony ordered one Electra in advance, for which he would pay out of his own pocket, and left an amount in cash with Lockheed as a down payment on the wider sales and license agreement. In return he received the exclusive rights to the Lockheed design in Europe for the next two years. But what he had really come for were the rights to sell the Electra in the Soviet Union. This required some additional massage, since Gross was acutely aware that delivering aircraft to the Soviet Union presented serious financial risks. After all, events after the Russian Revolution of 1917 had revealed that the Soviets were not to be trusted when it came to paying their debts. Yet Fokker was able to point out that they had duly paid him for his deliveries of fighter aircraft in 1924. This promoted trust. After studying the matter for a week, Bob Gross gave Fokker his way. After all, involving Fokker in Europe presented Lockheed with an opportunity to make money, while the risks involved appeared manageable.[8]

Early in February the agreement was ready to be signed, just at the time when President Franklin D. Roosevelt suddenly canceled the airmail contracts in the United States. This put the airline business in jeopardy, since it relied to a great extent on the income generated by the carriage of mail. Potential orders for new airliners would now be put on hold, all the more reason for Lockheed to agree to the contract with Fokker. Because there had thus far been no other contenders from Europe for the Electra, Anthony got the rights at a bargain price: $16,000.[9] Thus Fokker had positioned himself ideally to keep playing a pivotal role in European aviation, no matter how the fortunes of the Netherlands Aircraft Factory would evolve. It was tacitly agreed that any airplanes that Stalin ordered would be converted to bombers in Amsterdam before they would be shipped onward to the Soviet Union.[10]

The ink of the Lockheed contract was hardly dry when Anthony suffered acute appendicitis. He had to be committed to hospital in Los Angeles to undergo surgery, but he recovered quickly. In the California sun he consulted with his former company secretary, Herbert Reed, on the question whether and how to proceed with Elliott Roosevelt. Roosevelt himself was very much in favor of this. He proposed to use his position as the president's son to get access to Josef Stalin personally. On February 21, the parties reconvened, this time in Roosevelt's residence in Beverly Hills. Afterward Anthony returned to New York by plane.[11] He visited Roosevelt in Manhattan with Tiffany a week later to work out the details of the contract between them. If Roosevelt would manage to point the Soviet delegation to both aircraft they had on offer between them, the small band of go-betweens would find themselves to have not one but two aircraft in the offing. Anthony instructed Lockheed in Burbank to secretly make a model of a specially adapted Electra with provisions for carrying arms and dropping bombs.[12]

On February 28, 1934, Fokker, Roosevelt, and their business partners finally agreed that if the Soviets would order fifty Electras from them, they would split the proceeds fifty-fifty. There was potentially a lot of money to be made: $500,000 for each of the two signatories. They were convinced that selling the aircraft at such a profit presented a realistic scenario. In the end it was Fokker who dictated the terms of the agreement: "On any sales of airplanes similar to the Electra model airplane to the Soviet Union, a commission shall be paid to your corporation, provided the order is secured within one year from date . . . providing an order for a substantial number of airplanes is placed by the Soviet Union with the Lockheed Sales & Export Corporation prior to May 6, 1934, or shortly thereafter."[13]

Roosevelt assured Fokker that he was confident he would be able to swing the deal with the Soviet purchasing mission and with the Export-Import Bank in New York, which his father had founded. For his efforts Anthony paid him a cash advance of $5,000, plus a check for $6,666 that would enable Roosevelt to travel to Moscow, where, on the strength of his family name, he thought he would be admitted to the highest circles in the Kremlin.

In the end the plan fell through. When President Roosevelt heard of the scheme, he soon put a stop to his son's Soviet adventure. He had made repeated negative references in his election campaign to war profiteers and their exorbitant gains and could now hardly allow his son to rake in such profits.[14] Franklin Roosevelt bluntly forbade Elliott to use the family name to manipulate and sell arms to the Soviets.[15]

Now that Elliott Roosevelt was confined to remain in the United States on direct orders from the president, Anthony was left to fend for himself in the matter. He remained optimistic that he would be able to secure an order for the Electra from the Soviets. Arriving in Amsterdam on March 9, 1934, he was still considering various options. Arranging a visa for the Soviet Union and setting up a schedule for meetings took time. In the month that followed he traveled Europe with his old German friend and sales executive Friedrich Seekatz in order to secure commercial orders for the DC-2 and the Electra.[16] They sold six Electras to France and to the Republican government in Spain, for which Anthony had Tiffany deposit a down payment of $58,800 with Lockheed.[17] It was May 16 before he finally boarded a flight in Amsterdam that would eventually take him to Moscow. The plane made a stop in St. Petersburg, which he found a completely different city from the one he remembered from his first visit in 1912. The opulent richness that had depressed him then because he lacked the funds for luxury enjoyment had vanished completely. This time he had money to burn, but there was hardly anything for sale that was worth buying. Ordinary citizens sometimes owned next to nothing beyond the clothes they wore, which concealed empty stomachs. Luxury goods had long been transferred to warehouses controlled by the NKVD, Stalin's secret police, or had been sold off on the black market. Even for the formerly wealthy, the *kommunalka*, the typical Soviet apartment that several families were forced to share, had become the new norm.[18]

On May 18 Anthony flew on to Moscow. There things appeared to be somewhat better, at least at first sight. In large parts of the city construction was going on, not just for the metro—a prestige project—but also for houses, shops and department stores. It was Stalin himself who had proclaimed earlier that year that socialism did not stand for poverty and dearth, but on the contrary for the organization of a rich and cultured life for all members of the community.[19] Such assertions were, however, lost on Fokker, who encountered considerable difficulties to secure appointments with those in charge of aircraft procurement. None of the people he spoke to in Moscow appeared to be prepared for his arrival. To his frustration he discovered that, despite his fame, he stood very little chance of getting through to the right levels in Stalin's bureaucracy. No one he spoke to had the authority to do business with him. It must have troubled Anthony that his commercial interests dictated that he should not even complain about this. He tried to remain optimistic. In an interview with the Dutch newspaper *Handelsblad* he said, "This aircraft industry, it really makes you wonder! It must be something truly amazing, because when you arrive at the airport in Moscow, you see some three or four hundred aircraft lined up there: think about this and compare it to other European airports. . . . I have flown across a big part of Russia and have seen the signs everywhere of a new nation on the rise, and of the powerful will that is present to rid itself from the old system and become a great and powerful country."[20]

Anthony added that he thought it was about time for an official diplomatic recognition of the Soviet Union, although the Netherlands had voted against Soviet membership in the League of Nations only shortly before. It was the only time Anthony publicly commented on international politics. The attitude toward the Soviet Union was outdated, he said, and it prevented proper representation of Dutch commercial interests. In his view businessmen had been left to fend for themselves, which meant that all sorts of opportunities remained unexplored, especially for smaller industries.

Dealings with the Russians: Together with Elliott Roosevelt, the president's son, Fokker worked on a lucrative deal to sell airliners to the Soviet Union for conversion into bombers. This secret scheme was launched in 1934, but sales did not materialize. In August 1935, discovery of the scam led to a nationwide warrant for Fokker's arrest. Here Tony talks with Soviet officials under the wing of his F.XXXVI airliner in Holland.
N. V. NEDERLANDSCHE VLIEGTUIGFABRIEK FOKKER, LIQUIDATED 1996

Closer to home, he saw the vast distances within the Soviet Union as representing opportunities to sell a considerable number of fast Lockheed aircraft.

But of the wider implications of what was happening in the Soviet Union Anthony had little idea. Save for the unmistakable scarcity of goods in the shops, the nature and consequences of Stalin's repressive regime were completely beyond him.[21] Perhaps he had been shown only those things the Soviets wanted him to see. Although he had spent a full week in Moscow, the Russians had not presented him much besides airfields and parts of the aviation industry. Like other foreign visitors he had seen only the regime's success stories—and these were inviting. Anthony saw considerable markets in the making for such things as "home furnishings, such as furniture, lamps, paper, writing materials, radios, medicines, sanitation, canned foodstuffs, metalware, photocameras, electrical appliances, automobile parts, shoes (though not army boots), etcetera, in short goods for daily use which make life more pleasant in Western Europe, but of which one sees very little evidence in the Soviet Union."[22]

Nonetheless, Anthony returned from his eleven-day trip empty-handed. On May 28 he took residence at the luxurious Carlton Hotel in Amsterdam, his usual domicile when in Holland. At first instance the lack of tangible results from his visit did not bother him, because he had been told to expect a high-ranking Soviet delegation to pay a visit to Schiphol Airport on July 7. The delegation chief, Yakov Alksnis, Commander of Red Air Forces, even piloted Fokker's giant F.XXXVI and proclaimed himself enthusiastic about the aircraft. Indeed, Anthony entertained hopes that the Russians might even be prepared to order some.[23] But nothing came of it. Gradually it became clear that the Russians were well aware that the aircraft offered to them came at exorbitant prices. Evidently Fokker was not going to sell even a single machine in Moscow at the prices agreed earlier with Elliott Roosevelt, and thus the deal was off—much to Anthony's disgust. He deeply regretted having gone into business with Roosevelt.[24] To Donald Douglas he wrote an angry letter calling Roosevelt and his entourage a bunch of profiteers.[25] Tiffany even entertained the idea of approaching President Roosevelt directly to have the contract between his son and Fokker canceled, so that Fokker might be able to sell aircraft to the Soviets at a more reasonable price just in case they changed their minds.[26] But matters never got that far, and the whole scheme fell through without there ever having been any real prospect of a sale of aircraft. Anthony fretted: he personally lost more than $11,000 in the affair.

He was even less amused when Senator Nye and his commission confronted him again with the issue in September 1935 and subpoenaed him to appear before the congressional committee. Clearly an investigation that would involve a public statement from Fokker on the role of the president's son in the intended arms deal with the Soviets would evoke political turmoil. So Anthony was dead set against being dragged into playing a role in any such scenario. Negotiations with the Nye Commission ensued, which resulted in an agreement that Anthony would be allowed to make his statement behind closed doors before two members of the commission and thus avoid attracting public attention to the role of the president's son in the prospective arms deal. Having returned from his summer holidays, Anthony appeared before the committee members in the company of Tiffany on September 12.[27] They arrived well prepared, carrying an array of documents to prove that it had never really been his intention to sell arms to the Soviets. About the bomber mockup that Lockheed had secretly shown to the Soviet delegation, Fokker wisely kept quiet.[28] In time the affair blew over, and the 20,000-page printed report of the Commission Investigating the Munitions Industry did not even mention Fokker's testimony, or Roosevelt's role for that matter.

ɢ

The events around the sales rights for the Douglas and Lockheed aircraft illustrated that Anthony was trying to redefine his position in international aviation. Now that it appeared that his leading role in aircraft construction was over, he cast himself as the ideal liaison to connect the rapidly developing American aircraft industry with the European market for commercial transport aircraft. It was a turn that was at first not perceived in Holland, but it would have dramatic consequences.

The contracts with Douglas and Lockheed were profitable to both parties. They enabled the American firms to expand the market for their products for free. Anthony personally bought ten DC-2 aircraft straight off Douglas's production line for prices ranging from $71,700 to $74,265, depending on the version of the aircraft. They were to be delivered between June 15 and December 8, 1934. For another $100,000 he now also bought all rights for production of the DC-2 and possible future derivatives for a period of five years.[29] He clearly saw the potential and the technological leaps that the DC-2 and the Lockheed Electra represented. Although he was by no means sure of being able to keep his Amsterdam firm going and recover the time and effort that had been lost there before the name Fokker were history, buying the license rights proved a brilliant move. This way his firm not only acquired know-how of the most recent technological developments, but Fokker's new personal position also precluded that his European competitors would gain such knowledge. It showed that Anthony was years ahead of the competition in operating on a worldwide basis. He also he bought time to think about the future of his own factory.

In Holland, Fokker's strategy produced conflict. The first problems already announced themselves by the end of January 1934. That month the Dutch Aeronautics Study Service, responsible for issuing certificates of airworthiness, announced that the construction of the tail section of the DC-2 did not comply with the national demands for airworthiness. Without a Dutch national certificate KLM would not be allowed to operate the DC-2 trial machine it had ordered. The question was, who was to foot the bill for the necessary modifications: Fokker or KLM? A cynical Anthony telegraphed from California that, if KLM did not wish to pay for the modifications, he could always cancel the sales agreement, close his factory, and spend his time any way he liked. At KLM, Plesman was once again outraged: "And now it is an outright scandal, how our interests are treated by someone who is half-German, half-Dutch, half-American. The aircraft industry has to be bolted to the Dutch soil. It ought to be impossible that mister Fokker can just go off to America and 'close the shop' here, as he likes to put it."[30]

Anthony was not impressed. He was much more concerned with the question of whether he should keep his Amsterdam company going at all. After the development of three commercial aircraft models for which there were hardly any buyers, his company balanced on the verge of bankruptcy. The government was aware of this danger. Having an indigenous national aircraft industry, able to put out machines of its own design, was of prime strategic importance for a neutral country. At the behest of the government a special Commission to Advance the Aircraft Industry was installed on February 3, 1934, chaired by the former Treasurer General of the Finance Ministry, Anton van Doorninck. Top-ranking civil servants from the Ministries of Finance, Waterworks, Colonies, and Defense also had seats on the commission, which received instructions to investigate whether nationalization of the aircraft industry was called for.[31]

Anthony utterly detested this mission. In it he saw a concerted attempt to take away his only remaining aircraft factory and an uncalled for, unnecessary interference in his business affairs. Nonetheless, he showed up for the commission's first scheduled meeting with him on April 10, although he made no attempt to hide his resentment that such a committee had been called into existence in the first place and now wanted to meet with him in person. The distrust was mutual. Several members of the committee referred to the long history of Fokker's lack of cooperation with the War, Defense, and Navy Departments. Not surprisingly, the atmosphere of the meeting was tense. Committee members criticized Fokker for not keeping up with the latest technological developments in aviation and for being late time and again delivering new aircraft. Anthony defended himself with vigor: *Never* had his company received timely information on changes in specifications. How then could he be expected to meet governmental objectives? Under the circumstances it could hardly be surprising that his aircraft sometimes fell short of expectations, he said. By the time the Netherlands Aircraft Factory received the final papers, it was often just too late to make changes in the design. Anthony maintained that government interference was not the answer to the problems his company was experiencing. All that was needed were firm orders for new aircraft.[32]

In the end Fokker received commission to build thirty C.X light reconnaissance and ground attack aircraft for the Dutch Army Air Service. With that order the company could be kept afloat while the Van Doorninck Commission studied the matter. It even enabled a small expansion of Fokker's workforce. In June 1934 employment at Fokker stood at 435 people, which was up 300 from the all-time low of December

1932.[33] Nonetheless, the fundamental issue of the lack of modernization in Fokker's latest designs remained unresolved. Anthony explained, "The reduced turnover . . . and with it reduced income makes it . . . harder every day and in fact impossible to put up the funds necessary to continue the work of development and progress."[34]

It was therefore not surprising that he took an inflexible position vis-à-vis KLM in the discussions on the costs of adaptations to the DC-2 design. Fokker understood perfectly well that his adversary, Plesman, had no option but to try to reach some kind of settlement, although it took the two men half a year to resolve the issue. In August 1934 the Dutch Aeronautical Service announced it would admit the DC-2 on the basis of a special, once-only "Certificate of Equality" with the U.S. Air Transport Certificate. The solution came just in time, for on September 13 the trial machine arrived in the port of Rotterdam to be hoisted ashore. Both Fokker and Plesman were present for the occasion, avoiding each other as much as possible without attracting attention from the press to their behavior.

In the past month they had been discussing a follow-up order for the DC-2, talks that had evolved in a particularly bad atmosphere. By then Plesman was adamant that KLM would in future only operate modern Douglas equipment. Calculations had proved that an expansion of capacity on the famous route to the Dutch East Indies could be achieved more efficiently, and therefore cheaper, operating DC-2 aircraft than flying the big Fokker F.XXXVI that KLM had insisted Fokker would develop. Now that a resolution to the issue of the Certificate of Airworthiness was within reach, Plesman had secured approval from his board to approach Fokker on the possible order of no less than fourteen DC-2 aircraft—eight for the route to the colonies, and six for the expansion of KLM's European services.[35]

Ever since, the two adversaries had been at loggerheads again. At the heart of the matter was the issue of the price of the DC-2s. To provoke Plesman, Anthony had waved his contract at him containing his exclusive rights to trade in Douglas aircraft in Europe. He offered the DC-2, which he personally bought from Douglas for an average price of around $73,000, for the equivalent base price of $97,000 in Dutch guilders. This would leave him a profit margin of around 33 percent per aircraft. Plesman nearly had a fit when he heard of this, and the meeting between him and Fokker ended in a screaming row. Fokker was wise to take a few days off and allow the matter cool down.[36] That same afternoon he boarded a flight to London, where he planned to confer with British aeronautical friends. Four days later Plesman came with a counteroffer: $76,000 per aircraft. He believed this would still leave Fokker a margin of around 10 percent. But of course it was not in Fokker's interest to seek a compromise. As so often in his life, his perspective was that of the immediate future only: to achieve a rapid return on the investment he had made when buying the sales license from Donald Douglas. He suggested that arbitration might bring parties closer together. Plesman even refused to discuss such an option, fearing this would inevitably result in some compromise that would likely be an average between what

The aircraft salesman: In the 1930s Fokker could not keep up with technological developments in aircraft construction without large investments. Instead he staked his reputation on becoming the principal sales agent in Europe for the Douglas and Lockheed companies. His efforts were instrumental in the American aircraft industry's achievement of global dominance. Here he pitches the capabilities of the Fokker-Douglas DC-2. **N. V. NEDERLANDSCHE VLIEGTUIGFABRIEK FOKKER, LIQUIDATED 1996**

Fokker was asking and what KLM was willing to pay. The longer the two adversaries negotiated, the further they drifted apart.

Matters were to become much more complicated still. Far away in Australia the wealthy confectionery manufacturer and philanthropist Macpherson Robertson, a contributor to Melbourne's centennial celebrations, had unfolded a bold plan to commemorate the city's anniversary by staging an international air race from London. When Plesman heard about the plan, he saw it as an opportunity to further one of the long-term goals of KLM. Since 1929 the Netherlands had been negotiating fruitlessly with Australia and Great Britain to acquire Australian landing rights for a KLM airmail service to Sydney. Both in London and in Canberra, pride dictated such a route should be flown by a British or an Australian company, even if this meant much slower service. Plesman intended to break the continued Anglo-Australian rebuff by a public demonstration of the speed that a KLM service might offer for mail delivery. He was even willing to risk using the brand new DC-2 to participate in the air racing adventure and registered KLM's one and only DC-2, named *Uiver* for the race.[37]

Fokker was fiercely opposed to the idea. If the machine would somehow be lost in the endeavor, he stood to lose all of his investment in the sales rights for the machine. To a Dutch news reporter he commented, "'Neither the aircraft industry, nor commercial aviation will profit from races such as the one from London to Melbourne. The only party to harvest the fruits from this, is the Australian chocolate manufacturer who put up the prize money. . . . Every racing event of this kind is a huge risk. Most participants are daredevils that squander the money of others while risking their own neck."[38]

Such observations did not go down well at all at KLM. Repeatedly Anthony demanded that KLM desist from participating.[39] It put his relationship with Plesman under even more strain. Meanwhile, the test program for his own F.XXXVI was not at all going according to plan: "I know that all kinds of rumors have been going around about this plane and that is why I will tell you exactly what the situation is. The F.XXXVI, with which test flights will continue next week, has been out of service for a few weeks to enable some improvements to its technical installations."[40] That was a euphemism, since the F.XXXVI suffered multiple malfunctions. On the evening of August 22, a new fight erupted between the two men. Anthony refused to budge on the price of the DC-2. With barely concealed rage, Plesman wrote to him the next day, "You *will* understand that this way of conducting business—the way you propose—is not at all usual and that it will cost considerable effort to convince our board of the acceptability to treat orders in the way you suggest."[41]

But Anthony would not move. He knew all too well that KLM's choice for the DC-2 could bring the end to his role in aircraft construction. Had not Plesman actually conducted a vitriolic campaign against the Netherlands Aircraft Factory in the preceding months, using phrases like "a worthless factory" and "an old dump for a building"?[42] Now it was Fokker's turn, and he would have Plesman pay the bill as he presented it. Then Plesman made a crucial error. Pushed on by irritation and by his conviction that he would get his way in the end anyhow, Plesman sold off eight of his Fokker aircraft to foreign buyers. Was it to spite Fokker and make a point? Likely, but the effect was that he had given away all his room for maneuver in his negotiations with Fokker over the price of Douglas aircraft. His temper and hurry were to cost the airline dearly.[43]

Long before the final scores were settled, KLM's *Uiver* appeared at Mildenhall Airfield, fifty-five miles north of London. In the early hours of the morning of October 20, the aircraft of the participants were pushed out of the hangars the Royal Air Force had provided. Around 6:30 a.m., the starter signal sounded. After a sleepless night on two uncomfortable folding chairs in an unheated tent at the airfield, Anthony watched the participants take off one by one, pretending to be no more than meekly interested and glancing up from the pages of the aeronautical journal he feigned to be reading.[44] At 6:35 KLM's entry, its DC-2 *Uiver*, started and climbed into the morning light. Anthony held his breath, hoping for the best. The next day, one of his fears about the race materialized. The other Dutch participant, the fast, privately owned three-engine Pander S.4 *Panderjager* mail plane, hit a tractor on takeoff and burned in Allahabad, India. Fokker commented, "In general, I can say this, that the Melbourne Race—even if it hasn't finished yet—has resoundingly shown that the margin between success and catastrophe is very small indeed. Furthermore the race has proved that what a good crew really needs is a reliable airplane and reliable engines. As far as the *Panderjager* goes, it was bad luck for the pilot . . . that he had a bird with feeble legs. Moreover, it is a fact that cannot be denied that young birds first have to learn to fly. But above all: birds are born, while aircraft are built and need a long period of development. They have to be made reliable, both by people and by experience!"[45]

Nonetheless, the Melbourne adventure ended on a bright note for him. KLM's DC-2 *Uiver* finished second, after the purpose-constructed de Havilland Comet racing plane piloted by Charles Scott and Tom Campbell Black, and thus made history.[46] After that airlines were almost lining up to place orders for Douglas's fast airliner. The acquisition of the rights for the DC-2 was turning into Anthony's best business decision ever. On the other hand, the remarkable achievement of the *Uiver* and its crew did KLM more harm than good. The Dutch success strengthened the British and Australian resistance against allocating landing rights—the very reason for KLM's participation in the event. Moreover, it tied KLM even more firmly to its decision to reequip with Douglas aircraft. On October 30, the board decided to allow Plesman to continue his discussions with Fokker while increasing the maximum price KLM was willing to pay for the DC-2 to $107,000 per aircraft.[47] That was 10 percent above what Fokker was asking, but now that the Melbourne Race had brought the aircraft's potential fully to light, the airline realized that Fokker's price was bound to go up in the course of the negotiations.

Meanwhile, the Fokker factory was still in trouble. Modernizing the company would be costly. On November 2, 1934, the management saw itself forced to request financial assistance from a government program aimed to counter the effects of the economic crisis. Fokker needed a million guilders (about $675,000) to build a new factory, equipped for metal production, at Schiphol Airport.[48] The request for subsidy was relayed to the Van Doorninck Commission for advice. Its members were sceptic. The commission was by no means convinced that the Netherlands Aircraft Factory was in such bad financial shape as Fokker would like them to believe. If the government were to step in on Fokker's behalf, it had to be the government, and not Anthony Fokker, that would henceforth call the shots. After a brief discussion, the Cabinet in The Hague agreed with this conclusion on November 12.

Anthony heard about the outcome of the discussions only later. In October he had embarked upon a second tour of Europe to sell Douglas and Lockheed aircraft to the European airline industry. When he returned in Holland, Van Doorninck approached him with the question whether he would agree to a government takeover of his company in some form or other. Anthony indicated he was willing to discuss the issue. As far as he was concerned, there was room to talk, as long as he would be kept on as constructor and director of engineering. It was the beginning of a prolonged cat-and-mouse game. Before long it transpired that there was a consensus within the Van Doorninck Commission—and indeed within the Dutch aeronautical establishment—that a rescue operation for the Netherlands Aircraft Factory that involved the government in some form or other would only make sense if Anthony were permanently removed from exercising any influence on company affairs. In a meeting on December 12, 1934, Van Doorninck stipulated why:

> Fokker has to be expelled from his present factory . . . because Fokker is not fit to be a director. . . . It is an established fact that he is not fit to be in charge. The mood among the workforce is bad. Things in the factory run better when Fokker is not there. But Fokker has other exceptional qualities, which we would like to keep. . . . The most obvious plan would be to keep him on as a director. But we hear from all sides that he is no good for this. Nobody is satisfied about him. There is no order and no discipline in the factory. It is rife with the mistakes of every company that is badly managed. Therefore, if Fokker is to become director of the new factory, things will run aground. Nonetheless, he has very good qualities as a constructor and as a salesman.[49]

But what was Anthony to do in the light of such heavy criticism? He really did not know—and besides, he was too busy conducting talks in Britain and in France on possible cooperation and airplane deliveries. To be able to think things through at his leisure and come to grips with all the fuss surrounding his person, he boarded the train to Basel, Switzerland, a week later, intending to use the clean mountain air to clear his head.

ST. MORITZ, SWITZERLAND
JANUARY 1937

High up the slopes of the Engadin Valley just outside St. Moritz, Switzerland, snow-covered Chalet Oberalpina appeared like a scene from a picture book. Ever since Anthony bought the house in October 1934, Christmas and New Year's visitors had loved it there. Fokker's hospitality was legendary. On the first page his guest register read, "In this book, my friends / you will find all, young and old, small and tall / who enjoyed their stay in the land of snow and ice and sun / in Oberalpina, the chalet of Ton. / Celebrated in his generosity / he distributes pleasure / and all his friends visit. / The house fills with joy and laughter / while worldly worries disappear."

Even Anthony's ex-wife Tetta was welcome to visit and enjoy the distinctive atmosphere. Often a "crew" of up to ten people at a time stayed at Oberalpina. No effort was spared to make their stay memorable. The in-house staff of chamber-maids, cooks, and general servants worked long hours to get everything just right. Sweets, smoker's requisites, wine, and other alcoholic beverages were plentiful. The meals were especially famous: "The guests eat and eat as if it were hard-earned booty. Because after sports, eating is one's duty."[1] Most visitors were family-related: uncles, aunts, nephews and nieces, friends and acquaintances from the four corners of the earth. But Fokker also welcomed business contacts, movie types like Charlie Chaplin, and politicians such as Dutch Prime Minister Hendrik Colijn. Anthony enjoyed sharing his material possessions and loved having people around him. He himself would typically arrive during the week before New Year's Eve so that he might treat his guests to grand fireworks and champagne to celebrate the new year.

Days began early at Oberalpina. Although Anthony often worked into the night, he needed but a few hours of sleep and was generally a morning person. Most of his guests were there for winter sports: skiing on one of the slopes of the Suvretta, riding a boblette (a low, multiperson sled), or, for the true daredevils, riding a skeleton sled on the Cresta Run. Anthony was a member of the St. Moritz bobsled club and a skeleton fanatic with considerable experience. With his leather helmet, nickel elbow plates, and heavy, metal reinforced gloves to protect his limbs, he looked like a warrior. Metal pins on his shoes for braking completed the outfit. "I do things at leisure" he told a Dutch journalist a few years before: "I'm here for my own amusement and I don't need to go top speed." Nonetheless, he easily made 75–80 miles an hour on his skeleton. In one race, the local paper recorded him as one of the three fastest to finish. He also loved challenging his guests to accompany him down the track in the bobsled: "The first time you just don't know where you are in one of them. In the curves you feel like a fly on the ceiling; yet the second run isn't quite such a dare, and the third time around it's just boring normality."[2] For the slightly less adventurous guests, attractions included ice skating on the large open air rink in front of the Hotel Kulm, mountain hikes, playing with Anthony's English sheepdog, or simply going for a drive with as many people as could fit into Anthony's Lancia convertible.

For evening entertainment Anthony liked to show films that he had taken himself. Many, but not all, had to do with aviation. He spent hours to get just the right shots of the ice skating maneuvers of Angela Anderes, the Swiss ice skating champion, when she performed in St. Moritz in February 1937.[3] To take his guests to a festive evening in the bar of the Palace Hotel, Anthony organized horse-drawn sleigh rides. On other occasions the company went dancing in evening wear at the Kulm, where "uncle Tony" liked to demonstrate the rumba to his younger guests. There was no escaping such activities when staying at Oberalpina, if Anthony was present. As a memento, he presented all guests with a Delft blue pottery plate that depicted the various activities from their stay. Anthony had the plates made especially by the Dutch pottery factory Sphinx in Maastricht after a design by Bernard van Vlijmen.[4] Those who didn't like exercise, like Anthony's mother, Anna; his sister, Toos; or their former neighbor Catharina de Leuw-Stolp from Haarlem, preferred to come in the summer so that they could enjoy the mountain view in peace and quiet. For them the evenings unfolded at a more tranquil pace.

⚓

After ten years of spending his winter holidays in Davos, in Hotel Kulm, and the Palace Hotel in St. Moritz, Anthony had bought the Oberalpina chalet for the equivalent of $57,500 in October 1934. Beautifully situated, the house overlooked St. Moritz with its lake, and beyond it the Engadin Valley. After the transfer of ownership, Anthony had the house altered to suit his preferences. In the end it had ten bedrooms, four bathrooms, servants' quarters, and a large garage. He also altered and expanded the

Chalet Oberalpina: In October 1934 Fokker bought a large chalet in St. Moritz, Switzerland, his favorite winter sports resort. He spent several months there each year in the company of family, friends, and business contacts. Here the crew of 1937 prepares for skeleton sledding.
FOKKER HERITAGE TRUST, HUINS, THE NETHERLANDS

grounds around it until it encompassed almost ten acres, although his desire to have his own private landing strip did not materialize.[5] Inside the chalet, the atmosphere was typically Swiss, with walls, doors, floors, and ceilings made of unpainted pine. Old Dutch paintings of cityscapes in big ornamental frames decorated the walls. The furniture was eclectic, a mixture of traditional and more modern styles, with various cloth-covered and leather seats and sofas with low side tables. In the salon stood a large old Dutch fireplace.[6]

The house had four permanent staff members. To supervise them Anthony appointed someone from his inner circle of personal friends and relatives, as was his usual recruiting practice. One was the youngest daughter of Catharina de Leuw-Stolp, his mother's former neighbor in Haarlem. Johanna Hendrika de Leuw, nicknamed "Jojo," had been born on March 3, 1906, in the Dutch village of Vaassen, where her father Max de Leuw was the director of an ironware and sheet metal factory. Jojo held a Gymnasium-B diploma, Holland's highest level of secondary education, graduating from an Amsterdam school in June 1925. The year after her graduation her father had died after a long disease, after which she decided to get a degree in education and attend classes for a teacher's license in English, which she obtained in August 1931.[7]

Jojo was twenty-seven years old, a vivacious young woman whom Anthony had met at various social outings, such as a horse riding party at the Noordwijk beach in June 1933. Known for her joyful mood and friendly composure, Jojo had been one of the younger people that had stood out among the small group.[8] Since then she had repeatedly acted as Anthony's companion at official dinners and other social functions, like the IATA meeting in The Hague in August 1934.[9] A week after closing the deal on Oberalpina they met again. The conversation touched upon the newly acquired house in Switzerland, which Anthony planned to have remodeled and for which he was looking for a caretaker when he was not there. He suggested that Jojo might take to the job if she was available and accompany him to St. Moritz to see the property herself. He paid for her airfare.[10] Despite an age difference of sixteen years, Anthony and Jojo got on very well from the start. Before returning to Holland and to his customary altercations with Albert Plesman and with the Van Doorninck Commission, Anthony took her on an extensive tour of the area. From St. Moritz they drove to Tirano and Chiavenna across the Italian border.[11] When he took his leave, her position as Anthony's official hostess and head of the household in St. Moritz had been settled. In August 1935 he wrote to her, "I have had little opportunity to tell you how highly I appreciate your help, administration and company, how it is a load off of my mind to know that I can go for my pleasure to Ober Alpina and always find a home there with a pleasant atmosphere. I have enjoyed myself there without reserve and have had peace, and I thank this for a great part to you."[12]

It was not just the high altitude of Oberalpina—situated at over 6,000 feet, its clear air a boon for his sinus ailments—that made Anthony go to St. Moritz more often than he had in the past. Between Anthony and Jojo a romance was in the making.

Ʂ

Meanwhile, Anthony tried to reinforce his position in the European aircraft industry, despite the problems he encountered in Holland. From 1922 onward he had been a regular visitor to Britain, where he held good contacts. Despite the successes British racing aircraft had celebrated in recent years in various international contests, the British aircraft industry had trouble keeping up with developments in aerodynamics and construction technology that had occurred in the United States. For that reason, several British aircraft constructors were interested in a possible cooperation with Fokker, especially since he owned the European production rights for the latest American commercial transport aircraft. On November 12, 1934, he landed at London's Croydon Airport to confer the next day with Norman Blackburn, director of the aircraft and engine factory of that name in Yorkshire. He also met with executives of the small Airspeed outfit in Portsmouth, which had hitherto specialized in the construction of wooden aircraft. Anthony hoped to sell the rights to manufacture the Lockheed and Douglas models in the United Kingdom.[13]

Anthony's last muse: In 1934 Fokker hired Jojo de Leuw as his hostess at Chalet Oberalpina. The relationship between Anthony and the lively Jojo soon went further than they would admit to the outside world. Defying the conventions of the time, they began living together.
FOKKER HERITAGE TRUST, HUINS, THE NETHERLANDS

Airspeed had been a recent addition to his circle of British contacts. Anthony's first talks with its director and chief engineer, Nevil Shute Norway (later the best-selling novelist known by his first two names), and his partner, Hessell Tiltman, dated only from October 1934. Indeed, Airspeed itself was new. Just four years before, Norway and Tiltman had started their venture in a garage in York. Now they were looking for an association with an established name in aviation that could help them make Airspeed more visible in the field.[14] After a stock issue, Norway had approached Fokker in the wake of the success of the DC-2 in the Melbourne Race. What he was after was a sublicense to build the Douglas machines, yet he indicated that Airspeed might also be interested in building Fokker aircraft. Anthony understood very well that what the two engineers were after was the Douglas design. He managed to steer the discussions in such a way that Airspeed felt obliged to buy the rights to his old patents first. Given the modest size of the Airspeed outfit, he bit his lip when reporters asked him about it. Several larger cities, he said, had offered factory buildings to work in, but the deal was not done yet: "Politics also plays a role in this matter. There is a group in England that wishes to establish Fokker factories in Britain, though others are out to prevent this."[15]

In a series of conversations that were, in typical Fokker style, conducted at impossible hours in empty restaurants in London, Newcastle, and Amsterdam and in Fokker's chalet in St. Moritz, he managed to reach an agreement with Norway and his new commercial director, George Richardson, on January 25, 1935. For a modest £20,000 Airspeed received the license rights for fifteen types of Fokker aircraft. Anthony must have been pleased at the outcome. He managed to stipulate the sublicense for the DC-2 in such a fashion that the marketing rights for any airplane thus built by Airspeed would be strictly limited to the British Isles.[16] This represented a serious impingement on any possibility of Airspeed actually making any money on the deal with Fokker. and Norway's hopes that the connection would somehow prove helpful to the expansion of Airspeed therefore came to naught. It even proved impossible to overcome British import restrictions on foreign aircraft materials, and Airspeed did not build or sell even a single DC-2. For the same reason Fokker's plan fell through to use the Airspeed connection to circumvent the trade barriers that the United Kingdom had put up around the British Empire in 1932 to mitigate the effects of the world economic recession. As a result, the collaboration between Fokker and Airspeed remained primarily a paper bond. Asked about his role within Airspeed, Anthony, who had himself appointed in his favored guise of "technical and aeronautical adviser," admitted that the work involved was minimal.[17]

The link with Airspeed was not the only strategy that Fokker employed to counter the attempts to halt his course in Holland. In the first two months after the Melbourne Race he traveled around Europe in his personal DC-2 demonstration machine with Friedrich Seekatz, looking for customers for the Douglas aircraft.

The furthest destination of the trip was Turkey, where the Netherlands Aircraft Factory already possessed good contacts. Mustafa Kemal Pasha, or Atatürk, the country's strong leader, had a fascination for aeronautics. Anthony hoped to tap into this interest and set up some form of cooperation with the Turks. In that context negotiations were ongoing on the possible sale of up to five hundred Fokker fighter aircraft for the Turkish armed forces, to be built under license in Turkey.[18] The talks on the order, however, were not going as well as had been hoped in Amsterdam, and Anthony imagined that a personal intervention might lead to a breakthrough. The Netherlands Aircraft Factory really needed such a break. Yet, given his total lack of affinity with Turkish customs and culture, his six-day sojourn in Istanbul and Ankara proved much too short to effect the breakthrough he came for. Nor did his demonstration flight with the DC-2 at the Turkish military airfield at Eskişehir result in a sale. Anthony left it to his factory director, Bruno Stephan, to continue the negotiations, but even then no orders ensued.

On December 4 Anthony left Istanbul with the demonstration machine, bound for Athens. Along the route he thoroughly enjoyed the sun-drenched southern landscape. From the plane he shot several reels of film of the clouds and the landscape that passed under him. So avid were his filming efforts that one of the guests he had invited to accompany him onboard became suspicious: was he really just interested in the cloudscapes, as he said, or did his interest extend to the ground? After all, conflicts between Greece and Turkey had run high after 1918. In 1921 and 1922 the two countries had fought a short but intense war, bitter memories of which lingered. Anthony's strange filming interests were reported to the Greek authorities after the plane landed at Athens. While he did his best to interest the Greeks in the new DC-2 and spent some of the time that remained after the talks to tour and film the Acropolis and other ancient sites, the information on his aerial filming interests was passed around to various authorities. When Anthony reported at the Athens airfield on Friday morning, December 7, 1934, to board his demonstration machine and continue his tour to Rome, he was accosted by uniformed officials. To his immense surprise, he was arrested on charges of espionage for Turkey. The arresting officer charged him with illegally filming several weapons depots and army facilities in eastern Greece and expressly forbade him to leave the country. His film camera and his footage were taken into custody. Later that day, examination of the developed film reels revealed that Anthony really had been interested in filming only cloudscapes. At the end of the afternoon he was released again from custody, his passport was stamped, and he was given permission to leave and continue his voyage to Rome. The matter thus ended with a warning only, although the arrest did make the international press.[19]

In Italy the DC-2 was also demonstrated, and again Anthony was engaged in several days of talks with people from Mussolini's aeronautical establishment. He also visited his nephew Timon Fokker, a former Dutch diplomat who had been living in Rome since 1921 and had made a name for himself as an art expert. After five days

Anthony boarded a flight to Paris where he spent the night before continuing his journey to Rotterdam, and on by ferry boat to Harwich in Britain the next day.

In the meantime, Cornelis Vattier Kraane, Fokker's chairman of the board, had been busy negotiating Anthony's future position with the Van Doorninck Commission. It appeared almost certain that Anthony would lose control over his Dutch companies too. But what if that happened? He wanted to get out of Holland anyhow. What was keeping him? He pondered over the options in Britain. If all went well, a new factory where Fokker and Airspeed could build Douglas aircraft might be erected in Tyneside in cooperation with the shipbuilding firm Swan, Hunter and Wigham-Richardson. The mayor of Newcastle had even sent a congratulatory telegram ahead: "Delighted to hear you are likely to build a new factory near Newcastle. Very pleased to be of service to you. Welcome to Newcastle."[20] Although more than a few details remained to be clarified, especially those concerning the finances of the plans, the affair itself was gratifying for Fokker. It was the last time he managed to sell the rights for licensed production of aircraft carrying his name. It was also the last time he was asked to act as aeronautical engineering consultant. Still, it could not be denied that his technological know-how was becoming outdated. The cooperation with Airspeed would not last.

In Holland the financial consequences of the plans that were under discussion also bothered him. Would he even be able to retain control over his own corporate money, given the strengthened role that the government now pursued in aeronautics? Toward the end of 1934 Anthony instructed his financial adviser, Frits Elekind, to transfer nearly all the money in his corporate account to his private account. Of the company's 3.8 million guilders in liquidities (then approximately $2,568,000), some 3 million ($2.03 million) went into Anthony's private accounts. The members of the Van Doorninck Commission were appalled, since the move put extra pressure on the discussions.[21]

Anthony was unconcerned. While the talks continued in Holland, he preferred to spend his time at Oberalpina in the company of Jojo de Leuw. They passed Christmas and New Year of 1935 there with a group of invited guests. Not before mid-January did Anthony find time to bother with his financial interests. A month later he was again conferring with the Van Doorninck Commission. It must have been painful for him to see the course of action that the commission had embarked upon in his absence. In a meeting on February 28, 1935, Anton van Doorninck cautiously suggested that Fokker might occupy the position of "technical and aeronautical adviser," a vaguely defined function. Van Doorninck made an effort to underline the positive aspects of such an arrangement. In his view it would free Anthony to concentrate on aircraft development and sales, without being distracted by the run-of-the-mill issues of the company. Yet, after nearly twenty-five years of entrepreneurship in aeronautics, the mere proposal was an affront that, to add insult to injury, came from a group of civil servants with whom Fokker shared very little indeed.

To everybody's surprise, however, Anthony fully agreed with the proposal. He presented himself as "the most accommodating man in the world." In the end he didn't care much about which course of action to take, as long as he was not forced "to work in the factory from nine to five. . . . The main thing is that I can continue to orientate myself freely. I sometimes feel the disadvantage of being in Holland. In America everything moves much quicker."[22]

Nonetheless, the day had been tiring and disappointing for Anthony. When he finally got out of the meeting, he took the next available train to Switzerland to seek solace in Jojo's arms. But within two days his various obligations caught up with him. On March 3 customs officers stamped his passport at London's Croydon Airport as he disembarked from the flight from Switzerland to resume his discussions with Norway and the other people from Airspeed. The speed at which he cut across Europe was growing faster than ever. This was not without risk. On March 26 his flight from Le Bourget in Paris ended in an emergency landing on the little sports airfield of Stapleford Abbotts northeast of London.[23]

It was not just Fokker's plane that failed to fly. His whole British adventure was moribund. In 1936 the agreement was officially canceled when Airspeed received military commissions from the Air Ministry as part of Britain's rearmament program. The Official Secrets Act prohibited the admission of foreigners to any defense establishments.[24]

Anthony did not lose much sleep over the matter. What had now become far more important to him was that Jojo had managed to give him the feeling of having a real home to return to at Oberalpina. The more they saw of each other, the more his inner life blossomed. He was back in love. In April and May 1935 they toured Switzerland, France, and Italy in Anthony's Lancia for a month and a half, like a true love couple. Never before had Fokker taken out so much time for a holiday. He spent further vacation time with her that summer. Having Jojo near clearly did him a lot of good.

He needed the extra holiday. After all, the spring of 1935 had ended in a vexing fashion when what was left of a once working relationship with Albert Plesman came to a total crash after a visit that Donald Douglas paid to the Netherlands. On May 16 Douglas had arrived in London from Santa Monica, California, with his wife Charlotte, their three children, and his parents. Douglas had come to deliver the Wilbur Wright Memorial Lecture on May 30 at the Royal Aeronautical Society, detailing the development of the high-speed airliner.[25] After spending a few days in London and a visit to his ancestral Scotland, Douglas took his family to The Hague on May 22 by invitation from KLM to visit their head office and form a firsthand impression of Douglas's launching customer in Europe. Strangely, he had not scheduled a visit to the Fokker factory in Amsterdam. The Dutch visit started the next morning in a relaxed atmosphere with a late family breakfast at Hotel De Witte Brug, a walk around The Hague, and a short courtesy visit to the American diplomatic legation. After that, business took over at the KLM head office.[26]

Douglas and Plesman made an instant connection when they met. It was inevitable that their conversations would touch upon Plesman's bad relations with Fokker and on the long history of bitter negotiations on the price of the DC-2 aircraft. Surprisingly, Douglas claimed he knew nothing about these troubles and professed amazement at Plesman's representation of how things had evolved. In reaction to Plesman's bitter complaints, Douglas said he could not remember having given Fokker a full sales monopoly. On the contrary, according to Douglas, what had been exchanged between him and Fokker was a contract that provided for Fokker to be an independent go-between in European sales, nothing more.

Plesman nearly had a fit. He got Douglas to sign an official testimony before a notary in The Hague that very afternoon, in which Douglas explicitly confirmed that Fokker did not have any European monopoly on the sale of Douglas aircraft.[27] After he had witnessed Douglas sign the statement, Plesman told the board of KLM later that day that his airline would never again buy any Fokker aircraft. From now on, KLM was to become a strictly Douglas operator.

Meanwhile, Douglas felt uneasy about the statement he had just signed. He was unpleasantly surprised to find reporters from *Het Vaderland* waiting for him upon his return to the KLM office. Although they did not have a clue about the afternoon's developments, he appeared to be exceedingly modest, soft-spoken, and ill at ease when interviewed about his career in American aviation and plans of the Douglas Corporation.[28] After the interview he hurried to make himself scarce and go to dinner. The next morning he rented a small yacht in Rotterdam and left with his sons on a sailing trip through the Dutch coastal waters to Antwerp in Belgium, while his wife and daughter took a flight to Berlin to go shopping and sightseeing. In the best of moods, the family reunited on May 28. In a short press statement in Belgium before boarding the KLM flight to London, a Fokker F.XXII, Douglas stated the next morning to be "really delighted" about his Dutch visit.[29] His delight would be short-lived.

While Douglas was sailing the coastal waters, Plesman couldn't wait to send a copy of the notary testimony to Fokker, announcing the end of all business relationships between them. Never being one for correspondence in the first place, it took a while before Anthony could be bothered to read the incoming mail. He and Douglas had met at Croydon Airport on May 30 and jovially posed for the customary press photograph in front of the KLM plane before going to the Science Museum together for Douglas's lecture.[30] It was only after his return from London that Anthony saw the copy of the notary statement that Plesman had sent him. Now he was livid. How could Donald Douglas have possibly gone along in this matter and committed such a statement to paper, after the prolonged discussions they had had in California in

January 1934? This was not just a false, dirty trick, but an outright lie! And why had Douglas said nothing about this when they met at Croydon?

The more Anthony thought about it, the angrier he became. On June 5 he stormed into the Dorchester Hotel in London, where the Douglas family was staying. A fierce row between the two aircraft manufacturers followed. In his hand Fokker held a copy of the contract he and Douglas had signed on January 15, 1934. He waved it in Douglas's face, threatening to take him to court in the United States and sue him for his very last penny unless Douglas categorically revoked the testimony he had signed with Plesman in The Hague. Fokker not only had a strong case and a history of never giving up in lawsuits, but he could also point to a new act of foolishness on Douglas's part in going behind his back and accepting an offer from the French aircraft constructor Marcel Bloch to buy the licensed production rights for the DC-2. This made matters even worse. Unless Douglas repealed his statement, Fokker said, he would destroy Douglas's reputation and that of the Douglas Aircraft Factory. He meant it. Confronted with what could only become a major scandal, Douglas had no option but to back down. Nonetheless, Fokker filed a claim against Douglas for $50,000 to compensate him for the sale, against the clauses of their 1934 contract, of the license rights to Bloch—half the amount he had paid Douglas a year and a half before.[31]

The dust had not settled when, in July 1935, three KLM aircraft crashed within a single week. None of these crashes had any survivors. KLM went through the darkest hour of its existence. Earlier, its first DC-2, *Uiver*, had also been lost when it flew into the ground at Rutbah Wells in Iraq on December 20, 1934. Another KLM plane, a Fokker F.XII, had been lost on April 6, 1935, near Kassel, Germany. Two and a half weeks after the disastrous series of July crashes, journalists interviewed Anthony. He declared that the recent crashes were due to airline procedures, remarks that made front-page news in almost every Dutch newspaper. Anthony repeated what he had said after the Rockne crash: airlines and their macho pilots took unnecessary risks in adverse weather conditions to stick to flight schedules. In his view the Melbourne Race had added to such pressures and had made flight schedules into altars on which the safety of passengers were sacrificed. Pilots flew in weather conditions that were far too dangerous for passenger operations: "The past six months have proved all too clearly . . . that reputation in aviation is too precarious a possession to be endangered by the wish to attain top achievements where the margin between catastrophe and success is very small."[32]

This time it was not just Plesman's anger that flared up. Deeply insulted, the board of KLM convened in an emergency meeting to discuss the Fokker interview. The members qualified his words as a heinous attack on KLM, his revenge for the string of conflicts over the DC-2 at a time when the airline's public image was at its most vulnerable. The chairman of the board, Shell CEO August Wurfbain, called Anthony directly at his hotel in London in the middle of the meeting and demanded an explanation. Again emotions ran high. If KLM's board so wished, Anthony reiterated with rage, he was perfectly willing to come over and restate his opinion about the plane crashes for their benefit. That was, however, the last thing the board wanted at that point.[33] Anthony did not leave it at that. In an unusually long, nine-page letter, he took great trouble to spell out in detail what he had meant in the interview and why he had spoken out in public about the plane crashes: "On the grounds of my very special knowledge of aviation, both in the technical and in the organizational field, and because of my personal experience as a pilot and my familiarity with the flying characteristics of the aircraft involved and the mentality of the pilots, I think I am most qualified to express my opinion. Indeed I find it irresponsible *not* to do so, because I wish to avoid being blamed later on that I should have spoken out as an expert, instead of having remained silent BECAUSE I AM AN INTERESTED PARTY."[34]

Indeed he was an interested party. The number of American commercial aircraft he sold was rising fast. By the end of 1935 the count already stood at sixty-two planes.[35] Still, the matter spoiled his holiday feeling that summer and still further strained his relations with KLM. Between him and Plesman all conversation had become impossible. Fokker was in no hurry to make amends or seek a compromise, either. Gradually it became evident that he used the existing grudges to inflate all sorts of technical details to stall negotiations on the price of new American aircraft and their terms of delivery. He absolutely did not intend to invest any of his own money into modernizing his factory and readying it for licensed production of the DC-2, as Plesman would have liked. Instead, he preferred to order complete aircraft directly from Douglas and assemble them in Europe. This attitude brought further delays to the talks. Although the basic contract for the order of fourteen DC-2 aircraft was signed on August 15, Fokker continued to put up new hurdles on prices and the terms of sale. In the end Plesman saw no other option but to agree to go ahead with a base price of $88,380 per aircraft, which put the final delivery price (including packing, handling, and transportation) at $100,600 each. A victory for Fokker, although perhaps the only thing for Anthony to rejoice about was the profit he made on the base price of the aircraft: $215,000.[36]

In need of relaxation, Anthony did not stay for the act of signature and left for the United States with Jojo and his friends Wim and Nel van Neijenhoff on August 14, hoping for a holiday without fuss. Onboard the brand-new French liner *Normandie*, they let the worries of the past month slip away. In the four days it took the *Normandie* to cross the Atlantic, they enjoyed the combination of luxury, design, and cuisine that already made the ship famous. Nonetheless, the trip did not bring what they had hoped for. First there was the unpleasant episode with the subpoena from the Nye Commission, and then Anthony found himself in the ward of the Los Angeles Eye and Ear Hospital suffering from his usual symptoms of sinusitis. Not before the end of October did he return to Holland. It was bad luck for him that he should travel onboard the same ship, the German liner *Bremen*, that carried Albert Plesman and his chief technology officer, Pieter Guilonard, back to Europe after they had paid an extensive visit to the Douglas factories in Santa Monica. But even though they were confined to the same ship for a week, none of them managed to make a move and sit down to talk.[37] Because of their public image—the conflicts that raged between KLM and Fokker remained carefully shielded from view—they did manage, however, to travel the final stretch of the voyage together onboard the KLM plane that Plesman had sent to Cherbourg to pick them up. When the plane landed at Amsterdam's Schiphol Airport, Anthony couldn't stop himself from playing yet another prank at his adversaries. When the plane stopped, he made sure he was the first to stick his head out the cabin door, merrily waving his hat at the photographers and generally attracting all attention. To reporters asking him about the progress in aviation he said, "One more and more comes to the conclusion that the times of embellishing the progress of speed in airplanes must come to an end. Reliability and a certain level of comfort, and a decent speed are the best factors. For that reason the British have not allowed themselves to be dragged into this race, but have quietly and consciously gone their own way of which they now begin to reap the fruits. . . . They focused on reliability and safety and a reasonable speed."[38]

Meanwhile, the talks about restructuring the Netherlands Aircraft Factory had continued without Anthony's participation. Vattier Kraane had managed to secure an attractive financial arrangement for Fokker. The share capital of the new company would be raised to 2.2 million Dutch guilders ($1.4 million). The government was to participate in the new venture and would provide just over half of the capital in the form of shares and in the form of new factory grounds north of Amsterdam. In return the government was to receive 1,200 ordinary shares. Anthony's shareholding would be restructured to encompass 1,000 preferential shares worth 1 million guilders. If the new general meeting of shareholders decided on a further expansion of the working capital within a time frame of five years, both parties were supposed to expand their holdings equally. Still, the government would be allowed to appoint the majority of the board members, while The Hague would also have the ultimate say-so in the appointment of the company director.[39]

General agreement on these issues appeared to be within reach until Fokker entered the discussions again upon his return from his winter holiday in St. Moritz in January 1936. To the exasperation of Van Doorninck as chairman, he now claimed the position of director after all.[40] In the weeks that followed, Anthony proved himself an able negotiator, managing to retain his title as director, albeit with most of the executive power stripped away from him. He also maintained an "advisory role" in aircraft construction and in foreign sales. For these services he was to receive a comparatively modest salary of 18,000 guilders per year ($11,600), plus the peculiar settlement sum of "three-fifths of 25 percent of the net annual profit."[41]

Now all that was needed was the formal consent from the government. But when the treasurer general of the Finance Ministry, Leopold Ries, read the final report of the Van Doorninck Commission, which carried the recommendation that the government should step into Fokker's Netherlands Aircraft Factory, he concluded that Van Doorninck, in his drive to reach some form of agreement, had completely passed by one crucial point: "That question is whether there are enough guarantees, that the new factory will, in its *constructive* capabilities, be able to compete with the best foreign factories on a permanent basis. . . . With this question one will have to keep clearly in mind right from the start, that the cooperation of mister Fokker *alone*, will in no way secure these guarantees, in the first place because the Fokker sun is on the decline and in the second place because one would not want to be dependent on Fokker *alone* in the matter."[42]

Ries's skepticism was echoed at the other ministries involved, Waterworks, Colonies, and Defense. Thus warned, the Cabinet weighed all the pros and cons at length, concluding that the risks were too great to accept. Thus, on February 22, 1936, everything was back to square one.[43]

℀

The long negotiations on the future of the Netherlands Aircraft Factory, and on Anthony Fokker's role in it, ended with the unexpected result that everything stayed the way it had been. On Saturday June 6, 1936, he celebrated his twenty-fifth anniversary as a licensed pilot as the full owner of his company. That morning before work, all personnel gathered in the assembly hall. Anthony received several gifts from them, and he had a gift in return for his employees: the founding of a corporate pension fund. In a gesture of appreciation, he read out the names of more than a hundred employees who had been with the company for over ten years. That afternoon there were festivities at Schiphol for Fokker employees, invited guests, and the interested public. After introductory words from company director Jacob van Tijen, from the Minister of Waterworks, and from the chairman of the Dutch Aeronautical Society, Anthony again publicly thanked several faithful employees. He also expressed special gratitude to his mother, from whom he read a lengthy telegram of congratulations, although he had just visited her earlier that day and spoken to her over the radio. Thereafter all eyes looked skyward for an air show: a D.VII, an F.II, and a formation of five C.V aircraft performing aerobatics. As a special treat for the public a demonstration had also been organized with Fokker's latest fighter aircraft, the D.21.

For Anthony, the top of the bill was a flying demonstration with a replica of his 1911 *Spider* that had been constructed in the Fokker workshops, intended to symbolize the distance that Anthony had covered since the dawn of his activities in aviation. Patience was called for, because it was 8:30 p.m. before his friend Wim van Neijenhoff dared risk a takeoff into what wind there remained. By then only a handful of spectators were left. Van Neijenhoff completed a few rounds over the aerodrome at a height of some 250 feet. After fifteen minutes he put the fragile machine down on the grass again.[44]

Anthony enjoyed it, as he had enjoyed the whole day. For the larger public, which had no knowledge of the serious problems that had been chasing him in years past,

Anthony projected a festive image in front of the Dutch cinema newsreel cameras: "And now I'm back in front of the old *Spider*, which I built 25 years ago. Then I was sitting, all in the open, on two wooden beams with fifty horsepower and now we sit with 36 passengers in an enclosed cabin, with every comfort, and several thousand horsepower.... And I'm very proud of this jubilee, not only because I learned to fly 25 years ago, but because I have been able to build up an industry in those 25 years that is, in my opinion, still only at the beginning of what we may expect, and I hope that this will be in the interest of the Dutch prosperity."[45]

It sounded peculiar coming from the mouth of a man who had made most his fortune in Germany and in the United States, not in Holland, and whose single remaining company had just been under serious investigation to prevent bankruptcy. On the other hand, Anthony tremendously enjoyed the occasion—and the replica of the *Spider*. He had relished assisting in preparing the little plane. And even though he preferred to leave the actual flying to his friend, he made sure that the guests who sat at the dinner in his honor that evening at the Carlton Hotel in Amsterdam had the *Spider* dangling above their heads, suspended from the ceiling.[46]

To commemorate his twenty-fifth anniversary as a pilot, Anthony also donated 100,000 guilders ($64,500) to establish a Netherlands Aviation Fund that carried his name. Its task was to stimulate Dutch aeronautics. Doing so for his own company, however, required serious thought. The future of the Netherlands Aircraft Factory remained bleak, and its director, Bruno Stephan, had left Fokker's employ at the end of 1935 to pursue his fortune as aeronautical adviser to the Turkish armed forces. Recognizing he needed someone with industrial experience to steer his company into a new future, Fokker had hired Jacob van Tijen, a former industrial export manager with a passion for flying, as a replacement. Co, as he was nicknamed, set about attracting new capital and modernizing the company.

ᑫ

Anthony steered clear as much as possible. As soon as the exhilaration of the jubilee had passed, he took the night train to Basel to spend time with Jojo in St. Moritz. Restless as always, he did not stay long. On June 30, 1936, he embarked in Cherbourg for his next crossing to the United States, this time onboard the new, fast Cunard liner *Queen Mary*. He still had an ax to grind with Donald Douglas. Arriving in New York on July 6, he took the next available flight to Los Angeles. Several talks with Douglas and with Lockheed's Robert Gross followed. The results were satisfying and confirmed the agreements signed in 1934. To be sure his interests in California would be looked after in his absence, Anthony now appointed his own personal liaison officer with Douglas and Lockheed, Richard Mock, whom he had known since 1929.

With Mock in place, Anthony believed he deserved a true break from ongoing business affairs. The bigger part of July and August he was to be found fishing and relaxing onboard his yacht *Helga* off Montauk Point, Long Island, and entertaining

American friends at dinner parties in the Montauk Yacht Club. The slow life suited him. Despite his many travels between coasts, he had never taken the time out to visit the Grand Canyon. Now, come September, he felt the time was right. He stayed for more than a week in the best suite of the El Tovar Hotel, right on the edge of the south rim of the Canyon. From there he made walking tours on various trails below the canyon rim, looking for the most spectacular spots and angles to film and photograph the bizarre and amazing landscapes that unfolded before the visitor. In September the temperatures—in the mid-70s on average—for such hikes were manageable. Nonetheless, he had come to lug more than a bit of extra weight over the years, and his forty-six years of age were beginning to show in several respects. On one of his hikes he had accidently left a tin of exposed film behind, and the hotel staff had to go out to look for it and retrieve the footage. His eyes were also giving him trouble. The years of 20/20 vision lay way behind him now, and the eye operation that Anthony had undergone at the Los Angeles Eye and Ear Hospital in 1935 had not improved matters. Wherever he went he was forced to take his glasses with him.[47] After his departure from the El Tovar on September 21, he discovered he had left his glasses on the breakfast table. (It was a typical oversight; in 1935 he had even forgotten to take his clothing with him upon release from the hospital in Los Angeles.) Anthony's liaison Mock went to great lengths to retrieve the glasses and have them sent to Alpine, New Jersey.[48]

Aging was clearly becoming a factor in Fokker's life. Following a trip to San Diego in September 1937, he returned home with an infection from which he felt so sick that he sent Mock a telegram to go and see his longtime specialist in Los Angeles, Simon Jesberg, describing the symptoms. Jesberg referred him urgently to a colleague in New York.[49]

Mock, who was sent on quite a few such errands, found he had a taxing employer. His freedom to act on Fokker's behalf was strictly limited, and he spent quite a bit of time and effort tracing his whereabouts. His boss was usually difficult to find, and Anthony loathed being chased by business affairs at his private address. To circumvent this, Carter Tiffany acted as an intermediary. If matters required an urgent answer from Fokker, Mock would send a telegram to Tiffany's office in New York. Tiffany, in turn, would then telephone Anthony in Alpine asking for instructions. These then had to be relayed again to Mock, either by telephone or by telegram. Only in very urgent situations was Mock allowed to send a telegram directly to the telegraph office nearest to Alpine, requesting that the operator phone Fokker to relay the message. Anthony sometimes communicated with Mock in the same roundabout fashion, sending him a telegram that he would call with instructions at a certain time. He preferred to do so either late in the evening, at around 11:30, or early in the morning. Because California was three hours behind, this meant he would keep Mock on the alert and near his telephone around the clock. Punctuality never was Anthony's thing.[50]

While he was hiking the Grand Canyon, the idea had grown on Anthony to make one final attempt to provide a new footing for American interests. To Gen. Oscar Westover, commander of the Army Air Corps, he wrote about his

> *desire of continuing my activities as airplane designer and manufacturer in this country. . . . In Holland I am the dominating and controlling stockholder of the Netherlands Aircraft Manufacturing Company, which manufactures airplanes largely for the Dutch Army, Navy, Colonial air forces, and the Dutch operating airline, KLM. Owing to a lack of policy of the Dutch Government, very limited development funds, export facilities restricted to the smaller countries in Europe, its dependence for engines, materials and accessories upon foreign industries, its industrial possibilities are limited and largely confined to local and national activities. Therefore this enterprise has always been of secondary interest to me.*[51]

Would there be more interest in America, he wondered, in a very large transport airplane with enough range for transatlantic operations, and from which a bomber version might also be developed? At the Stockholm aeronautical exhibition earlier that year, Fokker had first revealed detailed sketches for such a project, the Fokker F.56 "flying hotel" that was to offer accommodation for fifty-six passengers divided over two decks.[52] Westover said he was interested, but suggested that Fokker's ideas would stand a much better chance of success if put forward in cooperation with a large American aeronautical firm.[53] This of course required a lot of preparation beforehand, and without guarantee of success, as Fokker knew only too well. He therefore chose to let it go and focus on the more pleasant things in life instead.

The latter was difficult enough, since his earlier conflict with Elliott Roosevelt caught up with him again in the fall of 1936. In the run-up to the presidential elections of November 3, 1936, the chief editor of the trade journal *Aero Digest*, Frank Tichenor, had managed to lay his hands on various documents that Fokker and Carter Tiffany had provided to the Nye Commission the year before. Tichenor, a Republican and a staunch Roosevelt-hater, had waited to publish the documents until the month before the presidential election, hoping the machinations of the president's son might seriously damage the president and his chances for reelection.[54] On October 6, with Roosevelt's campaign barely a week old, *Aero Digest* made the case public. The very next day Elliott Roosevelt and Anthony Fokker saw themselves in the headline news nationwide, while the radio also gave the case a lot of attention.[55]

Senator Nye was forced to reveal the documents about the case, which had hitherto been kept under lock and key out of respect for the president. It was embarrassing for him that the official printed report of the Senate Committee on the Munitions Industry, over twenty thousand pages long, had carried not a word on the affair with the president's son and his involvement with Fokker and the Soviets.[56] Anthony himself was much annoyed to find his name in the headlines in this fashion. In an interview with the *Los Angeles Times* he made no effort to diminish Elliott Roosevelt's role in the matter, which caused Elliott to threaten Fokker with a court action over slander.[57]

They were only words. The harder Elliott denied having had anything to do with the intended aircraft sale, the higher the evidence against him stacked. His former business associate George Stratton tried in vain to convince the press that Elliott had never received any money from Fokker for his involvement.[58] Elliott also vehemently denied that his father had known about the deal, although the *Chicago Tribune* quoted Carter Tiffany as stating that Elliott had telephoned his father at the White House with the terms of the agreement but had been forbidden to travel to Moscow by the president.[59] President Roosevelt remained silent, hoping the matter would blow over quickly if he refrained from commenting. And although First Lady Eleanor Roosevelt made a special detour on the campaign trail to visit Fort Worth, Texas, where her son had found a new domicile, she maintained that she had "nothing to say" about the airplane contract differences and that her visit was for private reasons only.[60] Chased by journalists who wanted to know the details of the case, Fokker finally indicated that, as far as he was concerned, the matter had been "an ordinary business deal that has been misinterpreted for purposes of political propaganda . . . [hoping] to clear any misapprehension that I am interested in politics; that I was in any way responsible for the current news releases on this subject or that I have any desire now or ever to embarrass the President of the United States or his family."[61]

For him that settled the matter, although his claim that he had let the contract expire because the prices of the airplanes quoted to the Soviets had been unrealistically high was not quite true. But because no new facts surfaced after the first reactions to the allegations in the *Aero Digest*, the attention from the media soon shifted elsewhere. Anthony must have been relieved, just as the Roosevelts were. Franklin Delano Roosevelt's presidential reelection campaign resulted in one of the biggest electoral victories in American history ever.

NEW YORK, NEW YORK
JUNE 1938

The shrill sound of the ship's electric bell was hard to miss. "I baptize you with the Latin letters QED," said Anna Fokker, calling from Villa Atlas in Bergen, Holland. Her voice was difficult to hear because of the static on the transatlantic telephone line. Under the bow of the ship, decked with flags and flowers, Anthony was touched by the moment. A bottle of Dutch water that he had brought from Haarlem for the occasion was smashed against the ship's hull. He nodded. One of the officials present at the wharf of the Consolidated Shipbuilding Corporation in New York gave the order, "Now let her go!" Lines were cut, blocks drawn away. Slowly the ship slid backward into the water of the Harlem River. While he exchanged a few more words with his mother beyond reach of the sound system, his 200 guests clapped and cheered. The day was June 20, 1938, at 3:15 p.m. The ceremony with the telephone was unusual, but at her age Anna Fokker had shown no inclination for transatlantic travel.[1] Thus Anthony had come up with the idea of a phone connection. His long-cherished dream—at $300,000 dollars his biggest and most expensive project ever—was finally being launched. Naturally there was no one more suited to share this moment with him than his cherished mother, who had supported him throughout his life. His eyes gleaming at his hypermodern, streamlined ship with its contrasting dark blue-gray and silver tones, Anthony told a *New York Times* reporter, "I know that many yachtsmen are skeptical of this ship. That is why I want it. I wish to prove to these skeptics that my ship, by introducing new principles, will revolutionize and give new impetus to the shipbuilding industry. I do not think my ship will last forever.

I hope it will be obsolete within two years. . . . That is good. That is progress. Today there are too many yachts which outlive their owners."[2]

He had hardly spoken the words when things went awry. At the end of the slope, the *QED*'s stern ran aground and got stuck in the mud of the Harlem River, even though the hull only reached just over five feet below the water line. The rejoicing stopped. But Consolidated had reckoned with such a turn of events; when launching a previous ship, the same thing had happened. In the middle of the river the tug *Russell 18* revved its engine and carefully moved in to connect a line. But when the tug started pulling, the tow line snapped. Twice more the *Russell 18* tried, but with the same result. The only thing left to do was to wait for high tide, around 3:30 a.m., and then have a final go. Anthony bit his lips.

Since Consolidated Shipbuilding had announced its unique order to build Fokker's revolutionary ship at the National Motor Boat Show in January 1938, six busy months had passed.[3] The 111-foot-long, 25-foot-wide superyacht, displacing 145,500 pounds of water, was still partly unfinished. Designer William Starling Burgess had made the *QED* into something really special. A former aviation pioneer, Burgess had achieved renown in the United States as the designer of advanced sailing yachts. Yet the *QED* would not depend on wind but rather on no less than three engines: a regular 800-hp Vimalert ship's engine for normal propulsion and two 600-hp specially adapted Wright Typhoon aircraft engines for high-speed operations. Together the power plants delivered 2,000 horsepower, which gave the ship a top speed of around 35 miles per hour. It was a luxury yacht and a racing vessel combined. Such a ship had never before been built, and Anthony derived great pride from the attention and admiration it received from the American press and the nautical community.

In March, Anthony, who was closely involved in the ship's construction, had his own private office installed on the premises at Consolidated to be able to monitor progress from day to day. His involvement could be traced to the choice of materials. The *QED* was built completely from wood. The hull and topside were made of thick mahogany plywood, chosen for its strength-to-weight ratio. As an aircraft constructor, Anthony was bent on keeping the ship's weight in check. In the course of construction he had it adapted repeatedly to save as much weight as possible. For example, the foundation for the ship's engines had initially been planned in 1,000-pound heavy oak, but Fokker substituted plywood girders that, in the end, weighed no more than 55 pounds.

The list of ideas and solutions that he proposed was long. The only thing for which he did not favor a lightweight solution was comfort onboard. The *QED* was designed to accommodate six to ten overnight guests. From the large stern of the yacht they entered a roomy, comfortable salon that resembled a modern living room, decorated in light colors, with blue and green settees facing each other on the port and starboard sides. On the floor between them lay a woven black-and-white checkered carpet. A few steps further toward the bow was the dining room, with a large table and matted chairs in a natural hue. There Anthony's guests enjoyed dinner while observing the carefully reproduced seventeenth-century world map painted on the far wall. As always with Fokker, food was important. Dishes were brought up from the ship's kitchen using a small lift.[4] Midship, under the steering hut, were the sleeping quarters, similarly equipped with every convenience and luxury. Anthony had his own stateroom onboard with a double bed, desk and work space, sitting furniture, and even a fireplace. The QED had showers and bathrooms for both salt- and freshwater bathing. For extra comfort in the bedrooms the ship was equipped with electric heating and air-conditioning. Even a refrigerator and an electric washing machine were provided.

Farther forward the guests would arrive in the more technical part of the vessel, from where small canoes, a light sailboat, and even a full-size speedboat could be launched. Anthony, who had always liked to name his boats after the women he was in love with, named the speedboat Jo-jo. For those who didn't mind getting wet from spray when the QED moved at speed, the bow had a separate partly open deck where guests could gain a lively impression of the yacht's capabilities. For communication with the shore, the ship had a wireless telephone. Much attention had been paid to reducing engine noise and vibrations. Eleven crew members ensured that the owner and his guests would have a great time onboard.[5] Like the Helga, the ship itself was registered in Amsterdam: the whim of a rich man seeking attention.

Early in August 1938 the boat was finally ready. On its maiden voyage Anthony took her to Montauk Point, Long Island, to demonstrate the QED to his nautical friends. It was no coincidence that he arrived there just in time to participate in the annual event for the well-to-do water sports community: the party at Montauk Manor, at which stylish New Yorkers could marvel at each other's latest acquisitions. On the way back, early in September, Anthony and Jojo stopped at the Playland jetty near Rye on Long Island, where they took great pleasure in riding the various attractions, among them the Rye Playland Airplane Coaster, which even proved fun for the experienced aviator.[6] After that the QED set course for New York, and Anthony cruised along Manhattan and up the Hudson River to moor at the tiny village of Upper Nyack.

After Violet's death Fokker had continued to live in his rented house in Alpine, New Jersey, which he dubbed "The Hangar." Having abandoned the large mansion project and then given up the apartment on Riverside Drive that was filled with the memories of the drama that had unfolded there, there had been little reason to move. Untainted by the drama with Violet, the house in Alpine had grown into a refuge full of good memories of happier times. It was conveniently close to the Forest Boat Basin at the foot of the cliffs, where the ferry across the Hudson docked and where he kept the Helga at the local marina.

Quod Erat Demonstrandum: A lifelong water sports enthusiast, Anthony dreamed of constructing a supermodern yacht after his own designs, matching shape with speed. When launched in New York in June 1938, the *QED* was the sensation of the American nautical community. Fokker spent more money on the boat than he ever invested in any plane.
FOKKER HERITAGE TRUST, HUINS, THE NETHERLANDS

But now that Jojo had come into his life, the world looked different. With her Anthony wanted to rebuild and move forward. In November 1936 he therefore bought the Jean Adriance Dole estate on North Broadway, just outside Upper Nyack, some twelve miles upstream from Alpine. Through his Pulpit Rock Corporation he paid $50,000 for the house, which had stood empty for several years before he stumbled across it. Sleepy Nyack was just what Anthony was looking for. There the high cliffs along the river made way for an earth-covered slope, where a picturesque village had grown from two older settlements, Lower and Upper Nyack. It was a fitting spot for New York businessmen hoping to escape the rigors of city life. Undercliff Manor, as the house was locally known, was a three-story, red-brick house built in 1900. The sale included nineteen acres of land stretching all the way to the shore of the Hudson. About 380 feet of private river bank enabled Anthony to have his own jetty constructed, along with a private boathouse.[7] To be able to moor the *Helga* in the river's shallow waters, he had a section of the Hudson dredged. Undercliff Manor itself derived its name from the 300-foot cliff that towered high above the house. Although the house was inconspicuous from the road, it offered a magnificent view over the Hudson from the back terrace. That view became Anthony's pride and joy.

Shortly after completing the sale, Fokker contacted the architectural firm that had designed the house, requesting significant modifications. Next he took the boat to Europe on November 13, 1936. He was expected at the Paris International Aeronautical Salon that opened at the Grand Palais that month, and where his Netherlands Aircraft Factory claimed major attention for the first time in many years with its newly developed, revolutionary two-engine fighter-bomber, the G.1—the result of changes that Jacob (Co) van Tijen had introduced at the factory. Anthony did not return to Nyack before June 1937, but then he engaged himself intensively with the house renovations. At the rear he had a sunroom added to the ground floor, with large glass windows on three sides, requiring the removal of two full floors of the back wall of the central hallway. On top of the sunroom he had a similar glass-enclosed addition constructed for his bedroom. Upon getting up in the morning, he would thus have a panoramic view of the Hudson.[8] This was where he planned to retire with Jojo, and privacy became of overriding importance. Anthony was always one to shield his private life from his public presence. And since money no longer played a role, he bought the house and barn of the neighbors across the road as well, so that he would be sure that his "sinful" partnership with Jojo would not give rise to gossip.

Anthony spent roughly $120,000 on the new estate after buying Undercliff Manor. Given that he had lived ten years in relatively modest seclusion, Undercliff Manor represented a real break with the past. Visitors entered the house via a two-story carpeted central hallway, the walls of which were decorated with large nineteenth-century paintings. The hallway instantly offered a spectacular view of the garden and beyond to the Hudson Valley. To the left and right double doors gave access to wood-paneled rooms with beautiful plaster ceilings and thick carpets displaying oriental patterns. The ambience was that of the previous century, like the houses Anthony had bought in Berlin at the end of the war, although the furniture provided modern comfort. Apart from the living room and the sunroom, the ground floor offered a breakfast room, a dining room, a pool room, a kitchen, and a separate dining room for the ten to twenty staff serving the house. The rooms in the living areas had marble-paneled fireplaces, with large painted portraits of former nobility hanging above them in the fashion of European country houses. On the second floor were five bedrooms, four bathrooms, and a storage room. At the top floor, under the roof, another four bedrooms and a bathroom catered to the needs of the permanent female in-house staff. The cellar held a washroom, a firing range, and a drawing room, where Anthony spent many hours working on sketches for the QED. Next to the house was a detached large double garage with sleeping quarters above for the male staff. The built-in pipe organ in the hallway was something Anthony inherited from the previous owner.[9]

In all, Undercliff Manor had twenty-two rooms. Thus Anthony had all the space he needed for his extensive furniture and sundry art objects, some of which he had acquired during his time in Germany. To top these off, he searched for a truly classical

Undercliff Manor: Fokker's reduced involvement in aviation paralleled his increasing need for rest and comfort. In 1937 he bought a large estate in Nyack, New York, on the shore of the Hudson River. He renovated the house to suit his wishes and had a jetty built for his yachts. **AUTHOR'S COLLECTION**

painting to complete the house's decoration. On the advice of his nephew Timon Fokker, an art expert, he bought the painting *An Elegant Shepherdess Listening to a Shepherd Playing the Recorder in an Arcadian Landscape*, a large canvas painted in 1649 by the Dutch artist Govaert Flinck, one of Rembrandt's disciples.[10] The rest of the interior design and the furnishings he left to the care of Jojo.

ℱ

Thus the pilot and aviation magnate became more of a settled man. The private domain occupied an ever greater part of his life. Time, or rather the control over it, was gaining importance by the year. In the second half of 1937 he was more involved in renovating his house, designing his superyacht, and generally enjoying the easy life than he was in the aviation business. That winter much of his energy in St. Moritz was spent on tinkering with a motorized snowplow and perfecting one of his older ideas, a "snowcycle." His changing priorities were reflected in his applications for reentry visas into the United States. In 1937 and 1938 he no longer filled in "business" as the purpose of his transatlantic travels, but rather "pleasure." He also began to delegate the sales activities for the Douglas DC-3, successor to the DC-2, to the staff at his factory in Amsterdam. He did manage to personally land the European sales rights for Consolidated aircraft, although his negotiations with Boeing, which he had hoped would result in a complete European sales monopoly, faltered.[11]

Little by little Anthony began to withdraw from his Dutch enterprise. In May 1937 he agreed to a proposal from his board to restructure the Netherlands Aircraft Factory into an open venture that was listed on the Amsterdam Stock Exchange. That same month Fokker shares were introduced in regular trading. The company's working capital was enlarged with the issue of new shares and rose to 2.5 million Dutch guilders (roughly $1.4 million). Anthony himself sold 65 percent of his personal holdings to the Netherlands Trading Company (NHM), although he kept 90 percent of the preferred shares. On the advice of Carter Tiffany, who was increasingly worried about the possible repercussions of political developments in Europe, Anthony began to prepare the transfer of a large part of his private assets to the United States. In 1938 and 1939 he had a total of $2,850,000 transferred to several banks and investment funds in New York. He also transferred the equivalent of about $1 million to America.[12]

After the slump that had lasted more than half a decade, his Dutch company now showed a profit again. From 1937 to 1939 the Netherlands Aircraft Company made about $2.1 million in net profit. The company was logging longer shifts and was even hiring new staff. In 1937 the number of employees stood at 750, rising to over 1,200 in 1938.[13] The strategy of steady modernization that Anthony's new director Co van Tijen had introduced was working. Fokker condoned the new course but largely refrained from direct involvement. He found it difficult to admit that his decline as an aircraft constructor had been caused by his parsimonious financial policies and his limitations as a self-styled engineer. His personal influence, exercised during occasional visits to the factory while traveling between the United States and Switzerland, was disruptive rather than helpful to the company. Never much interested in politics, he confessed to being confused and worried by developments in Europe. On March 18, 1938, he was interviewed when arriving in New York aboard the German liner *Europa*. Echoing the ideas of Brig. Gen. Billy Mitchell, Fokker said he was convinced that future wars would be decided primarily by massive use of aircraft. He anticipated attacks by aerial fleets of hundreds of bombers: "These machines will fly high and fast and will darken the sky over any city they pick, and there will be no adequate defense against them." Anthony was also pessimistic about the chances for a peaceful future, adding "that the possibility depends on Germany and Hitler, who is doing what he pleases."[14]

Yet Anthony's heart still lay with commercial aviation. In this area the Fokker company was faring as badly as it had before. Since 1934 KLM had not bought, nor indeed wanted to buy, a single airplane from Fokker. Late in February 1938 Albert Plesman even decided to scrap his two remaining F.XXII aircraft.[15] Unable to exercise any influence, Anthony remained an involuntary witness at a distance. He raised the subject with the Dutch Prime Minister Hendrik Colijn, one of the returning guests at his chalet in St. Moritz, only to learn that Colijn was unwilling to involve himself in the long-running dispute between the nation's two aeronautics leaders. Dissatisfied and brooding on how to effect some change in the situation, Fokker left again for New York with Jojo.

After returning to the United States on March 18, Anthony buried himself in the work on his *QED* at the Consolidated wharf in Morris Heights, New York. In the month that followed all he could think or speak about was his new yacht, but in the second week of May, with progress being satisfactory, he managed to break away and devote some time to aviation. With Jojo he traveled to Ottawa to discuss the possibility of selling the G.1 fighter-bomber to the Canadian armed forces. From there he went on to Montreal to confer with his former associate Bob Noorduyn on the possibility of Noorduyn Aviation's building the G.1 under license, should Canada decide to buy the aircraft. Unfortunately, nothing came of this notion.[16] With Jojo, Fokker returned to New York by ship as the guest of honor on the last section of the maiden voyage of the Holland-America Line's new steamer, the *Nieuw Amsterdam*. More partying soon followed, for Anthony had agreed to host the wedding party of his nephew and namesake Anthony J. Fokker, the son of his favorite uncle, Eduard. On May 28 Anthony J. married Heyda Jolanda de Haan from Laredo, Montana, at Undercliff Manor. Young Anthony worked as a mechanical engineer at Sikorsky Aircraft in Bridgeport, Connecticut, while Heyda was the younger sister of the chief engineer of Pan American Airways, André Priester, one of Fokker's Dutch friends in the States.[17]

After the wedding, water ruled. Anthony invested $25,000 in the S. M. Development Company, a small firm that traded in shipping technologies and had agreed to market products resulting from Anthony's ideas on maritime construction. The latter interests were furthered through one of Anthony's earlier ventures into shipbuilding, the Oertz International Streamline Rudder Company Ltd., which he had founded in 1929 with Johan Carp and Wilhelm Horter in London to sell streamlined ships' rudders.[18] With the invitations for the launch of the *QED* sent, he spent most of his days at Consolidated's wharf.

On the day of the launching ceremony, something happened that made his Dutch heart jump with pride and joy. From the crowd that had come to witness the event, a somewhat roguish-looking elderly man whom Anthony could not quite place thrust forward and pushed a note into his hand. Amateur sailor Jacob "Ko" Kuyt, who carried the note, was a fifty-nine-year-old former planter from the Dutch East Indies. In August 1937 Ko Kuyt had set out to sea for an adventurous trip around the world via Cape Horn in the company of his young shipmate Dirk Hofman, with 200 tins of kale, carrot and onion hotchpotch, tinned beans, pork sausage, and cutlets. They took only the most basic instruments and other necessities with them for the underfunded venture. Their small secondhand wooden pilot's boat, the *Holland* (built in Norway in 1898), had sailed from IJmuiden and hardly been heard of since. After a series of unlikely adventures, the two travelers and their third crew member, Eugène

Heinze, whom they had picked up on Curaçao, had come in to port at Staten Island on June 19, 1938, after a general change of navigational plans. However, the three had no American visas, only a stamp from the American consul on Curaçao on their health passports, and were therefore forbidden from entering the United States. Such a minor triviality did not stop Ko Kuyt, who somehow managed to report to the Dutch consul general in New York the next day. Assuming that Anthony Fokker might be just the kind of person for Kuyt to talk to for assistance, Consul Wilhelm Montijn gave him his personal invitation for the QED launch, along with an introductory note to Fokker. Indeed, after Kuyt handed him the note, Anthony quickly wrote down his telephone number: "Nyack 840. You just call me."[19]

The sailors' story appealed to Anthony's sense of adventure and heroics. On his instructions the captain of the *Helga* towed Kuyt and his crewmates to Nyack the day after the QED's launch. The *Holland* was then moored at the Petersen Boatyard, where the QED had also been taken out of the water to inspect possible damages from towing. Anthony was there too, Kuyt later recalled, "in his shorts, a pair of rough shoes and a hat I would not have liked to receive from him as a present."[20] While the *Holland* was being overhauled at Fokker's expense, Kuyt and his men were received as his special guests at Undercliff Manor. They were also asked to come along on the first trial sailings of the QED. When the *Holland* was finally ready to risk the seas again, Anthony suggested that Kuyt and his crew first sail their "secondhand oyster vessel" to Montauk, at the end of Long Island. There he wanted to film the departure of his Dutch guests before the crème de la crème of the American water-sports world. The three adventurers had made a deep impression on him. When the *Holland* finally put to sea, Anthony circled it with his speedboat *Jo-jo* while filming. He promised Kuyt a job at the Fokker factory in Amsterdam if he made it home safely.[21]

ᵍ

On December 2, 1938, Fokker boarded the *Queen Mary* with Jojo to return to St. Moritz well before Christmas. Once across the Atlantic, messages reached him that, although business for his company was looking up in military aviation, the prospects for building commercial airliners still looked extremely bleak. In the event that the war everyone now feared would not break out after all, recuperating some of the Netherlands Aircraft Factory's lost position in commercial aviation was of considerable importance.

To obtain a clearer view of where his company stood, Fokker hired the young Dutch economist Gerrit van der Wal to compile an overall corporate analysis. When the report came out early in 1939, Anthony was so impressed by the results, and by Van der Wal's perceptions, that he soon commissioned him to monitor his personal finances as well.[22] Van der Wal's report confirmed the wisdom of not exclusively relying on the development of military aircraft. Yet in The Hague, Anthony's adversary Albert Plesman, by now completely oriented toward American manufacturers, persisted in his refusal to talk with Fokker about the possibility of future orders for commercial airliners. On February 11, 1939, Anthony made an urgent appeal to Prime Minister Hendrik Colijn to help make KLM reconsider ordering Fokker aircraft: "Since 1934 more than 50 aircraft with a total value of almost ten *million* guilders have been ordered *abroad by KLM.* . . . Now the time has come *to decisively influence the position of the Fokker factory on the world market* for future times, which should lead *to the recapture* of its *preeminent independent place* among production companies, or effect a *lasting degradation* to an agency dependent on foreign ventures."[23]

That month Fokker repeated his plea several times. In circles of the Ministry for Waterworks, home of the government's Aviation Service, his move was not appreciated. Its director, Henri van Ede van der Pals, maintained that it was Fokker's own responsibility to stay in the forefront of aeronautical developments, instead of chasing domestic orders. To his minister, Jan van Buuren, he stressed that obligating KLM to buy nationally "might cause irreparable damage to a prosperous development of the airline."[24] Nonetheless, Van Buuren showed a degree of understanding for Fokker's position. In a time of rising political and military tensions, it was hard to ignore Fokker's appeal. The Fokker factory played a crucial role in the national defense, and Anthony had already covertly intimated that he might halt work on military aircraft if nobody listened to him. To show its goodwill, the Cabinet decided to appoint an Interdepartmental Advisory Commission on National Aircraft Construction. Like the Van Doorninck Commission before it, this advisory group consisted of representatives from the Ministries of Waterworks, Defense, Economic Affairs, and Colonies. Its mission was "to come up with proposals, in the interest of employment and of the national aircraft industry, to involve Dutch industry more closely in addressing the kinds of aircraft that the Netherlands might need."[25]

Early in March Van Buuren instructed Plesman to meet directly with Fokker and discuss the various aircraft types that his company had to offer.[26] But Plesman refused to cooperate. Thereupon Fokker reverted to the press, publicly complaining that KLM was again considering ordering aircraft from abroad: "Time and time again we have made designs for passenger aircraft these past years, without anything being built. It is clear that one cannot continue down this road. One cannot allow to pass up a single opportunity to have the national airlines place orders with the national industry. . . . Additionally, building our own trusted aircraft will enable us to obtain a share on the world market. . . . That is why we have said: now or never. The moment to take action has arrived."[27]

The leading Dutch business newspaper, *Algemeen Handelsblad*, cried blackmail. Nonetheless, the sworn adversaries sat down together on March 13, flanked by their respective legal counsels. The meeting was convened at the neutral territory of the Shell head office in The Hague, but the atmosphere was extremely tense, which Anthony's public comments had exacerbated. If Albert Plesman had not received specific instructions from his board, he would not have come. Across the table, Fokker was only too aware that this might well be the last opportunity for his company to get back into the construction of commercial airliners. Now that the government urgently needed his company's military aircraft, he finally held the crowbar with which to force the door at KLM that Plesman had hammered shut.

Fokker proposed two different types of aircraft. For short-haul flights he offered "design 175," a two-engine commercial transport that would seat eighteen passengers; this concept was related to the design of the American Douglas DC-5, which Plesman was contemplating buying for the domestic network. Plesman lost no time indicating that he was not at all interested. He also rejected a second Fokker project, "design 177," offering a rapid, three-engine plane for European routes. The days of three-engine aircraft were long gone, Plesman argued. The center engine obstructed the pilots' forward view, might spill oil on the windscreen, produced extra noise and vibrations in the cabin, and added to fire risk because of the fuel lines that would need to be integrated into the fuselage design.

On the other hand, Plesman was realistic enough to understand that he could not send Anthony home completely empty-handed. He therefore agreed to discuss the Fokker project that was least likely to come to fruition: "design 173," for a large, four-engine, long-range transport plane with engines in tandem arrangement. It featured a pressurized cabin for twenty-four passengers. Plesman demanded that Fokker offer a precise price and a set delivery date. Anthony was unable to provide these, as the 173 project was still in its infancy and had not even been finished on the drawing boards. Therefore the meeting broke up without any prospects for a possible accord.[28]

But the ice had been broken, and future talks seemed possible. Anthony regarded this outcome with some satisfaction, viewing it as a victory over his old opponent. Yet progress proved extremely difficult to achieve and was badly hampered by deeply rooted mutual distrust. Anthony's optimism was wounded when he read his private take on KLM's director on the front pages of De Telegraaf: "But my biggest objection to this most remarkable figure is that Plesman has proved to be just as effective a constructive force, as a *destructive* one. All interests must bow to his own. And I think this is wrong. . . . Again we offer to build transport aircraft for the Netherlands. This cannot be allowed to run aground on the basis of a single man's ill will."[29] Anthony's apologies, expressed in writing not to Plesman but to KLM's mediator, Gijsbert Bruins, and the KLM board the next day, almost sounded sincere: "Now tonight another piece against Plesman has appeared in de Telegraaf and was printed against my wish and my explicit instructions to avoid any personal element, while this piece has not been shown to me prior to publication and I would surely not have agreed to its appearance in this form."[30]

For once, Plesman chose not to retaliate. Talks between representatives of the two parties were continued, although progress proved difficult. Satisfied that he had at least been able to pry open the door at KLM and knock a dent into the airline's aircraft procurement program, Anthony left with Jojo for London and New York in early May. Plesman tried his best to obstruct the process, but in July 1939 he had to accept the services of a special liaison committee, acting as an intermediary between KLM and Fokker's Netherlands Aircraft Factory. KLM received permission from the government to order ten large airliners from Douglas and Lockheed, but the go-ahead came with a price tag: four all-metal, two-engine Fokker F.24 aircraft, plus a single Fokker F.180 Intercontinental. For the latter aircraft, intended for scheduled transatlantic services, the government allocated a subsidy for both parties. Even so, the agreement had shortcomings, and negotiations between Fokker and KLM dragged on until January 1940.[31]

ᚷ

Fokker was involved in these negotiations only at a great distance. Back in Nyack he tried to relax, indulging in the luxury lifestyle he believed he was now entitled to. In June he was one of the sponsors of the Rockland County Day at the New York World's Fair that had started on April 30.[32] Still a man with celebrity status, he liked being seen at high-society luncheons and dinners. On July 31 he collected his Dutch guests George and Svea Gleichman, their teenage daughter Betty, and Gerrit and Janna van der Wal on the QED when they arrived aboard the liner *Zaandam* at New York Harbor. He even managed to persuade the immigration authorities to let his guests transfer directly from the steamer to his yacht.

At his invitation and expense they spent a month with him for their summer holiday. It proved to be an unforgettable experience. First the party sailed up the Hudson to Nyack on the QED for a two-day visit to Undercliff Manor. On August 3 the "Dutch gang" sailed to New York, to visit the World's Fair at the Flushing Meadows–Corona Park to see the wonders of the "World of Tomorrow" and the various pavilion exhibits. They were quite impressed by the radio-controlled boats in the pond. Then they embarked for serious boating, traveling all the way up to Bar Harbor, Maine, a voyage interspersed with excursions to aviation companies such as Hamilton Standard Propeller in Hartford, Connecticut, to the Playland amusement park in Rye, New York, and visits to the superyachts of Anthony's most affluent sailing friends. Above all, it was a trip with a lot of physical activities. "Every Day Another Thrill" was Anthony's motto, and he expected his guests to follow this to the full. A month onboard thus included canoeing, fishing, swimming, rowing, waterskiing, underwater excursions with Anthony's diving bell, hunting sea eagles, horse riding, and picnics on beaches. Anthony was filmed while riding, although he appeared not to be an eminent cook: the T-bone steaks he prepared over a campfire burned.[33]

Along the way they picked up another of Anthony's old friends, the polar explorer Hubert Wilkins. Anthony threw a special party in his honor and went shark and tuna fishing with Wilkins at Montauk Point.[34] Wim and Nel van Neijenhoff joined the party later.

The summer was beautiful, and initially peace and happiness prevailed. Yet the radio and newspapers bought at marina grocery stores carried ever more disconcerting messages. In Europe political and military tensions were mounting by the hour.

As the days went by, news reports described Poland's surrender of the "free city" of Danzig, in response to Hitler's demands that supposedly were to safeguard German minorities in and around the city. The Germans were clearly preparing a military escalation, and army units assembled on both sides of the border. Fokker, however, remained hopeful that the crisis might blow over. Interviewed at one of the QED's stops in Boston Harbor at the end of August, he speculated that war was still years in the future.[35]

Nothing was further from the truth. While Anthony and his guests partied merrily, pressures across the Atlantic reached the point of explosion. On August 28 even the politically neutral Netherlands announced the mobilization of its armed forces. Four days later the German army invaded Poland. World war, which had been in the air for so long now, was unleashed. As an officer with the Dutch army reserve, Lieutenant Van Neijenhoff was required to report for duty as soon as possible. Anthony booked a ticket for him on the *Dixie Clipper*, one of Pan American's brand new giant Boeing 314 flying boats, with which Juan Trippe had started a scheduled transatlantic air service earlier that year. On September 7 the QED moored at the Pan Am jetty of Port Washington, Long Island, where Wim van Neijenhoff boarded the *Dixie Clipper*. Jojo filmed his departure. Now the other guests also wanted to go home as quickly as possible, while there was still time. George Gleichman needed to attend to his business. Gerrit van der Wal wanted to finish his dissertation in trade economics. His wife Janna longed for home. Anthony gave them a large wooden chest as a parting gift, with instructions only to open it when *really* necessary. That moment came in Holland's terrible "Hunger Winter" of 1944. The Van der Wals were overjoyed to find the chest stuffed with canned foods.[36]

᛭

Thus the holiday trip on the QED that had started in such high spirits ended sadly. Without their guests, Anthony and Jojo returned to Undercliff Manor. They followed the events unfolding in Europe with mounting anxiety. After the British and French declarations of war on Germany and the Soviet invasion of Poland on September 17, war held Europe in its grip.

In the Fokker residence an ever stronger desire for diversion manifested itself. A good opportunity arose when Paul Borchard, owner of a chain of drugstores in Manhattan and a prominent Republican politician in New York, told Anthony of his daughter's wedding plans. Anthony and Borchard knew each other from the time when Anthony had lived on Riverside Drive. Paula Borchard had fallen in love with the owner of a small flower shop in Westfield, New Jersey, Richard Vance. Perhaps inspired by Jojo, Anthony saw a beautiful romantic story in the love between the two young people from such very different backgrounds, and he offered to let them start off their honeymoon to Niagara Falls, Canada, on the QED. Thus he was the guest of honor at the wedding in the Good Shepherd Presbyterian Church on West 66th Street on October 7, and on the reception that followed at the Whitehall Hotel.

That evening some twenty-five guests, led by Fokker, waved off the newlyweds on the quayside at 79th Street. The ship's crew had everything in readiness for an immediate departure. In the corner of the stateroom the open fireplace was lit, and the flames sparkled. At 10:15 the QED cast off and slowly began to proceed up the Hudson toward Nyack. The party was over for the wedding guests, and they each went home.

The Vances retired for the sweet promises of their wedding night on the yacht. About an hour later, their bliss was violently interrupted near Yonkers. Capt. Lawrence Ganage suddenly saw sparks and flames emerge from the ship's port side and immediately sounded the alarm. He went to investigate, armed with a fire extinguisher, but found the fire was already too advanced to save the wooden yacht. There was nothing he could do but give the order to abandon ship. In a panic Richard and Paula Vance dove overboard in their night clothes into the Hudson. Shivering, they managed to climb onboard a collapsible life raft the crew had put overboard. Several crew members also had to jump into the river to save their skins. They were rescued by a group of young Yonkers Sea Scouts who had hurried to the scene of the disaster in a small boat. One crew member got lost in the dark, however, and could not be found in time; sadly, he drowned and was not found until the morning. The ship itself burned completely and then sank. There was little Anthony could do but offer the unfortunate couple the comforts of his home at Undercliff Manor so that they might recuperate somewhat from the horrors they had endured.[37]

The loss of the QED must have been a severe blow to Anthony, but he took the bad tidings in stride. The evening after the fire he and Jojo threw a surprise party for the Sea Scouts who had been so brave in coming to the rescue. As a token of his gratitude, he gave the boys a new outboard engine for their boat. He also donated an inflatable life raft and bought them all modern life vests. Among those who were directly involved in the rescue of his crew and guests he divided $1,000. Three days after the disaster he went to inspect the sunken wreckage onboard the Helga and had to agree that there was nothing left to salvage. Defiantly, he told press reporters he was already working on plans for a new superyacht.[38]

Indeed, within a week Fokker met with William Starling Burgess. This time around, Anthony was looking for a yacht that would harbor the ideal combination of engine power and sail and that might be transformed instantly from a motor yacht into a sailboat. He envisioned a ship with hollow masts that would release sails at the touch of a button. A month later, Burgess presented three concepts for such a trimaster motor yacht. By the end of November the two men, friends by now, had progressed a long way toward a partnership in shipping design.[39]

WESTERVELD, HOLLAND
FEBRUARY 1940

Saturday, February 3, was freezing cold. Snow had been on the ground for weeks. The wind cut through heavy winter coats. That morning a long line of people assembled at the entrance of the Westerveld Cemetery between Haarlem and IJmuiden in Holland. The railway company had made a special stop for the occasion to carry all those who wished to pay their respects. The complete workforce of the Nederlandsche Vliegtuigenfabriek, nearly 1,500 people, had arrived by special train from Amsterdam. In the mourning chamber in the middle of the cemetery, the family gathered with specially invited guests around the urn holding Anthony Fokker's remains. At long last it was time for the final goodbyes. The film cameras ran, the orchestra played. In front, behind the bier with the ashes, strode Anna Fokker-Diemont, her back straight despite the ordeal she had been through in the past two months. Tony's sister Toos walked next to her to offer comfort. Family and friends followed. All were dressed in black. In between them and next to her mother, Jojo stood out in her cream-colored coat. Her sister Fré was also present with her husband, Hans. A few steps behind them followed Tetta, by herself. She had traveled from Germany for the occasion. Slowly, holding their collars against the freezing cold, the party moved to the open grave.[1]

Neither Anna nor Toos had volunteered to speak, although Anna did write the envelopes for all those invited personally. It had been the last thing she could do for her son, although the task had weighed heavily on her.[2] The social conventions of the time made it impossible for Jojo to speak, although she had been with Tony for five years. On this very public occasion, she was no more than accepted in her silent grief, the price she paid for an extramarital relationship. Anthony J., uncle Eduard's son, spoke briefly for the family. He had been with Anthony when he died and had traveled from Connecticut. The dignitaries were next to speak. Amsterdam's mayor Willem de Vlugt talked about Anthony's meaning for his city as an industrialist and as an employer. Co van Tijen, Fokker's director, spoke of Anthony's role in building the company. Wim van Neijenhoff addressed the assembly as Anthony's friend. Albert Plesman also stepped forward, reviewing the long relationship between Fokker and KLM; for the occasion he minimized the many differences they had had.

After the eulogies, the bier with the urn was carried out over the carpet of snow that smothered every sound. Friedrich Seekatz and August Nischwitz, Fokker's oldest employees, who had been with him from before the Great War, served as the forward pallbearers. The others had been selected from the Fokker management and factory workers. Flowers from Anna, Toos, Jojo, her mother Catharina de Leuw-Stolp, Fré and Hans Wieringa, and on behalf of the company board and management adorned the bier. Then Toos's son Ton Nijland stepped up to the microphone as the last to speak, despite his young age. His solemn declamation of the poem "A Cross with Roses," written by Petrus Augustus de Génestet in 1859, ended the ceremony: "May each earthly flower / wither away / the fruit of Life / matures from it."[3]

ᚷ

After the disastrous session at the osteopath on December 1, 1939, Anthony had hovered between life and death for more than three weeks. That same afternoon he had been transferred to Murray Hill Hospital on 40th Street, near New York's Grand Central Station. Doctor Cushing accompanied him there as his treating physician. Initially there were some hopeful signs of improvement, and at one stage Anthony had even been able to answer a few simple questions, but after two weeks the fevers suddenly returned with great force and he had slipped into a coma, the result of increased pressure in the brain from the combined effects of encephalitis and the anesthesia. The situation looked grim. Wim van Neijenhoff was allowed to interrupt his army duties and travel back to the States on the next ship that sailed. Because of the restrictions on civilian shipping that had been imposed as a result of the war, the journey took longer than usual. It was the evening of December 23 before he finally stepped ashore on the pier in Hoboken.

Meanwhile, the bedside visits of Jojo and nephew Anthony J. had turned into a deathwatch. None of the things Cushing and his colleagues tried brought the patient any improvement. Even the administration of recently developed antibacterial drugs were to no avail. The coma appeared irreversible. As a last resort the doctors tried several more new drugs and five blood transfusions, but these too produced no effect. After Cushing declared Fokker's condition to be critical on December 21, the coma deepened even further. Anthony's responses to stimuli were gradually diminishing. Without even realizing it, he was losing his ultimate struggle.[4] Around 8:30 a.m. on December 23, he made his final soft landing.

Jojo was left with nothing but the sorrow of the irreversible. As the only blood relative living in the United States, Anthony J. informed the authorities of his uncle's death. Fokker's body was taken to the city mortuary for a full autopsy. By 5:10 p.m. this effort brought clarity on the fatality: acute suppurative *leptomeningitis pneumococcus*, with an extra complicating factor of chronic sinusitus.[5] Jojo returned home to Undercliff Manor to initiate the inevitable preparations. Anthony's body followed later. There, at the end of the road and in the shelter of the high rocks, his body was laid out in the spacious hallway of the house in which he had taken such pride. His coffin was surrounded by flowers that Jojo had selected with Frank Campbell, the owner of the funeral home that had also taken care of Violet's last journey. On December 26 Jojo and a group of Anthony's close friends, among them Violet's sister Lillian, gathered around the coffin for a private farewell. The Reverend James Mitchell of St. Paul's Episcopal Church in Englewood, New Jersey, who had joined Jojo's and Anthony's inner circle over the past year or so, led them in prayer. After the service the rose-covered coffin was taken to the Ferncliff Crematory in Albany to be incinerated.

Jojo then traveled alone back to Holland to seek comfort from her mother and sister Fré. Having completed various formalities, Wim van Neijenhoff followed suit with Anthony's ashes. On January 29, 1940, he arrived in Amsterdam. Shortly thereafter Fokker's personal belongings were also shipped to Holland, to be stored at Amsterdam's Municipal Bonded Warehouse.[6]

ℊ

In the meantime initial preparations had begun to effect Anthony's inheritance. When he had made his last will and testament, in September 1935, Anthony had named his mother Anna as his sole heir.[7] His personal fortune at the time of his death was estimated at approximately $6.5 million. Most of this money was in the United States, although Fokker had also kept around 1.1 million Dutch guilders ($585,000 dollars) in Holland as stock in his Dutch company. Apart from that were company assets in Amsterdam, estimated at 10.7 million guilders (about $5.7 million); it was unclear to what extent these included funds from Fokker's personal fortune. Anthony was also known to have bank accounts, investments, and property in Great Britain and Switzerland.[8] To sort out the full value of his possessions and take care of the inheritance, Anthony's trusted friend Carter Tiffany was appointed as the main—and after June 1940, the only—executor of Fokker's estate.

Fokker's usual solicitors in New York, the law firm of Cahill, Gordon & Zachry, received instructions for the estate's many legal aspects and for determining succession rights. This was far from simple because, apart from the geographical spread of Fokker's holdings, the war interfered. In May 1940 the German occupation of the Netherlands complicated matters enormously. In the five days it took the Wehrmacht to overrun the small country, the Dutch cabinet fled to London and set up a government-in-exile as the Netherlands' international and legal representation. Subsequently, the government-in-exile maintained that Fokker's Netherlands Aircraft

Factory, now under the control of the Germans, had to be classified as a hostile entity. The company's assets were therefore regarded as hostile funds, claimed by the exiled government. On top of this it was intimated that Anthony's will might not stand up to legal challenge. When it was drawn up in 1935, Fokker had been living in Alpine, New Jersey. Later he had moved to Nyack, New York, which implied that not all legal clauses were beyond challenge under the laws of the state of New York. And there was yet another complication: the American will was not recognized as valid under Dutch law, since it did not comply with Dutch legal forms and requirements. Failing a valid Dutch testament, all of Anthony's worldly possessions therefore automatically went to his mother.[9]

In Switzerland and in Great Britain, succession rights were levied on the sales of Fokker's possessions and real estate in these countries. In the interests of Anna Fokker, Carter Tiffany challenged such claims, supported by the New York lawyers. He also challenged succession rights claimed in the United States. To evade relatively high American taxes, Tiffany tried to prove that Fokker's principal residence had not been Nyack but rather St. Moritz, Switzerland. After years of deliberations and lengthy proceedings, the court of New York's Rockland County finally ruled against Tiffany's claim in 1948. As a result of these complications, the war, and the slow pace of the proceedings, the cumulative bill of Cahill, Gordon & Zachry ran very high indeed: around $200,000.[10]

After Tiffany had been appointed as sole executor of the will on June 3, 1940, he duly reported to the Netherlands' ambassador in Washington, Alexander Loudon. Together they filed a petition with the court of Rockland County that Tiffany would also be recognized as the Netherlands government's curator for the $2.7 million in assets that the Netherlands Aircraft Factory held in the United States.[11] Although such an arrangement appeared practical at the time, it meant that the private and business aspects of everything to do with Fokker's estate generated problematic internal conflicts.

⚓

Meanwhile, the German occupation of the Netherlands brought changes at the top of the Fokker company in Amsterdam. On direct instructions from Reichsmarschall Hermann Goering, Fokker's director Jacob van Tijen was ousted in favor of Friedrich Seekatz. Goering even traveled to Amsterdam in July 1940 to ensure that his old comrade received all necessary powers—and an attractive salary. Seekatz now suddenly made five times the money he had previously brought home as director of sales. He tried to take things easy and change as few things as he possibly could without antagonizing the occupation authorities. Much of his energy was spent in organizing elaborate drinking parties at the Amstel Hotel and the Hotel Americain, Amsterdam's most expensive accommodations. At these parties, which were frequented by the upper echelon of the occupation authorities, women passed from hand to hand.

Between 1940 and 1945 these festivities cost the company a grand total of 500,000 guilders ($266,000 in 1940 exchange value).[12]

Still, Seekatz, who had filed for Dutch citizenship in 1938, was not a mere collaborator. His drinking parties helped foil plans to march off a considerable part of the Fokker workforce for conscript labor in Germany. Precisely how he managed to avert this has remained a well-kept secret, but Seekatz liked to refer to his personal friendship with Goering. Goering's favor came at a price: Seekatz bought him four large American automobiles, one of which he parked in his own private garage. He also acquired about $10,000 worth of diamonds for Goering from the Jewish Asscher's Diamond Company in Amsterdam.[13] Moreover, with people from Goering's Stabsamt (staff office), Seekatz acquired nearly the complete collection of art held by the Jewish art trader Jacques Goudstikker, and had the works transported to Germany. Seekatz also bought some of Goudstikker's paintings for himself. But his biggest wartime pursuit was, perhaps, collecting girlfriends, until he was arrested for his role under the occupation in May 1945. After three years of legal proceedings, he was extradited to Germany in December 1948.[14]

ℱ

The other people belonging to Anthony's circle of friends and family made less controversial choices during the war. Anna Fokker continued to live in her house in Bergen, Holland. There she received a visit from Charles Parlin, one of the partners of Fokker's New York law firm, in January 1941, to consult with her on the settlement of the estate. The main topic of their conversation was the "desire" that had been expressed in July 1940 by the German authorities, on Goering's instructions, to obtain control over the stock of the Netherlands Aircraft Factory.[15] (Goering had an old score to settle with Fokker, who had refused to hire him as a sales representative for Scandinavia in 1919.)[16] Parlin indicated that it appeared to be in Anna's best interests to comply with this request, despite the fact that the estate was not yet legally settled. In April 1941 she therefore sold her shares in her son's company to Goering's Bank der Deutschen Luftfahrt (German Aeronautical Bank) for 1.6 million guilders (about $850,000), an amount that was later considered "fair" by Tiffany.[17] The deal was effected through a Dutch Nazi front man and was supposed to be paid for with money in the factory's corporate accounts in the United States, which meant that the money would remain in the United States and not be transferred to Anna Fokker.

Nonetheless, the sale gave rise to considerable difficulties. In July the Netherlands government-in-exile in London challenged the deal as an unlawful transfer of funds to the enemy. Such transactions had been forbidden under a Royal Decree of May 24, 1940. Dutch authorities in the United States took legal steps to block the transfer and thus impede the expansion of German interests in the Fokker company. Partly as a result of the legal controversies, the shares were never physically transferred to Goering's bank; instead they went into safekeeping at the Netherlands National Bank, where they remained for the duration of the war.[18]

The whole affair left Anna Fokker most unhappy. At her advancing age she wanted nothing more than to be left in peace.[19] Then, in 1944, the Netherlands government-in-exile claimed the shares under a special law that provided for confiscation of hostile funds. The stalemate was now complete, and Anna did not live to see it resolved. She died on March 6, 1945, at the age of seventy-nine, two months before the country's liberation at the end of the Dutch "Hunger Winter."

Because Anna left everything to her only surviving child, Toos, and her three grandchildren, Ton, Ina, and Anneke, the Fokker inheritance now took on new dimensions. After the liberation of May 1945, Toos and her children filed a legal request with the Dutch Council for Reinstatements to regain possession of the Fokker company shares. Because of obstruction on the part of the government, which now had an interest in recapitalizing the Netherlands Aircraft Factory without cost to the state, their case proceeded very slowly indeed, and in 1949 the family withdrew the request.[20] In legal terms this meant that they abandoned the appeal for reinstatement, which in turn meant that the government had solidified its claim to the Fokker shares.[21] Like her mother, Toos did not live long enough to witness the end of the legal wrangling or to enjoy her inheritance. She died on August 23, 1953, after which the legal rights and claims were passed on to her three children. Not before 1954, fifteen years after Anthony had passed away, was the matter conclusively settled and did the surviving heirs receive what was due to them.

Ϙ

Although she had shared her life with Anthony for five years, Jojo did not share in the inheritance. The social and legal conventions of the time and the character of their relationship did not provide for this. It was therefore fortunate that she had some independent means from her father's estate.

In the first months of 1940 her life took a wholly unexpected new course. William Winslow Dulles, a partner in the law firm of Cahill, Gordon & Zachry, traveled on the same ship to Europe that took Jojo home in January 1940. He had been commissioned to sort out Fokker's affairs with Carter Tiffany and compile the initial valuation of the estate. Jojo, who was well-informed regarding Anthony's various dealings and interests, accompanied Dulles and Tiffany on their mission. The three of them stayed for a while at Oberalpina, where Jojo was still running the household. She and William Dulles got on very well. In fact, in the weeks that followed they fell in love with each other.

Dulles had to return to New York in April 1940, having more or less completed the preliminary valuation of Fokker's European assets. Jojo journeyed to Amsterdam to live with her mother for the time being. In the summer of 1940 she received a peculiar telegram from New York, through the law firm that dealt with the Swiss aspects of the estate, but addressed to Fokker's lawyers in Amsterdam. It read, "My client would like to enter into a long-term relationship with your client." Jojo needed no explanation. She sent a reply telegram from Amsterdam through the same route:

"My client agrees." Jojo then approached the German authorities with a request for an exit visa. In the first months of the occupation, this was still possible, provided one had the right contacts. Nonetheless, she had to travel to Berlin to obtain a U.S. entry permit from the American embassy. Next she managed to purchase a seat on a Lufthansa flight that took her from Berlin to Lisbon in neutral Portugal, where she obtained passage on a liner to New York. On December 21, 1940, almost a year to the day after Anthony's passing, she arrived in New York. Six days later she married William Dulles. They went to live in Riverdale Park, a quiet part of the Bronx. The marriage, however, did not last, and in 1945 Jojo returned to the Netherlands with her three-year-old son Frederick.[22]

SCHWERIN, GERMANY
A CENTURY LATER

Schwerin is an appealing, quiet town in northeastern Germany, bordering on a large lake. The lakeshore is dominated by a large, picture-book palace, built on a small island, once home to the Grand Dukes and Duchesses of Mecklenburg. Well preserved, Schwerin's inner city has the look and feel of a bygone era. On the edge of town, where Bornhövedstrasse bends around the old Jewish cemetery, the surface changes to uneven cobblestones that date back a century. They lead to the buildings of the former Fokker factory, still standing on the edge of the lake.

In Halle 2 the silence of time lingers between the old walls. Filtered light shines from odd angles into the empty building. The gray-painted bricks appear fragile and dusty. The walls reach about twelve feet high. The crest of the roof, supported by wooden beams, sits another ten feet higher. The section in between has been closed by simple wooden planking, perhaps as long as a century ago. Some of the planks have come ajar, others hang loose. Sunlight falls onto an empty seasoned cement floor, measuring about a hundred by fifty feet. Leaning against the walls, a series of old wooden closets remain from the busy factory that once operated here. They show signs of paint and bird droppings, like all the woodwork. Only the swallows are still flying here. At the back of the factory floor, a long disused winch sits in its housing, its cast-iron wheels corroded. From there two iron rails run to the double sliding doors in the wooden lakeside of the building. In the middle they disappear under the doors and into the water of the Schweriner Lake, fifty yards further. The planks in the doors also show chinks. The resulting backlight patterns merge with the rays finding their way through the broken triangular windows. In a corner of the building a door opens to a narrow, unlighted corridor with white and brown floor tiles, separating the work floor from the offices.

To the left several old doors lead to the former rooms of the factory administration. These too are empty, apart from lamps that have been hanging from the low ceilings for a century. The traditional tiled stone hearths have remained where they always were. The windows have for the most part been nailed shut, and the smell of mold is strong. One room, halfway down the corridor, is larger than the others. This must have been Anthony Fokker's office. It is here that he must have been seated when the phone call from Berlin came in early August 1914: Germany was at war, and the army urgently needed reconnaissance aircraft—how many could he deliver?

This was where Fokker's success story began. Without the First World War, the name of Anthony Fokker would likely have remained only a footnote in the history of aviation: one of those who first engaged in the construction of airplanes and risked their lives trying to fly them, dreaming of fame and fortune. Most of the names of those young people no longer ring any bells. Anthony Fokker is one of the exceptions.

⚐

Fokker was a man who defied conventions. No one who encountered him in the street would have recognized the millionaire he was. Anthony paid little attention to his looks. He ate sweets until his last tooth had rotted. He seldom left the house without first stuffing his pockets with *Haagsche hopjes*, a traditional Dutch coffee-flavored candy. If he had the choice, his favorite meal would consist of soup stock, two kinds of pie, four flavors of ice cream, and an additional dessert. Putting on weight was something he took for granted. He ate when it suited him, preferably in company, for he liked having people about.

He was partial to getting up quite early in the morning, but other than that any semblance of a daily routine was foreign to him. Any room he entered he would shortly turn into chaos, with all sorts of papers and possessions lying around on the floor. Anthony loved and nurtured his eccentricity. One might find him tinkering with the engine of his Lancia sports car while wearing his best suit, or reclining in the back seat of his Cadillac covered in oil stains while his driver drove down Fifth Avenue. He would not walk twenty yards if he could find a car.[1] His odd behavior took its toll on the upkeep of steady relationships. Fokker apparently couldn't help getting into severe quarrels with all his business partners, even if it was clearly to his disadvantage. In love, matters were even worse. His two spouses left him: Tetta through a divorce, Violet in the most dramatic fashion. These were tragedies that hurt him deeply indeed, and they fed into his eccentricity. After both crises he found it extremely difficult to give his life new meaning and direction.

Fokker loved pranks and practical jokes. Using a battery and copper wiring hidden in the carpet, he ran an electric current over the floor of his bedroom in Oberalpina and then invited female guests to come and examine the new carpet—barefoot, since he did not want it soiled. He derived enormous pleasure from their shrieks and giggling when they touched each other and thus closed the electric circuit.[2] No one was spared from his pranks. He encouraged Dutch Prime Minister Hendrik Colijn to have dinner on his own so that Fokker could take Colijn's two young female assistants out.[3] He enjoyed shocking guests, for example by welcoming them stark naked in his bathtub, albeit hidden under a layer of foam.[4] Even newborn babies were subject to his odd sense of humor. In March 1938 he and Jojo visited Jojo's sister Fré, who had just given birth. Fré asked him to be quiet because her little son was asleep. Instead, Fokker banged his fist on the door of the baby's room as hard as he could, shouting enthusiastically, "He'll have to get used to it sometime!"[5] On the other hand, he could be generous to those he liked. A plea to "Uncle Tony" seldom went unheeded. As time went by, money, which had dominated his daily life when he was getting started in aviation, meant less and less to him. He volunteered to continue supporting his first wife, Tetta, after their divorce for the rest of her life. It did not bring her back.

The single-minded aviator and constructor worked day and night. The only place where he managed to relax was on the water; when he boarded one of this boats, he left workaday concerns on the shore behind him. Much of the time he was away on travel, mostly by train or by ship. His life was truly restless. He crossed the Atlantic at least forty-three times to connect his European and American interests. He traversed both continents several times, and the passports that he kept were covered with visas and stamps.

At his death American papers noted his restlessness: "He carried his office in his hat."[6] The results of Fokker's ceaseless traveling, however, were questionable. People in his employ were usually glad to see him leave, because he disrupted all normal procedures without offering explanations. To continue to be in control, he gave his associates only limited powers of attorney. Time and again they had to phone or telegraph him to ask for instructions. Making up his mind and sticking to a course of action was something he found difficult. In his American autobiography, he told his readers, "My life has been paced by the airplane. Hurtling through space on what now seems a predestined course, I had no idea what that course was. Most of the time I merely hung on."[7]

This pattern showed itself most clearly in business issues. Fokker was far from a born entrepreneur. Although the owner, or at least a major shareholder, of the companies that bore his name, he favored himself in the role of technical adviser. Perhaps as a result of his experiences in the First World War, his view was that of the short term. Corporate investments he tried to avoid, even if he must have known that he would suffer the consequences of such policies. He rented his factory buildings rather than owning them. Instead of investing in technological innovation, he wanted his new aircraft developed on the basis of yesterday's practical experience. Eventually, this lack of innovation cost him his leading position in international aviation.

After the First World War he set his sights on creating a future in the United States, convinced that he could succeed in America. But his plans, executed in a haphazard fashion, ultimately ran aground in General Motors' board room in 1931. Here too Fokker's limited technological savvy played a crucial role. His strategic position as the world's most important aircraft constructor came to a sudden dead end when he was ousted from the American company he had founded. He let it happen as if it did not concern him, and then remained silent about the causes of this business disaster.

Suddenly, all that remained was his company in Holland, which he had been willing to sell to General Motors less than a year before. What it was exactly that he now wanted to achieve with the Netherlands Aircraft Factory he did not know. Discussions on which course to take lasted years and ultimately remained without result. Long before that, Anthony had embraced a new business approach: rather than constructing aircraft under his own name, he began to focus on marketing aircraft built by his American competitors. This activity resulted in his biggest success: Anthony Fokker played a crucial role in bringing about the world dominance of the American aerospace industry that remains to this day. Strangely, for one to whom publicity mattered so much, he never claimed recognition for this important contribution to American aviation. On the contrary: having achieved this new and important goal, he gradually began to withdraw from his career in aviation to indulge in the leisurely pursuits of a multimillionaire. He spent more money on his superyacht QED than he ever invested in the development of any airplane.

As an entrepreneur and as a person, Anthony Fokker was an enigma to those around him—and maybe also to himself.

ACKNOWLEDGMENTS

I first stumbled across the historical figure of Anthony Fokker when doing research in Holland for my dissertation more than thirty years ago. My interest in this peculiar character was aroused instantly. Years later it resulted in the book *Fokker: A Transatlantic Biography*, published by the Smithsonian Institution Press in 1997. However, Fokker did not disappear from my radar after that. Indeed, his story resurfaced repeatedly in various writings and in documentary film projects, both in Holland and in the United States. The consequence was that I began to look at his story from a new perspective. Would it be possible, using the vastly increased resources of the digital information age, to get closer to my protagonist than had been possible twenty-five years ago, when I relied on tracking historical sources on paper? This was the starting point for this new biography. Nonetheless, compiling a coherent story from a multitude of loose bits and pieces of information was no easy matter.

To begin with, only a handful of personal documents from Anthony Fokker survive. Altogether they do not even fill a single archive box at the Dutch aviation museum Aviodrome, which keeps what records are left of the former Fokker factory and its founder. Fokker was no writer, and he preferred to deal with issues on the phone or through in-person contacts. To further complicate matters: most of Fokker's company archives that once existed have been destroyed over time. After the liquidation of the Schweriner Industrie Werke (Schwerin Industrial Works) in 1926, Fokker's German records went missing. In 1947 the complete archive of his Netherlands Aircraft Factory was given to the Amsterdam Fire Department for training purposes—an effective way of wiping out the fact that the company had flourished while working for the Third Reich between 1940 and 1945. After this, all that remained of the historical record was what individuals had kept in their desk drawers and office closets and had thus escaped the flames. Even some of these documents were lost after the Fokker Aircraft Company went bankrupt in 1996, and all remaining assets had to be sold off for scrap value. (What a contrast to the situation in the United States, where crucial parts of the archives of Fokker's Atlantic Aircraft Corporation and of the Fokker Aircraft Corporation of America / General Aviation Corporation have survived in the Boeing Historical Archive near Seattle.)

This situation meant that this biography had to be compiled from a large number of fragments of historical information found elsewhere: people and institutions with which Fokker had relations. These pieces of the puzzle were distributed over half the globe. On top of the research I did for my 1997 book, I visited several archives in Germany that held additional information: in Schwerin I called at the City Archive and at Mecklenburg's Main Country Archive. In Koblenz I spent time at the German

National Archive (Bundesarchiv). I also visited the archive of the German Museum of Technology in Berlin.

Beyond these sources, the Internet provided truly new leads to the story. In the past two decades we have been inundated by a flood of digital information that has radically changed historical research. Obscure information that used to be beyond view or reach can now be retrieved at the touch of a fingertip and from one's own easy chair. Forgotten books and journals have found a new virtual distribution and readership, as have the inventories of archives with previously unknown holdings. And it is not just the access to information that has improved, consultation itself has become easier as well. If travel in person is expensive, digital information is cheap and traverses distance easily. Scanning and transmitting source material have made a tremendous difference to this project. They enabled me to review far-away files in the comfort of my home study, which was especially fortuitous because Fokker's life evolved in four countries and on three continents. Archival institutions proved willing to provide many documents digitally, making it possible to dig into stories that I could not have uncovered previously.

This research benefited particularly from the digitization of old newspapers. Anthony Fokker may not have been much of a writer, but journalists usually found him willing to share his opinions verbally. Wherever he went, reporters followed him. In interviews he could be quite frank. I made extensive use of the digital newspaper collection in the Netherlands National Library in The Hague (www.delpher.nl), which offers access to most newspapers in the Netherlands and its former colonies. The same library pass gave me digital access to the archival issues of the *New York Times*, the *Wall Street Journal*, and the *Washington Post*. The *New York Times* always had an especially keen eye for Fokker's exploits. Some of the news that did not make it into the big papers I was able to retrieve from the amazing wealth of old local newspapers available at www.fultonhistory.com, covering communities in upstate New York. I also benefited from the Library of Congress National Digital Newspaper Program (www.loc.gov/ndnp), reaching up to 1924 at the time of this writing. Digitized issues of British papers such as the *Times*, the *Daily Mail*, and the *Guardian* also provided elements of the story, while the Europeana Newspapers effort includes German and French publications. Closer to home, the digitized issues of Fokker's hometown *Haarlems Dagblad* at the Noord-Hollands Archief provided several eyewitness reports to Anthony's early exploits, as did the newspapers of the Zeeuws Archief in Middelburg.

In addition to the various still photography collections that I consulted in Holland, Germany, and the United States, access to film images has been particularly helpful to this project. Fokker was an avid amateur filmmaker, and he left hours of footage for posterity. In Holland I consulted digitized film reels (from 1930 onward with sound) at Beeld en Geluid in Hilversum, the Eye Film Institute in Amsterdam, and the Digital Film Center Europe in Arnhem. Other images reached me through cooperation with Lucasfilm in San Francisco on a Fokker documentary. From Germany I received a compilation of film images that Fokker had taken when making visits to the Western Front in 1917 and 1918. Today they are kept at the Bundesarchiv. In the United States I was happy to obtain access to the University of South Carolina Moving Image Research Collection of former Fox Movietone newsreels; I am grateful to Benjamin Singleton for his cooperation. I also consulted American moving images at www.criticalpast.com.

⚓

Apart from the sizable list of people who were kind enough to help me with my research in the 1980s and 1990s, I have received support for the current book from various people with collections of material concerning Fokker. First and foremost I must mention Marc Smeulers from Bronkhorst, Holland, the grandson of Anthony's sister Toos. We got to know each other through our involvement in a television documentary. Marc allowed me to read and use unique family documents no one else had seen before, and he liberally shared his collection of family photos of his famous relative. This truly enriched the biography. Thanks, Marc!

I also owe much to Will Porrio of the Aviodrome Historical Archive in Lelystad, Holland, who was extremely helpful in tracing what is left of the paper trail on Fokker's life. Erik Haverkorn, who lives in the house where Anthony grew up in at Kleine Houtstraat, Haarlem, allowed me to look around for an afternoon. He even had a digital copy of the original construction plans for the house. In Santpoort, Holland, Gert and Lies Blüm opened their doors for me to consult the vast, rich collection of documents and photographs that Gert has assembled, over the course of more than fifty years, on Anthony's exploits in the United States. Without Gert, I would not have learned that part of the former American Fokker company archives had survived dozens of moves, mergers, and corporate takeovers and had come to rest at the Boeing Archives in Bellevue, Washington. There archivist Michael Lombardi was kind enough to dig deep into the old Fokker files and come up with near complete sets of photocopies of the board meetings of the Atlantic Aircraft Corporation and of the Fokker Aircraft Corporation of America / General Aviation Corporation. Thanks to Michael we now know more about the development of Fokker's businesses in the United States than in Europe over the same period.

In Germany, Michael Schmidt from Schwerin generously shared everything he had gathered in years of research on Fokker's development until 1918. It turned out he had also assembled an impressive collection of old photographs from various private collections. Some of them are reproduced in this book. But a true biographer also wants to get a direct sense of the locations where the story played out. Michael took me on several tours in Schwerin to the spots from Fokker's past that still survive. These visits filled in some of the blanks and enabled me to add extra detail to the German episodes. Stefan Schlick and Frau Kässler of the Schwerin City Hall let me look around at my leisure in the former *Halle 2* of the Fokker factory, which remains standing after a hundred years, while the Schwerin Fishery Club, housed in another part of the former Fokker complex, also opened its doors.

The Internet put me on the trail of research that Manfred Penning had undertaken on Fokker's apprenticeship days in Mainz, Germany, between 1910 and 1912. He kindly shared difficult-to-read documents that he had discovered in local archives. Fortunately, one of my colleagues at the Huygens Institute, Jan Gielkens, happens to be a recognized authority on German handwriting. Jan was able to decipher the *Kurrentschrift* that had remained opaque to Manfred and me. I would also like to mention René Demets of the European Space Agency, through whose enthusiastic cooperation and knowledge of Russian I was able to trace the background of Anthony's 1912 adventure in St. Petersburg and his love affair with Ljuba Golantschikova. Without his efforts we would still know little about this episode. My gratitude also goes to the Fokker Heritage Trust and its secretary, Michael Zwartelé, for his mediation, advice, and permission to reproduce examples from their photographic collection in this book. In Switzerland, Dora Filli of the St. Moritz Documentary Library was very helpful in tracing addresses, documents and other evidence on Fokker's chalet, Oberalpina. Christiane Sibille of the Documents Diplomatiques Suisses in Bern also advised me, pointing me toward several other archives in Switzerland.

Also thanks to the Internet, I got in touch with Eric Nelsen, the Palisades Interstate Park Commission's historical interpreter in New Jersey. He put me on the trail of Fokker's mansion construction plans, the groundwork for which can still be seen and visited at Pulpit Rock. Debbie Douglas of the MIT Museum in Cambridge, Massachussetts, sent me copies of the house's design. Laura Kissel of the Ohio State University Library's Byrd Polar and Climate Research Center Archival Program traced and copied documents for me on the relationship between Fokker and Richard Byrd. Simone Munson of the Wisconsin Historical Society in Madison searched the archives for information on Fokker and his publicity agent, Harry Bruno. I thank my late friend Glenn Feldman at the University of Alabama in Birmingham for his efforts to get me copies of the death certificates of Anthony and Violet Fokker.

In Holland, retired aeronautical consultant Hisco Baas got in touch with me several years ago. He happened to have friends who were near eyewitnesses (through now deceased family members) of some of Fokker's exploits. Hearing the stories that Fokker's friends later told to their families on their encounters with this strange man brought me a whole new perspective. I am very grateful to Hisco for putting me in touch with Maria Wolff-Wieringa, Lisajanna van Weel–van der Wal, and David van Weel in Amsterdam. David even gave me a digital copy of the beautiful color film that his parents made in 1939 of their holiday trip with Fokker on the QED. When we met, Carin Meerburg-Wieringa was also present. With her sister, Helen, she shared the family stories and memories of Fokker passed on by her mother Fré and her aunt Jojo, Anthony's last muse. They even allowed me to sit in Anthony's chair, originally from his chalet in St. Moritz. Their brother Jon Wieringa provided me with me several documents and authentic film footage of a visit to Oberalpina in 1937. Carin went out of her way to get me in touch with Jojo's son, Frederick Dulles of Charleston, South Carolina, and Montpellier, France. I had a long, productive conversation with him during a stopover of his at Schiphol Airport, Amsterdam.

Later still, when preparing this English edition of the book, I was contacted by Ronald Winckel from Kapellen, Belgium, whose mother, Betty, and grandparents, George and Svea Gleichman, also belonged to Fokker's circle of close friends. This encounter too brought several new sources to light, including old photo albums and more film footage. Further into the preparations for this English edition, I was introduced to Sabine Witzier, granddaughter of Fokker's sister, Toos—and to Anna Fokker's 1892 painting of the plantation and the film reels that she kept in her attic, yet another chance discovery. All in all, it might almost seem that coincidence has taken precedence over systematic research methodology, but I gladly leave it to the reader to judge how these serendipitous discoveries have enhanced the contents of this book.

NOTES

1. NEW YORK, NEW YORK, DECEMBER 1939

1. "The Merchant's Point of View," *New York Times*, November 19, 1939; "Holiday Gains Put at 10% for Stores," *New York Times*, November 23, 1939.
2. Thomas Kessner, *Fiorello H. La Guardia and the Making of Modern New York* (New York: McGraw-Hill, 1989), 48–59, 432–35.
3. J. B. Hubrecht, the Netherlands' envoy in Washington, to Minister of Foreign Affairs, July 26, 1922, Netherlands National Archive (henceforth NA), 2.05.37, Ministry of Foreign Affairs, DEZ, inv. no. 1760.
4. "A. H. G. Fokker Critically Ill," *New York Times*, December 22, 1939.
5. Simon Flexner, "The Results of the Serum Treatment in Thirteen Hundred Cases of Epidemic Meningitis," *Journal of Experimental Medicine* 17 (1913): 553–76.
6. *Het Vaderland*, December 23, 1939.

2. JAVA, NETHERLANDS EAST INDIES, APRIL 1890

1. C. W. Wormser, *Ontginners van Java* (Deventer: W. van Hoeve, 1942), 69–70.
2. Liesbeth Hesselink, *Genezers op de koloniale markt: Inheemse dokters en vroedvrouwen in Nederlands Oost-Indië, 1850–1915* (Amsterdam: Vossiuspers UvA, 2009), 44–45, 151.
3. *Het nieuws van den dag: Kleine courant* (newspaper in the Dutch East Indies), March 26, 1889. Hesselink, *Genezers op de koloniale markt*, 344.
4. Fiona van Schendel, *Djolotigo: Ontginning en exploitatie van een particuliere koffie-onderneming op Java, 1875–1898* (Amsterdam: NEHA, 2000), 47–84.
5. *Algemeen Handelsblad*, August 30,1874; family messages in *Het nieuws van den dag: Kleine courant*, September 2, 1874; for Fokker genealogy, see A. A. Vorsterman van Oyen, *Stam- en Wapenboek der Aanzienlijke Nederlandsche Familiën*, vol. 1 (Groningen: Wolters, 1885), 284–86.
6. "Telegrammen van Batavia," *De locomotief: Samarangsch handels- en advertentieblad* (newspaper in the Dutch East Indies), March 19, 1878; *Regeerings-Almanak voor Nederlandsch-Indië—1880* (Batavia: Landsdrukkerij, 1880).
7. *Regeerings-Almanak voor Nederlandsch-Indië—1893*, vol. 1, 418–19.
8. Herman Fokker, letter to the editor, *Soerabaijasch Handelsblad*, February 15, 1889.
9. Taxation report, Njoenjoer coffee plantation, April 29, 1893, NA, 2.20.01, Archive of the Nederlandsche Handel Maatschappij, inv. no. 7955.

10. Van Schendel, *Djolotigo*, 25.

11. *Het nieuws van den dag*, March 31, 1888.

12. *Java-bode: Nieuws, handels- en advertentieblad voor Nederlandsch-Indië*, July 28, 1888.

13. "Eenige flauwe herinneringen van ons verblijf op 't koffieland Njoenjoer bij Wlingi," school essay by Toos Fokker, October 31, 1904, family collection of Marc Smeulers, Bronkhorst, Holland.

14. I gratefully acknowledge Sabine Witzier and her husband Bart for letting me examine the painting that is in their private possession.

15. Anthony H. G. Fokker and Bruce Gould, *De vliegende Hollander* (Amsterdam: Van Holkema & Warendorf, 1931), 19.

16. Van Schendel, *Djolotigo*, 75–98.

17. Ibid., 118–19.

18. Observation on the basis of survey in *Regeerings-Almanak voor Nederlandsch-Indië—1893*, vol. 1, 402–12.

19. Brieven uit den Oosthoek, *Soerabaijasch Handelsblad*, March 4, 1891.

20. Taxation report, Njoenjoer, April 29, 1893, NA, 2.20.01, Nederlandsche Handel Maatschappij, inv. no. 7955.

21. *De locomotief: Samarangsch handels- en advertentie-blad*, December 20, 1893.

22. Founding papers of the 's-Gravenhaagsche Koffie Cultuur Maatschappij, September 30, 1895, NA, 2.09.46, Justice Ministry, Companies Founded, inv. no. 4444; see also *De locomotief: Samarangsch handels- en advertentie-blad*, April 1, 1896.

23. *Regeerings-Almanak voor Nederlandsch-Indië—1894*, vol. 1, 400–401; *Regeerings-Almanak voor Nederlandsch-Indië—1895*, vol. 1, 428–29; *Regeerings-Almanak voor Nederlandsch-Indië—1896*, vol. 1, 304–5; *Regeerings-Almanak voor Nederlandsch-Indië—1897*, vol. 1, 358–59.

24. Wormser, *Ontginners van Java*, 69–70.

3. NAARDEN, HOLLAND, MARCH 1910

1. Anthony Fokker to his mother, undated [March 1910], Aviodrome Historical Archive, Lelystad, Holland, collection A. H. G. Fokker, box 12.

2. Ibid.

3. Ibid.

4. Ibid.

5. A. H. G. Fokker and Bruce Gould, *Flying Dutchman: The Life of Anthony Fokker* (New York: Henry Holt, 1931), 16.

6. Toos Fokker, "Eenige flauwe herinneringen van ons verblijf op 't koffieland Njoenjoer bij Wlingi," school essay, October 31, 1904, Collection Smeulers, Bronkhorst.

7. Cor Wiegel, *Haarlem in oude ansichten* (Zaltbommel: Europese Bibliotheek, 1982), 74–75.

8. Note, Department of Public Administration, Municipality of Haarlem, December 17, 1918, Noord-Hollands Archive, Gemeente Haarlem, New Archive, inv. no. 126–1.

9. Construction drawing for Kleine Houtweg 39/41, Municipality of Haarlem, terrain map KH, sections 458 and 459 (1894; copy, March 17, 1910). Thanks to Erik Haverkorn, Haarlem.

10. Ibid., 21.

11. "Bill for Mrs. Fokker, Februari 14," Aviodrome, collection A. H. G. Fokker, box 12.

12. Authorized copy of Anthony Fokker's school results, October 21, 1955, Collection Thijs Postma, Hoofddorp, Holland, Hegener Papers, Fokker material.

13. L. J. de Lagh, "Fokkers laatste halfjaar op onze HBS," *De Resultante: Officieel orgaan van "De Garde" Vereniging van oudleerlingen van de voormalige 1ste HBS-b en het huidige Laurens Coster Lyceum te Haarlem* 13 (August 1961), 2–4, Aviodrome, collection A. H. G. Fokker, box 11.

14. Anthony Fokker, in *HBS Feestblad* (Haarlem), September 4, 1924, Aviodrome, collection A. H. G. Fokker, box 11.

15. Anthony H. G. Fokker and Bruce Gould, *De vliegende Hollander* (Amsterdam: Van Holkema & Warendorf, 1931), 31.

16. Fokker, *HBS Feestblad*.

17. Fokker and Gould, *Flying Dutchman*, 22–23.

18. Fokker's school results.

19. De Lagh, "Fokkers laatste halfjaar op onze HBS," 2–3.

20. Fokker and Gould, *Flying Dutchman*, 28.

21. *Haarlems Dagblad*, August 12, 1911, http://nha.courant.nu/issue/HD/1911-08-12/edition/0/page/1.

22. Guus van Ditzhuijzen, *De Loods*, August 2011; *Haarlems Dagblad*, March 25, 1919. http://nha.courant.nu/issue/HD/1919-03-25/edition/0/page/2.

23. Fokker and Gould, *Flying Dutchman*, 33–34.

24. Correspondence on Frits Cremers's school problems, NA, 2.21.043, Collection Cremer Family, inv. no. 204.

25. Frits Cremer to his father, February 1 and March 18, 1910, NA, 2.21.043, Collection Cremer Family, inv. no. 205; "An Improved Resilient Wheel for Road Vehicles," patent requested by Herman Fokker, May 24, 1909, admitted in London, May 12, 1910.

26. Fokker and Gould, *Flying Dutchman*, 26–32; photos of Fokker and Cremer with their Peugeot, undated [1909], Aviodrome, collection A. H. G. Fokker (photo album Bernard de Waal), box 15.

27. Fokker and Gould, *Flying Dutchman*, 31–32.

28. Jacob Cremer, undated memo [1909], NA, 2.21.043, Collection Cremer Family, inv. no. 364.

29. Frits Cremer to his father, February 1, 1910, NA, 2.21.043; Cremer to his father, April 26, 1910, NA, 2.21.0\3, Collection Cremer Family, inv. no. 205.

30. J. T. Cremer to States' Deputies of Noord-Holland, December 6, 1910, NA, 2.21.043, Collection Cremer Family, inv. no. 364.

31. Anthony Fokker to his mother, undated [March 1910], Aviodrome, collection A. H. G. Fokker, box 12.

32. Fokker and Gould, *Flying Dutchman*, 35.

33. Fokker to his mother, undated [April 24, 1910], Aviodrome, collection A. H. G. Fokker, box 12.

34. Ibid.

35. Fokker and Gould, *Flying Dutchman*, 35–36.

36. Fokker to his mother, May 9, 1910, Aviodrome, collection A. H. G. Fokker, box 12.

37. Ibid.

4. MAINZ, GERMANY, JULY 1910

1. A. H. G. Fokker and Bruce Gould, *Flying Dutchman: The Life of Anthony Fokker* (New York: Henry Holt, 1931), 37.
2. Ibid., 36.
3. "Belgian Aero Salon," *Flight*, January 23, 1909, 53, http://www.flightglobal.com/pdfarchive/view/1909/1909%20-%200051.html.
4. Fokker and Gould, *Flying Dutchman*, 34.
5. Herman Fokker to Henri Hegener, April 22, 1923, Collection Thijs Postma, Hegener Papers.
6. "Wo der Erfinder des Reißverschlusses studierte," *Allgemeine Zeitung Rhein Main*, December 14, 2010.
7. Anthony Fokker to his mother, July 30, 1910, Aviodrome, collection A. H. G. Fokker, box 12.
8. Ibid.
9. Ibid.
10. Jahresbericht Automobil Fachschule Mainz, 1911, http://tudigit.ulb.tu-darmstadt.de/show/Gm-311/0002.
11. Manfred Penning, "Die Erste Deutsche Automobilfachschule Mainz," *Mainzer Vierteljahres Hefte*, 2012, no. 2, 1–4; Penning, "Die Erste Deutsche Automobil Fachschule Mainz, Teil 2: Wo Fokkers erstes Flugzeug entstand," *Mainzer Vierteljahres Hefte*, 2012, no. 4, 37.
12. Anthony Fokker to his mother, July 30, 1910, Aviodrome, collection A. H. G. Fokker, box 12.
13. Jahresbericht Automobil Fachschule Mainz, 1911, http://tudigit.ulb.tu-darmstadt.de/show/Gm-311/0002; Michael Schmidt, "A. H. G. Fokker: Der niederländische Flieger und Flugzeughersteller in Deutschland" (unpublished manuscript, Schwerin, 2013), 15.
14. Penning, "Die Erste Deutsche Automobilfachschule Mainz," 1–4; Penning, "Die Erste Deutsche Automobil Fachschule Mainz, Teil 2," 38.
15. Anthony Fokker to his parents, October 12, 1910, Aviodrome, collection A. H. G. Fokker, box 12.
16. Ibid.
17. Penning, "Die Erste Deutsche Automobil Fachschule Mainz, Teil 2," 98–105; Michael Schmidt, "A. H. G. Fokker: Der niederländische Flieger und Flugzeughersteller in Deutschland" (unpublished manuscript, Schwerin, 2013), 15.
18. "Eine deutsche Fachschule für Flugwesen," *Flugsport*, 1910, no. 21, 700.
19. Fokker and Gould, *Flying Dutchman*, 43; author's correspondence with Manfred Penning, Mainz, 2012.
20. Bürgermeisterei Mainz, official report, "Erste Deutsche Automobil Fachschule," Kriegsminsterielle Verfügung 292/10, December 20, 1910, Stadtarchiv Mainz, Germany; Penning, "Die Erste Deutsche Automobil Fachschule Mainz, Teil 2," 98–105.
21. Fokker and Gould, *Flying Dutchman*, 44–47; Henri Hegener, *Fokker: The Man and the Aircraft* (Letchworth, UK: Harleyford Publications, 1961), 14; A. R. Weyl, *Fokker: The Creative Years* (London: Putnam, 1985), 10–12.

22. Manfred Penning, "Sie flogen am Grossen Sand: Die Anfänge der Fliegerei in Mainz," *AOPA Info* (Aircraft Owners and Pilots Association, Germany), newsletter 3 (2001), 30–34.

23. Carl Ries, "Määnzer Gefladdscher," *Mainzer Vierteljahreshefte* 3 (1981), no. 1, 130 ff.

24. Penning, "Sie flogen am Grossen Sand," 30–34.

25. Franz von Daum to Oberbürgemeister R. Fieser, December 4, 1910, Stadtarchiv Baden-Baden, inv. no. A 26/29–711 (copy via Manfred Penning, with thanks to Jan Gielkens for the transcription).

26. Memo, Oberbürgemeister R. Fieser, December 6, 1910, Stadtarchiv Baden-Baden, inv. no. A 26/29–711.

27. Während seines Aufenthaltes in Baden Oos bewohnte Fokker ein Zimmer in der Pension "Landhaus Rösch." Dort war er vom 19. Dezember 1910 bis 3. Februar 1911 und vom 23. bis 28. Februar 1911 angemeldet. Main Country Archive Schwerin, Ministerium des Innern 5.12–3/1 Signatur 10573, Blatt 456, Großherzogliches Bezirksamt Baden an Staatsministerium des Innern, February 6, 1915; Alexander Kauther, Paul Wirtz, and Michael Schmidt, *Anton Fokker: Ein niederländischer Flieger und Flugzeughersteller in Johannisthal* (Berlin: Johflug, 2012), 47; Heft 32, Dokumentenreihe Flugplatz Berlin-Johannisthal 1909–1914.

28. Von Daum to R. Fieser, December 15, 1910, Stadtarchiv Baden-Baden, inv. no. A 26/29–711; Von Daum to R. Fieser, December 20, 1910, Stadtarchiv Baden-Baden, inv. no. A 26/29–711.

29. Naturalization file for Anthony Fokker, Main Country Archive, Schwerin, Ministerium des Innern 5.12–3/1 inv. no. 10573, Blatt 456, Großherzogliches Bezirksamt Baden an Staatsministerium des Innern, February 6, 1915. Also see Kauther, Wirtz, and Schmidt, *Fokker*, 47. Fokker himself was erroneous later when he believed that this had happened around Christmas 1910; see Fokker and Gould, *Flying Dutchman*, 49–51.

30. Naturalization file for Fokker. The "apple tree" against which Von Daum reportedly crashed cannot be seen on any contemporary photo of Baden-Oos.

31. Anthony Fokker to his mother, April 1911, Collection Thijs Postma, Hegener Papers. Fokker, for whom names were often unimportant, erroneously referred to Grünberg as "Grunwald."

32. Interview with De Waal and Kuntner, *Algemeen Handelsblad*, May 31, 1913.

33. Anthony Fokker, postcard to his father, May 4, 1911, Aviodrome, collection A. H. G. Fokker, box 12; Fokker and Gould, *Flying Dutchman*, 52–53.

34. Newspaper report after a *Mainzner Anzeiger* clipping submitted by Anthony Fokker, *Haarlems Dagblad*, May 19, 1911.

35. Manfred Penning, "Die Erste Deutsche Automobil Fachschule Mainz, Teil 3: Wo Fokkers erstes Flugzeug entstand," *Mainzer Vierteljahres Hefte*, 2013, no. 1, 103.

36. Hans Karl Rehm, "Der fliegende Holländer, die Wahrheit im Fall Fokker," *Mainzner Anzeiger*, July 21, 1933; Kurt Ries, "Määnzer Gefladdscher: Eine kleine Geschichte der Fliegerei in und um Mainz," *Mainzer Vierteljahresheft für Kultur, Politik, Wirtschaft und Geschichte* 2 (1982), no. 3, 114–39.

5. HAARLEM, HOLLAND, AUGUST 1911

1. *Haarlems Dagblad*, September 1, 1911.
2. *Haarlems Dagblad*, September 1 and 4, 1911; *De Telegraaf*, September 1, 1911.
3. *Haarlems Dagblad*, August 24 and 28, 1911.
4. *Haarlems Dagblad*, August 31, 1911.
5. *De Telegraaf*, August 31, 1911; *Haarlems Dagblad*, September 5, 1911; A. H. G. Fokker and Bruce Gould, *Flying Dutchman: The Life of Anthony Fokker* (New York: Henry Holt, 1931), 57–61.
6. *Haarlems Dagblad*, September 2, 1911.
7. *Haarlems Dagblad*, September 4, 1911; Fokker and Gould, *Flying Dutchman*, 62.
8. Frank van Dalen, *Licensed to Fly for One Hundred Years: Anthony Fokker en zijn vlieg- tuigenfabriek* (Papendrecht: Fokker Technologies, 2014), 14–15.
9. Fokker and Gould, *Flying Dutchman*, 46–47, 53–56.
10. Ibid., 57.
11. Anthony Fokker to his mother, July 2, 1911, Aviodrome, collection A. H. G. Fokker, box 12.
12. "Vliegdemonstratie A. H. G. Fokker" ("Flying Demonstration A. H. G. Fokker," written by Herman Fokker and glued to a wooden cigar box), September 4, 1911, Aviodrome, collection A. H. G. Fokker, box 15.
13. Herman Fokker to Anthony Fokker, September 30, 1912, Aviodrome, collection A. H. G. Fokker, box 12.
14. Postcard, Anthony Fokker to his mother, September 15, 1911, Aviodrome, collection A. H. G. Fokker, box 11; photo in Bernard de Waal album, Aviodrome, collection A. H. G. Fokker, box 15. Fokker to his father, November 29, 1911, Aviodrome, collection A. H. G. Fokker, box 12.
15. Postcard, Fokker to his mother, September 19, 1911, Aviodrome, collection A. H. G. Fokker, box 12; *Berliner Tageblatt*, September 24, 1911.
16. Postcard, Fokker to his mother, postmarked September 18, 1911, Aviodrome, collection A. H. G. Fokker, box 12.
17. Fokker to his father, November 29, 1911.
18. Postcard, Fokker to his mother, October 5, 1911, Aviodrome, collection A. H. G. Fokker, box 12.
19. Fokker to his father, November 29, 1911.
20. Ibid.

6. BERLIN, GERMANY, MAY 1912

1. Günter Schmidt, *Als die Oldtimer flogen: Die Geschichte des Flugplatzes Johannisthal* (Oberhaching: Aviatik, 1995), 154.
2. Ibid., 152–55.
3. *Haarlems Dagblad*, June 1, 1912.
4. *Berliner Zeitung*, May 28, 1912; *Hamburgischer Correspondent und neue hamburgische Börsen-Halle*, May 28, 1912.
5. A. H. G. Fokker and Bruce Gould, *Flying Dutchman: The Life of Anthony Fokker* (New York: Henry Holt, 1931), 86–90.

6. *Flugsport*, no. 12 (1912), 460.

7. *Flugsport*, June 19, 1912, copy in Deutsches Technik Museum Berlin (DTMB), 1.4.146, Nachlass Peter Grosz, inv. no. 0311.

8. *Haarlems Dagblad*, June 10, 1912.

9. H. A. Somberg, "Fokker, Anthony Herman Gerard (1890–1939)," *Biografisch Woordenboek van Nederland*, http://resources.huygens.knaw.nl/bwn1880-2000/lemmata/bwn1/fokker.

10. *Flugplatz Johannisthal, Juli–September 1913*, Aviodrome, box "Fokker Johannisthal." See also Schmidt, *Als die Oldtimer flogen*, 11, 17–20, 28–33, 133.

11. Anthony Fokker to August Nischwitz, December 7, 1912, Archive Thijs Postma, Hoofddorp, Holland, file Correspondence Fokker.

12. Alexander Kauther, Paul Wirtz, and Michael Schmidt, *Anton H. G. Fokker: Ein niederländischer Flieger und Flugzeughersteller in Johannisthal* (Berlin: Dokumentenreihe zum Flugplatz Berlin-Johannisthal, 1909–1914, vol. 32),15.

13. Anthony Fokker to his mother, undated [May 1912], Aviodrome, collection A. H. G. Fokker, box 12.

14. *Haarlems Dagblad*, May 7, 1912, 6; interview with Jan Hilgers, *Algemeen Handelsblad*, December 27, 1912.

15. *Flugsport*, no. 12 (December 28, 1911), 755; *Flugsport*, no. 3 (January 31, 1912), 126.

16. *Utrechts Nieuwsblad*, February 6, 1912, 5; February 21, 1912, 6.

17. Borchardt, on behalf of Fokker Aviatik GmbH, to the German War Office, February 21, 1912, copy in DTMB, 1.4.146, Nachlass Peter Grosz, inv. no. 0313; *Berliner Börsenzeitung*, February 27, 1912.

18. Kauther, Wirtz, and Schmidt, *Fokker*, 48; interview with Claus Goedecker, in Frido Troost, Sytze van der Zee, and Willem Zoetendaal, *Salto Mortale: Fokker in bedrijf, 1911–1996* (Amsterdam: Basalt & d'Arts, 1998), 11–13.

19. Borchardt to German War Office, February 21, 1912.

20. Anthony Fokker to his father, May 3, 1912, Aviodrome, collection A. H. G. Fokker, box 12; John Roosendaal, letter to the editor, *De Luchtvaart*, August 3, 1912, 319–21; Herman Fokker to Anthony Fokker, September 30, 1912, Aviodrome, collection A. H. G. Fokker, box 12; Fokker and Gould, *Flying Dutchman*, 96–104.

21. Fokker and Gould, *Flying Dutchman*, 64–68.

22. *Flugsport*, no. 6 (March 1912), 226.

23. The German edition of Fokker's autobiography contains additional details on the general atmosphere at Senftleben's, although these comments are different in tone from the rest of the book and appear to have been added by the German editor, Carl Heinz Pollog. See A. H. G. Fokker, *Der fliegende Holländer: Die Memoiren des A. H. G. Fokker* (Frankfurt: Wunderkammer, 2010), 82–87. See also Alexander Kauther and Paul Wirtz, *Cafe und Conditorei Senftleben: Geschichten um und über das "Cafe Senftleben," dem Treffpunkt der Flugzeugführer vom Flugplatz Berlin-Johannisthal*, Dokumentenreihe zum Flugplatz Berlin-Johannisthal 1909–1914, vol. 3 (Berlin: GRIN, 2012).

24. Willy Hahn, *Aus meinem Fliegerleben: Erinnerungen und Gedanken eines deutschen Fliegers*, quoted in Kauther and Wirtz, *Cafe und Conditorei Senftleben*, 10.

25. Kauther, Wirtz, and Schmidt, *Fokker*, 20; A. R. Weyl, *Fokker: The Creative Years* (London: Putnam, 1985), 26–31.

26. Manfred Penning, "Sie flogen am Grossen Sand: Die Anfänge der Fliegerei in Mainz," *AOPA Info* (Aircraft Owners and Pilots Association, Germany), newsletter 3 (2001), 30–34.

27. Fokker to his father, undated [first week of April 1912], Collection Thijs Postma, Hegener Papers.

28. Ibid.

29. Postcard, Anthony Fokker to Tom Reinhold, postmarked May 10, 1912, Aviodrome, collection A. H. G. Fokker, box 12; *Flugsport*, no. 11 (May 22, 1912), 438.

30. Herman Fokker to Anthony Fokker, May 24, 1912, Aviodrome, collection A. H. G. Fokker, box 12.

31. *Berliner Börsenzeitung*, June 27, 1912.

32. Reinhold Platz, "19 Jahre Flugzeugbau bei Fokker," DTMB, Nachlass Grosz, inv. no. 0394; Kauther, Wirtz, and Schmidt, *Fokker*, 27.

33. Fokker to his father, undated [first week of April 1912]: Collection Thijs Postma, Hegener Papers; "Der Fokker-Eindecker," *Flugsport*, no. 7 (March 27, 1912), 239–41.

34. Peter Grosz and Volker Koos, *Die Fokker Flugzeugwerke in Deutschland, 1912–1921* (Königswinter: Heel, 2004), 20; Herman Fokker to Anthony Fokker, May 24, 1912, Aviodrome, collection A. H. G. Fokker, box 12.

35. *Flugsport*, no. 16 (July 31, 1912), 612.

7. ST. PETERSBURG, RUSSIA, SEPTEMBER 1912

1. John Roosendaal and J. Schriere, letters to the editor, *De Luchtvaart*, August 3, 1912, 319–23.

2. A. H. G. Fokker and Bruce Gould, *De vliegende Hollander* (Amsterdam: Van Holkema & Warendorf, 1931), 107–8. Only the Dutch edition of Fokker's autobiography contains the story of his first great love. Fokker himself must have added the paragraph after reading the text of the Dutch translation. In the American original, the story is not mentioned at all; the German translation of the Dutch edition carries only a short summary of his romance with Ljuba.

3. V. Semenov, "Aviatrix," *Rabotnitsa* [The female worker, a Soviet women's magazine], no. 8 (1978), 18–19. Special thanks are due to René Demets for the translation.

4. Interview with Ljuba Galantschikoff, *New York Evening Post*, December 13, 1930.

5. *Rigasche Rundschau*, Friday May 3, 1912; Frederik Gerdessen, Toivo Kitvel, and Johannes Tilk, *Aeg, mehed, lennukid: Eesti lennunduse arengulugu kuni 1940 aastani* (Tallinn: Eesti Entsüklopeedia-kirjastus, 2001), 22–26.

6. Scott W. Palmer, *Dictatorship of the Air: Aviation Culture and the Fate of Modern Russia* (New York: Cambridge University Press, 2006), 43–47.

7. Anthony Fokker to his mother, undated [mid-May 1912], Aviodrome, collection A. H. G. Fokker, box 12; Fokker to his father, May 3, 1912, Aviodrome, collection A. H. G. Fokker, box 12.

8. Interview with Jan Hilgers, *Algemeen Handelsblad*, December 27, 1912; Gerdessen, Kitvel, and Tilk, *Aeg, mehed, lennukid*, 31–34, 341–42.

9. W. Bruce Lincoln, *Sunlight at Midnight: St. Petersburg and the Rise of Modern Russia* (New York: Basic Books, 2000), 149–70.

10. A. H. G. Fokker and Bruce Gould, *Flying Dutchman: The Life of Anthony Fokker* (New York: Henry Holt, 1931), 93.

11. Anthony Fokker to his sister Catharina, August 27, 1912, Collection Thijs Postma, Hoofddorp, dossier Fokker correspondence.

12. Palmer, *Dictatorship of the Air*, 48.

13. Fokker and Gould, *Flying Dutchman*, 93.

14. *Flugsport*, no. 21 (October 1912), 813.

15. Fokker and Gould, *Vliegende Hollander*, 106; see also Fokker and Gould, *Flying Dutchman*, 94.

16. Fokker to Catharina, August 27, 1912.

17. Palmer, *Dictatorship of the Air*, 48; Andrei Alexandrov and Gennadi Petrov, *Die Deutsche Flugzeuge in russischen und sowjetischen Diensten, 1914–1951* (Eggolsheim: Nebel, 2004), 8–10.

18. My special thanks go to René Demets of the European Space Agency, who was indispensable for reconstructing the story of the St. Petersburg competition on the basis of primary sources in Russian. René Demets, "Roebels, ruzies en rivaliteit: De vliegwedstrijd van Sint Petersburg in 1912," *All Clear* no. 21 (2014), 26–27 (publication of the Dutch Aeronautical Association KNVvL).

19. *Flugsport*, no. 21 (October 1912), 813; postcard, Anthony Fokker to Tom Reinhold, September 18, 1912, Aviodrome, collection A. H. G. Fokker, box 11; *Algemeen Handelsblad*, October 4, 1912.

20. Fokker and Gould, *Flying Dutchman*, 94–95.

21. Palmer, *Dictatorship of the Air*, 48–50.

22. According to Fokker's own reporting in *Haarlems Dagblad*, December 11, 1912; see also *Berliner Börsenzeitung*, October 1, 1912.

23. Postcard, Anthony Fokker to Tom Reinhold, postmarked November 13, 1912, Aviodrome, collection A. H. G. Fokker, box 12.

24. Report of Ljuba's recollections available at http://www.igor-sikorsky.ru/skyman/aviatrisa-rekordsmen-lyubov-golanchikova.html.

25. *Flugsport*, no. 24 (November 19, 1912), 915; *Flugsport*, no. 25 (December 4, 1912), 947–48 (photographic print of the flight instrument readings shown on p. 948); see also *Haarlems Dagblad*, December 11, 1912, and *Berliner Börsenzeitung*, November 23, 1912.

26. Michael Schmidt, "A. H. G. Fokker: Der niederländische Flieger und Flugzeughersteller in Deutschland" (unpublished manuscript, Schwerin, 2013), 22–26.

27. Anthony Fokker to Tom Reinhold [undated, autumn 1912], Aviodrome, collection A. H. G. Fokker, box 12.

28. Herman Fokker to Anthony Fokker, September 30, 1912, Aviodrome, collection A. H. G. Fokker, box 12.

29. Fokker and Gould, *Vliegende Hollander*, 110.

30. Telegram, Anthony Fokker to his parents, October 12, 1912, Aviodrome, collection A. H. G. Fokker, box 12; *Haarlems Dagblad*, October 14, 1912.

31. Postcard, Anthony Fokker to Reinhold, postmarked November 13, 1912.

32. Contract between Anthony Fokker and Jan Hilgers, December 20, 1912, Aviodrome, collection A. H. G. Fokker, Fokker Schwerin, box 1; freight papers, Ostasiatischer

Frachtdampferdienst, Hamburg-Amerika Linie, December 25, 1912, Aviodrome, collection A. H. G. Fokker, Fokker Schwerin, box 1.

33. *Het nieuws van den dag voor Nederlandsch-Indië*, January 22, February 11, and March 6, 1913; *De Sumatra Post*, February 3, 1913; *Bataviaasch Nieuwsblad*, April 29, 1913; *Algemeen Handelsblad*, May 2, 1913; C. C. Küpfer, "Gedenkboek NV Koninklijke Nederlandse Vliegtuigenfabriek, 1919–1964" (unpublished manuscript, n.d.).

34. Postcard, Anthony Fokker to his sister Toos, postmarked November 23, 1912, Aviodrome, collection A. H. G. Fokker, box 12.

35. Adalbert Norden, *Weltrekord, Weltrekord* (Berlin: Drei Masken, 1940), 21.

36. Postcard, Anthony Fokker to his mother, November 27, 1912, Collection Postma, dossier Fokker correspondence.

37. Fokker, *Vliegende Hollander*, 110 (translated from the Dutch edition).

38. Ibid., 111 (translated from the Dutch edition). Among the few papers of this period that have survived from Fokker's early period are several remarkably merry postcards from female employees that suggest relationships extending beyond that of employer-employee.

8. SCHWERIN, GERMANY, JUNE 1913

1. Anthony Fokker to his mother, May 1912, Aviodrome, collection A. H. G. Fokker, box 12.

2. Jacob Cremer to Provincial Government of the Province of North Holland, December 6, 1910, NA, 2.21.043, Cremer Archive, inv. no. 364; Gerrit Cremer to Jacob Cremer, November 11, 1913, April 4, 1914, and June 21, 1914, Cremer Archive, inv. no. 206.

3. *Mecklenburgische Zeitung*, June 28, 1913.

4. Bernd Kasten and Jens-Uwe Rost, *Schwerin: Geschichte der Stadt* (Schwerin: Thomas Helms, 2005), 60, 96–102.

5. Bernd Kasten, "Zur Geschichte des Flugplatzes Schwerin-Görries, 1912–1945," in *Wege übers (Bundes-) Land: Zur Geschichte der Land-, Wasser-, Schienen-, und Luftwege in Mecklenburg und Vorpommern*, ed. Kathrin Möller and Wolf Karge (Schwerin: Atelier für Porträt- und Historienmalerei, 2002), 128.

6. John H. Morrow Jr., *German Air Power in World War I* (Lincoln: University of Nebraska Press, 1982), 7; John H. Morrow Jr., *The Great War in the Air: Military Aviation from 1909 to 1921* (Washington, DC: Smithsonian Institution Press, 1993), 37–38.

7. Peter Grosz and Volker Koos, *Fokker Flugzeugwerke in Deutschland, 1912–1921* (Königswinter: Heel, 2004), 10.

8. Chamber of Commerce Register, Berlin-Köpenick, (copy dated February 2, 1920): City Archive Schwerin, inv. no. M850; booklet, *Flugplatz Johannisthal, Juli–September 1913*, Aviodrome, box "Fokker Johannisthal."

9. Anthony Fokker, Nederlandsche Club address in New York on the occasion of Evert van Dijk's ocean crossing flight, July 1930, quoted in *Limburgsch Dagblad*, July 24, 1930; A. H. G. Fokker and Bruce Gould, *Flying Dutchman: The Life of Anthony Fokker* (New York: Henry Holt, 1931), 101–2; Marc Dierikx, *Fokker: A Transatlantic Biography* (Washington, DC: Smithsonian Institution Press, 1997), 19.

10. Michael Schmidt, "A. H. G. Fokker: Der niederländische Flieger und Flugzeughersteller in Deutschland" (unpublished manuscript, Schwerin, 2012), 27.

11. Postcard, Anthony Fokker to his mother, January 15, 1913, Collection Thijs Postma, Hoofddorp, dossier Fokker correspondence.

12. Postcard, Anthony Fokker to his parents, postmarked February 13, 1913, Aviodrome, collection A. H. G. Fokker, box 12; booklet, *Flugplatz Johannisthal, Juli–September 1913*, Aviodrome, box "Fokker Johannisthal."

13. Friedrich Seekatz, "In Memoriam A. H. G. Fokker," *Vliegwereld*, December 28, 1939; Schmidt, "A. H. G. Fokker," 23; *Flugsport* no. 4 (1914), 126–27.

14. Otto Weltzien to the Schwerin City Council, June 17, 1913, Stadtarchiv Schwerin, inv. no. M5025; Kasten and Rost, *Schwerin*, 102.

15. Volker Koos, *Die Fokker Flugzeugwerke in Schwerin: Geschichte, Produktion, Typen* (Schwerin: Reinhard Thon, 1993), 8; Grosz and Koos, *Fokker Flugzeugwerke*, 11.

16. Fokker and Gould, *Flying Dutchman*, 84–86.

17. *Algemeen Handelsblad*, May 19, 1913; *Rotterdamsch Nieuwsblad*, May 23, 1913; and *Flugsport* no. 11 (1913), 389–90. In his 1931 autobiography Fokker suggested he was present in The Hague, having arrived there by train, but this did not feature in the newspaper reporting; see Fokker and Gould, *Flying Dutchman*, 71–72.

18. *Het Centrum*, May 26, 1913; reporting with photo in *Revue der Sporten*, May 27, 1913, 26.

19. Peter Grosz, unfinished manuscript, "Fokker: The Early Years" (September 15, 2004), Archive Deutsches Technik Museum Berlin (DTMB), inv. no. 394.

20. Grosz and Koos, *Fokker Flugzeugwerke*, 11; Grosz, "Fokker: The Early Years, Part I," *World War I Aero* (2005), 41–48; City Magistrates to the Schwerin City Council, February 13, 1914, City Archive, Schwerin, inv. no. M2931.

21. Hans Haller to the Railway Board, May 16, 1914, Main Country Archive, Schwerin, 9.2–17, Reichsbahndirektion Schwerin, Altaktenbestand, inv. no. 344.

22. Schwerin Magistrates to the Mecklenburg Ministry of the Interior, January 20, 1915, Main Country Archive, Schwerin, 5.12–3/1, Mecklenburg-Schwerinisches Ministerium des Innern, inv. no. 10573; Fokker and Gould, *Flying Dutchman*, 144; Schmidt, "A. H. G. Fokker," 30; Gerrit Cremer to Jacob Cremer, June 24, 1914, NA, 2.21.043, Cremer Archive, inv. no. 206.

23. Anthony Fokker, letter to the editor, *Avia*, April 29, 1914.

24. Contract, "Ausbildung zum Flugzeugführer," October 19, 1913, Aviodrome, collection A. H. G. Fokker, box 12; "Flüge eines alten Adlers (Von Bismarck)," *Flugwelt*, no. 2 (1962), 124–26.

25. On the procurement of the Morane-Saulnier and the development of the Fokker M.5, see Alfred Weyl, *Fokker: The Creative Years* (London: Putnam, 1965), 61–82.

26. Grosz and Koos, *Fokker Flugzeugwerke*, 24–29.

27. *Mecklenburgische Zeitung*, February 11, 1914; photo of the accident in Bernard de Waal's private album, Aviodrome, collection A. H. G. Fokker, box 15.

28. Aircraft sales contract, signed by A. von Bismarck, May 11, 1914, Aviodrome, collection A. H. G. Fokker, box 12; see also "Flüge eines alten Adlers (Von Bismarck)."

29. Newspaper clippings, "Fokker flog dem Kriegsminister am 2. Juni," *Flugsport* (1914), 516; "Dank an Fokker," *Die Luftflotte*, August 1916, DTMB, Nachlass Grosz, inv. no. 0313.

30. Günter Schmitt, *Als die Oldtimer flogen: Die Geschichte des Flugplatzes Johannisthal* (Oberhaching: Aviatrik, 1995), 127–30.

31. Fokker and Gould, *Flying Dutchman*, 74–75.
32. Postcard, Fokker to his parents, June 1, 1914, Aviodrome, collection A. H. G. Fokker, box 12; Nordmark-Verein für Motorluftfahrt, *Fokker und Sablatnig Kopf- und Sturzflüge* (folder, June 28–29, 1914), Aviodrome, collection A. H. G. Fokker, box 15; "Fokker flog dem Kriegsminister am 2. Juni."
33. Chamber of Commerce Register, Berlin-Köpenick; Schmitt, *Als die Oldtimer flogen*, 72.
34. Summary, Founding Papers of the Fokker Aeroplanbau GmbH, October 23, 1917, DTMB, Nachlass Grosz, inv. no. 0313; IOU, Frits Cremer, February 18, 1914, Aviodrome, collection A. H. G. Fokker, box 13.
35. Duplicate, Schwerin Trade Register of Fokker Aeroplanbau, Schwerin City Archive, inv. no. M850.

9. STENAY, FRANCE, JUNE 1915

1. A. H. G. Fokker and Bruce Gould, *Flying Dutchman: The Life of Anthony Fokker* (New York: Henry Holt, 1931), 133–35.
2. J. H. J. Andriessen, ed., *De oorlogsbrieven van Unteroffizier Carl Heller, geschreven tijdens de Eerste Wereldoorlog* (Soesterberg: Aspekt, 2003), 26–28.
3. A. H. G. Fokker and Bruce Gould, *De vliegende Hollander* (Amsterdam: Van Holkema & Warendorf, 1931), 128–32; Peter Grosz and Volker Koos, *Fokker Flugzeugwerke in Deutschland, 1912–1921* (Königswinter: Heel, 2004), 38.
4. Volker Berghahn, *Der Erste Weltkrieg* (Munich: C. H. Beck, 2003), 64–66, 76; Roger Chickering, *The Great War and Urban Life in Germany: Freiburg 1914–1918* (Cambridge: Cambridge University Press, 2007), 60–63; Friedrich Seekatz to Marius Beeling, February 25, 1969, formerly in NV Fokker company archive, Schiphol Airport, Beeling Papers, miscellaneous correspondence.
5. City of Schwerin (M. Baller) to Mecklenburg Finance Ministry, July 25, 1914, Schwerin City Archive, inv. no. M2931.
6. Kurt Witgens letter, March 25, 1915 (copy), Collection Michael Schmidt, Schwerin.
7. Anthony Fokker to Friedrich Seekatz, telegram, August 21, 1914, Aviodrome, collection Seekatz; Fokker, *Flying Dutchman*, 117–18; A. R. Weyl, *Fokker: The Creative Years* (London: Putnam, 1985), 83–85; John H. Morrow Jr., *The Great War in the Air: Military Aviation from 1909 to 1921* (Washington, DC: Smithsonian Institution Press, 1993), 73; R. J. Castendijk, "A. H. G. Fokker," in *Het Vliegveld* 1 (1917), no. 2, 28–29; Hugo Hamacher to Anthony Fokker, October 30, 1914, formerly in NV Fokker company archive, Schiphol Airport, box A. H. G. Fokker 2.
8. Photographic postcard, Obotrit rowing society to Anthony Fokker, February 16, 1914, Aviodrome, collection A. H. G. Fokker, box 12.
9. Anthony Fokker to Friedrich Seekatz, April 21, 1914, Aviodrome, collection Seekatz; photographic postcard, Anthony Fokker to his sister Toos, February 18, 1917, Aviodrome, collection A. H. G. Fokker, box 12; photographic postcard, Anthony Fokker to his mother, July 21, 1915, Aviodrome, collection A. H. G. Fokker, box 12.
10. Vicki Baum, *Menschen im Hotel* (Berlin: Ullstein, 1929), 5–18; advertisement for Conrad Uhl's Hotel Bristol, *New York Times*, March 14, 1910; Egon Jameson, *Berlin so wie es war: Ein Bildband* (Düsseldorf: Droste, 1969), 32.

11. Granville Fortescue, *At the Front with Three Armies* (London: A. Melrose, 1915); Marcus Funck and Roger Chickering, eds., *Endangered Cities: Military Power and Urban Societies in the Era of the World Wars* (Boston: Brill, 2004), 111–26.

12. Fokker, *Flying Dutchman*, 202–3.

13. Circular, Chancellor's Office, Berlin, October 16, 1914, Mecklenburg Country Archive, Schwerin, 5.12–3/1, Mecklenburgisch-Schwerinisches Ministerium des Innern, inv. no. 20755.

14. Anthony Fokker to the Grossherzoglich Mecklenburgische Contingent-Kommando, December 22, 1914, formerly in NV Fokker company archive, Schiphol Airport, Beeling Papers.

15. See the correspondence between Anthony Fokker and his legal counsel, A. S. Oppenheim, regarding the naturalization issue. For example: A. S. Oppenheim to Anthony Fokker, February 22, 1919, Haarlem Municipal Archive, New Archive, no. 126–1. "Fokker is geen Nederlander meer!" [Fokker is no longer Dutch!], *De Telegraaf*, March 1, 1915. Summary, Trade Register Schwerin, February 2, 1920, Schwerin City Archive, inv. no. M850. See also Fokker, *Flying Dutchman*, 113–14, 120.

16. Correspondence, Fokker Flugzeugwerke with the Mecklenburgische Flugplatz Gesellschaft Görries-Schwerin [Airfield Society], 1916–17, Aviodrome, collection A. H. G. Fokker, box Fokker-Schwerin 1.

17. Letter Felix Wagenführ (formerly of IdFlieg) to Lieutenant Hildebrand in Goslar, November 21, 1929, Aviodrome, collection A. H. G. Fokker, box 11.

18. Interview with Friedrich Seekatz, May 6, 1918, *AZ Aëro* 6 (1918), no. 10 (May 25, 1918), 203–6, Deutsches Technik Museum Berlin (DTMB), Nachlass Grosz, inv. no. 0313.

19. Fokker production statistics, compiled by Peter M. Grosz on the basis of authentic delivery reports and shipping lists, DTMB, Nachlass Grosz, inv. no. 330, 331, 332; John H. Morrow Jr., *German Air Power in World War I (Lincoln: University of Nebraska Press, 1982)*, 47; Morrow, *Great War in the Air*, 75.

20. Michael Schmidt, "A. H. G. Fokker: Der niederländische Flieger und Flugzeughersteller in Deutschland" (unpublished manuscript, Schwerin, 2013), 43.

21. Film footage of aircraft production at Fokker in Schwerin, undated [1915–16], author's collection; *Berliner Volkszeitung*, April 26 and July 16, 1916.

22. Film footage of aircraft production in Schwerin.

23. Friedrich Seekatz to Anthony Fokker, April 6, September 4, and October 4, 1917, DTMB, Nachlass Grosz, inv. no. 0339.

24. Statement, Magistrate's Office, Schwerin, March 22, 1918, Mecklenburg Main Archive, Schwerin, 9.2–17, Reichsbahndirektion Schwerin, Altaktenbestand, inv. no. 344.

25. Anthony Fokker to the German Navy Office, January 16, 1917, DTMB, Nachlass Grosz, inv. no. 0348.

26. Robert Wohl, *A Passion for Wings: Aviation and the Western Imagination, 1908–1918* (New Haven, CT: Yale University Press, 1994), 207–10; Morrow, *Great War in the Air*, 90–92.

27. Alex Imrie, *The Fokker Triplane* (London: Arms and Armour Press, 1992), 11; Jörg Kranzhoff, *Fokker Dr.I* (Stuttgart: Motorbuch, 1994), 40–43, 46.

28. Patent, August Euler, no. 248601, May 25, 1912, German National Archive (Bundesarchiv), Koblenz, Euler Nachlass, N1103/052, N1103052020000; Patent, Franz Schneider,

no. 276396, July 10, 1914, Fokker-Schneider patent suit, 1916–1926, formerly in NV Fokker company archive, Schiphol Airport, series V/Alg. Secr., no. 67.

29. Kranzhoff, *Fokker Dr.I*, 42–46.

30. Fokker, *Vliegende Hollander*, 123–30; Henri Hegener, *Fokker: The Man and the Aircraft* (Letchworth: Harleyford Publications, 1961), 23–26; Kranzhoff, *Fokker Dr.I*, 43–46; Weyl, *Fokker*, 95–97.

31. Franz Immelmann, *Immelmann, "The Eagle of Lille"* (Philadelphia: Casemate, 2009), 67–68, 91; Schmidt, "Fokker," 40; Johannes Werner, *Knight of Germany: Oswald Boelcke, German Ace* (Philadelphia: Casemate, 2009), 114–15.

32. Volker Koos, *Die Fokker Flugzeugwerke in Schwerin: Geschichte, Produktion, Typen* (Schwerin: Reinhard Thon, 1993), 13; Grosz and Koos, *Fokker Flugzeugwerke in Deutschland*, 36–38; Schmidt, "Fokker," 40.

33. August Euler to War Ministry Patent Office, December 15, 1915, German National Archive, Koblenz, Euler Nachlass, N1103/059, N1103059069000; August Euler to Anthony Fokker, August 20, 1915, German National Archive, Koblenz, Euler Nachlass, N1103/059, N1103059093000; Anthony Fokker to August Euler, September 1, 1915, German National Archive, Koblenz, Euler Nachlass, N1103/059, N1103059092000.

34. Report of meeting at the German War Office, January 6, 1916, German National Archive, Koblenz, Euler Nachlass, N1103/059, N1103059064000 and N1130059065000.

35. Note, August Euler, May 8, 1916, German National Archive, Koblenz, Euler Nachlass, N1103/059, N1103059023000; August Euler to German War Ministry, July 10, 1916, German National Archive, Koblenz, Euler Nachlass, N1103/059, N1103059006000; Michael Düsing, *Abenteur gelber Hund: August Euler, Deutsche Luftfahrt ab 1908* (Stuttgart: Ergonomia, 2008), 166–69.

36. August Euler, notes of a meeting at Hotel Bristol, June 7, 1916, German National Archive, Koblenz, Euler Nachlass, N1103/059, N1103059010000.

37. Fokker, *Flying Dutchman*, 179–81.

38. Rental agreement, Gustav Lüderitz with Anthony Fokker, June 22, 1916, Aviodrome, collection A. H. G. Fokker, box Fokker-Schwerin 1; Wilhelm Horter to Flugzeug Waffen Fabrik, September–December 1916, Aviodrome, collection A. H. G. Fokker, box Fokker-Schwerin 3; German Patent Office, Patentschrift no. 302578, Anthony H. G. Fokker in Schwerin i.M., Abzugsvorrichtung für Feuerwaffen auf Flugzeugen (patented February 18, 1917), issued May 8, 1920, DTMB, Nachlass Grosz, inv. no. 0346.

39. Wilhelm Horter to IdFlieg Weapons Department, January 12, 1917, Aviodrome, collection A. H. G. Fokker, box Fokker-Schwerin 3.

40. Anthony Fokker to Friedrich Seekatz, October 17, 1917, DTMB, Nachlass Grosz, inv. no. 0313; production statistic in DTMB, Nachlass Grosz, inv. no. 0346. For further discussion of the weapons system, see Fokker, *Flying Dutchman*, 180–90.

41. Correspondence, 1916–33, on the Fokker-Schneider patent suit, formerly in NV Fokker company archive, Schiphol Airport, series V/Alg. Secr., no. 67 and series KW, nos. 22, 23, 24, 25, 26. See also "Memoires Franz Schneider" (unpublished manuscript), Archive Deutsches Museum, Munich, Franz Schneider Collection.

42. *Manchester Guardian*, January 21 and 24 and March 12, 1916; Michael Paris, *Winged Warfare: The Literature and Theory of Aerial Warfare in Britain, 1859–1917* (Manchester: Manchester University Press, 1992), 78.

43. Photograph of Anthony Fokker with moustache and cap, dated June 1915, Döppler Album, Heitzman "Stuffinder" Collection, Deansboro, New York.

44. Series of photographs of Anthony Fokker behind his desk, undated [1916], Smeulers Collection, Bronkhorst.

45. Copy of film footage made at Schwerin, undated [ca. 1915], author's collection.

46. Avner Offer, "The Blockade of Germany and the Strategy of Starvation, 1914–1918," in *Great War, Total War: Combat and Mobilization on the Western Front, 1914–1918*, ed. Roger Chickering and Stig Förster (Cambridge: Cambridge University Press, 2000), 169–188; Berghahn, *Erste Weltkrieg*, 82–83; Ulrich Kluge, *Die deutsche Revolution, 1918/1919: Staat, Politik und Gesellschaft zwischen Weltkrieg und Kapp-Putsch* (Frankfurt: Suhrkamp, 1985), 40.

47. Fokker, *Flying Dutchman*, 144–45. The American edition referred to the dog's name as "Zeiten."

48. Fokker film footage, author's collection.

18. SAINT-QUENTIN, FRANCE, AUGUST 1918

1. Curt von Morgen, *Meiner Truppen Heldenkämpfe: Aufzeichnungen von Curt von Morgen, Generalleutnant* (Berlin: Ernst Siegfried Mittler und Sohn, 1920), 147.

2. Some of this film footage can be seen at http://resources.ushmm.org/film/display/detail .php?file_num=3354 (Story RG-60.3352, Tape 2547). For a description of the film images, see: https://collections.ushmm.org/film_findingaids/RG-60.3351_Historian%20Lance %20Bronnenkant%20on%20Fokker%20films_en.pdf. See also Von Morgen, *Meiner Truppen Heldenkämpfe*, 143–47.

3. A. H. G. Fokker and Bruce Gould, *Flying Dutchman: The Life of Anthony Fokker* (New York: Henry Holt, 1931), 156–59.

4. Correspondence of lieutenants Kurt Wintgens and Otto Parschau with Anthony Fokker, January–July 1915, Collection Michael Schmidt, Munich.

5. Anthony Fokker to his father, October 10, 1917, Aviodrome, collection A. H. G. Fokker, box 12; interview with Anthony Fokker, *Az Aëro* 6, no. 13 (July 10, 1918), 265–66, Deutsches Technik Museum Berlin (DTMB), Nachlass Grosz, inv. no. 0313.

6. Michael Schmidt, "A. H. G. Fokker: Der niederländische Flieger und Flugzeughersteller in Deutschland" (unpublished manuscript, Schwerin, 2013), 46.

7. Reinhold Platz, "19 Jahre Flugzeugbau bei Fokker," undated, DTMB, Nachlass Grosz, inv. no. 0394.

8. Anthony Fokker to Friedrich Seekatz, October 10, 1917, Aviodrome, collection A. H. G. Fokker, Fokker Schwerin, box 2.

9. Villehad Forssman to Anthony Fokker, April–September 1916, DTMB, Nachlass Grosz, inv. no. 0355; Frank van Dalen, *Licensed to Fly for One Hundred Years: Anthony Fokker en zijn vliegtuigenfabriek* (Papendrecht: Fokker Technologies, 2014), 42–47; Mike Tate, "The Fokker Cantilever Wing," *Cross & Cockade International: The First World War Aviation Historical Society Quarterly Journal* 41 (2010): 3–19; Peter Grosz and Volker Koos, *Die Fokker Flugzeugwerke in Deutschland, 1912–1921* (Königswinter: Heel, 2004), 56–57.

10. Agreement between the German Army Office and Fokker-Flugzeugwerken m.b.H., Schwerin, January 30, 1917, DTMB, Nachlass Grosz, inv. no. 0340.

11. Anthony Fokker, passport data, Aviodrome, collection A. H. G. Fokker, box 11; color poster of the June 26, 1917, flight, Photo Archive, Aviodrome; *Volksblatt*, August 8, 1917.

12. Schmidt, "A. H. G. Fokker," 37.

13. Anthony Fokker to Friedrich Seekatz, October 10, 1917, Aviodrome, collection A. H. G. Fokker, Fokker Schwerin, box 2; Peter M. Grosz and A. E. Ferko, "The Fokker DR.I: A Reappraisal," *Air Enthusiast*, no. 8 (October 1978), 9–26; Alex Imrie, *The Fokker Triplane* (London: Arms and Armour Press, 1992), 23–25.

14. Grosz and Koos, *Fokker Flugzeugwerke*, 49.

15. Hendrik Walaardt Sacré, diary entries, October 3, 1913 to October 15, 1919 in Rolf de Winter, *Hendrik Walaardt Sacré, 1873–1949: Leven voor de luchtvaart* (Den Haag: Sectie Luchtmachthistorie van de Luchtmachtstaf, 1992), 53; Muller Massis, Netherlands military attaché in Berlin, to Gen. Cornelis Snijders, December 24, 1917, NA, 2.13.70, Generale Staf (Algemeen Hoofdkwartier), 1914–1940, doss. no. GG.151b, 240 (former CAD number); R. A. F. Hezemans, "To Fly or Not to Fly, That's the Question," A. P. de Jong, ed., *Vlucht door de tijd: 75 jaar Nederlandse luchtmacht* (Houten: Unieboek, 1988), 40; Dirk Starink, *De jonge jaren van de Luchtmacht: Het Luchtwapen van het Nederlandse leger, 1913–1939* (Amsterdam: Boom, 2013), 111; Wim Klinkert, *Defending Neutrality: The Netherlands Prepares for War, 1900–1925* (Leiden: Brill, 2013), 146.

16. Anthony Fokker to his father, October 10, 1917, Aviodrome, collection A. H. G. Fokker, box 12.

17. Ibid.

18. Ibid.; Schmidt, "A. H. G. Fokker," 36.

19. Anthony Fokker to Friedrich Seekatz, October 10, 1917, Aviodrome, collection A. H. G. Fokker, box 12; Michael Schmidt, "Die Geschichte der Schweriner Pianofortefabrik Perzina" (unpublished manuscript, Schwerin, 2012), 15–18.

20. Anthony Fokker to Friedrich Seekatz, October 10, 1917, DTMB, Nachlass Grosz, inv. no. 0339; Schmidt, "A. H. G. Fokker," 57; Heinrich Beauvais, Karl Kössler, Max Mayer, and Christoph Regel, *Deutsche Luftfahrt: Flugerprobungsstellen bis 1945* (Bonn: Bernard & Graefe, 1998), 150.

21. Imrie, *Fokker Triplane*, 114–15, attachments with translated reports of the crash investigation's committee; Jörg Kranzhof, *Flugzeuge die Geschichte machten: Fokker Dr.I* (Stuttgart: Motorbuch, 1994), 70–89; Grosz and Koos, *Fokker Flugzeugwerke*, 58.

22. Gerald D. Feldman, *Hugo Stinnes: Biographie eines Industriellen, 1870–1924* (Munich: C. H. Beck, 1998), 437–38.

23. Wolfgang Wagner, *Hugo Junkers, Pionier der Luftfahrt—seine Flugzeuge* (Bonn: Bernard & Graefe, 1996), 79–89; Richard Byers, "An Unhappy Marriage: The Junkers-Fokker Merger," *Journal of Historical Biography* 3 (Spring 2008): 1–30; protocol of the negotiations between Anthony Fokker and Hugo Junkers in Berlin and Dessau on December 16, 18, and 22, 1916, and Junkers's response to Fokker's proposal regarding payment to obtain a license to use Junkers's patent rights, February 1, 1917, Archive Deutsches Museum, Munich, Junkers Archive, inv. no. 0201/T11.

24. Protocol of the Fokker-Junkers negotiations; Byers, "Junkers-Fokker Merger," 8.

25. Hugo Junkers to Anthony Fokker, January 12, 1917, Archive Deutsches Museum, Munich, Junkers Archive, inv. no. 0201/T11.

26. Albert Vögler (Deutsch-Luxemburgische Hütten- und Bergwerksgesellschaft) to Hugo Stinnes, May 3, 1917, DTMB, Nachlass Grosz, inv. no. 0348.

27. Minutes of a meeting between Wilhelm Horter and Kurt Lottmann of the Junkers Werke, February 2, 1917; Anthony Fokker to Hugo Junkers, April 16, 1917, Archive Deutsches Museum, Junkers Archive, inv. no. 0201/T11.

28. Agreement between Anthony Fokker and Hugo Junkers, June 19, 1917, Archive Deutsches Museum, Junkers Archive, inv. no. 0201/T11.

29. Byers, "Junkers-Fokker Merger," 13.

30. Founding contract of the Junkers-Fokker Werke AG Metallflugzeugbau, drawn up between Hugo Junkers and Anthony Fokker, August 20, 1917, Archive Deutsches Museum, Junkers Archive, inv. no. 0201/T11.

31. Hans Schmidt to Hermann Schleissing, October 21 and 24, 1917, Aviodrome, collection A. H. G. Fokker, Fokker-Schwerin, box 2; Wagner, Hugo Junkers, 93–95.

32. Anthony Fokker to IdFlieg, December 10, 1917, and April 12, 1918, Aviodrome, collection A. H. G. Fokker, Fokker-Schwerin, box 2.

33. Peter M. Grosz, "Archive Celebrating the 70th Anniversary of the Fokker V.1," World War I Aero, no. 113 (1987), 28–39; Peter M. Grosz, "Reinhold Platz and the Fokker Company," Over the Front 5, no. 3 (1990), 213–22.

34. Junkers's patent application for aircraft, no. J.18073 XI/77h5, August 8, 1917, Archive Deutsches Museum, Junkers Archive, inv. no. 0201/T.11. Correspondence and documents concerning various lawsuits between Junkers and Fokker regarding the use of Junkers patents on the construction of the cantilever wing were kept until 1996 in the Fokker Archive, series KW, boxes 22–26; part of this dossier now resides in Aviodrome, collection A. H. G. Fokker.

35. Hans Schmidt to Friedrich Seekatz, December 16, 1917, Aviodrome, collection A. H. G. Fokker, Fokker Schwerin, box 2.

36. Weekly reports, Junkers-Fokker Works, January–December 1918, formerly stored in the Fokker Factory Archive, series KW, box 67; Peter M. Grosz and Gerard Terry, "The Way to the World's First All-Metal Fighter," Air Enthusiast no. 25 (August 1984), 60–76; Byers, "Junkers-Fokker Merger," 15–21.

37. Fokker Works to the Mecklenburgische Flugplatz Gesellschaft (Aerodrome Society), January 17, March 6, and December 13, 1917, Aviodrome, collection A. H. G. Fokker, Fokker Schwerin, box 1.

38. Peter März, Mythen, Bilder, Fakten: Auf der Suche nach der deutschen Vergangenheit (Munich: Olzog, 2010), 206–7; Volker Koos, Die Fokker-Flugzeugwerke in Schwerin: Geschichte, Produktion, Typen (Schwerin: Thon, 1993), 18.

39. Volker Berghahn, Der Erste Weltkrieg (Munich: C. H. Beck, 2003), 82–86, 101; Avner Offer, "The Blockade of Germany and the Strategy of Starvation, 1914–1918," in Great War, Total War: Combat and Mobilization on the Western Front, 1914–1918, ed. Roger Chickering and Stig Förster (Cambridge: Cambridge University Press, 2000), 178–80; F. W. Borchert, Beiträge zur Geschichte der Arbeiterbeweging in der Stadt Schwerin, Heft 12, Verlauf der Ergebnisse der Novemberrevolution im Bereich der Stadt Schwerin, November 1917 bis May 1919 (Schwerin: Kommission zur Erforschung der Geschichte der örtlichen Arbeiterbewegung, 1988), 3.

40. Friedrich Seekatz to Anthony Fokker, July 21, 1930, Aviodrome, dossier Seekatz.

41. Note, Grand Duke's Cabinet, March 18, 1918, and Fokker Aircraft Works to the Grand Duke's Cabinet, April 5, 1917, Main Country Archive, Schwerin, 5.2–1, Grossherzogliches Kabinett III, inv. no. 1309; Fokker emergency money, in Aviodrome, collection A. H. G. Fokker, box Fokker-Schwerin 2; Fokker and Gould, *Flying Dutchman*, 209–10; Schmidt, "A. H. G. Fokker," 59.

42. Anthony Fokker to Friedrich Seekatz, October 17, 1917, DTMB, Nachlass Grosz, inv. no. 0313.

43. Schmidt, "A. H. G. Fokker," 45.

44. Anthony Fokker to his father, October 10, 1917, Aviodrome, collection A. H. G. Fokker, box 12.

45. Theodore von Kármán, *The Wind and Beyond: Pioneer in Aviation and Pathfinder in Space* (Boston: Little, Brown, 1967), 85.

46. Anthony Fokker to his nephew, May 31, 1916, and to his father, October 10, 1917, Aviodrome, collection A. H. G. Fokker, box 12.

47. Correspondence, B. Urbich, secretary of the Seglerhaus am Wannsee, with Fokker, 1917–1918, Aviodrome, collection A. H. G. Fokker, box 11.

48. Anthony Fokker to his father, October 10, 1917, Aviodrome, collection A. H. G. Fokker, box 12.

49. B. Urbich to Anthony Fokker, June 21, 1918, Aviodrome, collection A. H. G. Fokker, box 11.

50. Fokker and Gould, *Flying Dutchman*, 228. In the Dutch edition, the story of their first encounter is curiously missing, although the story reappears in the German translation (otherwise mainly based on the Dutch version of the autobiography): A. H. G. Fokker, *Der fliegende Holländer: Die Memoiren des A. H. G. Fokker* (Frankfurt a.M.: Wunderkammer, 2010), 250–51.

51. Police report, Schwerin, May 25, 1916, in F. W. Borchert, *Beiträge zur Geschichte der Arbeiterbeweging in der Stadt Schwerin*, Heft 9, *1900–1917* (Schwerin: Kommission zur Erforschung der Geschichte der örtlichen Arbeiterbewegung, 1987), 45, 46–47.

52. Borchert, *Geschichte der Arbeiterbeweging*, Heft 12, 6–16; Schmidt, "A. H. G. Fokker," 60.

11. BERLIN, GERMANY, NOVEMBER 1918

1. A. H. G. Fokker and Bruce Gould, *Flying Dutchman: The Life of Anthony Fokker* (New York: Henry Holt, 1931), 215–20.

2. Sebastiaan Haffner, *De Duitse revolutie, 1918–1919: De nasleep van de Eerste Wereldoorlog* (Amsterdam: Mets & Schilt, 2007), 100–14.

3. Julius Stahn to Anthony Fokker, October 28, 1918, Aviodrome, collection A. H. G. Fokker, box 11.

4. F. W. Borchert, *Der Verlauf und die Ereignisse der Novemberrevolution im Bereich der Stadt Schwerin, November 1917 bis Mai 1919, Beiträge zur Geschichte der Arbeiterbewegung in der Stadt Schwerin*, Heft 12. (Schwerin: Kreisleitung SED, 1987), 6–16; Michael Schmidt, "A. H. G. Fokker: Der niederländische Flieger und Flugzeughersteller in Deutschland" (unpublished manuscript, Schwerin, 2013), 60.

5. Fokker and Gould, *Flying Dutchman*, 219–20.

6. Ibid., 218.

7. Ibid., 218–19.

8. Adrian Stahlecker, *Film en kunst in ballingschap, 1933–1945: Duitse artiesten en kunstenaars op de vlucht voor het naziregime* (Voorburg: De Nieuwe Haagsche, 2000), 210–11.

9. Haffner, *Duitse revolutie, 1918–1919*, 123–37.

10. Fokker and Gould, *Flying Dutchman*, 219.

11. Official French text of the armistice agreement of November 11, 1918, *Der Waffenstillstand 1918–1919: Das Dokumenten-Material der Waffenstillstands-verhandlungen von Compiègne, Spa, Trier und Brussel, herausgegeben im Auftrag der Deutsche Waffenstillstands-Kommission* (Berlin: Deutsche Verlagsgesellschaft für Politik und Geschichte, 1928), Band I, 75.

12. Tactical reports, Hermann Goering to General Command of the Air Force, Berlin, September 1, 1918, notes on BMW IIIa engine, November 1, 1918, Aviodrome, collection A. H. G. Fokker, Fokker-Schwerin, box 4; Anthony Fokker to Friedrich Seekatz, October 10, 1917, Aviodrome, collection A. H. G. Fokker, Fokker Schwerin, box 2.

13. Peter Grosz and Volker Koos, *Die Fokker Flugzeugwerke in Deutschland, 1912–1921* (Königswinter: Heel, 2004), 63–65, 102–3, 108.

14. Reinhold Platz, "19 Jahre Flugzeugbau bei Fokker," Deutsches Technik Museum Berlin (DTMB), Nachlass Grosz, inv. no. 0394.

15. A. H. G. Fokker and Bruce Gould, *De vliegende Hollander* (Amsterdam: Van Holkema & Warendorf, 1931), 193–98; Greg van Wyngarden, *Richthofen's Circus: Jagdgeschwader 1* (Oxford: Osprey, 2004), 27, 77.

16. John H. Morrow Jr., *German Air Power in World War I* (Lincoln: University of Nebraska Press, 1982), 79, 124; A. R. Weyl, *Fokker: The Creative Years* (London: Putnam, 1985), 268–86.

17. *Die Fokkerflugzeuge: Katalog der Fokkerwerke Schwerin* (Schwerin, 1918), in Schmidt, "A. H. G. Fokker," 61.

18. Sealed copy of notary act, signed by Hugo Alexander-Katz, December 4, 1918, Aviodrome, collection A. H. G. Fokker, Fokker-Schwerin, box 2; Richard Byers, "An Unhappy Marriage: The Junkers-Fokker Merger," *Journal of Historical Biography* 3 (Spring 2008): 19–20.

19. Memorandum of the U.S. envoy in The Hague regarding the ban on exports of financial assets from Germany, June 9, 1919, U.S. National Archives, State Department, record group 84, Netherlands Post File, General Correspondence 1919, 711.7; Fokker and Gould, *Flying Dutchman*, 221–23, 229–30.

20. Friedrich Seekatz to Marius Beeling, February 25, 1969, formerly in NV Fokker company archive, Schiphol Airport, Beeling Papers, miscellaneous correspondence.

21. Fokker, *Flying Dutchman*, 228–31; Schmidt, "A. H. G. Fokker," 62; Wolfgang Jansen, . . . *und Abends in die Scala* (Berlin: Bildarchiv Preussischer Kulturbesitz / Nicolai, 1991), 55.

22. Seekatz to Beeling, February 25, 1969.

23. Haffner, *Duitse revolutie, 1918–1919*, 141–57.

24. Anthony Fokker to Hans Bartsch, December 18, 1918, Main Country Archive, Schwerin, 5.12–3/1, Mecklenburgisch-Schwerinisches Ministerium des Innern, inv. no. 10573.

25. Jacob Wolff to the mayor of Haarlem, December 14, 1918, Haarlem Municipal Archive, New Archive, doss. no. 1261–1; news article about Wolff, *De Tijd*, November 19, 1936.

26. Correspondence between Fokker factory manager (Karl Hackstetter) and Otto Weltzien, November 1918, Aviodrome, collection A. H. G. Fokker, Fokker-Schwerin box 1.

27. Travel permit in Fokker's Mecklenburg passport, issued by the Schwerin police, December 16, 1918, Aviodrome, collection A. H. G. Fokker, box 11; German War Ministry statement, January 13, 1919, Main Country Archive, Schwerin, 5.12–3/1, Mecklenburg-Schwerinisches Ministerium des Innern, inv. no. 10573.

28. Anthony Fokker to Justice Ministry, Schwerin, January 16, 1919, Main Country Archive, Schwerin, 5.12–3/1, Mecklenburg-Schwerinisches Ministerium des Innern, inv. no. 10573.

29. Anthony Fokker to Justice Ministry, Schwerin, January 19, 1919, Main Country Archive, Schwerin, 5.12–3/1, Mecklenburg-Schwerinisches Ministerium des Innern, inv. no. 10573.

30. Wim Klinkert, *Defending Neutrality: The Netherlands Prepares for War, 1900–1925* (Leiden: Brill, 2013), 149–53; Dirk Starink, *De jonge jaren van de Luchtmacht: Het Luchtwapen van het Nederlandse leger, 1913–1939* (Amsterdam: Boom, 2013), 105–14.

31. *Het volk,* January 7, 1919.

32. Haffner, *Duitse revolutie, 1918–1919,* 161–68; Fokker and Gould, *Vliegende Hollander,* 219.

33. Report, Willem Gevers to the Netherlands Foreign Minister, January 9, 1919, National Archive, 2.05.19, Cabinet Archive Ministry of Foreign Affairs, Political Reports by Dutch Diplomatic Envoys Abroad, 1871–1940, inv. no. 204.

34. Haffner, *Duitse revolutie, 1918–1919,* 168–91.

35. Hermann Goering to Anthony Fokker, July 12, 1919, DTMB, Nachlass Grosz, inv. no. 0340; Klinkert, *Defending Neutrality,* 157.

36. Transcript, diary of Hendrik Walaardt Sacré, October 3, 1913, to October 15, 1919, The Hague, Netherlands Institute for Military History.

37. Marital certificate, A. H. G. Fokker and S. M. E. von Morgen, March 25, 1919, North Holland Archive, Haarlem, Burgerlijke Stand.

38. Workers representatives at Schwerin to General Management, Fokker Works, January 30/31, 1919, Aviodrome, collection A. H. G. Fokker, Fokker-Schwerin, box 2.

39. Memorandum, U.S. envoy in The Hague, re prohibition of the exports of financial assets from Germany, June 9, 1919, U.S. National Archives, Record Group 84, Department of State, Netherlands Post File, General Correspondence 1919, dossier 711.7.

40. "Het reizigersverkeer uit Duitschland," *De Telegraaf,* November 21, 1918.

41. Fokker and Gould, *Vliegende Hollander,* 232–35; interview with Fokker, *The World,* New York, November 9, 1919.

12. HAARLEM, HOLLAND, MARCH 1919

1. Postcard, Count and Countess Bassewitz to Mrs. Elisabeth Fokker, "released foreign Station Emmerich," postmarked in Amsterdam, April 16, 1919, Aviodrome, collection A. H. G. Fokker, box 12.

2. Film footage of the marriage, author's collection; *Haarlems Dagblad,* March 25, 1919.

3. Marriage certificate, A. H. G. Fokker and S. M. E. von Morgen, March 25, 1919, North Holland Archive, Haarlem, Burgerlijke Stand, registry card March 25, 1919.

4. *Haarlems Dagblad,* March 26, 1919.

5. Announcement in *Haarlems Dagblad,* March 26, 1919 (spelling error: Von Morken).

6. Frits Gerdessen, Nico Geldhof, Harm Hazewinkel, *Spijker: De eerste Nederlandse vliegtuigfabriek* (Voorburg: KNVvL, 2002), 9–10.

7. Overview of Fokker shipments, January–October 1918, Aviodrome, collection A. H. G. Fokker, Fokker Schwerin, box 4.

8. Fokker Works to Mayor Weltzien of Schwerin, May 10, 1920, Aviodrome, collection A. H. G. Fokker, Fokker-Schwerin, box 1.

9. Wim Klinkert, *Defending Neutrality: The Netherlands Prepares for War, 1900–1925* (Leiden: Brill, 2013), 157.

10. Fokker-Schwerin, survey of the 2nd to 4th airplane transport, March 10, 1920, Aviodrome, collection A. H. G. Fokker, Fokker-Schwerin, box 1. In his autobiography, Fokker later told an imagined story of "smuggling" the aircraft. He erroneously thought there had been six shipments: A. H. G. Fokker and Bruce Gould, *Flying Dutchman: The Life of Anthony Fokker* (New York: Henry Holt, 1931), 221–27. Initially, Heinrich Mahn appeared in the printed text as "Wilhelm Hahn" (224–26). The story of the smuggling originated with him; in 1930 Fokker paid him $100 for his memories: Heinrich Mahn to the Fokker factory in Amsterdam, August 16, 1930; Seekatz to Mahn, August 19, 1930, Aviodrome, collection Seekatz.

11. "Vliegtuigen voor Nederland," *Rotterdamsch Nieuwsblad*, April 2, 1919; Minutes of the joint Boards of Control of the Dutch railway companies Maatschappij tot Exploitatie der Staats-Spoorwegen and Hollandsche Yzeren Spoorweg-Maatschappij, December 1918, Archive Netherlands Railways, Utrecht, Minutes of the Boards of Control.

12. Fokker and Gould, *Flying Dutchman*, 221–27.

13. Klinkert, *Defending Neutrality*, 157–58.

14. Ambassador Graham to British Foreign Office, May 4, 1920, London (Kew), National Archives, Foreign Office Papers, FO 371, inv. no. 4289.

15. Frits Gerdessen, Nico Geldhof, Harm Hazewinkel, *Spijker. De eerste Nederlandse vliegtuigfabriek* (Voorburg: KNVvL, 2002), 10.

16. Heinrich Mahn to Friedrich Seekatz, August 16, 1930, Aviodrome, collection Seekatz.

17. Netherlands Parliamentary Papers, *Handelingen der Staten-Generaal*, 1919–1920, no. 553. 2–3: Wijziging en verhooging van het VIIIste hoofdstuk-der Staatsbegrooting voor 1920, 6; Klinkert, *Defending Neutrality*, 155.

18. Fokker Works to Mayor Weltzien of Schwerin, May 10, 1920, Aviodrome, collection A. H. G. Fokker, Fokker-Schwerin, box 1.

19. Fokker and Gould, *Flying Dutchman*, 230–35; Fokker, interview with *The World*, New York, November 9, 1919.

20. Fokker and Gould, *Flying Dutchman*, 232–34.

21. Request for a Declaration of Citizenship, signed by Consul Wolff in Berlin to the Mayor of Haarlem, December 14, 1918, North Holland Archive, Haarlem Municipal Archive, Nieuw Archief, 126–1; Wet op het Nederlanderschap van 1892, artikel 7, lid 5: J. C. Meijer, *Nederlandsche Staatswetten* (Sneek: Van Druten & Bleeker, 1893).

22. Statement from the German War Office, January 13, 1919, Main Country Archive, Schwerin, 5.12–3/1, Mecklenburg-Schwerinisches Ministerium des Innern, inv. no. 10573.

23. Consul Wolff to the Mayor of Haarlem, January 31, 1919; A. S. Oppenheim to Anthony Fokker, February 22, 1919, North Holland Archive, Haarlem Municipal Archive, Nieuw Archief, 126–1.

24. Telegram, Mayor of Haarlem to Consul Wolff, February 6, 1919; Mayor of Haarlem to the Queen's Commissioner in North Holland, March 10, 1919, North Holland Archive, Haarlem Municipal Archive, Nieuw Archief, 126−1.

25. Minister Heemskerk to Prime Minister Ruys de Beerenbrouck, March 25, 1919, North Holland Archive, Haarlem Municipal, Nieuw Archief, 126−1.

26. Proof of Citizenship of the Netherlands of Anthony Herman Gerard Fokker, April 24, 1919, NA, 2.05.37, Archive Ministry of Internal Affairs, inv. no. 1730.

27. De Telegraaf, April 9, 1919.

28. Transcript of the diary of Hendrik Walaardt Sacré, October 3, 1913 to October 15, 1919, Den Haag, Nederlands Instituut voor Militaire Historie; Leeuwarder Courant, April 24, 1919.

29. Haarlems Dagblad, April 28, 1919, and De Telegraaf, April 27, 1919.

30. Haarlems Dagblad, May 2, 1919.

31. Haarlems Dagblad, May 7, 1919, and July 8, 1919.

32. De Telegraaf, June 1, 1919.

33. Leeuwarder Courant, June 14, 1919, and Haarlems Dagblad, June 24, 1919.

34. Haarlems Dagblad, May 30, 1919, and De Telegraaf, May 31, 1919.

35. De Telegraaf, June 7, 1919.

36. Anthony Fokker, letter published in Haarlems Dagblad, June 28, 1919.

37. Minutes, meeting of Fokker's management with employee representatives, February 1, 1919, Aviodrome, collection A. H. G. Fokker, Fokker-Schwerin, box 2.

38. Schwerin Industrial Works, letter re compensations, October 4, 1921, Schwerin City Archive, inv. no. M850.

39. Fokker management to workers' council, May 17, 1919, Aviodrome, collection A. H. G. Fokker, Fokker-Schwerin, box 2.

40. Abstract, Schwerin Trade Register, 1920, City Archive Schwerin, inv. no. M850.

41. Joint workers' councils to Anthony Fokker in Amsterdam, May 30, 1919, Aviodrome, collection A. H. G. Fokker, Fokker-Schwerin, box 2.

42. Work order, Schwerin, by Anthony Fokker, June 13, 1919, Aviodrome, collection A. H. G. Fokker, Fokker-Schwerin, box 2.

43. Workers' representatives to Anthony Fokker in Amsterdam, August 21, 1919, Aviodrome, collection A. H. G. Fokker, Fokker-Schwerin, box 6.

44. Fokker Works to Aerodrome Society, November 25, 1918, Aviodrome, collection A. H. G. Fokker, Fokker-Schwerin, box 1.

45. Statement, SIW to German Transport Ministry in Berlin, October 4, 1921, DTMB, Nachlass Grosz, inv. no. 0313.

46. German Finance Minister to SIW, July 20, 1926, Aviodrome, collection A. H. G. Fokker, Fokker-Schwerin, box 1.

47. Günter Schmitt, Hugo Junkers und seine Flugzeuge (Stuttgart: Motorbuch, 1986), 35−39; Fokker and Gould, Flying Dutchman, 147−48; Lutz Budrass, Flugzeugindustrie und Luftrüstung in Deutschland 1918−1945 (Düsseldorf: Droste, 1998), 67.

48. Correspondence, Junkers-Fokker, Aviodrome, collection A. H. G. Fokker, series Junkers Patent (6 boxes).

49. Fokker Works to Aerodrome Society, November 25, 1919; subpoena, Aerodrome Society to Fokker Works, January 5, 1920, Aviodrome, collection A. H. G. Fokker, Fokker-Schwerin, box 1.

50. Official announcement impounding decision, September 19, 1919, City Archive Schwerin, inv. no. M728; *Berliner Tageblatt*, 23 September 1919.

51. Notes, based on Main Country Archive, Schwerin, 5.12–3/1, Mecklenburg-Schwerinisches Ministerium des Innern, inv. no. 20759.

52. Fokker and Gould, *Flying Dutchman*, 235–36; Fokker, interview with *The World*, New York, November 9, 1919; correspondence from 1919, Aviodrome, collection A. H. G. Fokker, Fokker-Schwerin, box 1. See also Horter to Schwerin Industrial Works, January 5, 1920, Aviodrome, collection A. H. G. Fokker, Fokker-Schwerin, box 1. Miscellaneous correspondence, 1919–23, formerly in NV Fokker company archive, Schiphol Airport, series V/Alg. Secr., no. 67.

53. Justizrat Werthauer to City Authorities of Schwerin, January 30, 1920, City Archive Schwerin, inv. no. M850. On Lioni, the ELTA, and Fokker, see *Algemeen Handelsblad*, August 16 and 23, 1919. After this, Lioni had been briefly involved in the founding of the Neluma (Nederlandsche Luchtvaart Maatschappij) in the east of the country: *Algemeen Handelsblad*, November 12, 1919.

54. Correspondence, Weltzien with the Fokker Works/SIW, spring 1920, City Archive Schwerin, inv. no. 850. Land Trading Agreement City of Schwerin with SIW, July 5, 1920, City Archive Schwerin, inv. no. M5038.

55. Carl Burgtorff to Anthony Fokker, December 20, 1919; sales contract, SIW (represented by Platz) with Eduard Schmidt, Schwerin-Görries, June 26, 1920, Aviodrome, collection A. H. G. Fokker, Fokker-Schwerin, box 1.

56. Correspondence, secretary of the sailing club Seglerhaus am Wannsee, B. Urbich with Fokker, 1918–19, Aviodrome, collection A. H. G. Fokker, box 11.

57. Wolfgang Jansen, . . . *und Abends in die Scala: Fotografien von Josef Donderer* (Berlin: Nicolaischen Verlagsbuchhandlung Beuermann, 1991), 55, 72.

58. Michael Schmidt, "A. H. G. Fokker: Der niederländische Flieger und Flugzeughersteller in Deutschland" (unpublished manuscript, Schwerin, 2013), 64.

59. "Juweel aan het Rokin," *Bouwen aan monumenten* 5 (2011): 38–43.

60. Act of Foundation, "Naamlooze Vennootschap Nederlandsche Vliegtuigenfabriek," in Amsterdam, July 21, 1919: Appendix to the *Nederlandsche Staatscourant* 216, no. 1548 (October 9, 1919). As in the founding papers of the Scala Theater in Berlin, Fokker's domicile was mentioned as Schwerin.

61. Founding Act of the NV Nederlandsche Vliegtuigenfabriek, *Bijvoegsel tot de Nederlandsche Staatscourant van donderdag 9 October 1919*, no. 216, Bijvoegsel no. 1548, article 2.

62. Bruno Stephan to Henri Hegener, August 30, 1958, Collection Thijs Postma, Hegener Papers, correspondence.

63. Report, Commission Fostering the Aircraft Industry regarding the NV Nederlandsche Vliegtuigenfabriek, presented to the Minister of Waterworks, June 21, 1935, 26: NA, 2.16.5240, Archive Netherlands Aeronautical Service (henceforth: Rijksluchtvaartdienst), inv. no. 1554.

64. *Algemeen Handelsblad*, August 4, 1919.
65. Anthony Fokker, in *De Gooi- en Eemlander*, September 3, 1919. The same message appeared, shortened, in *Algemeen Handelsblad*, August 9, 1919, and in *Het Centrum*, August 11, 1919.
66. Herman Fokker, in *Haarlems Dagblad*, August 19, 1919.
67. Report, Commission Fostering the Aircraft Industry to the Minister of Waterworks, June 21, 1935, 27: NA, 2.16.5240, Archive Rijksluchtvaartdienst, inv. no. 1554. Fokker paid 800,000 Dutch guilders for the ELTA complex; the annual rent for the land was 18,000 guilders.
68. E. B. Wolff, D. Vreede, A. Plesman, H. Walaardt Sacré, Advies inzake steunverleening Nederlandsche Vliegtuigindustrie, January 19, 1921, NA, 2.16.47, Government Commission on Aviation, inv. no. 21.
69. Bruno Stephan to Henri Hegener, July 17, 1957, Collection Thijs Postma, Hegener Papers, correspondence. Platz's successor, Marius Beeling, held the same opinion. He described Platz as a humorless man. Beeling, "Herinneringen van oud-directeur en hoofdconstructeur Ir. Marius Beeling," *Avia* 18, no. 7 (1969): 326–29.

13. NEW YORK, NEW YORK, NOVEMBER 1920

1. Henriëtte Kuyper, *Een half jaar in Amerika* (Den Haag: Daamen, 1918), 35–37; American travel impressions by Emanuel Moresco, vice president of the Council of the Dutch East Indies, in *Bataviaasch Nieuwsblad*, February 18, 1922.
2. *New York Evening Telegram*, November 10, 1920.
3. *Washington Herald*, April 12, 1919.
4. Copy memorandum, "interview with Mr. Fokker," Major Brett and Lieutenant Keller to the Chief of the Air Service, April 14, 1919, Collection Blüm, Santpoort, Holland.
5. Anthony Fokker, in *De Telegraaf*, October 30, 1920.
6. Anthony Fokker quoted in the *Buffalo Evening News*, November 11, 1920.
7. Dutch travel report, "Rondom de Wereld," in *Nieuws van den Dag van Nederlandsch-Indië*, July 24, 1920.
8. Film footage, in author's collection.
9. Anthony Fokker to Christine Döppler, undated (December 1920), Heitzman "Stuffinder" Collection, Deansboro, N.Y., Döppler Album.
10. *Washington Post*, November 16, 1920.
11. Anthony Fokker to Maj. Gen. Charles Menoher, Chief of the Air Service, December 4, 1920; copy letter, Menoher to Thurman H. Bane, McCook Field, Dayton, December 9, 1920, Collection Blüm, Santpoort.
12. Telegram, Frits Cremer to Jacob Cremer, January 28, 1921, NA, 2.21.043, Cremer Archive, inv. no. 202.
13. Frits Cremer to Jacob Cremer, August 25, 1922, NA, 2.21.043, Cremer Archive, inv. no. 209.
14. Frits Cremer to Jacob Cremer, February 1921, NA, 2.21.043, Cremer Archive, inv. no. 209.
15. Dora Cremer-van Spengler to Jacob Cremer, January 2, 1923, NA, 2.21.043, Cremer Archive, inv. no. 202.

16. Interview with Fokker *De Telegraaf*, January 18, 1921; Winckel family album, Kapellen, Belgium.

17. Accountants' survey of Fokker's private expenses, annex to the 1920 annual report of the Netherlands Aircraft Factory, Collection Blüm, Santpoort; advertisement in *Algemeen Handelsblad*, March 6, 1920.

18. Ignaz Matthey, *Roemer Visscherstraat 47: De geschiedenis van een Vondelparkvilla* (Amsterdam: Jan van der Steenhoven, Till Martin Kolle, 1994), 51–53.

19. Family residence and administration card, City of Amsterdam on Fokker, Amsterdam Municipal Archive, inv. no. 5422–0407–5100.

20. At the time of her death in the early 1960s in New York, Christine Döppler left three photo albums with letters, cards, and other mementos that ended up in the Heitzman Collection (see note 9). I was able to read them in 1994.

21. C. C. Küpfer, "Gedenkboek N V Koninklijke Nederlandse Vliegtuigenfabriek, 1919–1964" (unpublished manuscript), 90–91.

22. Anthony Fokker to the Dutch Navy Minister, August 5, 1920, Collection Blüm, Santpoort.

23. Anthony Fokker to Colonel Hendrik Walaardt Sacré, commander of the Dutch Air Service, June 11, 1920; Walaardt Sacré to the Chief of the General Staff, June 19, 1920, NA, 2.13.85, Archive of Military Aviation and Defense, 1910–1940 (1944), inv. no. 54 1920/1876.

24. Anthony Fokker to Colonel Hendrik Walaardt Sacré, commander of the Dutch Air Service, June 11, 1920; Walaardt Sacré to the Chief of the General Staff, June 19, 1920, NA, 2.13.85, Archive of Military Aviation and Defense, 1910–1940 (1944), inv. no. 54 1920/1876.

25. Anthony Fokker to E. P. Westerveld (director general P&T), April 30, 1920, Archive Netherlands Postal Services, verbaal no. 7098H.

26. Frank van Dalen, *100 Years Licensed to Fly, 1890–1939* (Papendrecht: Fokker Aerostructures, 2014), 90.

27. Peter Grosz and Volker Koos, *Die Fokker Flugzeugwerke in Deutschland, 1912–1921* (Königswinter: Heel, 2004), 132–33.

28. *Leeuwarder Courant*, March 27, 1920.

29. Henri Hegener, "Herinneringen aan Fokkervlieger Bernard de Waal," *Avia* 12, no. 4 (1963), 216–18.

30. Minutes, 25th meeting of delegates from the Board of KLM, July 13, 1920, KLM Board Papers, series R-5.

31. Hans Martin (general secretary of KLM) to Minister for Waterworks, March 12, 1927, NA, 2.16.19.39, Archive Ministry of Waterworks, Aviation Desk (1911), 1920–29, inv. no. 1.

32. Albert Plesman to the Board of KLM, October 8, 1920, KLM Board Papers, series R-5.

33. G. J. Nijland, "Uit de jeugdjaren van de Nederlandsche Vliegtuigenfabriek," *Het Vliegveld* 12, no. 10 (1929): 365–66.

34. Marc Dierikx, "Albert Plesman, 1889–1953," in *Nederlandse Ondernemers 1850–1950: Noord-Holland en Zuid-Holland*, ed. Joop Visser, Matthijs Dicke, and Annelies van der Zouwen (Zutphen: Walburg Pers, 2013), 312–17.

35. Reinhold Platz to Alfred Weyl, December 22, 1956, DTMB, Nachlass Grosz, inv. no. 0394.

36. Albert Plesman to the Board of KLM, October 8, 1920, KLM Board Papers, series R-5.

37. Anthony Fokker to the commander of the Dutch Air Service, quoted in letter by Walaardt Sacré to the Chief of the General Staff, June 19, 1920, NA, 2.13.85, Archive of Military Aviation and Defense, 1910–1940 (1944), inv. no. 54 1920/1876.

38. Albert Plesman to Anthony Fokker, December 30, 1920, KLM Board Papers, series R-5.

39. Minutes, 42nd meeting of delegates from the Board of KLM, June 7, 1921, KLM Board Papers, series R-5.

40. Memorandum, Dr. Ir. E. B. Wolff re the construction of aircraft material, March 4, 1921, NA, 2.16.80, Archive Advisory Commission for the Government Aeronautical Study Service, inv. no. 58.

41. Customs documents re import of aircraft into the Netherlands between January 1, 1920, and June 1921, dated July 1921, summary of contract conditions by Schwerin Industrial Works, undated (December 1922), Aviodrome, collection A. H. G. Fokker, Fokker-Schwerin, box 2.

42. Indictment by German Military Fiscal Authorities (Department for the Air Force) against Schwerin Industrial Works, December 2, 1920, Aviodrome, collection A. H. G. Fokker, Fokker-Schwerin, box 1.

43. Ibid.

44. Legal response, Werthauer, Engelbert, and Pröll, attorneys at law, Berlin, to Country Court Schwerin, June 20, 1922, Aviodrome, collection A. H. G. Fokker, Fokker-Schwerin, box 1.

45. Letter, von Morgen to Fokker's lawyer in Schwerin, Konrad Albrecht, January 29, 1923, Aviodrome, collection A. H. G. Fokker, Fokker-Schwerin, box 1.

46. Letter, German Finance Minister to Albrecht, September 20, 1926, Aviodrome, collection A. H. G. Fokker, Fokker-Schwerin, box 1.

14. AMSTERDAM, HOLLAND, JUNE 1923

1. Norman Franks and Greg van Wyngarden, *Fokker D.VII Aces of World War I* (Oxford: Osprey, 2003), 1:73.

2. Request no. 430, submitted by Julius Keizer, attorney at law, June 27, 1923: case number 923/23, A. H. G. Fokker contra S. M. E. von Morgen: North Holland Archive, 200, District Court, Amsterdam, inv. no. 696A.

3. Verdict, District Court, Amsterdam, July 30, 1923, case number 923/23, A. H. G. Fokker contra S. M. E. von Morgen: North Holland Archive, 200, District Court, Amsterdam, inv. no. 416.

4. Ignaz Matthey, *Roemer Visscherstraat 47: De geschiedenis van een Vondelparkvilla* (Amsterdam: Jan van der Steenhoven, Till Martin Kolle, 1994), 68–69. It is unclear what has happened to the unsigned manuscript from the former historical collection of the Fokker Company Archive since 1994. Most likely the manuscript was lost in the 1996 bankruptcy of the NV Fokker company.

5. Film footage, author's collection (film number RVD 1–3081).

6. Design of the *Honey Moon* (undated), Aviodrome, collection A. H. G. Fokker, Fokker Schwerin, box 2.

7. Dutch passport of Anthony Fokker, issued in Haarlem, valid April 8, 1919, to April 3, 1920, Aviodrome, collection A. H. G. Fokker, box 12. See also *Algemeen Handelsblad*, July 11, 1919.

8. Minutes, District Court Haarlem, roll no. 4423, September 14, 1921, North Holland Archive, 49 Kantongerecht Haarlem 1921–1930, inv. no. 25.

9. Photo (undated), Anthony and Tetta with Wilhelm II and others, near Doorn House (the former emperor's residence in exile), Smeulers collection, Bronkhorst.

10. *Leeuwarder Courant*, June 14, 1919.

11. *Brooklyn Daily Eagle*, February 15, 1920.

12. *Goessche Courant*, June 16, 1921.

13. Copy, postcard, Anthony Fokker to Christine Döppler, August 20, 1921, author's collection.

14. Peter Fritsche, *A Nation of Fliers: German Aviation and the Popular Imagination* (Cambridge, MA: Harvard University Press, 1992), 107–8.

15. Interview, Anthony Fokker, *Algemeen Handelsblad*, August 17, 1921.

16. Postcard, Anthony Fokker to Christine Döppler, August 20, 1921, Heitzman "Stuffinder" Collection, Deansboro, New York, Döppler Album. See also Anthony Fokker, "De zeil-vliegtuigwedstrijden in de Rhön," *Het Vliegveld* 5, no. 18 (August 27, 1921), 256–57.

17. *Le Siècle*, November 21, 1921.

18. Interview, Anthony Fokker, *Algemeen Handelsblad*, November 17, 1921.

19. Report, W. Thorbecke (the Netherlands' chargé d'affaires in Paris) to Minister of Foreign Affairs, November 30, 1921, NA, 2.05.37, Archive Directorate of Economic Affairs, Ministry of Foreign Affairs, 1919–40, inv. no. 1731.

20. *Le Journal*, November 18, 1921.

21. Interview, Anthony Fokker, *Het nieuws van den dag voor Nederlandsch-Indië*, February 4, 1922.

22. Ibid.

23. *De Telegraaf*, November 28, 1921.

24. *Le Petit Journal*, December 4, 1922.

25. "Fokker Flies over City," *New York Times*, July 24, 1921.

26. *De Telegraaf*, August 31, 1921.

27. C. C. Küpfer, "Gedenkboek NV Koninklijke Nederlandse Vliegtuigenfabriek, 1919–1964" (unpublished manuscript), 76, author's collection.

28. Peter Bowers, "The American Fokkers—Part I," *AAHS Journal* 11 (1966): 85–89.

29. Bob Noorduyn to Anthony Fokker, February 2, 1923, Collection Blüm, Santpoort.

30. Burke Davis, *The Billy Mitchell Affair* (New York: Random House, 1967), 133; Douglas Waller, *A Question of Loyalty: Gen. Billy Mitchell and the Court-Martial That Gripped the Nation* (New York: HarperCollins, 2004), 162–63.

31. Bowers, "American Fokkers," 86–91.

32. Letter, Mitchell to General Mason Patrick, quoted in Davis, *Billy Mitchell Affair*, 140.

33. Postcard, Anthony Fokker to his mother, May 13, 1922, Aviodrome, collection A. H. G. Fokker, box 11.

34. E. V. Rickenbacker, "Introduction," Anthony H. G. Fokker and Bruce Gould, *Flying Dutchman: The Life of Anthony Fokker* (New York: Henry Holt, 1931), 3–4; W. David Lewis, *Eddie Rickenbacker: An American Hero in the Twentieth Century* (Baltimore: Johns Hopkins University Press, 2005), 297.

35. Frits Cremer to his father, Jacob Cremer, August 1922, NA, 2.21.043, Cremer Archive, inv. no. 209.

36. Dora Cremer-van Spengler to Jacob Cremer, January 2, 1923, NA, 2.21.043, Cremer Archive, inv. no. 202.

37. *New York Times*, July 23, 1922.

38. Dora Cremer-van Spengler to Jacob Cremer, July 7, 1922, NA, 2.21.043, Cremer Archive, inv. no. 202.

39. Film footage, author's collection.

40. Ibid.

41. Bob Noorduyn to Navy Department, November 17, 1922; Noorduyn to Fokker, December 15, 1922; Anthony Fokker to Noorduyn, January 25, 1923; Noorduyn to Fokker, March 16, 1923: Collection Blüm, Santpoort.

42. J. B. Hubrecht to Minister Van Karnebeek, July 26, 1922, NA, 2.05.37, Archive Directorate of Economic Affairs, Ministry of Foreign Affairs, 1919–1940, inv. no. 1760.

43. Ibid.

44. Frits Cremer to Jacob Cremer, August 25, 1922, NA, 2.21.043, Cremer Archive, inv. no. 209.

45. Telegram, Anthony Fokker to Aneta Press Agency, quoted in *Bataviaasch Nieuwsblad*, July 27, 1922.

46. *Evening Star* (Washington, DC), September 3, 1922.

47. *Het Vaderland*, July 18, 1922.

48. *Washington Times*, September 8, 1922.

49. Founding Act of the American Airway Transport Company, July 1922; telegram, Frits Cremer to Jacob Cremer, August 8, 1922; letter, Frits Cremer to Jacob Cremer, August 25, 1922, NA, 2.21.043, Cremer Archive, inv. no. 209.

50. Bob Noorduyn to Anthony Fokker, October 20, 1922, Collection Blüm, Santpoort.

51. Telegram, Frits Cremer to Jacob Cremer, December 20, 1922, NA, 2.21.043, Cremer Archive, inv. no. 209; Noorduyn to Fokker, October, 20, 1922, and January 26, 1923, Blüm Collection, Santpoort.

52. Anthony Fokker, in W. M. van Neijenhoff and C. W. A. Oyens, *Zweefvliegen: Theorie en Practijk* (Amsterdam: Meulenhoff, 1935), 7.

53. Seekatz, quoted in *Flugsport*, September 12, 1922.

54. *Flight*, October 12, 1922, 592–93.

55. Ibid., October 19, 1922. See also *De Telegraaf*, October 17 and 22, 1922; *Daily Mail*, October 17, 1922.

56. Anthony Fokker, foreword to Van Neijenhoff and Oyens, *Zweefvliegen*, 7–8; C. W. A. Oyens, "Historische Tweezitters," *Avia* 18, no. 6 (1969): 288–89. See also *Meraner Zeitung*, May 14, 1923.

57. Bob Noorduyn to Anthony Fokker, December 5, 1922, and January 23, 1923, Collection Blüm, Santpoort.

58. *Nieuwe Rotterdamsche Courant*, December 17, 1922.

59. *De Telegraaf*, December 24, 1922.

60. *Nieuwe Rotterdamsche Courant*, August 1, 1923.

61. *Bataviaasch Nieuwsblad*, February 12, 1923.

62. Fokker to KLM, May 25, 1923, KLM Board Papers, series R-5.

63. Verdict, District Court Amsterdam, July 30, 1923, case no. 923/23, A. H. G. Fokker against S. M. E. von Morgen, North Holland Archive, 200, Arrondissementsrechtbank Amsterdam, inv. no. 416.

64. Marriage certificate, A. H. G. Fokker and S. M. E. von Morgen, March 25, 1919, North Holland Archive, Haarlem, Haarlem Civil Register, March 25, 1919.

65. Ernst von Morgen to attorney Jan de Pont in Amsterdam, October 11, 1954, Collection Smeulers, Bronkhorst. In the final settlement of Fokker's estate, Tetta received the agreed-upon sum of 35,000 Dutch guilders (then $9,200).

66. Anthony Fokker to Wim and Nel van Neijenhoff, undated [May 29, 1929], Aviodrome, collection A. H. G. Fokker, box 13.

67. Maria Moslehner (Fokker's Berlin secretary) to Von Morgen, July 28, 1923, previously kept in the Fokker Company Archive (1994), series V/Alg. Secr, 67.

68. German Transport Minister to Schwerin Industrial Works, January 23, 1922, Aviodrome, collection A. H. G. Fokker, Fokker Schwerin, box 2.

69. Stamps in Anthony Fokker's passport (Dutch passport, issued in The Hague, March 15, 1923), Aviodrome, collection A. H. G. Fokker, box 11; *Algemeen Handelsblad*, August 6 and 7, 1923.

70. Menu card signed by Anthony Fokker, Iris Fagerström, Ruth Requello, and Henri Hegener, undated (August 7, 1923), Collection Postma, Hoofddorp.

71. *Rotterdamsch Nieuwsblad*, August 7, 1923.

72. Minutes, Van Doorninck Commission re Netherlands aircraft industry, February 2, 1934, NA, 2.08.41, Archive Ministry of Finance, inv. no. 4112.

73. Minister of Colonial Affairs, De Graaff, to Minister of Waterworks, July 3, 1925; Report, Director Government Study Service for Aviation, E. B. Wolff, to Minister of Waterworks, November 2, 1925, NA, 2.05.37, Archive Direction Economic Affairs, Ministry of Foreign Affairs, 1919–1940, inv. no. 1729.

74. Wolff to Minister for Waterworks, November 2, 1925.

75. Fokker to KLM, September 13, 1923, KLM Board Papers, series R-5.

76. Minutes, 72nd meeting of delegates from the Board of KLM, November 2, 1923, KLM Board Papers, series R-5.

77. Sales agreement between the Netherlands Aircraft Factory and KLM, December 10, 1923, KLM Board Papers, series R-5.

15. DETROIT, MICHIGAN, OCTOBER 1925

1. Lesley Forden, *The Ford Air Tours, 1925–1931: A Complete Narrative and Pictorial History of the Seven National Air Tour Competitions for the Edsel B. Ford Reliability Trophy* (New Brighton, MN: Aviation Foundation of America, 2003), 1, 182. See also Frank van Dalen, *Licensed to Fly for One Hundred Years: Anthony Fokker en zijn Vliegtuigenfabriek* (Papendrecht: Fokker Technologies, 2014), 139–43.

2. Forden, *Ford Air Tours*, 171; *Poughkeepsie Eagle News*, October 7, 1925.

3. *Haarlems Dagblad*, April 3, 1926.

4. Board minutes, Atlantic Aircraft, August 7, 1925, Boeing Archive.

5. *New York Times*, September 22, 1925.

6. Anthony Fokker to Christine Döppler, September 8, 1925, author's collection.

7. H. M. Hicken (War Department, Chief of the Air Service) to Noorduyn, November 6, 1922, Collection Blüm, Santpoort; *New York Times*, May 4, 1923.

8. *Time* magazine, December 31, 1923.

9. *Flight*, December 6, 1923, 733–34.

10. Draft articles of incorporation, Atlantic Aircraft, undated (December 1923), Boeing Archive.

11. Bob Noorduyn to Anthony Fokker, February 2 and 6 and April 22, 1923, Collection Blüm, Santpoort.

12. Anthony Fokker to the Board of Atlantic, December 24, 1923; minutes, Meeting of Incorporators, December 20, 1923, Boeing Archive.

13. Minutes, special board meeting, Atlantic Aircraft Corporation, March 14, 1924, Boeing Archive.

14. Bob Noorduyn to Anthony Fokker, November 6, 10, and 17, 1922, and March 2, 1923, Collection Blüm, Santpoort.

15. C. G. Grey, ed., *Jane's All the World's Aircraft, 1920* (London: Sampson, Low, Marston, 1920), 299; 1922 edition, 196b; H. A. Seyffardt, "De ontwikkeling van het Fokker-concern in Amerika," *Het Vliegveld* 13, no. 2 (1929), 58–61; Henri Hegener, *Fokker: The Man and the Aircraft* (Letchworth: Harleyford, 1961), 68; Peter Bowers, "The American Fokkers—Part 2," *AAHS Journal* 11, no. 4 (1966): 253–55; minutes, special board meeting, Atlantic, April 7, 1924; Walter C. Teter to Atlantic Aircraft, December 5, 1924, Boeing Archive.

16. Bob Noorduyn to Francis Arcier, May 22, 1924, National Air and Space Museum, Washington, Arcier Collection, box 1, correspondence. Arcier left Atlantic on February 1, 1928, and moved to the General Airplane Corporation of Buffalo, New York; see G. Allison Long Jr., "The Biography of A. Francis Arcier (1890–1969)," *AAHS Journal* 26, no. 2 (1981): 126–42.

17. Bob Noorduyn to Anthony Fokker, December 5, 1922, Collection Blüm, Santpoort; C. C. Küpfer, "Gedenkboek NV Koninklijke Nederlandse Vliegtuigenfabriek, 1919–1964" (unpublished manuscript), 76.

18. Seyffardt, "Ontwikkeling van het Fokker-concern," 58; John Sloan, "Fokker in the United States—Part 1," *Aeronautica: Official Publication for Historical Associates of the Institute of Aeronautical Sciences* 7, no. 1 (1955): 3–5.

19. Bob Noorduyn to American Bluefrieseveem, October 18, 1922, Collection Blüm, Santpoort.

20. Bruno Stephan to Henri Hegener, August 30, 1958, Postma Collection, Hoofddorp, Hegener Papers, correspondence.

21. "Fokker's Predictions," *Time* magazine, February 11, 1924.

22. Friedrich Seekatz to Hein During, May 27, 1949, Aviodrome, collection Seekatz; Anthony Fokker to Bob Noorduyn, April 10, 1923, Collection Blüm, Santpoort.

23. Secret report, Netherlands Central Intelligence Service to Minister of Foreign Affairs, February 7, 1922, NA, 2.08.05.02, Verbaalarchieven Financiën: Kabinets- en geheim verbaal met eigentijdse toegangen, 1831–1935, inv. no. 10209, no. 40.

24. *De Tijd*, October 22, 1923.

25. Contract between Netherlands Aircraft Factory and Nederlandsche Handel-Maatschappij, February 26, 1924, NA, 2.20.01, Archive of the Netherlands Trading Company (NHM), inv. no. 6241.

26. Ben Knapen, *De lange weg naar Moskou: De Nederlandse relatie tot de Sovjet-Unie, 1917–1942* (Amsterdam: Elsevier, 1985), 98–103, 125.

27. Contract between Netherlands Aircraft Factory and Netherlands Trading Company, February 26, 1924, NA, 2.20.01, NHM, inv. no. 6241.

28. Anthony Fokker to Bob Noorduyn and Ernst Robert von Morgen in New York, September 22, 1923, Collection Blüm, Santpoort.

29. A. R. Weyl, *Fokker: The Creative Years* (London: Putnam, 1985), 388–92; Lutz Budrass, *Adler und Kranich: Die Lufthansa und ihre Geschichte, 1926–1955* (Munich: Blessing, 2016), 34–35.

30. Edward L. Homze, *Arming the Luftwaffe: The Reich Air Ministry and the German Aircraft Industry, 1919–1939* (Lincoln: University of Nebraska Press, 1976), 9; Heinz J. Nowarra, *Die verbotenen Flugzeuge, 1921–1935: Die getarnte Luftwaffe* (Stuttgart: Motorbuch, 1980), 18–26.

31. Gerald D. Feldman, *Hugo Stinnes: Biographie eines Industriellen, 1870–1924* (Munich: C. H. Beck, 1998), 815–43.

32. Hanfried Schliephake, "Die geheime Flugerprobung in Lipetzk/Russland," in *Die deutsche Luftfahrt: Flugerprobungsstellen bis 1945. Johannisthal, Lipetzk, Rechlin, Travemünde, Tarnewitz, Peenemünde-West*, ed. Heinrich Beauvais, Karl Kössler, Max Mayer, and Christoph Regel (Bonn: Bernard & Graefe, 1998), 55.

33. Soviet-German agreement on the use of Lipetzk, April 15, 1925, released by the Bundesarchiv at http://www.bundesarchiv.de/oeffentlichkeitsarbeit/bilder_dokumente/00931/index-0.html.de (July 2012).

34. G. Freund, *Unholy Alliance: Russian-German Relations from the Treaty of Brest-Litovsk to the Treaty of Berlin* (London: Chatto and Windus, 1957), 1–140, 210–12; Homze, *Arming the Luftwaffe*, 1–18.

35. Weyl, *Fokker: The Creative Years*, 388–92.

36. Documentation issued with Iron Cross, 2nd Class, May 7, 1924, Collection Smeulers, Bronkhorst.

37. Quarterly reports, Netherlands Aircraft Factory, 1924, Collection Blüm, Santpoort.

38. Statements, Ministry of Finance, in dossier, NA, 2.16.19.39, Archive Ministry of Waterworks, Aviation Desk (1911), 1920–29, inv. no. 15.

39. Interview with Fokker sales director F. Rasch, *Algemeen Handelsblad*, February 20, 1926. Other reporting mentions 10 or even 12 million leu in bribes, in which the Romanian Crown Prince Carol was allegedly also involved.

40. *Nieuwe Rotterdamsche Courant*, March 4, 1926; *Het Vaderland*, March 14, 1926.

41. Inspector of Imports and Duties in Amsterdam to Minister of Finance, August 5, 1924, NA, 2.08.05.02, Archive Ministry of Finance: Kabinets- en geheim verbaal met eigentijdse toegangen, 1831–1935, inv. no. 10217, no. 333.

42. *Nieuwe Rotterdamsche Courant*, April 15, 1921.

43. Film footage, royal visit to the Fokker factory in Amsterdam, author's collection; *Nieuwe Tilburgsche Courant*, April 5, 1924; *Bataviaasch Nieuwsblad*, April 5, 1924.

44. Statements, Ministry of Finance, in dossier, NA, 2.16.19.39, Archive Ministry of Waterworks, Aviation Desk (1911), 1920–29, inv. no. 15.

45. Albert Plesman to Frits Fentener van Vlissingen, February 1, 1924, KLM Board Papers, series R-5.

46. Accountants' report, W. Kreukniet and R.A. Dijker re Committee for Netherlands–Indies Flight, April 30, 1925; copy in author's collection. See also Marc Dierikx, *Bevlogen jaren: Nederlandse burgerluchtvaart tussen de wereldoorlogen* (Houten: Unieboek, 1986), 41–44.

47. The flight was recounted in detail in A. N. J. Thomassen à Thuessinck van der Hoop, *Door de lucht naar Indië* (Amsterdam: Scheltens & Giltay, 1925).

48. "Fokker Arrives to Build Aircraft," *New York Times*, November 8, 1924.

49. "Fokker Dreams of Air Travel for the World," *New York Times*, November 23, 1924.

50. Minutes, board meetings, Atlantic Aircraft, December 16 and 22, 1924, Boeing Archive.

51. Photo with caption, *New York Times*, February 22, 1925.

52. *De Gooi- en Eemlander*, February 10, 1925.

53. *Algemeen Handelsblad*, February 24, 1925.

54. *Flight*, April 23, 1925, 239–44; film footage at http://www.britishpathe.com/video/crash-proof-aeroplanes-coming/query/Fokker (2014).

55. *New York Times*, May 24, 1925.

56. *Goessche Courant*, April 20, 1925.

57. *De Tijd*, April 27, 1925.

58. *New York Times*, May 24, 1925.

16. TETERBORO, NEW JERSEY, APRIL 1927

1. A. H. G. Fokker and Bruce Gould, *De vliegende Hollander* (Amsterdam: Van Holkema & Warendorf, 1931), 255–59; Richard E. Byrd, *Skyward* (New York: Putnam, 1928), 222–38. Film footage of the crash can be seen at http://www.criticalpast.com/video/65675031734 (December 2013).

2. *New York Times*, April 17, 1927.

3. Bill Bryson, *One Summer: America 1927* (London: Doubleday, 2013), 21–22.

4. Canadian Census Records, 1906 and 1911, Winnipeg District (#10) Subdistrict: 03 A (Ward three).

5. *Winnipeg Free Press*, July 7, 1910.

6. *Manitoba Free Press*, March 1, 1917; *Winnipeg Free Press*, February 27, 1924.

7. Anthony Fokker to Christine Döppler (undated, summer of 1925), Heitzman "Stuffinder" Collection, Deansboro, NY, Döppler album.

8. Reporting in the Icelandic immigrant paper *Heimskringla*, Winnipeg, May 18, 1927.

9. Photo, March 14, 1927, reprinted in *Verenigde Vleugels* 7, no. 4 (July 2005): 17.

10. Violet Fokker-Austman to Anna Fokker-Diemont, April 22, 1927, Collection Smeulers, Bronkhorst.

11. "The Fokker–Kansas City Company: Fokker Plans to Become Resident of the USA and Build Here," *Aviation*, August 31, 1925. See also Seekatz to Dr. A. Zimmermann (Fokker's lawyer in Berlin), May 3, 1933, formerly in NV Fokker company archive, Schiphol Airport, V/Alg. Secr. 67 (1994).

12. *Aviation*, August 31, 1925; Henri Hegener, *The Man and the Aircraft* (Letchworth: Harleyford, 1961), 70.

13. Theo Wesselink, *Amerikaanse Fokkers: Een productie-overzicht* (Haarlem: Dutch Aviation Publications, 2003).

14. Peter Bowers, "The American Fokkers—Part 2," *AAHS Journal* 11, no. 4 (1966): 258–60.

15. *New York Times*, December 6, 1925.

16. Helen Schunck, "Working with a Genius," *Aeronautics* (August 1929), 74.

17. Ibid., 76.

18. Doree Smedley and Hollister Noble, "Profiles: Flying Dutchman," *New Yorker*, February 7, 1931, 20–24.

19. Postcard, Anthony Fokker to his mother, undated (December 1925), Aviodrome, collection A. H. G. Fokker, box 12.

20. *Time* magazine, January 4, 1926.

21. Rosalie Schwartz, *Pleasure Island: Tourism and Temptation in Cuba* (Lincoln: University of Nebraska Press, 1997), xxi, 14–15.

22. Matthew Josephson, *Empire of the Air: Juan Trippe and the Struggle for World Airways* (New York: Harcourt, Brace, 1944), 24, 28–29; Wesley P. Newton, *The Perilous Sky: Evolution of United States Aviation Diplomacy Toward Latin America, 1919–1931* (Coral Gables: University of Miami Press, 1978), 110; Robert Daley, *An American Saga: Juan Trippe and His Pan Am Empire* (New York: Random House, 1980), 15–19.

23. *De Telegraaf*, March 23, 1926.

24. Ignaz Matthey, *Roemer Visscherstraat 47: De geschiedenis van een Vondelparkvilla* (Amsterdam: Jan van der Steenhoven, Till Martin Kolle, 1994), 51–53.

25. Anthony Fokker to Mrs. Wilhelmina Alida ("Kees") Bangert-Bakker, January 19, 1931, Aviodrome, collection A. H. G. Fokker, box 12.

26. Advertisements in *Haarlems Dagblad*, August 20, 1926, and *Bloemendaalsch Weekblad*, August 21, 1926.

27. Minutes, meeting of Weltzien with Haller, Von Morgen, and several others, December 10, 1924, Aviodrome, collection A. H. G. Fokker, Fokker-Schwerin, box 1.

28. Comments, Weltzien re conversation with Haller, May 28, 1926, City Archive Schwerin, inv. no. M2931.

29. *Nieuwe Rotterdamsche Courant*, April 11, 1926.

30. Ministère de la Guerre—Ministère des Traveaux Publics, *Les Aéronautiques Etrangères: Allemagne*, reports re activities of "German" aeronautical firms in the years 1924 and 1926, Paris, Archives Nationales. In an interview with the *New York Times* published on May 30, 1926, Fokker told a similar story.

31. Report, Government Work Expansion Commission to the Minister of Waterworks re employment in the aviation industry, March 23, 1927, NA, 2.16.19.39, Ministry of Waterworks, Aviation Desk (1911), 1920–29, inv. no. 14.

32. Bruno Stephan to Henri Hegener, July 17, 1957, Collection Postma, Hoofddorp, Hegener Papers, correspondence.

33. *Haarlems Dagblad*, April 12, 1926, 5; film footage of the flying demonstration at http://www.youtube.com/watch?v=4NmjEOsveHY (2014).

34. "Ice Pole," *Time* magazine, January 4, 1926; George Hubert Wilkins, *Flying the Arctic* (New York: Putnam, 1928), 13–15.

35. "Newspaperman," *Time* magazine, March 22, 1926.

36. Wilkins, *Flying the Arctic*, 29-48.

37. *New York Herald* and *New York Tribune*, May 17, 1926.

38. Richard E. Byrd, *Skyward: Man's Mastery of the Air as Shown by the Brilliant Flights of America's Leading Air Explorer* (New York: Halcyon House, 1928), 166-206; Raimund E. Goerler, *To the Pole: The Diary and Notebook of Richard E. Byrd, 1925-1927* (Columbus: Ohio State University Press, 1998), 84-85.

39. *New York Times*, June 24, 1926.

40. Estate of Fokker v. Commissioner, 10 T.C. 1225 (1948), Docket No. 111851, U.S. Tax Court, June 29, 1948, http://www.leagle.com/decision/1948123510fdtc1225_11076 (2014).

41. Charles Lindbergh, *Spirit of St. Louis* (New York: Scribner, 2003), 26-30; Charles A. Lindbergh, *De brede Zee: Met de Spirit of St. Louis over de Oceaan* (Amsterdam: Elsevier, 1953), 38-19; Anthony H. G. Fokker and Bruce Gould, *Flying Dutchman: The Life of Anthony Fokker* (New York: Henry Holt, 1931), 261.

42. Goerler, *To the Pole*, 102.

43. Byrd, *Skyward*, 239.

44. *New York Times*, April 19, 1927.

45. *New York Times*, May 15, 1927.

46. Carroll V. Glines, *Bernt Balchen, Polar Aviator* (Washington, DC: Smithsonian Institution Press, 1999), 39-42.

47. *New York Times*, May 17, 1927.

48. Glines, *Bernt Balchen*, 43-44.

49. *New York Times*, May 19, 1927.

50. *New York Times*, May 20, 1927.

51. *New York Times*, May 21, 1927; Fokker and Gould, *Flying Dutchman*, 260-61.

52. Anthony Fokker, quoted in *New York Times*, May 21, 1927.

53. *Brooklyn Daily Eagle*, June 18, 1927.

54. Glines, *Bernt Balchen*, 45 (based on Balchen's notes of the incident).

55. Fokker and Gould, *Flying Dutchman*, 262; Bernt Balchen, *Come North with Me* (New York: Dutton, 1958), 100.

56. Sales agreement between Netherlands Aircraft Factory and Richard E. Byrd for the three-engine F.VIIa, June 23, 1927; Anthony Fokker to Richard Byrd, August 10, 1927, Ohio State University, Richard E. Byrd Papers, inv. no. 1053; sales agreement between Atlantic Aircraft Corporation and Richard E. Byrd for the single-engine Fokker Universal, June 23, 1927, Ohio State University, Richard E. Byrd Papers, inv. no. 4700.

57. Image of envelope and Fokker's business card in *Algemeen Handelsblad*, July 4, 1927.

58. *Algemeen Handelsblad*, July 1, 1927. A detailed account of the flight, based on an interview with Noville, appeared in the Dutch trade journal *Het Vliegveld* 11, no. 7 (1927): 213-18. See also Byrd, *Skyward*, 222-78.

59. Interview with Evert Smits (head of public relations at Fokker in Amsterdam, who had spoken with Byrd on July 2 in Caen), *De Telegraaf*, July 3, 1927.

60. Atlantic Aircraft Corporation to Richard E. Byrd, October 24, 1927; Bob Noorduyn to Byrd, December 27, 1927, and January 24, 1928; Byrd to Noorduyn, March 20 and May 2, 1928; Byrd to Lorillard Spencer, June 11, 1928; Spencer to Byrd, June 15, 1928, Ohio State University, Richard E. Byrd Papers, inv. no. 1053.

61. Byrd to Atlantic Aircraft Corporation, October 7 and December 8, 1927, Ohio State University, Richard E. Byrd Papers, inv. no. 1053.

62. Fokker and Gould, *Flying Dutchman*, 262–64; Byrd to Adm. William Moffett, May 3, 1931, Ohio State University, Richard E. Byrd Papers, inv. no. 387.

17. ΠΕШ YORK, ΠΕШ YORK, FEBRUARY 1929

1. *Brooklyn Standard Union*, February 9, 1929.

2. Death certificate, Viola Fokker, State of New York, Department of Health City of New York, Bureau of Records, no. 4915, February 8, 1929, New York City Department of Records, Municipal Archives.

3. *New York Times*, February 9, 1929.

4. Ibid., February 10, 1929.

5. Ibid., February 9, 1929.

6. Joan Jacobs Brumberg, "Chlorotic Girls, 1870–1920: A Historical Perspective on Female Adolescence," in *Women and Health in America: Historical Readings*, ed. Judith Walzer Leavitt (Madison: University of Wisconsin Press, 1984), 190. See also B. Sicherman, "The Uses of Diagnosis: Doctors, Patients and Neurasthenia," *Journal of the History of Medicine and Allied Sciences* 32 (1977): 33–54.

7. Clayton L. Thomas, ed., *Taber's Encyclopedic Medical Dictionary* (Philadelphia: F. A. Davis, 1989), 1200.

8. *North Tonawanda Evening News*, February 11, 1929.

9. Violet Fokker-Austman to Anna Fokker-Diemont, April 22, 1927, Collection Smeulers, Bronkhorst.

10. Department of Commerce, Bureau of the Census, Fifteenth Census of the United States, 1930, April 21, 1930, http://www.censusfinder.com/1930-federal-census-search.htm (2014).

11. A. H. G. Fokker and Bruce Gould, *De vliegende Hollander* (Amsterdam: Van Holkema & Warendorf, 1931), 111.

12. Juanita Percy to Anthony Fokker, August 1, 1931, Collection Smeulers, Bronkhorst.

13. Marc Dierikx, "Wings of Silver, Wings of Gold: Money and Technological Change in the Aircraft Industry during the 1920s and 1930s," in *Around Glare: A New Aircraft Material in Context*, ed. Coen Vermeulen (Dordrecht: Kluwer Academic, 2002), 95.

14. Elsbeth E. Freudenthal, *The Aviation Business: From Kitty Hawk to Wall Street* (New York: Vanguard Press, 1940), 98–100; Grover Loening, *Our Wings Grow Faster* (Garden City, NY: Doubleday, 1935), 169–94; Claude E. Puffer, *Air Transportation* (Philadelphia: Blakiston, 1941), 514.

15. Agreement between Ohio Valley Industrial Corp., A. H. G. Fokker, and Atlantic Aircraft, November 22, 1927, Boeing Archive, Seattle, inv. no. C150.

16. *Nieuwe Rotterdamsche Courant*, December 1, 1927.

17. Minutes, meeting of incorporators, December 3, 1927; minutes, board of directors, December 6, 1927, Boeing Archive, Seattle, inv. no. C150; *New York Times*, December 19, 1927, and May 25, 1928; Bayard Young, "Ohio Valley Weekend 50th: First W. Va. Commercial Plane Flew in 1928," *Intelligencer* (Wheeling, WV), December 16, 1978.

18. Agreement between Fokker Aircraft Corporation of America and Anthony Fokker, December 6, 1927, Boeing Archive, Seattle, inv. no. C150.

19. "Majestic to Sail Decked for Holiday: Liner Leaves about Midnight for Southampton," *New York Times* December 23, 1927.

20. Anthony Fokker quoted in *Haarlems Dagblad*, January 6, 1928.

21. Ibid.

22. Ibid.

23. *Het Vaderland*, January 18, 1928.

24. *De Tijd*, January 16, 1928.

25. Anthony Fokker quoted in *Haarlems Dagblad*, January 20, 1928.

26. De Geer to Minister of Waterworks, May 24, 1928, NA, 2.16.19.39, Archive Waterworks, Aviation Desk, inv. no. 14.

27. Photograph in *Nieuwsblad van het Noorden*, February 2, 1928.

28. *New York Sun*, April 21, 1928.

29. W. David Lewis, *Eddie Rickenbacker: An American Hero in the Twentieth Century* (Baltimore: Johns Hopkins University Press, 2005), 296.

30. Interview with Anthony Fokker, *Syracuse Journal*, June 7, 1928.

31. *Brooklyn Daily Eagle*, April 29, 1928.

32. *New York Times*, May 27, 1928. See also Estate of Fokker v. Commissioner, U.S. Tax Court, Docket No. 111851, June 29, 1948, http://www.leagle.com/decision/1948123510fdtc1225 _11076 (2014).

33. A detailed sketch of the design of the house appeared in the December 1930 issue of *The Architect*, 108. Quote from A. H. G. Fokker and Bruce Gould, *Flying Dutchman: The Life of Anthony Fokker* (New York: Henry Holt, 1931), 57.

34. *New York Times*, May 25 and October 25, 1928; Young, "Ohio Valley Weekend 50th."

35. See Thomas O. James, "The Fokker Aircraft Legacy in West Virginia," 2003, http://www.wvgenweb.org/marshall/tomjames/fokker.htm.

36. Charles Kingsford Smith, *M'n ouwe kist* (Amsterdam: B. J. Smit, 1932).

37. Memorandum of agreement between Wilmer Stulz and Richard Byrd, April 6, 1928, Richard Byrd Papers, Ohio State University, inv. no. 4700.

38. Susan Wels, *Amelia Earhart: The Thrill of It* (Philadelphia: Running Press, 2009), 58–75.

39. Telegram, Anthony Fokker to Amelia Earhart, June 18, 1928, George Palmer Putnam Collection of Amelia Earhart Papers, Purdue University, 1928 Friendship—Correspondence Received (Box 1), http://www.lib.purdue.edu/spcol/fa/pdf/earhart.pdf (2012).

40. Freudenthal, *Aviation Business*, 88–92; Puffer, *Air Transportation*, 515; Henry L. Smith, *Airways: The History of Commercial Aviation in the United States* (1942; repr., Washington, DC: Smithsonian Institution Press, 1991), 131

41. Joseph J. Corn, *The Winged Gospel: America's Romance with Aviation, 1900–1950* (New York: Oxford University Press, 1983), 91–111.

42. Agreement between Fokker Aircraft Corporation of America and Anthony Fokker, September 27, 1928, Boeing Archive, Seattle, inv. no. C150.

43. *Morning Herald*, October 22, 1928.

44. Extract from minutes, special board meeting, Fokker Aircraft Corporation of America, September 27, 1928, Boeing Archive, Seattle, inv. no. C150.

45. R. E. G. Davies, *Airlines of the United States since 1914* (London: Putnam, 1972), 58–69. See also Robert Bluffield, *Over Empires and Oceans: Pioneers, Aviators and Adventurers—Forging the International Air Routes, 1918–1939* (Ticehurst: Tattered Flag Press, 2014), 177–80.

46. Minutes, board meeting, Fokker Aircraft, October 24, 1928, Boeing Archive, Seattle, inv. no. C150; *New York Times*, October 25, 1928.

47. Wall Street notations of "Over the Counter Quotations for Unlisted Securities," *New York Times*, October 24–31, 1928.

48. Wayne Biddle, *Barons of the Sky: From Early Flight to Strategic Warfare—The Story of the American Aerospace Industry* (New York: Simon & Schuster, 1991), 178.

49. Ibid., 156–93; Freudenthal, *Aviation Business*, 97–99.

50. Rate changes at the Wall Street Stock Exchange and related news items, *New York Times*, April 1–May 19, 1929; Baker, Simonds & Co., *The Aviation Industry* (Detroit: Baker, Simonds, 1929), 20–22.

51. Minutes, board meeting, Fokker Aircraft, February 23, 1929, Boeing Archive, Seattle, inv. no. C150; *Brooklyn Daily Eagle*, February 26, 1929.

52. *Algemeen Handelsblad*, April 20, 1929; *Voorwaarts*, April 24, 1929.

53. Minutes, board of directors, Fokker Aircraft, May 14, 1929, Boeing Archive, Seattle, inv. no. C150.

54. Minutes, board of directors, Fokker Aircraft, May 29, 1929, Boeing Archive, Seattle, inv. no. C150; *Utica Daily Press*, May 17, 1929; *Time* magazine, May 27, 1929.

55. Alfred P. Sloan, *My Years with General Motors* (Garden City, NY: Doubleday, 1963), 364; Wall Street daily stock rates between April 29 and May 19, 1929; reporting in the financial section of the *New York Times* on the General Motors takeover bid between May 17 and July 24, 1929.

56. General Motors Annual Report 1929, 6, http://www.library.upenn.edu/collections/lippincott/corprpts/gm/gm1929.pdf (2014).

57. Minutes, board meeting, Fokker Aircraft, May 29, 1929; Lewis, *Eddie Rickenbacker*, 296; *New York Times*, July 24 and 27, 1929; Edward V. Rickenbacker, *Rickenbacker: An Autobiography* (Englewood Cliffs, NJ: Prentice-Hall, 1967), 178–79; Peter Bowers, "The American Fokkers—Part 4," *AAHS Journal* 16, no. 3 (1971): 189.

58. Minutes, board meeting, Fokker Aircraft, May 29, 1929.

59. *New York Times*, June 23, 1929.

60. Minutes, board meeting, Fokker Aircraft, May 29, 1929.

61. Minutes, board meeting, Fokker Aircraft, July 17, 1929, Boeing Archive, inv. no. C150.

62. General Motors Annual Report 1929, 10.

18. NEW YORK, NEW YORK, JULY 1931

1. General Motors Corporation (signed by Harris Hanshue) to Wallace P. Zachry, July 9, 1931; minutes, Board Meeting General Aviation, July 10, 1931, Boeing Archive, inv. no. C150.

2. William F. Trimble, *High Frontier: A History of Aeronautics in Pennsylvania* (Pittsburgh: University of Pittsburgh Press, 1982), 154–61.

3. Minutes, board meeting, General Aviation, July 10, 1931, Boeing Archive, inv. no. C150. See also *New York Times*, July 7, 1931.

4. Minutes, board meeting, General Aviation, June 26, 1931, Boeing Archive, inv. no. C150.

5. Minutes, board meeting, General Aviation, July 10, 1931; cancellation of employment contract with A. H. G. Fokker, July 10, 1931, Boeing Archive, inv. no. C150.

6. General Motors Corporation to Wallace P. Zachry, July 9, 1931, Boeing Archive, inv. no. C150.

7. *New York Times*, July 11, 1931.

8. Telegram from Anthony Fokker, *Het Vaderland*, July 12, 1931.

9. Anthony Fokker to Wim and Nel van Nijenhoff, May 29, 1929, Aviodrome, collection A. H. G. Fokker, box 13.

10. Minutes, board meeting, General Aviation, March 14, 1930, Boeing Archive, inv. no. C150.

11. *New York Times*, July 24 and 27, 1929; Edward V. Rickenbacker, *Rickenbacker: An Autobiography* (Englewood Cliffs, NJ: Prentice-Hall, 1967), 178–79; Peter Bowers, "The American Fokkers—Part 4," *AAHS Journal* 16, no. 3 (1971): 189.

12. Fokker to Wim and Nel van Nijenhoff, May 29, 1929.

13. *New York Times*, October 23, 1929.

14. *New York Times*, October 24, 1929.

15. Photograph and caption in *Voorwaarts*, October 26, 1929.

16. Doree Smedley and Hollister Noble, "Profiles: Flying Dutchman," *New Yorker*, February 7, 1931, 20–24.

17. *New York Times*, June 23, 1929.

18. Interview with Anthony Fokker, *New York Times*, May 30, 1926.

19. W. T. Whalen, vice chairman of the board, on the occasion of the launch of the first Fokker F-32, Fox Movietone News, March 21, 1930:, University of South Carolina, Fox Movietone News Collection, MVTN 5–624.

20. Interview with Anthony Fokker, *New York Times*, December 2, 1928.

21. Fokker to Wim and Nel van Nijenhoff, May 29, 1929.

22. Jim King to the office of Western Air Express in Los Angeles, November 23, 1929, quoted in Robert H. Schleppler, "The Fokker F-32," *AAHS Journal* 11, no. 2 (1966): 111.

23. Schleppler, "Fokker F-32," 112; Rickenbacker, *Autobiography*, 179.

24. René de Leeuw, ed., *Fokker Verkeersvliegtuigen: Van de f.i uit 1918 tot en met de Fokker 100 van nu* (Amsterdam: NV Koninklijke Nederlandse Vliegtuigenfabriek Fokker, 1989), 132.

25. Cis van Rhijn to Henri Hegener, April 16, 1957, Collection Postma, Hegener Papers, correspondence.

26. Interview by the author with Fokker's nephew Ton Nijland, February 19, 1987.

27. Estate of Fokker versus Commissioner, U.S. Tax Court, Docket No. 111851, http://www.leagle.com/decision/1948123510fdtc1225_11076 (2014).

28. *Brooklyn Daily Eagle*, November 29, 1929.

29. Overview of going rates in *Algemeen Handelsblad*, December 28, 1929.

30. Fokker Aircraft Corporation of America, sale brochure, prices entering into force on April 7, 1930, Aviodrome, Fokker collection.

31. "Bayard Young, Ohio Valley Weekend 50th: First W. Va. Commercial Plane Flew in 1928," *Intelligencer* (Wheeling, WV), December 16, 1978.

32. *New York Times*, May 26 and June 19, 1930.

33. R. E. G. Davies, *Airlines of the United States since 1914* (London: Putnam, 1972), 593–601.

34. Film footage, Fox Movietone News, March 21, 1930, University of South Carolina, Fox Movietone News Collection, MVTN 5–624.

35. *Brooklyn Daily Eagle*, March 22, 1930.

36. *Batavia Times* (Batavia, NY), December 12, 1925.

37. *Brisbane Courier*, June 20, 1927.

38. *Brooklyn Daily Eagle*, July 2, 1930.

39. *Rochester Democrat and Chronicle*, July 3, 1930.

40. Minutes, meeting of executives, General Aviation, July 10, 1930, Boeing Archive, inv. no. C150.

41. *New York Times*, April 7, 1930.

42. Minutes, board meeting, Fokker Aircraft, May 21, 1930, Boeing Archive, inv. no. C150.

43. Minutes, meeting of incorporators, Fokker Aircraft, June 16, 1930, Boeing Archive, inv. no. C150.

44. Minutes, meeting of stockholders, General Aviation, June 18, 1930, Boeing Archive, inv. no. C150.

45. *New York Sun*, June 28, 1932.

46. Minutes, meeting of executives, July 10, 1930, Boeing Archive, inv. no. C150.

47. Minutes, meeting of executives, March 5, 1931, Boeing Archive, inv. no. C150.

48. Friedrich Seekatz to the chief editor of the *Mainzer Tagesblatt*, December 23, 1929, Aviodrome, collection Seekatz.

49. Bruce Gould to the author, April 1, 1987; Bruce Gould, "Herinneringen aan Tony Fokker," *Het Vliegveld* 25, no. 1 (1941): 14; Hugo Hooftman, "Het leven van Anthony Fokker," *Cockpit* 1, no. 3 (1960): 100–102.

50. Admiral William Moffett to Richard Byrd, April 25, 1931, Byrd Papers, Ohio State University, inv. no. 387, and correspondence from Byrd with various people in the same archive; *New York Evening Post*, April 21, 1931; *Time* magazine, May 4, 1931.

51. Minutes, meeting of executives, March 23, 1931, Boeing Archive, inv. no. C150.

52. M. E. H. Warendorf to Friedrich Seekatz, February 26, 1931; Seekatz to Warendorf, June 4, 1931, Aviodrome, collection Seekatz.

53. Netherlands Parliamentary Papers (Handelingen der Staten-Generaal), 1931–1932, Tweede Kamer 1931–1932, kamerstuk 2 IV ondernummer 8; Verslag, 12 November 1931, 473–474.

54. Witness statement by C. H. McCracken, April 1, 1931, National Air and Space Museum, Washington, DC, Rockne Crash file.

55. Dominick A. Pisano, "The Crash That Killed Knute Rockne," *Air & Space Smithsonian* 6, no. 5 (1991–92), 88–93.

56. Leonard Jurden (supervising inspector on the scene) to G. C. Budwig (Director of Air Regulation, Department of Commerce), April 8, 1931, National Air and Space Museum, Rockne Crash file.

57. Admiral William Moffett to Richard Byrd, April 25, 1931; Nick Komons, *Bonfires to Beacons: Federal Aviation Policy under the Air Commerce Act, 1926–1938* (Washington DC: Smithsonian Institution Press, 1989), 185.

58. Interview with Anthony Fokker, *Geneva Daily Times*, April 2, 1931; Anthony Fokker to the executive committee of TWA, April 6, 1931, National Air and Space Museum, Rockne Crash file.

59. Leonard Jurden to the Chief of the Inspection Service of the Aeronautics Branch, April 7, 1931, National Air and Space Museum, Rockne Crash file.

60. Young, "Ohio Valley Weekend 50th."

61. Komons, *Bonfires to Beacons*, 185–88; Pisano, "The Crash That Killed Knute Rockne," 93.

62. Anthony Fokker quoted in *Time* magazine, May 18, 1931.

63. Minutes, board meeting, General Aviation, June 26, 1931, Boeing Archive, inv. no. C150.

19. THE HAGUE, HOLLAND, NOVEMBER 1933

1. C. C. Küpfer, "Gedenkboek NV Nederlandse Vliegtuigenfabriek Fokker, 1919–1964" (unpublished manuscript, in author's collection), 121–22.

2. Bouman to Anthony Fokker, Vattier Kraane, Friedrich Seekatz, and others, December 14, 1932, Aviodrome, collection Seekatz.

3. Albert Plesman Jr., *Albert Plesman, mijn vader* (The Hague: Nijgh & Van Ditmar, 1977), 41–42.

4. Albert Plesman to Minister of Waterworks, November 29, 1933, NA, 2.16.5240, Archive RLD (Government Aeronautical Service), inv. no. 6255.

5. Minutes, board meeting, General Aviation, August 19, 1931, Boeing Archive, inv. no. C150.

6. Minutes, board meetings, General Aviation, July 1931 to January 1933, Boeing Archive, inv. no. C150.

7. Minutes, stockholders meeting, General Aviation, October 27, 1931, Boeing Archive, inv. no. C150.

8. *New York Times*, March 24 and April 25, 1933.

9. Anthony Fokker to the Mayor of Schwerin, June 17, 1930, City Archive Schwerin, Magistrat, 16.16 Spenden und Schenkungen, inv. no. 4749.

10. Checkbook, City of Schwerin, 1931–1933, City Archive Schwerin, Magistrat, 16.16 Spenden und Schenkungen, inv. no. 4749.

11. Second report, Van Doorninck Commission, Annex 2, June 21, 1935, NA, 2.16.5240, RLD, inv. no. 1554. All exchange rate amounts from http://measuringworth.com/exchangeglobal (2015).

12. Correspondence in Archive Ministry of Foreign Affairs, NA, 2.05.37, Directorate of Economic Affairs, inv. no. 3114.

13. Willem Oudendijk to Minister of Foreign Affairs, October 1931, NA, 2.05.90, Archive Netherlands Legation in China, inv. no. 379; see also NA, 2.05.37, Directorate of Economic Affairs, inv. no. 5700.

14. Minutes, sixteenth meeting of the Van Doorninck Commission, May 21, 1935, NA, 2.08.41, Archive Ministry of Finance, inv. no. 4112. Financial data based on Küpfer, "Gedenkboek," 96.

15. Interview with Anthony Fokker, *De Telegraaf,* January 13, 1931.

16. Anthony Fokker to the Van Doorninck Commission, September 6, 1934, NA, 2.08.41, Archive Ministry of Finance, inv. no. 4106.

17. *De Tijd*, April 2, 1931.

18. Dirk Starink, *De jonge jaren van de luchtmacht: Het luchtwapen in het Nederlandse leger, 1913–1939* (Amsterdam: Boom, 2013), 186–87, 189, 198, 206.

19. Minutes, 100th meeting of the board of KLM, September 1932; Fokker to Plesman, October 13, 1932, KLM Board Papers, series R-5.

20. Report, Van Doorninck Commission, Annex 2, June 21, 1935, NA, 2.16.5240, Archive RLD, inv. no. 1554; Wayne Biddle, *Barons of the Sky: From Early Flight to Strategic Warfare—The Story of the American Aerospace Industry* (New York: Simon & Schuster, 1991), 183.

21. Interview with Anthony Fokker, *Het Vaderland*, December 21, 1931.

22. Bert Slotemaker (KLM's head of legal services) to the Minister of Waterworks, December 1, 1933, NA, 2.16.5240, Archive RLD, inv. no. 6339.

23. Interview with Anthony Fokker, *Het Vaderland*, December 21, 1931; report on the NV Nederlandsche Vliegtuigenfabriek, Tekelenburg & Van Til Accountants, March 7, 1935, NA, 2.08.41 Archive Ministry of Finance, inv. no. 4114.

24. *Het Vaderland*, September 24, 1933.

25. Anthony Fokker to Albert Plesman, October 13, 1932, KLM Board Papers, series R-5.

26. Confidential report by government accountant A. H. J. Schmitz regarding the financial policies of the Netherlands Aircraft Factory, issued on commission from the Van Doorninck Commission, May 13, 1935, NA, 2.08.41 Archive Ministry of Finance, inv. no. 4114.

27. *New York Times*, June 20 and July 20, 1931.

28. Anthony Fokker in the Dutch "Polygoon" cinema newsreel, September 29, 1931.

29. *Algemeen Handelsblad*, October 4, 1931.

30. Commercial statement (letter) by Anthony Fokker, November 6, 1931, printed in *De Sumatra Post*, July 26, 1932.

31. *New York Times*, December 8, 1931; press release, Aneta News Agency, January 4, 1932, in *De Indische Courant*, January 7, 1932.

32. Film footage by Anthony Fokker of tourist visits to Rome, Bremen, Budapest, Berlin, Prague, Paris, Munich, and Geneva, Fokkerfilm 01–3092, Archive Beeld en Geluid, Hilversum, the Netherlands.

33. *New York Sun*, June 28, 1932; *Brooklyn Daily Eagle*, June 30, 1932.

34. Photograph in *Algemeen Handelsblad*, November 4, 1933.

35. Interview with test pilot Emil Meinecke in *Bataviaasch Nieuwsblad*, February 21, 1939.

36. KLM Maintenance Department, report no. 10 on the F.XXXVI, September 13, 1934; confidential overview of the problems with the PH-AJA [as the aircraft was registered] between March 16, 1935, and approximately October 1, 1935, dated November 20, 1935, KLM Board Papers, series R-5.

28. MONTAUK POINT, LONG ISLAND, SEPTEMBER 1935

1. Anthony Fokker quoted in *New York Times*, September 5, 1935.

2. *New York Times*, September 4, 1935; *Troy Times Record*, September 5, 1935.

3. Agreement between Donald Douglas and Anthony Fokker, January 15, 1934, formerly in NV Fokker company archive, Schiphol Airport, series V/Alg. Secr. 15 (1994).

4. Wilbur H. Morrison, *Donald W. Douglas: A Heart with Wings* (Ames: Iowa State University Press, 1991), 76–78.

5. Minutes, board meetings, General Aviation, December 6, 1932, and January 12, 1933, Boeing Archive, inv. no. C150.

6. John B. Rae, *Climb to Greatness: The American Aircraft Industry, 1920–1960* (Cambridge, MA: MIT Press, 1968), 65–66.

7. Anthony Fokker to Van Doorninck Commission, August 16, 1934, NA, 2.08.41 Archive Ministry of Finance, inv. no. 4106.

8. Robert E. Gross to Courtlandt S. Gross, January 23, 1934, Library of Congress, Manuscript Division, Robert E. Gross Papers, box 4.

9. Report by Tekelenburg & Van Til Accountants, March 7, 1935, NA, 2.08.41 Archive Ministry of Finance, inv. no. 4110.

10. Chris Hansen, *Enfant Terrible: The Times and Schemes of General Elliot Roosevelt* (Tucson, AZ: Able Baker Press, 2012), 96.

11. Ibid., 94.

12. Ibid.

13. Contract, Fokker-Roosevelt, February 28, 1934, quoted in ibid., 95–96.

14. Conrad Black, *Franklin Delano Roosevelt: Champion of Freedom* (London: Weidenfeld & Nicolson, 2003), 909.

15. Testimony by Anthony Fokker before the U.S. Senate Special Committee Investigating the Munitions Industry, September 12, 1935, National Archives, Record Group 46, Executive File, box 156; see also Hansen, *Enfant Terrible*, 99.

16. Wayne Biddle, *Barons of the Sky: From Early Flight to Strategic Warfare—The Story of the American Aerospace Industry* (New York: Simon & Schuster, 1991), 203. Biddle quotes a letter from Anthony Fokker to Donald Douglas written during his European sales trip.

17. Robert E. Gross to Courtlandt S. Gross, May 3, 1934, Library of Congress, Manuscript Division, Robert E. Gross Papers, box 4.

18. Orlando Figes, *The Whisperers: Private Life in Stalin's Russia* (London: Allen Lane, 2007), 169–71, 174–86.

19. Ibid., 157–58.

20. Interview with Anthony Fokker in *Algemeen Handelsblad*, repr. in part in *Leeuwarder Courant*, June 7, 1934, and in *Nieuwsblad van Friesland: Hepkema's Courant*, June 13, 1934; see also NA, 2.21.081, Collection J.A. van Hamel, inv. no. 223.

21. Anthony Fokker to J. A. van Hamel, September 25, 1934, NA, 2.21.081, Collection J. A. van Hamel, inv. no. 222; interview with Anthony Fokker, undated, *Algemeen Handelsblad*, 1934, NA, 2.21.081, Collection J. A. van Hamel, inv. no. 223.

22. Undated clipping from *Algemeen Handelsblad*, 1934.

23. *Algemeen Handelsblad*, July 8, 1934.

24. Hansen, *Enfant Terrible*, 104–6.

25. Testimony of Fokker before Senate Special Committee, September 12, 1935.

26. Hansen, *Enfant Terrible*, 106.

27. Fokker's testimony, typed up and signed on September 19, 1935, National Archives, Record Group 46, Executive File, box 156; see also Hansen, *Enfant Terrible*, 98.

28. Hansen, *Enfant Terrible*, 94.

29. Agreement between Donald Douglas and Anthony Fokker, January 15, 1934, formerly kept in Fokker Corporate Archive, series V/Alg. Secr., 15 (1994).

30. Minutes, second meeting of the Van Doorninck Commission, February 15, 1934, NA, 2.08.41, Archive Ministry of Finance, inv. no. 4112.

31. Anton van Doorninck to Minister of Finance, November 27, 1933, NA, 2.08.41, Archive Ministry of Finance, inv. no. 4111.

32. Minutes, fourth meeting of the Van Doorninck Commission, April 10, 1934, NA, 2.08.41, Archive Ministry of Finance, inv. no. 4112.

33. Report of the Van Doorninck Commission, June 21, 1935, NA, 2.16.5240, Archive RLD, inv. no. 1554.

34. Anthony Fokker to Anton van Doorninck, August 16, 1934, NA, 2.08.41 Archive Ministry of Finance, inv. no. 4115.

35. Albert Plesman to the Board of KLM, June 21, 1934; minutes, 130th and 131st meeting of the board of KLM, June 26 and July 28, 1934, KLM Board Papers, series R-5.

36. Fokker to Van Doorninck, August 16, 1934.

37. Marc Dierikx, *Begrensde horizonten: De Nederlandse burgerluchtvaartpolitiek in het interbellum* (Zwolle: Tjeenk Willink, 1988), 116–32.

38. Interview with Anthony Fokker, *Nieuwsblad van het Noorden*, August 17, 1934.

39. Anthony Fokker to Anton van Doorninck, September 12, 1934, NA, 2.08.41, Archive Ministry of Finance, inv. no. 4115.

40. Interview with Anthony Fokker, *Het Vaderland*, August 18, 1934.

41. Albert Plesman to Anthony Fokker, August 23, 1934, KLM Board Papers, series R-5.

42. Minutes, second meeting of the Van Doorninck Commission.

43. Minutes, 134st meeting of the board of KLM, October 30, 1934, KLM Board Papers, series R-5.

44. "Mildenhall to Melbourne?" *Time* magazine, October 29, 1934.

45. Interview with Anthony Fokker, *Het Vaderland*, October 27, 1934.

46. Koene D. Parmentier, *In drie dagen naar Australië: Met de Uiver in de Melbourne Race* (Amsterdam: Scheltens & Giltay, 1935).

47. Minutes, KLM board meeting, October 30, 1934, KLM Board Papers, series R-5.

48. Minutes, 9th meeting of the Van Doorninck Commission, November 8, 1934, NA, 2.08.41, Archive Ministry of Finance, inv. no. 4112.

49. Minutes, 11th meeting of the Van Doorninck Commission, December 12, 1934, NA, 2.08.41, Archive Ministry of Finance, inv. no. 4112.

21. ST. MORITZ, SWITZERLAND, JANUARY 1937

1. Contributions in the guest book of Chalet Oberalpina, Aviodrome, collection A. H. G. Fokker, box 12; private film footage, Wieringa family, Oberalpina, January 1937, author's collection.

2. *De Telegraaf*, January 13, 1933.

3. Film footage, private possession of Sabine Witzier, granddaughter of Fokker's sister Toos.

4. Group interview by the author with the Van der Wal and Wieringa families, July 25, 2012.

5. *Estate of Fokker v. Commissioner of Internal Revenue*, 10 T.C. 1225 (1948), Docket No. 111851, U.S. Tax Court, June 29, 1948, http://www.leagle.com/decision/1948123510fdtc1225_11076 (2014); floor plan of Oberalpina, Aviodrome, collection A. H. G. Fokker, box 12.

6. Photos of Oberalpina, Aviodrome, collection A. H. G. Fokker, box 12.

7. *Nieuwe Rotterdamsche Courant*, June 25, 1925; *Algemeen Handelsblad*, August 8, 1931.

8. Fokker family photographs in Collection Smeulers, Bronkhorst.

9. Photo collection in Netherlands National Archive, http://proxy.handle.net/10648/6a332e34-1ad9-102f-a76c-003048944028 (2017).

10. Interview with Jojo's son, Frederick Dulles, November 28, 2012.

11. Netherlands passport, issued to Anthony Fokker at The Hague, July 7, 1934, Aviodrome, collection A. H. G. Fokker, box 11.

12. Anthony Fokker to Jojo de Leuw, August 19, 1935, quoted in *Estate of Fokker v. Commissioner of Internal Revenue*.

13. Interview with Anthony Fokker, *Het Vaderland*, November 15, 1934.

14. Nevil Shute, *Slide Rule: The Autobiography of an Engineer* (London: Heinemann, 1954), 7–9.

15. Interview, *Het Vaderland*, November 15, 1934.

16. Shute, *Slide Rule*, 219–21; minutes, thirteenth meeting of the Van Doorninck Commission, February 5, 1935, NA, 2.08.41, Archive Ministry of Finance, inv. no. 4112; report, Van Doorninck Commission, June 21, 1935, NA, 2.16.5240, Archive RLD, inv. no. 1554.

17. Minutes, special meeting of the Van Doorninck Commission with Anthony Fokker, Vattier Kraane, and Frits Elekind, February 28, 1935, NA, 2.08.41, Archive Ministry of Finance, inv. no. 4109.

18. Bruno Stephan to Henri Hegener, January 5, 1956, Collection Postma, Hegener Papers, correspondence.

19. *Deutsche Allgemeine Zeitung*, Berlin, December 8, 1934; *Het Vaderland*, December 7, 1934.

20. Telegram quoted in *Manchester Guardian*, January 11, 1935.

21. Minutes, sixteenth meeting of the Van Doorninck Commission, May 21, 1935, NA, 2.08.41 Archive Ministry of Finance, inv. no. 4112.

22. Minutes, special meeting, Van Doorninck Commission.

23. Fokker passport (see note 11).

24. Shute, *Slide Rule*, 229.

25. Wilbur H. Morrison, *Donald W. Douglas: A Heart with Wings* (Ames: Iowa State University Press, 1991), 83–84.

26. *Het Vaderland*, May 24, 1935.

27. Official statement of Donald Wills Douglas, May 23, 1935, KLM Board Papers, series A-9/A-950, R-506–2.

28. *Het Vaderland*, May 24, 1935.

29. Ibid., May 29, 1935.

30. *Flight*, June 6, 1935, 618.

31. Anthony Fokker to Donald Douglas, June 5, 1935, formerly in Fokker Corporate Archive, series V/Alg. Secr., 15.

32. Interview with Anthony Fokker, *De Maasbode*, August 6, 1935.

33. Minutes, KLM board meeting, August 6, 1935, KLM Board Papers, series R-5.

34. Anthony Fokker to the Board of KLM, August 22, 1935, KLM Board Papers, series R-5 (italics and capitalization by Fokker).

35. *Estate of Fokker v. Commissioner of Internal Revenue.*

36. Contract between KLM and Fokker regarding the acquisition of the DC-2, August 15–December 31, 1935, KLM Board Papers, series A-950. For an overview of price negotiations between KLM and Fokker regarding the DC-2, March 14, 1939, see NA, 2.16.5240, Archive RLD, inv. no. 13290.

37. Anthony Fokker to the Board of KLM, November 30, 1935, KLM Board Papers, series R-5.

38. Interview with Anthony Fokker, *Het Vaderland*, November 2, 1935.

39. Third Report, Van Doorninck Commission, February 4, 1936, Appendix E (Concept Agreement between the Netherlands and Fokker), NA, 2.08.41, Archive Ministry of Finance, inv. no. 4111.

40. Minutes, 22nd Meeting, Van Doorninck Commission, January 27, 1936, NA, 2.08.41, Archive Ministry of Finance, inv. no. 4112.

41. Third Report, Van Doorninck Commission, Appendix D (Concept Employment Contract with Anthony Fokker), February 4, 1936, NA, 2.08.41, Archive Ministry of Finance, inv. no. 4109.

42. Treasurer-General R. A. Ries to Minister of Finance, February 12, 1936, NA, 2.08.41, Archive Ministry of Finance, inv. no. 4111.

43. Minister of Defense to Minister of Finance, March 12, 1936, NA, 2.08.41, Archive Ministry of Finance, inv. no. 4108.

44. *Het Vaderland*, June 6 and 7, 1936; *De Gooi- en Eemlander*, June 8, 1936.

45. Film footage, "Polygoon" newsreel, June 6, 1936.

46. Wim van Nijenhoff, "Memories of Anthony Fokker," March 1, 1940, Collection Postma, Hegener Papers, correspondence; *De Tijd*, May 17, 1936.

47. Richard Mock to Geneva Carr, Los Angeles Eye and Ear Hospital, November 4, 1935, formerly in Fokker Historical Collection, Schiphol Airport, A. H. G. Fokker, box 2 (1994).

48. Richard Mock to the El Tovar Hotel, September 29, 1936, formerly in Fokker Historical Collection, A. H. G. Fokker, box 2 (1994).

49. Mock to Fokker, September 20, 1937, formerly in Fokker Historical Collection, A. H. G. Fokker, box 2 (1994).

50. Telegrams between Mock and Fokker, June–August 1936, formerly in Fokker Historical Collection, A. H. G. Fokker, box 2 (1994).

51. Anthony Fokker to Gen. Oscar Westover, October 16, 1936, quoted in *Estate of Fokker v. Commissioner of Internal Revenue.*

52. *De Tijd*, May 14, 1936.

53. Correspondence quoted by Carter Tiffany in *Estate of Fokker v. Commissioner of Internal Revenue.*

54. Chris Hansen, *Enfant Terrible: The Times and Schemes of General Elliot Roosevelt* (Tucson, AZ: Able Baker Press, 2012), 97.

55. See *New York Times*, October 7, 1936; *New York Post*, October 7, 1936.

56. *Report of the Special Committee on Investigation of the Munitions Industry* (Nye Report), U.S. Congress, Senate, 74th Congress, 2nd sess., February 24, 1936.

57. *Los Angeles Times*, October 7, 1936; *Los Angeles Illustrated Daily News*, October 8, 1936.

58. *New York Times*, October 8, 1936.

59. Hansen, *Enfant Terrible*, 101–2; *Chicago Tribune*, October 13, 1936.

60. *New York Times*, October 9, 1936.

61. *New York Times*, October 11, 1936.

22. NEW YORK, NEW YORK, JUNE 1938

1. *Het Vaderland*, June 21, 1938, and October 9, 1939.

2. *New York Times*, June 21, 1938.

3. Carter Tiffany, "Een persoonlijke herinnering aan Anthony Fokker" (undated memoir, 1940), Collection Thijs Postma, Hoofddorp, Holland, Hegener Papers, correspondence; *New York Times*, January 14, 1938.

4. Color design drawings for the QED interior, https://www.georgeglazer.com/archives/prints/sports/maritime/fokker.html.

5. Michael Zwartelé and Jan Briek, "Quod erat demonstrandum: Het wonderlijke jacht van Anthony Fokker," *Waterkampioen*, no. 9 (2001), 74–77.

6. *Brooklyn Daily Eagle*, August 7, 1938; *Mount Vernon (NY) Daily Argus*, September 7, 1938.

7. *New York Times*, November 20, 1936.

8. Estate of Fokker v. Commissioner of Internal Revenue, 10 T.C. 1225 (1948), Docket No. 111851, U.S. Tax Court, June 29, 1948, http://www.leagle.com/decision/1948123510fdtc1225_11076; Tiffany, "Een persoonlijke herinnering aan Tony Fokker."

9. Estate of Fokker v. Commissioner of Internal Revenue; photo album, "Voyage on the QED, August 1939," Winckel Collection, Kapellen, Belgium.

10. Sotheby's *Old Master Paintings*, auction catalog, Amsterdam, May 8, 2007, 112.

11. Estate of Fokker v. Commissioner of Internal Revenue.

12. Agreement signed by Anthony Fokker in Paris on May 25, 1937, with Van der Mandere and Van Til; sealed statement by J. Lubbers (attorney at law) and J. J. B. van der Mandere, June 1, 1937, NA, 2.20.01, Nederlandsche Handel Maatschappij, inv. no. 5554, Documents concerning the introduction of shares of the Netherlands Aircraft Factory at the Amsterdam Stock Exchange, 1937; Estate of Fokker v. Commissioner of Internal Revenue; testimony of Carter Tiffany before Supreme Court of Rockland County, January 29, 1943, formerly in Fokker Corporate Archive, series V/Alg. Secr., no. 13. On the advice of Tiffany, the management of the Netherlands Aircraft Factory transferred an additional $1.5 million to its U.S. accounts in the last months before the German invasion of the Netherlands in May 1940. With these transfers, approximately 36 percent of the gross assets of the company were relocated to American banks.

13. Annual reports, Netherlands Aircraft Factory, 1937, 1938, and 1939, profit and loss accounts, formerly in Fokker Corporate Archive (1994); figure for 1937 from a Fokker advertisement in *Het Vliegveld* 21, no. 8 (1937), v; figure for 1938 from Johannes de Vries, *Met Amsterdam als brandpunt: Honderdvijftig jaar Kamer van Koophandel en Fabrieken, 1811–1961* (Amsterdam: Ellerman Harms, 1961), 84.

14. Interview with Anthony Fokker, *New York Times*, March 19, 1938.

15. *De Gooi- en Eemlander*, February 25, 1938.

16. *Het Vaderland*, May 10, 1938, and *New York Times*, May 10, 1938.

17. *New York Times*, May 29, 1938.
18. Estate of Fokker v. Commissioner of Internal Revenue; *Nieuwe Rotterdamsche Courant*, July 15, 1929; NA, 2.09.06, Ministry of Justice, London Archives, 1936–1945, inv. no. 2823.
19. J. G. Kuyt, *De "Holland": Zaandijk–New York v.v.* (Amsterdam: P. N. van Kampen, 1938), 136.
20. Ibid., 137.
21. *De Groene Amsterdammer*, December 24, 1938, 7.
22. Group interview by the author with the Wieringa and Van der Wal families, Amsterdam, July 25, 2012; Estate of Fokker v. Commissioner of Internal Revenue.
23. Anthony Fokker to Hendrik Colijn, February 11, 1939, NA, 2.16.5240, Archive Rijksluchtvaartdienst (RLD), inv. no. 13290 (italics by Fokker).
24. Memorandum, Van Ede van der Pals to Van Buuren (Minister of Waterworks), February 16, 1939, NA, 2.16.5240, Archive RLD, inv. no. 13290.
25. Formal decision by the Interdepartmental Commission of Advice regarding the construction of aircraft in the country, May 5, 1939, NA, 2.16.19.30, Archive Interdepartmental Commission, inv. no. 1.
26. Jan Van Buuren to Albert Plesman, March 4, 1939, NA, 2.16.5240, Archive RLD, inv. no. 13290.
27. *Algemeen Handelsblad*, March 13, 1939; *De Telegraaf*, March 14, 1939.
28. Anthony Fokker to Albert Plesman, March 9, 1939, KLM Board Papers, series A-9/A-950, R-506.2; account of the meeting between KLM and Fokker on March 13, 1939, NA, 2.16.5240, Archive RLD, inv. no. 13290.
29. "Fokker on Plesman," *De Telegraaf*, March 15, 1939.
30. Anthony Fokker to G. W. J. Bruins, March 15, 1939, KLM Board Papers, series A9/A950; R-506.2.
31. Contract between the Government of the Netherlands and the NV Nederlandsche Vliegtuigenfabriek Fokker, January 22–23, 1940, and contract between the Netherlands Aircraft Factory and KLM, January 25–26, 1940, NA, 2.16.5240, Archive RLD, inv. no. 10290.
32. *New York Times*, May 7, 1939.
33. Private film footage of the Van der Wal family, August 1939, author's collection.
34. *New York Times*, August 7, 1939.
35. *Warrensburg (NY) Lake George News*, September 14, 1939.
36. Interview with the Van der Wal and Wieringa families, July 25, 2012.
37. *Poughkeepsie Star-Enterprise*, October 9, 1939; *Herald Statesman*, Yonkers NY, October 10, 1939; *Westfield Leader*, October 12, 1939.
38. *Herald Statesman*, October 10, 11, 20, and 24, 1939.
39. Bartlett Gould, "The Last Days of Anthony H. G. Fokker," *World War I Aero*, no. 89 (April 1982), 26–27 (based on papers from the estate of William Starling Burgess).

23. WESTERVELD, HOLLAND, FEBRUARY 1940

1. Official photo album of the interring of Anthony Fokker's ashes, compiled by the Netherlands Aircraft Factory Fokker, Aviodrome Historical Archive, Lelystad.
2. Anna Fokker-Diemont to Christine Döppler, January 27, 1940, Heitzman "Stuffinder" Collection, Deansboro, NY, Döppler album.

3. *Het Vaderland*, February 3, 1940.

4. *Syracuse Herald Journal*, December 22, 1939, and *New York Sun*, December 23, 1939.

5. Certificate of Death, Anthony Herman Gerard Fokker, Bureau of Records, Department of Health, Borough of Manhattan, no. 26149, December 25, 1939, 7.06 a.m., New York City Department of Records, Municipal Archives.

6. Act of Taxation, July 13, 1949, Collection Smeulers, Bronkhorst.

7. Last Will and Testament of Anthony H. G. Fokker, September 26, 1935, carbon copy, author's collection (with gratitude to Jon Wieringa).

8. Estate of Fokker v. Commissioner of Internal Revenue, 10 T.C. 1225 (1948), Docket No. 111851, U.S. Tax Court, June 29, 1948, http://www.leagle.com/decision/1948123510fdtc1225_11076.

9. Carter Tiffany to Anna Fokker, January 29, 1940, author's collection.

10. William Dulles (Cahill, Gordon, Zachry & Reindel, New York) to J. van der Mandere (attorney at law, Amsterdam), February 9, 1949; G. E. A. van Til (Fokker's accountant) to Inspector of Internal Revenues, June 8, 1954, Collection Smeulers, Bronkhorst.

11. Estate of Fokker v. Commissioner of Internal Revenue.

12. Head of the Government Migrants and Aliens Service to the Netherlands Control Institute, Amsterdam, August 9, 1952, National Archive (NA), 2.09.49, Archive NBI (Netherlands Control Institute), inv. no. 167997.

13. Copy of Hermann Goering's instructions to Friedrich Seekatz, January 3, 1941; invoice, Asscher's Diamond Company for Goering, February 14, 1941, NA, 2.09.09, Archive CABR (Central Archive Special Justice), inv. no. 24519.

14. J. C. van Dijk, acting director, Netherlands Control Institute, to Goudstikker's successor, Alois Miedl, October 15, 1962, NA, 2.09.49, Archive NBI, inv. no. 167997; formal interview and statement, Friedrich Seekatz, December 9, 1948, NA, 2.09.09, Archive CABR, inv. no. 24519.

15. Formal interview and statement, Henri van Maasdijk, Leeuwarden Prison, February 14, 1947, NA 2.09.48.02, Archive Council for the Restoration of Justice, Process Department, Amsterdam Chamber, inv. no. 1949/1246.

16. Marc Dierikx, *Fokker: A Transatlantic Biography* (Washington, DC: Smithsonian Institution Press, 1997), 62–63.

17. Estate of Fokker v. Commissioner of Internal Revenue.

18. Netherlands Legation in Washington, DC (Charles J. H. Daubanton) to Minister Eelco van Kleffens in London, July 3, 1941, and Secretary-General of Justice in London to Van Kleffens, NA, 2.09.06, Ministry of Justice, London Archives, 1936–1945, inv. no. 2823, Anthony Fokker, testament [J 2376], 1941; Van Maasdijk, formal interview and statement, February 14, 1947,.

19. Letters, Anna Fokker-Diemont to Christine Döppler, Heitzman "Stuffinder" Collection; legal plea, E. van Haersma Buma (on behalf of NBI), Council for the Restoration of Justice, Process Department, Amsterdam Chamber, February 23, 1950, NA 2.09.48.02, inv. no. 1949/1246.

20. Verdict, Council for the Restoration of Justice, Process Department, Amsterdam Chamber, July 17, 1950, NA 2.09.48.02, inv. no. 1949/1246.

21. Verdict (R14357 1245/49), Court Chamber, Council for the Restoration of Justice, June 15, 1950, NA, 2.16.5240, Archive Netherlands Civil Aviation Service (RLD), inv. no. 5568.

22. Author's interview with Frederick Dulles, November 28, 2012; marriage announcement, *Algemeen Handelsblad*, December 27, 1940.

24. SCHWERIN, GERMANY, A CENTURY LATER

1. Doree Smedley and Hollister Noble, "Profiles: Flying Dutchman," *New Yorker*, February 7, 1931, 20–24.

2. "Recollections of Anthony Fokker," written for journalist Henri Hegener by Anthony's sister, Toos, undated (ca. 1951), Collection Thijs Postma, Hoofddorp, Holland, Hegener Papers, Fokker dossier.

3. Special thanks are due to Robert Boonstoppel, who was willing to share the stories of his mother, Colijn's secretary. Interview by the author, May 15, 2013.

4. Interview by the author with Anthony Fokker's nephew, Ton Nijland (born 1917), February 19, 1987.

5. Group interview by the author with the Wieringa and Van der Wal families, Amsterdam, July 25, 2012.

6. *Rochester Democrat and Chronicle*, December 24, 1939.

7. Anthony H. G. Fokker and Bruce Gould, *Flying Dutchman: The Life of Anthony Fokker* (New York: Henry Holt, 1931), 10.

SOURCES AND BIBLIOGRAPHY

ARCHIVAL SOURCES

CANADA

Canadian Census Records, 1906 and 1911, Winnipeg District #10, Subdistrict 03 A (Ward 3)
http://automatedgenealogy.com/uidlinks/Links.jsp?uid=150592767 (2014)
http://archives.winnipegfreepress.com (2012)

GERMANY

Archive, Deutsches Museum, Munich
Junkers Archive
Franz Schneider Collection

Archive, Deutsches Technik Museum, Berlin
1.4.146, Nachlass Peter Grosz

Archive, Ministry of Foreign Affairs (Auswärtiges Amt), Berlin
Cat. R: Auswärtiges Amt des Deutschen Reiches, ZS 40778

Collection Michael Schmidt, Schwerin/Munich

German National Archive (Bundesarchiv), Koblenz
N1103 Euler Nachlass
http://www.bundesarchiv.de/oeffentlichkeitsarbeit/bilder_dokumente/00931/
    index-0.html.de (2012)

Main Country Archive (Landeshauptarchiv), Mecklenburg, Schwerin
5.2–1 Grossherzogliches Kabinett III
5.12–3/1 Mecklenburg-Schwerinisches Ministerium des Innern
9.2–17 Reichsbahndirektion Schwerin

Municipal Archive (Stadtarchiv), Baden-Baden
A 26 Bürgermeisterei

Municipal Archive (Stadtarchiv), Mainz
Bürgermeisterei-Archiv Mainz

Municipal Archive (Stadtarchiv), Schwerin
Archiv Magistratur

GREAT BRITAIN
National Archive, London (Kew)
Foreign Office Papers, FO 371, inv. no. 4289

ICELAND
http://timarit.is (2014)

LATVIA
Rigasche Rundschau, May 3, 1912
http://www.theeuropeanlibrary.org/tel4/newspapers/search?title=Rigasche+Rundschau&
   query=1912

NETHERLANDS
Aviodrome Historical Archive, Lelystad
Collection A. H. G. Fokker
Dossier Platz
Dossier Seekatz

Beeld & Geluid, Hilversum
Fokker film footage

Collection Blüm, Santpoort

Collection Smeulers, Bronkhorst

Collection Thijs Postma, Hoofddorp

Former Company Archive, Nederlandsche Vliegtuigenfabriek NV Fokker, Schiphol-Oost/
   Rijk (1994)

KLM Royal Dutch Airlines, Amstelveen
Board Papers, series R-5

Municipal Archive, Amsterdam
Gezinskaarten, inv. no. 5422–0407–5100

National Archive, The Hague
2.05.19   Archive, Ministry of Foreign Affairs, 1871–1940
2.05.37   Department of Economic Affairs, Ministry of Foreign Affairs, 1919–40
2.05.90   Archive, Netherlands Legation in China
2.08.05.02   Archive, Ministry of Finance (verbaal archief)
2.08.41   Archive, Ministry of Finance
2.09.06   Justice Ministry, London Archive, 1936–45

2.09.09	Justice Ministry, Central Archive, Special Justice (CABR)
2.09.46	Justice Ministry, Companies Founded, 's-Gravenhaagsche Koffie Cultuur Maatschappij
2.09.48.02	Archive, Council for the Restoration of Justice (Raad voor Rechtsherstel)
2.09.49	Archive, Netherlands Control Institute (Nederlands Beheers Instituut)
2.13.70	General Staff (General Headquarters), 1914–40
2.13.85	Archive of Military Aviation and Air Defense, 1910–40
2.16.19.30	Interdepartmental Advisory Commission Regarding the Construction of Aircraft Material
2.16.19.39	Archive, Ministry of Waterworks, Aviation Desk, 1920–29
2.16.21	Directorate of the Post Office and Telegraphy, 1893–1926 (verbaal archief)
2.16.47	Government Commission on Aviation (Staatscommissie inzake Luchtvaart)
2.16.80	Archive, Advisory Commission of the Government Study Service for Aviation (RSL)
2.16.5240	Archive, Government Aviation Service (Rijksluchtvaartdienst), 1919–82
2.20.01	Archive, Netherlands Trading Company (Nederlandsche Handel Maatschappij)
2.21.043	Collection, Cremer Family Papers
2.21.081	Collection, J. A. van Hamel

Nederlandse Spoorwegen, Utrecht
Minutes, Board of Control, 1918–19

Noord-Hollands Archive, Haarlem
49 District Court Haarlem (Kantongerecht), 1921–30
200 Supervisory Court Amsterdam (Arrondissementsrechtbank)
Municipality of Haarlem, Civil Register (Burgerlijke Stand)
Municipality of Haarlem, Nieuw Archive 126–1

UNITED STATES

American digital archival documents
http://www.criticalpast.com/video/65675031734 (2013)
http://www.leagle.com/decision/19481235l0fdtc1225_11076 (2014)
http://www.censusfinder.com/1930-federal-census-search.htm (2014)

Boeing Archive, Seattle, WA
Board Minutes, Atlantic Aircraft Corporation
Board Minutes, Fokker Aircraft Corporation/General Aviation

Heitzman "Stuffinder" Collection, Deansboro, NY
Döppler Album

Library of Congress, Manuscript Division, Washington, DC
Robert E. Gross Papers

National Air and Space Museum, Smithsonian Institution, Washington, DC
Arcier Collection

Rockne Crash File

National Archives, Washington, DC / College Park, MD
Senate Special Committee Investigating the Munitions Industry, Record Group 46, Executive
    File
State Department, Record Group 84, Netherlands Post File, General Correspondence 1919

New York City Department of Records, Municipal Archives, New York
Department of Health, City of New York, Bureau of Records

Ohio State University, Columbus, OH
Richard E. Byrd Papers

Purdue University, Lafayette, IN
George Palmer Putnam Collection of Amelia Earhart Papers

University of South Carolina, Columbia, SC
Fox Movietone News Collection

LITERATURE

Alexandrov, Andrei, and Gennadi Petrov. *Die deutsche Flugzeuge in russischen und sowjetischen Diensten,
    1914–1951.* Eggolsheim: Nebel, 2004.
Andriessen, J. H. J., ed. *De oorlogsbrieven van Unteroffizier Carl Heller, geschreven tijdens de Eerste Werel-
    doorlog.* Soesterberg: Aspekt, 2003.
Balchen, Bernt. *Come North with Me.* New York: Dutton, 1958.
Baum, Vicki. *Menschen im Hotel.* Berlin: Ullstein, 1929.
Beauvais, Heinrich, Karl Kössler, Max Mayer, and Christoph Regel. *Die deutsche Luftfahrt: Fluger-
    probungsstellen bis 1945. Johannisthal, Lipetzk, Rechlin, Travemünde, Tarnewitz, Peenemünde-West.* Bonn:
    Bernard & Graefe, 1998.
Berghahn, Volker. *Der Erste Weltkrieg.* Munich: C. H. Beck, 2003.
Biddle, Wayne. *Barons of the Sky: From Early Flight to Strategic Warfare: The Story of the American Aerospace
    Industry.* New York: Simon & Schuster, 1991.
Black, Conrad. *Franklin Delano Roosevelt: Champion of Freedom.* London: Weidenfeld & Nicolson,
    2003.
Borchert, F. W. *Beiträge zur Geschichte der Arbeiterbeweging in der Stadt Schwerin,* Heft 9, *1900–1917.*
    Schwerin: Kommission zur Erforschung der Geschichte der örtlichen Arbeiterbewegung,
    1987.
———. *Beiträge zur Geschichte der Arbeiterbeweging in der Stadt Schwerin,* Heft 12, *Verlauf der Ergebnisse der
    Novemberrevolution im Bereich der Stadt Schwerin, November 1917 bis May 1919.* Schwerin: Kommis-
    sion zur Erforschung der Geschichte der örtlichen Arbeiterbewegung, 1988.
Bowers, Peter. "The American Fokkers." Parts 1–4. *AAHS Journal* 11–16 (1966–71).
Bryson, Bill. *One Summer: America 1927.* London: Doubleday, 2013.
Budrass, Lutz. *Flugzeugindustrie und Luftrüstung in Deutschland, 1918–1945.* Düsseldorf: Droste, 1998.
Byers, Richard. "An Unhappy Marriage: The Junkers-Fokker Merger." *Journal of Historical Biogra-
    phy* 3 (Spring 2008): 1–30.

Byrd, Richard E. *Skyward. Man's Mastery of the Air as Shown by the Brilliant Flights of America's Leading Air Explorer.* New York: Halcyon House, 1928.

Chickering, Roger. *The Great War and Urban Life in Germany: Freiburg, 1914–1918.* Cambridge: Cambridge University Press, 2007.

———, ed. *Endangered Cities. Military Power and Urban Societies in the Era of the World Wars.* Boston/Leiden: Brill, 2004.

Chickering, Roger, and Stig Förster. *Great War, Total War: Combat and Mobilization on the Western Front, 1914–1918.* Cambridge: Cambridge University Press, 2000.

Corn, Joseph J. *The Winged Gospel: America's Romance with Aviation, 1900–1950.* New York: Oxford University Press, 1983.

Dalen, Frank van. *Licensed to Fly for One Hundred Years: Anthony Fokker en zijn vliegtuigenfabriek.* Papendrecht: Fokker Technologies, 2014.

Daley, Robert. *An American Saga: Juan Trippe and His Pan Am Empire.* New York: Random House, 1980.

Davies, R. E. G. *Airlines of the United States since 1914.* London: Putnam, 1972.

Davis, Burke. *The Billy Mitchell Affair.* New York: Random House, 1967.

Dierikx, Marc. *Begrensde horizonten: De Nederlandse burgerluchtvaartpolitiek in het interbellum.* Zwolle: Tjeenk Willink, 1988.

———. *Bevlogen jaren: Nederlandse burgerluchtvaart tussen de wereldoorlogen.* Houten: Unieboek, 1986.

———. *Fokker: A Transatlantic Biography.* Washington, DC: Smithsonian Institution Press, 1997.

Düsing, Michael. *Abenteur gelber Hund: August Euler—deutsche Luftfahrt ab 1908.* Stuttgart: Ergonomia, 2008.

Encyclopaedie van Nederlandsch Oost-Indië. Parts 1 and 2. Den Haag/Leiden: Nijhoff/ Brill, 1921.

Feldman, Gerald D. *Hugo Stinnes: Biographie eines Industriellen, 1870–1924.* Munich: C. H. Beck, 1998.

Figes, Orlando. *The Whisperers: Private Life in Stalin's Russia.* London: Allen Lane, 2007.

Fokker, A. H. G. *Der fliegende Holländer: Die Memoiren des A. H. G. Fokker.* 1933. Reprint, Frankfurt: Wunderkammer, 2010.

Fokker, A. H. G., and Bruce Gould. *Flying Dutchman: The Life of Anthony Fokker.* New York: Henry Holt, 1931.

———. *De vliegende Hollander.* Amsterdam: Van Holkema en Warendorf, 1931.

Forden, Lesley. *The Ford Air Tours, 1925–1931: A Complete Narrative and Pictorial History of the Seven National Air Tour Competitions for the Edsel B. Ford Reliability Trophy.* New Brighton, MN: Aviation Foundation of America, 2003.

Fortescue, Granville. *At the Front with Three Armies.* London, A. Melrose, 1915.

Franks, Norman, and Greg van Wyngarden. *Fokker D.VII Aces of World War I.* Part 1. Oxford: Osprey, 2003.

Freudenthal, Elsbeth E. *The Aviation Business: From Kitty Hawk to Wall Street.* New York: Vanguard Press, 1940.

Freund, G. *Unholy Alliance: Russian-German Relations from the Treaty of Brest-Litovsk to the Treaty of Berlin.* London: Chatto and Windus, 1957.

Fritsche, Peter. *A Nation of Fliers: German Aviation and the Popular Imagination.* Cambridge, MA: Harvard University Press, 1992.

Gerdessen, Frederik, Toivo Kitvel, and Johannes Tilk. *Aeg, mehed, lennukid: Eesti lennunduse arengulugu kuni 1940 aastani.* Tallinn: Eesti Entsüklopeediakirjastus, 2001.

Gerdessen, Frits, Nico Geldhof, and Harm Hazewinkel. *Spijker: De eerste Nederlandse vliegtuigfabriek*. Voorburg: Koninklijke Nederlandse Vereniging voor Luchtvaart, 2002.

Glines, Carroll V. *Bernt Balchen: Polar Aviator*. Washington, DC: Smithsonian Institution Press, 1999.

Goerler, Raimund E. *To the Pole: The Diary and Notebook of Richard E. Byrd, 1925–1927*. Columbus: Ohio State University Press, 1998.

Gould, Bruce. *Skylarking: The Romantic Adventure of Flying*. New York, H. Liveright, 1929.

Grey, C. G., ed. *Jane's All the World's Aircraft, 1920*. London: Sampson Low, Marston, 1920.

Grosz, Peter, and Volker Koos. *Die Fokker Flugzeugwerke in Deutschland, 1912–1921*. Königswinter: Heel, 2004.

Haffner, Sebastiaan. *De Duitse revolutie 1918–1919: De nasleep van de Eerste Wereldoorlog*. Amsterdam: Mets & Schilt, 2007.

Hansen, Chris. *Enfant Terrible: The Times and Schemes of General Elliott Roosevelt*. Tucson: Able Baker Press, 2012.

Hazewinkel, Harm, Loet Kuipers, Hans Willem van Overbeek, Roger Soupart, and Prudent Staal. *Een eeuw Fokker: Verhalen en anekdotes uit 100 jaar Fokker geschiedenis*. Hilversum: All Media Productions, 2011.

Hegener, Henri. *Fokker: The Man and the Aircraft*. Letchworth: Harleyford Publications, 1961.

Hesselink, Liesbeth. *Genezers op de koloniale markt: Inheemse dokters en vroedvrouwen in Nederlands Oost-Indië, 1850–1915*. Amsterdam: Vossiuspers UvA, 2009.

Homze, Edward L. *Arming the Luftwaffe: The Reich Air Ministry and the German Aircraft Industry, 1919–1939*. Lincoln: University of Nebraska Press, 1976.

Immelmann, Franz. *Immelmann: "The Eagle of Lille."* Philadelphia: Casemate, 2009.

Imrie, Alex. *The Fokker Triplane*. London: Arms and Armour Press, 1992.

Jameson, Egon. *Berlin so wie es war: Ein Bildband*. Düsseldorf: Droste, 1969.

Jansen, Wolfgang. *. . . und Abends in die Scala: Fotografien von Josef Donderer*. Berlin: Bildarchiv Preussischer Kulturbesitz/Nicolai, 1991.

Jong, A. P. de, ed. *Vlucht door de tijd: 75 jaar Nederlandse luchtmacht*. Houten: Unieboek, 1988.

Josephson, Matthew. *Empire of the Air: Juan Trippe and the Struggle for World Airways*. New York: Harcourt, Brace, 1944.

Kamphuis, J. *Bouwhistorische documentatie en waardebepaling: Vesting Naarden, Promerskazerne*. Den Haag: Ministerie van VROM, 1994.

Kármán, Theodore von. *The Wind and Beyond: Pioneer in Aviation and Pathfinder in Space*. Boston: Little, Brown, 1967.

Kasten, Bernd, and Jens-Uwe Rost. *Schwerin: Geschichte der Stadt*. Schwerin: Thomas Helms, 2005.

Kauther, Alexander, and Paul Wirtz. *Cafe und Conditorei Senftleben: Geschichten um und über das "Cafe Senftleben," dem Treffpunkt der Flugzeugführer vom Flugplatz Berlin–Johannisthal*. Berlin: GRIN, 2012.

Kauther, Alexander, Paul Wirtz, and Michael Schmidt. *Anton Fokker: Ein niederländischer Flieger und Flugzeughersteller in Johannisthal*. Berlin: Johflug, 2012.

Kessner, Thomas. *Fiorello H. La Guardia and the Making of Modern New York*. New York: McGraw-Hill, 1989.

Kingsford Smith, Charles. *M'n ouwe kist*. Amsterdam: B. J. Smit, 1932.

Klinkert, Wim. *Defending Neutrality: The Netherlands Prepares for War, 1900–1925*. Leiden: Brill, 2013.

Kluge, Ulrich. *Die deutsche Revolution, 1918/1919: Staat, Politik und Gesellschaft zwischen Weltkrieg und Kapp-Putsch*. Frankfurt: Suhrkamp, 1985.

Knapen, Ben. *De lange weg naar Moskou: De Nederlandse relatie tot de Sovjet-Unie, 1917–1942*. Amsterdam: Elsevier, 1985.

Komons, Nick. *Bonfires to Beacons: Federal Aviation Policy under the Air Commerce Act, 1926–1938*. Washington, DC: Smithsonian Institution Press, 1989.

Koos, Volker. *Die Fokker Flugzeugwerke in Schwerin: Geschichte, Produktion, Typen*. Schwerin: Reinhard Thon, 1993.

Kranzhof, Jörg A. *Flugzeuge die Geschichte machten: Fokker Dr.I*. Stuttgart: Motorbuch, 1994.

Küpfer, C. C. "Gedenkboek NV Koninklijke Nederlandse Vliegtuigenfabriek, 1919–1964." Unpublished manuscript.

Kuyper, Henriëtte. *Een half jaar in Amerika*. Den Haag: Daamen, 1918.

Kuyt, J. G. *De "Holland": Zaandijk–New York v.v.* Amsterdam: P. N. van Kampen, 1938.

Leavitt, Judith Walzer, ed. *Women and Health in America: Historical Readings*. Madison: University of Wisconsin Press, 1984.

Leeuw, René de, ed. *Fokker Verkeersvliegtuigen: Van de F.I uit 1918 tot en met de Fokker 100 van nu*. Amsterdam: NV Koninklijke Nederlandse Vliegtuigenfabriek Fokker, 1989.

Lewis, W. David. *Eddie Rickenbacker: An American Hero in the Twentieth Century*. Baltimore: Johns Hopkins University Press, 2005.

Lincoln, W. Bruce. *Sunlight at Midnight: St. Petersburg and the Rise of Modern Russia*. New York: Basic Books, 2000.

Lindbergh, Charles A. *De brede zee: Met de Spirit of St. Louis over de oceaan*. Amsterdam: Elsevier, 1953.

Loening, Grover. *Our Wings Grow Faster*. Garden City, NY: Doubleday, 1935.

März, Peter. *Mythen, Bilder, Fakten: Auf der Suche nach der deutschen Vergangenheit*. Munich: Olzog, 2010.

Matthey, Ignaz. *Roemer Visscherstraat 47: De geschiedenis van een Vondelparkvilla*. Amsterdam: Jan van der Steenhoven, Till Martin Kolle, 1994.

Möller, Kathrin. *Lilienthal, Fokker & Co.: Fliegerei an der deutschen Ostseeküste*. Rostock: Hinstorff, 2012.

Möller, Kathrin, and Wolf Karge, eds. *Wege übers (Bundes-) Land: Zur Geschichte der Land-, Wasser-, Schienen-, und Luftwege in Mecklenburg und Vorpommern*. Schwerin: APH, 2002.

Mommsen, Hans. *Die verspielte Freiheit: Der Weg der Republik von Weimar in den Untergang, 1918 bis 1933*. Frankfurt: Ullstein/Propyläen, 1990.

Morgen, Curt von. *Meiner Truppen Heldenkämpfe: Aufzeichnungen von Curt von Morgen, Generalleutnant*. Berlin: Ernst Siegfried Mittler und Sohn, 1920.

Morrison, Wilbur H. *Donald W. Douglas: A Heart with Wings*. Ames: Iowa State University Press, 1991.

Morrow Jr., John H. *German Air Power in World War I*. Lincoln: University of Nebraska Press, 1982.

———. *The Great War in the Air: Military Aviation from 1909 to 1921*. Washington, DC: Smithsonian Institution Press, 1993.

Neijenhoff, W. M. van, and C. W. A. Oyens. *Zweefvliegen: Theorie en Praktijk*. Amsterdam: Meulenhoff, 1935.

Newton, Wesley P. *The Perilous Sky: Evolution of United States Aviation Diplomacy toward Latin America, 1919–1931*. Coral Gables, FL: University of Miami Press, 1978.

Norden, Adalbert. *Weltrekord, Weltrekord.* Berlin: Drei Masken, 1940.

Nowarra, Heinz J. *Die verbotenen Flugzeuge, 1921–1935: Die getarnte Luftwaffe.* Stuttgart: Motorbuch, 1980.

Palmer, Scott W. *Dictatorship of the Air: Aviation Culture and the Fate of Modern Russia.* New York: Cambridge University Press, 2006.

Paris, Michael. *Winged Warfare: The Literature and Theory of Aerial Warfare in Britain, 1859–1917.* Manchester: Manchester University Press, 1992.

Parmentier, Koene D. *In drie dagen naar Australië: Met de Uiver in de Melbourne Race.* Amsterdam: Scheltens & Giltay, 1935.

Penning, Manfred. "Die erste deutsche Automobilfachschule Mainz." *Mainzer Vierteljahres* 32 (2012–13): 2:36–39 and 4:36–43.

Plesman Jr., Albert. *Albert Plesman, mijn vader.* Den Haag: Nijgh & Van Ditmar, 1977.

Postma, Thijs. *Fokker: Aircraft Builders to the World.* London: Jane's, 1980.

Puffer, Claude E. *Air Transportation.* Philadelphia: Blakiston, 1941.

Rae, John B. *Climb to Greatness: The American Aircraft Industry, 1920–1960.* Cambridge, MA: MIT Press, 1968.

Regeerings-Almanak voor Nederlandsch-Indië, 1880–97. Batavia: Landsdrukkerij, 1880–98.

Rickenbacker, Edward V. *Rickenbacker: An Autobiography.* Englewood Cliffs, NJ: Prentice-Hall, 1967.

Schendel, Fiona van. *Djolotigo: Ontginning en exploitatie van een particuliere koffie-onderneming op Java, 1875–1898.* Amsterdam: Nederlands Economisch-Historisch Archief, 2000.

Schmidt, Günter. *Als die Oldtimer flogen: Die Geschichte des Flugplatzes Johannisthal.* Oberhaching: Aviatik, 1995.

Schmidt, Michael. "A. H. G. Fokker: Der niederländische Flieger und Flugzeughersteller in Deutschland." Unpublished manuscript, Schwerin, 2013.

Schmidt, Michael. "Die Geschichte der Schweriner Pianofortefabrik Perzina." Unpublished manuscript, Schwerin, 2012.

Schmitt, Günter. *Hugo Junkers und seine Flugzeuge.* Stuttgart: Motorbuch, 1986.

Schwartz, Rosalie. *Pleasure Island: Tourism and Temptation in Cuba.* Lincoln: University of Nebraska Press, 1997.

Shute, Nevil. *Slide Rule: The Autobiography of an Engineer.* London: Heinemann, 1954.

Sloan, Alfred P. *My Years with General Motors.* Garden City, NY: Doubleday, 1963.

Stahlecker, Adrian. *Film en kunst in ballingschap, 1933–1945: Duitse artiesten en kunstenaars op de vlucht voor het naziregime.* Voorburg: Nieuwe Haagsche, 2000.

Starink, Dirk. *De jonge jaren van de Luchtmacht: Het Luchtwapen van het Nederlandse leger, 1913–1939.* Amsterdam: Boom, 2013.

Thomas, Clayton L., ed. *Taber's Encyclopedic Medical Dictionary.* Philadelphia: F. A. Davis, 1989.

Thomassen à Thuessink van der Hoop, A. N. J. *Door de lucht naar Indië.* Amsterdam: Scheltens & Giltay, 1925.

Trimble, William F. *High Frontier: A History of Aeronautics in Pennsylvania.* Pittsburgh: University of Pittsburgh Press, 1982.

Troost, Frido, Sytze van der Zee, and Willem Zoetendaal. *Salto mortale: Fokker in bedrijf, 1911–1996.* Amsterdam: Basalt & d'Arts, 1998.

Vermeulen, Coen, ed. *Around Glare: A New Aircraft Material in Context.* Dordrecht: Kluwer Academic, 2002.

Visser, Joop, Matthijs Dicke, and Annelies van der Zouwen, eds. *Nederlandse Ondernemers, 1850–1950: Noord Holland en Zuid-Holland.* Zutphen: Walburg, 2013.

Vorsterman van Oyen, A. A. *Stam- en Wapenboek der Aanzienlijke Nederlandsche Familiën.* Vol. I. Groningen: Wolters, 1885.

Vries, Joh. de. *Met Amsterdam als brandpunt: Honderdvijftig jaar Kamer van Koophandel en Fabrieken, 1811–1961.* Amsterdam: Ellerman Harms, 1961.

Der Waffenstillstand, 1918–1919: Das Dokumenten-Material der Waffenstillstandsverhandlungen von Compiègne, Spa, Trier und Brussel, herausgegeben im Auftrag der Deutsche Waffenstillstands-Kommission. Vol. I. Berlin: Deutsche Verlagsgesellschaft für Politik und Geschichte, 1928.

Wagner, Wolfgang. *Hugo Junkers: Pionier der Luftfahrt—seine Flugzeuge.* Bonn: Bernard & Graefe, 1996.

Waller, Douglas. *A Question of Loyalty: Gen. Billy Mitchell and the Court-Martial That Gripped the Nation.* New York: HarperCollins, 2004.

Wels, Susan. *Amelia Earhart: The Thrill of It.* Philadelphia: Running Press, 2009.

Werner, Johannes. *Knight of Germany: Oswald Boelcke, German Ace.* Philadelphia: Casemate, 2009.

Wesselink, Theo. *Amerikaanse Fokkers: Een produktie overzicht.* Haarlem: Dutch Aviation Publications, 2003.

Weyl, A. R. *Fokker: The Creative Years.* London: Putnam, 1985.

Wiegel, Cor. *Haarlem in oude ansichten.* Zaltbommel: Europese Bibliotheek, 1982.

Wijling, G. *Ploegen en zaaien: Een eeuw Haarlems middelbaar onderwijs.* Haarlem: Tjeenk Willink, 1964.

Wilkins, George Hubert. *Flying the Arctic.* New York: Putnam, 1928.

Winter, Rolf de. *Hendrik Walaardt Sacré, 1873–1949: Leven voor de luchtvaart.* Den Haag: Sectie Luchtmachthistorie van de Luchtmachtstaf, 1992.

Wohl, Robert. *A Passion for Wings: Aviation and the Western Imagination, 1908–1918.* New Haven, CT: Yale University Press, 1994.

Wormser, C. W. *Ontginners van Java.* Deventer: W. van Hoeve, 1942.

Wyngarden, Greg van. *Richthofen's Circus: Jagdgeschwader 1.* Oxford: Osprey Publishing, 2004.

Zweig, Stefan. *Die Welt von Gestern: Erinnerungen eines Europäers.* 1941. Reprint, Frankfurt: Fischer Taschenbuch, 2012.

INDEX